Date Due

a list of the ten plays selected each year for the previous ten volumes of the "Best Plays" series. My thanks to him for his interest and to you for your continuing support.

B. M.

Forest Hills, L. I., 1930.

CONTENTS

atalogue of the "ten best plays" of the Chicago season, ing to the opinions and preferences of this writer, would no special value here, for it would certainly include a r of titles from this and last year's blue ribbon announce- in Manhattan. It would be marked, however, by the on of three plays that have been premiated by many of stern colleagues—"Strictly Dishonorable," "Holiday," and Moon." To compensate for my eccentricity of taste, I award "Strictly Dishonorable" a teddy bear, as a thin, uasive comedy of prurient appeal; "Holiday" an orchid, as mple of affected and "precious" dialogue written in a vich Village state of mind; and "June Moon" a night- ng cereus, as a technical Broadway satire whose cleverness ot carry with much vitality across the Hudson.

most vivid incidents of the year—premieres which had of emotion or the thrill of new adventure in playgoing— he appearances of Mr. Cohan in "Gambling"; of Mr. in his *Ave atque vale,* with the revival of "Sherlock s"; and of Mei Lan-fang, exquisitely revealing the mys- f the Chinese drama. These were first nights that deserve called memorable occasions. In Mr. Cohan's case, the asm with which he was received, after twelve years' from the Chicago stage, caused a change in his destiny. night the retreating drama won a victory against the although it may have been only an affair of outposts. han found that the old fire of the stage was still burning, was so deeply moved by the experience that he imme- canceled a Hollywood contract for the exploitation of ks, and plunged into theatrical production with renewed

long runs in Chicago were few, and several plays of distance records were expected—for example, "Journey's nd "Street Scene"—disappointed their managements. The in the race were "Strange Interlude," with seventeen "Nina Rosa," an operetta, with sixteen; "Your Uncle ," with sixteen (at two theatres and on a cut-rate basis); trictly Dishonorable," with fifteen.

1 marked the end of first-class, or two-a-day, vaudeville ago. The Palace, a Chicago institution for almost twenty the present theatre, however, is new), succumbed to the y of the times and became a "continuous" house, offering bills of vaudeville and films. Thus the Palace of New st its only surviving sister.

Eugene O'Neill's "Strange Interlude"; and Karel Capek's good old "R. U. R."

The Dramatic League of Chicago: "Thunder in the Air"; St. John Ervine's "The First Mrs. Fraser"; "The Infinite Shoe-black"; "The Matriarch," with Constance Collier; and "Dear Old England."

The Goodman Theater repertory company: "Romeo and Juliet"; Capek's "The Makropoulos Secret"; "Tour du Monde"; Paul Green's "The Field God"; Sheridan's "The Rivals"; "Kol-pak Must Dance," by Hellmuth Unger; "Ariadne," by A. A. Milne; and "Escape," by John Galsworthy.

The Civic Theater: Fritz Leiber's company in ten plays by Shakespeare, as follows: "Hamlet," "Julius Cæsar," "The Mer-chant of Venice," "Macbeth," "The Taming of the Shrew," "Twelfth Night," "Richard III," "As You Like It," "King Lear," and "Othello." Late in the season the Civic also staged a series of light opera classics by the American wing of the Civic Opera company—"The Bohemian Girl," "The Chimes of Normandy," "The Gondoliers," and "The Yeomen of the Guard."

The appearance of the Dramatic League and the Chicago Civic Shakespeare Society (Mr. Leiber's sponsorship) represented new developments. The former entered the field of subscription-list plays in fairly direct competition with the Theatre Guild, and after its debut in Chicago extended its operations to Philadel-phia, where the title, the Professional Players, was used. Other cities, among them Boston, Cincinnati, Pittsburgh, Cleveland and Detroit, will be added to the circuit next season.

The Dramatic League proclaims itself an expression of experi-enced professional management, and promises its subscribers the high skill in acting and authorship that characterize the "com-mercial" stage at its best. It has been a transparent secret that Mr. Lee Shubert is the director-in-chief of the organization. His associates in the venture (various New York producers of estab-lished reputation) and the members of his board of strategy remain unnamed.

The five plays of the Dramatic League's season were of British origin. They varied in merit, but none of them represented a misspent evening in the theatre. They were effectively staged, according to the standard methods of scene-design, and they were excellently acted. The list provided the national season with one signal success—"The First Mrs. Fraser." The sub-scribers to the League were pleased with their investment, and plans for a second season were begun with nearly 8,000 subscriptions on the books.

The Chicago Civic Shakespeare Society sprang full-fledged out of the mind and purse of Harley L. Clarke, a utilities magnate. Fritz Leiber, as the only available die-hard of the classic repertories, was placed in command of a twelve weeks' season of Shakespeare at the Civic—a small, handsome playhouse in the new Opera building. Moreover, he was given a contract for five years, with guarantees. His company was inadequate to the severe task of staging ten of the major tragedies and comedies in a period of three months, and most of the work was in the rough-edged vein of Shakespearean "stock." The "Hamlet," however, was an organically sound and unified production, with settings in a gay *moderne* style, designed by Herman Rosse. Mr. Leiber's first season, although filled with flaws, gratified playgoing appetites that were famished for the neglected classics, and it must be regarded as laudable pioneering for the future.

The Theatre Guild ended its third formal season in Chicago with a subscription list that gladdens the hearts of its directorate. It looks forward to the fourth with nearly 15,000 signatures on the dotted lines. This city has become such an important factor in the Guild's plans that the establishment of a branch executive office here is not unlikely, and the acquisition of a theatre all its own, either by renting or building, is a distant possibility. The run of "Strange Interlude" was a notable box office affair. It kept the Blackstone filled for four months.

The Goodman Theater repertory company, born and bred in Chicago, a native product in every way, went through its fifth season with gratifying results. Its young people began to grow up; its acting became more stageworthy; its grasp of the art theatre ideal strengthened. First nights at the Goodman were pleasant affairs, although "Kolpak Must Dance" was a surly specimen of the Da-da glooms, and "Ariadne" was negligible fluff. Its "Romeo and Juliet" had alternating heroines, Katherine Krug and Joan Madison, both young; the former fair and crystalline, the latter dark and pensive. Its "Makropoulos Secret" was an admirable illustration of modern decorative stagecraft. Its "Holiday" had definite rights of comparison with the Broadway original.

In the early spring, the Goodman began a campaign (somewhat belated, it seemed) for subscribers to its next year's program. The objective was 10,000, and by June 1 about 4,000 of them were in the bag. The close of the season was given a

surprising turn by the sudden resi
Stevens, director of the Goodman and
tion, on the ground that the trustees
whose wing the theatre exists) were
of remote control which conflicted wi
repertory. Hubert Osborne, of his s
put on "The Makropoulos Secret,"
Dance" and "Ariadne"), was promp
and the trustees promised an impr
stars, for the coming year.

Taking up the Chicago stage "ex
market experts would say, one finds
comparatively infrequent; that gilt-
scarce; and that revivals seemed to
In the field of drama, the following e
with the star of significance:

"Journey's End"; "The Perfect
God" and "The Love Duel," both w
Age of Innocence," because Kathari
in Hand"; "June Moon"; "Street S
"Gambling," because it brought C
Chicago as an actor after years of a
able"; William Gillette's farewell i
Stratford-upon-Avon company, from
Theatre, in nine of the classic plays
the Chinese marvel of hermaphroditis
with a perfect cast; "Candle Light,
as its rising star; and "Solid South
a picturesque character study.

The best musical shows—of exc
numerous—were: "Follow Thru";
Boat"; "Animal Crackers," with t
Rosa"; "Whoopee"; "A Wonderfu
shamefully neglected by playgoers)
Queenie Smith; and "The Little Sh

A list of the Chicago theatres r
time, to the flesh-and-blood drama,
tions they have housed during the p
statistical interest. Here it is: Ad
stone, 4; Cort, 7; Civic, 2 (reperto
8; Grand Opera House, 8; Goodman
runs); Harris, 6; Illinois, 3; Majesti
7; Selwyn, 6; Studebaker, 4; Wood

A c
accord
be of
numb
ments
omissi
my E
"June
would
unpers
an ex
Green
bloom
does n
The
the sti
were
Gillett
Holme
teries
to be
enthus
absenc
That
talkies
Mr. C
and h
diately
his wo
vigor.
The
which
End"
leaders
weeks
Dudley
and "
June
in Chi
years
tenden
mixed
York l

"Now then," I can hear people who think of the theatre as merely show business, saying, "this talk of plays and their worthiness and art theatres and such is all very well in its way; but what about the box offices? How did they fare during the season of 1929-30 in Chicago?"

Well, what with the stock market debacle of November, and Chicago's public pay roll moratorium of February, and the menace of the talkies, and everything, there is not much to be said for show business in Chicago during the period under discussion. I didn't help to count the money, but I heard the groans, the wails, the shrieks of dismay, that came from the managers' offices; and I gathered the impression that the traffic in amusements was no laughing matter. To put it bluntly, show business in Chicago was terrible.

SAN FRANCISCO YEAR, 1929-30

By George C. Warren
Drama Editor *San Francisco Chronicle*

SAN FRANCISCO and Broadway were brought much nearer to each other during the theatrical year which ended May 31. Many of the New York plays were done here within a few weeks of their Broadway premieres or immediately after the close of runs there, and with players of the original casts in the principal rôles.

This factor of the year was perhaps its most significant and vital feature. As it ends, the collapse of the Henry Duffy producing-stock venture, five and a half years old, is the sensation of the moment, and a great loss to the drama on the Pacific Coast. Duffy's productions have grown better and better, his casts finer with the passing seasons, with guest stars of importance the order of the day.

The activity of the police censors has been another thing that has been notable, and the increasing number of original productions has given agreeable novelty to the year.

Perhaps the most important of these plays tried out in San Francisco was Noel Coward's "The Queen Was in the Parlour," which Edward Belasco and Home Curran produced handsomely, with Pauline Frederick, Vernon Steel and William Stack in the cast. The play is several years old but had not before been done professionally in the United States—there was, I think, a performance or two by a Boston Little Theatre group.

As this is written, Paul Bissinger's intimate revue, built along the lines of "The Little Show," with which Bissinger was connected as assistant stage manager and player of bits, is being got into shape for a New York opening in August. It is called "Hi-There!" has Odette Myrtil and Ken Murray at the head of the cast, and was staged by Alexander Leftwich. It was produced at Erlanger's Columbia Theatre, the new playhouse on the San Francisco amusement map, a handsome house, made out of the old Orpheum Theatre, richly and tastefully decorated and furnished by Albert Herter, the artist.

The house was opened March 10 by Charles L. Wagner, who presented Madge Kennedy in A. A. Milne's "The Perfect Alibi," bringing out several of the players who were in the piece during its season's run at the Charles Hopkins Theatre, New York—Alan Bunce, Richie Ling, Carson Davenport, Leo G. Carroll and A. P. Kaye.

An original play that will probably have further production, as Leo Carrillo finds in one of its characters a rôle that suits him, was Dr. Charles D. McGettigan's "Quien Sabe?" a romantic melodrama dealing with the bandit, Joaquin Murietta, founded on legends and information that came from Mrs. McGettigan, who was a daughter of General Vallejo, an official in California under Mexican dominion.

The play, produced by the College Players of St. Ignatius College, under the direction of James J. Gill, had a week's run in a downtown theatre and attracted much attention from the public. Carrillo, now on his way from a year in Australia, wants to produce it with himself as Murietta, on his return to America.

This same body of amateurs made two other original productions during the year. One was a farce, called "Stop! Go!" by Marion Short and Pauline Phelps; and the other a mystery melodrama, "The Sky Train," by Paul Cruger, a writer for talking pictures in Hollywood.

Henry Duffy staged H. H. Van Loan's and Lolita Westman's comedy, "Cooking Her Goose," with Nydia Westman starred, at his Alcazar Theatre, afterward presenting it over his circuit in Hollywood, Oakland and Portland.

Two ambitious musical pieces were staged here, one of them a comic opera called "Bambina," written, book and music, by Myrta Bel Gallaher, and staged by Edward Royce, with Nancy Welford, Al St. John, the movie comedian, Marie Wells, and Edwin Woods in the cast. It was well done, but failed to click. The other, "Oh, Susanna," had the days of '49 for its theme, and Bernard McConville for its author. Aubrey Stauffer wrote the score. It was tried in Los Angeles as well as San Francisco, but did not make the grade, although it was handsomely staged.

Oliver Morosco put on a play, "The Woman in White," which had Charlotte Walker for its star, but it failed utterly. Mrs. Fremont Older, wife of the editor of the San Francisco *Call*, was the author. Two other plays, done by amateurs, had first performances on any stage: Edna Higgins Strachan's "The

McMurray Chin," a domestic comedy of promise, and "To Serve the Queen," which retells the legend of King Arthur, Queen Guinevere and Sir Launcelot, written by Roland English Hartley of the University of California. The first of these was produced in Oakland, the other in Berkeley.

Police censorship was exercised on four plays. George Scarborough's "Bad Babies" was raided twice at the Capitol Theatre, but the cases were dropped when the producer closed the show to save the young actors and they were hardly more than children representing school boy and girl bandits and harlots—from further arrests. Sidney Goldtree's tiny upstairs theatre, the Green Street, was made a mark. Two raids were made on a farce called "Easy for Zee Zee"; two on the farce, "The Flat Tire," both adaptations from the French, and eight on the Viennese farce by Dr. Julius Horst, "The Peephole." Goldtree escaped with verdicts of "Not Guilty" or hung juries, but the police under Corporal Peter Peshon, morals censor, and Captain Layne, of the morals squad, kept arresting the actors until Goldtree took off the Horst farce, and substituted "The Married Virgin," an adaptation of Edouard Bourdet's "The Rubicon," which is now running.

There is some hope of a reorganization of the Henry Duffy Players and a continuation of its activities on a smaller scale. There is a receiver in charge and performances continue. Too great expansion and bad business for six months are given as the reasons for the failure of the organization. Duffy had two theatres in San Francisco, two in Oakland, two in Hollywood and one each in Los Angeles and Portland, Ore.

During the year he had among his guest stars Mary Boland, Violet Heming, Frances Starr, Dale Winter, Leo Carrillo, Robert McWade, Eugene O'Brien, Taylor Holmes, May Robson, Tom Moore, Kay Hammond, Frank Craven, Charlotte Greenwood, Kolb and Dill, Nydia Westman, Guy Bates Post, Violet Kemble Cooper and Mabel Taliaferro. In several cases he brought out supporting players from the New York casts of such plays as "Ladies of the Jury," "Let Us Be Gay," "Remote Control," "Salt Water" and "Holiday."

Belasco and Curran have made a number of handsome productions besides "The Queen Was in the Parlour." They staged, for the first time in the West, W. Somerset Maugham's "East of Suez" with Lenore Ulric starred; "The Criminal Code," for which they brought Arthur Byron, Russell Hardie, Leo G. Curley, Thomas Findlay, and Walter Kingsford of the New York cast;

"Lulu Belle," which had Dorothy Burgess in the Ulric part; and "Follow Thru," done in association with Schwab and Mandel, and with Zelma O'Neal, Allen Kearns and Mary Lawlor featured.

Few traveling attractions visited the Pacific Coast, but those that came were well received. Ethel Barrymore had the biggest engagement she has ever done here with "The Kingdom of God" and "The Love Duel," each for two weeks; and "Journey's End," with Basil Gill as Lieutenant Osborne, played six weeks to sell-out business. "Bird in Hand," presented by the company which afterward went into New York, replacing there the actors who were the American originals, did four big weeks. "After Dark" had a hilarious engagement of six weeks, and "June Moon," with the Chicago cast, did well. Mae West in "Diamond Lil" did not fare well.

The Stratford-upon-Avon Festival Players had a big two weeks, selling out often, and giving fine, smooth performances of nine of Shakespeare's plays; and Ben Greet brought his company for a week, presenting the quarto "Hamlet," "Everyman," "Much Ado About Nothing" and "Twelfth Night." Another English company, headed by Maurice Colbourne and Barry Jones, played repertory for two weeks, offering Shaw's "Arms and the Man," Milne's "The Dover Road" and Oscar Wilde's "The Importance of Being Earnest." Their performances were fairly even and interesting and the business about of the same type.

Early in the year Fay Bainter was seen in "Jealousy," to fair business, and Helen Hayes came in "Coquette," but the engagement was spoiled by Mary Pickford's preceding her in the talking picture of the play. Edna Hibbard appeared in two plays not suited to her style, Rachel Crother's "Let Us Be Gay" and "The Door Between," by Vincent Lawrence, whose "Among the Married" made some impression recently, acted by a Pacific Coast cast.

"Little Accident" was liked here, and Fay Marbe appeared for a week in her "one girl revue," to fair business. An interesting engagement was that of Noel Madison, son of Maurice Moscovitch, who played Cadell in Patrick Hamilton's "Rope's End." He made an excellent impression, but did not draw the crowds.

The Little Theatre groups have been active with two of the San Francisco bodies taking possession of their own theatres as this goes to press. One of these, the Players' Guild, has a pretty theatre seating 500 persons. Stanley MacLewee has worked long and hard to get this theatre open. His first offering was Frederick Lonsdale's "On Approval," followed by "Children of Darkness" by Edwin Justus Mayer. Professional casts are employed, and each play runs two weeks. The theatre will close for the summer after the third production, not yet announced. This group has a subscription list of 2500.

The Reginald Travers Players will take possession of the Travers Theatre, a very intimate playhouse, financed for two years, installed in the Fairmont Hotel. It will seat 172 persons, and is on a subscription basis. The opening play will be "The Affairs of Anatol."

The playhouse of Berkeley has kept open through the year in its reconstructed old church for a theatre, and the Playmakers, a group of University of California people who write, stage and act their own one-act plays, has given its regular four performances. It proposes to produce original three-act plays by its members next season, if manuscripts of sufficient merit are submitted. The group is seven years old.

At the University of California the Little Theatre has done its regular list of plays, and the Dramatic Council of Stanford University, under the direction of Harold Helvenston, has kept up its work, presenting two original musical things during the year, and offering standard plays. Clemence Dane's "Granite," well done, was one of them.

Theatre Arts, Inc., an organization now seven years old, directed by Talma-Zetta Wilbur, and Community Playhouse Productions, with Baldwin McGaw directing, are other bodies that keep alive the amateur spirit, as has the Community Players of the Young Men and Young Women's Hebrew Association, which will have a home of its own some time during the new year.

Business on the whole has been fair, with heavy attendance for some of the attractions, while others, as good, have suffered.

THE SEASON IN SOUTHERN CALIFORNIA

By Monroe Lathrop

Drama Editor of the *Los Angeles Express*

RIGHT at the citadel gates of its dearest enemy, the vocal celluloid, the living theatre of Southern California made its most defiant gesture in the year ending June 1, 1930.

Something more than two hundred plays reached the footlights of the thirteen legitimate theatres of Los Angeles—a number much in excess of the record of any previous twelvemonth. Perhaps the citation of one fact will make it clear that in quality the average was as high as any of previous record.

That fact is that of the Ten Best Plays chosen by Mr. Mantle for this volume, which are foreknown as this is written, five made a prompt appearance here, if we count "Rebound," which was in rehearsal before the above date. The others were "The Criminal Code," "Strictly Dishonorable," "June Moon" and "The Last Mile."

Still further attesting the high average, came also five of Mr. Mantle's selections for the previous year—"Journey's End," "Wings over Europe," "Holiday," "Little Accident" and "The Kingdom of God." When to these are added such long-term plays of the metropolitan stage as "Bird in Hand," "The Bachelor Father," "Follow Thru" and "Brothers," no further pressing of this point of quality is necessary.

It has been a year of color and variety. It has had its distinct Oriental tinge. It has had a liberal portion of classics. There have been several revivals of the favorites of the Mauve Decade. The London stages have sent direct many of their best exponents of British authorship and thespian training. A generous sprinkling of musical pieces has enlivened the season.

Then there have been special events of the theatre out of the ordinary, such as a visit from the "Chauve Souris"; the return to the stage of George Fawcett after a silence of seventeen years; recitals from the classics by E. H. Sothern; the appearance in a one-man show of Maurice Chevalier, the French artist, with vast success, and a similar affair by Fay Marbe, after her European tours.

The practical annihilation of "the road" seems to have had no ill effect upon the supply of good quality dramatic entertainment here. It is now the custom of New York successes to venture over the Great Divide with the promise of good reward in the growing cities of the coast; and such reward has come to Ethel Barrymore, with her two plays, "The Kingdom of God" and "The Love Duel"; to Mr. Belasco's "The Bachelor Father"; to Mr. Woods' "Jealousy," the two-character tragedy; to "Coquette," with Helen Hayes; to Mr. Drinkwater's English company in "Bird in Hand"; to Maurice Browne's London company in "Journey's End"; to Mae West and her "Diamond Lil";

to Mr. Pemberton's "Strictly Dishonorable," and to "The Criminal Code," starring Arthur Byron.

But the coast no longer relies upon adventurous managers of New York to fill most of its playgoing needs. With a wealth of the best acting talent of the world now resident here, drawn by the opulent rewards of the studios, original production of plays has become a fixed habit.

Evidence of this was to be found in more than thirty new plays tested out among treble the number that had their inception and execution entirely from local initiative. Of these new ones it is sufficient to say that few proved worthy of permanent record. "Top o' the Hill," by Charles Kenyon, presented with Helen Menken and William Boyd, ventured to New York, where the shortcomings of this piece by the author of "Kindling" were as promptly discerned as at home.

Arthur Goodrich's dramatization of Booth Tarkington's "The Plutocrat" had its premiere at the Pasadena Community Theatre and, with the talent of Mr. and Mrs. Charles Coburn in its favor, probably fared best of the productions that moved on to the Atlantic seaboard.

"Cooking Her Goose," a new comedy by H. H. Van Loan and Lolita Westman, survived a mere three weeks at a Duffy house and got no farther than a Hollywood studio where it found a welcome in the talkie maw.

Martin Flavin's "Spendthrift" was another maiden bow from the stage of the Pasadena theatre. It was anything but a worthy sister to this author's "Broken Dishes" and "Criminal Code," and returned to Mr. Flavin's fat portfolio of dramas for doubtful disposition.

Two productions at least new to the American stage were Noel Coward's "The Queen Was in the Parlour," presented for the first time in this country by Belasco and Curran, with Pauline Frederick; and "To What Red Hell," which Lucille La Verne brought back from London and tested out with similar indifferent results.

"Bad Babies" created the most commotion of any of the new ventures. This tale of errant youth by George Scarborough, hectic alike in dialogue and action, ran afoul of the police and courts and brought the law's fist down on author and actors in the shape of stiff fines. Its notoriety brought eight weeks of seeming success quite unwarranted by any dramatic merit.

Other failures included "Her First Night," by Sidney Toler and Charles McDermott; "Maternally Yours," a wild farce on the humors surrounding childbirth, by Clarence Odell Miller, a Pasadena attorney; "The Latest Murder," a mystery melodrama by Hampton Del Ruth; and "Come Seven," a comedy of Negro life by Octavus Roy Cohen, with colored players.

With meagre support, the Civic Repertory carried on in its second season. Its most praiseworthy contributions were Gilbert Emery's "The Hero," with Grant Mitchell as guest artist, and Ransom Rideout's "Goin' Home," with white and colored players. The English plays, "A Bill of Divorcement" and "And So to Bed," Molière's "Imaginary Invalid," Sierra's "Romantic Young Lady" and "Wound Stripes," a new play of no distinction, were in its list.

The Pasadena Community Theatre gave its usual thirty or more varied productions, ranging from minstrels to classics. Its most notable things were the New York Theatre Guild's English importation, "Wings Over Europe"; the Russian Soviet play, "The Armored Train"; Shaw's "Candida" and "Man and Superman"; "The Blue Bird"; and "Julius Cæsar." It has now in rehearsal an elaborate staging of O'Neill's "Marco Millions."

Most pretentious of the year's musical offerings were Schwab and Mandel's "Follow Thru" and Lillian Albertson's large and colorful presentation of "The New Moon." Of like scope were two new operettas of local authorship. "Oh, Susanna," by Bernard McConville and Aubrey Stauffer, and "Bambina" were richly staged but lacked the spark that insures real success. "Harry Carroll's Revue" was a failure, but Fred Waring's "Rah, Rah, Daze" had eight weeks of popularity. A brief revival of "The Desert Song" and "The Student Prince" by Miss Albertson had fair prosperity.

Three dramatic streams flowed incessantly through the year, because of the activity of Henry Duffy, Edward Everett Horton and Franklin Pangborn as actor-managers. Mr. Duffy, the most prolific, with three theatres, presented over 40 plays, chiefly light popular hits of the previous New York season, with some revivals of older pieces. Most notable of the Horton presentations were Vincent Lawrence's "Among the Married," and "Serena Blandish"; these, like the Duffy offerings, handsomely mounted and expertly cast. Mr. Pangborn contented himself with revivals of plays of tested appeal.

The Oriental tinge was given to the season, first by Mr. and Mrs. Coburn, who brought their production of "The Yellow Jacket," including several of the eastern company, from New York. If it did not prove of large popularity, it served as a fitting prologue to the genuine thing which came soon after—a company from the Osaka Theatre in Japan, with native plays and sword-dances. Later in the season came Mei Lan-fang, China's foremost actor, and company, whose engagement had to be extended.

The British representation, already referred to, was furnished by the Stratford-upon-Avon Players from the Shakespeare Memorial Theatre, with a repertory of the Bard's done with fine team work and gusto; by London companies, with "Bird in Hand" and "Journey's End"; by the Ben Greet Players, in classics done in the old style; and by the Coburn-Jones company from England, in Shaw and Wilde revivals.

Southern California, like New York, had its outbreak of revivals of the favorite plays of our grandparents. The best of these, "The Streets of New York," was so well done by Edward Horton that it had a prosperous run of five weeks. Rivaling it in merit and interest was the reproduction, in the exact original manner, at the Pasadena theatre of "Our American Cousin," the play which mingled comedy with the tragedy of Lincoln's assassination. The Pasadena stage also had revivals of "Nellie the Beautiful Cloak Model," "Ten Nights in a Barroom" and "Trilby." A traveling company from the East brought "After Dark."

John Steven McGroarty's pageant-play had its annual season and added seventeen weeks to its remarkable record, and the outdoor Pilgrimage Play, before a mountain fire destroyed its theatre, which is being replaced by a larger and better one, had its summer presentations.

Long-run records for the year went to the Mission Play, with 17 weeks; "She Couldn't Say No," with Charlotte Greenwood, 13; "New Moon," 10; "Let Us Be Gay" (in two houses), 11; "Follow Thru," 7; "Rah, Rah, Daze," 8; "Rope's End," 6; "The Sap," 6; "Among the Married" (at two houses), 8; "Bad Babies," 8; "The Boomerang," 6; "Your Uncle Dudley," 6.

THE GREEN PASTURES

A Fable Play in Eighteen Scenes

By Marc Connelly

ONCE or twice in the lifetime of every playgoer there occurs an adventure such as that of the first performance of "The Green Pastures." It is an occasion, usually, for which he is little prepared, and which he accepts, even with its attendant satisfactions, a little doubtfully. Probably the seeming perfections of the play will fade with the morning, when the memory of it cools and the mood of it is dissipated.

But in this instance the memory of the play was immeasurably strengthened with a majority of its devotees as time passed. The definite success of the first night was repeated with each succeeding performance until "The Green Pastures" became the talk of the city in all its sections.

Probably no other people could accept this naïve retelling of the story of the Old Testament, as a colored preacher in Louisiana might relate it to his Sunday school class, as the American people have accepted and will accept it.

It demands, first, something of the background a majority of the American people experienced in living with their puritan and essentially religious forbears. It demands, second, a knowledge of and a kindly sympathy for the Southern Negro and his trusting and childlike religious faith, to give it its best values as a recital in dramatic form.

But to those who have experienced the fullest reaction from it, there is no extravagance in the description attached to "The Green Pastures" by the critic who spoke of it as "the divine comedy of the modern theatre."

Like most plays demanding a particular brand of courage for their production, "The Green Pastures" was refused by several of the more important producers.

It reached the stage finally because a financier with a love of the theatre declared his willingness to produce it, even if he never had a penny in return for his investment. This broker-producer's name is Rowland Stebbins, but he prefers to label his theatrical ventures as being sponsored by Laurence Rivers, Inc. Earlier in the season he had produced George Kelly's "Maggie the Magnificent."

"The Green Pastures" was shown first at the Mansfield Theatre, New York, the night of February 26. Its press reception was varied, but mostly ecstatic, its general popularity immediate.

The play opens with a scene in the corner of a Negro church in what Mr. Connelly describes as the "deep South." Mr. Deshee, the preacher, is instructing a class of ten Negro children of assorted ages in the first chapter of the Old Testament.

Mr. Deshee is an elderly and a kindly man. The children are dressed as any group of children might be in any lower Louisiana town at Sunday school time, and they are listening to the words of the preacher with varying degrees of interest.

"Three or four are wide-eyed in their attention. Two or three are obviously puzzled, but interested, and the smallest ones are engaged in more physical concerns. One is playing with a little doll, and another runs his finger on all the angles of his chair."

Mr. Deshee is pretty well into the begats, starting with Adam. "An' Adam lived a hundred and thirty years, an' begat a son in his own likeness, after his image; an' called his name Seth. An' de days of Adam, after he had begotten Seth, were eight hundred years; an' he begat sons and daughters; an' all de days dat Adam lived were nine hundred and thirty years; an' he died."

Getting by Seth, Mr. Deshee skips to Enoch and Methuselah. And having disposed of Enoch and Methuselah, "de oldest man dat ever was," he comes to Noah. But Noah is being saved for another lesson.

"I'm gonter tell you all about him next Sunday," promises the teacher, in conclusion. "Anyway, dat's de meat an' substance of de first five chapters of Genesis. Now, how you think you gonter like de Bible?"

Opinions are varied. One little girl thinks it's wonderful. One boy can't quite understand why Bible folk lived so long. Carlisle, who is especially persistent, wants to know what the world looked like way back "when de Lawd begin." Who was in N'Orleans den?

"Dey wasn't nobody in N'Orleans on 'count dey wasn't any N'Orleans," explains Mr. Deshee. "Dat's de whole idea I tol' you at de end of de first Chapter. Yo' got to git yo' minds fixed. Dey wasn't any Rampart Street. Dey wasn't any Canal

Street. Dey wasn't any Louisiana. Dey wasn't nothin' on de earth at all caize fo' de reason dey wasn't any earth."

And if Carlisle wants to know, as Carlisle does, how the Lord decided he wanted the earth in the first place, and wanted it right here where it is, that's because the Book says so.

"De Book say, but at de same time dat's a good question," admits the teacher, "I remember when I was a little boy de same thing recurred to me. An' ol' Mr. Dubois, he was a wonderful preacher at New Hope Chapel over in East Gretna, he said: 'De answer is dat de Book ain't got time to go into all de details.' And he was right. You know, sometimes I think de Lawd expects us to figure out a few things for ourselves. We know that at one time dey wasn't anything except Heaven, we don't know just where it was but we know it was dere. Maybe it was everywhere. Den one day de Lawd got de idea He'd like to make some places. He made de sun, de moon and de stars. An' He made de earth."

Of course there was nobody around then, nobody but angels. And all the angels did, so far as Mr. Deshee knows, was to fly around and have a good time. Of course they had picnics. And fish fries. With boiled custard and ten cent seegars for the adults. Probably had a fish fry every week. Must have had a Sunday school, too, for the cherubs.

What did God look like?

"Well, nobody knows exactly what God looked like," admits Mr. Deshee, reluctantly. "But when I was a little boy I used to imagine dat He looked like de Reverend Dubois. He was de fines' lookin' ol' man I ever knew. Yet, I used to bet de Lawd looked exactly like Mr. Dubois in de days when He walked de earth in de shape of a natchel man."

Now it is time for the class to go home to dinner. But before they go they must review the main facts of the first lesson.

"What's de name of de book?"

"Genesis."

"Dat's right. And what's de other name?"

"First Book of Moses."

"Dat's right. And dis yere's Chapter One. (*The lights begin to dim.*) 'In de beginnin' God created de heaven and de earth. And de earth was widout form an' void. An' de darkness was upon de face of de deep.' "

SCENE II

Through the darkness come the voices of a choir singing "Rise, Shine, Give God the Glory."

When the lights are bright again the choir is seen to be a mixed company of angels. "That is, they are angels in that they wear brightly colored robes and have wings protruding from their backs. Otherwise they look and act like a company of happy Negroes at a fish fry. The scene itself is a pre-Creation Heaven with compromises. In the distance is an unbroken stretch of blue sky. Companionable varicolored clouds billow down to the floor of the stage and roll overhead to the branches of a live oak tree which is up left. The tree is leafy and dripping with Spanish moss, and with the clouds makes a frame for the scene. In the cool shade of the tree are the usual appurtenances of a fish fry; a large kettle of hot fat set on two small parallel logs, with a fire going underneath, and a large rustic table formed by driving four stakes into the ground and placing planks on top of the small connecting boards. On the table are piles of biscuits and corn bread and the cooked fish in dish pans. There are one or two fairly large cedar or crock 'churns,' containing boiled custard, which looks like milk. There is a gourd dipper beside the churns and several glasses and cups of various sizes and shapes from which the custard is drunk."

Those angels directly in charge of the fish fry are variously employed. Mammy Angels are ladling out the custard and fixing bread and fish for the cherubs; men angels are cutting fish and passing the pieces to the cooks. One Mammy Angel is occupied trying to extract a fish bone from one small cherub's throat by slapping her smartly on the back.

Some of the Mammy Angels wear their hats. Some of the men smoke cigars with evident satisfaction. There is much pleasant gossip and a general tendency to smile and count the occasion as altogether perfect. Even little bursts of temper are accepted pleasantly and laughed away an instant later. It is to be noted, however, that the arguments have an earthy tang. The men find it quite as difficult to impress the women in Heaven as elsewhere.

"You cain't tell dem nothin'," complains one who has tried. "Does you try to 'splain some simple fac' dey git man-deaf."

Experiences with the more playful cherubs are also familiar. "You fly down yere," excitedly calls one mammy to her adventuring offspring in a tree. "You wanter be put down in de sin book? . . . You want me to fly up dere and slap you down? Now, I tol' you!"

"Dat baby must got imp blood in him, he's so vexin'," she concludes.

There is some general discussion as to the probable whereabouts of Satan since the Lord put him out. If there is no other place but just Heaven, naturally Satan must be somewhere about, but as none of the travelers has seen him, it is reasonably concluded that the Lord has made a special place for Satan. It ain't much of nobody's business where.

"You bettah let de Lawd keep His own secrets, Lily," advises one stout angel. "De way things is goin' now dey ain't been no sinnin' since dey gave dat scamp a kick in de pants. Nowadays Heaven's free of sin an' if a lady wants a little constitutional she can fly 'til she wing-weary widout gettin' insulted."

An Archangel arrives with Sunday school cards for the cherubs and the choir softly sings "When de Saints Come Marchin' In," during their distribution.

Now there is some little flutter stirred by the appearance of the Angel Gabriel. "He is bigger and more elaborately winged than even the Archangel, but he is also much younger and beardless. His costume is less conventional than that of the other men angels, resembling more the Gabriel of the Doré drawings . . . In a moment the heavenly company is all attention.

"Gangway!" calls Gabriel, impressively lifting his hand. "Gangway for de Lawd God Jehovah!"

There is a reverent hush and God enters. He is the tallest and biggest of them all. He wears a white shirt with a white bow tie, a long Prince Albert coat of black alpaca, black trousers and congress gaiters. He speaks in a rich bass voice.

"Is you been baptized?" the Lord demands.

"Certainly, Lawd!" the angels chant, in reply.

"Is you been baptized?"

"Certainly, Lawd!"

"Is you been baptized?"

"Certainly, Lawd. Certainly, certainly, certainly, Lawd!"

Two verses of the spiritual are sung and as the second is finished all heads are reverently bowed. For a moment God looks upon them and then solemnly raises His hand.

"Let de fish fry proceed," He says.

As the activities of the celebration are resumed, several of the children gather about the Lord as He talks with the Archangel.

They are hanging to His coat tails, some of them, but He doesn't object—not even to Herman, who is inclined to play a little rough. He just picks Herman up good-naturedly and gives him a couple of good spanks.

They offer God a fish sandwich, which He politely refuses. He will try the b'iled custard, however. And He is pleased to accept a ten-cent seegar to smoke later. He also seems pleased to hear them declare that the fish fry is goin' "fine and dandy," and that they have been "marchin' and singin' de whole mo'nin'."

"I heerd you," the Lord admits, and they are much gratified. "You gittin' better all de time. You gettin' as good as de one at de throne. Why don' you give us one dem ol' time jump-ups?"

"Anythin' you say, Lawd."

They sing "So High You Can't Get over It." He likes that one.

But when the Lord sips the custard a look of displeasure comes on His face. He takes another sip. It is no better.

Gabriel—What's de matter, Lawd?

God (*sipping again*)—I ain't jest sure, yit. Dey's something 'bout dis custahd. (*Takes another sip.*)

Custard Maker—Ain't it all right, Lawd?

God—It don't seem seasoned jest right. You make it?

Custard Maker—Yes, Lawd. I put everythin' in it like I allus do. It's supposed to be perfec'.

God—Yeah. I kin taste de eggs and de cream and de sugar. (*Suddenly.*) I know what it is. It needs jest a little bit mo' firmament.

Custard Maker—Dey's firmament in it, Lawd.

God—Maybe, but it ain' enough.

Custard Maker—It's all we had, Lawd. Dey ain't a drap in de jug.

God—Dat's all right. I'll jest r'ar back and pass a miracle. (*Choir stops singing.*) Let it be some firmament! An' when I say let it be some firmament, I don't want, just a little bitty dab o' firmament caize I'm sick an' tired of runnin' out of it when we need it. Let it be a whole mess of firmament! (*The stage has become misty until* God *and the heavenly company are obscured. As He finishes the speech there is a burst of thunder. As the stage grows darker.*) Dat's de way I like it. (*Murmurs from the others: "Dat's a lot of firmament." "My, dat is firmament." "Look to me like he's created rain," etc.*)

First Mammy Angel (*when the stage is dark*)—Now, look,

Lawd, dat's too much firmament. De Cherubs' is gettin' all wet.

SECOND MAMMY ANGEL—Look at my Carlotta, Lawd. She's soaked to de skin. Dat's *plenty* too much firmament.

GOD—Well, co'se we don' want de chillun to ketch cold. Can't you dreen it off?

GABRIEL—Dey's no place to dreen it, Lawd.

FIRST MAMMY ANGEL—Why don't we jest take the babies home, Lawd?

GOD—No, I don' wanta bust up de fish fry. You angels keep quiet and I'll pass another miracle. Dat's always de trouble wid miracles. When you pass one you always gotta r'ar back and pass another. (*There is a hush.*) Let dere be a place to dreen off dis firmament. Let dere be mountains and valleys and let dere be oceans an' lakes. An' let dere be rivers and bayous to dreen it off in, too. As a matter o' fac', let dere be de earth. An' when dat's done let dere be de sun, an' let it come out and dry my Cherubs' wings. (*The lights go up until the stage is bathed in sunlight. On the embankment upstage there is now a waist-high wrought iron railing, such as one sees on the galleries of houses in the French quarter of New Orleans. The Cherubs are being examined by their parents, and there is an ad lib. murmur of "You all right, honey?" "You feel better now, Albert?" "You all dry, Vangy?" until the* ARCHANGEL, *who has been gazing in awe at the railing, drowns them out.*)

ARCHANGEL—Look yere! (*There is a rush to the embankment, accompanied by exclamations, "My goodness!" "What's dis?" "I declah!" etc.* GABRIEL *towers above the group on the middle of the embankment.* GOD *is wrapped in thought, facing the audience. The choir resumes singing "So High You Can't Get over It" softly. The babbling at the balustrade dies away as the people lean over the railing.* GABRIEL *turns and faces* GOD *indicating the earth below the railing with his left hand.*)

GABRIEL—Do you see it, Lawd?

GOD (*quietly, without turning his head upstage*)—Yes, Gabriel.

GABRIEL—Looks mighty nice, Lawd.

GOD—Yes. (GABRIEL *turns and looks over the railing.*)

GABRIEL (*gazing down*)—Yes, suh. Dat'd make mighty nice farming country. Jest look at dat South forty over dere. You ain't goin' to let dat go to waste, is you, Lawd? Dat would be a pity and a shame.

GOD (*not turning*)—It's good earth. (GOD *turns, room is made for Him beside* GABRIEL *on the embankment.*) Yes. I ought to have somebody to enjoy it.

Suddenly God makes a decision. He will go down to the earth. Gabriel can be His working boss while He is away. Gabriel can fix up that matter of the two stars, and that other matter of the sparrow that fell.

"I'll be back Saddy," promises the Lord, as He turns and quiets the choir. "I'm gonter pass one more miracle. You all gonter help me an' not make a soun' caize it's one of the most impo'tant miracles of all."

He turns and faces the sky, raising His arms above His head. "Let dere be man!" He calls.

There is a roll of thunder. The scene grows dark. The choir breaks exultantly into "Hallelujah!" They are still singing when the lights reveal

SCENE III

Here is a "heterogeneous cluster of cottonwood, camphor, live oak and sycamore trees, youpon and turkey berry bushes, with their purple and red berries, sprays of fern-like indigo fiera and splashes of various Louisiana flowers. In the middle of the stage, disclosed when the mistiness at rise grows into warm sunlight, stands Adam. He is a puzzled man of 30, of medium height, dressed in the clothing of the average field hand. He is bareheaded. In the distance can be heard the choir continuing 'Bright Mansions Above.' "

A bird sings and Adam is pleased. Slowly, as he awakens to life, Adam senses his strength. The muscles of his arms are pleasing to him. He glances down at his feet, firmly planted on the ground and lifts and stamps them in joy. Then God enters.

"Good mo'nin', son," calls God.

"Good mo'nin', Lawd," answers Adam, a little awed.

"What's yo' name, son?"

"Adam."

"Adam which?"

"Jest Adam, Lawd."

Everything is going fine with Adam. Of course, he points out, the work is new, but as soon as he learns the ropes—

Still there is one thing wrong. Both the Lord and Adam admit as much. Adam can't be quite right, thinks God, until he has a family. Because, in his heart, Adam is a family man.

Adam, to tell the truth, hadn't thought much about a family, because he didn't know what a family was. But now the Lord is going to pass another miracle and show him.

Again there is darkness, and out of the darkness the Lord calls

Eve. When the lights go up the first woman is standing beside the first man.

"She is about twenty-six and quite pretty. She is dressed like a country girl. Her gingham dress is quite new and clean. God is now at the other side of the stage, looking at them critically. Eve looks at Adam in timid wonder and slowly turns her head until she meets the glance of God. Adam stands beside Eve. They gaze at each other for a moment. God smiles."

"Now I'll tell you what I gonter do," He says to them, "I'm gonter put you in charge here. I'm gonter give you de run of dis whole garden. Eve, you take care of dis man, an', Adam, you take care of dis woman. You belong to each other. I don' want you to try to do too much caize yo' both kind of an experiment wid me an' I ain't sho' whether you could make it. You two jest enjoy yo'self. Drink de water from de little brooks an' de wine from de grapes an' de berries, an' eat de food dat's hangin' for you in de trees. (*He pauses, startled by a painful thought.*) Dat is, in all but one tree. (*He pauses. Then, not looking at them.*) You know what I mean, my children?"

"Yes, Lawd," they answer, but slowly they turn their heads in the direction of the forbidden tree. "Thank you, Lawd!"

"I gotter be gittin' along now. I got a hund'ed thousan' things to do 'fo' you take yo' nex' breath. Enjoy yo'selves—"

The Lord is gone. Adam and Eve stand looking after him. Suddenly they are conscious of their hands that seek each other in a lingering clasp. And then again they are conscious of the tree.

"Adam!"

It is Eve who calls. And again, as he answers, with a look almost of terror in his eyes:

"Adam!"

The light is fading. From afar the choir's voices swell into "Turn You Round."

It is dark, and from the darkness come the voices of Mr. Deshee and the children, back in the Sunday school.

"Now, I s'pose you chillun know what happened after God made Adam 'n' Eve? Do you?"

"Why, den dey ate de fo'bidden fruit and den dey got driv out de garden."

"An' den what happened?"

"Den dey felt ver bad."

"I don' mean how dey feel, I mean how dey do. Do dey have any chillun or anything like dat?"

So the matter of Cain and Abel is settled. Probably they weren't born until a long time after Adam and Eve settled in the garden, the children agree. But one thing everybody knows, and that is "dis boy Cain was a mean rascal." The lights fade.

SCENE IV

By the side of a road "Cain, a husky young Negro, stands over the body of the dead Abel." There is a rock in his hand.

God finds them thus and is displeased. Cain has his defense. He was working in the field, he says, and minding his own business, and Abel was sitting in the shade and insulting him.

"Me, I'd be skeered to git out in dis hot sun," Abel had said, tauntingly; "I be 'fraid my brains git cooked. Co'se you ain't got no brains so you ain' in no danger."

At that Cain had "flang" the rock, and was willing to take what came.

What Cain has done is to commit a crime, the Lord tells him; a crime for which he will be dragging a ball and chain all the rest of his life. The best thing he can do now is to get out of the county. He had better go, advises the Lord, and find himself a wife and raise himself a family. Nothin' can make a man forget his troubles like raising a family.

Cain starts walking. The choir is singing "Run, Sinner, Run" as the lights go down.

SCENE V

Cain walks and walks, passing considerable scenery on the way, until finally he comes to a fence. Above the fence there is a tree and on the tree a sign reading: "Nod Parish. County Line."

Cain would rest under that tree. He feels as though he had been walking fully forty years. But he is not permitted to rest long. From out the branches of another tree near by comes a voice, the voice of a girl.

"Hello, Country Boy!" she calls.

"Hey-ho, Good lookin'!" Cain calls back. "Which way is it to town?"

That is the way it starts, and before Cain hardly knows it, the girl is sitting beside him. "She is as large as Cain, wickedly pretty, and somewhat flashily dressed."

"I bet you kin handle a gal mean wid dem big, stout arms of your'n," she ventures. "I sho' would hate to get you mad at me, Country Boy."

"Come yere," smiles back Cain. "Don't be 'fraid. I ain' so mean."

They grow confidential and discover much in common. Cain thinks he may ask the girl's folks if they wouldn't like to take in a boarder. And the girl thinks that would be great.

"I guess—I guess if you wanted to kiss me an' I tried to stop you, you could pretty near crush me wit' dem stout arms," she suggests.

"You wouldn't try too much, would you?" he counters.

"Maybe, for a little while." But she isn't at all sure.

The choir is singing "You Better Mind" as Cain and Cain's girl start walking toward the town.

The Lord appears at the end of the road and watches after them as they disappear.

"Bad business," says He, shaking His head. "I don' like de way things is goin' *a*tall."

The lights fade.

SCENE VI

In God's private office in heaven a large window at back looks out upon a vast blue sky. God's desk is a battered roll-top, with an old, leather-seated swivel-chair in front of it. There are writing materials on the desk, a cuspidor and a waste basket alongside. There are law books on the shelf above the desk, a calendar on the wall, and Gabriel's trumpet hangs on the hat rack.

"The general atmosphere is that of the office of a Negro lawyer in a Louisiana town. As the lights go up God takes a fresh cigar from a box on the desk and begins puffing it without bothering to light it. There is no comment on this minor miracle from Gabriel, who is sitting in one of the chairs with a pencil and several papers in his hand."

God and Gabriel have just finished most of the important business. There is still the minor matter of a Cherub over at Archangel Montgomery's house—"dat little two story gold house, over by de pearly gates"—to be attended to. "Wings is moltin' out of season." Gabriel will attend to that.

Gabriel would also like to get in a little secret practice on his trumpet, which he takes caressingly from the hat rack. But the Lord, without even turning around, warns him to be careful.

There is the matter of a complaint from the moon people. The moon's beginning to melt a little from the heat of the sun. But the Lord knows about that. The heat is caused by those angels that have got in the habit of flyin' over to the moon for the Saddy night dances. They beat their wings when they dance and that causes the heat. Let it be known that dancing around the moon after this will be considered sinnin', suggests the Lord. That'll cool off the moon.

There have also been a good many prayers from mankind down on the earth lately. That worries the Lord a little. He isn't any too well pleased with that earth job. What He saw the last visit He made down there three or four hundred years ago didn't please Him at all.

He thinks perhaps He had better go down again. He needs a little holiday.

"I'll go down an' walk de earth ag'in an' see how dem poor humans is makin' out," He decides finally. "I'll be back Saddy."

The lights fade.

SCENE VII

The choir is singing "Dere's No Hidin' Place" when the lights go up. God is trudging along a country road, pleased with the scene and the sound of church bells that comes over the fields.

But now He has met Zeba, sitting on a stump strumming a ukulele and singing a blues song. That doesn't please Him so well. "Zeba is a rouged and extremely flashily dressed chippy of about eighteen."

She laughs at the Lord when He tells her the song she sings is not fit for the Sabbath. She laughs because there ain't no Lord's day no more.

"People jest use Sunday now to git over Saddy," laughs Zeba.

"You a awful sassy little girl," declares the Lord.

"I come fum sassy people! We even speak mean of de dead!" impertinently answers Zeba.

God is impelled to speak sharply to Zeba. Then she admits that she is the great-great-gran' daughter of Seth. Also, she may be on the road to hell, as the preacher says, but she thinks she's on the road to the picnic grounds to meet her sweet papa.

Soon the sweety has appeared. He is Cain the Sixth, and tough. Cain isn't interested in anybody at the moment except his baby, her ukulele and the song she is singing sitting on his lap.

They can't see God by the time the song is finished. They're too occupied with their own business. There are rumors, Cain allows, that Zeba has been foolin' around with some of those creeper men. He just wants her to know that he carries a guarantee that she's his gal and his only. The guarantee is a revolver.

"Bad business!" echoes God, as He resumes His walk. Zeba and Cain continue on to the picnic grounds.

Now God is alone on the road again. The birds are singing and from a clump of bushes a patch of "black-eyed Susans" (pickaninnies ranging in age from 3 to 5) look smilingly out at Him.

"How you flowers makin' out?" God calls.

"We O.K., Lawd."

"Yes, an' you look very pretty."

"Thank you, Lawd."

"It's only de human bein's make me down-hearted," muses God as He continues His walk. "Yere's as nice a Sunday as dey is turnin' out anywhere, an' nobody makin' de right use of it."

Now He is cheered by the sight of a group of boys in a circle and on their knees. Prayin' probably! Why not in a church? But as God approaches the kneeling group a boy, "his head bent, swings his hands rhythmically up to his head three or four times. There is a hush."

"Oh, Lawd, de smoke-house is empty," shouts the boy. "Oh, Lawd, lemme git dem groceries. Oh, Lawd, lemme see dat little six!" He casts the dice. "Wham! Dere she is, frien's!"

"Gamblin'!" ejaculates the Lord, disgustedly. "An' wid frozen dice!"

The gamblers are too intent upon their game to notice Him. One does look up to greet Him, impudently, as "Ole Liver Lips." He ignores the crowd, but He is interested in the youngest boy. A little boy gamblin' and sinnin'! And chewin' tobacco like he was his daddy! He oughta be 'shamed. And all those gamblers oughta be 'shamed leadin' him to sin.

"He de best crap shooter in town, mister," one of the gamblers reports.

"I'm gonter tell his mammy," announces God. "I bet she don' know 'bout dis."

"No, she don' know," they laugh. "She don' know anythin'."

"If you fin' my mammy you do mo'n I kin," insists the boy.

Down the road apiece God comes upon the cabin where the boy lives. A voice inside refuses to open the door without a search warrant. The gamblin' boy? His mother done elope with a railroad man. His father is dead drunk under the table. Everybody that was at the party the night before is drunk. And the owner of the voice would be if the new white mule he'd made hadn't burned his throat so he had to stop drinkin'.

God sadly resumes his walk, talking to Himself as He goes along.

GOD—Dis ain't gittin' me nowheres. All I gotta say dis yere mankind I been peoplin' my earth wid sho' ain't much. (*He stops and looks back.*) I got a good min' to wipe 'em all off and people de earth wid angels. No. Angels is all right, singin' an' playin' and flyin' around, but dey ain' much on workin' de crops an' buildin' de levees. No, suh, mankind's jest right for my earth, if he wasn't so doggone sinful. I'd rather have my earth peopled wit' a bunch of channel catfish, dan I would mankin' an' his sin. I jest cain't stan' sin. (*He is about to resume His walk when* NOAH *enters.* NOAH *is dressed like a country preacher. His coat is of the "hammer-tail" variety. He carries a prayer book under his arm.*)

NOAH—Mo'nin', brother.

GOD—Mo'nin', brother. I declare you look like a good man.

NOAH—I try to be, brother. I'm de preacher yere. I don't think I seen yo' to de meetin'. (*They resume walking.*)

GOD—I jest came to town a little while ago an' I been pretty busy.

NOAH—Yeh, mos' everybody say dey's pretty busy dese days. Dey so busy dey cain't come to meetin'. It seem like de mo' I preaches de mo' people ain't got time to come to church. I ain't hardly got enough members to fill up de choir. I gotta do de preachin' and de bassin', too.

GOD—Is dat a fac'?

NOAH—Yes, suh, brother. Everybody is mighty busy, gamblin', good-timin', and goin' on. You jest wait, though. When Gabriel blow de horn you gonter fin' they got plenty of time to punch chucks down in Hell. Yes, suh.

GOD—Seems a pity. Dey all perfec'ly healthy?

NOAH—Oh, dey healthy, all right. Dey jest all lazy, and mean, an' full of sin. You look like a preacher, too, brother.

GOD—Well, I am, in a way.

NOAH—You jest passin' through de neighborhood?

GOD—Yes. I wanted to see how things was goin' in yo' part of de country, an' I been feelin' jest about de way you do. It's enough to discourage you.

NOAH—Yeh, but I gotta keep wres'lin' wid 'em. Where you boun' for right now, brother?

GOD—I was jest walkin' along. I thought I might stroll on to de nex' town.

NOAH—Well, dat's a pretty good distance. I live right yere. (*He stops walking.*) Why don' you stop an' give us de pleasure of yo' comp'ny fo' dinner? I believe my ol' woman has kilt a chicken.

God—Why, dat's mighty nice of yo', brother. I don't believe I caught yo' name.

Noah—Noah, jest brother Noah. Dis is my home, brother. Come right in. (God *and* Noah *start walking towards* Noah's *house which is just coming into view on the treadmill.*)

(*The stage darkens, the choir sings "Feastin' Table."*)

SCENE VIII

God and Noah are in the combination living and dining room of Noah's house. It is a clean and cheerful room, with a checked tablecloth on the table. Mrs. Noah, "an elderly Negress simply and neatly dressed," finds them there.

Mrs. Noah is glad to have another preacher stop for dinner and everything's about ready. The chicken's in the pot. Won't be five minutes. She'll call Shem, Ham and Japheth.

"Dey's our sons," Mrs. Noah explains. "Dey live right acrost de way, but always have Sunday dinner wid us."

God is much pleased with Mrs. Noah. Likes Noah's home, too. In fact, He grows quite expansive about it, and gives Noah one of His ten-cent seegars. Then they settle back to a serious talk.

God—Jest what seems to be de main trouble 'mong mankind, Noah?

Noah—Well, it seems to me de main trouble is dat the whole district is wide open. Now you know dat makes fo' loose livin'. Men-folks spen's all dere time fightin', loafin', and gamblin', and makin' bad liquor.

God—What about de women?

Noah—De women is worse dan de men. If dey ain't makin' love powder dey out beg, borrow and stealin' money for policy tickets. Doggone, I come in de church Sunday 'fo' las' 'bout an hour befo' de meetin' was to start, and dere was a woman stealin' de altar cloth. She was goin' to hock it. Dey ain't got no moral sense. Now you take dat case las' month, over in East Putney. Case of dat young Willy Roback.

God—What about him?

Noah—Dere is a boy sebenteen years old. Doggone, if he didn't *e*lope with his aunt. Now, you know, dat kin' of goin' on is bad fo' a neighborhood.

God—Terrible, terrible.

Noah—Yes, suh. Dis use' to be a nice, decent community. I been doin' my best to preach de Word, but seems like every time

I preach de place jest goes a little more to de dogs. De good Lawd only knows what's gonter happen.

GOD—Dat is de truth.

Suddenly Noah has a twitch in his knee. Thinks it may be his buck-aguer. And it might be a sign of rain.

That, allows God, is exactly what it is. Such a rain as they never have seen before in those parts.

"What would you say was it to rain for forty days and forty nights?" asks God.

"I'd say dat was a *complete* rain," admits Noah.

"Noah, you don' know who I is, do you?"

"Yo' face looks easy," Noah admits, "but I don't think I recall de name."

Then, as God slowly rises and reaches his full height, "there is a crash of lightning, a moment's darkness and a roll of thunder."

When the lights go up Noah is kneeling before the Lord.

"I should have known you," the old man confesses, "I should have seen de glory . . . I'm jes' ol' preacher Noah, Lawd, an' I'm yo' servant. I ain' very much but I'se all I got."

The Lord's plans for the flood are complete. Of all the human beings in the world only Noah and his family are to be saved.

"I ain't gonter destroy you, Noah," says God. "You and yo' fam'ly, yo' sheep an' cattle, and all de udder things dat ain't human I'm gonter preserve. But de rest is gotta go. (*Takes a pencil and a sheet of paper from His pocket.*) Look yere, Noah. (NOAH *comes over and looks over His shoulder.*) I want you to build me a boat. I want to call it de 'Ark' and I want it to look like dis. (*He is drawing on the paper. Continues to write as He speaks.*) I want you to take two of every kind of animal and bird dat's in de country. I want you to take seeds and sprouts and everything like dat and put dem on dat Ark, because dere is gonter be all dat rain. Dey's gonter be a deluge, Noah, and dey's gonter be a flood. De levees is gonter bust and everything dat's fastened down is comin' loose, but it ain't gonter float long, caize I'm gonter make a storm dat'll sink everything from a hencoop to a barn. Dey ain't a ship on de sea dat'll be able to fight dat tempest. Dey all got to go. Everythin'. Everythin' in dis pretty world I made, except one thing, Noah. You an' yo' family and de things I said are gonter ride dat storm in de Ark. Yere's de way it's to be."

Noah is a little puzzled about the animals. Two of every kind means a lot of animals. Especially two of every kind of snakes.

And if he is going to take all kinds of snakes Noah thinks he had better take along a "kag of likker," too. God agrees to the kag. Noah thinks perhaps he had better take two kags, to be on the safe side. He could put one on each side of the Ark to balance it. But God is firm about the one kag. Let Noah take one kag and put it in the middle of the ship.

Mrs. Noah has brought in the dinner. The choir is singing "I Want to be Ready." There is a distant peal of thunder as Noah and God draw their chairs up to the table.

SCENE IX

Noah, Shem, Ham and Japheth are building the Ark. On the hillside below them a group of curious townspeople are amusedly watching. Noah has found himself a boat captain's uniform, a silk hat and a slicker. He is doing most of the ordering but practically none of the building.

The crowd, particularly the women, are inclined to joke Noah about his ark. A lot of people are thinking him crazy. But Noah pays little attention to them. He is building an ark and he hasn't any time to waste.

It is about time, too, for the animals to be arriving. Perhaps Ham had better go down to the foot of the hill and wait for them and bring them up as soon as they get there.

Zeba, the wicked one, has joined the group with a new boy friend—one Flatfoot, big and black and ugly. Flatfoot is sure Noah's crazy. Sane folks build boats down where the water is. They don't expect the water to come up to the boat, like Noah says it's going to.

Now Cain the Sixth, and the gambling boys, have also joined the crowd. They are in great good spirits. But Zeba senses trouble when her eye catches the look in Cain's eyes. Quickly she warns Flatfoot that Cain is carrying a gun. Cain denies the charge. Lets her search him to see. He hasn't brought a gun for Flatfoot, he announces, throwing his arms around that surprised young man. Not a gun—just a little knife, which he sinks into the small of Flatfoot's back.

"It's all right, folks," calls Cain the Sixth, as he tosses the knife away and puts out his arms for Zeba. "I jest had to do a little cleanin' up."

Flatfoot's body lies where it fell. There's no use burying it, the crowd is agreed. Nobody ever comes up there. Flatfoot wasn't any good, anyway.

Now there is a spatter of rain. It's no surprise to Noah. Rain is what he expected. But he thinks those po' chillun standing out there laughing at him had better be praying.

The crowd is convinced there may be a shower. It begins to disintegrate. Down below the hill the animals have arrived. Ham reports that he is ready to herd them into the ark as soon as the gangplank is in place.

"God's give us His sign," shouts Noah, as the rain grows heavier. "Send 'em up de gangplank . . . De Lord is strikin' down de worl'!"

Ham cracks his whip. The heads of two elephants, their trunks flapping against the branches of the trees, appear at the end of the gangplank. The choir is singing "Dey Ol' Ark's a-Movering." The rain increases. Darkness falls. There is the swish of water as the choir continues singing.

SCENE X

The Ark is at sea. Rows of stationary waves prove it. All about, save around the Ark, there is darkness. Only Shem, smoking his pipe on deck, is on watch.

A steamship whistle blows. The blast startles Shem. Not until Ham appears and explains that the whistling is being done by Daddy, and that Daddy has been getting a heap of comfort out of the kag of likker, which is pretty nearly almos' gone, is Shem satisfied.

"How long you think dis trip's gonter las'?" he wants to know.

"I don' know," answers Ham. "Rain fo'ty days 'n' fo'ty nights and when dat stop' I thought sho' we'd come up ag'inst a san' bar or somethin'. Looks now like all dat rain was jest a little incident of the trip. (*The whistle blows again.*) Doggone! I wish he wouldn't do dat. Fust thing we know he'll wake up dem animals again."

Japheth brings the latest news from Noah. The old man says he has had a dream. He thinks they're nearly somewhere. But nobody can see any hope in that. Mrs. Noah is quite out of patience with Noah.

"You boys go stop yo' paw pullin' dat cord," she orders. "He so full of likker he think he's in a race."

"He claim he know what he's doin'."

"I claim he's gettin' to be a perfec' nuisance," insists Mrs. Noah. Nor is she any gentler with Noah when he comes on deck, his high hat at a rakish tilt. But Noah finally asserts himself.

o, suh. Man is a kind of pet of mine an' it ive up tryin' to do somethin' wid him. Dog- e all right at de core or else why did I ever e firs' place? (*Sits at desk.*) t dat I hates to see yo' worryin' about it,

e ain' anythin' worth while anywheres dat ody some worryin'. I ain' never tol' you de in' things started up yere. Dat's a story in e more I keep on bein' de Lawd de more I know rovin' things. And dat takes time and worry. wid mankin' is he takes up so much of my time. ble to help hisself a little. (*He stops suddenly* Hey, dere! I think I got it!

erly)—What's de news?

itating)—Yes, suh, dat seems an awful good idea. ll me, Lawd.

l, have you noticed dat every now and den, man- some pretty good specimens?

Dat's de truth.

suh. Dey's old Abraham an' Isaac an' Jacob an' all

Dat's so, Lawd.

every one of dem boys was a hard wukker an' a good got to admit dat.

—Dey wouldn' be up yere flyin' wid us if dey hadn'

o, suh. An' I don' know but what de answer to de ble is right dere.

—How do you mean, Lawd?

Why, doggone it, de good man is de man what keeps busy. been goin' along on de principle dat he was somethin' angels—dat you ought to be able to give him somethin' jest let him sit back an' enjoy it. Dat ain't so. Now collec' I put de first one down dere to take keer o' dat nd den I let him go ahead an' do nothin' but git into mis- (*He rises.*) Sure, *dat's* it. He ain't *built* jest to fool and not do nothin'. Gabe, I'm gonter try a new scheme.

RIEL (*eagerly*)—What's de scheme, Lawd?

—I'll tell you later. Send in Abraham, Isaac and Jacob. *ice outside calls: "Right away, Lawd."*) You go tell dem t dem bolts back in de boxes. I ain't gonter use dem ag'in ile.

"Look yere," he demands, "who's de pilot o' dis vessel?"

"Ol' Mister Dumb Luck," ventures Mrs. Noah.

"Well, see dat's where you don't know anythin'."

"I suppose you ain't drunk as a fool?"

"I feel congenial," admits Noah, cordially.

Furthermore he is quite satisfied that the Lord knows who's running the boat and how.

Noah thinks it is time to send off another dove, and Shem brings one up from the hold. Ham throws out the sounding line. There's only about an inch of water!

It is also getting light in the east. Far off a choir is singing "My Soul Is a Witness for the Lord."

"An' de boat's stopped," shouts Noah. "We've landed! Shem, go down an' drag de fires and dreen de boiler. Yo' go help him, Ham!"

Now the dove is back with an olive branch in its mouth. Noah sends her down below to tell the other animals. There is much excitement and good feeling. Even Mrs. Noah is contrite.

"It was jest gettin' to be so tiresome. I'm sorry, Noah," she pleads.

"Dat's all right, old woman." Noah understands.

The water has disappeared. The Ark is again on the hillside. In the distance mountains have appeared out of the haze. The singing grows louder as a rainbow appears over the Ark.

Old Noah stands at the rail slowly taking in the glory of the change. "Thank you, Lawd!" he mutters. "Thank you very much indeed. Amen."

Even as he speaks God appears beside him. He has come to congratulate Noah on the way the ship has been handled. He didn't mind the cussin' and the drinkin'—much.

"I figure a steamboat cap'n on a long trip like you had has a right to a little redeye, jest so he don't go crazy," says the Lord.

"Thank you, Lawd. What's de orders now?"

God—All de animals safe?

Noah—Dey all fin' an' dandy, Lawd.

God—Den I want you to open dat starboard door, an' leave 'em all out. Let 'em go down de hill. Den you and de family take all de seeds 'n' de sprouts an' begin plantin' ag'in. I'm startin' all over, Noah. (Noah *exits.* God *looks around.*)

God—Well, now we'll see what happens. (God *listens with a smile, as noises accompanying the debarking of the animals are heard. There are the cracks of whips, the voices of the men on the Ark, shouting: "Git along dere." "Whoa, take it easy." "Duck yo' head." "Keep in line dere," etc. Over the Ark there is a burst of centrifugal shadows, and the sound of a myraid of wings.* God *smiles at the shadows.*) Dat's right, birds, fin' yo' new homes. (*Bird twitters are heard again.* God *listens a moment and rests an arm on the railing. He speaks softly.*) Gabriel, can you spare a minute? (Gabriel *appears.*)

Gabriel—Yes, Lawd? (*The sounds from the other side of the Ark are by now almost hushed. The Lord indicates the new world with a wave of the hand.*)

God—Well, it's did.

Gabriel (*respectfully, but with no enthusiasm*)—So I take notice.

God—Yes, suh, startin' all over ag'in.

Gabriel—So I see.

God (*looking at him suddenly*)—Don' seem to set you up much.

Gabriel—Well, Lawd, you see— (*He hesitates.*) 'Tain't none of my business.

God—What?

Gabriel—I say, I don' know very much about it.

God—I know you don'. I jest wanted you to see it. (*A thought strikes Him.*) Co'se, it ain' yo' business, Gabe. It's my business. 'Twas my idea. De whole thing was my idea. An' every bit of it's my business 'n' nobody else's. De whole thing rests on my shoulders. I declare, I guess *dat's* why I feel so solemn and serious, at dis particklar time. You know *dis* thing's turned into quite a proposition.

Gabriel (*tenderly*)—But, it's all right, Lawd, as you say, it's did.

God—Yes, suh, it's did. (*Sighs deeply. Looks slowly to the right and the left. Then softly.*) I only hope it's goin' to work out all right.

(*The curtain falls.*)

PART TWO

Two cleaning women are straightening up God's office and gossiping as they work. Outside there is the whirr and distant boom of an explosion that breaks in upon the singing of a choir engaged somewhere with the rendering of "A City Called Heaven."

The booming is a long way off, but it means trouble for some-

If Gabriel happens to be passing the Big Pit, the Lord suggests, he might just lean over the brink and tell Satan he's just a plain fool if he thinks he can beat anybody as big as God.

Gabriel will take pleasure in delivering God's message and he thinks that he will also take advantage of the occasion to spit right in Satan's eye.

The Lord has just time for a little miracle while He is waiting for Abraham, Isaac and Jacob. He finds the new polish on the sun has made it a little too hot and He cools it off.

"Men," says God when Abraham, Isaac and Jacob are comfortably seated in the office, "I'm goin' to talk about a little scheme I got. It's one dat's goin' to affec' yo' fam'lies and dat's why I 'cided I'd talk it over wid you, fo' it goes into ee-fect. I don' know whether you boys know it or not, but you is about de three bes' men of one fam'ly dat's come up yere since I made little apples. Now I tell you what I'm gonter do. Seein' dat yo' human bein's cain't 'preciate anythin' lessen you fust wukk to git it and den keep strugglin' to hold it, why I'm gonter turn over a very valuable piece of property to yo' family and den see what dey kin do with it. De rest of de worl' kin go jump in de river fo' all I keer. I'm gonter be lookin' out fo' yo' descendants only. Now den, seein' dat you boys know de country pretty tho'ly, where at does yo' think is de choice piece of property in de whole worl'? Think it over a minute. I'm gonter let you make de s'lection."

ABRAHAM—If you was to ask me, Lawd, I don' think dey come any better dan de Land of Canaan.

GOD (*to* ISAAC *and* JACOB)—What's yo' feelin' in de matter?

JACOB (*after a nod from* ISAAC)—Pappy an' me think do we get a pick, dat would be it.

GOD (*goes to window again; looks out*)—De Land of Canaan. Yes, I guess dat's a likely neighborhood. It's all run over wid Philistines and things right now, but we kin clean dat up. (*He turns from the window and resumes His seat.*) All right. Now who do you boys think is de best of yo' men to put in charge down dere? Yo' see, I ain't been payin' much attention to anybody in pa'tic'lar lately.

ISAAC—Does yo' want de brainiest or de holiest, Lawd? (*Men look up.*)

GOD—I want de holiest. I'll make him brainy. (*Men appreciate the miracle.*)

ISAAC (*as* ABRAHAM *and* JACOB *nod to him*)—Well, if you want a Number One, goodness, Lawd, I don' know where you'll git more satisfaction dan in a great-great-great-great grandson of mine.

GOD—Where's he at?

ISAAC—At de moment I b'lieve he's in de sheep business over in Midian County. He got in a little trouble down in Egypt, but t'wan't his doin'. He killed a man dat was abusin' one of our boys in de brick works. Of co'se you know old King Pharaoh's got all our people in bondage.

GOD—I heard of it. (*With some ire.*) Who do you think put dem dere? (*The visitors lower their heads.*) It's all right, boys. (*All rise.*) I'm gonter take dem out of it. An' I'm gonter turn over de whole Land of Canaan to dem. An' do you know who's gonter lead dem dere? Yo' great-great-great-great grandson. Moses, ain't it?

ISAAC—Yes, Lawd.

GOD (*smiling*)—Yes. I been noticin' *him.*

ABRAHAM—It's quite a favor fo' de fam'ly, Lawd.

GOD—Dat's why I tol' yo! You see, it so happens I love yo' family, an' I delight to honor it. Dat's all, gen'lemen. (*The three others rise and cross to the door, murmuring, "Yes, Lawd," "Thank you, Lawd," "Much obliged, Lawd," etc. The choir begins "My Lord's A-writin' All de Time" pianissimo.* GOD *stands watching the men leave.*) Enjoy yo'selves. (*He goes to the window. The singing grows softer. He speaks through the window to the earth.*) I'm comin' down to see you, Moses, and dis time my scheme's *got* to wukk.

(*The stage is darkened. The singing grows louder and continues until the lights go up on the next scene.*)

SCENE II

At the mouth of a cave Moses is sitting on the grass eating the lunch Zipporah, his wife, has brought to him. "Moses is about forty, Zipporah somewhat younger."

They are both a little worried over the darkness that seems to have centered on the cave. Everywhere else the sun is shining, but it certainly looks like rain where they stand.

Zipporah thinks this may be God's way of warning Moses that there are 'Gyptians hanging around. It may be the new Pharaoh is mean enough to be sending soldiers even this far after Moses.

But Moses isn't worried. The Lord has taken care of him for many years and he has a feeling He isn't going to fail him now.

It is a confidence well bestowed. Zipporah is no sooner gone than God Himself appears out of the darkness. He is standing back of a turkey-berry bush and speaks to Moses. At first Moses only hears His voice, and thinks it is his brother, Aaron. But when God makes the bush to glow with a consuming fire that does not consume, he knows it is God.

The burning bush was just a trick, God explains. He is going to teach Moses much more wonderful tricks than that. And when He has made him the most wonderful tricker in all the world God is going to send Moses down into Egypt and lead his people out of bondage.

"Yo' people is my chillun, Moses," the Lord explains. "I'm sick an' tired of de way ol' King Pharaoh is treatin' dem, so I'se gonter take dem away, and yo' gonter lead dem. You gonter lead dem out of Egypt and across de river Jordan. It's gonter take a long time, and you ain't goin' on no excursion train. Yo' gonter wukk awful hard fo' somethin' yo' gonter fin' when de trip's over."

"What's dat, Lawd?"

"It's de Land of Canaan. It's de bes' land I got. I've promised it to yo' people, and I'm gonter give it to dem."

"Co'se ol' King Pharaoh will do everything he kin to stop it."

"Yes, and dat's where de tricks come in."

Moses would like to have Aaron go with him, if God is agreeable. God was going to suggest Aaron and now, as another little trick, He summons him and there is Aaron standing between them.

God begins the instructions about the tricks with a rod that looks just like a walking stick until He lays it on the ground. Then—

The lights fade. Somewhere the choir is singing "Go Down, Moses."

SCENE III

Pharaoh's throne room plainly suggests a Negro lodge room. The walls are hung with huge parade banners bearing such inscriptions as "Sublime Order of Princes of the House of Pharaoh, Home Chapter," "Mystic Brothers of the Egyptian Home Guard Ladies Auxiliary No. 1," "Supreme Magicians and Wizards of the Universe," etc.

The throne is an ordinary armchair on a dais with a drapery over its back. "Pharaoh is seated on the throne. His crown and garments might be those worn by a high officer in a Negro lodge during a ritual. About the throne itself are high officials, several of them with plumed hats, clothing that suggests military uniforms, and rather elaborate sword belts, swords and scabbards. A few soldiers carrying spears are also in his neighborhood and one or two bearded ancients in brightly colored robes with the word 'Wizard' on their conical hats. In the general group of men and women scattered elsewhere in the room Sunday finery is noticeable everywhere. Most of the civilians have bright 'parade' ribbons and wear medals."

In the space in front of the throne a Candidate Magician is performing a card trick. Pharaoh does not think much of the trick. Nor does the committee of magicians about him. The Candidate is advised to go back and study some more.

The Head Magician is called to make his report. Everything, he says, is being carried out according to Pharaoh's orders. The Hebrew babies are being killed with success and expedition.

"Betwixt de poleece and de soljahs we killed about a thousan' of 'em las' night. Dat's purty good," ventures the Head Magician.

"Yeh, it's fair," agrees Pharaoh. "I guess you boys is doin' all you kin. But I fin' I ain't satisfied, though."

HEAD MAGICIAN—How yo' mean, Yo' Honor?

PHARAOH—I mean I'd like to make dose Hebrew chillun realize dat I can be even mo' of a pest. I mean I hates dem chillun. An' I'm gonter think of a way of makin' 'em even mo' mizzable.

HEAD MAGICIAN—But dey *ain't* anythin' meaner dan killin' de babies, King.

PHARAOH—Dey must be sump'n. Doggone, you is my head tricker, you put yo' brains on it. (*To the others.*) Quiet, whilst de Head Magician go into de silence.

HEAD MAGICIAN (*after turning completely around twice, and a moment's cogitation*)—I tell you what I kin do. All de Hebrews dat ain't out to de buryin' grounds or in de hospitals is laborin' in de brick wukks.

PHARAOH—Yeh?

HEAD MAGICIAN (*after a cackling laugh*)—How would it be to take de straw away from 'em and tell 'em dey's got to turn out jest as many bricks as usual? Ain't dat nasty?

PHARAOH—Pretty triflin', but I suppose it'll have to do for the time bein'. Where's de extreme inner guard? (*One of the military attendants comes forward.*) Go on out and tell de sup'intendent to put dat into ee-fect. (*The attendant bows and starts for the door. He stops as* PHARAOH *calls to him.*) Wait a minute! Tell 'im to chop off de hands of anybody dat say he cain't make de bricks dat way. (*The attendant salutes and exits, the door being opened and closed by one of the soldiers.*) Now, what's de news in de magic line?

HEAD MAGICIAN—I ain't got very many novelties today, King. I been wukkin' too hard on de killin's. I'm so tired I don' believe I could lift a wand. (*There are murmurs of protest from the assemblage.*)

PHARAOH—Doggone, you was to 'a been de chief feature of de meetin' dis mawnin'. Look at de turn-out you got account o' me tellin' 'em you was comin'.

HEAD MAGICIAN—Well, dat's de way it is, King. Why don' you git de wizards to do some spell castin'.

PHARAOH—Dey say it's in de cyards dat dey cain't wukk 'til high noon. (*He glances at the* WIZARDS.) Think mebbe you kin cheat a little?

FIRST WIZARD—Oh, dat cain't be done, King.

PHARAOH—Well, we might as well adjourn, den. Looks to me like de whole program's shot to pieces.

The arrival of Moses and Aaron prevents the threatened adjournment. They come barging in, despite the protests of the soldiers, and stand confidently, a little defiantly, before Pharaoh. When he orders the soldiers to put them to the sword Aaron calmly produces the rod and swings it around in a circle which he advises them to respect.

As they feel the sting of a mysterious electrical force the soldiers draw back. Pharaoh, bewildered, orders his magicians forward. Let them put a spell on these intruders. But even the magicians are helpless before this new kind of magic. Evidently it is a time for compromise. If these boys are trickers they may be an addition to the court. Suppose they do a little tricking that Pharaoh may judge of their big talk.

"I s'pose you know I'm a fool for conjurin'," says Pharaoh. "If a man can show me some tricks I ain't seen, I goes out of my way to do him a favor."

Moses and Aaron show Pharaoh the walkin' stick trick first. When Aaron lays it on the first step of the throne, the walking stick turns into a wriggling snake.

Pharaoh is pleased, but not pleased enough to grant Moses the favor he asks. Will Pharaoh let the Hebrew chillun go?

Pharaoh will not. Don't they know the Hebrews are his slaves?

Can't they tell by the groaning they hear that the Hebrews are being treated like slaves? No, Pharaoh will not let the Hebrews go. But do they know any more tricks?

Again Aaron swings the rod. The room grows dark and a great buzzing of flies is heard, mingled with the slaps and protests of the crowd.

"All right—stop de trick," yells Pharaoh.

"Will you let de Hebrews go?"

"Sho' I will. Go ahead, stop it!"

The lights come up, the buzzing stops, and Pharaoh smiles. That *was* a good trick. But, being a tricker himself, Pharaoh knows a better one. He has changed his mind about letting the Hebrews go. That's out-trickin' the trickers. Has they got any more tricks?

"Yes, suh," answers Moses. "Dis is a little harder one. (AARON *lifts the rod.*) Gnats in de mill pon', gnats in de clover, gnats in de tater patch, stingin' all over."

Again the darkness and the buzzing, the slapping, the protests and expressions of general misery. Pharaoh's cries for relief are louder this time, and his promise more positive. A gnat has stung him on the nose and his interest is personal.

Moses bids the gnats begone. Pharaoh is still smiling. And again he has changed his mind. Now a new light comes in Moses' eyes.

"Listen, Pharaoh," he says, "you been lyin' to me, an' I'm gittin' tired of it."

"I ain't lyin', I'm trickin', too. You been trickin' me and I been trickin' you."

MOSES—I see. Well, I got one mo' trick up my sleeve which I didn't aim to wukk unless I had to. Caize when I does it, I cain't undo it.

PHARAOH—Wukk it an' I'll trick you right back. I don' say you ain' a good tricker, Moses. You is one of de best I ever seen. But I kin outtrick you. Dat's all.

MOSES—It ain't only me dat's goin' to wukk dis trick. It's me and de Lawd.

PHARAOH—Who?

MOSES—De Lawd God of Israel.

PHARAOH—I kin outtrick you an' de Lawd, too!

MOSES (*angrily*)—Now you done it, ol' King Pharaoh. You been mean to de Lawd's people, and de Lawd's been easy on you caize you didn' know no better. You been givin' me a lotta say-so an' no do-so, an' I didn' min' dat. But now you've got to braggin' dat you's better dan de Lawd, and dat's too many.

PHARAOH—You talk like a preacher, an' I never did like to hear preachers talk.

MOSES—You ain't goin' to like it any better, when I strikes down de oldes' boy in eve'y one of yo' people's houses.

PHARAOH—Now you've given up trickin' and is jest lyin'. (*He rises.*) Listen, I'm Pharaoh. I do de strikin' down yere. I strike down my enemies, and dere's no one in all Egypt kin kill who he wants to, 'ceptin' me.

MOSES—I'm sorry, Pharaoh. Will you let de Hebrews go?

PHARAOH—You heard my word. (AARON *is lifting his rod again at a signal from* MOSES.) Now, no more tricks or I'll—

MOSES—Oh, Lawd, you'll have to do it, I guess. Aaron, lift de rod. (*There is a thunderclap, darkness and screams. The lights go up. Several of the younger men on the stage have fallen to the ground or are being held in the arms of the horrified elders.*)

PHARAOH—What have you done yere? Where's my boy? (*Through the door come four men bearing a young man's body.*)

FIRST OF THE FOUR MEN—King Pharaoh. (PHARAOH *drops into his chair, stunned, as the dead boy is brought to the throne.*)

PHARAOH (*grief-stricken*)—Oh, my son, my fine son. (*The courtiers look at him with mute appeal.*)

MOSES—I'm sorry, Pharaoh, but you cain't fight de Lawd. Will you let His people go?

PHARAOH—Let them go. (*The lights go out. The choir begins "Mary Don't You Weep," and continues until it is broken by the strains of "I'm Noways Weary and I'm Noways Tired." The latter is sung by many more voices than the former and the cacophony ends as the latter grows in volume and the lights go up on the next scene.*)

SCENE IV

The singing has continued through the darkness, and now it swells in volume as the lights come on. Stretched across the stage in solid phalanx the children of Israel are marching and singing.

"They are of all ages and most of them are ragged. The men have packs on their shoulders, one or two have hand carts . . . It is nearing twilight and the faces of the assemblage are illumined by the rays of the late afternoon sun . . . The foot of a mountain appears; a trumpet call is heard, the marchers halt . . . A babel of 'What's de matter?' 'Why do we stop?' 'What dey blowin' for?' etc. Those looking ahead begin to murmur: 'It's Moses, it's Moses!'"

Moses comes, leaning on the arm of Aaron. They are old men now, their beards long and gray. And Moses is weary. Something has happened that never had happened before, and he can't understand. He knows he is an old man, but the Lord had said he was to show his children the Promised Land.

"Fo'ty years I bin leadin' you," he mutters. "I led you out o' Egypt. I led you past Sinai, and through de wilderness. Oh, I cain't fall down on you now!"

"Le's res' yere fo' de night," advises Aaron. "Den we'll see how you feel in de mo'nin'."

MOSES—We tol' de scouts we'd meet 'em three miles furder on. I hate fo' 'em to come back all dis way to repo't. 'Tis gettin' a little dark, ain't it?

AARON—It ain't dark, brother.

MOSES—No, it's my eyes.

AARON—Maybe it's de dust.

MOSES—No, I jest cain't seem to see. Oh, Lawd, dey cain't have a blind man leadin' 'em! Where is you, Aaron?

AARON—I'se right yere, Moses.

MOSES—Do you think— (*Pause.*) Oh! Do you think it's de time He said?

AARON—How you mean, Moses? (*Crowd look from one to another in wonder.*)

MOSES—He said I could lead 'em to the Jordan, dat I'd *see* de Promised Land, and dat's all de further I could go, on account I broke de laws. Little while back I thought I *did* see a river ahead, and a pretty land on de other side. (*Distant shouts "Hooray!" "Yere dey are!" "Dey travelled quick," etc.*) Where's de young leader of de troops? Where's Joshua? (*The call "Joshua" is taken up by those on the right of the stage, followed almost immediately by "Yere he is!" "Moses wants you!" etc.* JOSHUA *enters. He is a fine-looking Negro of about thirty.*)

JOSHUA (*going to* MOSES' *side*)—Yes, suh.

MOSES—What's de shoutin' about, Joshua?

JOSHUA—De scouts is back wid de news. De Jordan is right ahead of us, and Jericho is jest on de other side. Moses, we're dere! (*There are cries of "Hallelujah!" "De Lawd Be Praised!" "De Kingdom's Comin'!" etc. With a considerable stir among the marchers, several new arrivals crowd in from right, shoutin'*

"Moses, we're dere!" JOSHUA, *seeing the newcomers.*) Yere's de scouts. (*Three very ragged and dusty young men advance to* MOSES.)

MOSES (*as the shouting dies*)—So it's de River Jordan?

FIRST SCOUT—Yes, suh.

MOSES—All we got to take is de City of Jericho.

FIRST SCOUT—Yes, suh.

MOSES—Joshua, you got to take charge of de fightin' men, an' Aaron's gotta stay by de priests.

JOSHUA—What about you?

MOSES—You are leavin' me behind. Joshua, you gonter get de fightin' men together an' take dat city befo' sundown.

JOSHUA—It's a big city, Moses, wid walls all 'round it. We ain't got enough men.

MOSES—You'll take it, Joshua.

JOSHUA—Yes, suh. But how?

MOSES—Move up to de walls wid our people. Tell de priests to go wid you with de ram's horns. You start marchin' round dem walls, and den—

JOSHUA—Yes, suh.

MOSES—De Lawd'll take charge, jest as He's took charge ev'y time I've led you against a city. He ain't never failed, has He?

SEVERAL VOICES—No, Moses. (*All raise their heads.*)

MOSES—An' He ain't gonna fail us now. (*He prays. All bow.*) Oh, Lawd, I'm turnin' over our brave young men to you, caize I know you don't want me to lead 'em any further. (*Rises.*) Jest like you said, I've got to de Jordan but I cain't git over it. And yere dey goin' now to take de City o' Jericho. In a little while dey'll be marchin' 'round it. An' would you please be so good as to tell 'em what to do? Amen. (*To* JOSHUA.) Go ahead. Ev'ybody follows Joshua now. Give de signal to move on with ev'ything. (*A trumpet is heard.*) You camp fo' de night in de City of Jericho.

When the marchers have disappeared and the singing has died away in the distance, God comes to Moses in answer to his call. And God is not displeased with Moses.

"Moses, you have been a good man," He says. "You have been a good leader of my people. You got me angry once, dat's true. And when you anger me I'm a God of Wrath. But I never meant you wasn't gonter have what was comin' to you. And I ain't goin' to do you out of it, Moses. It's jest de country acrost de River dat you ain't gonter enter. You gonter have a Promised

Land. I been gettin' it ready fo' you fo' a long time. Kin you stand up?"

"Yes, suh, Lawd."

"Come on, I'm gonter show it to you. We goin' up dis hill to see it. Moses, it's a million times nicer dan de Land of Canaan."

As they walk up the mountain Moses is worried afresh. How can the Lord be there with him, and with Joshua and the fighting men, too? It can be done, God explains. It is Moses' faith that is helpin' him up the hill. It is God who is even now helpin' Joshua's men.

From the distance there comes the blast of rams' horns and the sound of crumbling walls. Nearer the choir is singing "Joshua Fit de Battle of Jericho."

"You did it, Lawd! You've tooken it! Lissen to de chillun—dey's in de Lan' of Canaan at last! You's de only God dey ever was, ain't you, Lawd?"

The Lord does not answer. "Come on, ol' man," He says. He is smiling as He helps Moses up the hill. They are near the top when the darkness descends.

Out of the darkness comes again the voice of Mr. Deshee in the Sunday school.

"But even dat scheme didn' work," he is telling the children. "Caize after dey got into de Land of Canaan dey went to de dogs again. And dey went into bondage again. Only dis time it was in de City of Babylon."

The choir is singing "Cain't Stay Away."

SCENE V

In what might be the public room of a night club in New Orleans a flashy crowd of young people is assembled. "Their costumes are what would be worn at a Negro masquerade to represent the debauchees of Babylon."

There are long tables stretched across the room, but at one end there is a special table on a dais, with a canopy over it, "Reserved for King and Guests." A jazz orchestra is furnishing music for the dancing, which is free and familiarly modern.

The dancing has not been going on long before the master of ceremonies brings the crowd to attention. The King of Babylon and party are arriving. The King is wearing an imitation ermine cape over his evening clothes and sports a diamond tiara. The five girls with him are gaudily arrayed, and as he escorts them proudly to his table he suggests that they remind him to send them a peck o' rubies in the morning.

The King is pleased that the party is going fine, and he is expectin' a Jew boy, a particular friend, who is the High Priest and who may drop in later. Expanding with the joy of the dance, the King is glad he can show the Jew boys in general that there ain't nobody in the world like the Babylon girls.

His satisfaction is momentarily depressed by the appearance of a prophet, "a patriarchal, ragged figure," who would halt the party. Does halt it, in fact, long enough to issue a warning.

"Listen to me, sons and daughters of Babylon," he cries. "Listen, you children of Israel dat's given yo'selves over to de evil ways of yo' oppressors! You're all wallowin' like hogs in sin, an' de wrath of Gawd ain' gonter be held back much longer. I'm tellin' you, repent befo' it's too late. Repent befo' Jehovah casts down de same fire dat burned up Sodom and Gomorrah. Repent befo' de—"

The High Priest is an interruption. He is a "fat voluptuary, elaborately clothed in brightly colored robes. He walks hand in hand with a gaudily dressed 'chippy'."

"Aw, he's one of dem wild men, like Jeremiah and Isaiah. Don't let him bother you none," the High Priest advises the King.

The King is for having "the ol' bum" thrown out. But on second thought he decides to have him shot instead.

"Smite 'em down, Lawd, like you said. Dey ain' a decent person left in the whole world." It is the prophet's last prayer. The master of ceremonies is his executioner.

They have carried the body out and the King is in negotiation with the High Priest about a little bribe of two hundred pieces of silver that shall guarantee the Babylonians the favor of the Hebrews' God when there is a sudden clap of thunder and the lights go out.

When the lights are on again God is standing in the center of the room.

"Dat's about enough!" He thunders. "I'se stood all I kin from you. I tried to make dis a good earth. I helped Adam, I helped Noah, I helped Moses an' I helped David. What's de grain dat grew out of de seed? Sin? Nothin' but sin throughout de whole world. I've given you ev'y chance. I sent you warriors and prophets. I've given you laws and commandments, an' you betrayed my trust. Eve'ything I've given you you've defiled. Ev'y time I've fo'given you you've mocked me. An' now de High Priest of Israel tries to trifle wid my name. Listen, you chillun of darkness, yo' Lawd is tried. I'm tired of de struggle to make you worthy of de breath I gave you. I put you in bondage ag'in to cure you and yo' worse dan you was amongst de flesh pots of Egypt. So I renounce you. Listen to de words of your Lawd God Jehovah, for dey is de last words yo' ever hear from me. I repent of dese people dat I have made and I will deliver dem no more."

(*There is darkness and cries of "Mercy!" "Have pity, Lawd!" "We didn't mean it, Lawd!" "Forgive us, Lawd!" etc. The choir sings "Death's Gwine to Lay His Cold Icy Hands on Me" until the lights go up on the next scene.*)

SCENE VI

God's in His Heaven, writing at His desk, but all is far from right with the world. Outside the door of God's office the prophet Hosea, "a dignified old man with wings like Jacob's," passes and repasses restlessly. God doesn't like that. Hosea interferes with God's work.

Gabriel announces the arrival of a delegation. It is made up of Abraham, Isaac, Jacob and Moses and the Lord wearily receives them.

They have come about the same old business. They want the Lord to go back to their people. For hundreds of years they have been coming and asking the same thing, and always God's answer has been the same.

"I repented of de people I made," the Lord reminds them. "I said I would deliver dem no more. Good mo'nin', gen'lemen."

Slowly the four file out. Why do they keep comin'? Gabriel thinks probably it is because they expect the Lord to change His mind. But they don't know Him.

Again the presence of Hosea irritates the Lord, but He doesn't know what to do about it. Hosea has a right in Heaven or he wouldn't be there. And God can't find it in His heart to stop him.

"He never has spoke to me," God admits, "an' if he don' wanta come in, I ain't gonter make him."

But that isn't the worst of it. Every time Hosea passes God hears a voice—the voice of Hezdrel talkin' in such a way that God has to hear. Down on the earth they are getting ready to take Jerusalem and Hezdrel is one of the defenders. But God ain't comin' down!

"I hates to see yo' feelin' like dis, Lawd," sympathizes Gabriel.

"Dat's all right," wearily answers God. "Even bein' Gawd ain't a bed of roses. (GABRIEL *exits.* HOSEA's *shadow is on the wall. For a second* HOSEA *hesitates.* GOD *looks at the wall. Goes to window.*) I hear you. I know yo' fightin' bravely, but I ain't comin' down. Oh, why don' yo' leave me alone? Yo' know yo' ain't talkin' to me. *Is* you talkin' to me? I cain't stand yo' talkin' dat way. I kin only hear part of what yo' sayin', an' it puzzles me. Don' yo' know yo' cain't puzzle God? (*A pause. Then tenderly.*) Do you want me to come down dere ve'y much? You know I said I wouldn' come down? (*Fiercely.*) Why don' he answer me a little? (*With clenched fists, looks down through the window.*) Listen! I'll tell yo' what I'll do. I ain' goin' to promise you anythin', an' I ain't goin' to do nothin' to he'p you. I'm jest feelin' a little low, an' I'm only comin' down to make myself feel a little better, dat's all."

(*The stage is darkened. Choir begins "A Blind Man Stood in De Middle of De Road," and continues until the lights go up on the next scene.*)

SCENE VII

In a shadowed corner beside the walls of the temple in Jerusalem, Hezdrel, who was Adam in an earlier scene, stands where Adam stood. He holds a sword in his right hand. His left hand is in a sling.

Around Hezdrel are the bodies of men who have fallen in the fight, and in the distance sounds of the battle continue. There is a trumpet call. A detail of men reports to Hezdrel that the fighting has stopped for the night.

"Dey're goin' to begin ag'in at cockcrow," the corporal adds. "Herod say he's goin' to take de temple tomorrow, burn de books an' de Ark of de Covenant, and put us all to de sword."

Hezdrel is ready. And the men, too. "We'll be waitin' for 'em. Jest remember, boys, when dey kill us we leap out of our skins right into de lap of God."

The men have taken the wounded back and Hezdrel is alone when God appears from the deep shadows. He comes as an old preacher from back in the hills to learn how Hezdrel is makin' out, and Hezdrel is suspicious that He may be a spy in his brain.

Things aren't going so well with Hezdrel. He and his men know they are going to be killed, but they are ready. They are ready because they have faith in their dear Lord, "de Lawd God of Hosea." Which puzzles God a little.

GOD—Ain't de God of Hosea de same Jehovah dat was de God of Moses?

HEZDREL (*contemptuously*)—No. Dat ol' God of wrath and vengeance? We have de God dat Hosea preached to us. He's de one God.

GOD—Who's he?

HEZDREL (*reverently*)—De God of mercy.

GOD—Hezdrel, don' you think dey mus' be de same God?

HEZDREL—I don' know. I ain't bothered to think much about it. Maybe dey is. Maybe our God is de same ol' God. I guess we jest got tired of His appearance dat ol' way.

GOD—What you mean, Hezdrel?

HEZDREL—Oh, dat ol' God dat walked de earth in de shape of a man. I guess He lived with man so much dat all He seen was de sins in man. Dat's what made Him the God of wrath and vengeance. Co'se He made Hosea. An' Hosea never would a found what mercy was unless dere was a little of it in God, too. Anyway, He ain't a fearsome God no mo'. Hosea showed us dat.

GOD—How you s'pose Hosea found dat mercy?

HEZDREL—De only way he could find it. De only way I found it. De only way anyone kin find it.

GOD—How's dat?

HEZDREL—Through sufferin'.

God is still puzzled. If they do kill Hezdrel in the morning, and Herod makes good his threat to burn the temple and the Ark of the Covenant and the books, then that will be the end, won't it?

But those books, Hezdrel explains, are only copies. There are other sets. One in the mind of Hezdrel. Others in the minds of those who have escaped from the beleaguered city. These are scattered safe over the countryside ready to set down the word again.

"Dey cain't lick you, kin dey, Hezdrel?" God is proud of His fighting son.

"I know dey cain't," answers Hezdrel . . . "Tell de people in de hills dey ain't nobody like de Lawd God of Hosea."

"I will. If dey kill you tomorrow I'll bet dat God of Hosea'll be waitin' for you."

"I *know* He will."

"Thank you, Hezdrel."

"Fo' what?"

"Fo' tellin' me so much. You see I been so far away, I guess I was jest way behin' de times."

God has gone. The corporal is back to report the cock's crow. The fighting has been resumed. The men are eager and ready.

"Dis is de day dey say dey'll git us," Hezdrel reminds them. "Le's fight 'em till de las' man goes. What d'you say?"

"Le's go, Hezdrel!"

"Give 'em ev'ything, boys!"

Above the sound of battle the choir is singing "March On!" triumphantly. The lights are out.

SCENE VIII

There is another fish fry in heaven. The same angels are there and the choir, less restless than before, is still singing confidently the warrior's song, "March On!"

Seated in an armchair near the center of the grounds God is staring thoughtfully into space. His pensiveness worries Gabriel. He has been sittin' that way an awful long time. Is it somethin' serious that is worryin' God? It is, God admits, very serious.

GABRIEL (*awed by his tone*)—Lawd, is de time come fo' me to blow?

GOD—Not yet, Gabriel. I'm just thinkin'.

GABRIEL—What about, Lawd? (*Puts up hand. Singing stops.*)

GOD—'Bout somethin' de boy tol' me. Somethin' 'bout Hosea an' himself. How dey foun' somethin'.

GABRIEL—What, Lawd?

GOD—Mercy. (*A pause.*) Through *sufferin'*, he said.

GABRIEL—Yes, Lawd.

GOD—I'm tryin' to find it, too. It's awful impo'tant. It's awful impo'tant to all de people on my earth. Did he mean dat even God must suffer? (GOD *continues to look out over the audience for a moment and then a look of surprise comes into his face He sighs. In the distance a voice cries.*)

THE VOICE—Oh, look at him! Oh, look, dey goin' to make him carry it up dat high hill! Dey goin' to nail him to it! Oh, dat's a terrible burden for one man to carry! (GOD *rises and murmurs "Yes!" as if in recognition. The heavenly beings have been watching Him closely, and now, seeing Him smile gently, draw back, relieved. All of the angels burst into "Hallelujah, King Jesus."* GOD *continues to smile as the lights fade away. The singing becomes fortissimo.*

THE CURTAIN FALLS

THE CRIMINAL CODE

A Drama in Prologue and Three Acts

By Martin Flavin

EVER since he stepped hopefully but hesitantly out of the commercial world of Chicago, to test his fortune as a dramatist on Broadway, and offered as his first play the somewhat weird but impressive drama called "Children of the Moon," any play by Martin Flavin has been awaited with more than customary anticipation by the professional and seriously interested playgoers of New York.

It happened, also, that "The Criminal Code," which was produced by William Harris, Jr., at the National Theatre in early October, was the first production that that producer had made in some seasons; which gave additional interest to this particular first night.

When the Flavin play was threatened with success, many persons were made happy. The reviews ranged from modest praise to a freely spoken acclaim. Here, declared many, was the finest serious American play the theatre had revealed in seasons.

The public, slow to accept tragedy, was at first a bit timid about attending Mr. Flavin's prison drama; but as the season rolled on, and it became apparent that "The Criminal Code" would be at least a serious contender for Pulitzer prize honors, interest was stimulated and the run automatically lengthened.

The first scene of Mr. Flavin's play, a prologue, is laid in the office of Martin Brady, State's Attorney. Mr. Brady, "A big, broad-shouldered man past 50 years of age," is interrogating a witness, "a bald, bleary-eyed, wizened little man with a cringing manner and a whining voice," while a clerk at the other end of the desk, "with heavy, shell-rimmed glasses and a bored, weary manner," is taking notes.

The wizened little man is a waiter from Spelvin's café. He has about finished his account of a fight that had taken place in the cafe the night before. A boy, a stranger apparently, had struck one of the town's better known young men—the son, in fact, of the town's wealthiest and most influential citizen—with a water carafe and knocked him senseless.

The boy, it appears from the waiter's account, had been crazed by something he had drunk and something the young man, (Parker by name) had said to the girl with whom he (the boy) had been dancing.

"He shouts out: 'You've insulted this lady,'" reports the waiter. "Mr. Parker stood up then and motioned him away. 'Beat it, kid,' he says. But the boy keeps on shouting, crazy-like: 'You apologize—apologize—apologize!' and a lot of other things like that. Then Mr. Parker cursed him, sir, and he reached back to his hip pocket. 'Twas only for his handkerchief, sir; he'd nothing else there. And the boy picks up the carafe from the table, and strikes before any one could stop him."

The next witness is a girl—the girl who was with the boy at the night club. Merwyn Fontaine is what she calls herself, but she is quick to change this to Gertrude Williams when Attorney Brady impatiently demands her real name.

Gertrude was just walking along the streets the night before, she reports, stopping now and then to look in the shop windows, when a young man spoke to her. Passing over the fact that she might have been insulted, Gertrude recalls that the young man said he was lonesome, that he hadn't been in town long and that this was his birthday. He asked her to go somewhere with him and Gertrude suggested that they go up to Spelvin's place.

There they danced awhile and had some ginger ale—and gin—a pint of gin. The gin was Gertrude's suggestion, too, she admits, although any one can buy gin at Spelvin's. Then they danced some more and young Parker began to get fresh.

BRADY—You knew Parker?

GIRL (*hesitating*)—I—I'd seen him.

BRADY—Had you ever been—out with him? (*She looks down at the floor.*)

GIRL—Yeah. (*A pause.*)

BRADY—Go on! What'd he do?

GIRL—He— He was just making remarks and—and putting his hands on me while I was dancing with the young man. He wanted me to come over to his table, and—and when I wouldn't, he got sore, and—and called me a name. That's what started everything. The young man that was with me, he was a perfect gentleman; he wouldn't stand for that. He went right over to Mr. Parker's table then, and—and—

BRADY—Yeah, yeah, I know all about that, Gerty. That's all. (*He waves her away.*) Come back here at five o'clock. Don't forget now, five o'clock.

GIRL (*backing away*)—Yes, sir.

BRADY—And don't do any talking. Keep your mouth shut.

GIRL—Yes, sir. (*She goes out.*)

BRADY—Is that all of 'em, Lew?

LEW (*checking back through his note book*)—Three—five—six—seven. Yeah, that's all.

BRADY (*calculating with pursed lips*)—Seven eyewitnesses, and they all check on material points.

LEW—Open and shut, eh?

BRADY—Like a knife.

LEW—If young Parker should die— (*A pause.*)

BRADY—Parker's dead.

LEW (*with a flash of interest*)—Yeah? That right? What is it, Mart? Second degree murder?

BRADY (*considering*)—By God, it might be at that! (*He picks up a sheepskin book from the desk, and opens it, murmuring to himself.*) Malice . . . malice . . . express or *implied*— Deliberate intent . . . no considerable provocation . . . provocation . . . provocation . . . Hum— (*The phone rings. He drops the book, and picks up the receiver.*) Yeah?— Yeah— Certainly I know all about it. Do you think we're asleep down here?— Yeah— Yeah— Yeah I'm taking personal charge— Don't know! Can't tell yet. Call me up at six o'clock, and I'll give you a statement— Yeah— Yeah— Yeah— Sure, I understand— So long, Al. (*He hangs up the receiver.*) Goddam yellow press! How they love the smell of blood!

LEW—Yeah.

BRADY—They're all alike. They'll squeal themselves deaf over this, and—old Thad Parker spends more money for advertising than any other man in this town.

LEW—That's right, Mart. I never thought of that.

BRADY—Yeah— And an election coming on. (*He ponders through a pause. Briskly:*) Send in the boy.

Robert Graham is "a clean, wholesome-looking, slender lad, pale of face now and frightened." He is in charge of "a heavy-looking officer in plain clothes."

Robert, although a little shaken, answers Attorney Brady's questions promptly and frankly. He is 20 years old. Yesterday was his birthday. He came from Hood Valley, where his mother still lives. He is a clerk in the brokerage firm of Price and

Hatton. He has worked there a month, which is all the time he has been in town. He has no friends in town—no particular friends—and he never has been arrested before.

The attorney's attitude toward him is severe but not unkindly so.

"Well, Bob, you're in a jam," he says.

GRAHAM (*faltering*)—Yes, sir.

BRADY (*licking the loose wrapper of his cigar*)—Young Parker died this afternoon.

GRAHAM—Oh! (*And he sits down abruptly, and covers his face with his hands.* BRADY *opens a drawer of the desk, and takes out a flask.*)

BRADY (*gently*)—Would you like a little drink, Bob?

GRAHAM (*shuddering*)—No, sir.

BRADY (*doubtfully*)—Yeah? (*He returns the bottle to the drawer, watching the boy with anxious, troubled eyes.*) Bob! You can make a statement to me, if you want to, but anything you say may be used against you. I want you to understand that.

GRAHAM—Yes, sir.

BRADY—It looks to me like the best thing for you to do is to come clean; plead guilty and take your jolt. But your lawyer might advise you differently. Have you got a lawyer?

GRAHAM (*in a choking voice*)—The firm I work for sent their lawyer to see me this morning.

BRADY—What'd he say?

GRAHAM—He—he told me not to talk.

BRADY—Yeah? Then don't you say a word. You haven't said anything yet that'll do you any harm— All right, Mike, I'm through. It's tough luck, Bob. But that's the way things go. That's the way they break sometimes. You have to take 'em the way they fall.

GRAHAM (*numbly*)—Yes, sir. (*He goes slowly across the room and out.*)

Attorney Brady is impressed with Robert Graham. The boy has a nice personality. A smart criminal lawyer taking his case could make it pretty tough for the state. "Say, if that kid belonged to me," he says, half to Lew, the clerk, and half to himself, "I'd make a plea of self-defense and fight it out."

"But Parker didn't have a gun."

"He *thought* he had—he thought he was fighting for his life. It's what you think that counts."

"And he was full of gin."

"Yeah? Suppose he was. What of it? I'd get a disagreement at the worst—a year's delay, and a new trial. The witnesses would fade away. They always do. The whole mess would get cold. The papers would have something else to yawp about—I'd get him off. He'd never serve a day."

"I guess you could, Mart," agrees Lew, admiringly.

"A thing like this could happen to anyone—to me, to you, to anyone— It's just a rotten break, that's all—"

A man named Nettlefold has called. He is of the firm of Nettlefold, Lambskin and Kroll. They are attorneys for Price and Hatton, who have asked him to look after the interests of one of their young men who appears to have become involved in an unfortunate affair. Mr. Nettlefold, however, is not a criminal lawyer, and is therefore somewhat at sea as to how to proceed. Still, he could not disregard the request of an old friend and client—

The case, the State's Attorney assures Mr. Nettlefold, is open and shut like a knife. The boy Graham picks up a prostitute on the street, takes her to a notorious joint, buys and drinks a pint of gin with her within an hour. The girl runs into Parker, an old flame, Graham is jealous, Parker tries to avoid a quarrel, Graham picks up a water bottle and caves in Parker's skull. That's the state's case in a nutshell. Confirmed by the testimony of no less than seven witnesses.

"We propose to ask for a verdict of second degree murder," concludes Mr. Brady.

Mr. Nettlefold is gravely concerned. The boy seems such a nice boy. And murder— A conviction, says Attorney Brady, means a sentence of from ten years to life. That's the law of the commonwealth as set down in the criminal code.

But the State's Attorney is not without feeling. He is, taking all the circumstances into account, willing to let Mr. Nettlefold plead the boy guilty to manslaughter and let it go at that. Graham will get a maximum sentence of ten years, and the newspapers will roast hell out of Mr. Brady, with an election coming on. Still Mr. Brady will do it.

"But ten years is a long time, Mr. Brady," Mr. Nettlefold pleads; "a big piece out of a boy's life—and—the stain on him—"

BRADY (*passionately*)—My God, man, what do you want? There's a boy laying on a slab in the morgue! There's a big piece out of his life—all of it. Somebody's got to pay for that —something!

NETTLEFORD (*rising*)—But—

BRADY—The old Mosaic law, Mr. Nettlefold: "An eye for an eye." That's the basis and foundation of our criminal code—Somebody's got to pay. (*He thumps the desk with his fist.*)

NETTLEFOLD—Yes, yes, I quite see your point. (*He sighs.*) But I can't help thinking of the effect of imprisonment—what it may do to this youth—how it may blight his life—

BRADY—Think it over. Talk it over with the boy, and with your office.

NETTLEFOLD—A very grave responsibility—very!

BRADY—Think it over, carefully. Take your time, and let me know in a day or so.

NETTLEFOLD (*backing away*)—Yes, I'll do that, Mr. Brady. Thank you very much for your—er—courtesy. Good day.

BRADY—'S all right— Pleased to have met you— Good day. (NETTLEFOLD *goes out.* BRADY *sits down by the desk; and for a moment seems to reflect. He smiles; and murmurs to himself.*) Like taking candy from a child, yeah! (*Absently he picks the book up from the desk, and turns the pages; the smile fades from his face. He puts the book down on the desk; grimly, to himself*). Christ! (*The curtain falls.*)

ACT I

We stand before the grim walls of a prison, a massive section of which rises within a false proscenium to reveal the laboratory of a state's prison, "a gray, grim room with lofty, steel-barred windows at the back." Six years have passed.

A hooded light is suspended in the centre of the room. Beneath the light, seated on a low stool, is Convict 23499, once known as Robert Graham. "He wears the coarse gray convict uniform. Across the pocket of his shirt is sewn a white strip of cloth on which is stamped his number."

Graham is being examined by the prison physician, Dr. Rinewulf, "a thin, frail-looking man with restless eyes and a harsh unfeeling voice, with just a trace of foreign accent. He wears a white laboratory coat." At one side, holding a history chart, stands the doctor's convict assistant, "a pale-faced, tight-lipped, old-looking young man."

It is Dr. Rinewulf's conclusion, which he voices aloud to the prisoner, that Graham is not sick. He may have no appetite, he may not be able to sleep and he may have bad dreams—still he is not physically sick. There is nothing wrong with him. He is neurotic and—outside—the doctor would prescribe a change of scene—the mountains or the sea. It is not medicine that Graham needs.

Laboriously the Doctor drags from the all but inarticulate boy that he works in the jute mill and that he has been in prison six years. When he is dismissed Graham shuffles listlessly from the room. The Doctor looks after him as he mutters:

"Jute mill—jute mill—six years. Breaking of morale— You see it in his eyes— Environmental— Mechanistic occupation—Sex starvation— God knows what. You cannot find them with a stethoscope!"

Rather a pity, cases like this, the Doctor thinks. There is something there worth saving—and it is almost gone.

. . . .

A group of men enter the office. They are led by MacManus, secretary of the Prison Commission, "a burly, overfat, coarse man with a broad, flat face, a boisterous voice and the manner of a ward politician."

"Behind him is Martin Brady, nearing 60 now, quite gray—a bit less active physically, less sure of himself." With them are the chaplain of the prison, "a dull, weary-looking man of middle age, in mussy, semi-clerical garb," and Gleason, the captain of the yard, "a big, heavy, ponderous, stupid man in khaki-colored uniform, and carrying a loaded cane with a sharp, iron ferule."

MacManus is taking Brady, who is the new prison warden, on his first tour of inspection and introducing him to his staff. Brady used to be State's Attorney up in town, MacManus explains, and ought to be Governor by rights.

To MacManus this is a highly diverting tour. There are a lot of funny birds in a prison. That assistant of the Doctor's, for instance—that's Kellogg, the fellow who got a girl in trouble and then cut her up and packed her body in a trunk. Now he is one of the best surgeons in the jail. Operates on the Doc himself.

The scene changes. The party has passed on to the jute mill—"gray, concrete walls, and dull, gray light." The rattle and clang of machinery is deafening; convicts are carrying in bales of jute and stacking them against an iron bridge which crosses the room and from which the MacManus party surveys the scene.

MacManus is proud of the jute mill, too. Twenty-five hundred men working there and producing 5,000 bales of jute a day. Some factory!

"Speed 'em up! Speed 'em up! Make the crooks earn their keep. That's what I say."

"Pretty tough, eh?" suggests the new warden.

"Tough? They like it, Mart. Gives 'em something to do, something to think about. Eh, Captain?"

"That's right, Mr. MacManus."

Now MacManus notices Jim Fales, "a tall, slender man, 40 perhaps, but gray, with a lean, crafty face." Fales, who has slapped the dust out of his shirt and sat down on the bale of jute he has lugged in, is one of the prison's most famous residents—"yeggman, train robber. God knows what! Sharp as a trap and slippery as an eel," reports MacManus. It would be well for Warden Brady to look out for Fales.

The party moves on. The convicts are about to be fed. They get their feed at 3.30 on dark days, and it's a sight to see 'em eat.

Now Robert Graham has carried in another bale of jute and sunk wearily down beside Fales. "His voice is listless, empty; his eyes dull; his body sagging. The spirit within him is close to the breaking point." Fales is interested, and sympathetic.

"Don't let these bastards get your goat now, Bob," Fales warns. "You've done the long end of your stretch, and you're just a kid. You've got a life ahead of you. Pull yourself together. If you smash up now you're gone."

Graham is hopeless. He can't go on. Nor can Fales' stories of those others who have broken under the strain divert him—not even the story of Sam Price who was caught in a break and thrown into the dungeon when he wouldn't squeal; thrown into a dungeon with six feet of concrete all around him, bread and water once a day and a bucket meal on the seventh—"cold slop you wouldn't feed a dog!" Torture for Sam every day, until the day the boys smuggled a knife in to him—

The descending wall cuts off the story of Sam Price, "the gamest little cuss" Jim Fales ever knew.

. . . .

The same iron bridge that crossed the jute mill spans the mess hall. From it the MacManus party views a sweep of tables, two of which are within view, four convicts seated at each of them. At one are Graham, Fales, Runch, "a small, wiry, ferret-faced man of uncertain age," and a Negro. The men are eating and chatting among themselves; all but Graham, "who sits stolidly, his elbows on the table and his chin cupped in his hands. There is the buzz and drone of many voices—four thousand men stretched out into the vague space beyond the footlights; rattle of plates and spoons and cups, and scraping of feet and benches on the concrete floor."

MacManus' pride spreads over the scene; a building to be proud of, built by convict labor; a dinner party that looks like an uptown banquet and won't suffer from any after-dinner speeches.

MACMANUS—Quite a sight, Mart. Four thousand men in here, eh, Gleason?

GLEASON—Four thousand and seventy-nine, Mr. MacManus.

BRADY—Yeah?

MACMANUS—We got it down to twenty-three cents a day per head. That right, Captain?

GLEASON—Twenty-three and a half, sir.

MACMANUS—Some system, Mart! They can't feed the bears in the park for that.

BRADY—What are they eating?

MACMANUS—Spaghetti, coffee, bread—all the bread they want. No man goes out of here hungry.

BRADY—What've they got in those little bags?

MACMANUS—Sugar. They get it once a week. And they gamble with it, too. Sugar and tobacco, that's their wampum, Mart. (*He laughs.*)

BRADY (*half to himself*)—Tough! Pretty tough!

MACMANUS—Tough? Don't kid yourself, Mart. It's better grub than most of them ever had. Good wholesome food, plenty of vitamins and calories and all that stuff. I never see none of 'em losing any weight in here, eh, Captain?

GLEASON—That's right, Mr. MacManus.

BRADY—Yeah.

MACMANUS—See Jim Fales sitting over there?

BRADY—Yeah.

MACMANUS—Notice the bird the other side of him. He's an ex-hophead, name of Runch. Just an ordinary dip. But if you ever want an earful out of him, Mart, give him a shot of coke, and he'll go to hell for the second.

BRADY—Yeah.

MACMANUS (*chuckling*)—There's a group for you: Runch, a

hophead; Jim Fales, professional crook; that big buck nigger, just a plain moron; and that kid on the end—I don't know him—

BRADY—Just a bad break, maybe.

MACMANUS—Yeah, but there they are: Moron, hophead, professional crook, and—

BRADY—The whole history of a prison.

MACMANUS—Yeah, that's right, Mart; you said it. Well—(*He glances at his watch.*) Better be getting on, eh? I want you to see the lockup. To me, that's the greatest show of all.

Now they've gone and the conversation at the first table rises above the drone of voices. The hophead Runch is begging sugar from Jim Fales and being cursed for what he already owes. Runch himself is on the verge of hysteria, his stomach turned against the slop they've fed him. "I'd sell my soul for a plate of ham and eggs," he screeches, before they can squelch him.

Graham, too, can't stomach the food, for all Fales' pleading that he has got to keep up his strength or they'll get him. Again Fales tries the effect of reminiscence on Graham. The story this time is of Ned Galloway, the warden's butler, and the smartest, whitest guy in the place. Galloway was a steward on an ocean liner—that's the way he worked—and he wanted Fales to go along with him to Buenos Aires—

The descending wall again interrupts the story.

. . . .

In the cell house the MacManus party stands on a bridge facing tiers of cells. Warden Brady is beginning to show the strain of the inspection. "His arms are folded; his shoulders sag; there is a frowning, troubled look upon his face."

On narrow balconies before each cell two convicts stand, awaiting the signal to enter. Fales and Graham are together. "There is the murmuring, unintelligible hum of four thousand voices, talking, whispering," cut short by the clang of an electric gong.

"Well, here's our bird cage, Mart," expands MacManus.

"Yeah."

"The new cell block. A cage within a cage. The last word in modern prison construction. Steel and concrete. Why, a safe blower with a kit of tools couldn't work his way out of that, eh, Captain?"

"That's right, Mr. MacManus."

Two thousand cells, and every one with air and light. Once inside the convicts can do anything they like—talk, smoke, read, play cards, anything—until nine o'clock. Then the cell lights go out.

"Tough—pretty tough," ventures the new warden.

"Tough?" echoes MacManus. "They like it. They're champing at the bit to get in now. Am I right, Captain?"

"They like to get into their cells. Yes, sir, that's right."

"Why?" Warden Brady wants to know.

Gleason doesn't know just why, never having given the matter any thought, but—

The gong saves him. "The convicts step into their cells. Terrific, deafening crash of steel. Twilight has vanished and, in its place, the searing white of arc lights floods the scene. The hum subsides into the drone of swarming bees."

"That's system, Mart," exults MacManus. "One lever locks the door of every cell. I suppose I've seen this thing a hundred times, but I always get a kick out of it, Mart. . . . You're looking at four thousand men, and the next second—click!—they're gone!—Just as if they were wiped off the face of the earth."

"Yeah."

MACMANUS—Well—let's go—I want to see your daughter and your sister, Mart; and then I've got to beat it back to town.

BRADY—Is it always light like that?

MACMANUS (*as they descend the steps*)—All night. Light is the enemy of crooks, you know. And then these doors are locked. There's only two men left in the building besides the cons—a guard on the floor in case any one gets sick, you know, and a gun man on the bridge inside. Wherever the guard moves inside that block, the gun man follows him along the bridge, covering him with the gun. Some system, Mart! (*They disappear from sight. The wall descends.*)

. . . .

In their cell Jim Files is comfortably stretched out in the top bunk reading a newspaper by the light of a ceiling bulb. Graham sits on the edge of the lower bunk, his elbows on his knees, his face in his hands, staring at nothing.

Suddenly the boy's nerves snap and he cries out, shrilly, that he cannot go on; that he must be let out! Fales leaps from his own bunk and covers Graham's mouth with his hand to still his shrieks. From afar down the cell block come murmured protests. An outbreak like that could get a man jerked out of his cell and thrown into the cooler, Fales protests, hoarsely, as he quiets his hysterical mate.

To keep him quiet, to put into his mind again something that may restore an interest in keeping alive, Fales sits beside Graham and reveals in hoarse whispers the idea of a break that has been planned.

It is a long chance they are going to take, and it has to be thought over seriously. It doesn't mean so much to a man like Fales, on the shady side of forty and starting a twenty-year stretch. With the bad lungs the jute mill has given him he can't last half his term, anyway. Outside he has a stake planted, and a little place in Switzerland where he would be safe. But for Graham—

FALES—You think it over, kid. It's always a long shot. Nine out of every ten come back.

GRAHAM (*whispering passionately*)—I don't *care*, Jim. If I could only get one breath of air outside—one good, square meal! If—if I could see a woman's face again—I dream of those things, Jim, night after night— Oh, God! such dreams!

FALES—Yes, I know, but think it over, Bob—and take your time.

GRAHAM (*eagerly*)—But when, and how?

FALES—There's four in on it now: myself, Dutch Trask, Pete Grimes, and Runch.

GRAHAM—Runch?

FALES—I'm not very keen on him, myself. He was a hophead once. You can't ever count on them. But he's a pal of Grimes, and Grimes has framed the trick.

GRAHAM—But how?

FALES (*very softly*)—It's an inside job, of course. Those are the only ones that have a chance.

GRAHAM (*tense with eagerness*)—Yes?

FALES—There's a guard in here with an itching palm. Grimes got a line on him from outside. He thinks he's safe. For a thousand bucks he'd go to hell, Grimes says.

GRAHAM—Yes?

FALES—They've framed the whole thing up outside. It works like this . . . (*The descending wall interrupts his speech.*)

. . . .

The Warden's office, adjoining his living quarters, is "a bare, gray, cheerless room, built in the wall of the prison above the entrance gate."

It is peopled now by Miss Brady, the Warden's sister, "of middle age, a bit carping in speech and manner, decently and sedately dressed," and Mary Brady, his daughter, "a girl of 25, slender, not perhaps pretty, but good to look at, with black hair, and keen, blue eyes suggestive of her father's."

Miss Brady is plainly distressed by her surroundings. Neither does she think the prison is any place for Mary's father—who should be sitting in the Governor's mansion. Nor is her state of mind notably quieted by the catlike entrance of the Warden's clerk, come noiselessly from an alcove in which the files are kept, to inquire for the Warden.

Mr. Simpkins, the prison chaplain, offers some little comfort in his somewhat flabby way. He can assure them, at least, that they are quite safe. The main entrance to the prison yard is directly below the room they are sitting in and is guarded by huge barred gates. Outside their windows is the main courtyard in which Mary has discovered a quite lovely flower bed. Mr. Simpkins thinks probably the convicts appreciate all that is done for them. Still, he must confess they are not as penitent as might be wished.

From the windows Mr. Simpkins points out the various shops. The dungeons? Oh, they are beneath the hospital. The towers on the wall are where the machine guns are kept and the searchlights that flood the yard in case of an attempted escape. Yes, prisoners do escape, occasionally, but—

Dr. Rinewulf has come to look up the card of Prisoner 23499. He is pleased to meet the Warden's family. Prison doctoring, he assures them, has its compensations. At least his patients keep their appointments and pay their bills.

From the card the clerk brings him, Dr. Rinewulf learns that his prisoner's name is Robert Graham, that he was convicted of manslaughter, sentenced to serve ten years and that his record is clear of punishments.

Now MacManus has returned with Warden Brady. The tour of inspection is finished, "and the children all put to bed for the night." MacManus is of a mind to joke with the women of the Warden's family. They should not feel any sense of depression in their new home. They have the finest stone house in the state and such service as even a Henry Ford, with all his millions, could never buy. Their chef once worked for one of the larger hotels and drew ten thousand dollars a year as salary. His career was temporarily halted when he poisoned his wife. Their butler was a second steward on an ocean liner;

their house boy a porter on a Pullman; their chauffeur an aviator—which reminds Gleason that the Warden's chauffeur is about to be released. He will have to pick up another. And don't let him be afraid of murderers, insists MacManus—a thief is always a thief, but a murderer is a murderer only once.

The others have gone on into the living quarters when Dr. Rinewulf stops Warden Brady long enough for a report and a request. The Doctor is interested in a prisoner, a man in the jute mill. He feels that this man's morale is breaking down and that something might be done to save him. He wishes the Warden would see the boy himself. Which the Warden agrees to do.

MacManus is back for a parting word of advice. He doesn't have to tell the best State's Attorney the old town ever had anything about crooks, but he does think Brady will be an awfully wise man if he is careful not to let anything go wrong while he is in charge of the prison. The politicians who have shelved him temporarily by giving him this appointment (when by rights he ought to be Governor) will be watching him and hoping to get something on him. Let him be on the watch. The only way to run a prison is with "heels on their necks." Let him be particularly watchful of theorists like Rinewulf—always wanting to experiment with something; always talking about "sex starvation and God knows what."

"Gleason is your best bet," MacManus tells the warden; "level-headed, cold as ice; and he knows the game from A to Z. Eternal vigilance—that's the ticket. Don't let 'em pull no monkey tricks. A jail break or a killing, Mart—you know what that'd mean. The newspapers'd howl their heads off. They're laying for you, Mart, and waiting for a chance—and hoping that they get it."

MacManus has gone when Gleason brings in Number 23499. "Graham comes with slow and dragging footsteps . . . his vacant eyes stare straight before him, his shoulders sag, his step is noiseless."

GLEASON—Dr. Rinewulf said you wanted him brought here.

BRADY—Yeah, that's right. (*He seems uncertain what to do or say, and then goes slowly to the desk, seats himself, picks up the card and turns it in his hands.*) Yeah— Yeah— Your name is Robert Graham? (*A pause. The boy shifts his feet, but makes no answer.*) Did—did they ever call you Bob? (*A pause.*)

GLEASON (*in an ugly voice*)—D'you hear the Warden talking to you? (*He takes a step forward.* BRADY *checks him with a gesture.* RINEWULF *comes in and goes quickly to the desk.*)

BRADY (*in a kindly, reassuring tone*)—Well, Bob, I don't know what you're here for. These cards don't tell much of a story, but— (*He hesitates, turning the card in his hand.*)

GLEASON—It's the Parker case, Mr. Brady.

BRADY—Parker?

GLEASON—Yes, sir—young Parker that was killed six years ago.

BRADY—Yeah? Oh! (*He starts and looks sharply at the boy. Memory floods back.*) Yeah— Oh, yeah! Yeah, I remember now. Well, well . . . (*He stares at the card, and the furrows in his brow are deep.* MARY *comes into the room, and pauses just inside the door. She is facing* GRAHAM *across the room, and she looks straight at him into the blankness of his eyes, curiously and unafraid. He starts, catches his breath, his body stiffens, his head comes up; and his drooping shoulders straighten up and back.* RINEWULF *is missing nothing.* BRADY'S *eyes are on the card. A little, friendly smile touches the girl's lips.*)

MARY—We're having tea, father.

BRADY (*only now aware of her presence*)—Eh? Tea? (*He chuckles.*) Say, we're getting pretty stylish, aren't we, Mary? (*She laughs.*) All right, run along—I'll be there in a minute. (*She turns, and leaves the room. He looks back at the card.*) Change of occupation and environment . . . Hum! . . . (*The descending wall interrupts his speech. The curtain falls.*)

ACT II

In the Warden's living room, "a gray, cheerless room with barred windows at the back which look down into the prison yard," a tea table is standing with the remains of a lunch upon it. Back of the table Miss Brady is dozing in her chair. She does not hear Galloway, "a tall, stooped, raw-boned, powerful-looking man of middle age," as he comes noiselessly to take away the tea things. Miss Brady doesn't like Galloway, however good a servant he may be.

Mary Brady is preparing to take a journey, and the thought that her niece will be away for a week or ten days is not pleasant to Mary's aunt. Miss Brady does not like the thought of being left the only woman in the Warden's family. Dr. Rinewulf has become so interested in the success of his experiment—that of reclaiming the prisoner Robert Graham, the Warden's new chauffeur—that he hates to see it interrupted even for a week.

If Mary is a little conscious of this "miracle" in which she has taken part she tries not to show it, but she is interested in the Doctor's report that he has taken the trouble to investigate the crime for which young Graham was sentenced and is glad that it has been found to have been more an accident than a crime. He is hoping the Warden, who will doubtless remember the circumstances of the case, will be interested in confirming the record.

Graham bears out the Doctor's report of his complete reconstruction when he comes to carry Mary's suitcase and drive her to her train. "His step has the spring of youth in it, his shoulders are square, his head high. His hair is neatly combed and there is a sparkle in his eye." He is diffident in the presence of Dr. Rinewulf but glad to report that he is eating and sleeping fine and dreaming not at all.

It is while Mary is getting her hat from an inner room that Galloway, the butler, takes occasion to warn Graham of an impending danger.

"Don't let these bastards fool you, kid, just because you're sitting on a cushion now," he mutters out of the corner of his mouth. "Your friends are still inside."

Fales and Trask and Grimes are in solitary for eight months, Galloway reports. That's what they got for their attempted break, and somebody's going to get the squealer that told on them. There ain't walls thick enough nor guards enough to save Runch's life, even though the men know the poor dope fiend was tricked into a confession when the guards fed him dope and then took it away from him and held it out in front of him until he was half-crazed. Tough for Runch, sure; but what about Fales and the others?

So Runch will have to pay, according to the code, and the best thing Graham can do is to keep away from him and out of the corridor.

Now Mary is back and Graham is happily eager to help her with the last of her packing. "There is such obvious, doglike worship and devotion in his eyes that she looks away," when he talks with her about her trip.

Graham—Will—will you be gone—long?

Mary—Only a few days.

GRAHAM—Oh!

MARY—Is there anything I can do for you?

GRAHAM (*He thinks for a moment.*)—No, thank you.

MARY—Any one you'd like to have me see?

GRAHAM (*simply*)—There isn't anybody now. My mother died three years ago.

MARY—Oh!—I didn't know.

GRAHAM—She used to come to see me every month until she died. It—it kept my courage up. Something to look forward to, you see. Afterwards I began to slip, I guess. It's awfully hard to make yourself believe that it's worth while—to try. And that's what you've got to do—or break.

MARY—Yes.

GRAHAM—They all think they've had a rotten deal. That's all you hear. Bad luck, tough breaks; that's all they talk about. It gets under your skin in time, and fills you up with bitterness and hate. That's all there is in here.

MARY—And are you—bitter?

GRAHAM—No, not now. (*He shakes his head.*) I was. But I seem to see more clearly—now.

MARY—What?

GRAHAM—I don't think I can put it into words. But, well, you see they've got laws in here just like they have outside. Somebody's got to pay. That's at the bottom of it all—and—well, I guess we've got to make the most of it. It may be wrong, but—I guess it's all there is.

MARY (*nodding gravely*)—I see.

GRAHAM—Most everybody's trying to do what seems to them, right. Inside and out, I mean. They just think differently, that's all.

MARY—Yes. (*A pause.*) My father is trying to get you a parole.

GRAHAM—Yes, I know. It doesn't matter so much to me, now.

MARY—Why do you say that?

GRAHAM—I—I mean if you stay here.

MARY—You don't mean that.

GRAHAM (*doggedly*)—Yes— Yes, I do. It isn't like it was before at all. If I can see you every day—just see you! And when they lock me up at night there's something to think about —to—to wait for till tomorrow. I—well— (*A pause.*)

MARY—What will you do when you are free again?

GRAHAM—I don't know. I've thought about it a lot, too. (*Anxiously.*) Don't you think it will make a difference to people?

MARY—What?

GRAHAM—That I have been in prison.

MARY—It shouldn't.

GRAHAM (*with simple eagerness*)—No, it shouldn't, should it? When a thing is paid for, that should end it, but—(*He shakes his head.*)—they don't think that in here. They say it does. They say that's why so many who go out, come back. (*A pause. He searches her face.*) Would—would it make a difference to you?

MARY (*evenly*)—I don't think so.

GRAHAM (*a little breathlessly*)—Oh! (MISS BRADY *comes into the room. She has a bit of sewing in her hand.*)

MISS BRADY—Haven't you gone yet? Whatever are you thinking of? You'll miss the train, Mary.

MARY—I'm going now. Good-by. (*And she hurries out into the corridor.* GRAHAM *picks up the bag and follows her.*)

MISS BRADY (*communing with herself*)—Well, I don't know, I'm sure— (*She sighs and sits down on the sofa. And she sews a stitch or two, then pauses to yawn and tap her lips as if quite overcome with drowsiness, then rubs her eyes and sews again.* GALLOWAY'S *face appears in the doorway, and regards her steadily. The wall descends.*)

Mary and Graham stop in the Warden's office on their way out, so Mary may say good-by to her father. The Warden is not keen to see his daughter go, but, as MacManus says, the prison isn't much of a place for a young girl and it probably has got under her skin a little.

MacManus is paying the prison and the Warden one of his periodical visits. He is in very good spirits, and glad to report that the stunt the Warden pulled in the Fales break has caused a lot of favorable comment in town.

"The papers had to hand it to you for that," MacManus reports. "One of them said the other day it was a crime wasting Mart Brady on a prison job. There's been a lot of talk in town, I tell you. You picked the proper moment for it, Mart—just when an election's coming on. What've you done with Runch?"

"I've got him in here as my clerk, and he can barely read and write. He sleeps in there (the alcove). I have his food sent in. He never sets a foot outside."

"He's safe enough in here."

"Yeah? He's petrified, scared stiff. He's like a rabbit in a trap. It hurts to look at him. He's gotten on my nerves. I can't sleep nights for thinking of him, Mac—I want to get him out of here. I do!"

MacManus, a little puzzled by the Warden's vehement earnestness, is quick to promise that he will do what he can. He realizes that a killing in the prison just now would be bad.

There is also the matter of the parole for Graham. What's MacManus doing about that?

Well, that is also going through the regular channels. It still has to come before the Board. Those things take time—

"Yeah, yeah," agrees Brady, impatiently. "But I want to get him out of here, that kid. He's been here nearly seven years for—for nothing."

"You sent him up yourself."

"I did, God pity me," admits Brady, passionately. "And justly, too, according to our criminal code. All right, he's done enough and paid enough. I want to get him out."

"Yeah—well, I'll try to rush it through."

With MacManus gone and Runch in to return the papers to the files the Warden tries to allay the plainly apparent fears of his clerk. He is perfectly safe there. There are eight feet of stone between him and the yard. None of the clerks in the turnkey's office could possibly get by the guards and certainly none of the Warden's servants would risk their soft jobs, or their necks, to get Runch.

It sounds safe enough, but Runch knows. "They'll get me, sir, they'll get me. I know they will," he whines. Runch wants to get away. He didn't want to squeal. He was framed. He was promised freedom. A guy that squeals is entitled to a break—

The Warden is doing what he can—he can't do more.

. . . .

Graham is back with the car, as ordered. The Warden wants to talk with him, too. As the boy sits near the desk a "far off droning sound begins, so faint at first that one is almost unaware of it. It has the quality of swarming bees and of the surf. There is a rhythm in it, and a beat, and it will mount by almost imperceptible degrees into a roar."

Brady—I'm trying to get you out of here.

Graham—Yes, sir. I know.

Brady—It isn't as easy as it sounds. Prisoners think the Warden is God, but there's a lot of gods stuck over him, and rules and laws. The system's like a big machine: you go in one end and come out the other. See?

Graham—Yes, sir.

Brady—It has to be like that, I guess—it has to be. (*A pause.*) There's four thousand men in here, Bob, and every one of them wants me to do something.

Graham—Yes, sir.

Brady—You've done six years out of your ten. Your record's clean. You're eligible for parole. I'm doing what I can to get you out.

Graham—Yes, sir.

Brady—You're pretty bitter, maybe. I don't know.

Graham—No, sir—not now.

Brady—So much the better for you. Most prisoners are, and then the fight goes on forever. You've only paid according to the law. That's all. A State's Attorney has to fight like hell for that. For every man he puts behind the bars, a dozen slip between his fingers. He has to fight a dirty yellow press, and maudlin public sentiment, and shyster lawyers that'll stoop to anything for money, and juries of sentimental women and plain morons. That's all part of the game. And— (*He breaks off abruptly; listening. The distant roar rises and surges. It has now the semblance of a chant, a jeering college yell.*)

The Roar—Yah, yah, yah— Yah, yah, yah— Yah, yah, yah— Yah, yah, yah. (*It goes on, rising and falling, and gaining volume.*)

Brady—What's that? (*He gets up and strides to the window.*)

Graham (*at his side*)—I think it's in the recreation yard behind the jute mill, sir.

Brady—Yeah.

Graham—A fight, perhaps.

Brady—Yeah. (*He strides to the door.*) Wait here till I come back. (*And he goes out.* Graham *remains standing by the window, looking out. In a moment* Runch *comes into the room. He is shaking with terror.*)

Runch—Christ! What's that noise? (Graham *starts, turns, moves back.*)

Graham—I don't know— A fight, maybe.

RUNCH—A fight? A fight? (*He shuffles to the window.*) What would they yell like that for?

GRAHAM—I don't know. (*He draws farther back. The sound subsides a little.*)

RUNCH (*furiously*)—You think the touch of me'd foul you, eh? God damn you, you're sitting pretty now. You may be in a jam like this yourself, some day. I'm just as square a guy as you—as any one. They framed me, and I fell for it—that's all. I got a rotten break—a rotten break. (*The noise swells up.*) Christ! They're starting in again— What is it— What? (*He presses his face against the window.*) The guards are running back there, every one! . . . I can see the machine guns on the wall. . . . They got 'em trained that way. Maybe it's a riot, eh?

GRAHAM—I don't know.

RUNCH (*whining*)—I've always been a friend of yours, Bob. Remember when we lived up in the block, you and Jim Fales, and me next door? And we messed together, too—the three of us, eh, Bob?

GRAHAM—Yes.

RUNCH—I never done you any dirt. You ain't got anything against me, Bob?

GRAHAM (*hesitating*)—No.

RUNCH (*pleading*)—Give me a tipoff, kid. Have they got me framed?— Are they going to get me— Eh?

GRAHAM—I don't know.

RUNCH (*furiously*)—The hell you don't! You're down there in the yard. You know what's going on. You're holding out on me. Why don't you show your eyes, and look me in the face? (*Whining again, and clasping his hands in supplication.*) Have a heart, kid!— Have a heart!— Give me a chance—a break— (*The noise swells up again.*) God!— God!— (*He turns to the window, and turns back.*) Go find out what they're yelling for!

GRAHAM—I can't. He told me to stay here.

RUNCH—You're lying to me. (GRAHAM *shakes his head.*) Just down the stairs, and ask the guards down there.

GRAHAM—No.

RUNCH—By God!— I think you're in on it, yourself.

GRAHAM—No—I don't know anything, I tell you.

RUNCH (*pleading again*)—Then go out there, and listen in the hall. You might hear something, Bob. I only want to know what's up. I can't stand waiting here like this— Please, Bob—please. (*The sound is louder. He can scarce be heard. He goes toward* GRAHAM, *who backs from him toward the door.*) I'd do the like for you. I'd do it for a dog. (*And now his voice is drowned. The roar submerges everything. He seizes* GRAHAM *by the arm, and* GRAHAM *pulls away from him, and bows his head, and goes out into the hall.* RUNCH *turns back, cursing and mumbling to himself. He covers his ears with his hands, and shuffles to the window and looks out.* GALLOWAY *appears at the entrance to the corridor; in his hand is the haft of a knife, the blade of which is in his sleeve. He stands there for a moment; then, as if impelled by some psychic power,* RUNCH *turns deliberately and stares straight into his face. A pause. Suddenly, with a little squeal like a frightened animal, he breaks for the stairs; but* GALLOWAY *is swifter of foot, and blocks him at the door. He stops and cowers back, looks desperately about, then squeals again, and darts into the alcove.* GALLOWAY *follows him; some moments pass; the roar begins to fade.*)

Galloway is coming slowly from the alcove when Graham, returning from the hallway, sees him. The butler is furious. Why couldn't Graham have the sense to stay away? He was warned! Perhaps he was planted there? Probably the only safe thing to do now would be to slit Graham's throat, too—

But Galloway is convinced, after a searching look into the boy's eyes, that Graham is not lying.

"Beat it, you fool!" he yells, darting toward the corridor. "Get out! Don't let them find you here, you sap!—you dumbbell! Go on! Go on! Get out!"

Now the noise in the courtyard has faded. Graham has taken a quick look into the alcove and there is horror in his eyes as he staggers back to the centre of the room. Warden Brady, followed by Gleason, comes bursting through the hall door.

At first they do not see Graham. Then, as the Warden tells him to put the car away, he is conscious of a change in the boy's attitude. What's wrong with him? Is he sick, or what?

There's nothing wrong with him, Graham answers, and they let him go.

Gleason is puzzled about the racket in the yard. There wasn't a fight. Gleason couldn't discover what started it or where it started. But prisoners are like that. Once they get a thing going it spreads through 'em all.

"It's not a pretty sound," agrees Brady.

"No, sir, it's not. It drives the guards near wild, sometimes. I've known them to keep it up all night, to kick about the grub. But what can you do when there's four thousand of 'em?"

"Nothing—I guess."

Sometimes, Gleason has found, it is pure orneriness. Sometimes they'll pull a stunt like that to cover something else.

Warden Brady had thought of that. Now, with a sudden tenseness in his voice, he calls: "Runch!" There is no answer. Now the Warden has entered the alcove and is calling Gleason, and Gleason knows.

"By God! They got him!"

There are hurried calls for Dr. Rinewulf, and for the Chaplain. Gleason can be heard trying to extract a confession from the dying man. It avails him nothing. When Rinewulf arrives he is able to keep Runch's heart beating a few minutes, but not long enough for the dying man to receive the consolations of the church. By the time Chaplain Simpkins reaches him Runch is dead.

The investigation is hurriedly pressed. It is Gleason's first thought that Graham, the chauffeur, has done the job, but the Warden can't believe that. However, he sends for Graham. Also for the guards who were on the gate—Kurtz and Stolper—one a man of middle years, the other young; both with "dull, stupid faces."

Quick questioning reveals that, during the excitement, Stolper had left his post at the outer gate for a minute and crossed to see what was happening. The gates were locked. The door of the turnkey's office! Stolper never thought of that! A man could have come out of that office and gone up the Warden's private stairway. But Stolper didn't see any one either go up or come down.

Now Gleason, sent to find out where Miss Brady has been the last half hour, and what she's been doing, is back to report that he found the Warden's sister asleep; that she had been asleep ever since Mary Brady had left and that her sleeping is suspiciously like that of a person who has been drugged.

So, whoever killed Runch had access to the room from either entrance—each arranged to alibi the other. Again Gleason suggests Graham, but the Warden dismisses the idea impatiently—

"Use your nut," he shouts. "Why plant these alibis and then leave some one to be caught red-handed? He blundered into it, the boy—just blundered into it."

"Well, anyway, he knows who done it."

There is an expression of pain in the Warden's eyes as he answers, slowly:

"Yeah, I guess that's right, Gleason—I guess he does."

The Warden is gentle with Graham, when he reports. His tone is sober, almost sad, as he interrogates him. That Bob did not do the murder he is ready to believe from the boy's firm denial. It was "just a happenstance—the way things break sometimes—" that he should have blundered into it. Those who did the planning had thought of everything but that. But that Bob knows who did do the killing the Warden is also convinced. Nor is Graham's faltering denial of that charge at all convincing.

"I'm afraid you can't get away with that, my boy," he warns. "I go out of this room, and leave you here, and Runch is alive. When I come back, you're still here, white as chalk, and Runch is dead or dying— You knew that, didn't you?"

"Yes." Graham's answer is almost inaudible.

BRADY—Yeah. And you were in here when the man was killed.

GRAHAM (*desperately*)—No, no, I wasn't here.

BRADY—What?

GRAHAM—I wasn't here. I went— (*He hesitates, seeing the trap into which he is about to fall.*)

BRADY—Went where?

GRAHAM (*stammering*)—Nowhere.

BRADY—What do you mean?

GRAHAM—Nothing—I— (*He takes a deep breath.*) Nothing.

BRADY—And yet you say you don't know who did that. You're lying, Bob—lying to shield a murderer, a man who crept in here with a knife and struck that poor, defenseless creature down. (*A pause.*) Is that worth while? (*No answer.*) A man is dead in there, Bob. The law says some one has to pay for that.

GRAHAM (*doggedly*)—I didn't kill him.

BRADY—I know that, Bob.

GRAHAM—I didn't even know. I wasn't even in on it. I'll swear to that.

BRADY (*soothingly*)—Yeah, yeah, sure, Bob, I understand. But there'll be an inquest.

GRAHAM (*startled*)—An inquest?

BRADY—Yeah, that's right. The long arm of the law will reach right through these gates—the same law that's outside. You didn't think of that?

GRAHAM—No, sir.

BRADY—What will you say to the coroner's jury then?

GRAHAM (*taking a deep breath*)—Nothing. (*A pause.*)

BRADY—You can't get away with that. They'll yank you out of here and put you in the county jail. I've got no jurisdiction then, no more than you or any one. I'm just a witness in the dock. What can I say? They'll hold you as an accessory before the fact, or after it, or God knows what. You might get ten or twenty years for that.

GRAHAM—No! (*He staggers.*)

BRADY (*rising quickly to his feet*)—Sit down, my boy—sit down. (*He takes his arm, and* GRAHAM *sinks down in a chair.*) I've got to tell you this. You've got to know. A free man has nine chances out of ten to cheat the law. A prisoner hasn't one chance in a hundred. Opinion is against him from the start. (*A pause. He sits on the edge of the desk chewing his cigar.*) They could indict you for this, Bob. Men have been hung on slimmer evidence.

GRAHAM—No— No!

BRADY—Yeah, that's right. (*He picks up the code from the desk, turns to a page, and reads:*) ". . . except that a prisoner serving a sentence for homicide, who shall be convicted of murder, shall be hanged . . ." (*He closes the book, and puts it down.*) That's our criminal code, Bob.

GRAHAM—It isn't fair. It isn't just.

BRADY—It's the law— That's all we've got— (*A pause.*) I doubt if they'd convict you, Bob, but—you can never tell which way those things will jump. The State's Attorney here is a young man. He's out to make a record for himself. The papers will be at his back. They'll leave no stone unturned to punish somebody for that. (*A pause.*) It's tough—tough—but you see the way things lie. You'd better tell me, Bob.

GRAHAM—I can't do that— I can't do that. (*He shakes his head.*) There's a law inside here, too. A man can do anything but squeal. He can't do that. I'll have to take my chance, I guess.

BRADY—Chance! You've got no chance. You're in a net. You're caught. You've got to clear this up to save yourself.

GRAHAM—I can't.

BRADY—You must. Good God, boy, stop and think! You may get ten or twenty years.

GRAHAM—No, no, I'd rather die than that. I couldn't stand it. No.

BRADY—Your parole's up in town. It's due here any day. The prison board will cancel that.

GRAHAM—I didn't kill him. I have done nothing wrong.

BRADY—The time you've earned for good behavior will be lost. That leaves you three more years to serve—three years at least.

GRAHAM—It isn't right. It isn't fair.

BRADY—And I can't keep you here with me. They'd never stand for that. You'd go back in the jute mill, Bob.

GRAHAM (*wildly*)—No, no, I can't. I won't.

BRADY—You've not forgotten the smell of jute in six short months?

GRAHAM—God!— No.

BRADY—You see, you're up against it, boy. You've got to tell. (*Suddenly he slams his fist down on the desk, and shouts:*) Who killed that man? Who killed him, Bob? Come clean now! Quick! Speak up! Who killed him? Who? Who? (*A pause.*) Yeah? (*Gently, pleadingly.*) Just tell me where he came from, Bob. From there?—or there? (*He indicates the corridor and hall.*) You can't be doing any harm by that. I know it was one way or the other. It's just a detail that I'd like to know. From there, eh, Bob? (*No answer.*) Or over there?— (*No answer.*) Come now, be reasonable. It won't be violating your code to tell me that—Bob!

GRAHAM (*stolidly*)—I don't know.

Still patiently the Warden sits on the edge of his desk close to Graham. Pleadingly he confesses his friendship for the boy. And yet he has an obligation toward the dead man, too. It was his duty to protect Runch. Having failed in that duty, he will be attacked. It's a tough break for Graham, a rotten piece of luck that sent him there. But the cards have to be played the way they lay. Graham is up against the wall and there is only one way out. Who killed Runch?

Graham can't tell.

"You'll trade your life away to live up to a code that's made by murderers and crooks to cheat the laws of honest men? You're not a crook. That's not your code."

"It's all I've had."

"No," shouts Brady, snatching up the book from the table. "This is your code and mine. Hold fast to it. You can't be faithful to them both. Stick with the law. You're not a crook. Don't turn one now. Don't turn your back on this. (*He slams the book down on the desk.*) Who killed that man?"

"No."

A kind of dumb defiance shines through the boy's speech. He shakes his head and stumbles on. "I—I can't forget so quickly what I've learned in here—I can't do that. I think it's right, their code, for them— I can't go back on it—or them. I can't—

I wouldn't be anything then, don't you see? Not anything—I—I'd be like that thing in there— No! No!"

Gleason is back from the corridor. There is anger and hatred in his frown as he glares at Graham and asks the progress of the examination. There is a threat of hell to come in his tone as he swears that by God they'll take all the defiance out of the suspect.

Again Warden Brady interferes. He would give Bob one more chance. Let the boy consider. His parole is on the way. In another week he can be outside the walls free to go and come, to do as he will, to have a home and a wife and kids—

Or will he rot in prison for another three, or ten, or twenty years? Or hang, perhaps? Or go back to the jute mill, even the smell of which sickens him?

And to the dungeon now—"a bucket meal each seven days—cold slop. And bread and water in between. No ray of light, no air, no sound, no human voice. Black emptiness, that's all."

There is terror in Graham's eyes as he arises and backs away from his tormentors.

"God, no!" he cries. "For what? For what?"

BRADY—The prison rules. A prisoner must obey. Come now! (*He follows the boy, and grips him by the shoulders.*) Who killed that man?—Who killed that man? Think fast, Bob! For God's sake, think fast! Who killed him? Eh? (*The boy cowers back. His eyes are suddenly expressionless.*) Yeah? (*He stares at the blank eyes for a long moment, and a baffled, tired look comes into his face. His shoulders droop, and he turns away. To* GLEASON; *harshly:*) Take him away!—Put him in the dungeon!—Lock him up!

GLEASON—Yes, sir. (*He raps with his cane on the floor.*) Come now, get out!—On your way! (GRAHAM *turns and goes slowly from the room—with dragging step, his shoulders bent, his body sagging,* GLEASON *following him.*) He'll not be so cocky in a week.

BRADY—Wait! No violence to that boy! Let no one lay a hand on him! You understand?

GLEASON (*doubtfully*)—Yes, sir.

BRADY—I'm doing this for him—for him. I've got to save him, do you see? To save him from himself. He's got to tell. He must. He must. (*He strikes the desk with his fist.*)

GLEASON (*vaguely impressed*)—Yes, sir—he will. A week of bread and water in the dark'll loosen up his tongue.

BRADY—You think so, eh?

GLEASON—It mostly always does.

BRADY—Yeah— Yeah. (*A pause; abruptly; savagely:*) Get the Bertillon man! Finger-print everything up here—the hall, the stairs, the corridor, the body there! Don't miss a bet. You understand? I've got to get that bird. I've got to get him!

GLEASON—Yes, sir. (*He starts to go.*)

BRADY—Wait! Send Galloway in here—the cook, the nigger, too; and all that gang down there. I want 'em all. By God, I'll grill it out of them. I'll get the bird that turned this trick. I'll get him.

GLEASON—Yes, sir. Is that all?

BRADY—Yes. Go. Be quick. Put everybody on this job. Don't miss a bet, you understand? Don't miss a bet!

GLEASON—No, sir. (*And he dashes from the room.*)

BRADY (*sinking down in the chair beside his desk; wildly to himself*)—A week of bread and water in the dark— A week of bread and water in the dark! . . . The dark! The dark! . . . Christ! (*Then, steadying himself, he snatches up the telephone.*) Warden talking— Get me the coroner— Yeah . . . (*The descending wall interrupts the speech. The curtain falls.*)

ACT III

In the living room of the Warden's quarters Miss Brady is seated on the sofa, "a shawl about her shoulders, and an air of mild invalidism." Dr. Rinewulf is facing her.

Miss Brady has been ailing for some days. She has not been able to sleep the whole week that has passed since Runch was murdered. She really has wanted to go away, but has hesitated to add anything more to her brother's anxieties.

It has been a terrible week—with the newspapers attacking Warden Brady shamefully, accusing him of all manner of impossible things; of even knowing more about the case than he will tell.

Dr. Rinewulf does what he can to reassure Miss Brady. She should not let the prison get on her nerves.

"These men have no concern with you," he points out to her. "They will not harm you—no. Their quarrel is with the law. They are like animals—like—like—rattlesnakes. They will not strike unless you interfere with them." Still, Miss Brady is not entirely reassured as she goes back to her room.

At the door, as he is leaving, Dr. Rinewulf meets Mary Brady, returned from her trip. Back of her a new chauffeur, a boyish-looking convict, named Jerry, carries in her bag and leaves.

Dr. Rinewulf stops long enough to tell Mary that he is particularly glad she is back. Things have happened since she has been away, as she doubtless has seen if she has read the papers. Mary has paid but little attention to the papers. She is so used to attacks upon her father—he has been crucified so many times—that she automatically lays all such things to dirty politics.

She is, however, puzzled by the absence of the Robert Graham who had been the Warden's chauffeur when she left. What has become of him? As to that, the Doctor thinks probably either her aunt or father had better tell her.

Mary has gone when Galloway slides cautiously into the room and is met a second later by the new chauffeur. The appointment has been prearranged and Jerry is late, but he is inclined to resent Galloway's dictation of his movements. Nor is his resentment helped by the butler's further orders.

On his next trip to the garage, Galloway instructs him, Jerry is to be careful to pass the cookhouse door at exactly three minutes after four. At the door he will meet Joe MacNamee going in. He will stop and speak to Joe and slip him the knife that Galloway now draws from his sleeve.

It is a shoemaker's knife; there will be no tracing it back to Jerry, even if all the plans fail. He is to give the knife to MacNamee, who, so long as he insists on knowing, is going to slip it into the bucket feed that is to go to the kid in the cooler that afternoon.

If the knife gets by the leather-headed cop who inspects the feed, it will get to Graham. Graham has had a tough time of it the last week. He's entitled to something.

Jerry, however, isn't prepared to believe it has been so tough for Graham.

"They haven't put the lash on him or beat him up," he insists.

GALLOWAY—Suppose they haven't. Have you ever been down there, where he is?

JERRY—No.

GALLOWAY—Well—I have! A straw tick on a stone floor—in the dark. You don't know what that feels like, Jerry.

JERRY—No.

GALLOWAY—They'll come down a dozen times a day and try and pry it out of you. They'll threaten anything, and promise anything.

JERRY—The bastards!

GALLOWAY—They'll stand there in your cell, and tell you what they had for dinner, and blow tobacco in your face, and talk to you about the sunshine, and the trees—and women.

JERRY—Christ!

GALLOWAY—They'll wait until you go to sleep, then snap a flashlight in your face, and kick and cuff you to your feet, and yell into your ears! Oh, they got lots of bright ideas!

JERRY—God!

GALLOWAY—You think it's not so tough for him, eh, Jerry?

JERRY—I guess I didn't think about it, Ned.

GALLOWAY—I'm only asking you to take the short and easy end of this.

JERRY—Yeah? (*A pause.*) What good's a knife to him down there?

GALLOWAY—Not much, perhaps, but it's an out—a two way out—to end the torture, or—

JERRY—Yeah, yeah—I see.

GALLOWAY—The kid's been game—dead game. We owe him something.

JERRY—Yeah.

GALLOWAY (*after a long pause*)—Well—? (*He breaks off, conscious of some one coming from the right.*)

JERRY (*whispering*)—O.K. Slip it to me.

GALLOWAY (*slipping him the knife*)—Beat it! Be quick! (JERRY *runs into the corridor;* GALLOWAY *goes quickly to the table as* MARY *comes in from the right. The wall descends.*)

. . . . . .

In his office Warden Brady is in conference with Sheridan, the new State's Attorney, "a young man, thirty-five perhaps, rather countrified in dress, a bit self-conscious now and therefore somewhat pompous in manner and in speech."

Mr. Sheridan has come to have a showdown with Warden Brady as to what he is doing in the murder case and why there has been no coroner's inquest. He gets but little satisfaction. The Warden realizes Mr. Sheridan's position; he knows how the yellow press is riding the State's Attorney's office and demanding action. There's an election coming on, too—

But the Warden is conducting his own investigation in his own way and he doesn't purpose being interfered with. Suddenly, angered by certain of Sheridan's slurs respecting his motives, Brady lashes out at the young man.

"Don't try to tell me how to run my job," he shouts. "I learned this game when you were in the cradle. I'm moving heaven and earth to get the bird that turned this trick. Well, give me a chance! Lay off! You and your coroner and inquest—what the hell can you do? You'll only ball things up."

"I only want to do my duty," Sheridan shouts back; "to serve the law and justice—"

"Justice! That's what I want, too. That's what I'm after."

If Mr. Sheridan is not satisfied with what is happening he will have to take such action as he sees fit. Let him report the case to the Attorney-General, as he threatens, and see that an inquest is called the next morning.

. . . . . .

Gleason is back from another visit to Graham. The boy still refuses to talk. He's got so now he won't even shake his head.

"We're at him every hour of the day and night," reports Gleason. "We hardly let him get no sleep at all. I've tried most everything I know. He's stubborn as a mule. I took him in a bucket feed just now, the first he's had. I tried a little stunt that works sometimes—to leave him smell the food, and then just snatch it back."

"Yeah."

"It didn't do no good. I yelled at him until I was hoarse."

"Did you tell him what I said?"

"Word for word. I told him: his parole's here; it came this morning; it's laying on your desk; he could be out and free in half an hour. Yes, sir, I told him that."

"My God, there must be something in a faith like that!"

Dr. Rinewulf has come to report to the Warden that Graham naturally shows the effects of a week on bread and water, but that he is more seriously concerned with the breaking of the boy's spirit and morale—of the man himself.

"He is sullen now," the Doctor reports. "It is difficult to see into his eyes. And when one does, one sees that they are filled with bitterness and hate. There is no trace of what I found in them before—that spark worth saving. It is a pity—yes, a pity!"

The phone rings. In answer the Warden barks his refusal to make a statement. Let the papers print what they like.

"To hell with all that tripe," he shouts, as he hangs up the receiver. "God damn yellow press! The only thing they give a whoop about is circulation. To hell with them! They'd put Christ on the cross again to get an extra on the street."

There is apparently nothing more to be done, Brady admits. The inquest will be called at 10 next morning and the law will have to take its course. Graham stands a good chance of getting the rope. But they'll do nothing more to force the boy's tongue. It is just possible they have done too much already. Let Gleason lay off him. . . .

The wrinkles are smoothed out of the Warden's face at sight of his daughter. "It's like a breath of heaven to have you back here, Mary," he sighs, as he kisses her.

But there are only solemn looks on Mary's face. Her voice is quiet and even as she demands to know what her father has done with Robert Graham, and her questioning is persistent.

The Warden tries to put her off at first, but she knows too much to be put off. Her aunt has told her what has happened in the prison. She knows, too, that her father was responsible for the boy's imprisonment. Now she wants to know what has been done with him.

Graham, the Warden admits, is in the dungeon. He was put there, technically, for an infringement of the prison rules, but practically to save his life.

MARY—What good is it to save a man, father, if you destroy him while you're doing it?

BRADY (*The crease deepens in his brow. Slowly.*)—Yeah—that's right, Mary . . . I thought of that myself.

MARY—A broken thing—what good is that to any one or to itself? Prisons are filled with broken men—with broken minds and souls—twisted and distorted! What good is it to save a man for that? He would be better—dead!

BRADY (*His chin is heavy on his chest.*)—Yeah . . . I thought of that.

MARY—This man was clean and fine—and—*straight*. What would he be when you had broken him?

BRADY (*standing up, with passionate impatience*)—Yeah, yeah, that's all right. I see your point. I've thought of all that stuff, myself. But what am I going to do? His parole's laying there. (*He picks it up from the desk, and slaps it with his hand.*) It's taken me six months to get it—I want to get him out of here. I want to turn him loose. Well, then, I can't. He's tied my hands— I can't. (*He throws the paper down, and strides across the room.*)

MARY (*tensely*)—You can! You must!

BRADY—Yeah? What would you do?

MARY—I'd set him free tonight.

BRADY—Yeah? (*He laughs, harshly.*) You're just a kid. You don't know anything about these things.

MARY (*passionately*)—I do. I do. I'd set him free, and then I'd fight for him. I'd get behind him, and I'd see him through. If he were free, he'd have a chance. He has done nothing wrong. He's only doing what he thinks is right. It's only what you think that counts.

BRADY (*listening with narrowed eyes*)—Yeah.

MARY—A man like you could find a way to save him. Delays and disagreements, and what not. You know the way those things are done, father. You've often told me of the things they've done to you. He'd be outside and free. He'd have a chance. You'd get him off, father. You know you could.

BRADY (*calmly*)—You're crazy, Mary.

MARY—I'm not. You could do that. You know you could.

BRADY—Yeah—and what would they do to me—for that?

MARY—What does it matter?

BRADY—Matter? (*He stares at her.*) You don't know what you're saying, girl. You don't know what it means. They'd just bust me higher than a kite. I'm only hanging by a shoe-string now. They're after me. They're only waiting for a chance. Well, you know that— And an election coming on. . . .

MARY—But, if it's right—

BRADY (*interrupting passionately*)—Right!— Yeah, what's that?— You talk as if I'd done a crime, myself. I've only done my duty all my life—my duty by the public and the law. I'm not God. I didn't make things right or wrong. I didn't make the law. There's nothing on my head. I don't owe any man the scrap of future left to me. (*She tries to speak; he drowns her out.*) No, no, you're crazy. You're just a kid. You don't know what it means. I've done the best I could for him— I'm through— I'm done— The law must take its course.

MARY (*gasping*)—No. (*She runs to his side, and grasps his sleeve; desperately.*) No. You can't do that— You can't— (*He stares at her, suddenly startled and oppressed by vague concern, and very gently he disengages her hands from his sleeve, and holds them in his own.*)

BRADY (*gently, but with a tremor in his voice*)—Say—what's gotten into you? What do you mean? What's back of all this stuff?

MARY (*stammering*)—I— (*She turns away her head.*)

BRADY—Yeah? (*He holds fast to her hands.*) Come on,

sweetheart, let's get right down to cases on this thing. What's up?

MARY (*bravely; looking him squarely in the eyes*)—I love him, father.

BRADY—Yeah? (*He drops her hands.*) Yeah? (*A long pause.*) Is that on the level, Mary?

MARY—Yes.

BRADY (*evenly; wearily*)—Why didn't you tell me at first?

MARY—I wanted you to do it, because it was right—not just for me!

BRADY—Yeah— I see. (*He nods slowly. A pause.*) How long has this been going on?

MARY—It hasn't gone at all. He's never said a thing to me, but—well, I read it in his eyes. That's why I went away: to see, to find out just how much I cared—and whether it would make a difference to me that he had been—in prison.

BRADY (*nodding*)—Yeah.

MARY—And I know now that it doesn't. (*A pause.*) I'm sorry if it hurts you, father, but—

BRADY (*with an effort*)—No. (*A pause.*) No. You can't help that, Mary. Love—you have to take it when and where it comes. You're not a child. You've always had a level head. I wouldn't set myself against a thing like that. That's up to you. Yeah. (*He sighs.*) I guess that's one thing that the law don't cover.

MARY (*searching his eyes, tremulously*)—What—what will you do, father?

BRADY—There's just one answer left to that, Mary—I'd turn the demons out of hell—for you.

MARY—Oh! (*And she sways a little on her feet.*)

BRADY—Don't you worry, sweetheart. (*He goes to her, and puts his arm around her shoulders.*) We'll see him through, somehow—some way. He'll never serve another day—if we can help it! And I guess we can. Yeah, I guess we can—some way. (*He kisses her on the forehead. She is close to tears.*) Buck up, old girl, now! Steady!

MARY (*smiling into his eyes*)—Yes—father.

BRADY—Yeah. (*He nods, smiles back at her through all the creases in his face, but his teeth are set, and his lips tight. He turns away and crosses slowly, and heavily, to his desk, and sinks into his chair, stifling a groan, turning it off into a cough. And he picks up the telephone. His voice is level, unnaturally so.*) Warden talking. Find Captain Gleason, and tell him to send

Number two-three-four-nine-nine up to my office . . . Yeah . . . That's right . . . Yeah.

MARY—Thank you, father. (*The wall descends.*)

. . . . . .

The dungeon row is in total darkness when Gleason and Kurtz come with Graham's bucket feed. Not until Kurtz finds the light switch with his pocket flash are even the steel doors revealed—doors "with perforations through the steel no bigger than a lead pencil forming crosses in the centre of each."

Kurtz unlocks a dungeon and growls a command for the inmate to come out. There is no reply. Kurtz plunges into the cell and backs out to report that Graham is huddled in a corner as though he were sick. Or he might be unconscious—

"You smashed him pretty hard today," he reminds the Captain.

"I only hit him once, and with my fist!" protests Gleason. "Give me that flash! By God, I'll give him something to be sick about!"

There are curses inside the dimly lighted cave, and the sound of blows struck. Now even Gleason is forced to admit his prisoner may be sick. He'd like to have his way with him once—But they had better send for the Doctor now.

Kurtz leaves the stair door unlocked as he hurries away for Rinewulf. Gleason spends the time pacing up and down the narrow space, mumbling his disgust of the way things are run around here.

"You can't do nothing with these mollycoddle ways—a crook's a crook—that's all there is about it. Spare the rod and spoil the child—"

Now Graham's face, dirty and contorted, appears in the doorway directly at Gleason's back. "His clothing is torn; his feet bare. A knife blade glitters in his hand. Slowly his other hand steals around the corner feeling for the light switch. Click, the lights are out."

"Eh? What's that? God!"

A choking, strangling sound; and the thud of a falling body. Gleason is down.

The concrete prison wall towers high in the darkness. "Angles in the wall create black shadows. In one of these there is, invisible, a steel-barred gate." The sound of voices high up on the wall is heard. It comes from the guards protesting the bitter cold of the night and the monotony of their jobs.

There is a shadow against the wall, groping its way from left to right. Suddenly, by a blinding flash of searchlight, the shadow is revealed to be Graham. The light blinds him and he throws his arm across his eyes.

"Pull up there, you!—Don't move!—I've got you covered with a 30-30, bo! Now, where the hell do you think you're going—strolling around the yard this time of night? Look up here at me, you!"

"Lay off— That's the bird that drives the Warden's car!"

"I thought they had him in the cooler."

"They did. I guess they let him out."

"O.K."

Across the yard there is another flash of light and another inspection. They know him now. He's Bob and he's out of the cooler. Well, he can tell the world about coolers now.

"Jesus, but you look tough," a guard shouts down at him. "You need a shave. The Warden said you were to come right up."

There is a crash of drawn bolts as the light goes out.

In the office Warden Brady is seated back of his desk, writing. Mary is waiting. There is an old brown suitcase by the door to the stairs.

When Jerry, the chauffeur, comes, the Warden gives him particular instructions. He is to take the suitcase, put it in the car and wait.

"I'm turning a man out tonight," the Warden explains. "I'll send him down in a few minutes. You will drive him to the station."

The Warden has slipped a bill into the envelope with the letter he has been writing, Mary watching him narrowly, when the door opens and Graham shuffles into the room.

At sight of him Mary steps forward, and then stops abruptly. Graham cringes before the sight of her and fixes his gaze upon the floor. There is an embarrassed moment before the Warden thinks to relieve the situation with his good news.

"I'm sorry for what happened," the Warden is saying, jerkily, painfully. "I've done the best I could for you—for every one—"

Graham does not lift his eyes from the floor.

"Your parole has come. I'm going to send you out tonight. Yeah—that's right, Bob. I've got it here. It only came this evening. And here's a pass to take you through the gate. My driver's waiting there. He'll take you to the station. Your—your clothes are in the car—"

Graham tries to speak. He can only shake his head.

"Yeah. Sure!" the Warden hurries on. "There's some money in this envelope. You go to the address that's on it, and just wait there until you hear from me—"

A hoarse "No!" escapes the trembling lips of the boy. "It's too late," he says. "You can't—"

Dr. Rinewulf has rushed into the room.

"Gleason is dead—stabbed in the back—here's the knife. A shoemaker's knife, I think," he reports.

"I killed him!" adds Graham, dully. And as Mary shudders, "I killed him," he repeats. "I didn't know, you see. I thought he's only come to torture me again. I couldn't stand it any more. I didn't have the strength. He's come so many times to coax and plead and threaten. And in the night he's waked me up to try to make me tell. I couldn't stand it any more. I was afraid I might give up."

"Oh, God!" Mary has covered her eyes with her hands and turned her head away.

"I killed him," Graham repeats, a note of defiance coming into his voice. "I'm not sorry. No one has any right to make another being suffer as I did—in there."

The telephone is buzzing. There is no other sound. Across the table Mary looks dully, appealingly into the eyes of Dr. Rinewulf. He answers the query she cannot voice.

RINEWULF (*gently*)—Already it is known. The prison in alarm.

MARY (*turning back to her father*)—No! God! There must be some way—some way—

BRADY (*thickly*)—We're whipped, my child.—I can't beat this. Nothing can save him now. The law— (*His lip quivers. He looks at the parole slip in his hand, tears it across and drops the pieces on the floor. Faintly at first but growing steadily stronger, the dismal wail of a siren. Slowly the boy's face turns toward the window.*)

MARY (*despairingly*)—Father! Father!

BRADY—It—it's just the way things break sometimes. The way—they break. (*The siren drowns his voice. It shrieks and screams. The whole house rocks with it. The curtain falls.*)

BERKELEY SQUARE

A Play in Three Acts

By John L. Balderston

THE somewhat discouraging collapse of the native drama at the close of the theatre season of 1928-29 left the theatrical gates wide open for the entrance of imported London successes in the spring and fall of 1929.

The first of these proved to be Sherriff's "Journey's End"; the second, Drinkwater's "Bird in Hand"; the third, John Balderston's "Berkeley Square." For although Mr. Balderston is an American, born in Philadelphia, his play was written in London and was numbered with the London successes previous to its importation by Gilbert Miller in association with Leslie Howard, the English actor.

"Berkeley Square" is somewhat difficult of classification. It is neither fantasy nor straight drama, but an artful combination of the two. To speak of it as fantastic drama is to appear to ignore its finer qualities, its delicate and most appealing spiritual realities.

Mr. Balderston's play undertakes to project the spirit of Peter Standish, a 1928 American, back into the year 1784 when his namesake and most distinguished ancestor, also an American, first visited the ancestral home of the Standish-Pettigrew family in Berkeley Square, London.

Thus in the late afternoon of October 23, 1784, we are introduced to the morning room of the house in Berkeley Square. It is a formal and handsome room, "panelled and painted a creamy white. There are two long recessed windows at the back, with pelmets and curtains of rose-coloured Italian brocade that fall to the window seats. They look out into the trees of the enclosed garden, now drenched with rain."

There is a large fireplace set at an angle across the corner of the room, and in the centre panel between the windows at back, a tapestry hangs. "The room is lit by five glass sconces of two lights each," and as the curtain rises a maid "wearing a blue-gray dress with frilled mob-cap," is lighting these candles. There is a fire in the grate, and the deep tones of a grandfather clock in the hall can be heard striking five.

There is the sound of a horse stopping outside. The maid, going to the door, returns with a letter. She is followed by Tom Pettigrew, "a youth in his twenties, clothed as a town buck of the period. He has aristocratic features; mouth normally twisted into a sneer; naturally coarse, brutal, disagreeable under the veneer of good breeding," and he is slightly tipsy.

There is an arrogant authority in the manner in which Tom takes the letter from the maid. He will himself give it to her ladyship to whom it is addressed, he announces. He would also steal a kiss from the maid if she did not protest too effectively, or if he had not at the moment been interrupted by his sister, Kate Pettigrew. Kate, at 25, is "dressed fashionably; a cool, competent, handsome, self-assured" young woman, one who is quite naturally contemptuous of her brother's show of familiarity with the maids and of his habits of life in general.

Tom's attitude is particularly aggravating to Kate in that he boasts of news he will not tell her; news of the coming of her Cousin Peter from America, from whom, he suspects, comes the letter that has but now arrived for their mother. Tom has talked with Bill Clinton within the hour, and Bill had crossed with Cousin Peter in the *General Wolfe*.

Kate should be more than moderately excited at this news, thinks Tom, seeing that it is practically settled that she is to marry the approaching Peter and, by the acquisition of a settlement of some fifteen thousand pounds a year, which sum has been named in the preliminary arrangements, successfully relieve the Pettigrew family from the beggary that threatens.

Lady Anne Pettigrew, "50, stout, high-nosed, determined, rather a dragon," comes soon to confirm Tom's news. The letter is from Cousin Peter. He is in London, at the Blue Boar Tavern in Jermyn Street.

"Honoured madam," reads Lady Anne. "Having arrived within the hour, travelling by post from Plymouth, I make haste to dispatch you this intimation that I shall do myself the honour to wait upon yourself, my fair cousins, and Mr. Pettigrew, at a half after five this evening, in Berkeley Square. I subscribe myself, Madam, your most obedient cousin and humble servant, Peter Standish. To the Lady Anne Pettigrew."

KATE—Our cousin's letter is well bred.

LADY ANNE—Mr. Standish's letters from New York have already vouched for his parts.

TOM—And Messrs. Barings' discreet replies, for his substance.

LADY ANNE (*surveying* KATE *thoughtfully*)—You look charming, my child.

TOM—Such blushes, too. Art or nature?

KATE—More natural than wit in you.

TOM—Your husband will find you sharp of tongue, my lass. (*Clock outside on landing strikes once.* TOM *looks at his watch.*)

TOM—A quarter after five o'clock. The cavalier should be here ere long.

LADY ANNE (*after a moment's thought*)—Tom, you will greet him below and bring him up the stairs. (*To* KATE.) And *you* will welcome him, on my behalf.

KATE—Not—alone? Surely you will present him to me?

TOM—My sister fears that she would make herself cheap.

LADY ANNE—Hold your tongue! (*To* KATE.) You will do as I tell you. When I return, I shall know—

TOM—The baggage is bashful! Where learnt you this trick, Kate? Gad's blood, if only he'll have you!

LADY ANNE—He wants an English wife, and he commends Kate's miniature. Where else could he aspire to such a connection?

TOM—Our mother is ingenious. If you fail to please in person, as you did by post, there's still another daughter. . . .

LADY ANNE—What insolence is this?

TOM (*a bit cowed, but pressing on*)—My poor friend Throstle's fifteen hundred a year is scarcely to be set against ten thousand. . . .

LADY ANNE—Enough of your crude jesting. You well know whom Helen is to marry.

KATE—But Helen's disposition, ma'am. . . . (*Sits by mother on settee.*)

LADY ANNE—You may safely leave Helen's fancies to me, and trust her mother to act in her interests.

TOM (*to* KATE)—Ay, and in ours too. And as for your prejudices against my friend Throstle . . .

KATE—Your friend, while you can borrow from him!

TOM—Gad, even tailors have to be paid somehow.

KATE—The disgusting little man.

LADY ANNE—Kate!

TOM—What's wrong with him? Teeth none too good, perhaps, but an artist, a man of parts, not without generosity.

KATE—Such as you hope to find in Mr. Standish! (*To* LADY ANNE.) He'll ruin everything! (*To* TOM.) I wish you'd go racing at Newmarket for the week!

TOM—And who then would drynurse Master Colonial?

LADY ANNE—You are not to say Colonial. The Colonists are now independent.

TOM—Yankee puppy, then.

LADY ANNE—Peter Standish is your cousin!

TOM—What was his father? A fur dealer, a tradesman!

LADY ANNE—His grandfather built this house.

TOM—And lost his money—fled to America with the scum o' the country and married God knows whom there.

KATE—Drynurse indeed! You think to find him drink, women, and cards, so that he pay for yours.

TOM—I shall. But I will get you your husband.

KATE—And is it likely that such a man as our cousin will put himself in your hands?

TOM—Such a man! His polite letters have foxed you, Kitty.

LADY ANNE—What do you know of him?

TOM (*mischievously*)—Bill Clinton told me he's a devil of a temper. Got cashiered from the rebel army for insubordination.

LADY ANNE (*anxiously*)—Every woman likes a man of spirit. What else did Clinton say?

TOM (*laughing*)—That he can drink any two men of us here under the table! That the mothers in the Yankee villages locked up their daughters when Captain Peter Standish was looking for billets!

LADY ANNE (*angrily, anxiously looking towards* KATE)—These are monstrous lies!

KATE—He thinks to disturb me, ma'am, with absurd inventions.

TOM (*indignant*)—Inventions! (*Laughs again.*) I leave those to your Yankee! Clinton says he's always inventing things—strange machines to do all our work.

KATE (*indifferently*)—Our cousin has written me of his hobbies.

TOM (*embarrassed*)—I had thought to put him down at White's, ma'am; we might lighten his load of dollars there. But at the moment that attention is beyond me.

LADY ANNE (*suspiciously*)—Indeed! And why?

TOM—Because of a slight put upon me by the committee.

KATE—He's been posted at his club.

TOM (*sheepishly*)—If I am to show him proper civility, I must beg a hundred pounds of you, ma'am.

LADY ANNE—You had fifty but Tuesday!

KATE—Gambling again!

TOM—Am I to parade our wretched poverty before the town? I am a gentleman and do as my equals.

KATE—Need you scatter months of our pin money in an evening?

TOM (*to* KATE)—Think you I'd begrudge you a hundred pounds had I a settlement of fifteen thousand all but in my hands?

LADY ANNE—You are insupportable: I know not where to turn for money.

TOM—After this once, ma'am, I'll not need to trouble you more.

KATE—He means to rob our cousin.

TOM (*snarling, turning on her*)—How dare you!

KATE—Rook, then.

TOM—D'you mean I play unfairly, wench?

LADY ANNE—Kate! Thomas!

Throstle, "a dandified, fussy, precious little man of forty odd," now arrives, and is also full of the news of the arrival of Peter Standish and eager to be of assistance in introducing him to London. Throstle's immediate concern, however, is Helen Pettigrew, "a girl of about twenty, simply dressed, a wistful, sensitive face," who has joined the group. Helen, who is in all respects a contrast to her polished and worldly sister, is also prey to the excitement of Cousin Peter's approach. She is, however, more confident of Peter's character than the others. Her sister Kate, Helen feels, will find Peter all that she may wish for, in manner and in devotion.

Now there is the rumble of a second coach outside and the family has fled, leaving Kate to do the honors. Kate, flustered and at a tension, prepares herself hastily for the expected entrance.

There is a knock at the door—but it is only Tom. He has been to the outer door looking for Peter and found no one. Probably Peter has gone around to the back. "Knows his place," laughs Tom. "I'll bring him up the back stairs."

The noise of the wind and the rain rises to greater intensity. Outside the clock is heard to strike twice. Slowly the door begins to open, and Kate resumes her position facing it. The light from the hall streams into the room, casting the shadow of a man on the opposite wall. Slowly Kate curtseys a welcome. The lights grow dim. The curtain is down.

. . . .

Time has now sped ahead 144 years. It is 1928. The scene is still the room in Berkeley Square, "but the tone of time has descended upon it, and there are some changes. The windows now have curtains and different shaped pelmets of flowered linen, a copy of a Georgian pattern on a blue ground, and between them, in place of the tapestry, is a three-quarter length of a young man in Eighteenth Century costume, by Sir Joshua Reynolds."

There are electric lights now, and though the room gives but little indication of having been recently lived in, the writing bureau is open and littered with books and papers. Among these there is an Egyptian antique, a crux ansata. From the landing the slightly wheezy chime of the old clock is heard again striking five.

The door is opened by Mrs. Barwick, an elderly housekeeper. She admits the Ambassador, "a man in the late sixties, distinguished, suave, urbane, sensitive."

The Ambassador has called to see Peter Standish, about whom he is confessedly anxious. That the young man is a creature of moods Mrs. Barwick feels there is no reason to doubt, but that there is anything particularly strange about him, save that he does spend a good share of his time reading and walking about restlessly at night, she is quick to doubt.

Peter, appearing at the moment, is discovered to be a "nervous, sensitive young man of about 26. He wears a long, black dressing gown. His manner is feverish, his impatience at being disturbed by an unwelcome visit is tempered by his respect for the visitor."

While Mrs. Barwick serves tea the Ambassador is also at some pains to draw Peter out, though not with great success. The facts concerned with his arrival in England are simple. A relative, Standish Pettigrew, having read a paper of Peter's on architecture, and knowing of the Queen Anne house in Berkeley Square, called his attention to it. It turned out that an earlier Standish, the first Peter Standish in fact, had built the house—the same Peter Standish whose portrait, by Reynolds, hangs on the wall and to which, curiously enough, the living Peter Standish bears a strong resemblance.

The property has now come to Peter as a legacy from old Standish Pettigrew, and he has found it practically as it was 200 years before, furniture and all. Even the crux ansata on the desk, the Egyptian symbol of life, and Mrs. Barwick, the housekeeper, came with the house.

It isn't Peter's intention to do much entertaining in the old place, even though he does open it up. He won't be able to afford that. True, he is planning to marry Marjorie Frant, and Marjorie may be more intent on a social life, but for a time they will devote themselves principally to doing the place over and making it livable again. Peter and Miss Frant are to be married as soon as Miss Frant returns from America. She has been called home on some family matter and Peter has planned to stay in the house and continue going over the fascinating old books and papers he has found. It is Peter's absorption with the papers that worries the Ambassador.

AMBASSADOR—Too many old papers, Standish. People get morbid and musty, when they shut themselves up all alone in old houses. Marjorie is really quite disturbed about you.

PETER—I wish she wouldn't be. I can't go out just now. I've most important work to do here.

AMBASSADOR—Your studies in the eighteenth century are fascinating, no doubt, but surely not so pressing—

PETER (*raising voice*)—But I've just got to stay here in the house!

AMBASSADOR (*perplexed*)—Well, I mustn't bore you with questions. But you *are* making your friends a bit uneasy. Of course if there were anything I could do—though if you *will* make a hermit of yourself there probably isn't—

PETER (*walks to tea-table*)—Well, as a matter of fact—(*Stops.*)

AMBASSADOR (*encouragingly*)—Yes?

PETER—Well, if you could possibly manage to drop in here two or three times a week, regularly, while Marjorie is gone, I'd appreciate it enormously. Oh, but now I've said it I realise that for *me* to ask such a thing of *you* would be impertinent. And you probably haven't the time, anyway.

AMBASSADOR (*puzzled*)—But why shouldn't *you* come to see *me?* And make it as often as you like.

PETER (*struggling to avoid saying too much*)—Thanks, but, well, I don't know if I could. I mean, I might not want to!

AMBASSADOR (*really shocked*)—But surely—

PETER—Oh, I simply can't make it any clearer just now. (*Sits in armchair.*)

AMBASSADOR—Look here, Standish, don't you think you ought to get away for a bit?

PETER (*a little wildly*)—Ah! get away! It would be great to get away, really away, into the blue, wouldn't it? You think I'm a bookworm, don't you? But there still *are* adventures, inconceivable adventures—

AMBASSADOR (*after a pause*)—Won't you tell *me* what's the trouble?

PETER—I'd like to—it *isn't* trouble—it's—it's wonderful! (*Rises.*) Oh, I'd like there to be someone here who *knows*—but I *can't!* We can't talk without using words, so what's the use of talking when there are no words? I understood it all till just now, when you asked me about it, and *now* I don't understand anything about it at all! (*Sits beside him on settee.*) Now look here. Suppose you are in a boat, sailing down a winding stream. You watch the banks as they pass you. You went by a grove of maple trees, upstream. But you can't see them now, so you saw them in the *past,* didn't you? You're watching a field of clover now; it's before your eyes at this moment, in the *present.* But you don't know yet what's around the bend in the stream there ahead of you; there may be wonderful things, but you can't see them until you get around the bend, in the *future,* can you? (AMBASSADOR *nods; he listens politely.*) Now remember, *you're* in the boat. But *I'm* up in the sky above you, in a plane. I'm looking down on it all. I can see, *all at once,* the trees you saw upstream, the field of clover that you see now, and what's waiting for you, around the bend ahead! *All at once!* So the past, present, and future of the man in the boat are all *one,* to the man in the plane. Doesn't that show how all Time must really be one? Real Time—real Time is nothing but an idea in the mind of God! (PETER *is panting and excited. Clock without strikes once.* AMBASSADOR *rises, consults watch. Turns, looks at* PETER *reflectively.*)

AMBASSADOR—I suppose that old grandfather clock came with the house, too?

PETER—Yes, it's ticked away five generations—and it's ticking away now, back in that other time!

AMBASSADOR (*replaces watch*)—H'm. Other time. (*Walks toward picture, looking at it.*) A quarter past five already. Wasn't Marjorie coming to tea?

PETER (*tense, half-turned around on settee, watching him closely*)—Oh, yes, I think she was. She told you?

AMBASSADOR (*warily*)—That portrait now. (*Turns to* PETER.)

One might almost think that— (*He stops at* PETER'S *excited movement.*) Of course, none of us believes in ghosts at home, but over here, in these old houses—

PETER (*interrupting*)—Who said anything about ghosts? (*Jumps up.*) *He* isn't a ghost. He's alive, alive, alive! I don't mean now; he's dead now, of course; I mean then; I mean back there in his own time, back there where that clock's ticking, just as it's ticking here, now! (*Hurries excitedly to window, throwing back curtains.*) How would you like to walk the quiet streets of London in the eighteenth century? And breathe pure air, instead of gasoline? And ride in Sedan-chairs, instead of taxi-cabs? Seeing Sheridan at the first night of "The School for Scandal," or hear Dr. Johnson say the things Boswell wrote (*turning, looks at portrait*) or watch Reynolds at work on— (*Turns again and stops, meeting* AMBASSADOR'S *grave, steady look.*)

AMBASSADOR (*gently taking* PETER'S *arm*)—Yes, Standish, it does sound attractive, but it isn't a thing we'd really do, even if we could. And if we felt anything like *that* coming on, we'd clear out, even out of a wonderful house like this.

PETER (*impatiently throws off his arm*)—Oh, I'd like to see anybody try to clear me out, *now!*

AMBASSADOR—If we *could* get back, we'd seem worse than ghosts to all the people in the other time; we'd seem to them things that hadn't even been born yet!

PETER—They wouldn't know.

AMBASSADOR—They'd find us out, Standish—we'd make *slips.*

PETER—Oh, no, we wouldn't, we couldn't, don't you see, because what happened back there is real, does really happen, of course, it *has* happened. So if anybody *could* change places with somebody back there, it would only be a charade: he'd have to do all the things that the other fellow had done. He couldn't change anything in the eighteenth century that really *had happened* in the eighteenth century, could he?

AMBASSADOR—H'm. Change places.

PETER (*excitedly*)—Yes, *change places!* Oh, but I was a fool to tell you. And now I suppose you'll go and ring up a specialist.

AMBASSADOR (*ignoring this*)—I still don't see what credentials we could take back into the past that would make them accept us as even human.

PETER (*triumphantly*)—Ah, credentials! (*Rushes to writing-bureau, rummages among papers, comes back waving small book above his head.*) Here's my passport!

AMBASSADOR—What's that?

PETER—It's *his* diary! (*Sits by him on settee, opening leaves, speaks with feverish rapidity.*) He's put everything down! I've learned it almost word for word. That's what I've been doing! (*Looks in diary.*) His trip from New York took twenty-seven days, in a barque called the *General Wolfe.* No wonder he calls the trip "dreary." He fought under Washington. The war was just over, but he made friends with an English Major Clinton on the boat. Peter was an inventor, when all that was just beginning; that's why he wants to see into our wonderful new age of machinery that he senses ahead of him! (*Turning leaves.*) It says Reynolds wouldn't finish the portrait. (*Turns to picture.*) But he did finish it. It's obviously all Reynolds! (*Presses diary into* AMBASSADOR's *hands.*) Look! (*Points to passages.*) He married the elder sister, you see! Kate—that's Kate Pettigrew. They lived in this house. I've other papers about them—they had children, who died here. See! There was a younger sister, Helen. Her people tried to force her into a marriage she hated. The diary stops before that was settled. Look! There's even something about a Kashmir shawl that Helen's aunt in the country gave her just before Peter came over. Minute details about everything, you see! (AMBASSADOR *hands diary back.*) And I've got his letters, courting Kate before he'd ever seen her. (*Dashes to bureau, sits, rummages.*) They were in a secret drawer here. I've got the letter Peter wrote Lady Anne—the girl's mother—when he'd just arrived from New York. (*Jumps up.*) Oh, damn! I know where I left it! You *must* see that!

Peter has gone for the letter when Mrs. Barwick lets Marjorie Frant in. She is "an attractive girl in the late twenties, dressed with sensible good taste." Marjorie barely has time to thank the Ambassador for coming, and he to advise her to try and get Peter to take the trip back to America with her, before Peter is back with the letter which he excitedly hands to the Ambassador to read. He does not even see Marjorie. It is from the first Peter Standish, sent from the "Blue Boar" in Jermyn Street to Lady Anne Pettigrew in 1784, announcing the arrival of himself in England.

"The paper's yellow and the ink's faded," Peter declares, "and yet Lady Anne is reading that letter *now!*"

It is time, Marjorie decides, to make her presence known. Peter is pleased to see her, and hopeful that she will have a good crossing. But he couldn't think of going with her—even though she accuses him of caring more for the old house than he cares for her.

"If you love me you will come," insists Marjorie. And Peter answers, simply: "I can't."

MARJORIE—You won't, you mean. Peter, darling, I don't know what's the matter, but you're not well; you're not yourself. Well, if you won't come then I won't go. I'm going to stay in London!

PETER (*distressed*)—You told me you *had* to go!

MARJORIE—You want to get rid of me! You're so strange, you hold me off from you!

PETER—I must have this month here alone. Trust me!

MARJORIE—But, Peter, dear—you're so strange, you've never been like this. Why won't you tell me what it is? I *will* trust you, if you'll only just tell me—

PETER (*distressed. Turns from her*)—But I can't; you'd—no, no—you mustn't ask it— (*Stops, listens. Noise of coach. In a low, tense whisper.*) What's that? (*He crosses rapidly to window and holds back curtains.*)

MARJORIE—What's that? (*Faint noise of wind and rain.*)

PETER (*Turns at window.*)—Sounded like a wagon rattling over cobblestones. It seemed to stop here. (*Looking up at portrait.*) But there's only your car at the door.

MARJORIE—I didn't hear anything. Cobblestones, in Berkeley Square? Why, they've had wood blocks for ages; it's quieter even than our asphalt in New York. Peter, what's the matter with you? (*The electric lights go out. Noise of wind and rain increases.*) Oh, dear!

PETER—I'll light a candle. (*Lights candle on tea-table.*)

MARJORIE—Darling, your hand's shaking! Ring, Peter. Get somebody to fix the lights! (*Enter* MRS. BARWICK, *carrying candle. She stops a few steps inside door.* PETER *faces her behind tea-table, holding candle.*)

MRS. BARWICK—A gentleman to see you, sir. Just as he came in the lights went out all over the house. He's all muffled up.

MARJORIE—Who is he?

MRS. BARWICK—When I asked his name he only said again, "Mr. Peter Standish." I've shown him into the study. (PETER *walks slowly to door as if in a trance.*)

MARJORIE—Peter, who is it? (*He walks on, unheeding.*) Peter! It's my very last evening.

PETER (*speaking in a dead cold voice*)—There no time. No Time! (*He goes out, closing door behind him.*)

MARJORIE (*hysterical*)—Who is this man?

MRS. BARWICK—I don't know, miss.

MARJORIE (*crying*)—He heard noises in the street, when there were no noises.

MRS. BARWICK—He's not himself, miss. I'll get a lamp and see to the lights.

Slowly the door swings open, the pale light of a candle shining in. There is the sound of wind and rain. Marjorie, running to the door, recognizes Peter and calls. There is no answer. "Peter, I'm afraid of you!" she cries; then adds, with a little nervous laugh: "Isn't it absurd, to be afraid of my Peter!"

The curtains shut out the scene but not Marjorie's scream.

. . . .

Again we are back in 1784. Kate Pettigrew, having completed her curtsey before the slowly opening door, rises. There is no more noise of wind or rain and Peter Standish enters slowly, wearing the costume of the man in the portrait. At first Peter is dazed and shrinks back toward the closed door. When finally he demands incredulously to know who Kate is, and she answers quite simply that she is Kate Pettigrew, he is struck with awe and wonder. He is awkward, and still doubtful, as he kisses the hand extended him, and hesitant as he exchanges the formal commonplaces of a first meeting with her. He still is quite puzzled to find himself there, and would reassure himself as to whether Kate has ever seen him before.

PETER—I mean, am I—different from what you expected?

KATE—Indeed, I think you are, cousin. We were led to look for a bold, forward fellow.

PETER—I'm a little surprised, too—I thought that Kate would be—well . . .

KATE (*with a touch of spirit*)—Not so timid? I trust you will find me not always such a ninny, and my conversation not limited to the weather. But I'm sure you've had a tiring journey after your voyage. Come, sit down and tell me about it. (KATE *sits on settee;* PETER *remains standing.*) You said nothing of your voyage in your letter.

PETER—My letter!

KATE (*surprised*)—To my mother, from the "Blue Boar," where I hope they have made you comfortable.

PETER—My letter from the "Blue Boar"! (*Looking at her for confirmation.*) Of course, I went there when the coach came in, and I've just come over from America.

KATE (*surprised*)—We did not think you had come from Poland.

PETER—In the *General Wolfe.*

KATE—Really! In the packet? Did you not swim across?

PETER (*now reassured, laughs with her*)—In the *General Wolfe* —it took twenty-seven dreary days.

KATE—I suppose the sea is always dreary, but you had a swift passage.

PETER (*after pause*)—Yes, the wind was with us all the way; we must have almost beat the record.

KATE—Record?

PETER—Oh, that's an American word. I'm afraid you'll find that I use a lot of strange phrases. We're developing a new language over there.

KATE—You must instruct me in it.

PETER (*goes to settee, sits by her awkwardly, still a little afraid*)—Kate, forgive me for being such a boor.

KATE (*nervous, but coquettish, since she likes him*)—Your manners have been unexceptionable.

PETER—But hardly appropriate for a man who has just met his betrothed for the first time.

KATE—Are we betrothed? I had not heard of it.

PETER—Come, don't tease me. It's been practically all arranged in our letters. (*Clumsily steals a kiss.*)

KATE (*shrinking back*)—There's nothing settled yet, and this is more in keeping with what I have heard of your rough ways at home, sir.

PETER (*taking his cue from her coquettish tone, and rather awkwardly attempting to act as he imagines his rôle demands*)—Come, Kate, don't call me sir. I'll certainly not call you miss. (*Seizes her arm.*) Call me Peter! Say it!

KATE (*protestingly*)—Sir! Cousin! (*Both rise,* PETER *makes to kiss her again—she escapes, laughing.*) Peter, then! You'll think me a brazen creature to laugh at your clowning, but I'll have no more of it!

PETER—Come, Kate, it's all arranged. The settlement was to be—fifteen thousand pounds, wasn't it? That's all for the lawyers. We two needed only a kiss to make sure.

KATE—I vow you are the most abrupt man! You are but the audacious fellow I told Helen we must expect.

PETER—Helen? Oh, yes, your sister.

KATE—You've not even asked mother's permission to pay your addresses.

PETER—Must I do that?

KATE—Is it not invariably done?

PETER—Er—not in New York.

KATE (*chaffing*)—This is London. These are strange manners you bring us from the United States. And do visitors in New York walk into people's houses without so much as a by your leave?

PETER (*disturbed*)—I rang the bell.

KATE—Bell? What bell?

PETER—I mean, the knocker.

KATE—We saw you alight from your coach, but—who let you in?

PETER—The door was ajar. I walked in—to get out of the rain.

KATE (*accepting this*)—We wondered. . . . But your clothes are dry!

PETER—I wore a cloak.

KATE—Even your boots are dry! (PETER *turns from her, fumbling for cigarette-case in waistcoat pocket. Absent-mindedly opens and extends silver case to her.*)

KATE (*looking at it*)—*I* had no miniature of *you,* although I wrote and asked you for one.

PETER (*looks at miniature astonished, puts it back in pocket, fumbling in other pockets*)—Well, I preferred to present myself in the flesh. (*Brings jewelled bracelet out of pocket.*)

KATE—Oh, what is it? (PETER *gallantly hands it to* KATE.) Most charming. But . . . Is this not a little premature?

PETER (*puzzled*)—Premature?

KATE (*sits on settee*)—Does this not signify, in New York, what it does here?

PETER (*understanding*)—Of course. If you will have the declaration formal, I know how it was done—how it is done. (*Goes on one knee before her.*) Miss Pettigrew, fair cousin, will you be my wife?

KATE (*laughing*)—You go much too fast.

PETER—You'll not dislike me for that.

KATE—I've not said that I mislike you? (*She lets him slip the bracelet over her wrist.* LADY ANNE *enters.* PETER *springs up and back in alarm and confusion.*)

KATE (*rises*)—Ma'am, I present our cousin, Mr. Peter Standish. (PETER *stares at her;* LADY ANNE *curtseys; at length he kisses her hand.*)

LADY ANNE—Welcome, ten thousand welcomes, dear, dear cousin.

PETER—Lady Anne, forgive me. Kate's beauties have quite deprived me of my wits and speech.

KATE—A deceiving tongue you've brought with you from New York—Peter.

Now Helen Pettigrew and Mr. Throstle have joined the group. And Tom Pettigrew. They are all at some pains to make Peter feel at ease. Tom even goes so far as to approve the cut of his clothes and his choice of a scarf.

Peter meets their questions guardedly but with confidence. He has had a dreary twenty-seven days crossing in the *General Wolfe.* He is pleased to echo Tom's suggestion that now the Colonies are rid of English rule they will do very well by themselves.

"Our fathers—I mean, we—have brought forth on that continent a new nation, conceived in liberty and dedicated to the proposition that all men are created equal."

"All men—created equal!" echoes Lady Anne, in astonishment.

"That's the proposition."

"But, sir, that proposition is absurd," insists Mr. Throstle.

"Of course it is absurd," agrees Peter.

"I'm fascinated by your strange theories that life in the future is all going to be so changed—and so exciting," ventures Kate.

"Especially in the United States," adds Tom.

"Exciting?" says Peter. "Oh, very, for people who like bustle, and efficiency, but I'm sure people like—ourselves, in a hundred years, would give their eyes to get back here again!"

"We shall be damnably mouldy in a hundred years," laughs Tom. "But if the present interests you, sir, I'm your man. Cousin Tom will show you the town!"

Mr. Throstle is sure Peter would like to meet the President of the Royal Academy—Sir Joshua Reynolds. And Peter wonders if Sir Joshua would paint his picture.

He would, and gladly, they assure him—for a hundred guineas. It's a monstrous price, but then Sir Joshua's the fashion!

Peter admires the rare old Chelsea china, and the fine old Queen Anne chairs, rather to their surprised amusement. The wars have impoverished them so, Lady Anne explains, that they have been unable to get rid of the rubbish.

Peter will, he assures them, be very happy to attend the ball that is to be given the following week in honor of Helen's birthday. And they are considerably puzzled by his foreknowledge that this is the birthday dance at which Helen will receive a Kashmir shawl as a gift from her Aunt Willoughby. True, there is a parcel come from Aunt Willoughby, but it never has been unwrapped. By what conjuror's trick does Peter know that it contains a Kashmir shawl?

Such tricks are common in Scotland, Mr. Throstle has heard his friend, Mr. Boswell, say. But they are none the less mysterious. Peter tries to explain that he has, in some way, become muddled, but that does not explain. Nor could he have known by thought-reading, because Helen had no thought of what her present was to be. And he could not have heard from other sources, as he suggests, because he has but now arrived in London. Only Helen's interference, when she sees that Peter is worried, saves him from an increasingly embarrassing situation. Cousin Peter is still feeling the effects of the trip, Helen suggests, and Peter finds he has a sudden headache to make good her suggestion.

They all have left him now, Tom and Throstle to go into town, Kate to fetch him a compress for his head, Lady Anne to see to his room. Only Helen remains, and as they meet at the door they gaze steadily into each other's eyes.

HELEN (*moving back in front of settee*)—Won't you sit down, cousin?

PETER—Thanks so much for helping me out.

HELEN (*smiling*)—There wasn't anything really the matter with your head, was there?

PETER—No, not exactly, but you were the only one who saw—or, at any rate, you made them stop bothering me.

HELEN—I didn't see how you could know about my shawl.

PETER—Please be an angel and don't ask me any more about the confounded thing.

HELEN (*sits on settee*)—If you wish.

PETER—Oh, thank you. Just as soon as I saw you I felt, here's someone I can talk to. You'll help me out here, won't you?

HELEN—How can *I* help you, cousin?

PETER—It's all so strange.

HELEN—Strange?

PETER—All this.

HELEN—England? London?

PETER—Yes. I didn't think it would, but it makes me—uncomfortable. You see that, I see that you see it. I—I feel like a fish out of water.

HELEN—Kate will soon put you at your ease.

PETER—I'm sure she'll try. Oh, there's so much I want to ask you, I don't know where to begin.

HELEN—We're all most anxious to make you feel at home here.

PETER—Helen, are you really engaged to Mr.—Mr.—

HELEN—Mr. Throstle.

PETER—Forgive me. It's none of my business. But I thought your brother said—

HELEN (*flushing, turning from him*)—He had no *right* to say it!

PETER—I thought so! I could see that you weren't in love with him.

HELEN (*turns back to him*)—Do you think that's reason enough not to marry him?

PETER—Of course. Well, Helen, we'll make a bargain. You help me out and I'll back you up.

HELEN (*rising and speaking eagerly*)—Will you?

PETER—Yes, I will! . . . But—I'd forgotten. I can't interfere with things that happen, that really *do* happen. (*Lamely.*) My position here is so—so unusual.

HELEN—Oh, but you can. You don't realise yet what your position here is. They'll do anything you wish.

PETER—Yes, but . . . Oh, you can't understand this—whatever I may think or feel, everything's bound to go on as it did—I mean as it would—without my being here. Perhaps you really *do* marry him, after all.

HELEN—Never!

PETER—That's the spirit! I don't like the little fellow. And, anyway, I'm sure there isn't anybody good enough . . . why do you look at me like that?

HELEN—I don't know.

PETER (*earnestly*)—Is there anything strange, or wrong, about me?

HELEN—Strange, or wrong?

PETER—I'm an American, you know. Just come into this new world. That's why I'm so nervous.

HELEN—Is it? (*Picks up shawl.*) My sister will join you in a moment. (*Turns to go.*)

PETER (*following her, pleadingly*)—Don't go. Just to see you steadied me. I've nothing in common with the others.

HELEN (*turning to him at door, meaningly*)—*All* the others?

(*She leaves, closing door.* PETER *moves quickly as though to open door and follow her, checks himself. He stands a moment, disheartened and afraid, and looks around the room. He goes up to the writing-bureau as to an old friend, strokes it, looks at familiar chairs and the carpet. Standing back, he pulls out miniature case, opens it again absent-mindedly, snaps it shut in disappointment. Then he opens it again and gazes at the miniature. He looks at the door through which* KATE *has gone out, then, slowly putting case back in his pocket, at the door on the other side of the room. Musing, he turns, sees himself in the mirror beside the fireplace, touches wig and his collar, passes his hand over his coat. He goes up to the tapestry suspended over console table where the picture hangs in 1928, and as he is gazing at it the chimes from a neighbouring church tower are heard. He walks to a window and opens curtains, raises window. The chimes are louder.* PETER *looks out into Berkeley Square for some time motionless.*)

PETER (*the thrill of the adventure, and all his appreciation of what he sees in his voice*)—Berkeley Square! . . . I thought it would be like this! (*The chimes continue to play. The curtain falls.*)

ACT II

It is the night of Helen Pettigrew's birthday dance, back in the past. The morning room in Berkeley Square is brilliantly lighted by candles and from the adjoining drawing room there come the strains of a string orchestra. The room has been cleared of most of its furniture and the settee has been moved back.

From time to time the dancers wander in on their way to the banquet that has been spread below stairs. The Major Clinton who crossed with Peter Standish is among them, gay in his dress uniform. A Miss Barrymore, properly impressed with the social importance of this affair at the Pettigrews' and with the news of Kate making the splendid catch of her rich American cousin, is full of gossip about the younger sister, Helen—"the Cinderella Pettigrew" Miss Barrymore calls her—who has been enjoying this night dancing with the fairy prince.

But Lady Anne Pettigrew is agitated at the way things are going. She confesses as much to the beautiful and distinguished Duchess of Devonshire. His Royal Highness, it appears, is below stairs with the punch and refuses to be lured away. The Duchess advises composure in her hostess. "These fat German princelings," she reminds Lady Anne, "poison any entertainment. Be content with the honor of his presence among your bottles."

The Duchess, like so many of the other ladies present, has been greatly taken with Lady Anne's dazzling Yankee. She would have the tête-à-tête with Peter that she has been promised.

Peter has been successful with the ladies, but he has not done so well with the men, according to the report of his Cousin Tom.

"Mr. Standish, sir, is a man of rare parts," agrees Mr. Throstle, himself somewhat vexed by the attentions that Peter has paid to Helen Pettigrew.

"Too rare, by half," insists Tom. "'Tis no small honor for a Yankee to enter White's Club. He patronizes the bucks, sir. Told me the best quality in England were vulgar, brutal and dirty. He turned his back on the Prince of Wales. Thank God 'twas thought an accident!"

"Why did he do so?"

"Because His Highness blew his nose with his fingers."

"Sir, the first gentleman of Europe, in his cups, is something coarse."

"So. But he's the Prince."

Not the least of Tom Pettigrew's resentments concerning Peter is caused by Peter's insistence upon a daily bath. Throstle is quite astounded to hear that any man could possibly be so strange as actually to wash himself *all over* every morning!

The weirdest of all Peter's performances, however, is his apparent gift for predicting exactly what is going to happen. One day, while gambling, he told his fellow players that his losses would amount to a hundred and twelve guineas. And when they footed the reckoning that was the exact sum. It is little wonder, agrees Tom, that sister Kate should be worried by such reports.

"A woman may well mislike to live with a man who knows what she's going to do the day after tomorrow, eh, Kate?"

Kate is even more disturbed when, as Peter joins the group (he has just been assuring Lord Stanley that England should not grudge the American colonists their poor stretches of wilderness so long as she controls an empire upon which the sun never sets), he fails to recognize his old friend of the voyage, Major Clinton. Peter a little embarrassedly suggests that it probably is due to the fact that the Major has put aside his service uniform and is dressed up like a peacock. He does not seem the same man.

Now Kate, for the second or third time during the evening, avoids dancing with Peter, claiming a previous engagement with

Major Clinton, and Lady Anne takes advantage of the moment to present the Duchess of Devonshire.

"Ah, Duchess," says Peter, turning back from the drawing room, "I have disgraced myself. And I had three lessons."

"What was it you said about your American 'steps'?" she chaffs him.

PETER—Oh, we have forgotten your polite measure; *our* dances are modelled on those of the—Red Indians.

DUCHESS—If you are to take my scalp it must be by your wit, which they say is better than your dancing. I am told, sir, that you seem to regard this country as a museum, and ourselves as specimens in glass cases. (*Sits on settee.*)

PETER—Oh, I cannot leave you with that absurd impression.

DUCHESS—Do your best to make another, then. But, please, no politics; I should be no match for you there; you have overwhelmed Lord Stanley.

PETER—Upon one theme, in *your* company, I might do justice to what Lady Anne expects of me.

DUCHESS—Your tone of voice identifies the theme! If we are to speak of sentiment, let me congratulate you. Miss Pettigrew will make you a devoted wife.

PETER—There is nothing in the world like the devotion of a married woman. It's a thing no married man knows anything about.

DUCHESS—What! A cynic about marriage before you have reached the altar?

PETER—What is a cynic, Duchess?

DUCHESS—One who sneers at love, at romance.

PETER—Yes; one who knows the price of everything, the value of nothing! But we should face the facts. (*Sits on stool.*) In love one first deceives oneself and then others—and that is what is called romance.

DUCHESS—Sir, such views of romance are commonly entertained by that most ignoble work of God, a faithless husband.

PETER—Fidelity is a strange thing! When we are young we try to be faithful, and cannot; when we are old we try to be faithless—

DUCHESS (*delighted*)—And cannot! Oh, a delightful aphorism, sir! Your American pyrotechnics make me feel as stupid as a schoolgirl at her first ball. I can scarcely believe that I am—well, who I am—

PETER (*up*)—Georgiana, Duchess of Devonshire!

DUCHESS—You roll it out as though you were announcing me at Court.

PETER (*with real but wholly impersonal enthusiasm*)—All the charm of the period seems to centre in that name!

DUCHESS—Flatterer! Admit that in America you had never heard of me!

PETER—What barbarian has not heard of the Fifth Duchess? (*Sits on stool.*) Your name in English social history is the finest flower of the age of elegance. We know your face from—(*Anxiously.*) Gainsborough *has* painted you, hasn't he? (*She nods.*) All the legend and beauty of the age cling about you. All one's dreams of the time have you for their central figure—your receptions, those dinners at Devonshire House—as powerful in politics as irresistible in love, what can the eighteenth century offer that—(*breaks off, alarmed, continues self-consciously*) that can compare with—

DUCHESS—You speak of me so strangely. (*With a little laugh.*) I find your overwhelming compliments—a little disturbing. You're talking about me as we two might talk about Madame de Maintenon. In the past tense!

PETER—Oh, *no,* Duchess, I never once used the past tense! (*Rises.*)

DUCHESS—You have been *thinking* of me in the past tense. (*She rises.*) Now I know what it is! You've been talking about me—as though—(*she steps back*) as though I were already dead!

PETER (*discouraged*)—And I tried so hard to make an impression.

DUCHESS (*controlling herself and smiling*)—Sir, you *have* made an—indescribable impression.

Mr. Throstle would add his congratulations to those of the others who have spoken of Peter's success of the evening. He would also have Peter know that he bears him no resentment because of his marked attentions to Helen. True, Peter's self-assurance is magnificent, but it occurs to Mr. Throstle that he might do well to consider the possibility of Kate Pettigrew breaking with him. The suggestion causes Peter to laugh a bit nervously as he assures Throstle of its absurdity.

"Kate break with me!" he exclaims. "Listen, Throstle! We're going to get married and have three children—one of them dies of smallpox at the age of seven and is buried in St. Marks churchyard! That's absurd, isn't it? But you believe it, don't you?"

"Since you can read Miss Pettigrew's future, perhaps you'll inform me as to Miss Helen's," retorts Throstle, maintaining his composure with difficulty.

Peter is slightly staggered at this. No, he cannot tell Helen's future. And immediately he tries to be rid of the subject. "Look here, Throstle. Can't you take a joke? I don't know any more about the future than you do."

"My *reason,* sir, tells me as much," replies Throstle, but he is none too amiable in dismissing the matter.

Nor do Peter's worries end there. He is listening now to the story of the burning of a woman before Newgate that morning and is horrified to learn that as high as three guineas a seat was paid for points of vantage. Also that Dr. Johnson, the great lexicographer, was there. When he voices a protest he is irritated at their criticism of his squeamishness, and their references to his fondness for his bath. He might easily have been drawn into further and more acrimonious discussions if Helen Pettigrew had not again saved him.

Helen is concerned at the trouble Peter is having. What, for instance, had he been saying to the Duchess of Devonshire that that lady should gain so unhappy an impression of him?

PETER—Come and talk to me. (HELEN *sits on settee.*) Your mother begged me to impress the Duchess (*sitting on stool*)—so I dazzled her with some cheap epigrams made up by a fellow named Oscar Wilde.

HELEN—A friend of yours in New York?

PETER—Oh, no. He's dead. At least—well, never mind, it's rather complicated.

HELEN—You did indeed dazzle the Duchess, Peter. But, somehow you seem to have made her almost afraid of you, too!

PETER—I know. They all like me at first. But then I say something—wrong. I see it in their eyes. (*Intensely.*) Are you afraid of me?

HELEN—I couldn't be afraid of somebody I'm sorry for.

PETER—Why are you sorry for me?

HELEN—Oh, because I think you're unhappy with us, though you're so brave, and you try to hide it. You feel so strange here—

PETER—Yes, I do.

HELEN—I can't imagine what America's like. It's so far away. But I suppose everything's so different. And the people, too.

PETER—Yes, that's it. Everything's different.

HELEN—And as for what worries you so, people being afraid of you I mean, that's only—only—

PETER—Only what?

HELEN—You know, Peter. It's because you look through us; you seem to know what we think, even what we're going to do next. (*Slowly.*) I don't understand you. And I wish I could help you.

PETER—Oh, but you do! Just by your sympathy, even though you can't know how much I need it. The days are all right. I go about your old London—that's the most wonderful experience that ever came to a living man! But when I lie in bed and think! It all seems nightmare, until I remember you. You're not like the others; you're—real— (*Seizes her hand.*)

HELEN (*withdrawing hand*)—I am Kate's sister!

PETER (*humbly*)—Forgive me.

They have managed to arouse His Royal Highness and get him above stairs. He is "elderly, corpulent, many chinned, amiable. He wears the garter ribbon and star."

The Duke is apologetic for having been so long absent and pleased to meet Mr. Standish and his fiancée. They are, he insists, "A fine bair of loffers" and they have all his "gongratulations."

When the Duke leaves the party Peter walks to the door with him, explaining, as he goes, about the corn whisky native to America of which the Duke has heard interesting rumors.

When the others follow, Helen and Kate are left alone, and this offers Helen an opportunity to clear her mind of certain misgivings.

HELEN—What is it, Kate! We always tell one another everything.

KATE—Helen, dear, I don't know myself. I *meant* to dance with him—I was rude, ill-bred, anything you like—but I *couldn't*.

HELEN—He cannot understand why you slight him.

KATE—Then you were talking of me as you danced. (*Ironically.*) I suppose he complained of my cruelty.

HELEN—He doesn't seem to take your behavior—so seriously as I do.

KATE—Oh, so he doesn't take me seriously?

HELEN—He says there can't be any *real* disagreement, it isn't possible, because of course you *will* marry.

KATE—So; he thinks I *must* marry him, because we must have the money!

HELEN—Oh, Kate, you *know* such a thought could never cross his mind!

KATE—How do you know what thoughts cross his mind? About you, for instance? You're too good, Helen, to suspect anybody.

HELEN—Suspect Peter? Of what?

KATE—Oh, it doesn't matter.

HELEN (*earnestly*)—I want to compose this—estrangement. I shall be miserable until everything is settled—and over.

KATE—You think I'm being very unfair. But there's such a thing as instinct, Helen.

HELEN—Oh, Kate, just because he sees and knows things, strangely—

KATE (*interrupts*)—I can't help it, Helen, when I'm with him he makes me afraid. And when you're with him—I'm afraid for you!

Now Lady Anne and Tom Pettigrew have returned and the subject of Peter and the strangeness of him becomes a general family discussion. There is talk of Sir Joshua Reynolds having refused to finish Peter's portrait because of the mysterious something he has seen in his subject's eyes which he cannot fathom. He has ordered the canvas destroyed. Peter, however, returning in time to overhear this part of their comment, bids them not to worry. The picture will not be destroyed and Sir Joshua will finish it. Peter is more concerned about Kate Pettigrew's attitude.

PETER—Kate, what's the matter? You've been avoiding me all the evening.

KATE—You have not been avoiding my sister.

PETER—That fellow Clinton's been upsetting you, hasn't he? I know what he told you.

KATE—Of course you know what he told me.

PETER—You see, Kate, I let him bore me on the boat with talk about machines and what he thinks is going to happen when we'll all be dead, and now, just because I'm myself again on shore, he—

KATE (*interrupting*)—You know what he told me, you know what I am thinking now, you know what is going to happen next!

PETER (*steps nearer*)—This is just a mood, Kate, it will pass.

(KATE *shudders, moves back.*) There's nothing to be afraid of.

KATE—You attracted me; I thought I loved you.

PETER (*definitively*)—You mustn't talk like that. We're going to be married!

KATE—So, I am to marry you, when I am put to it to force myself to remain alone with you!

PETER—Oh, this is that cursed picture— (*Moves up to easel.*)

KATE—Sir Joshua saw it! (*Moves towards door.*)

PETER—Go to bed, Kate; you'll be yourself again in the morning.

KATE (*turns at door*)—In the morning I shall post to Budleigh. I cannot stay in this house with you! (*Slips bracelet from wrist, extends it to him.*)

PETER (*coming towards her*)—Kate, you mustn't break our engagement. (*Confidently.*) You *can't* do that!

KATE—Oh, I *can't* do that! How smugly you say it! So you think there are no limits to what a wizard can do with a woman? The women all press after you, don't they? But no woman wishes to dance with you twice—excepting Helen! I was never so afraid of anything in my life as I am of you (*laughs wildly*), and you think you can make me marry you, when I fear you as I fear the devil! (*Throws bracelet on the floor.*)

PETER—Kate, this can't be!

KATE—I leave London in the morning, and I'll not return while you are in this house. I hope I may never set eyes on you again. In God's name, go back to—to America, if that's where you come from!

PETER—But things *can't* happen that *didn't* happen!

KATE—You speak words without sense. Only God and the devil know what they mean.

PETER—Oh, Kate, be reasonable. (*Picks up bracelet.*) Please. I only mean it's all arranged. I've come over to marry you—

KATE—Sir, your self-assurance is almost ridiculous.

PETER—Oh, no, Kate, if you only knew. I haven't got any self-assurance at all. I wish I had. But we are going to be married, and have children, and live in this house. That *happens!* (*Pleadingly.*) You must feel that just as I do, don't you? It's *true!*

KATE—I've only this to say to you: I shall not return from Budleigh while you are in this house! (*Turns, to open door.*)

PETER (*advancing towards her, hysterically*)—No, Kate, don't go! (*She turns to him.*) We'll be happy together, and this marriage *has* to be. It *is!* (*Holding out bracelet.*) *This, this* is impossible! You *can't* do that! It *didn't happen* that way!

KATE (*advancing to him*)—Whatever you mean, I've a woman's simple answer to your "can't do that." Since that first day I've been afraid to look in your eyes. But now, look in mine and tell me that you love me!

PETER (*turns away, hand to head*)—Kate, that will be all right; we'll be happy together. (*She turns to door.*) Kate! You won't go to Budleigh tomorrow, for when you meet me in the morning I shall be—different. I won't seem the same man. I may feel differently about Helen and Throstle—promise me now that you'll stand by Helen against them all, even against—me. Help her, Kate! She'll be alone, and she'll need your help—

KATE—She will indeed need help, if *you* take such an interest in her!

. . . .

The family has a good chance to exercise its general consternation after Peter has left them. How dare Kate so much as think of defeating all their plans by refusing to marry Peter? The Pettigrew rehabilitation depends upon the match. Tom's personal re-establishment with his creditors hangs upon it, and he intends to see the marriage take place if he has to post the banns himself.

They have all gone to their beds when Peter returns to the room, wandering restlessly about in the half light in a state of complete abstraction. Now Helen appears in the door and calls to him.

HELEN—Peter.

PETER (*at length, in dazed voice*)—You know?

HELEN—We all know. (*He turns, walks away.*) Kate's not herself tonight. You mustn't think hardly of her, cousin.

PETER (*turns*)—Oh, it isn't Kate's fault.

HELEN—That's generous of you, Peter. I want you to tell me what all this mystery means, so that I can go to Kate—

PETER—No, I can't, you'd be afraid of me, too.

HELEN (*with quiet dignity and force*)—That's not true!

PETER—Oh, if I could only believe that!

HELEN (*gently pressing*)—How can you speak of things that haven't happened yet as though they had happened? How can you know things you couldn't know? First, about my shawl. And since, so many things? (*He sits on stool by settee,* HELEN *standing by him.*) Tell me!

PETER—The border line between what's just happened, and what's just going to, is—shadowy, for me. Things of tomorrow often seem as real as things of yesterday. And so, in fact, they are.

HELEN—Then it's true! You do see ahead!

PETER—You believe, when it's incredible, against nature?

HELEN—Can you see ahead just a day or two, or months and years?

PETER—Many months, and many years.

HELEN—I love life so! I want to see ahead, because I love it so.

PETER—So you're in love with the future, as I was in love with the— (*He breaks off.*) It's better just to dream about what's ahead—to dream *your* dreams—than really to know.

HELEN (*sits on settee*)—But, Peter, I want to make Kate understand about these powers of yours; I want to make her see how proud and happy she should be, instead of afraid.

PETER—She'd only be still more afraid. It wouldn't be any use. But I could tell you about things that are going to happen, just for yourself, if you really want so much to know. . . . You think she threw me over tonight just because she was afraid of me? It's more hopeless than that, Helen; she's found out that I don't love her.

HELEN (*after pause*)—But you want to marry her.

PETER—Don't let's talk about that. I had to go on with it, that was all.

HELEN—Then you don't love Kate any more than she loves you now, and it isn't about Kate you're unhappy, but because you feel lost here, and strange, and because people are afraid of you—

PETER—Yes, and as everything has closed in around me, your sympathy has kept me from going mad!

HELEN—You make me very happy.

PETER—You know how I feel, you must know, but try to believe, even though you can never understand why, that the beauty that is with us and about us now, though it's more lovely than all the real things that ever were, *isn't real,* Helen. It's only a mirage. It's like a vision of heaven; it couldn't exist in this world at all, or in any real world, it's—it's unnatural!

HELEN—Unnatural?

PETER—Yes, and impossible, *not real,* Helen. You must forget it and forget me, for your own dear sake.

HELEN—You know I can't do that, Peter.

PETER (*in agony and remorse*)—Oh, what have I done?

HELEN (*bewildered*)—Peter, you know the Future! Tell me ours!

PETER—Our Future! No, I don't know *that!* Oh, Helen try to understand—I come to you from—somewhere else. Another world.

HELEN—I know. It's all so different here.

PETER—But I'm not—one of you!

HELEN—I've always felt that, Peter. Peter, it's something you've done that's like a wild beast in your mind. Whatever it is—if you'd murdered someone— (*A thought strikes her.*) Peter! What price have you paid for the splendour about you? You've not sold your soul to—if the Fiend comes for you, he can have me too!

PETER—No, my soul's not damned, not what you mean by damned. (*Embraces her.*) I love you. Oh, God, help us both! I love you!

HELEN (*quietly and proudly*)—I loved you before I ever saw you, in my first dream of you, coming with a candle, from somewhere far away, to meet me.

PETER—Oh, but Helen, I'm not playing my part now. (*Breaks from her.*) I'm myself, you see. I'm *myself,* and I'm muddling everything up! This isn't possible, this isn't my world—or yours. It isn't my life—or yours!

HELEN—Then take me away with you, Peter.

PETER—I can't! I can't!

HELEN (*runs to him, clings to him*)—Then don't leave me!

PETER—*I won't!* (*Looks wildly behind him to where the picture hangs in the modern scene.*) When I kissed Kate, that was *his* kiss, to his betrothed! (*Straining her to him.*) But there's *never been* a kiss like *this,* since the world began! (*A long kiss.*)

CURTAIN

ACT III

A week has passed. We are again in the morning room in Berkeley Square in 1784. Tom and Lady Anne Pettigrew are there and Mr. Throstle is calling. Even though it has been a week since Mr. Throstle has looked in, there is, he feels, every reason why they should understand his absence.

Lady Anne professes not to understand, but Tom admits the situation is altered. Everyone in London must be talking of

Peter Standish's attentions to Helen Pettigrew. Since the birthday ball these two have been constantly in each other's company.

Peter and Helen are back now from another of their rides about the countryside. These appear not to have done Peter's health much good, seeing he is drawn and pale and seems to have aged noticeably within the week.

Being nervous and conscious of the covert criticism of Throstle, Peter is of a mind to resent that gentleman's presence. Lady Anne, sensing the gathering storm, carries Throstle away.

"I'd like to wring the little sneak's neck for him," explodes Peter, as they leave, and Tom follows after.

"But, Peter, we don't really care about what they say," protests Helen.

PETER—Of course we're always together, and Lady Anne keeps expecting me to say something—

HELEN (*a little strained*)—You *are* happy with me, Peter?

PETER (*embracing her*)—Divinely happy! This morning, in those enchanted Richmond woods—

HELEN—The sun on the red leaves!

PETER—Helen, dearest, forgive me, I don't want to drag in everyday practical things into this dreamland we've been living in—

HELEN (*pleadingly*)—Then don't, Peter! (*Walks to window, looking out.*) There's a thrush by the fountain! Come out into the Square, we musn't lose even the twilight of this day that was made just for us!

PETER—That Throstle—they're *all* talking about us, now! We can't go on like this. Why did you make me promise not to tell them we love each other?

HELEN—You try to keep away from them all. And they know you do, Peter. (*She comes away from the window.*)

PETER—Of course I try to keep away from them—to be with you. That's natural, isn't it?

HELEN (*They sit on settee.*)—When you *do* have to talk to them, you say things you shouldn't. Sometimes I'm afraid you'll even tell them—tell them the truth.

PETER—Oh, Helen, don't bring back the thoughts that are nightmare! Do you think I'm going out of my head? (*With nervous laugh.*) If I did tell them, it would certainly send *them* out of theirs!

HELEN (*sadly*)—Can't you think of it as I do, as a fairy story and not as a nightmare? Don't you see the difference? They're both impossible, but fairy stories are beautiful and nightmares are ugly.

PETER—What is the end of every fairy tale?

HELEN (*murmurs*)—And so they lived happily, ever afterwards.

PETER—Then make this a *true* fairy story! Let me go to Lady Anne!

HELEN—How can I, when even though you love me, your mind and body ache to get back?

PETER—They don't, Helen, they don't; I adore the peace of old things, the quiet and the charm—

HELEN—You can't deceive me. 'Tis true that you were fond of what's left in your world of our poor little London that is here now. But I feel the loathing and contempt in your heart, and the fear! Your whole soul yearns for your own life.

PETER—Helen, how can it matter to me where I am or what world I'm in, if I have you with me?

HELEN—You're like an angel who should put off his wings and give up his heaven to live on earth with a girl who loves him.

PETER—Heaven! I thought of it when I lived in it as all raw nerves and clatter and ugliness!

HELEN—But you don't think that now as you look back on it, Peter! Oh, I've watched you, and you've let things slip! When you were talking of the thrill of speed you said we all live here with chains on our feet—you said, if I thought your city was Paradise by day, I ought to see it in the winter evenings, when the lights come on—and even in the woods at Richmond, you said you wished you had a ci-ga-rette!

PETER—Oh, curse cigarettes! Give me yourself, and I can forget it all and be happy in our love.

HELEN (*suddenly*)—Peter, did you sleep last night?

PETER (*taken aback*)—Do people really *sleep,* in the eighteenth century?

HELEN (*distressed*)—Oh, my love, I knew it!

PETER—Why, that's nothing at all, Helen. I shall be all right when I really have *you!*

HELEN (*sadly, doubtfully, murmurs*)—When you have me.

PETER—My darling—the way you say that, as though it could never happen!—you make me afraid—tell me that you never think of this as a love of ghost for ghost! Even though you love me so, don't you think of me sometimes as a phantom who hasn't even been born yet, as a shadow?

HELEN (*kisses him passionately*)—Dear shadow!

PETER—Your kisses! You seem all spirit and white fire, not flesh and blood at all, excepting when you kiss me, and then I know that you want me as I want you, and that whatever else of terror and mystery there may be, our love is the old everlasting love of man and girl—

HELEN—Something more. (*Rises, turns from him.*) Perhaps something less.

PETER (*rises*)—Not something less! We're going to live our lives out here together!

HELEN (*turns to him, embraces him*)—I want to believe it, Peter. Make me believe it!

PETER—I will, Helen; I can and I will; I'll go to Lady Anne right away. (*Noise of coach.*) That's what I need: to feel that I've taken the plunge, that it's settled! And you want me, you need me too! Why else has this wonder happened?

The rumble of a coach sends Helen and Peter out of the room. They are not seeking visitors. Particularly this visitor, who happens to be Kate Pettigrew returned unexpectedly from Budleigh, where she has spent the week. She comes home with her mind made up respecting this Peter Standish. She has heard of what has been going on in her absence and she has come to correct it. Nor can the slurs and threats of her brother Tom alter her plan. Kate intends to save her sister, whom, she says, she had rather see dead in her coffin than the wife of Peter Standish.

When she finds herself opposed by both Lady Anne and Tom, and no more than mildly supported by Mr. Throstle, Kate still is obdurate, and determined to prove that Peter is not what he seems. When Major Clinton, who has called at Kate's request, persists in the statement that Peter Standish is in fact the man who crossed in the *General Wolfe* with him, she is angered but not undone. Having sent for Peter she herself undertakes his cross-examination.

KATE—Mr. Standish! When you came into this house, though the door was shut and locked, *did* you come from America?

LADY ANNE (*turning on her, furiously*)—To your room! To your room, I say!

KATE (*walks up to* PETER)—I remain till I've had my answer. Sir, do you *really* come from America?

PETER (*much upset by* KATE'S *direct attack*)—I do. That, at least, is true!

KATE (*laughing hysterically*)—I made a list of ten of his phrases—he said they were used in New York—on my way home I stopped in Grosvenor Square. Should not the American Minister, Mr. Adams, know what words are used in New York?

PETER—He's from Massachusetts.

KATE—I asked him. He had never heard one of the ten! So you see, those words are not used in America! They are not used in England! They are not used in this world! (*Violently.*) The devils use them, in hell!

TOM—Hark'ee, Kate, you mad wench! That Throstle skulking over there, who's as mad as you now, he spoke to Mr. Adams, and the Yankee Minister knew Peter in New York.

KATE—Peter Standish came from New York in the *General Wolfe*—his body stands there—(*to* PETER) but what have you done with *him?*

LADY ANNE—Poor abused cousin!

KATE (*turns on her*)—In the old days he'd have been burned, he'd have been burned at the stake!

PETER—Why not now? You burn people still—you burn women!

LADY ANNE—Physicians, straps, restraint, confinement!

PETER (*suddenly beside himself*)—Yes, *and whips!* . . . Whip her, if she's crazy, flog her, as you flog lunatics at Bedlam, flog them in public, with a crowd of your gaping Londoners looking on—you savages!

KATE—You have stolen his body, but what have you done with his *soul?*

PETER (*laughing hysterically, advancing on* KATE)—"John Brown's body lies a-mouldering in the grave, His soul goes marching on!"

TOM (*behind* PETER)—She's out of her head, never mind what she thinks about you!

PETER (*turning on him quickly*)—And what do *you* think about me? (TOM *steps back.*) You daren't look me in the eyes, yet you'd marry me to your sister! D'you think I don't know why! You—a gentleman! Insolence, ignorance and dirt! Your sport, the cockpit and bearpit, gambling and obscenity, making a beast of yourself with drink and debauching servant girls! And you're no worse than the rest, no worse than your

Prince—you *are* a typical English gentleman of your time—God! What a Time! You and your friends know it all, don't they, Throstle? So you despise your rude barbarian forbears, do you? Well, we who know better love them and despise you. No warmth in your blood, no soul in your art. God! What a Period! Dirt, disease, cruelty, smells! a new fire of London, that's what's needed here, yes and a new plague too! God how the Eighteenth Century stinks! You, Kate, you may be a fool, but you're the best of the lot, for you're trying in your silly way to help Helen now, and I love you for it! (*Turns to* LADY ANNE.) Madam, I've seen you in Sheridan's plays, I've read you in Jane Austen's novels. You know what you want, and you plough straight ahead in the storm, over everything, through everything, like a tank, lumbering through the mud! (*Laughs wildly.*) You hear that, Kate? Like a tank, lumbering through the mud! That's your eleventh strange word from the lexicon of Beelzebub. Go to the American Legation and ask Charles Francis Adams what "tank" means! No, it's not Charles Francis Adams who's Minister here now; it's his grandfather, John Adams, second President of the United States. Charles Francis Adams isn't born yet; he won't be Minister here until the Civil War in 1861. What's one blunder among so many? Peter Standish came from New York to Plymouth in the *General Wolfe*, did he? Peter Standish came from New York to Plymouth in the *Mauretania!* Shall I make a few more blunders for you to gibber at? (*To* KATE.) Shall I drive you back to Budleigh in my car, fifty miles an hour? No, not on a broomstick! (*To* LADY ANNE.) Shall I sell that portrait for you in America, madam, for thirty thousand pounds? (*Shouts as he rushes up to tapestry.*) The Americans buy all the Reynoldses! (*Stops dead, arms outstretched, gazing up at tapestry. The others exchange glances.* LADY ANNE *steps forward as though to go to him, when he turns, shrinking back against the console table.*) What do I care about you? You're all over and done with! (*Sidles along rear wall, afraid, grasping window curtains for support.*) You're all dead—you've rotted in your graves—you're all ghosts, that's what you are—ghosts!

When Peter turns his attack on Throstle that gentleman protects himself by grabbing candlesticks from the bureau, holding them before him in the form of a cross. Repeating the Latin exorcism, consigning Peter to hell, he runs in terror before Peter, now grown furiously menacing.

Now Peter stands at the window wondering audibly at his own state of mind. "And I was in love with the Past, he marvels, in shaking voice. "Is that a crime, is it as bad as murder? It must be, for see what my sentence is—imprisonment for life, for life, for life—in this filthy little pigsty of a world!"

Yet when Helen finds him here and is fearful lest *that other* Peter has replaced him he is happy again at being what he is. Nor will he listen without protest to her unhappy conviction that sooner or later he must go back to his own world. Now that he has told them all how he feels "buried alive—among the dead," he can never see them again. Nor does that mean that he and Helen can go away together, as he proposes. Peter must go alone.

"I'm strong now," Helen protests, even as Peter kisses her and would hold her to him. "Don't make me weak again. Each night I've said, 'He must go back!' But each morning, when we'd ride away together, I'd think, 'Let me have only one more day!' "

"No, we're going to tell them," persists Peter, sitting by her side. "You agreed, Helen."

Helen—My darling, I've known that you must go. Except when to be with you made me a coward again, when I let you convince me, only because I wanted to be convinced. But *after this*—

Peter—Don't, Helen! I was a fool, a weakling, it won't happen again. I couldn't face my own life without you.

Helen—What life is this for you? Be brave, Peter, and listen! My life, my London, are nightmare to you. No sad thoughts now, my Peter. We two alone have been chosen for this wonder out of all the millions of lovers since time began. Our Love is against nature, you said, and so it can't be real, but it *is* real, more real, Peter, than if you had been born in my world, or I in yours, because it is—a miracle. Think of what has been given us, not of what is taken away!

Peter—Nothing *can* be taken away; that we have come together at all, doesn't that prove that we weren't meant to lose each other?

Helen—Yes, yes, and we shall be together always, Peter—not in my time, nor in yours, but in God's.

Peter—Yes, but, Helen, I want you *now*—this is our one life on earth!

Helen—*Our* life on earth?

PETER—You *can't* want me to go back! You love me!

HELEN—With all my soul!

PETER—Then I stay here!

HELEN (*up*)—Stay, then, Peter! "For life—for life" a life of nightmare that never ends! So that I may watch you in torment, when I cannot help you! So that you may live on in my world, in a living death, *mad!* (*Kneels beside him.*) Because you love me, you condemn me to *that?* (PETER *buries his face in his hands.*) You *do* see *it!* Leave me, while our love is still beautiful! I ask it for *my* sake. (*She rises. Pause.* PETER *rises, turns slowly, takes a few mechanical steps towards the panel where the picture hangs in 1928. He stops, then goes up to console table, extends his hands to the panel, in gesture of surrender.*)

PETER (*turns, leaning against console table*)—But now *he* will be here, in my place, with this body! How can *you* bear *that?*

HELEN—Love will give me strength. (*Turns away, head in hands; as he walks slowly away she speaks half over her shoulder.*) You've your life to live out in the Future, Peter. Don't be too sad there about a girl who's been dead so long. (*Turns to face him.*) As I grow old, your youth will seem to me eternal youth, for you *will* come, won't you, young as I see you now, to my grave in St. Mark's churchyard. To you, that will be tomorrow. And yet, 'twill be generations after I am dead. I'll ask for a stone with the letters cut deep, so they won't wear away, before you come to me. And you must come—alone.

PETER—Alone?

HELEN (*turns away.*)—But if you love that girl, you must marry her.

PETER—Don't, don't.

HELEN (*turns to him.*)—You *can't* live in this house, with only that old woman to look after you. When that happens I shall be . . . And yet, I *am* jealous, even though I *will* be dead.

PETER—I love you only, now, and in my own time, and in whatever other times may come. (*She moves towards him, stops.*)

HELEN—I believe. Forgive me. (*The afternoon light has been gradually dimming. Clock on landing strikes once. They both start; he steps back, stops as* HELEN *speaks.*) If only you could take back with you just one thing that was mine! (*Turns, opens drawer in small table, takes out crux ansata.*) Father got this in Egypt, while the fleet was there. In some strange way it has meant so much to me. (Peter *looks up slowly.*)

Peter (*overwhelmed*)—The crux ansata!

Helen—What is it?

Peter—The symbol of life, and of eternity!

Helen—Then that's why I loved it so.

Peter—Helen! This was mine—long ago!

Helen—Yours—long ago?

Peter—It was standing over there, when I first entered this room—in the Future. (*It has now grown dusk.*)

Helen—This little thing—has crossed the great darkness between us. Mine while I live, yours in that world that I shall never see. (Peter *steps towards her; she holds out the Cross as though to ward him off, and takes step backwards.*) This was our parting!

Peter is standing facing Helen in the centre of the room when Lady Anne bursts in upon him. She, too, is terrified now, for she is sure that she has just left Peter drinking with Tom in the study.

"I passed you on the stairs as you turned your head," Peter offers by way of explanation.

"I vow you run like a cat," declares Lady Anne, and Peter backs out dazedly from the room.

Now the maid has lighted the candles, obliterating all the "dear shadows" that are still in Helen's mind. And now Tom has come to report boisterously that everything is clearing. Standish has been telling him in the study that at last his mind is clearing of the fever of which he has been ill ever since he arrived. That frenzy of the early afternoon was but the last of it and now he is quite like one of them.

"May God's mercy remember Kate as well!" prays Lady Anne. "I said all along it was superstitious gabble."

"I never could make the fellow swallow above half a bottle," continues Tom. "And now he's laid me five guineas he'll drink me under the table. (*At the door.*) Here he comes upstairs!"

"Leave me alone with him," pleads Helen.

"*You!* 'Tis Kate he wants to see."

Tom has disappeared in great good humor, calling boisterously down the hall: "You Yankee mystery-monger!"

"One of us—now!" repeats Helen, mechanically. The door opens slowly, and as Helen curtseys low the curtain falls.

. . . .

"The curtain rises in 1928 at the relative moment when it fell on the preceding scene in 1784." The portrait of Peter is again in place. A single candle burns on the desk. The crux ansata decorates the writing table.

Mrs. Barwick shows in the Ambassador and Marjorie Frant. She had called them the moment Peter left the house looking at her even as though he was seeing the last of her.

There are no electric lights, Mrs. Barwick explains, since Peter in a rage had smashed the main switchboard downstairs. It was quite wrong, Marjorie is now convinced, for them to have left Peter in his fevered state in the old house. He should have been sent to where he could have received proper attention.

That was the Ambassador's idea, but though both he and the specialist had kept a close watch of him, Peter had been too clever for them.

AMBASSADOR—My dear, I've been in touch with Sir William Briggs all along, but Peter has been one too many for us. He won't give himself away to the doctors—

MARJORIE—Won't give himself away! Why, those drunken scrapes, when he shouts old curses and drinking songs, his gambling and scattering I.O.U.'s all over London, telling people that he's ten thousand pounds a year but some other man has got hold of all his money—*surely*, any doctor with a grain of sense—

AMBASSADOR—Ah, no, Marjorie, of course we who know Peter—but to convince others there must be more definite symptoms.

MARJORIE—Anyway, we've got to find him now; we must follow him!

AMBASSADOR—But we haven't anything to go on yet. You mustn't be so upset, Marjorie. Of course he'll come back. Where could he go? And he didn't even say he wasn't coming back. Now, Mrs. Barwick, has anything in particular happened since I was here?

MRS. BARWICK—Well, sir . . .

MARJORIE—Go on, do you suppose I don't know?

MRS. BARWICK—*She* was here again, sir, and they quarrelled something dreadful. (AMBASSADOR *holds up warning hand to* MRS. BARWICK.)

MARJORIE—Oh, I'm not a baby; he doesn't know what he's doing any more than he knows who he is, and now that we've got her name we can buy her off if we have to.

MRS. BARWICK—And those people came again from that night

club. He was shouting at them, sir. I—I listened, sir, I thought it my duty, sir, so I could tell you, Your Excellency.

AMBASSADOR—Oh, quite, right, Mrs. Barwick.

MRS. BARWICK—He yelled at them, sir. He said they weren't alive, and they wouldn't be born for another hundred years. And when they laughed at him he hit one of them, and then they went away and I found him drunk on the floor, miss.

The door has opened slowly and Peter comes in, carrying a sheet of paper. "He looks pale and dazed and, without seeing the others, lays the paper down on writing-bureau, placing the crux ansata on it."

Peter turns as the Ambassador speaks to him. He recognizes them and his greeting of Marjorie is pleasant and reserved. She is greatly pleased that he remembers her, but is puzzled again the moment after when she holds up her face to be kissed and he kisses only her hand.

The Ambassador is also encouraged at the change in Peter, but his restored confidence is not quite strong enough to allow him to feel at ease when Peter suggests that he would like to talk with Marjorie alone. The Ambassador thinks perhaps he should sit in the corner with a book, until Marjorie, too, insists on his going.

It seems to Peter a long, long time ago that he and Marjorie were going to be married, but Marjorie is happy in even this delayed recollection of the plan. It proves that Peter is cured —that he can no longer think that he is that other Peter of the portrait. But Peter is a little distressed by her happy acceptance of his recovery.

PETER—Marjorie, something has happened, something you could never believe. And now I must live alone—here.

MARJORIE (*after a pause, turns away, her voice shaking*)—In this house, with only your old woman? Why, the place can't even be kept clean.

PETER—I'll shut up most of it.

MARJORIE—Peter, you know you can't afford it.

PETER—No—I'll keep this room—(*as though to himself*)—just as it was, always.

MARJORIE—Even when you're well, you can't look after yourself. (*She sees distress and begins again in a different voice.*) Never mind, Peter. But I can't break an old habit. I shall go on looking after you, even if it's from a long way off.

PETER—I feel such a beast.

MARJORIE (*sure of herself by now*)—It's all right. Tell me about your work. (*Crosses to writing-bureau.*) This used to be over there. (*She takes up the crux ansata, walks with it towards console table.* PETER *turns, almost snatches it from her, comes down to small table, puts it down, sits in armchair;* MARJORIE *astonished and hurt.*) Why, Peter, what's the matter? (*Turns, ruffles papers on writing-bureau.*) Is this the draft for your new architecture book? May I look? (*Picks up paper.*) Why, here's an epitaph.

PETER—I copied it just now, from a tombstone in St. Mark's churchyard.

MARJORIE (*coming to him with the paper*)—Whose epitaph is it?

PETER—A girl who died one hundred and forty-one years ago.

MARJORIE—Who was she?

PETER—A cousin of Peter Standish.

MARJORIE (*looking at paper*)—It's Latin. What's it all mean? (*Extends paper to him;* PETER *takes it mechanically.*) Peter! You're crying! . . . Who was that girl who's been dead for ages? . . . Peter, speak to me! (*Turns away; turns again to him.*) . . . Don't you know me, Peter? (*Moves toward door, hesitates, turns to him again.*) You want me to go? (MARJORIE *leaves.*)

PETER—"Here lies, in the confident hope of the blessed resurrection, and life eternal, Helen Pettigrew, beloved younger daughter of Sir William Pettigrew, K.B., Vice-Admiral of the Blue, and the Lady Anne Pettigrew, who departed this life June the fifteenth, 1787, aged twenty-three years . . ." (*His voice breaks down. The paper falls to the floor.* PETER *remains motionless in the same pose for some moments before the curtain falls slowly.*)

STRICTLY DISHONORABLE

A Comedy in Three Acts

By Preston Sturges

THE theatre season of 1929-30 had done itself considerable credit by the middle of September. Following the listless, discouraging close of the previous year not much was expected of the new season. And yet its first four weeks had revealed popularly successful plays in David Belasco's production of Laurence Johnson's "It's a Wise Child," George Cohan's production of his own "Gambling," and Arthur Hammerstein's production of the Kern-Hammerstein "Sweet Adeline."

Then, on September 18, Brock Pemberton produced a new light comedy written by Preston Sturges and called "Strictly Dishonorable." It was Mr. Sturges's second try. He had, the season previous, offered a first comedy, "The Guinea Pig," which had failed of success by a reasonably narrow margin, and Mr. Pemberton, having confined his experiments to the heavier or more unusual type of drama, had not had a success in several seasons.

When, therefore, "Strictly Dishonorable" was promptly hailed as the best light comedy of recent production, and a rushing business followed the hailing, a great many persons were made happy, including the professional reviewers.

This success continued through the season. When Muriel Kirkland, who rose to sudden prominence through her performance of the chief rôle, was taken ill during the holidays, Margaret Perry, 17-year-old daughter of Antoinette Perry, who was associated with Mr. Pemberton in the direction of the play, stepped into the rôle and duplicated the quick success of her predecessor, being sent west later to head a Chicago company by way of reward.

As the curtain rises on "Strictly Dishonorable" it is midnight, or near midnight, in West Forty-ninth street, New York. The day is Saturday, the time early autumn and the scene the interior of a speakeasy.

Rather a comfortable speakeasy, being small and friendly,

with a hat rack in the hall, a slot machine against the wall, a portable phonograph and a radio to give the place a tone. At one end of the room there is a neat little bar with a curved end, a brass rail, a high stool for short ladies and, the suspicion is strong, a very shiny mahogany top.

This is Tomaso Antiovi's speakeasy, run, so far as service is concerned, largely by Giovanni and Mario, waiters, watchers and helpful assistants to the proprietor.

On the floor above Tomaso's place are bachelor quarters, and one stairway by which they can be reached can be seen through an archway at back. Judge Dempsey, an amiable magistrate, red-faced and good natured, who occupies one of the upstairs apartments, is making his way slowly toward it when he is stopped by Antiovi in person. Tomaso is worried. Some one has sent him a paper. A summons, in fact, to appear and answer a charge of contempt of court. Why contempt? Tomaso has done nothing. Said nothing!

According to the paper, the Judge discovers, Tomaso, or Tom, as he calls him, has been summoned for speeding on Sunday and has ignored the invitation. But Tom was not even driving his car on Sunday—

And then suddenly the truth appears. It was Mario, the waiter, who had been driving Tom's car that Sunday. It was Mario who had been given just "a very little ticket" and thought no more about it.

The Judge thinks, under the circumstances, he may be able to explain the matter to the court so that Tom will have no more trouble. He also thinks, being tired, and a little weak, that he can stop long enough to drink one—but only one—of Tom's old fashioned cocktails.

They have a sort of neighborly interest in common—the Judge and Antiovi. The interest is an Italian singer living upstairs named Di Ruvo, over whom Tom feels that he has a right to exercise a sort of guardianship. Di Ruvo, a favorite at the Metropolitan, is much too popular with the ladies, Tomaso reports, and the Judge is amused by his fears for his charge. Surely Di Ruvo is now a grown man. What if he does keep late hours on occasion? Last night he had sung "Pagliacci" divinely and been rapturously acclaimed. Tonight he is attending a big party and is not yet home? What of it?

Still, Tomaso cannot help feeling that, as an old-time servant of the Di Ruvos in the old country, he still is in some way responsible for his old master's son.

Now there are belated customers at the door. A young man and a young woman. They have never been there before, Giovanni reports, but they have a card. And so they are admitted.

The young man, after a hasty inspection, does not care for Tomaso's place. It is dead, for one thing, he tells the girl, and it isn't the place he has been looking for. He must have mixed his cards. They will not stay.

But the young lady is interested. She never has seen a place just like this before—with a cute little bar and everything. She wants to stay—a little while anyway. It has taken them an hour to park the car and she is glad to get in any place, even if it isn't the place Henry is looking for. If she goes out she is a little afraid she may be taken home. Which, Henry admits, is what he had in mind. It is high time they *were* home. However, he agrees to stop a minute, and calls loudly for service.

MARIO (*crossing to table*)—You like a drink?

HENRY (*mimicking*)—Yes, I like a drink. What do you think I came here for? Bring me a double Scotch! What do you want, Izzy—a liqueur?

ISABELLE—Whatever you say, Henry. It's all the same to me.

HENRY—And a creme de menthe!

WAITER (*as he crosses to bar*)—One double Scotch—and one benedictine.

HENRY—I—SAID—CREME—DEE—MINT! Now get it straight.

MARIO—No got any. S'alla same, anyway.

TOM—Maybe I got! (*He goes out.* MARIO *starts to read tabloid.*)

HENRY—Well, make it snappy.

ISABELLE—Don't get angry, Henry. You never used to get cross so easily. Why—when I first knew you, you were always smiling and . . . and sweet. What's the matter with you, getting cross all the time?

HENRY—You didn't think I was going to be as sappy all my life as I was when I first met you, did you?

ISABELLE—Well, I hoped so. You said you'd be always like that and I'd . . . learn to love you 'cause you were going to be so good to me. You weren't just making believe, were you?

HENRY—Of course I wasn't. But when a fellow's courting a girl, naturally . . . he puts his best foot forward . . . and . . . puts up with a whole lot of damned nonsense he wouldn't stand for otherwise. Now when I sell bonds, I sell my personality first—

ISABELLE—You . . . you're not going to be nice to me any more?

HENRY—Of course I am, Isabelle. But you've got to be more *serious. Life* is serious. You Southerners are all alike. You think the sun shines just to make a nice day for you to go picnicking. It doesn't! It shines to germinate wheat kernels to make your bread. It shines so you can have vegetables—fresh squash, beans, spinach—

ISABELLE—I hate spinach! (TOM *enters.*)

HENRY—Well, you don't eat the right food. But you will! (*To* TOM.) Say, do I have to wait here all night?

TOM—Just a minute, mister. I got other customers. Must serve him first.

HENRY—You seem to be taking a long time about it.

TOM—An old fashioned take a lot of stuff.

ISABELLE—We're not in any hurry, Henry.

HENRY—Who said we're not. I want to get home.

ISABELLE—Not just yet, please. You know . . . New York thrills me so, I'm happy . . . just to be in it.

HENRY—Yeah? Well, it doesn't thrill me. (*Drums table and looks over at Tom.*) Hey!

TOM—In a moment, sir.

ISABELLE—Could we—could we have our drinks at the bar, Henry?

HENRY—The bar is for men; you'd better stay at the table.

ISABELLE—Oh, but I wanted to. (*Resignedly.*) Oh, all right.

It is the Judge's conviction, expressed in a hoarse whisper, that Henry and Isabelle must be married. But Isabelle, overhearing, is quick to assure him that they are not, although she is wearing a part of her trousseau.

In another minute Isabelle and the Judge would have been exchanging ideas on engagements and such things if Henry had not interfered. Henry, in fact, is right ugly about it, and insulting, and the Judge is quite ready to defend his honor if necessary. Only the presence of Isabelle, and the pleading look in her eyes, restrains him. Perhaps, after all, it would be better if he were to retire. He will go to the kitchen and help Tom paste on labels.

Isabelle is ready to go after this exhibition, but Henry isn't. Nobody is going to have the satisfaction of driving Henry out of any place. What he wants now is another drink. And why can't he get it? Tom is not keen to serve Henry, but he will, and does.

And now Henry would like to quarrel a little more with Isabelle. Something in her manner suggests that she is not altogether pleased with Henry and he would like to know what it is.

ISABELLE (*sweetly*)—Let's forget about it.

HENRY—Let's *not*. If you've got any private thoughts about me, I'd rather know them . . . *before* we're married. If I had any private thoughts or criticisms of you, I'd tell you about them.

ISABELLE—I'm sure you would, dear, you're so . . . frank.

HENRY—Well, you be frank, too!

ISABELLE—It's nothing really, except that I'm not used to all the ways up here.

HENRY—Well, the people are different.

ISABELLE—Oh, not really, I guess, but . . . down home everybody's sort of friendly like . . . that's all.

HENRY—That's only because it's a little town. You'll find the same thing once we're settled in West Orange. . . .

ISABELLE—I . . . I don't think we'll find it in West Orange, Henry.

HENRY—What's the matter with West Orange?

ISABELLE—Oh, nothing.

HENRY—Isn't everybody there friendly to you? The family's certainly been nice to you, hasn't it?

ISABELLE—Of course, Henry. Naturally everybody I've *met* has been nice. That isn't what I'm talking about. It's the whole *feeling* out there that isn't . . . cordial. Don't you see?

HENRY—Frankly, I don't.

ISABELLE—No . . . I don't suppose you do. But . . . but . . . that's why I don't want to live in New Jersey.

HENRY (*facing her across the table*)—You . . . you . . . don't . . . want . . . to . . . live . . . in . . . New Jersey!

ISABELLE—No, Henry, I don't.

HENRY—But that's . . . ridiculous! I've never *lived* anywhere else. I've never *considered* living anywhere else.

ISABELLE—I know, dear.

HENRY—All my family's lived there always. I was born there. Why, it's *beautiful* in New Jersey.

ISABELLE—Yes, Henry . . . But I don't like it.

HENRY—I suppose you're going to tell me Yoakum, Mississippi, is a better town than West Orange. That little dump!

ISABELLE—I never said I wanted to live in Yoakum all my life. . . . I don't boast about it.

HENRY—You don't bo— Well, I should say you wouldn't. Good Lord! You come from Yoakum to West Orange. . . .

ISABELLE—From Hell to Heaven?

HENRY—Well, I wouldn't have said it. . . .

ISABELLE—Of course not, dear, you're too polite. (*She smiles at him quizzically.*) Aw, listen to me, Henry. I'm not ungrateful. I think it was sweet of your mother to ask me to visit you all and give me those two pretty dresses. I think you're all just as nice as you can be: sweet and thoughtful and . . . and very elegant and . . . and . . . honorable (*she makes a hopeless gesture*) . . . but I don't want to live in New Jersey, Henry.

HENRY—Where *do* you want to live?

ISABELLE—Couldn't we have a tiny little apartment here? I've seen pictures in *House and Garden* of such cunning ones . . . with little kitchenettes and . . . and . . . built-in washtubs and things. Couldn't we afford that, Henry?

HENRY—Of course I could afford it . . . but you couldn't run it. You can't even take care of your own stuff, let alone manage a whole apartment!

In proof of Isabelle's inefficiency Henry cites her most recent shopping tour—when she bought him shirts with sleeves so long his mother had to sit up nights shortening them. She hadn't even called on the furnace people who claim they can heat an eight-room house all winter on one ton of coal.

As for their living arrangements, Henry refuses even to consider any home place outside of New Jersey. He hates New York, and, besides, he wants Isabelle to be near his mother, where she can learn to manage things. If he has to take a stand he can—and he does: Isabelle can live where she likes. He is going to live in West Orange. So Isabelle suspects meekly that she will live in West Orange, too.

Neither is Isabelle's next stand for independence much more successful. She decides now that she would like to sit on the stool at the bar, just for the experience. Anyway, she would like to put her foot on the rail. She is over there before Henry can stop her, and now her elbow has accidentally rung the bell, and in pops Tom.

"Gimme a drink!" demands Isabelle, acting, as she thinks, like any old souse.

"What do you want?" inquires Tom, in his best professional manner.

"What've you got?"

"Bacardi, Manhattan, Bronx, Silver Fizz, Golden Fizz—Old Fashioned—"

"Ooh! I think I'll go back to my boyhood days and have an Old Fashioned. Will you join me, Henry?"

Henry will not. Henry will stick to Scotch. And Henry is far from happy. Isabelle, he has an idea, wants to get drunk, though she assures him she doesn't. She is having a lovely time when the Judge returns, mellowed and forgiving. He is even anxious to buy Henry a drink now and Henry finally agrees to take one—one that shall be the last. It is getting late. Maybe not in New York, but in New Jersey, and it is possible that they—he and Isabelle—may be locked out.

The fact that Isabelle and Henry are living together in New Jersey before they are married is a little puzzling to the Judge. Sounds a little irregular, in fact, until Henry, with excessive particularity, explains that Isabelle, who is engaged to marry him, is, at the moment, visiting his parents. He, naturally, is also living with his parents. Which doesn't seem natural at all to the Judge. The Judge doesn't live with his parents and Tom doesn't live with his parents. Why should Henry? The Judge doesn't care for New Jersey, either. West Orange! Why not South Banana? Or Eas' Pineapple?

Henry has just made a new declaration that he is going home when Augustino Caraffa, the Count of Ruvo, arrives. The Count is tall, dark, handsome and genial. He is inclined to make fun of Tomaso's anxiety about his being out so late and he would joke with the Judge about it. But he has taken the precaution to bring Tomaso presents that should serve to soften his anger—a violet ray lamp for his rheumatism and a package of India figs, which are his passion.

Now Gus, as the Judge calls Di Ruvo, has met Isabelle—"Isabelle Parry, the flower of the South"—and Henry, "her fortunate escort." Gus is quickly attracted to Isabelle and she is not unmindful of a quickly awakened interest in Gus. Henry is playing the slot machine at the time.

Now that everybody knows everybody so much better, Isabelle is eager to have the truth about the Judge. Is he really a Judge? He is, they carefully assure her, a first-class Judge—of dogs. All kinds of dogs, including the Spitz.

Gus is ready to make the occasion something of a party. He

would have Tomaso find some champagne. Isabelle has never had any champagne. Many things are happening tonight that are new to Isabelle. Among other things, she seems to recognize Di Ruvo. She is sure that she has seen him or his picture—that's it. In a Lucky Strike ad! That's where she has seen him. Which is nothing compared to her surprise when they put a love song on the Victrola and she recognizes the voice, the heavenly voice, as that of Caraffa of the opera, and she hears Tomaso complimenting Di Ruvo as the singer of the song.

"But I thought you said Caraffa," she protests.

"Yes, but I am Tino Caraffa," Di Ruvo finally admits. "That is my stage name."

"You! How wonderful!"

"Thank you very much. May I give you a little more champagne?"

"If you please."

"Have you still . . . some illusion?"

"More than ever."

Henry is away from the slot machine now, and has added Di Ruvo to his dislikes. Before he can definitely proclaim the fact, however, there is a call for him from a policeman at the door. At least there is a call for the party who has left a car bearing a New Jersey license parked outside, and that is Henry.

Now Henry would settle his check (although the amount greatly displeases him) and have Isabelle hurry into her wraps. Again Isabelle is reluctant. She thinks she might stay at least while Henry is fixing up his automobile trouble. But Henry is firm, or would be if the impatience of the policeman did not force him to go ahead.

The silence following Henry's departure is a trifle embarrassing to all of them, especially to Isabelle, who feels that she should apologize for her young man from New Jersey.

ISABELLE (*pleadingly; a little ashamed*)—He isn't . . . always that way.

GUS (*consolingly*)—Of course not, my dear. We understand.

JUDGE (*at the bar*)—A charming fellow . . . at heart.

ISABELLE—Oh, yes, he really is, but— (TOM *enters.*)

TOM—They're having a lovely argument. They put the automobile in front of a water faucet.

ISABELLE—Perhaps we could help.

JUDGE—Aw, he'll get out of it all right.

ISABELLE (*getting cape and bag*)—Good-bye! It's been mighty nice to meet you both. I never met anybody famous before—I thought it would be different—

GUS—But why?

ISABELLE—Oh, I don't know. I always thought a famous person would be very grand . . . and . . . but you're just . . . like the people I like.

GUS—I am very glad you like such people . . . because I . . . like you . . . very much.

ISABELLE—Thank you.

GUS (*crossing to phonograph*)—Do you think we could dance once before you go? Or would Mr. Henry object.

JUDGE—Oh, Henry would be delighted.

ISABELLE—Well, Henry's outside . . . he isn't here . . . and I'd like to dance with you.

GUS (*starting phonograph*)—Will you then? (*She nods. They meet and dance.*)

JUDGE (*as he exits*)—Playing with dynamite—playing with dynamite.

GUS—You are very lovely!

ISABELLE—You shouldn't say that.

GUS—Why not?

ISABELLE—Because it isn't true.

GUS—But aren't you beautiful?

ISABELLE—No.

GUS—Very well, that's different then. (*He laughs.*) I . . . I love to dance with you, because you are very ugly. Is that better?

ISABELLE—I'm not so terribly ugly.

GUS (*in feigned astonishment*)—Aren't you?

ISABELLE—No. . . . I'll get by.

GUS—Really!

ISABELLE—Oh, yes. But I'm not beautiful.

GUS—To me, Miss Parry, you are more beautiful than . . . than . . .

ISABELLE—Than what?

GUS—Than I could ever imagine anyone to be.

ISABELLE—You shouldn't say that to me.

GUS—You are right. I shouldn't.

ISABELLE—And I ought not to like to hear it.

GUS—No.

ISABELLE—But I do. (*They both laugh.*) Aren't we wicked? (*She trips and hurts her ankle.*) Oh! (*She looks down at it.*)

GUS—Oh, my dear, did you hurt yourself?

ISABELLE—I've turned my ankle.

GUS—We must not let anything happen to something . . . so adorable. (*He is kneeling. Kisses finger tips and touches them to ankle.*) There. Now it is well again.

ISABELLE—I think you are a very bad man.

GUS—I? A bad man? But why?

ISABELLE—Well . . .

GUS—Do you really dislike me?

ISABELLE—I . . . I don't know. (*Tries to walk; ankle causes her to limp slightly.*)

GUS—It still hurts? I'm so sorry. (*He gets a chair.*)

ISABELLE (*sitting in chair*)—I think if I take my weight off—it'll be all right.

They exchange confidences. Gus assures Isabelle that the girl Lilli she heard him telephoning to a moment before is just nobody but a cousin. And Isabelle frankly tells Gus of her home in Mississippi and the awful things that happened to papa's income when women stopped wearing underwear. This is a surprise to Gus. He didn't know that women ever had worn cotton things.

There is a commotion at the door. Henry rushes back into the room. He is pretty mad.

"Just what I thought," explodes Henry. "A grafting cop sees a New Jersey car parked near a hydrant, so he pushes it up in front of it, and works a little blackmail."

"How do you know he pushed it?" gently inquires the Judge.

"Because I know he did. And (*to* ISABELLE) you want me to live in this rotten town! Come on, let's get out of here!"

Tomaso had no intention of starting a new row when he suggests that perhaps Isabelle would like to dance once more before she goes, but a row is what happens.

Henry is furious. So that is what Isabelle does as soon as his back is turned! That's why she wanted him to go out—so she could make a fool of him! A fine wife she would make!

ISABELLE—But, Henry! I didn't do anything.

HENRY (*sneering*)—Oh, no. Maybe it isn't anything where *you* come from. But the women of *my* family don't pick up with the drunken bums they meet in a speakeasy.

ISABELLE (*aghast*)—Henry . . . *please!* (MARIO *appears in the archway.*)

HENRY—You heard me. It's a good thing I wasn't gone longer. What do you *mean* by dancing with that lousy Wop? (MARIO *and* GIOVANNI *go forward angrily, talking in Italian.*)

GUS (*jumping to his feet*)—You—

ISABELLE (*turning to* GUS *and the* JUDGE *with a helpless gesture*)—I'm . . . I'm sorry.

GUS (*bowing to* ISABELLE)—It's perfectly all right. (*Then to* MARIO *and* GIOVANNI *who are talking angrily*)—No, no, *ragazzi.* That was for me. (*He waves them back.*)

HENRY—Yeah, that was for you, you Dago! (*He starts to cross and bumps against the chair. He falls to his hands and knees.* MARIO *and* GIOVANNI *laugh loudly. Beside himself.*) Shut up! You rats. (ISABELLE *intervenes.*)

GUS (*perfectly calm*)—Why not address your remarks to me? —MR.—GREENE!

HENRY—Did you think you weren't included? What I say goes for everybody.

GUS—Splendid!

HENRY—Yes . . . you're very brave, aren't you?

GUS—No . . . not unusually so.

HENRY—I'll say you're not!

GUS—You say so.

HENRY—*Yes!* And I'll tell you something else, you greaser!

GUS—Continue, please . . . don't hesitate.

HENRY (*advances menacingly. Then he looks back at the two and hesitates.*)—If there weren't so many Dagoes around here to stick knives in my back, I'd give you something to remember me by. (MARIO *and* GIOVANNI *threaten* HENRY.)

GUS—Just a moment, Mr. Greene. (*He turns to* TOM.) Tomaso, *porta via i ragazzi*— (MARIO *and* GIOVANNI *exit in hallway, followed by* TOM.) Now, Mr. Greene, I am at your service —you have only one *Dago*—to face.

HENRY—Yeah! I'm apt to trust you and your gangster friends. (*To* ISABELLE.) Come on. Get your things and get out of here. (ISABELLE *looks around helplessly and begins to gather her things very slowly.*) (*Savagely.*) Do you hear me? (HENRY *walks around.* ISABELLE *clenches her fists and doesn't move.*) *Do you hear me?* Get your stuff together and come on or by God I'll . . .

ISABELLE—You'll what?

HENRY (*toward her*)—I'll teach you to behave like a little tart!

ISABELLE (*furious*)—You'll *what?*

HENRY—You heard me. I'll give you one more chance. Now

snap into it or you can stay—for good! (ISABELLE *puts bag on table, defiantly.*)

HENRY (*somewhat less blusteringly*)—You—you know what this means?

ISABELLE—Perfectly.

HENRY—If you don't come now . . .

ISABELLE—I understand.

HENRY—I . . . won't come back . . .

ISABELLE—I know everything you're thinking; that I have no money . . . to go home . . . and that . . . Mother . . . hasn't any to send me. I'm glad. I'll . . . manage without you. Now . . . (*She takes off her engagement ring.*) . . . take your ring. (*Hands him ring.*) Take it, I say! (*Dazedly, he does so.*)

HENRY—Now wait a minute!

ISABELLE (*working herself into a frenzy*)—Now go back to *West Orange* . . . and tell them about me. That I wasn't good enough for you. And while you're at it, you can tell them I'd rather scrub floors than be married to such a . . . such a . . . gentleman.

HENRY—Yes, and it would suit you better too. You and all the other lazy white trash like you. (*He strides to the door and goes out.*)

ISABELLE—Thank you, Henry. (*The iron gate clangs.*) Well, now I've done it. (*She starts to laugh hysterically.*)

Di Ruvo, Tomaso and the Judge are all terribly sorry for Isabelle. Di Ruvo especially. But they needn't be. Isabelle is feeling fine. Finer than she has felt for months. She knows now what has been the matter with her. She's had too much Henry! And too much family in West Orange! What Isabelle needs right now is a drink! Perhaps two drinks, which they will not let her have.

Isabelle is happy and excited. She even kisses the Judge when he tries to apologize. Nor does she pay much attention to the Judge's suggestion that they will find a way to send her home. But she is still anxious to explain Henry.

"He seemed so different from everybody down home," she tells them. "I thought he was better than they were. And I just this minute woke up. They were lazy and he was industrious. They liked to make love, gamble and likker up. Oh, they were bad all right and compared to them he was upright and honorable. But I guess honor isn't everything . . . do you think so, Judge?"

"Well, I should say, speaking ex-officio, that honor . . . or righteousness . . . should be tempered with the milk of human kindness—that is, if you can temper anything with milk."

"Bravo, Judge," cried Gus.

"But I think too much honor is apt to curdle the milk."

Henry has returned and is at the door, Tom reports. He wants to talk with Isabelle. A little triumphantly Isabelle tells Tom to send him away. Her decision is made!

At first Henry refuses to go. Henry is "mad like Hell" and threatens to have an officer arrest them all for kidnaping the young lady. Tom had to push the door in Henry's face to get rid of him.

But Henry is as good as his word. He is right back with Officer Mulligan and demanding things in the name of the law. What shall they do now?

The Judge thinks perhaps he had better take charge of this situation. Let Gus take Isabelle to the dining room and keep quiet. Then let Tom send Officer Mulligan in, without Henry.

Mulligan, a typical representative of the finest Irish police force in the world, is officially curious and officially firm—until he sees his old friend Judge Dempsey. Then he becomes politely inquiring and genial.

He is, says Mulligan, pursuing a dangerous kidnaper. Two kidnapers, in fact—one of them a young Eyetalian, and the other "an old, broken down bar-fly, a regular bum," according to the young fella who has lost the girl. The Judge is interested in this complainant.

JUDGE—What does he look like? Tall man, with a beard?

MULLIGAN—No, your Honor, he's clean-shaven.

JUDGE—Broken-nose?

MULLIGAN—No, not at all, he wears glasses.

JUDGE (*thinking hard*)—With glasses, huh? . . . Oh! *that* fellow—that Orangeman.

MULLIGAN—That what?

JUDGE—That Orangeman.

MULLIGAN (*stiffening*)—Oh, he is, is he, now?

JUDGE—Yes. He was talking about it all the time he was in here.

MULLIGAN—And I thought he was a dacent young fella.

JUDGE—You never can tell.

MULLIGAN—That's a fact. (*He eyes the bottle surreptitiously.*)

JUDGE (*moving to bar*)—What do you say to a little drink, Mulligan?

MULLIGAN—Shure, your Honor, my tongue is like blottin' paper, but I never touch a drop whilst pursuin' a criminal.

JUDGE—And a very good rule, too. How about a little ginger ale, out of a non-refillable bottle? That's what I'm having.

MULLIGAN (*eyeing the bottle*)—Oh, ginger ale! With pleasure, your Honor. (*The* JUDGE *pours two stiff drinks.*) Well, here's to Prohibition, Sor: a noble law.

JUDGE—Experiment.

MULLIGAN—Whatever it is. (*They drink.*) And what a wonderful improvement they've made in these soft drinks since that law went in.

JUDGE—That's progress for you.

MULLIGAN (*He thinks for a second, then scowls.*)—An Orangeman, huh? And makin' all that trouble. (*He pounds on the bar.*) They *always* make trouble.

JUDGE (*tapping his forehead*)—I think he's crazy.

MULLIGAN—They all are.

JUDGE—He was a terrible nuisance, in here, always losing things.

MULLIGAN—Besides the girl, what else did he lose?

JUDGE—Besides the . . . Well, first, he lost a dog.

MULLIGAN—You're sure it wasn't a horse?

JUDGE—No, it was a dog! That's what he said, and we believed him.

MULLIGAN—Never believe an Orangeman.

JUDGE—Of course not. But we didn't know he was one then.

MULLIGAN—I'll bet there wasn't any dog.

JUDGE—That's what I suspect.

MULLIGAN—Just a liar.

JUDGE—Right! And when he came back from the street *he told* such a *story,* such a pre*posterous,* ri*diculous,* un*believable* story, that we *knew* he was lying.

MULLIGAN—What did he say?

JUDGE—Well, he said the *officer* on this *beat* . . . had deliberately, and with malice aforethought, pushed his car—

MULLIGAN—Pushed his car—

JUDGE—In front of a municipal hydrant.

MULLIGAN—With malice aforethought—

JUDGE—And then—you won't believe your ears, Mulligan—had tried to extract from him a certain amount of United States currency, in other words, held him up for a bribe—not to arrest him.

MULLIGAN—Oh, he said that, did he? Well, he'll be lucky this night if he doesn't lose some of his teeth.

JUDGE—Of course after that, we didn't believe anything he said.

MULLIGAN—Naturally! (*Bell and pounding heard outside; also* HENRY'S *voice.*) Well, I think I hear a disturbance on the public highway. . . . Some drunk, no doubt. Perhaps a few hours in the cooler. Well, good night, sir, and many thanks for the ginger ale.

There is a look in Mulligan's eye as he rushes out that prompts the Judge to follow him to see that he does not, accidentally, overdo anything. Let him not use his nightstick. He'll not, Mulligan calls back, reassuringly, "only in case of a tie."

It is while the Judge is looking after Henry and Mulligan that Gus and Isabelle solve a more immediate problem.

ISABELLE—I'm sorry to be such a nuisance.

JUDGE—It's no nuisance—it's a pleasure.

GUS (*crossing to* ISABELLE)—Isabelle—may I call you Isabelle?

ISABELLE (*She faces* GUS.)—Uh-huh.

GUS—Can you possibly forgive me? I'm terribly sorry for you, but very happy for me. To think—you are alone—with me. Do you know that you are adorable?

ISABELLE—Am I?

GUS (*very passionately*)—Yes. . . . I am mad about you.

ISABELLE—You're very convincing.

GUS—But now what are you going to do for tonight?

ISABELLE—I . . . I don't know.

GUS—You must . . . stay here.

ISABELLE—Huh?

GUS—With me.

ISABELLE (*looking into his eyes*)—What do you mean?

GUS (*slightly ill at ease*)—I mean I . . . I hope you will accept my hospitality—until you find what you wish to do.

ISABELLE—For tonight?

GUS—For so long as you will honor me as my guest.

ISABELLE (*very slowly*)—But . . . have you room for me?

GUS—Certainly! In my living room upstairs is a divan so

comfortable . . . so embracing . . . so soft . . . it longs for somebody to repose on it.

ISABELLE—Somebody like me?

GUS—Nobody else, Isabelle.

ISABELLE—But I don't want to be any more bother.

GUS—You—bother? Sweet child—will you be my guest?

JUDGE (*entering*)—Well, Mulligan pointed things out to Henry very, very clearly. And now, young lady, to find a place for you.

ISABELLE—Well, he just said—he was kind enough to offer me—he said I could stay in the living room of his apartment for tonight.

JUDGE—But you're not going to?

ISABELLE—Yes, I am.

JUDGE (*glancing from one to the other*)—Well, in that case, I wish you a very good night. (*He starts out.*)

ISABELLE—Judge!

JUDGE—Yes.

ISABELLE (*hesitating*)—Good night.

JUDGE—Good night. (*He goes upstairs.*)

ISABELLE (*to* GUS)—The Judge is afraid for me.

GUS—Yes.

ISABELLE—What are your intentions toward me?

GUS (*smiling*)—Strictly dishonorable, Isabelle.

ACT II

A few minutes later the Count Di Ruvo and Isabelle Parry open the door of Di Ruvo's apartment and enter. This is a handsomely furnished living room in which a grand piano takes up a good share of the room and a handsome divan another share. There is a love seat in the bend of the piano, a covered canary cage hangs in the French window, and a large teddy bear guards the picture of a handsome young woman on the piano.

It is all quite wonderful to Isabelle. This is the first time she has ever been in a man's apartment and she thinks it charming. She is, however, a little surprised to find a hairpin on the floor. She didn't know women wore them any more. And if it belongs to the cleaning woman, as Di Ruvo suggests, it occurs to Isabelle that she must be a blonde who also has acquired the habit of leaving cigarette butts about with lip rouge on them.

Isabelle is, however, prepared to accept things as she finds them. She is very happy, and would be happier if Gus would sing something for her. But Gus does not want to sing.

"I am not Caraffa now," he protests. "It is only me, Di Ruvo, Gus, who—who is so happy to be alone—with you. . . . No, no, no! Caraffa belong to everybody. He is hanging in his dressing room with his costumes. He waits for his sweethearts—for Mimi, for Tosca, for Manon. He is not lonely. It is Di Ruvo—Gus—who *was* lonely—until he found his Isabelle."

"Is it like that to be famous?"

"Yes, it is to be all alone, nearly always. To own a talent like singing is to own maybe a trained bear that dances to make people laugh. The owner, he is nobody, but the bear, he is everybody. The poor man is invited to a party. What happens? So soon he arrives, they say: Did you bring the bear? or: Will you sing for us a song? It is the bear, the talent they want. For him they care nothing."

"I never thought of that."

There is a knocking on the floor above. It is Judge Dempsey signaling to Gus and it frightens Isabelle out of Gus's arms. The Judge, calling down into the court, wants to know what date it is, and when he discovers it is the ninth he is greatly surprised.

Gus is not interested. Irritated, in fact. Gus is always irritated by busybodies. He wishes they would all mind their own business. Tomaso, he wants to tell Gus how he should live. The Judge, he tells Isabelle how she should love—and neither knows what he is talking about.

"Believe me, darling," Gus pleads. "Believe me and you will know happiness—"

Now the Judge is at the door, and when the door is opened ever so little he walks right in. He has made a surprising discovery. The date is the ninth and the ninth is his birthday. Being his birthday, the Judge has decided to celebrate. They are going to have a nice old-fashioned party—for which Tomaso is bringing up the champagne. They will have the party right there in Gus's room—with music—and—

But now there is more trouble. Tom brings the champagne, but he also brings the report that Officer Mulligan has returned—still looking for Isabelle. Henry has told the desk sergeant at the police station of the kidnaping and Mulligan has been sent to bring in the girl.

Mulligan finds his way to Gus's apartment even while they are thinking up ways to be rid of him. He is amiable enough, but he has been sent to find a young lady who is being held against her will by villains. Still, he can't seem to find her and while he is looking he is not averse to having another goblet of their ginger ale. Thus fortified the Judge thinks perhaps Mulligan had better run around to all the other speakeasies and see if he can find any kidnapers there.

"Who do you think I am?" demands Mulligan. "Paul Revere?"

With Mulligan gone and Tomaso finally satisfied that he can do nothing more for them—seeing they are not ready to give him their orders for breakfast—the Judge's party might have made headway if at the moment Gus's cousin, Lilli, who had previously telephoned, had not appeared downstairs in person. It is necessary for Gus to go down and get rid of her. He could not think of having Lilli come up, as Isabelle suggests. She is much too old to climb the stairs—

Judge Dempsey is worried. He confesses as much to Isabelle as soon as Gus is gone. And Isabelle is equally frank in confessing that she is in love with Di Ruvo.

JUDGE—Isn't this rather sudden?

ISABELLE—I don't know. I've never been in love before.

JUDGE—But . . . what about the other fellow?

ISABELLE—Henry?

JUDGE—Yes.

ISABELLE—I didn't love Henry.

JUDGE—Is that quite—fair?

ISABELLE—I told him I didn't love him.

JUDGE—Oh.

ISABELLE—He said I'd learn to love him—little by little.

JUDGE—Oh—an optimist.

ISABELLE—I think he read it in a book somewhere. I never heard of anybody learning to love little by little, like it was playing the piano or something. Did you?

JUDGE—I don't know. I played a silver cornet.

ISABELLE—I always thought it was *bang*—all at once, or not at all. And now, I know it's bang.

JUDGE—A big bang.

ISABELLE—Uh-huh. So much so that nothing else matters very much.

JUDGE—How did you ever get engaged to Henry—although it's none of my business.

ISABELLE (*sitting in arm chair*)—Well, I had to get married some time; and my sisters all got the pick of the boys 'cause they were prettier-

JUDGE—Aw . . .

ISABELLE—Oh, yes, they were. So that only left Willie Borelle and Chet Lee when it came my turn to pick, and Willie's got the jitters—

JUDGE—Jitters?

ISABELLE—You know, he makes faces all the time—like this. (*She distorts her face.*)

JUDGE—Oh, my God.

ISABELLE—It's awful. And both Chet's parents died in the State Asylum, and he said if I didn't marry him he'd shoot me, so I didn't marry him.

JUDGE—You were very brave.

ISABELLE—Well, he'd already told that to all my sisters, so I reckoned he was pretty safe. Besides, Poppa always said: Never let anybody bluff you.

JUDGE—Your father was right.

ISABELLE—Uh-huh—he played poker that way. By the time he died, our plantation was so small we didn't know whether to grow cotton on it or turn it into croquet grounds.

JUDGE—And then along came Henry.

ISABELLE—Uh-huh—in a big shiny Buick. He was visiting over at the Sawyers'. Went to college with the Buick. He liked me right away.

JUDGE—Can't blame him for that.

ISABELLE—Had to carry me up to show me to his parents right off. They're all right—if you like that kind of people. Think they're better than my family. He was so sweet to me down home and then, soon's he got me North you'd 'a' thought I belonged to him. (*She goes toward door and looks at it as if waiting for* GUS *to return.*) And I know now I couldn't belong to anybody—unless I loved him.

JUDGE—And now you think you're in love with Gus?

ISABELLE (*turning*)—I don't think, Judge. When I heard that record and I saw him standing there bashful like a little boy, I said: Woman, prepare to see your dreams come true.

JUDGE—Young woman (*she turns to him*), tonight you're going to a hotel—to the Martha Washington! And tomorrow you're going home!

Isabelle is determined and stubborn. When the Judge threatens to have her arrested she only laughs at him. When he tries to be really severe she pretends to sob convulsively—and smiles provokingly at his solicitude. She just *can't* go home.

"I can't go back like *damaged goods,*" Isabelle protests. "You can't do that. In a little town, you can't do that no matter how innocent you are. Why, the whole of Yoakum would sit with its eyebrows up in the air for nine months just waiting and hoping for the worst."

"They could wait as long as they wanted—nothing would happen."

"Then they'd say nothing *could* happen. I know my own home town."

Isabelle has made up her mind. She is going to stay where she is with Gus—no matter what happens.

"Of course you know he won't marry you," the Judge warns, seriously.

"I don't expect him to marry me."

"He'll never marry."

"He's probably right."

"I . . . won't . . . have . . . it!"

"Now, don't start again, darling," pleads Isabelle. "If I want to be foolish, let me be foolish . . . for once. I've always tried to be sensible and good . . . you know it isn't much fun to be a girl . . . sometimes . . . and now I'd just like to drift with the current and not struggle any more . . . and for a little while . . . be happy."

The Judge gives up finally. Nothing that he can say, by way of either warning or advice, has any effect. Isabelle's mind is set on her love and her adventure. She knows what she is doing. She has seen many movies and she has five married sisters. It may be that sometimes such adventures end happily. Perhaps we hear of them only when they end unhappily.

The Judge has gone back to his room. Gus, having disposed of the visiting cousin, has changed into pajamas and lounging robe in the adjoining bedroom and Isabelle is prepared to make a full report of all that she has been talking about with the Judge. They were discussing happiness, she says, happiness and things like that. And she adds:

"He wanted me to go away from you."

"And you?"

Isabelle—I didn't want to go. (*Pause.*) But I think I'd better.

Gus—Darling!

Isabelle (*warding him off*)—Don't you think I'd better?

Gus—Yes, I think you had.

ISABELLE—But I don't want to. If I stayed—would you promise not to say sweet things to me?

GUS (*holding her hands*)—But, darling, I won't say sweet things to you if you don't want me to.

ISABELLE—But I do want you to! (*He starts to embrace her.*) Gus, couldn't you overpower me?

GUS (*backs away a step in surprise*)—What!

ISABELLE—Then it wouldn't be my fault.

GUS—Darling, you must not say such things.

ISABELLE—But I think 'em.

GUS—Listen to me, darling! A great man once said, "Thought is the eternal rival of love." When you love, don't think—just drift with the current of your heart.

ISABELLE (*starting to back*)—But that's just it. I'm a little frightened.

GUS—Frightened? You? A great big girl like you? Who came from Missis—well, where you said—here to New Jersey to live with those cold storage family—and after weeks with these ice boxes, you had the courage to face Mister Henry. You are not frightened; I'll not let you be frightened.

ISABELLE—Stop scolding me—stop it, I say. I won't let you scold me. (*Defensively, she picks up music.*) Oh, it's in Italian. I always wanted to travel. Sing it for me!

It is a love song that Gus sings. It means "I adore you," and after the song is finished there is a demonstration with the translation. Isabelle finds herself in Gus's arms, still worried but very happy.

The divan is the guest bed, Gus explains. He keeps it made up—"pink sheets, ruffles and everything"—in case any of his friends should miss a train.

He keeps pajamas handy, too, and slippers! It must have been his sister who had left the small slippers. And the pajamas are a pair that have shrunk in the wash.

The hooks of Isabelle's dress are a little troublesome, but Gus manages them. It has been a long time since anyone has helped Isabelle undress, she admits. Of course, when she was little—But then she wore a lot more clothes than she does now. Her mother wore even more than she and grandma wore more than both of them together. It must have been awfully tiresome for the men in grandma's day, Isabelle thinks—waiting around for the women to get ready to go swimming. But probably they didn't swim much in those days.

Now the pajamas are on, the stockings are off, the lights are low, and confessions of mutual love have been repeated and registered.

ISABELLE—Oh, Gus, I am happy!

GUS—It is I who am so happy.

ISABELLE—I love you.

GUS—But, darling, you are trembling. Are you then so afraid?

ISABELLE—I'm a little bit afraid.

GUS—But you must not be. Life is beautiful . . . and its most beautiful moments are called . . . love. They are very rare, my Isabelle, such moments as this . . . to be accepted tenderly . . . and without fear.

ISABELLE—Don't let me go.

GUS—No, no—let you go? I'll hold you close—close to me. My baby—like a child— (*She breaks into sobs.*) But you are crying. (*They separate.*) But you are a baby!

ISABELLE—No, I'm not . . . don't girls usually cry?

GUS—Yes.

ISABELLE—Well . . . I'm no different from anybody else. (*Then, out of a clear sky.*) Do you think I'm pretty?

GUS—Hein?

ISABELLE—Do you think I'm pretty?

GUS—Of course I think you're pretty. You're lovely.

ISABELLE—Well, why don't you say so, then. (*Turns to him angrily.*) Isn't this the time to say sweet things to me? What are you staying over there for? Don't you like me?

GUS (*rather emotionally*)—It is because I like you so much . . . that I'm staying here. You little . . . foolish! (*Suddenly he makes up his mind.*) Come here! (*He crosses and takes her hand.*) Come here. (*Leads her to divan.*) Go to bed! (*She gets into bed and he stands over her. Angrily.*) Now listen to me. Never in my life before . . . have I done anything so stupid as now I am about to do. Do you understand? Never! Not once . . . I . . . I cover myself with ridicule . . . and I am . . . positive . . . that I will regret it forever. *All my life,* I will be angry for this moment. I know that I am *crazy!* (*He strides over to table and picks up the teddy bear, returns to the bed and puts it down beside her.*) *There!* So you won't be frightened.

ISABELLE (*clutching at the teddy bear*)—I'm not frightened.

GUS (*with an effort*)—Now . . . *Good night.*

ISABELLE—What do you mean?

GUS—I mean . . . that for tonight . . . I will sleep in the Judge's apartment. And you . . . *you* are going home tomorrow. Where your mamma can take care of you.

ISABELLE—I won't. (*Then she sobs.*) I hate you, you're horrid.

GUS (*at the door*)—Yes, I knew you would thank me. Good night. Come here, come here.

ISABELLE—Well, what do you want now? (*Crosses to him.*)

GUS—When I go (*picking up chain on door*) you will place this end of the chain in this receptacle . . . do you see? So if I change my mind, if I weaken, this chain will be stronger . . . than my resolutions. Do you understand?

ISABELLE (*mulishly*)—I won't do it. I hate you. You're horrid!

GUS—You are a very bad girl. Good night.

ISABELLE—Aren't you even going to kiss me?

GUS—No.

ISABELLE—Aren't you going to put me to bed?

GUS—No!

ISABELLE—Then I'll scream! (*She starts to scream. He picks her up and starts to divan.*)

GUS—*Dio mio!* Am I a nurse maid that I have to take care so of babies? (*Puts her on divan.*)

ISABELLE—Now kiss me!

GUS—Just a little one. (*He leans over. She grabs him and kisses him soundly. With difficulty he breaks away.*) *Now*—hook the chain on the door, Baby! (*He starts for the door. She picks up the teddy bear and throws it on the floor, crying as she does so.*)

ISABELLE—I'm not a baby! I'm not a baby!

CURTAIN

ACT III

The sun is trying to shine through the curtains of the Di Ruvo apartment next morning when Tomaso lets himself quietly in the door. His gentle knocking has not been heard. He wears the white jacket of a *valet de chambre* and carries a breakfast tray. Isabelle is asleep on the divan, stirring uneasily but not waking as Tom proceeds to draw the window curtains, uncover the canary and put the room in order. These tasks include his picking up and sorting out the silk things Isabelle has draped about the furniture. One stocking, he notices, has a small hole. He finds a new pair in the stand drawer and substitutes them for the others.

In fact, Tom finds everything he is looking for except the Count Di Ruvo. The Count is not in his bedroom, nor in the bathroom, nor under the covers of the divan. It is very puzzling. Tom needs Isabelle's help. To waken her he turns on the phonograph which proceeds to play, more or less violently, "The Stars and Stripes Forever."

Isabelle opens her eyes, sits up angrily, hurls the teddy bear off her bed, and commands that the music be stopped. She is not in good spirits this morning, and all she knows about "His Excellency" is that he spent the night upstairs in Judge Dempsey's apartment.

Tom is fairly, though modestly, nonplussed.

As for breakfast, Isabelle would like a cup of coffee. She hates eggs and she doesn't want to be bossed. Tom brings her plain tea, refuses her the cream and the sugar, and rather expects her to eat sausages.

Judge Dempsey is the first caller and he is beaming. He knew Isabelle was the right kind of a girl. It is pretty hard to fool him on character. When Gus appeared at his door asking a bed for the night because Isabelle had sent him away, the Judge's estimate of Isabelle was confirmed. There is something about a decent girl that shows in her eyes.

The Judge has been stirring this morning. Been as far as the Grand Central and bought Isabelle a ticket home—a yard or more of ticket entitling her to ride all the way from New York to Yoakum, Oregon. The fact that she lives in Yoakum, Mississippi, complicates matters slightly.

Furthermore, Isabelle does not like the idea of being sent home. She likes it even less when the Judge tells her the idea originated with Gus; that they bought the ticket as a joint present to their guest.

Now Henry has telephoned. He is apologetic over the phone, and Isabelle agrees to see him. She knows now what she has to do.

Isabelle is in the bathroom dressing when Gus bursts ecstatically into the room. He, too, has just made a most amazing discovery, he admits to the Judge. He is in love! Actually in love! He never expected it to happen again. But after he had lain awake all night he knew, and early this morning he had cabled his mamma for her permission.

"I take the telephone," explains Gus. "I say give me Western

Union, I say take a cable, please. And to my mother I say: 'Mamma Mia, I am in *love*. With the most beautiful, adorable, enchanting, exquisite, lovely, pure, intelligent, remarkable, educated' . . ."

"At fifty cents a word?"

"It was your telephone—'faithful, obedient and irreplaceable maiden in the entire world and I humbly beg your permission to marry her. Answer immediately. Urgent.' The answer should be here now . . . let me see: two o'clock here is seven o'clock in the morning in Italy . . . The cable would get there about nine . . . Mamma would faint once with excitement . . . that takes about an hour . . . then she composes her answer . . . that takes another hour . . . then Giulio the butler goes down to the telegraph office with the message . . . it isn't far, but he's old . . . that's another hour . . . then two hours for transmission, that makes nine o'clock . . . What time is it?"

"Eleven minutes past ten."

"One hour and eleven minutes late! My God, they have no consideration."

Now Gus is upstairs getting dressed. The Judge has retrieved the last of Isabelle's scattered belongings and passed them through the bathroom door to her. And then Henry arrives.

The Judge does not care to meet Henry, and Isabelle is quite formal. Henry is apologetic. He had said some rotten things but he was pretty drunk. He would like to have a lot of things overlooked, but he is not without his suspicions as to the sleeping arrangements made by Isabelle the night before. He is willing to take her word for it that everything was all right, of course. But—

"If I thought—" threatens Henry.

"You can think anything you like," counters Isabelle. "I know how your mind works."

"Naturally, I—"

"I still have my virginity, if that's what's worrying you."

"Isabelle!"

"Don't be a hypocrite . . . that's what you were thinking . . . though why they make so much fuss about it is more than I can understand."

"Fuss about it!"

"You heard me. As if it mattered to anybody but me. By the way, I forgot to ask you. Are *you* pure?"

"What? Why . . ."

"You needn't bother to answer. I'm not curious."

Henry hopes that everything is settled and that their engagement still holds. Isabelle supposes it does. She is at least sufficiently complaisant to let him kiss her.

Gus, bursting into the room, sees that kiss. Tom has brought him the answer to his cable and he has rushed back to read it to Isabelle when he finds her in Henry's arms. It is not an encouraging sight to Gus. He is quite depressed by it, in fact. He would, however, like to have a few words with Isabelle—alone—if she doesn't mind. She doesn't, and Henry's objection does not count.

ISABELLE (*turning coldly to* HENRY)—This gentleman has shown me the greatest courtesy, Henry. More than you can possibly realize. You have nothing to fear in leaving me alone with him.

HENRY—I didn't mean that.

ISABELLE (*still in the same level tone*)—Will you wait for me in the car, please?

HENRY—Yeah, but—

ISABELLE—Are you going to start all over again, Henry?

HENRY (*going to door*)—Oh—all right. But it's a damn funny idea.

ISABELLE (*looking at* GUS *uneasily*)—What is it, Gus?

GUS (*very gravely*)—I came here just now . . . to ask you to marry me.

ISABELLE—Oh!

GUS—Yes.

ISABELLE—When did you get that idea?

GUS—This morning . . . after I left you. I couldn't sleep. I lay in bed wondering . . . wondering . . .

ISABELLE—What to do with me?

GUS—Yes.

ISABELLE—Then you thought of this . . . solution.

GUS—Yes. Always you see, I thought marriage was not for me. For a woman, such life would be . . . Hell. Here a few months, then quick to Milan, a week at La Scala, then two, maybe three days at home, then a rotten trip to Spain (ISABELLE, *who has been only to Excelsior Springs, West Orange, N. J., and New York, listens to this itinerary breathlessly. She dreamily contemplates the wonders of such a trip.*) . . . one week in Barcelona, one week in Madrid, then off to South America for the season. *It's terrible!*

ISABELLE—Yes, it must be.

Gus—*It is. It's awful.* So always I put behind me thoughts of marriage, so that some poor woman would not have to . . . share my sufferings.

Isabelle—That was very thoughtful of you.

Gus—But bad as it would be for the woman, think what it would mean for the children.

Isabelle—Yes, I suppose it would be hard for the children.

Gus—*Terrible!* But I will *not* be separated from my wife and children. I am, by nature, a family man. All my ancestors, on both sides, had families.

Isabelle—I guess mine did too.

Gus—So you can see what it would be like . . . to travel? Nurses, valets, governesses, maids, toys . . . tutors, little boys, little girls, animals . . . it would be like traveling with a menagerie!

Isabelle—How many children did you expect to have?

Gus—I haven't decided yet.

Isabelle—Oh!

Gus—But then this morning, I said, what the Hell, we only live once. If I can travel, the family can travel. So I put on my best suit, and came to tell you. And I found you there . . . (*He extends his arm toward where she stood with* Henry.) So now . . . before you go . . . out of my life into the arms of . . . a younger man, I want you please to remember that I loved you, Isabelle.

Isabelle—You don't.

Gus (*unheeding*)— . . . that I loved you. Very real . . . very fine . . . very honorable love. And when I lose you, I am losing something . . . (*he taps his heart*) of me. Something . . . I am afraid I will not find any more. (*In a more matter-of-fact tone.*) Something I did not deserve, Isabelle, because I have been a very wicked man. But that is no consolation to me now. You must go now. You must not keep Henry waiting . . . the wife must be obedient and thoughtful. But if sometimes you hear me sing . . . you will know I am singing for you, Isabelle, only for you, and . . . and . . . that is all.

Isabelle—You don't love me. (*Facing him.*)

Gus—Would I then have asked you to marry me? The only time in my life I ask anybody.

Isabelle—And you were sure I'd say "Yes," weren't you?

Gus—No, Isabelle, but I hoped.

Isabelle—Oh, yes, you were.

Gus—No, my child.

ISABELLE—You were sure I'd say yes because I couldn't do anything else. You felt sorry for me, and out of the kindness of your heart, you said well, nobody else wants her, she's in trouble. *I'll t*ake her. Well, I don't want your charity. I won't have it, yours or anybody else's.

GUS—But, I loved you, Baby—

ISABELLE—You're just trying to make me unhappy by telling me this now. That's what you're doing. Well . . . it's too late. I *don't* love you . . . I . . . I love Henry. You saw me kissing him just now. You know what that means? It means . . . that for the rest of my life . . . I'm going to live . . . in WEST ORANGE . . . New Jersey!

GUS—But I loved you.

ISABELLE—You don't.

GUS—I do.

ISABELLE—*You don't!* If you did, you wouldn't have left me last night with that stuffed teddy bear. (*She leaves the room.*)

GUS (*putting out his hands*)—Baby! (*Now* JUDGE DEMPSEY *appears in the door, watching* ISABELLE *leave.*)

JUDGE—What does it say?

GUS (*reading*)—*Filio mio: tio ha mia permisso*— (JUDGE *interrupts— Yes, I read that version.*) Oh, excuse me, I will translate: My son—you have my permission and my blessing but . . . there cannot be no such person . . . you must be dreaming. I guess she is right . . . my mother. I was dreaming. (*The canary begins to sing.*) You can sing, Caruso, but I . . . I will never sing again.

JUDGE—Oh, for God's sake, let's have a drink. (*Phone starts to ring.*) I have something in my room. (*He leaves.*)

GUS (*at phone*)—Yes, who? Oh, hello, Lilli, but the conference has just ended. No, it was not a success. I had hoped it would mean a long contract, but it was a complete failure. Yes, Lilli. No, Lilli, I cannot see you. (JUDGE *enters, leading* ISABELLE. GUS *sees her and puts receiver on phone. Then he rushes to her.*)

ISABELLE—It wasn't true. I lied to you. I do love you. (*Telephone starts ringing in jerks, then begins to ring regularly. They embrace.*)

GUS—But I warn you—I must have four sons and seven daughters—

JUDGE (*starting out*)—Well, in that case, I'll tell Henry not to wait.

CURTAIN

THE LAST MILE

A Tragedy in Three Acts

By JOHN WEXLEY

IT has been a good many years since the production of a play has caused as much excitement in theatrical New York as did that of John Wexley's "The Last Mile," which was done at the Sam H. Harris Theatre February 14. Probably the production of "What Price Glory?" in 1924, the Stallings-Anderson war play, which created something of a sensation on its own account, is the nearest event of comparative significance.

"The Last Mile" is the tragedy of the death house in a state penitentiary. Its basis and inspiration were found by its author in a short play printed in the *American Mercury* in July, 1929, detailing, by verbatim report, death house conversations the night set for an electrocution, as they were set down by Robert Blake, who left the play as his only legacy for his mother. Blake died in the chair for a murder committed in Texas. This play was called "The Law Takes Its Toll."

Using the Blake manuscript as the basis of his first act Mr. Wexley added to it two acts devoted to such prison mutinies as had recently occurred in both the Canon City, Colo., and the Auburn, N. Y., prisons. The result is a tragedy so tense, so stripped of theatrical artificialities, and emotionally so moving that even calloused reviewers of plays were frank to admit its disturbing and unsettling effect upon their nerves.

The play was extravagantly praised in the press as a tragedy that might conceivably fail of popular support, but one that must be reckoned among the greatest theatre exhibits of the time.

A few weeks after the premiere Mrs. Ella Blake, the mother of the Robert Blake whose prison manuscript had inspired the play, having been counseled by friendly attorneys in the Southwest not to be content with that division of the royalties offered her by Mr. Wexley's agents, came personally to New York to demand her rights. A compromise was effected by which Mr. Wexley agreed to pay Mrs. Blake twenty per cent of all royalties and a proportionate share of book and picture rights. Mrs. Blake also attended the play on this visit and, far from sinking into the swoon expected, was frank to say she thought it quite mild as compared with life in the real prison in which her boy was held previous to his death.

The audience facing the stage at a performance of "The Last Mile" is sitting presumably across the corridor in cells evenly numbered, facing the odd row, or cells 1 to 13.

At one end of the corridor, that at the left of the audience, there is the barred and bolted steel door that leads to the offices and the prison yard. At the opposite end of the corridor is another steel door painted green, the entrance to the electrocution chamber.

Standing grasping the doors of their cells, unable to see each other, or pacing the space between the door and the back wall of their cells, are six prisoners. Cell 1 is temporarily empty. At the entrance door an armed guard, named Drake—"a cruel, mean, vicious, handsome, clean-cut American," of 28—leans back in his chair keeping a baleful and contemptuous eye on the cells before him.

It is about 9 o'clock in the evening of a May day. At 11 Richard Walters, Cell 7, a "tall, slender, romantic, good-looking boy," about 25 years old, is scheduled to "burn." Walters, as his author sees him, "has lots of guts, is religious and conventional; has a good sense of humor, but can be a real man, too; a blue-eyed type and inclined to be a trifle heavy."

At the moment Walters is beginning to react to an approaching nervous hysteria. He realizes that he has but a couple of hours left, and is trying desperately to appear brave and undismayed. His voice, in spite of him, rises a note or two above its normal pitch when he speaks.

The other prisoners are doing what they can to help him keep his spirits up. Red Kirby, his neighbor in Cell 9, is sure Walters will yet get a stay from the Governor. Such things have happened, and Kirby, being a man of 45, "a real bandit with years of experience," feels that he can speak with some authority. He already has had a couple of stays himself.

"The Governor gave a couple last week," calls Red. "No reason why you should not get one."

"You'll get it, white boy," echoes Sunny Jackson, Negro, from Cell 13. "You'll get it. Just you keep right on praying."

Sunny is coal black, a giant in stature, both religious and superstitious. On occasion he breaks into song and his voice is deep and melodious.

In Cell 11 Eddie Werner, a "thin, emaciated, ascetic, gray and bony" little man, who has lost his mind, recites in a fervent wail parts of a mysterious verse that is never finished—

"I have seen them come
I have seen them go—"

Werner is only awaiting the order of the Lunacy Commission to be taken away from the death house. Walters might have "gone nuts," too, but it is too late to try that now.

The guards bring in Walters' last meal. All the prisoners are interested in that. Especially Sunny.

JACKSON—What did you ohder, Seven? (*A guard opens the door, delivers the tray to* DRAKE *and exits.*)

WALTERS—I ordered a tenderloin steak, baked potatoes, fruit cocktail, bread and lots of butter, coffee and some mushroom soup. (*A guard gives him food through aperture.*)

JACKSON—That oughta be plenty.

WALTERS—Yea, I guess I'll be gettin' good and hungry on my way down.

JACKSON—Ah can't figah how yo' all came to think of that theah mushroom soup. (*Scratches his head.*) But Ah don't think Ah could eat it if Ah was yo'.

WALTERS (*testily*)—Aw, shut up. I got the chance to eat to-night, what I want and all I want, and I'm goin' to. I'm sorry I didn't order fried turkey and a lot of side dishes.

KIRBY—They'll give you anything you ask for.

MAYOR (*sarcastically*)—Yeah. Any reasonable request you make now will not be refused you.

JACKSON—Where do yuh think they got that theah mushroom soup from? Is it canned soup?

WALTERS (*eating*)—I dunno. It tastes too good to tell.

JACKSON—Ah wish Ah had some.

WALTERS—You'll have it, Thirteen. You'll have all you want.

JACKSON—Please woan't yuh stop callin' me Thirteen? How many times . . . ?

WALTERS—I'll stop. (*Ceases to eat suddenly.*) I'm feelin' sick. I don't think I can finish this all.

Someone has sent a handful of cigars for Walters and left no name. He divides them with "Killer" Mears, Cell 5, and Fred Mayor, Cell 3. Mears is "of the type that deserves the name.

Hard as nails, medium height; wiry; narrow, hard eyes; narrow mouth; illiterate but intelligent; dominant."

Mayor is only about 23, "hot-tempered, nervous, intelligent, cruel, handsome; women, perhaps, would call him sweet at times."

"Say, Fred Mayor," calls Walters shrilly. "I'm gonna ask them to let me hold your hand tonight."

"The hell they will," laughs Mayor.

"Sure they will, and you'll get the juice through you and we'll go to hell together."

The whole tier laughs at this—all except demented Eddie Werner. He goes on with his recitation—

"The death house's where they come and go,
They linger just a little time
Before they give you the electric chair
Sentenced for some awful crime—"

There are shouts and protests. "Fer Christ's sake, Eddie! Have a heart," cries the unhappy Walters, covering his ears with his hands to shut out the dismal verse. But there is no stopping Werner—

"When I hear the lonesome hum of the motor
That sends the high voltage to your chest,
I have a sad, unexplainable sensation
Running through my breast—"

"God, God, I'll go mad," shrieks Walters, and his protests are joined by those of Mears. But Guard Drake will do nothing to quiet Werner. Drake likes poetry.

They have changed guards now. O'Flaherty, a kinder man, has relieved Drake. And Werner is quiet for the moment. Then there is an ominous hum of electric current. The lights grow dim and lighten again. The men know what that means. They are testing the chair. They have been "playin' with it all the goddam day," according to Mears, just as though nobody had any nerves.

They are all nervous now. The hum of the machine has brought life closer to them—and death. The current has even attacked Walters' vitals. He doubles with the pain of it. It'll get worse, Red Kirby says.

Principal Keeper Callahan and Guard Harris bring in Tom D'Amoro, a "tough, dapper, curly-haired, short, dark Italian-American." D'Amoro is the new inmate for Cell 1.

D'Amoro pauses before the door of his cell. It is the concluding gesture of a long-drawn defiance. Harris would hurry him in. "What's your hurry? I got plenty of time," the Italian counters, cynically. And then, with gusto, he spits at the ceiling of his "ice-box."

The others are soon acquainted with D'Amoro. He gives his name in response to Mears' questioning, and admits his offense. Yeah, he's the dago that croaked the cop.

One by one the others introduce themselves. "My name is Mears, Cell 5." "Fred Mayor, Cell 3." "Vincent Jackson, in the last cell." "Red Kirby, Cell 9."

"Pleased to meet you, fellers. Who's goin' to burn tonight?"

"Number 7," shrieks Walters. "Seven is gonna burn . . . Richard Walters!"

Eddie Werner, the demented one, is at his poetry again. They explain Eddie to D'Amoro. He is quite in agreement with them in thinking that the authorities should get Werner to hell out of there!

There are a few other commissions that Walters has to take care of. His money for one thing. He's only got a coupla dollars, but they might as well go to someone. There are no takers at first, but finally Vincent Jackson thinks perhaps he might as well take the money, seein' it's botherin' Walters. If the stay comes he can send it right back—

There are four packs of cigarettes. They go to Mears and Mayor.

It is getting late. And yet there's still time for that stay—

Werner is off again—

> "When I hear the lonesome hum of the motor
> That sends the high voltage to your chest—"

And D'Amoro, the newcomer, catching the hysteria of the moment, is yelling his own defense ceaselessly—

"I couldn't help killing him. He shot at me on the roof and it was either me or him. Now what could I do! If a guy is pumpin' lead at you and you hear the bulls and dicks blowin' their whistles down below in the streets and people shoutin' and ya got a gun, why ya just shoot back. Ya just gotta shoot back."

Jackson is singing, low and feelingly—

> "Nobody knows the trouble I've seen,
> Nobody knows but Jesus,
> Nobody knows the trouble—"

Keeper Callahan is in with a telegram. It is for Walters. He reads it tremblingly and shouts an answer:

"Hell, no! Tell 'em I said, Hell, no!"

"Who are you yelling at?" demands Callahan.

"You! You!" shouts Walters. "Tell 'em I said, Hell, no!"

"That's what the Governor said for you, too," mutters Callahan, as he walks out the door.

Slowly the dread significance of that statement strikes Walters' consciousness. At first he tries not to hear. The others would reassure him. He's a mean skunk, that keeper. He's just tryin' to frighten Seven. Then Walters knows. And crumples under the blow.

Well, he told 'em Hell no, anyway! That was a telegram from the sheriff of some other county askin' if he and a friend might sit in on the execution. And Walters told 'em. The warden had explained that he could have five personal witnesses if he wanted them, in addition to the five for the State, but—

Father O'Connors, a priest of 35, "tall, well-built, religious," has come to hear Walters' prayers. The guard lets him in the cell, and as he adjusts the stole about his shoulders Walters reads—

"I confess to Almighty God, to blessed Mary ever Virgin . . . to blessed Michael the Archangel . . . to blessed John the Baptist . . . to the Holy Apostles, Peter and Paul, and to all the saints, and to you, Father, that I have sinned exceedingly in thought, word and deed, through my fault, through my fault, through my own grievous fault.

O'CONNORS—Sancti. Amen. Now, Walters, you believe in God?

WALTERS—I do, Father.

O'CONNORS—In his only Son, Our Lord . . .

MAYOR—Huh!

MEARS—Shh . . . Keep quiet.

O'CONNORS (*continuing*)—Forgiveness of sin through the resurrection of the body, and life everlasting?

WALTERS—I do, Father.

O'CONNORS—Taken the name of God in vain?

WALTERS—I have.

O'CONNORS—Committed robbery or adultery?

WALTERS—No, never, Father, never.

O'CONNORS—Procured, desired or hastened the death of anyone? (WALTERS *is still.*) Well, have you?

WALTERS—I have, Father, but I didn't mean it. Honest! I didn't. It was all an accident. So help me, Jesus. So help me. (*He commences to sob convulsively but quietly.*)

O'CONNORS (*places his hand on his shoulder consolingly*)—God is merciful, Walters, to those who have faith. Say a good act of contrition.

WALTERS—Here?

O'CONNORS—Yes, begin here.

WALTERS (*reads*)—O, my God, I am heartily sorry for having offended Thee and I detest all my sins, because I dread the loss of Heaven and the pains of Hell, but most of all because they offend Thee, my God, who art all, good and deserving of all my love. I firmly resolve, with the help of Thy Grace, to confess my sins, to do penance, and to amend my life. Amen.

O'CONNORS (*as* WALTERS *reads*)—*Dominus noster Jesus Christus te absolvat; et ego, auctoritate ipsius, te absolvat* (*in decreasing tones*) *ab omni vinculo excommincationis, et, interdisti, inquintum possum, et tu indignes. Deinde ego te absolve a peccatis tuis, in nomine Patris et Filli, et Spiritus. Amen.* All right. God bless you. I'll see you later, Walters.

Father O'Connors is not as successful in stirring the interest of the other prisoners. Mayor openly flouts his offers of spiritual help and Mears flings back in his face his statements of the peace and understanding that comes with faith. Nor is Mears convinced that Walters is any better off for the help the priest has given him.

"It seems to me he's very brave," insists Father O'Connors.

"Brave," sneers Mears. "Why—how the hell is he brave if I'm afraid, too? How is he feeling if my belly is turning over with the idea?"

"He has faith, John, he believes. I wish you would allow me to talk to you, too—about God—about—"

"Listen here, O'Connors—I look at you and I can't make you out. You look like a fellow that's read books and always kept your eyes open. You talk like a three-year old. You want me to believe—in what? In another world? So that I shouldn't fear to go on the week of the ninth? Eh? All right. What kind of a place is this next world of yours? What's in it? Did anyone ever see it? Where's your proof that it exists?"

"You've got to have faith—in the Lord, and believe in his Son—the Christ—he promised—he died—"

"That ain't faith. That's just closing your eyes and wishing

Say—I've been through too much. Maybe I never went to school. Maybe I never had no education, but I've thought a lot in my time—I had to, and I know this: I got to see it in black and white, I got to have two and two make four. I ain't talkin' myself into nothing. Say, don't you think I'd like to believe and so not be afraid of that in there . . . (*gestures to door on right*) not have to wait, and worry and wait—and go nice and peaceful, and smiling and have faith? Why sure—you can talk that way—you don't have to go—you're not waiting—afraid—afraid . . ."

"I would have no fear."

"You wouldn't?"

"I'm certain I wouldn't."

When the guards, Peddie and Drake, come to prepare Walters for the chair they let him bring the rest of his possessions from the cell and pass them among his cellmates. There are a few oranges, a pipe and a book.

Now they have shaved Walters' temples, slit the cloth of the left trouser leg and shaved the side of the calf. He will not let them shave the crown of his head, even when Drake warns him that he will get twice as much juice if he doesn't, so they soak the hair with alcohol.

He is a subdued and trembling Walters as he is locked back in his bare cell. He has joked with the others and promised frequently to meet them in Hell. He will be brave, all right. He'll do them credit. But it is 10 o'clock. It isn't easy to forget that. It isn't anything that sucking an orange will help, either.

"It ain't that, Red," Walters admits to Kirby. "You see, I just hate to go. I didn't know I hated anything so bad in all my life. I hate to leave you guys."

"This old life isn't any good anyway, Kid. Let's just hope you're goin' to a better one. Maybe there is a better place somewhere. There oughta be."

Now Walters is in the grip of hysteria again. What if he shouldn't get that stay? What if he shouldn't? What if he shouldn't?

Excitedly, faster and faster he repeats the query. Each time one of them assures him that he will, he will, he's sure to get it!

"Well—just keep by me, you damn guys."

It is a last appeal for support.

"Keep stickin' by me. I'll build me an air-castle—or somethin', to get my mind off it, off the chair. Hey, tell us how you slit his throat, Sunny. Tell us how you ripped up that high yaller."

"Lemme 'lone, white boy. Ah'm busy prayin' for you."

"Thanks. Keep it up. I'll pray for you later on. Wish I had a drink."

It is against the rules, but Guard O'Flaherty produces a flask and Walters gulps a drink.

An evangelist has called. He, too, would help to guide the departing soul. His assurances of salvation are as positive and as slangy as Billy Sunday's. He doesn't get a great deal of sympathy.

"Aw, can that stuff, Aimee MacPherson," sneers Mayor. "Don't think you can make us believe you're a man by using slang."

They have brought Walters the coffee he didn't drink with his last dinner. It quiets his nerves for the moment.

"Red, you were damned lucky to get that thirty-five-day stay," he tells Kirby. "Boy, I wish I had one. Looks like I ought to get one stay, at least. Just one."

"Seven, if it was possible for me to do it, I'd give you half of mine and we'd both have seventeen and a half days each. I wish I could do it."

"You wouldn't fool me, would you, Red? This ain't no time to do that."

"Not right here in town with my shirt on. Of course I got no way to prove my statement to you. I can see why you find it hard to believe; but just the same, I would do it. I would. I wish it was only possible, because I hate like hell to see you go, Seven."

"I wish you could do it, Red. If you ain't kiddin' me."

"He ain't," insists Mayor. "He'd do it. I believe him."

"Ya all think so, guys?" Walters finds it difficult to believe in such imagined generosity.

"Seven, we all think he means what he says," calls D'Amoro.

"Well, thanks a lot, Red." And Walters is deeply pleased.

Father O'Connors is back. A guard carries a portable altar, which is placed in Walters' cell. The candles are lighted. His preparations made, O'Connors leaves, but will be back shortly to administer holy communion.

"Seven, there must be something for you to look forward to," consoles Red Kirby. "It must be better than this life or it wouldn't be worth much. I don't think any of us is losin' much when we walk to that chair. Anyhow, there's bound to be a Heaven or something, and if there is something or somebody like a God, everybody'll have the opportunity to get in right."

Two reporters have arrived. They are the friendliest, the squarest of the lot. They come from the *News* and the *Post*. Walters had half promised to give them his whole story. He hesitates now, but little by little he blurts it out as they stand in front of his cell.

WALTERS—She wasn't no kid, like the D.A. said she was. She was over sixteen. You see her pictures. (*Pauses.*) I was makin' pretty good money. I was workin' then for the town gas company, as a meter-reader. I loved her. . . .

FROST—You did. (WALTERS *nods.*) You really loved her?

WALTERS (*slowly*)—Yes, I did. I was crazy over her, I guess. I'd been pretty wild, ya see, and I liked her, so much, I guess, because she was so, so . . . clean, a virgin, and very pretty.

FROST—Then what?

WALTERS—Well . . . I wanted to marry her . . . I asked her, ya might not believe me, but I did. I'd have done everything for her, but she kidded me and teased me along, and I—I couldn't sleep nights. I wanted her so. Well, that day I took her ridin'. You won't believe me, but it's true . . . true as God. I took her ridin' to elope with her. She asked me where I was goin'. I said, "Just ridin'." And she says, "It's time to go back," and I laugh and say, "Sure, Ethel, sure. We'll go back, and how." Well, she gets nervous. Ya see, she didn't give me much credit for honest intentions, and that was what . . . (*Catches himself.*) Well, I'll come to that, and here she is gettin' nervous. So I see she's gotta know and I drive into a side road, and park under a tree near a little brook. Well, very slow-like I take out the diamond engagement ring I had bought for her, and I tell her to shut her eyes. She does. I slip the ring on her finger. Now get this, cause you woulda done the same. I take and I kiss her hand with the ring on it. She opens her eyes and looks at me for a second, then she looks at her hand and says softly . . . "Oh!" . . . Then I kiss her on the mouth, and it was the first time, and . . . it was . . . wonderful. It was a nice, clear day, near about sunset. She lets me kiss her, but suddenly she begins to squirm and yell, "No, no. I don't want to. Let me go. I hate you. Take me home. I hate you. I hate you." And she rips off the ring and throws it into the little brook near us, right outa the car.

FROST (*makes a note*)—A little brook, eh?

BROOKS (*aside to* FROST)—Shh. Shh. Well, what happened?

WALTERS (*after a slight pause, speaking a bit faster*)—I don't know what. But I think to myself. Aw, what the hell. I'll give her the works. I don't care, and besides, I was sore. Jeez, figger throwin' away my ring, the ring that would have made her my own wife. I was sore. I pulled her out of the car and laid her on the grass and just . . .

FROST—Forced her.

WALTERS (*speaking quite rapidly now*)—Yea. Then she began to cry and yell. Then she said, "I'll have you arrested. I'll have you put in jail." And she called me all kinds of dirty names. Well, I don't know, I was sore. Now get this, cause you would have done the same, maybe. I get peeved and I hit her. She goes down. (*Slight pause.*) I'm sure it was that sharp rock under her head that did the killin', cause I couldn't hit hard enough to kill anybody, although maybe I could, but anyway it wasn't like that D.A. said, that I hit her with the rock, but I didn't mean it . . . honest, I didn't mean it. (*Stops abruptly.*)

BROOKS—Anything else? Any more?

WALTERS (*slowly, wearily*)—Huh? More? No . . . buddy . . . I'm tired. (*Apologetically.*) I don't feel like goin' on. You guys know the rest.

BROOKS—Sure, we do, sure. Well, thanks. I'll do something for you some day.

WALTERS—See what you can do for my mother. Will ya?

FROST—Sure we will. We'll run her a newspaper fund . . . O.K.?

WALTERS—Gee. Thanks.

FROST—Well, so long. Good luck.

WALTERS—So long, fellers. Thanks a lot for comin'.

BROOKS—So long.

Walters is still hopeful of that stay. The warden's secretary has promised him that he will stand right by the telephone. But—

Here is Principal Keeper Callahan with the death warrant. He has to read that. It is one of the rules. There is no life in Callahan's voice as he begins—

"People of the State of Oklahoma vs. Richard Walters. State of Oklahoma, County of Elmira. To the Agent and Warden of the Keystone Prison at Keystone, Oklahoma. Whereas, at a trial term of the County Court, held in and for—"

The voice drones on to the signature: "James Carney Leffingworth, County Judge of Elmira County, Oklahoma, presiding."

"That's all, Seven. Anything you want to say, say now. Your mother asked me to get your last words for her."

"I'd send her a telegram if I had the money, but I gave it all away to Thirteen."

Thirteen passes a bill back and Callahan writes the telegram.

"Tell her I'm laughin', and jokin', and singin'. Tell her I'm thinkin' of her. Tell her I'm all right. All right. Got that? That my thoughts are all of her . . ."

Callahan has gone. The guard has lighted a cigarette for Walters. Jackson is praying hard for him now, and Walters is trying desperately to hold on, as he said he would. He even tries to sing a little—

"A little white light will lead you to my blue heaven.
A smiling face, a fireplace, a cozy room—"

The tune is pathetically off key. The song is soon finished. Kirby and D'Amoro have voiced their last hope that if Walters has to go he will take it like a man and Walters has promised.

"They say that a fellow has never died here who didn't show weakness," he tells them. "I'm going to show them that I can go like a man. I can, all right! I can! I can!"

A guard brings the keys to the green door. The priest follows. In Walters' cell he administers the Holy Communion.

"Our Father, who art in Heaven, hallowed be Thy name—"

The priest repeats the Lord's prayer. Walters continues after him.

"Almighty God, unto whom all hearts are open, all desires known, and from whom no secrets are hid; cleanse the thoughts of our hearts by the inspiration of Thy Holy Spirit—"

With an effort the prayer is finished. There is still another. Father O'Connors is a gentle prompter.

"O Lord Jesus, God of my heart, and life of my soul," cries Walters, until his voice breaks and the sobs come. "Oh, Jesus Christ, get me out of here," he calls, desperately; "don't let me go, don't let me die—"

Again the gentle priest inspires a new and desperate courage. Walters' voice strengthens as he repeats the passages. And now the prayers are finished and Father O'Connors has taken his stand in front of the green door. Book in hand, he is reading softly aloud.

"I hate to go but it looks like it's gotta be done," calls Walters.

"Don't give up hope," repeats the ever hopeful Kirby.

WALTERS—I still got hopes but they're gettin' weak.

WERNER—Ho . . . lmes. When your time draws near, less than one hour.

WALTERS—Light me a cigarette. (*There is a tense air of expectancy that grows heavier and heavier. More and more intense. One can almost feel it, touch it.*) Let me out with the boys, O'Flaherty, I wanna tell 'em all good-bye.

O'FLAHERTY—I can't do it, Seven. I would if I could, but it would be against the rules. I'm awful sorry. I wish I could.

WALTERS (*with attempted nonchalance*)—Oh, I don't care; 'sall right. (*He is given one.*) I'm not takin' it as hard as I thought I'd be. I'm pretty nervous though; I never had anything to do with electricity before. Wonder how it feels? Wonder if a guy knows anything? I hope it won't take long. They say Skippy Woodworth turned all his insides red from the burning. His brain, too. Is that right about them keepin' the brains here in the hospital for findin' out things? I don't think my insides'll turn red. They got it perfected by now. Skippy was a long time ago. I hope my insides don't turn red . . .

MAYOR—Aw, ya never know what hits ya. It's all over in a few shakes. Brace up.

WALTERS (*speaking in a sort of strange monotone*)—Ya know it's funny. I was worse at my trial than I am now. I almost broke down at my trial. I lost fifteen and a half pounds, while my case was in court. (*Suddenly, as if in anguish.*) Give me some more coffee, fer Christ's sakes!

MAYOR—Oh, my God!

WALTERS (*Guard gives him coffee.*)—Huh! Well, here's to the old death house, boys!

CALLAHAN (*enters with more guards. Cell 7 is unlocked by one.*)—All right, Seven. Let's go. (*Seven exits cell slowly.*)

WALTERS (*wavers, but the guards hold him on either side. Gulps and swallows with difficulty*)—Good-bye, Sunny. I won't shake hands. It's bad luck.

JACKSON—Good-bye, Mr. Walters. Ah hope mah prayers done yuh some good.

WALTERS (*crosses to Eleven*)—Good-bye, Eddie. I don't know which of us is better off.

WERNER—Good-bye, son. Farewell. (*Beckons him with his finger to come closer.*)

WALTERS (*interrupts*)—O. K., Eddie.

KIRBY—Good-bye, kid. Stand right up.

WALTERS—Huh. I think I'm doin' about as well as you would do.

KIRBY—I know you are.

WALTERS—Good-bye.

KIRBY—S'long. Don't fergit to hold it.

WALTERS (*as he crosses slowly to Five, he looks down upon his split trouser leg*)—Huh. They split my pants, and I don't like it much. This is a new style boys. How do you like it? Hello, Five. Give me a drag, will ya? (*The guards seize him, as he bends over to take a puff.*) Don't worry. I ain't gonna run away.

MEARS—Good-bye, Seven. Stay with 'em.

WALTERS—I'll make it. Good-bye, Killer John Mears.

MEARS—Good-bye, Richard Walters. Give 'em my best regards. (*Laughs.*) Laugh at 'em.

WALTERS—I will. I will. I can do it. Good-bye, Freddie. I hope you get a stay.

MAYOR—Hope so. Good-bye. I'll meet ya in two weeks. Wait for me.

WALTERS—Uh-huh. S'long. Glad I met ya, One.

D'AMORO—Likewise. Good-bye. (WALTERS *is now again held by the guards.*)

WALTERS—This is the last mile. (*He is now at the green door, the* PRINCIPAL KEEPER, CALLAHAN *and the* PRIEST *behind him and a guard in front. The guard unlocks the green door, yanks at it but it fails to open. Almost hysterically.*) Say, Five. They can't get the damned door open. What d'ya think of that?

MEARS—Take those keys and open it for 'em, Seven. (*Laughs.*)

WALTERS (*slowly*)—I'd stay right here until next Christmas before I'd open it for 'em. (*The door is finally opened.*) Well, it's open. I'll say good-bye to everybody again. So long, everybody. (*Cries of "good-bye," "so long," etc.*) I wish I'm the last one who ever sits in that goddam, bastard chair. (*He exits. The lights suddenly grow dim after a pause and the whine of the motor is heard. There is a pause. Then* MAYOR *breaks down and sobs.*)

MEARS (*as the lights go dim again*)—They're givin' him the juice again. (*Shouts in a terrible rage.*) What the hell are they tryin' to do? Cook him?

ACT II

Two weeks later the inmates of the death house are the same. Sunny Jackson has been moved into Cell 7 and is playing a game of checkers with Red Kirby in Cell 9. The checker board is on a stool in the corridor placed in front of the partition dividing the cells. The men can both reach it through the bars, but neither can see the other.

Mayor, Werner, Mears and D'Amoro are either leaning idly against their cell doors or are stretched out on their bunks. It is late afternoon and a descending sun shines thinly through the cell windows at back. It is the day appointed for Mayor's execution.

Mayor is still outwardly calm. He has a pain over his heart, he admits to Mears, but he is hoping he will stand up. What is he thinking of? Of his girl mostly. His girl Elaine—

Elaine hasn't been to see him lately. She's sick. She'll be giving birth any day now. But it won't be a nameless kid she'll be having. Fred and Elaine were hitched in court, right after the sentence, he is quick to register. They're married, all right. And Elaine—

The name starts the crazed Werner reciting poetry again.

> "Elaine the fair, Elaine the lovable,
> Elaine, the lily maid of Astolat—"

This time Werner does not irritate Mayor. He likes this poem. He learned it once in high school. It's about King Arthur and his knights.

> "High in her chamber, up on a tower to the east
> Guarded the sacred shield of Launcelot—"

Werner can't remember more than that. They would all like him to go on now, but he can't remember. Keeper Callahan is in with a notice from the warden. It concerns the appeal of Mayor's case and, according to the rules, it has to be read, whether Mayor wants to hear it or not. The notice expresses the warden's regret that the appeal has been denied. The original sentence of death will be carried out.

MAYOR (*after a pause*)—You know, I once read, that when a man is about to die, he was drowning in this story, that he'd give anything in the world to live just another minute. He'd give anything. What do you think of that, Five?

MEARS—Huh? I wasn't listenin'.

D'AMORO—I believe that, Three.

MAYOR—It said that if a drowning man could have just a square yard of earth in the middle of an ocean, he'd be satisfied to stay there all his life instead of dyin' just that minute.

MEARS—That's right.

MAYOR—I'm afraid to die, honest. I got everything to live for. I got a good family, I got a good trade, and I got a wonderful girl. Why do I have to—die? I'm too young—I ain't lived at all. (*Pause.*) I always wanted to travel and see the world and I never got the chance. I worked so God damn hard. First I was a porter, when I was fifteen, and I had to leave school when my mother died. Then I was a shipping clerk, bossing fifteen men, and makin' good money.

KIRBY—But you did kill him, didn't you? I hope you ain't claimin' to us that you're innocent.

MAYOR (*wearily*)—No, I don't claim that. I admit it. I shot him. . . .

D'AMORO—Why?

MAYOR (*repeats*)—Why! Why! Christ! I don't know. I was nuts. Yeah. Why did I? Oh, sweetheart, my sweet girl! Poor kid, first she's my sweetheart, then she's my wife, and right away she's got to be my widow— Oh—Jesus—why—why the hell—

MEARS (*slowly*)—Sweetheart—wife and widow—all in three minutes. . . .

MAYOR (*dully*)—Sweetheart—wife—widow. . . . . (*Drake laughs.*)

KIRBY—Brace up, Three, don't let that screw laugh at ya.

MEARS—Shut your mug, screw.

DRAKE—Shut yourself, Mears. You don't give orders. You take 'em!

JACKSON—That white boy's lower than whale dung.

DRAKE—All right. I'll see you burn yet.

JACKSON—You keep your mouth shut, or you'll be feeling my black hands on your throat.

DRAKE—Wouldn't you like to, Boogey.

KIRBY—If that nigger ever got you between his hands, you'd need Holy Communion quick.

JACKSON—Need something.

Mayor has got out a picture of Elaine. He is proud of that picture. He wants the others to see it. Both Mears and D'Amoro agree that Elaine's a fine-looking girl. Mayor would go on talking about Elaine, but there are other thoughts that keep crowding in—thoughts of how Walters took it when it came his time, singin' ten minutes before, and makin' cracks about waitin' for Christmas when they couldn't get the door open.

Nerve? That wasn't nerve! Not as Killer Mears sees it. They're all scared stiff, swears Mears. They could save juice on a lot of 'em if they'd examine them before the switch is pulled.

JACKSON—I suah didn't wanna see that fellah Waltahs go.

KIRBY—That's all right. You'll meet him in Heaven, Sunny.

JACKSON—I'm thinkin' I won't even meet him, nor you, nor any white man up in Heaven, Red Boy. You know that song—I got shoes, you got shoes, goes like this—(*Begins to sing.*)—All Gawd's chillum got shoes. When Ah git to Heaven Ah'm gonna put on my shoes and Ah'm gonna walk all over God's Heaven—Well, that song is all one grand lie—and it's a fool nigger that believe it. Don't you all know theah is two Heavens, one foah the white man and one foah the black man. Why, if I could sneak mah way into that theah white man's Heaven by accident or somepin'—why youah keepahs up there would say to me—What for you want in this Heaven, anyhow? Who told you to come heah? Don't you all know this ain't youah place? Git ovah in your own nigger Heaven long by that theah toilet, you black bastard, before youah is sent to nigger Hell.

KIRBY—What—have you got a hell—too—for the niggers?

JACKSON (*bitterly*)—Suah—suah there is a nigger hell. Do you think they're gonna let us fry in the same fiah with yoh all?—No, sir, never no fry.

Guard Harris has brought in Mayor's supper. He passes it on to Drake and Drake takes it over to Mayor's cell. As he turns to go back to his station at the door Killer Mears' arms shoot out and circle his neck in a vise-like grip.

Drake is helpless. He struggles briefly. Slowly his body sags toward the floor.

Mears reaches through the bars, takes the prostrate guard's gun and keys and quickly lets himself out.

"It's a quarter past five, men," he calls to the others in muffled, excited tones; "we gotta work fast. We ain't got no time to waste. Just watch me! I'm the leader. I'm runnin' this!" He unlocks Cell 7. "Come out, Sunny!"

JACKSON—I'm with yuh, Boss.

MEARS (*unlocks Cell 3*)—Come on out, Mayor.

MAYOR—Mears, Mears. You're a man, Mears.

MEARS—All right. Keep your shirt on. Don't get excited. (*Unlocks Cell 1.*) All right, One, out. Maybe you won't be sittin' on that chair on the 29th.

KIRBY—Maybe he won't live to see the 29th.

MEARS—Sure, maybe he won't, but what of it. What's the matter? Ain't you joinin' with us?

KIRBY—The warden's a pretty good skate, Mears, you shouldn't try to make trouble for him or if you do, do it yourself, an' don't be draggin' us in with you.

MEARS—Draggin' yuh in? Why, you old heel. You oughta fall on your knees and beg me for the chance to let you in on this.

KIRBY—But the warden . . .

MEARS (*interrupting*)—To hell with the warden. (*Dominantly.*) Come on out now and join with us. (*Slight pause.*) Or, would you like to burn better? Didn't ya see enough? Ask Three here how he felt walkin' outa that cell instead of walkin' into that place. (*Points.*) How do ya feel, Mayor?

MAYOR—I can breathe now. I feel like I been born again. Let's get to work, Killer.

KIRBY—An' if we get shot?

MEARS—So ya will. At least you'll get it suddenly, when you don't expect it. At least you won't be hearin' a goddam clock beatin' away the minutes of your life. You won't have to walk up to it, and have a priest tellin' you to make yourself ready for God.

KIRBY—All right, Mears. I wasn't against yuh. I was only tryin' to look at it reasonable. I'm with yuh.

Werner won't come, even after Mears has beaten him. And Mears thought he was faking that crazy stuff. Well, let him stay locked in. And D'Amoro—D'Amoro is ready to join, but he would also like to have a hand in running the show—until Mears sticks a gun under his chin and advises him to keep his mouth shut and do as he is told.

Drake, the hated guard, still dazed by the effect of the choking, is thrown into one of the cells. With Mayor and Jackson, Mears makes a hasty search of the outer office. Then he outlines his immediate plan.

"Nobody in there yet," he reports. "We got the doors bolted down. Guess they're in the office next door. Now all of you remember. Got to rush. Sudden, quick. Before they can pull. D'Amoro, Kirby, stay, here. Git yourself one of those iron stools. Git stools, everybody. Remember don't hit too hard, fellows, I want 'em alive.

The three—Mayor, Jackson and Mears—have gone again to the outer office. D'Amoro and Kirby await results inside.

A moment later there are the sounds of shots and a fight in the office. Then the priest, O'Connors, Guards Peddie and O'Flaherty march into the room, followed by Mayor with two guns leveled at them. Keeper Callahan and Guard Harris come next, with Mears guarding them.

"Come on, ya damn screws. Git in there," commands Mears. "Put yer hands up, everybody. Frisk 'em, men. Get their cartridges. That's what we need."

Quickly the captives are searched. Their own handcuffs are put on them. Their money is appropriated. Their advice is profanely spurned.

Mears has no time to listen to priest's talk. Nor has he any fear of Callahan now. They may as well save their breath. Mears goes on with his orders.

MEARS—D'Amoro! Mayor! You two get to work loosening them bars in Cell 7. I gotta have one window clear. Don't stand looking at me! Grab that stool or something.

MAYOR—I saw an axe on the wall in the office—near the fire extinguisher. That would be . . .

MEARS—That's it, boy. Get it and get a pencil and some paper while you're in there. (MAYOR *exits. To the others.*)

O'CONNORS—You do not know what you are doing, John. The law demands—

MEARS—I have every right—I'm the law now!

D'AMORO—Say, Boss; where's Sunny?

MEARS—What?

D'AMORO—The nigger—where is he?

MEARS—Dead.

D'AMORO—Oh. (*Pause.*) Did you get them all? The screws?

MEARS—No—two got away. (*Noise outside, voices, shouts, footsteps running.*) Get on those windows, fellows. Plug anybody you see. We got almost three hours before it gets dark.

D'AMORO (*suddenly, loudly*)—Get down, Kirby. (*He shoots.*) I got 'em. The damn screw—had a sure bead on you.

KIRBY—Jeez. Thanks. One hand watches the other. Eh?

D'AMORO—Sure. That's the idea.

MAYOR (*enters carrying axe, and pencil and paper*)—Here it is, Killer. Which window?

MEARS—Give it to One. (MAYOR *gives axe to* D'AMORO.) Get those bars out, Tom, but keep low. Don't take no chances. (D'AMORO *gets to work.* MEARS *to* MAYOR.) Sit down—write. Warden—We the convicts of the death house (*The convicts at the windows listen attentively, much interested.* CALLAHAN *and* O'CONNORS *lean forward from the floor; the imprisoned guards come close to the bars of their respective cells; shooting outside has ceased.*) demand our liberty. We'll take with us O'Connors and your brother-in-law, the principal keeper. (*Repeating.*) Plenty of gas and oil—good tires. Four hours' start—no double crossing. Then we'll drop your men safely.

D'AMORO—We can. (*Shots outside.*)

MEARS—Now—*If* we do not get these conditions in full by . . . 9 o'clock tonight we're goin' to kill one of your guards. Signed. The C. C.'s of the Death House.

Harris is the most frightened of the guards. That threat to kill a guard sends him into hysterics. But Mears pays no attention to his wailing, save occasionally to shut him up.

There is a white flag being waved from the other side of the prison yard. The warden's men want to get the body of the guard D'Amoro has shot.

Mears lets them come for the body and calls down to them from Kirby's cell.

"Hey—there below. I'm throwin' a note down. Give it to Warden Stone. Tell him I want quick action. No funny works —a big closed car. Remember—I mean business. Now get back pronto and don't come near here unless you feel like being buried. Git! (*To the men.*) Shoot back, fellows, but be easy on your bullets."

Now Mears has apportioned the bullets. There are forty or fifty of them. He holds out six—one for each of the rebels if needed.

From across the yard comes the rattle of machine guns.

"Well, men, it's on!" shouts Mears. "The war's begun! Shoot—you bastards—shoot!"

There is a wail from the crazed Eddie Werner. The shriek

of the prison siren gradually rises above the din of the firing. The curtain falls.

ACT III

Two hours later the death house shows the effects of the battle. Cell windows are chipped, empty cartridge shells are scattered over the corridor floor.

Mears, a wound in his cheek on which the blood has dried, paces the corridor "like a caged leopard." Mayor is on watch at the window of Cell 7. D'Amoro on guard below him. Callahan and O'Connors, still handcuffed, are sitting in front of the door to the execution chamber. The imprisoned guards, Harris, Peddie, O'Flaherty and Drake, are two in a cell, and talking excitedly among themselves.

Kirby is the first to mention the time, though Mears has been looking anxiously at his watch with increasing frequency.

It is 9:35. The note read 9:30. If nothing was heard by 9:30 a guard was to be killed.

"Are you going to do it?" demands Kirby.

"Don't you know me, Red?"

"Then—who's first?"

"We'll take that guy Drake first."

Kirby is sent to relieve Mayor. Mayor is told to bring Drake out. The guard is brought protestingly from his cell. He can't understand. He won't believe Mears means to kill him, even after he hears the terms of the note.

There is no hesitancy on Mears' part. He always has hated Drake, the skunk. Seeing him grovel now fills the killer with loathing. He kicks and drags him into a cell. He doesn't want to litter up the corridor.

"I hope I'll miss you the first time, Drake," sneers Mears, "so you'll have to go through it a second time."

There is a shot. Drake crumples up in the cell.

"I had to hit him on the first shot, Callahan," Mears explains to the staring keeper. "I couldn't afford to miss him. We'll throw him out the window."

A dull thud follows the pushing of Drake's body through the cell window from which D'Amoro has broken out the bars. There is a note pinned to the body. This message reads that unless the warden accepts the terms of the death house men another guard will be killed at 10. It is now 9:55.

Kirby isn't weakening. He wants Mears to realize that. But he isn't quite satisfied that they are right in taking another chance. Look at it, for instance, from the warden's end, suggests Red. He's got a lot to lose—his job, and his reputation, and perhaps a little graft. There's bound to be an investigation and ugly things come out in investigations. He's got a job to consider, too.

"Don't you forget, too, that outside all those items I mentioned that that warden is sent here to keep us guys in here. That's his job. He can't go back on the men who give him the job—he can't—"

"It's 10 o'clock, Red." Mears speaks quietly. "Get this guy Peddie out here."

There are wails of protest from Peddie. He's got a wife and kids! Why not take a bachelor? Peddie's only twenty-nine, he cries. That's too young to die!

Mears is relentless. Kirby can't drag Peddie from the cell. In his panic the guard has thrown himself on the floor and is clinging to the steel uprights of the bed. Mears decides to shoot him where he lies. He raises his pistol and fires. The gun clicks, but there is no report.

This situation calls for an investigation of the ammunition. A count of bullets reveals only the six that Mears is holding in reserve and a few held by the others.

"We should have been more careful," suggests Kirby.

"We been here five hours," Mears ruminates. "If we had enough bullets we could hold out a couple of days, easy." A second later his decision is made. "All right," he agrees. "We'll play our ace now, before we're caught with our pants down."

The ace is Callahan. There are six bullets left. One for Callahan and five for the men. Mears goes into conference with Kirby. Which of the guards shall they send with a message to the warden?

O'Flaherty is picked. A white guy, O'Flaherty, now brought from the cell, pale and trembling, thinking he may be the one to follow Drake.

"Jesus—John—you ain't gonna do me, are ya?"

"No. Come here. Ya see we mean business, don't ya?" O'Flaherty sees. "Well, I'm leaving ya go—free; but I want you to tell that warden something, and I want you to tell him right. You know what was written on those notes, don't ya?"

O'Flaherty (*nods quickly*)—Yes, I know. I heard. (O'Flaherty *is frightened by* Mears' *quiet desperation.*)

Mears (*between his teeth*)—Well, I want you to tell that

warden that he ain't got no chicken-hearted sons-of-bitches here . . . that I'm prepared to carry out in every particular everything I say I'm gonna do. See?

O'Flaherty (*breathing heavily*)—Yeah. Sure.

Mears (*only pausing for breath*)—You tell him—now remember this—tell him that we got four men in here. Four—live—men. The guards Harris, and Peddie—

Harris (*interrupting wildly*)—No, no, not me! Not me! Don't let them kill me. Mears! Mears!

Mears (*continuing after looking at* Harris *for a minute*)—The priest and the principal keeper, his own brother-in-law. Tell him I'm going to kill every one of them. I'm prepared to kill every one of them. Hear that?

O'Flaherty (*assenting; he cannot speak*)—Mm. Mmm. Mmm.

Mears (*without stopping*)—Remember, if he don't come through with my demands, if he don't come through, say that Callahan goes in half an hour. (*Examines his watch.*) Principal Keeper Callahan at 10:45 o'clock. Get it? An' tell him I want that car in A-1 condition. Perfect. No funny works. See?

O'Flaherty (*relieved that this is the end of the torture*)—Yeah. Everything. I'll remember every blessed word. I thank ye for this, John. I'll never fergit ye for this. I'm thinkin' of retirin' anyway. My pension is beginning in a few months now, and—

Mears (*interrupts abruptly*)—All right. Beat it. Let O'Flaherty out. An' don't get hurt when you're openin' that door. Keep him in front of ya.

They watch O'Flaherty as he makes his way across the prison yard. Nervously they await results. No one appears.

"Get ready, Callahan," warns Mears.

"Me?"

"Yes, you. In fifteen minutes now—at 10:45. I just want to give you a taste of what we get in here. I want you to know that when this big hand here gets to 10:45 (*Shows him the timepiece.*) you're gonna get a thirty-eight size piece of lead in your head. See?"

"You don't mean that, Mears? You don't mean you're going to do that? Without a goddam chance—"

"Huh! I never meant anything more in my life, Callahan. Didn't ya hear what I told O'Flaherty, that I meant what I said? Now, listen, I'm willin' to give ya a chance though I hate the guts in all of ya. You write what you want to the warden, and tell him whatever you like, but remind him that he's got to 10:45 to make up his mind."

"All right. Give me a pencil."

Mayor volunteers to hold the paper while Callahan, trembling, manages to write the note:

"Stanley: Get me out of this. Mears' desperate. Give them what they want, or I'm a dead man at 10:45. Stan—for Rose's sake. My blood'll be on your head. Frank Callahan."

They have waved the shirt that is their flag of truce. They have dropped the note. Now it has been picked up and taken back to the warden.

Presently a trusty, his hands held above his head, is seen crossing the yard. He comes with a message for Mears. The warden is sending word that he can't give Mears what he wants. "He says he can't do nothin'," the trusty reports. "He just wants to call quits. He won't do ya anything for this if ya stop . . . immediately."

"Tell that guy to go to hell," is Mears' answer.

Let them all go to hell. The warden. The militia. Callahan. All of them.

Nor is Mears moved by Father O'Connors' appeal that he reconsider and give the warden a chance. Why should he? Mears wants to know that. "He's only gonna give me the electric chair. He's only gonna kill me. What do ya want me to do? Get down on my knees and thank him?

O'Connors—That's his job—his duty—

Mears—All right. This is my duty. To show the world that I don't like it. To show the world that I object to it. Do ya think I wanna die? You think I ain't a human being? Ya think I don't wanna live? Ya think it's very nice to wait in that goddam cell, day after day, week after week, month after month, and see men die, one after another, see lights go dim, hear the whine of that lousy motor, and wait, and wait and die a million times every goddam minute?

O'Connors—But, what did you start all this for? You have brains enough to know he will never let you through—even if you killed the whole force—

Mears (*passionately*)—Because I wanna show them. I wanna show them what it means. To die. I want to show what a man, what men will go through *not* to die. Do ya think these men here got any hopes of gettin' through? Do you? No. Do you think I got any? No! First we wanna show 'em, and second we wanna die like men, not like rats in a trap. That's why. Like men— (*Stops abruptly and glances at his watch.*) It's 10:37, Callahan. How does it feel? Do you think you understand a little bit of what we feel? Now?

CALLAHAN—Christ, Father. I've been working together with him for twenty years. Why, we're pals. I'm his own brother-in-law. He can't let me go this way. He can't. It's murder, Father. No. He wouldn't. What does it mean to him? A job. That's all.

O'CONNORS—It's his duty, Frank.

CALLAHAN—Duty? (*Slowly.*) To hell with it.

O'CONNORS—If these men succeed in obtaining their freedom this way—

CALLAHAN (*angrily*)—Well, what the hell of it? Isn't it better to let four men free than to have four of us killed? Isn't it better? They can catch them later on. These men are not going out to blow up the world. They only want to get away. That's all. They only want to get away.

O'CONNORS—But, it's setting a precedent—it would destroy the morale. Prisons couldn't exist without morale, without—

CALLAHAN (*suddenly shouting*)—Who in hell cares for morale or precedents, when it means our lives? Your life and my life!

O'CONNORS—No. They couldn't shoot me. A priest of God! No!

CALLAHAN—You don't think so? Well, ask him. Ask him. What are you afraid of? Is O'Connors next to go, or isn't he? (MEARS *nods.*)

MEARS—What'sa matter? What are ya afraid of? You're a believer. There's another world. A heaven. Quiet there. You're in God's path, ain't ya? Christ. He died for you, for mankind. Can't you die for us?

WERNER (*reciting*)—

I fight alone, and win or sink,
I need no one to make me free
I want no Jesus Christ to think
That he could ever die for me!

HARRIS—Don't let them kill me! Mears! Mears!

O'CONNORS (*stares dully at* MEARS).

MEARS—Callahan—you got about three minutes to live. Three

minutes. They stopped firin' to see what we'll do. The whole world is waitin' to see if we got the nerve to kill you. If we got the nerve to kill the P.K. of a prison and a priest of God. Huh! We'll show 'em.

D'Amoro (*with fire*)—Show 'em.

Mayor—We'll show 'em that being murdered is not so nice.

Callahan—Listen—Mears—I want you to know—

Mears—How do you feel, now? How many times did you read a death-warrant? How many times did you give the electrician the death-signal? Eh? How many guys did you hold a hose to, or laced up in a strait-jacket, eh?

Callahan—Mears! Men! Listen to me. For Christ's sake! I only worked here. I didn't put you here—

Mears—Why the hell did you have to work here?

Mayor (*sneering*)—What would you like to have for your supper, Keeper? Nothing will be refused you that's reasonable.

D'Amoro—Who would you like to have for your witnesses?

Callahan—Stop! Stop! For God's sake! He can't! Stan! I'm the father of her children—

Mayor—And I'm a father, too. I've never even seen my kid.

Mears—You've got two minutes, Principal Keeper, say your prayers. So ya wanta live, eh, well, so do I. I want to live. I want to be free. I want to see an ocean again. I want to walk in the sun. I want to lay with a woman again. One minute, Callahan. Do you feel your guts turnin' over like I have?

Werner—

> Flashed all their sabres bare,
> Flashed as they turned in the air.

Callahan—All right, Mears. Where do I stand?

Mears (*looking at watch*)—Right where you are. (*He fires.*)

Callahan's body falls into Cell 7. Father O'Connors softly intones prayers for the dead.

"I suppose—I'm next?" the priest inquires.

"You are, O'Connors."

But now rebellion within rebellion is started. D'Amoro won't stand for any guy's shootin' a priest. That's a lousy trick But a sharp blow in the stomach from Mears' gun quiets D'Amoro.

They have thrown Callahan's body into the yard, now, and as the guards come to take it away Mears shouts his decision that the priest shall be next to go. It is the quiet Mayor who rebels this time. And the cowed D'Amoro has recovered strength enough to add fresh protest. It's bad luck to kill a priest.

Mears weakens. Perhaps— Well, they'll not kill O'Connors—but they'll send word they're going to. Maybe that will work.

Mayor is at the window with the message when a sniper from across the yard gets him. He falls back with a groan. Though they try to revive him when he talks his thoughts are rambling. But he thinks it was a lousy trick—to wave a flag of truce and then shoot a guy. Mayor is in miserable pain and pleading for help.

O'Connors offers to do what he can. He knows a little something of surgery. Mears takes off the priest's handcuffs. He would like to help Freddy Mayor, Mears would.

Now a guard is sneaking across the yard with a box or something. And another guy a little way behind him. It's dynamite! They're bringing dynamite to blow up the Death House!

Two of the precious bullets are sent after the guards. Mears gets them both but not until after they have planted the dynamite.

An explosion rocks the building. No one is killed but the lights are out. Wires broken.

Now Father O'Connors is making another plea. It is for Mayor this time. The boy is suffering terribly. Mears can help him if he will give up now. The doctors can probably save Mayor if they can get him to the hospital. The boy will go mad with pain if they don't.

But what will it amount to if they do save him? Mears wants to know that. To get him well—to get him good and healthy—so they can kill him again? There's not choice in that.

The pain is too much for Freddy Mayor. He can't stand pain. Yet he wouldn't have Mears give up on his account. That wouldn't be fair.

"We're pretty near licked anyway, Freddy," Mears admits.

"It won't do no good," Mayor protests. "I'm goin' out like a light—"

MEARS—O'Connors says not for a long time, Freddy—it'll be hard—

MAYOR (*with fine simplicity*)—You don't understand—I couldn't go through it again—waiting—I've suffered so these last few weeks—you can't imagine—I couldn't do it again—don't make me—help me—

MEARS (*softly*)—What can I do, kid?

MAYOR (*deliberately*)—Don't you know, Killer Mears?

MEARS (*after a pause*)—That's a tough one, Freddy—that's an awful tough one.

MAYOR—My eyes are closed—and I'm thinkin' of Elaine—Elaine and the kid—I think I know what it looks like—I'm thinkin' of 'em both—John— (*There is a muffled shot—and silence. After an interval* MEARS *emerges from the cell.*)

WERNER—

Flashed all their sabres bare,
Flashed as they turned in the air—

MEARS (*standing in door of Cell 7*)—Christ, do you think I wanted to do that? Well, what the hell are you waiting for? Get on those windows. We haven't given up yet.

KIRBY—What's the use. There's only two bullets now.

MEARS—Yeah. That's right. I'd forgotten.

KIRBY (*pause*)—Well.

MEARS (*looking him straight in the eye*)—Well—what?

KIRBY—Well—maybe—we oughta wave a shirt.

MEARS (*snapping*)—What for?

KIRBY—Well—(*then blurting it out*) we're through, ain't we? We're all through.

MEARS (*repeating mechanically*)—Through?

KIRBY (*more confidently*)—You don't think we got a chance this way. (*No answer.*) But, if we pack in right now while there's still time, we're all right, maybe. Let's figure it out reasonable. It pays sometimes to figure a thing out before.

MEARS (*half-listening—thinking of something*).

KIRBY (*quickly, earnestly*)—Well, look. They can't give us more than the chair on our original sentence. See? Because this noise will have to be settled first and somebody's gotta be responsible. See that, don't ya? Now, look, there's gotta be, first the indictment, then the trial and investigation, and then the conviction, and all the regular red tape. Now that takes time. Plenty. And you can't tell. Why we might even get a chance on insanity. Christ. That's an idea. Sure. See? Think of that.

MEARS—That's the toughest, hard-boiled mob in the world out there. Prison guards and state troopers. We hate them. Well, they hate us. I'm telling you. They're just waiting to let scream at us a thousand machine guns.

KIRBY—But—with our hands up—

MEARS—They—hate—our—guts.

Kirby (*after a pause, slowly*)—Then we're through?

Mears (*echoes him*)—Through.

D'Amoro—What ja gonna do, Killer? (*There is an outburst of machine gun fire.*)

Werner (*commences to recite wildly, between bursts*)

Cannon to the right of them,
Cannon to the left of them,
Cannon in front of them,
Volleyed and thundered.

Kirby—I know that poem. I can remember it when I was a kid in school.

Mears—I used to know it, too.

Werner—

Flashed all their sabres bare,
Flashed as they turned in the air,
Sab'ring the gunners there,
All the world wondered . . .

Kirby—It's a good poem.

Mears—Yeah, Eddie, that's a good poem. That's a damn good poem. Eddie, you're right. That's it. (*Stands.*) Let 'em wonder out there. Let the whole goddam world wonder. (*Walks slowly across stage, takes* Kirby's *hand and puts gun with remaining two bullets in it, then crosses and opens door right and turns.*)

Mears—So long, fellows, meet you later. (*Exits slowly, the searchlight swinging across from right to left. The door slams. There is a burst from the machine guns and the priest intones in Latin as the curtain falls.*)

THE FIRST MRS. FRASER

A Comedy in Three Acts

By St. John Ervine

ST. JOHN ERVINE, the English play critic and novelist, spent the theatre season of 1928-29 in America as the guest critic of the New York *World*.

Shortly after his return to England word came that a new comedy of his had been produced at the Theatre Royal, in London, called "The First Mrs. Fraser," with Marie Tempest, W. Graham Browne and Henry Ainley in the three leading rôles. Speculation on the part of Mr. Ervine's friends as to the play's reception was shortly satisfied by reports of its unquestioned success.

During the summer Grace George saw the London performance and concluded negotiations for the American rights to the play, which she presented in November at the Princess Theatre in Chicago, with A. E. Matthews and Lawrence Grossmith as her leading men.

The London success of the comedy was repeated in Chicago. So well was the play received there, in fact, that it was not transferred to New York until holiday time. Starting at the Playhouse the last week in December it was played through to summer, weathering a series of as depressing spring weeks in the theatre as the theatre capital has known in twenty years.

Thus does "The First Mrs. Fraser" legitimately take its place with those other plays made in England which did much to tone up a droopy and none too creditable American season.

Conceived and written in the manner and with much of the technical facility expended upon those polite comedies which distinguished the middle nineties, when Arthur Wing Pinero, Richard Claude Carton, Henry Arthur Jones, Sydney Grundy and Clyde Fitch were providing the stage with its better plays, "The First Mrs. Fraser" declares a character of its own that is distinctly modern, particularly in relation to its treatment of the modern divorce and the younger generation's attitude toward life and their elders.

At the beginning of the play we are in Janet Fraser's flat in Knightsbridge. It is a pleasantly furnished room in which people in comfortable circumstances live comfortably. "It is the late afternoon, not quite tea time, but near enough to the hour to make the thought of tea very agreeable."

Ninian Fraser, "an attractive-looking lad, able to make disagreeable remarks in an agreeable manner," is sprawled upon the sofa reading a novel by Mr. Edgar Wallace "which is very wrong of him, for Ninian is in his last year at Oxford and his thoughts should be on sterner stuff."

Ninian's reading, however, is shortly interrupted. The maid announces a Mr. Fraser, who, it transpires, is James Fraser, Ninian's father but no longer the first Mrs. Fraser's husband.

James Fraser, "a tall, heavily-built man, with greying hair; an emotional man, in some respects, but quick to see where an advantage may be taken," is plainly a little fussed at being thus discovered by his younger son the first time he has dropped in to tea quite so informally since the Fraser divorce was granted.

And Ninian is plainly upset by the incident. He has known that his father and mother have seen each other occasionally but—does the second Mrs. Fraser know that his father is there?

She does, James assures him. She may not know that he is there at that precise moment, but she knows that he and Ninian's mother are friendly. He is there to consult Ninian's mother and, when she comes, he wants Ninian to clear out and keep anyone else out who tries to come in.

"But," demands Ninian, "will that be proper?"

"Damn it, man, don't be flippant," snaps James.

NINIAN (*suddenly serious*)—Listen, father! You're not going to upset her, are you?

JAMES—Upset her? Good God, no!

NINIAN—Because I can't allow any of that. You see, you're only my divorced father!

JAMES—All right, my boy, all right. I know how fond of her you are. You haven't much liking for me!

NINIAN—Oh, I . . .

JAMES—There's no need to alarm yourself. I'm not going to upset your mother. I want her advice.

NINIAN—But doesn't your wife . . . ?

JAMES (*irritable again*)—Don't keep on calling her my wife! Call her Elsie. You know damn well what her name is!

NINIAN—Well, doesn't . . . Elsie give you advice?

JAMES—Look here, Ninian, you'll have to know sooner or later, so you may as well know now. It's about Elsie I've come here.

NINIAN—I don't think I approve of that.

JAMES—Man, this is serious.

NINIAN—I'm sorry, father, but you married Elsie without your children's consent!

JAMES—Will you stop being clever? You're not at your damned kindergarten now. Keep that sort of smart talk for Oxford. They've time for it there. (*He pauses a moment and then goes on in a quieter tone.*) Elsie wants to divorce me.

NINIAN (*astounded*)—Divorce you! Father, have you been messing about again?

JAMES—No, she wants to marry some other body.

NINIAN—Already? How long have you and she been married?

JAMES—Close on five years.

NINIAN—She isn't as patient as mother was. She lived with you for twenty years. Of course, Elsie's a lot younger than you are. Twenty-four, isn't she?

JAMES—Thereabouts. I know what you're thinking, Ninian: no fool like an old one. But my mind's young, isn't it?

NINIAN—I'm sorry, father, but I can't work myself up into a state about you!

JAMES—Who's asking you to? All I want you to do is, to clear out when your mother comes in. (*He listens.*) Is that her, do you think? (*Voices are heard in the hall.*)

NINIAN (*rising and going toward the door*)—Yes. Someone's with her.

JAMES—Blast!

Janet Fraser "is an attractive woman of forty-eight or thereabouts. Her accent is not so markedly Scottish as James', but it has a slight twirl in it . . . She is a woman of character and decision, not intellectual in the sense that she is familiar with the clichés of cliques, but very intelligent. She has dignity and judgment, and there is laughter in her eyes. Janet is a thoroughly nice woman. Everyone wonders why James left her. So, sometimes, does James."

Janet's attitude toward James is cordial but formal. At the moment she is more particularly interested in the Philip Logan who has come home with her. She is sure James will want to see Philip but it is quite evident that James does not share this conviction.

Logan is "a handsome, well-dressed, well-cared-for bachelor, about the same age as James; an amiable, unassuming and likeable chap, who makes no enemies because he makes no effort. James does not care about him much, but that is chiefly because James despises him for living on private means and is jealous of his easy manners."

Philip, who is planning a fishing trip, will only have time to swallow a mouthful or two of tea, and James' anxiety that tea be promptly brought, so as not to delay Philip, convinces the bachelor that James is really trying to be rid of him. James does not deny the charge. In fact, when Janet sees Philip to the door, James is quite definite about his opinion of Philip. Nor does Ninian's explanation that the reason he calls Philip "uncle" is because he thinks if he calls him "uncle" loudly and often he will be spared the disagreeableness of calling him "father" later tend to allay James' irritation.

"Good God!" he explodes. "You don't mean to say your mother thinks of marrying him?"

"*He* thinks of marrying her," Ninian explains. "I doubt if he thinks of anything else except . . . fishing."

JAMES—But she can't marry him?

NINIAN—Why not, father?

JAMES—Well, I mean she's! . . . Oh, of course, I know she has a perfect right to marry anybody she likes.

NINIAN—But you can't understand her wanting to?

JAMES—Not Philip anyway. I've often wondered why he was so eager to help with the divorce.

NINIAN—It must puzzle you to understand how any woman who has been married to you, can dream of marrying him.

JAMES—I don't think higher education has improved you, Ninian.

NINIAN—Do you know why I don't want mother to marry again? I'll tell you. Because I find a fatherless home very pleasant to live in. I've had one father, father, and I don't want another, thank you!

JAMES—You . . . you pup you!

Janet returns in time to prevent a row. She is anxious to hear of James' trouble, but she cannot develop a very deep concern regarding Elsie Fraser's state of mind.

Elsie, it appears, wants to marry Lord Larne. His lordship is young and not overbright, but he is the son of the Marquis of Ballymena, who will one day come into the title and Elsie fancies herself as a peeress. But before Elsie can marry Lord Larne she must divorce James Fraser, and there's the rub. James has come to Janet for advice. He and Janet are, apart from anything else, old friends, James reasons, and he wants to consult her.

Janet cannot see it quite that way. She is flattered, but she is much inclined to let James get himself out of his own difficulties.

James doesn't want a divorce. At least James doesn't want to be divorced. And Elsie doesn't want to be named as a respondent. Elsie reasons, says James, that it's his place to let her divorce him because she is young and a woman and he is old and a man. And nothing that James has said has altered this opinion.

It is Janet's final conviction that the only sane solution for Elsie would be to elope with Lord Larne. But James is shocked by that suggestion.

JAMES—The Ballymenas are very pious people. They could make a lot of difficulty for her, if she was not perfectly respectable. That's what she says, and she hopes that I'll behave like . . .

NINIAN—A little gentleman! What cads some women are! They want to lead a rackety life and remain perfectly respectable, and some poor noodle has to provide them with the respectability by making himself look like a blackguard.

JAMES—Meaning me, I suppose, when you say noodle.

NINIAN—Meaning you, father!

JAMES—You haven't much respect for me, Ninian?

NINIAN—No, father, I haven't. As a successful business man, you're no doubt it, but as a parent you're a wash-out! I can't think why mother married you!

JANET (*firmly*)—I can!

JAMES (*angrily*)—I won't be talked to like that by my own son!

NINIAN—Now, look here, father, it's not a bit of good trying to come the outraged parent over me. The only way in which you can get my respect is by earning it. You treated mother damned badly!

JANET—Ninian, Ninian, dear!

NINIAN—And you think you've only got to come here and say, "I'm your father!" and I'll instantly forget how you insulted and humiliated mother! Well, you can't! I'm not sorry at all to hear that this woman for whom you deserted my mother! . . .

JANET (*trying to restrain him*)—Please, Ninian, please!

NINIAN (*refusing to be restrained*)—I'm only trying to make my feelings plain, mother. I'd be sorry if father left the house thinking I admired him.

JAMES—I haven't any doubt about your feelings for me, Ninian. In a way I can understand them, and I respect you for them. But I think I'm entitled to some thanks from you. I worked for you, worked damned hard for you!

NINIAN—And mother helped you when you needed help, didn't she?

JAMES—Yes, she did. I admit that. Nobly and loyally she helped me!

JANET—Thank you, James.

NINIAN—But when you had made your position with her help, and were a very rich and important man, you chucked her for a damned little flapper that hadn't the brains to do anything but spend the money mother'd helped you to make. Pretty, isn't it?

JAMES (*miserably*)—Janet, speak to him!

JANET—Well, it's true, isn't it, James?

JAMES (*rounding on* NINIAN)—Anyway, I was generous to you and Murdo. I sent you both to expensive schools, and gave *you* a college education.

NINIAN—Yes, you robbed us of our good Scotch accent, and gave us a common English public school one in its place. When we go back to Scotland, people think we're English. I suppose it has never occurred to you, father, that Murdo and I suffered a good deal at school while you were prancing through the Divorce Court.

JAMES—Suffered?

NINIAN—Yes, suffered. Boys used to come and read spicy bits out of the Sunday papers to us. Out loud, so that all the other boys could hear. One chap asked me to find out how much you paid for the woman you took to Brighton! . . . That wasn't so damned pleasant! Murdo had to fight a fellow who made a dirty joke about you. Do you think that was fun for us, father?

Again Janet is obliged to interfere. This time she takes Ninian by the arm and leads him gently to the door. There "she gives him a little pat on the shoulder and pushes him out of the room."

James has really come as much for comfort as for advice, he admits to Janet, when they are alone. Janet, he admits, is a very comfortable woman.

And now the real truth as to James' feelings respecting Elsie's demand for a divorce comes out. He does not want to be a respondent a second time. It would do his reputation no end of harm, seeing there is a growing prejudice against divorced people.

"I know for a fact that I was taken off the Honours List through it," James admits.

"Oh, James, should I have been a lady if I hadn't divorced you?" The thought is exciting to Janet.

"Aye. I was to have had a baronetcy, but after the divorce . . . (*He shrugs his shoulders.*) Mind, I offered to pay a bit more, but they said I couldn't figure in the Honours List and the Divorce List in the same year."

Elsie is aware that there is no hope, now, of a title for James and that, naturally, strengthens her interest in Lord Larne.

And so the situation resolves itself to this: James cannot afford to let Elsie divorce him, because it would make him look like a libertine. And if he divorces her he will look ridiculously like an old man unable to hold his young wife. Of the two he'd rather look like a libertine than a fool, but he greatly prefers not to look like either.

As to his losing Elsie—well, he is fond of her, of course, but sometimes young women do seem a bit foolish. They always want to be on the move . . .

James thinks perhaps if Janet would talk with Elsie it would help. Elsie has a great respect for Janet.

Ninian, back for his tea and hearing this, flouts the idea of his mother talking with her successor. His father has made his bed and he must lie on it. But Janet is quite capable of making her own decision.

"I think that proverb is such a silly one," she corrects Ninian. "If my bed weren't comfortable I should get up and remake it. Elsie is evidently a very astute young woman. She knows you can't feather your bed with mud."

"Aye! That's very true, Janet," agrees James. "I'll repeat that remark to her. And if you'll excuse me now, I'll just run along. I'm very grateful to you, Janet."

"It's been very nice to see you again, James. You haven't been here for a long while. You must come again soon."

"I will. When Ninian's not here."

Before James can leave the Murdo Frasers are announced. Murdo is James' elder son. He is about twenty-four, "less sensitive than Ninian, a little stodgy, too, and more like his father than his mother, but quite a decent, thick sort of chap." Alice, Murdo's wife, is "a pleasant-looking girl of twenty-three, with very candid eyes, and a very quiet but assured and direct manner."

Alice and Murdo are plainly surprised at meeting James Fraser, but he escapes before the surprise can register. Janet takes him to the door.

It now appears that the younger Frasers have also come to talk with Ninian and Janet about the elder Frasers, or more particularly about Elsie Fraser. And they are more than a little surprised to learn that James had come for advice about giving Elsie a divorce so she could marry Lord Larne. Why Lord Larne? Elsie's real attachment, they are assured, is a certain Mario, a specialty dancer at the Half and Half club.

Mario or Larne, Murdo is all for getting his father away from Elsie so they can get him married to Janet again, but he has little support from the others. There's Uncle Philip, they remind him. Murdo doesn't worry much about Uncle Philip. He is all right for tea-parties and carrying parcels, but he is sure his mother would never marry Philip.

Now Janet is back. And greatly surprised to hear of Elsie's interest in a dancer at the Half and Half club. Janet did not even know there was such a place. It's such a curious name. The Half and Half club!

"The women members are half men and the men members are half nothing," Ninian explains.

"That must make it very confusing," Janet thinks. "But everything is very mixed nowadays. I had a letter this morning which began 'Dear Sir or Madam.' "

In this family council Janet agrees with Murdo that divorces are a fairly disagreeable business whoever gets them.

"If I had known the misery I'd have to endure before the decree was made absolute," Janet insists, "I'd have let him divorce me."

"Was it very awful?" asks Alice.

"Awful! My dear, it was horrible! I was watched and followed by an evil-minded person called the King's Proctor, who treated me as if *I* had committed the adultery. Twice I was called to his office and cross-questioned because some ill-natured person had written anonymous letters about me. I didn't dare to be seen with Philip after six o'clock in the evening. Whenever I went out, a man, who looked like something out of a sewer, followed me. He began to get on my nerves! . . . James and Elsie suffered nothing. She wasn't even mentioned in the proceedings. I don't think it's right that the innocent person should be treated like a criminal."

Ninian is hopeful that Elsie will get her share of misery when she tries the divorce court and Murdo reiterates his hope that his father will be freed one way or another so he can remarry Janet. But Janet is not so sure she feels that way about it.

"My dears," she protests, "I think you must allow me to settle my own affairs. It is not customary for children to arrange their parents' wedding."

The next moment a small bombshell is thrown into the midst of the group by the maid's announcement of Mrs. James Fraser. Following close upon the announcement Elsie appears. She is "aged about twenty-four, very pretty, very smart, as hard as nails."

Elsie is a bit disconcerted by finding herself in the presence of so many of the enemy, but quickly recovers her composure. She had hoped, she frankly admits, that she would find Janet alone. She had wanted to have a private conversation with Janet.

"About your divorce from father?" impudently suggests Ninian.

"How did you know?"

"My hus . . . I mean your husband was here about half an hour ago," explains Janet.

The children are reluctant to go, but they do depart finally.

ELSIE—They weren't a bit pleased to see me, were they?

JANET—No, not very. I don't know that I'm pleased to see you myself.

ELSIE—I don't blame you. I should feel just as you do. You know, I'm fair-minded. I do see other people's point of view. Of course, I know it's very odd, my being here at all. I mean, even in these times it isn't quite usual for one wife to call on the other wife.

JANET—I've known it to be done.

ELSIE—Oh, so have I. I know a girl who took the first wife up to her bedroom and showed her some of her wedding presents. I must say I thought that was a bit thick.

JANET—Yes, a little ostentatious.

ELSIE—Still, people don't feel about these things now as they used to do in your young days, do they?

JANET—No—not quite the same.

ELSIE—What I really came for was to talk to you about James.

JANET—Yes?

ELSIE—He's not happy.

JANET—No.

ELSIE—No, he's not at all happy. I have to confess that I've failed to make him happy. James is miserable with me.

JANET—Really?

ELSIE—Of course, I've tried—heavens, how I've tried—but it's all been useless. The difference in our ages is too great.

JANET—There is exactly the same difference between your ages now that there was when you married.

ELSIE—Yes, but I didn't realize it then.

JANET—You're quite certain that you're not making James happy?

ELSIE—Oh, quite! The truth is, Mrs. Fraser, he still loves you. I've known it for quite a while now. I'm too young and inexperienced for him, and I can feel him comparing me to you . . . to my disadvantage.

JANET—You aren't so very young.

ELSIE—I'm under twenty-five.

JANET—Murdo was born before I was that age.

ELSIE—But people are younger today than they were then. Everybody knows that. There are quite a lot of statistics about it. But I'm not thinking of myself, I'm thinking of James' happiness. I'd like him to be happy again, and there's only one way to do it.

JANET—What's that?

ELSIE—I must give him up. Oh, I know, it isn't going to be very nice, but I'm prepared to make the sacrifice!

JANET—I don't quite follow you. I understood from James that you wanted to divorce him.

ELSIE—Well, yes, of course, but that's only a formality. It doesn't matter so much for a man as it does for a woman, and a woman has to think of her reputation sometimes. Now, listen, Mrs. Fraser, I've thought of an idea. You see, I've realized only too well that James loves you; not me. I only roused his passion!

JANET (*a little shocked*)—Oh, did you?

ELSIE—I'm sure of it. Now wouldn't it be wrong of me to keep you two apart? I've always said that it is a crime to make a couple who do not love each other live together.

Janet is interested, but a little angered by Elsie's suggestion that she should take James back. And she is quick to make it clear to Elsie that she understands why she is so anxious to be rid of James. She wants to marry Lord Larne. However, Elsie is not going to be allowed to divorce James, Janet assures her. James has been divorced once and he does not wish to be divorced again.

Which, Elsie is convinced, is pure selfishness on James' part. There is no sense in their trying to live together. She can't make James happy. He is much too old.

As for Lord Larne—of course she loves him, else she would not want to marry him. She may be a lot of things, Elsie admits, but she is not a snob. Lord Larne has his virtues. He dances well and he never fusses with Elsie when she dances with other men. James dances like an elephant and is always complaining about the modern dances and modern dancers. Elsie doesn't see why. So long as she doesn't run down the schottische and the waltz why should James run down the Charleston and the Black Bottom?

Neither can Elsie understand why Janet dislikes her, which Janet is frank to confess she does. It should be possible, Elsie thinks, for one woman to like another, even if that other has run off with a husband. Elsie has always liked Janet. Ask James!

Janet is tired of talk and would clear the situation as it stands. Elsie wants to be rid of James, Janet knows, so she can marry Lord Larne, not because she has any thought of James' happiness. Janet is also quick to resent Elsie's suggestion that James is an old man, and if he is older than Elsie, if she sees her future now as that of a young woman playing nurse to an old man, she should have thought of that before she married James.

"How could I?" demands Elsie heatedly, "I was nineteen and very poor, and he was rich. I couldn't think of anything else. I consider that I have given him all that he's entitled to. Five years of any girl's life are enough for a man of his age."

JANET—I can't tell you how I despise you.

ELSIE—You think I'm cheap.

JANET—Yes, I do.

ELSIE—Well, that's frank anyhow. But I can't see it. I've only got that much of life. (*She indicates a small space with her hands.*) I want to get all I can out of it. That isn't wrong, is it? I'm young, aren't I?

JANET—Stop talking about your youth. Everybody's mad about the young, as if there'd never been any young before.

ELSIE—Well, there haven't been any like us before. We're a new sort of young.

JANET—The best thing you can do is to elope with Lord Larne. Then James will divorce you, and Larne will have to marry you.

ELSIE—No, I won't do that. I've a right to ask James to let me divorce him.

JANET—He won't do it.

ELSIE—Won't he? He'll be glad to do it before I've finished with him. I've a nasty little nature when I'm roused.

JANET—I don't doubt that.

ELSIE (*conciliatory again*)—Look here, he'll do it if you ask him.

JANET—Do you expect me to?

ELSIE—Yes. Why not?

JANET—There's only one thing that would make me willing to help you to a divorce: the thought that James would be rid of you.

ELSIE (*snatching at a straw*)—Well, why don't you do it for that reason, then?

JANET—Oh, no, my girl! If you want a divorce you must get it in the way that he got his. Go to some hotel with your fancy man!

ELSIE—Oh, how dare you suggest such a thing!

JANET—You and all your generation . . . you're greedy and mean and horribly cruel. You think of nothing but luxury and easy life and what you call fun, and you don't care whose feelings you hurt so long as you get your fun. There isn't one of you that's worth that! (*She snaps her fingers.*) You can't do anything, you know nothing, you are nothing, and presently, when your prettiness begins to fade, there'll be nothing left of you but a bitter memory. You come here and lie to me about your wish for James' happiness!

ELSIE—Lie!

JANET—Yes, lie. You think of nothing and no one but yourself and your own happiness. You've taken all you can get out of him and now you want to take all you can get out of some one who has a little more to offer. But you aren't going to give anything! Oh, no! You'll go on taking and taking until there is nothing left to take.

ELSIE (*with a great effort at being dignified*)—Of course, if you're going to insult me!

JANET—Insult you! Is that possible?

ELSIE—Have you anything else to say?

JANET—Yes. If I can separate James from you, I will, but don't imagine that I shall try to make life easier for you. I won't. I hope it will be hard. I hope it will be damned hard.

ELSIE—Good afternoon, Mrs. Fraser! (*She stalks toward the door.*)

JANET—Good afternoon! (*Exit* ELSIE, *shutting the door with a bang.*) I hope it will be damned hard!

THE CURTAIN FALLS

ACT II

A fortnight later James Fraser is again calling on Janet. When he finds her out, he suspects that she is with "that ass, Logan." The suspicion is irritating.

Philip, as it happens, is not with Janet but seeking her. He, too, calls presently and James' disgust is complete. He is even surly. But Philip overlooks that. He is a little put out himself. Why, Philip would like to know, is James hanging about Janet's flat so much? People are quite sure to talk, and Philip doesn't like the idea at all. As a man of the world James should know that a single woman has to be ever so careful about the sort of man she lets into her house. Finally, says Philip, if James had any sense of decency he wouldn't come there at all.

James, if not purple with rage, is at least flushed with anger. But he does not purpose losing his temper. Let Philip have a care. James will not be provoked beyond his endurance.

Philip finally agrees to go. If James' business with Janet is both urgent and private Philip does not mind leaving James there. But he does not want his agreement to be accepted as a precedent. And before he goes he leaves a message for Janet with the maid.

"Will you please tell Mrs. Fraser when she returns," says Philip, "that I have two tickets for the theatre tonight and that I'd like her to dine with me."

"Very good, sir."

"I'll call for her at a quarter to seven! Then we can dine in comfort."

"Yes, sir."

James writhes a little hearing this invitation and as soon as

Philip has gone he recalls Mabel and tells her that she needn't mind about Mr. Logan's message to Mrs. Fraser. He (James) will see that she gets it.

Now Janet is home. She is not at all surprised to find James, but he is prompt with an explanation for being there.

JAMES—I just happened to be passing, and I thought I'd drop in. As a matter of fact, Janet, I've got a couple of tickets for a theatre tonight, and I wondered if you'd care to have a bite of dinner with me and go on to play afterwards.

JANET—I'd love it, James, but what about Elsie? Won't she want to go with you?

JAMES—She has something else on tonight.

JANET—Well, if you're quite sure you'd like me to, and that Elsie won't mind, I will.

JAMES—I'm perfectly sure, Janet. Thank you.

JANET—What's the name of the play?

JAMES (*confused*)—Oh, I don't rightly remember its name. You see, the tickets were given to me, and I didn't like to ask for the name of the piece. I thought it 'ud be like looking a gift horse in the mouth!

JANET—We'll look it up in the paper. (*Picking up the newspaper.*) What's the name of the theatre?

JAMES—Tt, tt, tt, I've forgotten that, too! The tickets are at home, but I'll come for you at half after six, Janet, and take you out to dinner somewhere. You'll be sure to be ready then, won't you? You'll not keep me waiting?

JANET—I'll be quite ready.

JAMES—Good! I suppose you've seen a lot of these plays?

JANET—No, not many. Philip takes me to some now and again.

JAMES—Aye. Well, I don't suppose his taste amounts to much.

JANET—I hope the tickets are for that new piece at the Haymarket. I hear it's very good.

JAMES—That's the theatre. I remember now.

JANET—Do you know what Philip wanted?

JAMES—Philip? No.

JANET—Mabel told me he left a few minutes before I got in.

JAMES—Oh, aye, he did. I think he got tired of waiting for you. He's an impatient man, I'm thinking. There's no stability in him.

JANET—Did he say he'd come back?

JAMES—No, no. He just passed the time of day and went.

JANET—Perhaps he'll come in later. He lives quite near!

JAMES—Perhaps. Mind you, Janet, if he should happen to come in and suggest going to the theatre to you, you'll recollect that you're going with me.

JANET—Of course, James. But what makes you think he'll want to take me tonight?

JAMES—He's the sort of a man that if he knew you were in the notion of going to the theatre with somebody else, would manœuvre to get you to go with him. I don't like that sort of spirit.

Elsie Fraser, James reports, is back from a four-day visit to the country. Elsie is also being very difficult, and he sees no end to the business but misery and anxiety. James is still determined, however, not to let Elsie divorce him. As Elsie refuses to be divorced Janet can see no way out. Elsie and James will probably have to stay just as they are.

James is depressed by the prospect. He thinks, considering what he has done for her, that the least Elsie owes him is gratitude. He has made allowances. He has tried desperately to be young. He has even tried to learn the modern dances, "wriggling up and down the room like a lop-sided crab, slapping myself!"

"I wish you'd let me see you dancing the Black Bottom, James," sweetly suggests Janet.

"You're making fun of me, Janet, and I'm terribly unhappy."

JANET—But, James, you must have known it couldn't go on.

JAMES—I did in a kind of way, but I wanted to make it go on as long as possible. I've always had a great love of youth, Janet. I like to feel that I'm young, and somehow Elsie turned me into a boy again. I'd go to dances with her, and force myself to do all the things that the young men were doing until I began to imagine I was as young as they were . . . and then suddenly I'd see myself in a looking-glass, an old, sweating man with a sagging face that was beginning to wither . . . and that sight took all the fun out of me! I learned then that it's useless pretending to be young. I'd look at Elsie, and say to myself, "If I live another twenty years, she'll be in the prime of her life, a fine, vigorous woman, and I'll be an old man!" And then I'd think to myself, "That's how I seem to her now—old and tired and ridiculous!" There's no equality, Janet, between the young and the old. I daresay we're hard on them, sometimes, but, my God, they're cruelly hard on us.

JANET—Well, how can there be equality between us, James? We start by taking care of them, and finish with them taking care of us. They're down when we're up, and they're up when we're down. There can't be any equality there.

JAMES—But there can be kindness, Janet.

JANET—You didn't ask Elsie for kindness. You asked her for love.

JAMES—Do you feel any ill-will against me, Janet?

JANET—Yes, sometimes.

JAMES—I don't wonder at that.

JANET—But sometimes I feel quite kindly towards you. My ill-will gets less and less, and I'm far happier now than I ever imagined I could be.

JAMES (*almost shocked, for his vanity is wounded*)—Happier! Then you don't miss me?

JANET—I did miss you at first, and when I missed you, I hated you. It's lucky for you, James, I miss you less now. You'd never get inside that door if I didn't.

JAMES—I'm not so sure that wouldn't please me better—in a way.

JANET—But I've a good deal of affection for you, James.

JAMES—I'm glad of that.

JANET—I often think how queer it is that people dislike growing old when they love old things everywhere else. I suppose a young face is very attractive and pretty, but I think that an old face, with all the marks of life on it, is more beautiful still. I like the wrinkles round an old man's eyes, and the deep lines down his face and the quietness of his ways and the calm look he has. There's some compensation in age, James, if you only knew it. (*She changes her tone quickly to a lighter one.*) And now you must run along home if you're to change and get back here in time.

JAMES (*rising*)—All right! I'll be back here at half after six! Where shall we dine?

JANET—Somewhere very expensive. I'd like you to take me to some place where you can't really afford to go. But I suppose you're so wealthy that there isn't such a place in the world. Doesn't it sound dreadful?

JAMES—I'll ring up all the restaurants in London and ask them which charges the most. Bye-bye for the present, Janet.

When Philip calls on the telephone to confirm his theatre engagement he is much upset to hear that Janet has another engagement with James. And Janet is shocked by the language Philip uses over the telephone. Philip should think of the telephone girl, even if he does not think of her! Of course he can come in and explain— But how was Janet to know?

Ninian Fraser, who has met his father on the stairs, repeats his determination not to permit James to fuss Janet and reports, among other things, that he has had an encounter of sorts with Lord Larne. He had even spoken to his lordship about Elsie and Larne's reaction was anything but happy. Ninian wishes ever so strongly that the whole thing might be cleared up. He doesn't like his mother going out with his father, and he is not particularly happy about his Uncle Philip's continued attentions.

Philip is none too happy at the moment. He comes with a bouquet of flowers for Janet and a strong protest against the dirty trick that James has played on him by taking over the invitation to the theatre.

"That's how James made his fortune, Philip," Janet explains, not without a touch of pride.

"But you're not going with him!" protests Philip.

"Indeed I am," declares Janet. "It isn't every evening a woman gets a chance of going out with her former husband. I'll go with you another night."

"He ought to have his head punched," says Philip.

Philip has picked up a copy of the *Tatler* and in it he comes suddenly upon a picture of Mario, the dancer in whom the younger Frasers had accused Elsie of being interested. Philip has quite a story to tell about Mario which seems to confirm the other gossip.

PHILIP—This chap, Mario . . . I'm certain of *him* now . . . turned up at the fishing inn where I was staying, late at night . . . about midnight . . . with a lady.

JANET—Yes.

PHILIP—I'd been out fishing pretty late . . . there was good water and I thought the fish would rise . . . but damn the rise they did!

JANET—Leave out the technical details, Philip, and get on with the human interest.

PHILIP—Yes, but it's a bit thick when a chap goes off fishing in the dark and comes home with nothing. So I stood myself a good stiff glass of grog, and just as I was saying, "Here's to you, Philip!" this couple came in.

JANET—Aha!

PHILIP—I couldn't see her face distinctly . . . she was all muffled up, and the minute she saw me, she looked away, but she was the dead spit of James' second. I heard him asking if they could have a room for the night, and I said to myself, "Ho, ho!"

JANET—You would, Philip, you would!

PHILIP—Well, I ask you. I said, "Bless you, my children!" and went upstairs, and, as I tumbled into bed, I thought to myself, "If that pretty lady should turn out to be James' second! . . ."

JANET—Don't keep calling her "James' second." Call her Elsie.

PHILIP—No. That would be familiar, that would! "If she should turn out to be James' second," I said to myself, "this chance encounter would be a bit awkward for her if James started being snorty about things!" And then I went to sleep. In the morning ere yet came the dawn!

JANET—If you attempt to be funny, Philip, I shall scream.

PHILIP—In the morning then, about six o'clock, I was awakened by the noise of a motor car and, being of a suspicious nature, I hopped out of bed and ran towards the casement window. I looked out, and saw our friend Mario and the lady departing. They didn't see me!

JANET—Did you recognize her?

PHILIP—I wouldn't like to take my affy-davy on it!

JANET—But you're pretty certain in your own mind?

PHILIP—Yes. Pretty certain!

JANET—Do you know Elsie well?

PHILIP—Not what you'd call well, but I know her. I mean I've seen her several times.

JANET—Wasn't there a big charity ball at St. Albans while you were at that place, fishing?

PHILIP—Yes, it was that very night.

JANET—You're sure?

PHILIP—Absolutely. Some people from the inn went, but they spent the night at St. Albans. If this couple were at it, they must have left pretty early.

JANET—Did they sign the register?

PHILIP—Yes. "Mr. and Mrs. Hopkinson." Damned silly to use a name like that. Absolute give-away! I say, wouldn't it be funny if it was Elsie!

JANET (*grimly*)—Yes. Ha, ha!

PHILIP—Well, that's a lugubrious sound, if you like! I've a good mind to ask somebody to invite me to dine at the Half and Half one night so's I can go up to Mario and say, "Hillo, Hoppy, old boy, and how's Mrs. Hopkinson tonight?" I bet I'd have some fun.

JANET—More than he would. Now, it's time you went.

Philip is of a mind to repeat his protests about James, and to express wonder that Janet, the adorable, ever could have married such a man. Philip would also repeat his proposal of marriage to Janet if she would listen, but Janet refuses to be proposed to between tea and dinner. After dinner's different—

The maid announces Elsie Fraser. Here is a chance for Philip to confirm or correct his suspicions about Elsie and Mario. Let him take a good look at Elsie as he goes out, suggests Janet—he can see her without her seeing him—and if she is the same woman he thinks she is he can send a note back to Janet. With this trap set Philip leaves.

Elsie is angry. She has come to protest against Ninian Fraser's insulting her to her friends. Specifically she objects to what Ninian had said to Lord Larne. She is not sure she could not bring action for libel if she were one who wanted to make a fuss, or one who believed in washing dirty linen in public.

Janet is interested in hearing that Elsie admits the linen is dirty. She is also interested in hearing what it was that Ninian said to Lord Larne that was so insulting to Elsie.

"Well," reports Elsie, with spirit, "he went up to Button . . . that's my name for Lord Larne . . . who had a headache . . . he often has headaches . . . and he said, "I hear you want to marry my father's wife! . . ."

"Well, that's true, isn't it?"

"That wasn't all he said. While Button was trying to think of something to say, Ninian added, 'I heartily congratulate my father!' Right out in front of everybody! Such a rude thing to say . . . and in public, too! Mrs. Fraser, you simply must put a stop to this sort of thing. I'm sure I've never expected much consideration from Murdo *or* Ninian, but I did at least expect that they would behave like gentlemen. After all, they've both been to public schools, and that does count even in these days. No matter what a man's private feelings may be, he should always behave like a gentleman . . . in public anyhow."

Janet is of the opinion that ladies should always behave like ladies, too, and she thinks it quite natural that Ninian should be interested in Elsie's plans.

"A boy likes to know how long he may expect his step-mother to continue to be his step-mother," suggests Janet sweetly. "I think what he said about you was most filial."

"Well, I don't," snaps Elsie. "It was meant to be nasty and it was nasty."

Janet is of the further opinion that Ninian is a gentleman and that the Home Chat notion that gentlemen always talk about women in a chivalrous manner is foolish because they don't.

Elsie, though far from mollified, is prevailed upon to sit down and have a cigarette. She is also impelled to repeat her conviction that James will do the right thing about letting her divorce him. The conviction is strengthened in Elsie's mind because she is a determined woman and always gets what she wants—always—because if she can't get what she wants she stops wanting it. Her motto, admits Elsie, is to get all she can and give as little as possible for it.

She will marry Lord Larne, too. For that matter she could marry him any minute she wanted to. All she would have to do would be to call him and say, "Button, let's bolt!" and he'd meet her at the station with tickets for Paris.

Elsie prefers, however, to wait until James is ready to do as she wants him to do and make it possible for her to divorce him. The delay will serve merely to make Lord Larne the more anxious. Janet is seriously interested in Elsie's point of view.

JANET—Tell me . . . this is just curiosity . . . do you love anybody but yourself?

ELSIE—I love lots of people. I'm quite fond of James, when he isn't stuffy and obstinate, and I'd really be quite fond of you, if you'd let me. *I'm* not vindictive!

JANET—I said "love," Elsie.

ELSIE—I don't follow you.

JANET—Isn't there someone you *love?*

ELSIE—Really, Mrs. Fraser!

JANET—A man?

ELSIE—Well, Larne, I suppose! I mean to say, I don't actually dislike him, so I suppose I must love him. I mean to say, when a woman's willing to live with a man, and have children by him, because, of course, I shall have to have children . . . the succession, you know . . . and I don't mind having them, when it's really necessary, I mean . . . well, if a woman's willing to do all that for a man, I suppose you'd call that love?

JANET—No, *I* shouldn't, but I can imagine that you would.

ELSIE—I really think there's far too much talk about love, and most of it is *so* sloppy. Either you get on with people or you don't get on with them. That's all there's to it!

JANET—Listen, Elsie, is there anybody in this world whom you love so much that you'd go hungry for them and work for them until you were sore and not care what became of you if only they were safe, even if you got nothing from them but disappointment and misery and pain?

ELSIE—I say, what a way to talk! Whatever do you mean?

JANET—Do you love James like that? (*A shrug from* ELSIE *as much as to say, "Don't be silly!"*) Or Lord Larne? (*She picks up the* Tatler *and opens it at the page where* MARIO'S *photograph appears.*)

ELSIE—Good heavens, no!

JANET (*passing the* Tatler *to her*)—Or Mario?

ELSIE (*taking it*)—Mario? (*She is wondering what all this means.*)

JANET—The dancer!

ELSIE (*recovering herself*)—Oh, yes, dear old Mario! Do you know him?

JANET—No, but *you* do.

ELSIE—Oh, yes, well. This is a terribly good phctograph!

JANET—Do you love him?

ELSIE—Mrs. Fraser!

JANET—You *do* love him, don't you?

ELSIE—I don't understand what you mean.

JANET—Listen! You don't love James. You never have loved James. You don't love Lord Larne. You never will love Lord Larne. But even in the meanest heart there is some love for somebody, and you love Mario. That's the only decent thing in your worthless life.

Elsie would run from this charge. She doesn't purpose staying there to be insulted. But she changes her mind when Janet suggests that perhaps it would be better if she were to continue the discussion with Lord Larne himself. It may be true, as Elsie intimates, that Larne knows of her friendship with Mario, but does he know that Elsie spent the night with the dancer at a fishing inn after the charity ball at St. Albans?

Elsie is wild with rage at the mere suggestion of such a filthy lie, but less positive of herself after Janet has telephoned the Half and Half club and learned that Mario, while he danced there the night of the charity ball, left early and motored to St. Albans.

"I didn't know he was at St. Albans," protests Elsie. "I didn't see him."

"You're in love with him, aren't you?"

"No . . ."

JANET—You are! You're in love with him. (*But* ELSIE *does not answer.*) Shall I tell you what happened at the Charity Ball? You were staying with the Falders, weren't you? (*No answer.*) You went to the Ball with their party. Mario motored down from London, and met you there. You danced with him and one or two other people, I suppose, just so that you should be seen, and then you and Mario disappeared. The Falders never ask questions after dances. You stopped at the fishing inn. You were given a room, and you both slept in it. Mario signed the register, "Mr. and Mrs. Hopkinson!" (*Another gasp from* ELSIE.) Not a very distinguished name, is it? The next morning at six o'clock, you and Mario left, and I presume he drove you to the Falders' house, and said he had brought you from St. Albans!

ELSIE—There isn't a word of truth in it, not one word of truth. I shall go straight to my lawyers!

JANET—Why not go straight to Larne?

ELSIE—You're a horrible woman! You want to ruin me because you hate me! It wasn't my fault, was it, that James liked me better than he liked you? You're too old! (*She stops, feeling that she has said too much.*)

JANET (*frigidly calm*)—Lord Larne is at his club, isn't he? What is his club?

ELSIE—I shan't tell you. Find out!

JANET—Very well. I shall ring up his father, Lord Ballymena, and ask him! (*She reaches for the telephone book, and begins to turn over the leaves. She finds the place, and reads the information aloud. Reading.*) Baltic, Baly, Baly . . . ah, here it is, Ballymena, the Marquis of, Regent 44444. (*She puts down the book and reaches for the receiver.*)

ELSIE (*before she can take it up*)—Wait! . . . There's no need to . . . to bring other people into it.

JANET (*sitting back*)—Very well! If you're prepared to be sensible and discuss the subject intelligently, all right!

ELSIE—Of course, I don't admit anything you've said . . . I feel so shocked that I hardly know what I'm saying or doing. You must admit that it's a most serious charge, this!

JANET—I do. It's a terrible charge. You've not only committed adultery, so far as James is concerned, but you've, so to speak, committed it in the eyes of Lord Larne!

ELSIE (*whose nerve is rapidly failing her*)—You mustn't say that!

JANET (*without any pity*)—Listen, Elsie. You are Mario's mistress!

ELSIE—No! No, I'm not!

JANET—You are. Why tell lies about it? (*A convulsive gulp from* ELSIE.) You know you love him. That's why you want to marry Larne. That poor noodle can be more easily deceived than James can. You will have Larne for his title, and you'll have Mario for your lover!

ELSIE (*in tears*)—No, no, no!

JANET—Yes! (*Then softening her voice a little.*) Come, Elsie, you do love Mario, don't you? (*There is a silence for a moment or two, and then* ELSIE, *recovering herself and speaking with some dignity, says quite simply*):

ELSIE—Yes, I love him.

JANET (*sitting back with a sense of victory*)—Ah! Does he love you?

ELSIE (*shaking her head*)—No. I'm only one of a crowd!

JANET—I can almost pity you now.

ELSIE—Well, that's that! What are you going to do?

JANET—That depends a great deal on you.

It is Janet's idea that the case against Elsie is complete. The meeting with Mario at the fishing inn was observed by a third party in all its important details. Therefore it is Janet's suggestion that Elsie allow James to divorce her. Let her elope with Lord Larne, as she suggested it would be easy for her to do, and Larne can be named as the corespondent.

Elsie protests a little weakly, but she agrees finally to talk with Lord Larne at his club and, with Janet's prompting, to tell him over the phone that she is miserable with James; that they have had a furious row; that she can stand it no longer and that Lord Larne must take her away now, this very night. There is a train from Victoria station at 8:20 and they can go to Dieppe—

"Tell him to go home and pack, and meet you at the station," prompts Janet, a little too close to the phone.

"No, darling, it was just a buzzing noise," Elsie is obliged to explain. "Listen, Button, go home now, straight home, and pack whatever you need for the present and meet me at Victoria. You'll get the tickets!"

JANET—Tell him not to forget his passport. And don't you forget yours.

ELSIE—And don't forget your passport, darling! No, I won't be late. Thank you so much, Button. What should I do without you! No, I shouldn't . . . I should just kill myself! (*She puts the receiver back on its holder and turns to* JANET *and continues in a perfectly calm voice.*) He's coming!

JANET—That's all right, then! This is the first elopement I've ever had anything to do with, and really it's quite enjoyable. Now, you'd better go home and pack, too.

ELSIE—How do I know you won't give me away?

JANET—You'll have to chance that.

ELSIE—You won't, will you?

JANET—Not if you do as you're told. Don't forget, by the way, to leave a note for James, telling him you've left him, and that you've gone to Paris with Lord Larne. You'd better get the chambermaid in the hotel to take a good look at you, and keep any bills!

ELSIE—You seem to know all about it.

JANET—Well, you taught me, didn't you?

ELSIE—You'll never tell!

JANET—My dear Elsie, what happens to you after James has divorced you is of no interest to me! (*The door opens and the maid enters.*)

MABEL—Mr. Fraser.

ELSIE—Oh! (*Enter* JAMES *in full evening dress. Exit the maid.*)

JAMES—Elsie! What are you doing here?

JANET—She and I have been having a little chat. She's just going. Good-bye, Elsie.

ELSIE—Goo-good-bye! (*Out she goes, almost running.*)

JAMES—That's damned queer!

JANET—Yes, quite a coincidence, husband and wife meeting, and at the house of number one, too.

JAMES—I say, Janet, you're not ready! I asked you to be ready! You know how I hate to be kept waiting!

JANET—Well, James, I got very interested in something Elsie told me, and then I had to telephone!

JAMES—Telephone! Women are always telephoning. (*He picks up Philip Logan's note to* JANET.)

JANET—I shan't be long. Sit down and look at the *Tatler*. There's a good photograph of Mario in it.

JAMES—That damned dago! (*Reading the note.*) What does this mean?

JANET (*at the door*)—What does what mean?

JAMES (*reading the note aloud*)—"I'm not quite sure, Philip." (*She doesn't reply. She waves her arms in the air and laughs and laughs—and the curtain falls.*)

ACT III

Six months later Janet Fraser is alone in her living room trying with some little difficulty to keep her mind on her reading. Being restless, her attention is easily distracted. Hearing voices in the hall she turns, eagerly, toward the door and there is a trace of disappointment in her voice as she greets Philip Logan.

Philip has been a little disappointed himself. The maid has been, he noticed, reluctant to let him in. Nor is Janet's explanation that she had given instructions that she was at home to no one altogether a satisfying explanation. Philip has a feeling, which Janet rather confirms, that everybody about the Fraser flat has promptly taken it for granted that Janet and James are to be remarried once James has his decree.

This, it appears, is the day on which the decree is to be granted, and Philip has taken the precaution to come early that he may get in a final proposal of marriage before James arrives with the tidings. It is the first time, Janet notes, that Philip ever has got ahead of James and Philip doesn't care for the note of pride that creeps into that statement, either.

About the only satisfaction Philip is able finally to extract from the situation is that the decree of divorce cannot be made absolute for another six months, and during that time at least he will be on even terms with the ex-husband. Janet insists she will not marry Philip, but she hopes he will continue to be, as he always has been, her dear friend, and take her to a theatre and to dinner on Tuesdays.

Now the younger Frasers, Ninian, Murdo and Alice, are back from the court. James Fraser's divorce has been granted with admirable expedition and very little fuss. James himself is to follow later. They have come on ahead to sort of clear the way for him.

Of the children, Murdo is still hoping that his mother and father will remarry at the earliest possible moment, and Ninian is quite opposed to anything that would seem to interfere with his mother's doing what she wants to do. He is particularly displeased with his brother's attitude of smugness and his constant harping on his mother doing something just to make him (Murdo) happy.

Janet is interested in their varied viewpoints but also convinced that the question of whether or not she shall remarry James is one that he alone is entitled to ask.

The maid is pleasantly flustered as she announces the arrival of "the master," which the children promptly accept as a hint that they should get out.

They are gone now and James, quite relieved, both by their departure and the fact that the divorce business is finally over, settles comfortably into a good talk with Janet—a good talk about James. It has been a very wearing business for James. Nobody, in all probability, will ever realize all that James has gone through. But just now he is thinking about the future.

JAMES—As you perfectly appreciate, Janet, this has been a very upsetting and exhausting affair for me. I'm not showing all I've felt, but it isn't the people who show their feelings who suffer the most. I need change and rest, I want to get away from everything and everybody, and I think it would be a good plan for me to take a trip around the world. That'll do me a bit of good . . . take my mind off things . . . and, of course, it'll give people time to forget about the divorce.

JANET (*feeling awful*)—Yes.

JAMES—I can't bear to think of people talking about me, and I'd rather they got it over and done with while I'm out of the country. Don't you think that's a good plan?

JANET—Oh, quite, James, quite!

JAMES—I've always had a great fancy to go round the world, but somehow I've never had time. Now's my chance! I can knock about the East for a while, look at India and China and Japan and Australia—and then, mebbe, go on to America and have a look at it.

JANET—That'll be very nice for you!

JAMES—That's what I thought. Do you know, Janet, when I was sitting in that court today, listening to the lawyers droning my marriage away, I said to myself: "I haven't deserved this! I *have not* deserved it!" You'd nearly think, to hear lawyers, that the break-up of a man's marriage was nothing but a formality.

JANET—Yes, wouldn't you?

JAMES—However, it's done, and what's done can't be undone. I never was one to cry over spilt milk.

JANET—You haven't very often had to cry over it, James.

JAMES—Oh, I've had my fair share of trouble, Janet. You mustn't think that *our* divorce—yours and mine—was any pleasure to me. Oh, no! It was not, indeed. You've had your trouble, but I've had mine, too. Of course, I've faced it. Whatever I am, Janet, I'm not what you'd call a flabby sort of a fellow that lets himself be down-faced by adversity. Oh, no! I can stand up to things, and give as good as I get. That's a fact, isn't it?

JANET—Yes, I'd agree to that.

JAMES—There are plenty of men who'd be knocked out by such a blow as I've had, but it'll take a lot more than this to knock *me* out! I don't want to pat myself on the back or blow my own trumpet, but I must say I've taken this stroke with great fortitude.

JANET—Yes, James.

JAMES—When I come back from this trip, I think I'll live in the country. I've always had a fancy for country life—you know, chickens and bees and homegrown vegetables. It's a fine thing to be able to take your own lettuces straight off the ground. You know they're fresh, anyway! And then, there's no need now for me to work so hard as I have done hitherto. Elsie was a very expensive young woman to maintain, and I shall be able to live more economically now! . . . Well, that's my idea—to come back and live in the country. Will that suit you?

JANET (*astonished*)—Me!

JAMES—Yes.

JANET—Are you making me a delicate offer of marriage, James, or are you just asking for information about country life?

JAMES—Of course I'm asking you to marry me. I thought you understood that. It occurred to me that it would be very nice for us both to grow old together in the country, settle down in peace and quietness . . .

JANET—I didn't quite grasp the idea!

JAMES—Do you think you could overlook the past, and marry me again? Of course, you understand that this must be kept strictly between ourselves. If the King's Proctor got to hear about it, my decree would be rescinded and there'd be no marriage for you or me. Or Elsie. But in six months' time, everything will be all right, and we can get married without any bother or hindrance whatever.

Janet does not answer him directly. This is, she reports, the second proposal of marriage she has had that day. Philip, too, had urged his suit.

It was damned nerve on Philip's part, James is convinced, Philip being what he is—an angler.

"Anybody with an active mind 'ud go mad if he had to sit for hours holding a worm in front of a fish." That's James' opinion of Philip.

"Don't be ignorant, James," Janet corrects him. "Philip doesn't use worms; he uses flies."

"What difference does that make when it's the same fellow at the other end of the stick?" demands James.

When they do get back to the subject of marriage Janet has made up her mind quite firmly. She has decided not to marry James. Which is distinctly a shock to James. Janet shouldn't permit herself to be foolish.

JANET—. . . It must be very difficult for you to believe that I've not been waiting here for you to come and propose to me, and I won't deny that I've thought about it. I've thought a great deal about it. I've lain awake at night wondering what I should do.

JAMES—What's there to wonder about?

JANET—Oh, a hundred and one things, James.

JAMES—Of course, I know that I'm a damaged specimen . . .

JANET—Don't business men call it "loss through depreciation"?

JAMES—Still I was good enough to be your husband before.

JANET—And you see no reason why you shouldn't be my husband after? You're rather vain, James.

JAMES—I wouldn't have called myself that.

JANET—No, you wouldn't, but I should!

JAMES—Well, perhaps I am. After all, a man with any stuff in him is always a bit conceited. Will you marry me?

JANET—No.

JAMES—Why? Because I ran off with Elsie? (*She doesn't answer.*) But supposing I hadn't been divorced, and had just gone off with Elsie or some other woman for a while? Would you have taken me back?

JANET—Probably!

JAMES—Well, then! What's the difference?

JANET—There is a difference, James. Any man may be unfaithful to his wife and not care a snap of his fingers for the other woman. But Elsie was not your mistress, James; you married her. You gave me no peace until I had agreed to divorce you. That was deliberate. You meant to get rid of me. Even now, if Elsie would come back to you, you would forgive her!

JAMES—No. I can never forgive her!

JANET—But you expect me to forgive you . . . You frightened me when you first came in, James. I thought you weren't going to ask me . . .

JAMES—But I did.

JANET—Yes, you remembered just in time, didn't you. But it was too late then. While you were talking of your plans and your sufferings, I began to change my mind about marrying you. You didn't say a single word, James, that showed any consideration whatever for me. You only asked me to marry you as a sort of afterthought . . . when you'd settled your trip around the world. You'll go to China and India and Japan, and, perhaps America, and then you'll come home and marry poor old Janet. That'll please the old girl!

JAMES—Really, Janet, is that fair? I ask you.

JANET—You almost made me feel that you wanted to economise on me.

JAMES—No, that's not fair. That's catty, and just like a woman, too.

JANET—Well, what am I to think? You talked of going to live in the country. I prefer London. You said you wouldn't have to work so hard now you'd got rid of Elsie. Apparently, I shall be much cheaper to maintain. But that's where you're mistaken. I'm just as costly as she is, every bit. You once gave her a very beautiful pearl necklace. Perhaps I'd like one, too.

JAMES—You can have it.

JANET—But that's not the point.

JAMES—Well, what is?

JANET—Why do you want to marry me?

JAMES—I'm fond of you. Besides, it seems right. Everybody expects us to marry. Murdo's got his heart set on it.

JANET—Have you got yours?

JAMES—Of course I have.

James' confidence in his own sentiments apparently does not impress Janet overmuch. She was married to him for twenty years, she recalls. She was a devoted and faithful wife. And when she was discarded at the end of that time it seemed very much as though her life was ended.

True, she did have the boys, but they were away at school and there were few friends. Mostly, they were James' friends or friends made because they were of importance to James' business. Gradually Janet has reclaimed the friends she had given up, and made new friends. She joined societies. She renewed her interest in music. She found that she was able to see something in the theatre beside musical comedies, which were the only thing James had cared for. And there were her Tuesday dinners with Philip.

"So, you see, James, I've succeeded in making a very pleasant and agreeable life," Janet concludes. "I'm valued for myself, and not merely as somebody's wife. You would cut no ice at all with my friends. I cut a lot."

JAMES—A gang of highbrows, I suppose?

JANET—No—just ordinarily nice intelligent people. If I married you, I should have to give up that life, and all I shall get in exchange is a cottage in the country where I can help you to economise. I'm to feed the chickens and hive the bees and gather me cabbages while I may, and be grateful for a quiet home and a repentant husband . . .

JAMES—Well, everything seems to be thoroughly messed up. I suppose this is the end of things for us.

JANET—Oh, no! You can take me out to dinner and a theatre once a week. Any day except Tuesday. That's Philip's evening.

JAMES—I don't think I want to share you with Philip.

JANET—Oh! Isn't that selfish of you?

JAMES—This last while back, I've been cheering myself up with the thought that you and I would settle down again, but of course, if you're determined not to marry me— (*He waits for her to say something, but she does not speak. Then a little bewildered he goes on.*) This isn't quite what I expected from you, Janet, but, of course, I can't reasonably complain. You're entitled to get a bit of your own back. (*He pauses again, but she does not speak. He gets up.*) Well, I'll say "good-bye." (JANET *rises too.*)

JANET—Good-bye, James.

JAMES—I mean to say, Janet, this is "good-bye." For good!

JANET—For good?

JAMES—Yes.

JANET—Very well, James. (*The telephone bell rings. Answering.*) Hillo! Oh, hillo, Philip . . .

JAMES—Tell him to go to hell!

JANET (*into the telephone*)—No, that was James. He says you're to go to hell. No, I shouldn't if I were you. Well, yes, if you want to, but I'm too tired to go out or to see anybody . . . Something for me! Yes, all right, send it along. No. No, I'm not . . . not to anybody. Yes, I know, Philip, you've said all that before.

JAMES (*seizing the receiver from her*)—Ring off, blast you. (*He bangs the receiver back on its receptacle.*)

JANET—That was very rude of you, James. You mustn't treat Philip like that. You'd better go now.

JAMES—All right. I'm going. (*He walks to the door, but stops before he reaches it.*) Good-bye, Janet. (*They shake hands.*) It's a pity, of course. (*He turns to go.*) A great pity! (*He stands at the door, with his hand on the handle for a moment. Then he turns to look at her. They do not speak. Then he opens the door.*) Did that fellow Philip say he was sending you a present or something?

JANET—Yes.

JAMES—What is it?

JANET—I don't know. He said it was a little surprise for me.

JAMES—I'll surprise him one of these days. (*He goes out so suddenly that* JANET *is left aghast.*)

(*She waits for a moment and then goes toward the door. As she does so, the sound of the street door shutting is heard. She gives a little gasp, and then shuts the door and goes to the window and looks out. Then she gazes around the room and murmurs: "Yes, you've made a very pleasant and agreeable life for yourself,* JANET, *you fool!"—and returns to her seat.*)

Mabel, the maid, is plainly worried by the abrupt departure of Mr. Fraser and still more distressed by Janet's belief that he will not be back at all. She manages, however, to get the tea things in.

Ninian, in for tea, is also surprised, but rather pleased, that Janet is able to report that James had asked her to marry him and that she refused. Ninian, in fact, is much more pleased than Janet, which surprises him a little.

"But, mother, you don't mean to say—" Her expression stops him.

JANET—Yes, I do mean to say. There's your tea. Drink it and don't talk so much. I'm getting very tired of garrulous children. One of these days, there will be a terrible revolt of the old against the young.

NINIAN (*properly abashed*)—I'm very sorry, mother. Of course, I'm only thinking of your happiness.

JANET—Too many people are only thinking of my happiness. They're making me thoroughly miserable. (*The maid enters with a parcel.*) What is it, Mabel?

MABEL—A special messenger brought this, ma'am.

JANET—Oh, yes. I know what it is. Put it down, please! (*The maid does so and retires.*) It's from Philip. He said he was sending me a surprise.

NINIAN—I suppose you're not going to marry *him?*

JANET—You can suppose anything you like! More tea?

NINIAN (*passing his cup to her*)—Thanks. (*He glances at the parcel.*) This is from Jones, the jeweler round the corner.

JANET—Round the corner!

NINIAN—Yes.

JANET—Here, take your tea and hand me that! (NINIAN *does so and she nervously undoes the parcel.*) You know, you're much too inquisitive, Ninian. Always prying into other people's business.

(*The parcel is undone. It contains a jewel-box which she opens. Inside is a lovely pearl necklace. She takes it out and looks at it, momentarily unable to speak.*)

NINIAN—Great Scott, it's a pearl necklace!

JANET—So it is!

NINIAN—Uncle Philip's splashing his money about, isn't he?

JANET—It isn't your Uncle Philip, you fool. It's your father.

NINIAN—Father!

JANET—Yes. He's beginning to court me all over again . . . and I rather like it, Ninian . . .

(*She gives a little gurgle of joy as she fastens the necklace round her throat*) and—

THE CURTAIN FALLS

JUNE MOON

A Comedy in Three Acts

By Ring Lardner and George S. Kaufman

THERE was happy promise in the announcement that Ring Lardner and George S. Kaufman had made a play from Mr. Lardner's short story "Some Like 'Em Cold," and called it "June Moon." Each is outstanding in his achievements as an American humorist, Mr. Lardner preëminent as a representative of the homely native wit of the Middle West, Mr. Kaufman a leader of those Eastern satirists who have grown up in the sophisticated atmosphere of a smartly artificial New York and come recently into wide popularity.

If the promise were happy its fulfillment was even happier. One of the major triumphs of the theatre season in the matter of first nights was the first performance of "June Moon" at the Broadhurst Theatre October ninth. An audience typical of early season New York, being a third professional, a third resident and a third wide-eyed tourist, fairly rocked the theatre with its laughter. From which propitious beginning "June Moon" played on and on to a succession of other happy audiences straight through the season. In the minds of a few, this editor being one of them, there was some doubt that the play would do as well outside the city in which its characters and scenes flourish, but reports from the back country would seem to indicate otherwise.

In the prologue of "June Moon" we meet Edna Baker and Fred Stevens in the chair car of a train nearing New York. It is early evening and the car shades are drawn. Fred and Edna are pretty much average as to type. She is small and trim and modestly dressed. He is above average height and might be a clerk. They are both in their early twenties.

Fred has practically finished the Sunday papers, which are scattered about the floor of the car between their chairs. Edna is reading a magazine, but is quite conscious of her seat mate's restlessness. She probably suspects that he would like to start a conversation if he could think of something to say. And she would quite as probably like to help him.

When Fred does suggest that she might like to look over his paper she is, however, properly formal. This does not discourage him and soon he is talking volubly, mostly about himself.

He comes from Schenectady, he tells her. In Schenectady he had had a job in the General Electric plant, but gave it up because he wanted to go to New York and write songs. The boys in the shipping department of the G.E. gave him a farewell banquet, and a suitcase with his initials on it.

EDNA (*a bit too eagerly*)—Is that what you are? A song writer?

FRED (*Nods.*)—Not the music part; just the words. Lyrics, they're called.

EDNA—It must be wonderful to have a gift like that.

FRED—That's what Benny Davis called it—a gift. I guess you've heard of him—he's turned out a hundred smash hits.

EDNA—I guess I must have.

FRED—He wrote, "Oh, How I Miss You Tonight!" It was a song about how he missed his mother—he called her his "Old Pal."

EDNA—That's sweet!

FRED—Well, he happened to be playing in Schenectady in vaudeville, and I happened to meet him and I happened to show him some of my lyrics. And he said a man like I with the song-writing gift was a sucker not to go to New York, because that's where they have the Mecca for a man if you got the song-writing gift. So he gave me a letter to the Friars' Club, asking them to give me a two weeks' card, they call it. The Friars' Club is where they have the Mecca for songwriters. And he give me a letter of introduction to Paul Sears, the composer. He wrote "Paprika." You remember "Paprika"? (*He sings a strain of it.*) "Paprika, Paprika, the spice of my life—"

EDNA (*with quick concurrence*)—I think so.

FRED—When you write a song like "Paprika" you don't ever have to worry again. He's one of the most successful composers there is, Paul Sears. I bet you, I and he will turn out some hits together.

EDNA—Are you going to be partners with him?

FRED—If he wants me to, and I guess he will when I show him Benny Davis's letter. That's the hard part, getting acquainted. I'd have broke away a long time ago only for my sister. I couldn't leave her alone.

EDNA—Is she in Schenectady?

FRED (*Nods.*)—She got married a week ago Saturday. A fella I been working with in the shipping department—Bob Gifford.

EDNA—She'll miss you just the same. I know how sisters feel, especially when their brother is like you or Dick.

FRED—Well, anyway, she got married, and I give them a pair of book-ends.

EDNA—She'll love them!

FRED—She always done everything for me—I mean, cooked my meals and sewed things for me. Look! (*Dives for his bag and starts opening it.*) She made me a half dozen shirts before I left. Different colors. Here's one of the blue ones. I bet if you was to buy a shirt like that, you couldn't buy a shirt like that under a dollar seventy-five.

EDNA—I'll bet it would cost more than that.

FRED—Marion can sew, all right. My mother used to say she was a born seamstress.

EDNA—I love to sew. (*Looks at the shirt.*) Has it got your monogram, your initials?

FRED—No. She was going to put a "F" on the sleeve, but she was too busy.

EDNA—It's too bad you're not my brother and I'd embroider your whole initials.

FRED—You don't have to be a man's sister to embroider their shirt.

EDNA—I don't want you to misjudge me, Mr. Stevens. I'm not the kind of a girl that talks to strangers. My friends would die if they knew I was talking to a man whom I had not been properly introduced.

FRED—You don't need to be scared of me, girlie. I treat all women like they was my sister. Till I find out different.

EDNA—A girl alone in New York can't be too careful, especially a girl in my position. You take at Dr. Quinn's, where I work—he's one of the best dentists there is, and he has lots of men patients that would be only too glad to start a little flirtation. Why even Doctor himself was fresh, the first day I met him. It turned out he wasn't really, but it seemed that way. He put his arm around my shoulders and I jumped away from him like he was a leopard or something, and I told him, I said, "Doctor, I guess I don't care to work here after all." Then he laughed and said forget it, that he was just testing me. He said he didn't want an assistant who was inclined to flirt. And from that day he's never made any advances, except once or twice.

Fred is of the opinion that what Edna may find she needs in New York is a protector and he knows where she can find one if such should prove to be the case. Soon they are exchanging opinions as to what may be and what should be expected of men—and of girls—especially of girls who have any thought of getting married some time and making things attractive and homelike for their husbands.

Edna is just naturally a great home girl. She makes practically all her own clothes, she admits. She doesn't like going out nights much, either. She had a lot rather sit at home and sew, or read, or maybe just sit and dream. Edna likes babies, too, though she blushes to confess it, which certainly is nothing against a woman in Fred's estimation. Women ought to like babies. They disagree mildly upon only one subject. Fred doesn't altogether approve of a woman's working after she's married, as Edna says she would be willing to do until her husband established himself.

FRED—The girl I marry won't never have to work. I don't believe God ever meant for a woman to endure a life of drudgery.

EDNA—Oh, Mr. Stevens, if only all men felt the same way!

FRED (*a look at his watch*)—My, it's nine twenty-six already.

EDNA—It's been a shorter trip than usual, for some reason.

FRED (*trying to peer out the window*)—I wonder where we're at now?

EDNA (*also peering*)—Pretty near Yonkers, I guess.

FRED—If we was on the other side we could see the Hudson River.

EDNA—My, but it's dark!

FRED—There's a moon out.

EDNA—Yes, I love it.

FRED—June—moon.

EDNA—What?

FRED—I just said June moon.

EDNA—It isn't June. It's October.

FRED—I know, but June and moon go together. They rhyme. I'm always thinking of words that rhyme, even when I ain't working.

EDNA—That'd be a catchy name, June Moon. For a song, I mean.

FRED—Yes, you could get other words to go with it. Spoon, and croon, and soon. Marry soon, or something.

EDNA—And macaroon.

FRED—Yeah. I wish I had some. I'm hungry.

EDNA—I am, too, kind of. . . . Some day when that song is published and people are singing it everywhere, I'll say to my friends, "I knew the man that wrote that. We were riding on a train and he looked out and saw the moon, and he thought of this song, and then the train got to New York and he never saw poor little me again."

FRED—You won't be telling the truth, because I'm going to see you again.

EDNA—You say that now. But you'll forget all about me.

FRED—No, I won't. Are you going right home when we get in?

EDNA—Why—I intended to. (*She sits up, expectantly.*)

FRED—I thought I'd go and get something to eat some place, only I wouldn't know where to go if I didn't have somebody with me that knowed where to go.

EDNA—I can tell you a place where I go once in a while, the Little Venice. Though most of the time I stay home and cook my own dinner, just because I love to cook.

FRED—It'll be a little late to cook tonight. I was wondering if you wouldn't go along to this place, and maybe we could eat together.

EDNA—I'd love to.

FRED—It ain't a very expensive place, is it?

EDNA—Oh, no. The last time I went, there was two of us and we had hot roast beef sandwiches, and peas, and coffee, and it only came to a dollar-twenty.

FRED (*with vast relief*)—All right. I guess we can each afford sixty cents.

END OF PROLOGUE

ACT I

Ten days later, in one of those Riverside Drive apartments in New York that have become a little bit *déclassé* since people began moving to the East Side, Paul Sears and Lucille, his wife, are spending a more or less quiet evening at home.

Paul, in his middle thirties, is a composer of popular songs and he works at it rather persistently. He is at the piano now, "in his shirt sleeves, and is alternately hitting a few discouraged keys and then making penciled notations on the music sheet in front of him. Paul is not a two-finger pianist, but he falls short of it by only one finger."

Lucille, "a spare but still attractive woman, on whom three

years of marriage have left their mark," bears the monotonous repetition of the one phrase with which Paul is struggling with considerable fortitude but not much patience. She cares little more for his chatter, or his complaints.

Paul, it appears, is disgusted with his current working partner, a man named Fagan, whose lyrics are evidently not what they used to be, and who is getting so he refuses to change even a line to help the melody. Still, Paul thinks the new song he has been doing with Fagan will be something of a knockout and probably another "Paprika."

"The silliest thing in the world to me," counters Lucille, "is a man trying to be a composer when he can't even play 'Chopsticks.' "

That does not worry Paul any. Irving Berlin can't play much either. And Gershwin! Ain't Boston right now complaining that he hasn't given them even one tune in "Pretty Polly"? It ruins a composer to play the piano too good.

This particular evening in the Sears home is to be devoted to a conference with a new lyric writer Paul has just dug up, a young fella with a fresh slant. A nice kid, too, and he's got money. But lyric writers are pretty much all alike to Lucille. She gets no kick out of this new promise.

Eileen is Lucille's sister. She is staying home, too, waiting for a telephone call from her friend Hart, but she keeps pretty much to her room and away from Paul. There is not much love lost between Paul and Eileen. What she thinks of him is sufficient, and what he thinks of her is that she should get out and find herself a job. Also, it is his private opinion that Mr. Hart is also getting tired of her.

Lucille is naturally on her sister's side. At the moment, when Eileen is drawn into the room by a telephone ring that she thought might be for her, Lucille reminds her that the evening gown she has been mending is getting worn and should be replaced.

LUCILLE—Why don't you look around Monday? See what you can find.

EILEEN—Maybe I will. I've just been putting it off. I'm lazy, I guess.

LUCILLE—I'd never be too lazy to shop, if I had anything to shop with.

PAUL—You wait till this number gets over.

LUCILLE (*quite pleasantly*)—By that time I'll only want a shawl.

PAUL (*finally flaring up*)—There's nothing helps a man like being married to a woman that always encourages you and looks on the bright side. I'm going to write an article for the *American Magazine,* saying I attribute my success to my wife.

EILEEN—Why don't you try writing articles? They might be pretty near as good as your tunes.

PAUL—You don't have to worry about my tunes. Anyhow, I was talking to Lucille.

EILEEN—It's time you did something more for Lucille besides talk to her!

PAUL—If I was in your place, I'd keep pretty still in this house. That is, unless I was paying board.

EILEEN (*It's a good battle by this time.*)—Don't you dare say I'm dependent on you, because I'm not!

PAUL—Only for your meals and a place to sleep!

EILEEN—You wouldn't even have a job if it wasn't for me! Do you think Hart is keeping you on the staff because you wrote a hit three years ago?

LUCILLE—Now!

EILEEN—Well, make him lay off me, if he knows what's good for him. If he keeps riding me, he'll be looking for a new job!

PAUL—Swell chance of them letting me out when I've got a number like "Montana." I'd run right to Harms with it.

EILEEN—Harms wouldn't let you in their elevator!

PAUL (*as he goes proudly into the next room*)—I was in it this afternoon!

EILEEN (*A long, long sigh.*)—Is Hart going to phone or isn't he? It gets me crazy, this waiting.

LUCILLE—I wouldn't mind waiting if there was something to wait for. I nearly go out of my mind, just sitting. You hear women brag about the nice, cozy evenings they spend at home with their husband. They're not married to a piano tuner with ten thumbs.

EILEEN (*hoping against hope*)—Maybe he didn't get back from Philadelphia. He might still be over there.

LUCILLE—What time was he going to call up?

EILEEN—Six o'clock. He said he'd call me the minute he got in. Maybe the train was late.

LUCILLE—They aren't late very often, from Philadelphia.

EILEEN—It's the only evening we'll *have* for three weeks, with him going away again tomorrow. (*Restlessly pacing.*) If he was going to be late you'd think he'd try to reach me.

LUCILLE—Of course, you know him better than I do, but when

a man's really crazy about a girl, he calls her up, I don't care what he's doing. It's only when he begins cooling off that he finds excuses, like being in Philadelphia.

EILEEN—But he was in Philadelphia.

LUCILLE—I know, but they've got phones there now, too.

EILEEN—If you think he's cooling off you're crazy! He's insanely jealous. When I told him I was thinking of going out with Bert Livingston he was sore as hell. He said, "All right, go ahead and go out with him." I asked him if he meant it, and he said, "Sure! Go out with the whole Lambs Club!" He's insanely jealous and tries to hide it.

LUCILLE—I'd go out with the janitor if he asked me. God, I'm sick of this place.

EILEEN—Why don't you go to a picture?

LUCILLE—They charge admission. (*A little sardonic laugh.*) Remember the way I used to figure when Paul first came along? I thought marrying a song writer meant going to all the first nights, meeting everybody that was worthwhile, going down to Palm Beach—

EILEEN—You would, too, if Paul was any good.

LUCILLE—I wonder what it'd be like if we'd stayed in Stroudsburg. I'd probably be married to Will Broderick, and we'd have a car—

EILEEN—To drive over to Scranton in.

LUCILLE (*A sigh.*)—I suppose I ought to get consolation out of one thing. I never expect a phone call or a mash note or an invitation or even a half pound box of candy. Whatever happens is velvet.

It is Eileen's opinion that Lucille is a fool to stick around with Paul. She should ship Paul while there is still time. Grounds? She wouldn't need any grounds—just let the Judge look at him.

But Lucille is hesitant. She never could fool anybody, least of all Paul. He'd know if she ever tried to fool him. Besides, "women can't go wrong if they're not invited." So far there haven't been any volunteers. Also, Lucille is a little superstitious. If she did quit Paul he'd probably write ten smash hits in a week.

Furthermore, Lucille has an idea that Eileen would be wise to do a little worrying about her own affairs. Hart may be insanely jealous, but he has a queer way of showing it. Especially if he has any ideas about marrying Eileen. Perhaps it would be a good idea for Eileen to go around with some of the other boys while

Hart is away on one of his trips. But Eileen wouldn't dare. She might get herself murdered.

Maxie has called. "He is a man in his late forties, easy-going, kindly, and wears a dinner coat. He is an arranger for Goebel's, and he knows the popular song business backwards."

Maxie is also something of a Broadway cynic. He sees so much, hears so much, likes so little. Disappointed in his own career—he might have been a song writer himself if he hadn't got into the business of fixing up other people's tunes—he fails to react with any enthusiasm to the persistently threatened success of the egoists he works with. Nor can they fool him.

So far as this new song of Fagan's and Paul's is concerned, Maxie thinks it is a great idea of Fagan's to write a lyric about the Northwest for a change. But it never was because Fagan once lived in Montana. "If song writers always wrote about their home state," says Maxie, "what a big population Tennessee must have." And the one encouraging thing he hears about the expected Fred Stevens is that he comes from Schenectady, because, thank God, he can't get that in a lyric.

"You'll like this fella," promises Paul. "He's young yet. He's got a fresh slant."

"What does he do—write about countries instead of states?"

"I've been thinking maybe he and I could do something together, if I can get rid of Fagan."

"Fagan isn't so bad. Only he's using up his ideas too fast. 'Montana Moon.' He puts a state and a moon all in one song."

Paul insists on singing "Montana Moon" as Maxie plays it over. That doesn't help a great deal. Not with Lucille.

"Golden West that seems so far away,
Golden girl for whom I'm always pining,
Don't you know I love you night and day,
But chiefly when the full bright moon is shining."

And then the chorus:

"Montana moonlight,
As bright as noonlight,
Oh, may it soon light
My way to you!
I know you're lonely,
My one and only,
For I am lonely,
Yes, lonely, too."

Lucille calmly goes back to her sewing, but Paul keeps on:

"My heart is yearning
For kisses burning,
For lips as sweet as a rose in June.
I'm always dreaming
Of your eyes gleaming,
Beneath the beaming
Montana Moon!"

The enthusiasm following is again confined mostly to Paul. It may be a good number, but Lucille is satisfied that Berlin will still refuse to kill himself over it. There's some sympathy behind a Berlin song. So there might be behind his songs, Paul agrees, if he got a little sympathy at home.

Maxie is anxious to reëstablish harmony in the home, but even he cannot promise Paul too much for "Montana." It seems Hart and Goebel, the publishers, were talking about it that afternoon.

Eileen overhears that. So Hart was in the office that afternoon! And not in Philadelphia! And she waiting home for a call!

Paul urges Maxie on, and he reluctantly finishes his report of a growing fear that Goebel and Hart are not thinking of buying "Montana" right now. Which Paul simply cannot believe. It's a great tune. Even if the lyric kills it it should get a great mechanical break. . . .

Now Fred Stevens arrives. He has found the Sears apartment after some little difficulty with the subway. He is pleased to meet everybody, and equally glad to assure them that he is feeling fine. He is not, he admits modestly, much of a song writer. He only does the words. But words, Lucille assures him, pleasantly, are all Paul needs—words and music.

FRED—I've always been one of Mr. Sears' greatest admirers. I've admired Mr. Sears ever since he wrote "Paprika."

LUCILLE (*gently*)—You've got a good memory.

PAUL—Maybe Stevens and I will turn out another "Paprika."

FRED—I'm anxious to get started all right. Since I got to town, all I've done so far is spend money.

LUCILLE (*expansively*)—Well, you're quite a stranger!

PAUL—Sit down.

FRED—Thanks. I guess I'm a little late. I got off the wrong subway station and there was an old woman selling papers, and

I stopped and talked to her because I knew she must be somebody's mother.

MAXIE (*who has never stopped playing*)—A fresh slant.

FRED—I was right, too, because she told me she has six sons. I feel sorry for old women that has to earn their living.

LUCILLE—What do the boys do—rent her the stand?

FRED—No, most of them are in a hospital and two of them had their foot cut off. She told me all about it and I give her a dollar.

PAUL—You want to be careful in a place like New York. There's all kind of people waiting to take your money away from you.

FRED—It's a great city, all right. Today I took the ferry boat over to Staten's Island and back. (*He explains it to* LUCILLE.) It's an island and you have to take a ferry boat. But I suppose you been there.

LUCILLE—I go there a lot—just for the trip.

FRED—I seen the Goddess of Liberty, too—I mean the statue. It cost a million dollars and weighs 225 ton.

MAXIE (*gently*)—She ought to cut out sweets. (*He indulges in a fancy run.*)

FRED (*gesturing in the direction of* MAXIE)—He can play the piano! . . . And I seen some of the big ocean liner steamboats. I seen the *President Harding* just coming in from London or Europe or somewheres, and the other day I seen the *Majestic* tied up to the dock. She's pretty near twict as long as the *President Harding* and weighs 56,000 ton. The *President Harding* only weighs 14,000 ton.

LUCILLE—Imagine!

FRED (*to* LUCILLE)—Have you been through the Holland Tunnel?

LUCILLE—No, I haven't.

FRED (*to* PAUL)—Have you been through the Holland Tunnel?

PAUL—No.

FRED (*not for a minute giving up*)—Have you been through the Holland Tunnel, Mr. Schwartz?

MAXIE—I've been waiting for somebody to go with.

FRED—I'll go with you!

MAXIE—Fine!

FRED—I want to go every place so as to get ideas for songs. I was telling Mr. Sears about one idea—I haven't got it written yet—it's a song about the traffic lights. Green for "Come ahead!" and red for "Stop!" Maybe a comical song with a girl signaling her sweetheart with different colored lights in the window; a green light when it's all right for him to call—

LUCILLE—And a red one when her husband's home.

FRED (*shocked*)—No, I was thinking about her father. I wouldn't write about those kind of women—I got no sympathy for them.

LUCILLE—I guess you're right.

FRED—I was thinking of another idea on the way up here. Maybe a song about the melting pots—all the immigrants from overseas who've come to the Land of Liberty. Take the Jews—do you know there's nearly two million Jews in New York City alone?

MAXIE—What do you mean—alone?

FRED—And then there's the Hall of Fame, up to Washington Heights. They got everybody up there. Washington, Lincoln, Longfellow—they got two dozen—what do you call 'em—busts?

LUCILLE (*sweetly, to* PAUL)—That's the place for you, dear.

FRED—No. A man's got to be dead for twenty-five years.

LUCILLE—Well, that fits in.

MAXIE (*It's too much for him.*)—I've got to be going along.

PAUL—Wait. I want Stevens to show you one of his lyrics—have you got that one with you? About the game?

MAXIE—I've got to be downtown at ten.

PAUL—This won't take a minute. (*To* FRED.) Go ahead.

FRED—I'll have to explain first, so you'll understand. The idea come to me at a football game between Syracuse and Colgate. They beat them, and they felt pretty bad, so the idea come to me for this little song. I call it "Life Is a Game."

MAXIE—A novelty!

FRED—Here's the verse. Are you ready?

PAUL—Yeah.

FRED—

"I don't know why some people cry
When things appear to go wrong;
I always say 'Laugh and be gay!'
Things cannot always go wrong!
No use to pine, no use to whine,
Things will come right if you just give them time."

That's the verse.

LUCILLE—Uh-huh!

FRED—Then here's the refrain:

"Life is a game; we are but players"—

MAXIE—Hey, bring it here! Maybe we can put some music to it.

FRED—Just play some chords.

MAXIE—I'll see if I know any.

FRED (*sings as well as he can to* MAXIE'S *improvisation*)—

"Life is a game; we are but players
Playing the best we know how.
If you are beat, don't let it wrangle;
No one can win all the time.
Sometimes the odds seem dead against you;
What has to be, has to be,
But smile just the same, for life is a game,
And God is a fine referee."

Maxie picks up the last line and sings it again, tacking on a rousing musical finale to fit. It is really the finish of "All Those Endearing Young Charms," but so far as Fred is concerned it has been composed especially for his lyric. He is beaming with pleasure.

FRED—I haven't got the second verse yet.

MAXIE—You won't need one.

Lucille suggests that she likes a song with love interest. Fred has one of those too, though it is not quite worked out. So far he has practically only got the title—"June Moon." Certainly doesn't sound, Maxie admits, like a war song.

"June Moon," Fred explains, is to be a song about a fella who has met a girl in June when there was a moon shining, and then she went away, or perhaps he went away, and then whenever he looks at the moon after that he thinks of her.

Paul is a bit dubious about another moon song, but Maxie is already setting it to a tune and Fred, all aflutter, is thinking up original rhymes—like spoon—

It was while he was coming to New York in the train that he got the idea, Fred admits. He happened to look out the window—

But he has no chance to go on with the story. The phone call for Eileen has come at last and she flounces in to answer it.

Maxie, noting the expression in Eileen's eyes, considers this an excellent time for him to withdraw—he's due at the Orchard at 10, anyway. Paul sees Maxie to the door, which leaves Fred a little embarrassedly in the presence of Lucille, Eileen and Eileen's telephone conversation—

"Yes, I can imagine," she is saying, sarcastically. "It must have been terribly tiresome in Philadelphia all day. . . . What? . . . Oh, really? . . . I thought you were leaving tomorrow. . . . What time tonight? . . . My, it must be important! . . . Then —I won't have a chance to say good-bye before you go. . . . Oh, no, don't trouble yourself—it's quite all right. . . . Yes, I'm sure you are. . . . No, I don't mind a bit. . . . I'm just sorry you have to spend the night on a train, that's all. . . . Oh, perfectly! . . . Have a pleasant trip." But she doesn't mean ". . . a pleasant trip." A look flashes between Eileen and Lucille.

Now Fred has been introduced to Eileen and been visibly impressed, though it is not at all apparent that Eileen greatly cares.

Mr. Stevens, Lucille explains, is new to New York, having come from Schenectady, and has been all over town getting ideas for songs. Fred confirms the statement and admits that he likes New York a lot, except for the expense of living. That very morning he had spent 90 cents for a breakfast that really didn't have anything to it except some salt mackerel, mashed potatoes and a cup of Instant Postum.

Lucille is afraid he soon will run out of money at that rate, but Fred assures her that he still has plenty. And at the sound of those welcome words Lucille has an idea which, being a good sister, she flashes immediately to Eileen.

Mr. Stevens, agrees Lucille, may have seen many things in New York, including, as he admits, the Goddess of Liberty, but he never will have lived until he has seen the night places. Why shouldn't they, just the four of them, make up a nice little party and show Mr. Stevens the town? Eileen would love to go, wouldn't she? Of course she would. Why not?

Fred is fairly excited by the thought but unfortunately he has another engagement. Still, with Eileen's urging, he is induced to break that. Especially after they assure him that he doesn't have to be dressed for a swell place. They will take him some place like the Orchard, where Maxie plays. What a surprise that will be to Maxie! It is Fred's first experience with a real New York girl like Eileen. He thinks she's great.

PAUL (*doing a little work*)—Maybe it wouldn't be a bad notion for you to knock around a few nights—I mean, before we start working. Might give you some ideas.

FRED—I'm willing.

PAUL—Great!

FRED—Say, can I use your phone a minute?

PAUL—Sure. Do you want the book?

FRED—No, I know the number . . . Rhinelander 4160.

PAUL—I'd better clean up a bit.

FRED—Look! They was talking about this Orchard. That ain't one of them expensive places, is it?

PAUL—No, just about average.

FRED—Hello . . . . I want to speak to Miss Edna Baker, please. . . . Yes. (*To* PAUL.) (I mean, what do you think it would be likely to come to for the four of us? More than ten dollars?

PAUL (*vaguely*)—No—not unless we go on to some other place. You've got more with you, haven't you?

FRED—What other place?

PAUL—One of the other clubs.

FRED—But I don't— Hello. . . . Hello. . . . Eddie? . . . I want to tell you something.

PAUL—I'll go and wash up. (*He leaves the room.*)

FRED—Well, I'm up there now, but that isn't— Sure . . . Yeah, it looks all right. . . . No, I'm still here. There was a piano player from Goebel's here. He liked my stuff and made up a tune to some of it. . . . Yeah. . . . He said it was all right. But that isn't . . . what I called up to say was I can't get around till late. . . . No, it'll be later than that. There's no telling what time it'll be. . . . We got to study some songs. . . . Paul Sears and his wife. . . . No, no, don't think that. It's a business proposition. They're taking me to a place where we'll get some ideas. . . . Just the three of us. . . . But you know I'd rather be with you. (EILEEN *comes back, with coat over her arm.*) But I can't . . . I can't . . . *They're* taking *me.* I'll tell you all about it in the morning. That's all I can say now. . . . I can't . . . In the morning . . . Good-night. (*Hangs up.*)

EILEEN—You seem to be having your troubles.

FRED—No, that wasn't anything. Just a—friend of mine.

EILEEN—Is she nice?

FRED—It isn't—anybody. Just a little girl I happened to meet.

EILEEN—I understand.

FRED—She's just a—a girl from a little town.

(LUCILLE *comes back, full of life, pulling on gloves, etc.*)

LUCILLE—Listen—it's kind of early for the Orchard anyhow. So why don't we take in the second show at the Capitol?

PAUL (*coming into the room*)—Is everybody ready?

EILEEN—Oh, that's fine! And I know what you'd love! After the Orchard what do you say we go to the Cotton Club? (*She throws a quick explanation to Fred.*) That's Harlem!

LUCILLE—Great!

EILEEN—They've got a wonderful tap dancer up there! Better than Bill Robinson!

PAUL—But say, the Cotton Club doesn't get hot till three!

FRED—What time?

EILEEN—Oh, that's all right! We can go to the Madrid or Richman's in between.

LUCILLE—Oh, great!

PAUL—But say, Richman's burned down the other night!

FRED—Let's not go there.

LUCILLE—I'll tell you where I haven't been for a long while! The St. Regis Roof!

EILEEN—Grand!

LUCILLE—They've a wonderful view!

FRED—Where?

LUCILLE—The St. Regis Roof.

FRED—I get dizzy if I climb a ladder.

(*The voices of the others pick up in a confused jumble as*

THE CURTAIN FALLS

ACT II

A month later, in a room at Goebel's music publishing house, furnished with music shelves along one wall, a piano and a few chairs, Maxie, the arranger, is playing idly and mostly for his own amusement. Goldie, "who may have got her name because of the color of her hair, or it may be because she is really Miss Goldberg," is filing sheafs of songs in the shelves and carrying on a desultory conversation with Max, from which it appears that everything is getting along as well as might be expected.

Mr. Hart is just back from the West and a little disappointed in business. They are, he found, still singing "The Rosary" out there and Maxie thinks perhaps it may be a hit yet.

Maxie is waiting for Paul Sears and Fred Stevens. He has to play their new "June Moon" song, and he is not at all surprised that he has been kept waiting. He has been in the song business for twenty-two years and nothing has happened yet.

Fred is the first to arrive, all hot and excited. He has made one important change in the lyric of "June Moon." It has previously read "Sweet nightbird, hovering above." Now it reads "winging aloft," which means practically the same thing, Maxie admits, only higher.

FRED—I wish I'd known Mr. Hart was going to be late. I could have slept some more. I had to get up at twelve.

MAXIE—That must be tough after working for the General Electric, where a man's hours are practically his own.

FRED—No. I had to be on the job at eight, every morning. But I went to bed about ten, except Saturday nights, when I seen a picture or something. I didn't know what life was, in Schenectady.

MAXIE—I bet it's an open book to you now.

FRED—Imagine—only going out one night a week and then just to a moving picture show! Down here it's like as if every night was a special night—there's always new places to go to. Miss Fletcher—she's always locating new ones! We was in three last night! Wound up at half past seven this morning, in the Bucket of Blood! There's a lively place! We was the last ones there. Paul and Lucille, they went home at seven, but I and Miss Fletcher stayed and she made the proprietor sell me six bottles of gin. It's a real gin what they call pro-war. You got to have good gin. It's one of the things they put into what they call a Bronx cocktail.

MAXIE—Is that so?

FRED—Didn't you ever have one?

MAXIE—I don't drink. After I listen to songs all day I don't want liquor. I just go home and take a general anæsthetic.

FRED—I like Bronxes best. They're nothing but gin and orange juice. I don't know why they call it a Bronx.

MAXIE—It's a great orange country, up there.

FRED—Anyway, I got a bargain—six bottles for sixty bucks. I give Miss Fletcher three bottles for a present, because if it hadn't been for her I wouldn't have got them. She made the man do it. When you're around with her you just can't resist doing things.

MAXIE—I know. That's why I don't carry a gun.

FRED—She's a great sport all right. She'd make a wonderful

wife—she's such a good pal. I think a man's wife ought to be their pal as well as their sweetheart.

MAXIE—You ought to patent that.

FRED—Say—how much money do you think a fella ought to be making before he could get married? In New York, I mean?

MAXIE—It depends on the girl.

FRED—Buddy De Sylva makes pretty near a half million dollars a year out of just writing lyrics. I guess a man could support a wife on that!

MAXIE—If she was satisfied to ride a bicycle.

FRED—Well, suppose "June Moon" is a big smash? What's the most we could make out of it?

MAXIE—It's hard to say. Take a song like "Swanee River" and it's still going big.

FRED—Yeah, but that's because it was in a big production like "Show Boat."

MAXIE—How's that?

FRED—And with that girl to sing it, that sits on the piano.

MAXIE—You're thinking of Ruby Keeler in the "Wild Duck."

FRED—Well, whoever it was. (*Turns away; suddenly remembers.*) Oh, say! I was over to the tailor's today. I'm getting a new suit. Miss Fletcher took me.

MAXIE—That so?

FRED—It's a blue search, with a hair-bone strip. He took my measures all over. Like I was a fighter. I'm thirty-eight inches around my chest, and thirty-three around my stomach, and—I forget my thigh. Anyway, he's got it all wrote down.

MAXIE—I must get a copy.

FRED—If they like "June Moon" I'm going to have an evening dinner coat made, with a Tuxedo. I been wearing an old suit of Paul's, but it's too big. Miss Fletcher says it would hold two like me.

MAXIE—There couldn't be two.

FRED—She was just joking.

MAXIE—I see.

FRED—They've given me a wonderful time, all right. They've introduced me to all the big stars! Gil Boag, and Earl Carroll, and Texas Guinan! I met Texas Guinan!

MAXIE—She's kind of hard to meet, isn't she?

FRED—No. She's one of the friendliest women I ever seen. When the girls told her who I was she said it was a big night in her life—she said she'd always wanted to meet a lyric writer. I wonder what my friends in Schenectady would say if they knew I sat around and talked to Texas Guinan! I didn't know nothing when I lived there. Even the first few weeks I was in New York, I was kind of a sap.

MAXIE—That sounds incredible.

FRED—I went sightseeing to places like the Aquarium, and Grant's Tomb, and the Central Park animal zoo, and thought I was having a great time. A little friend of mine, she took me around places she'd been to and I thought I was seeing New York because I didn't know no better. She was from a small town, too—she didn't know no better either. Only now I've learned.

MAXIE—What's become of her? Did she go home?

FRED—No, she lives here. She works for a dentist. I must call her up sometime and see how she's getting along.

There are many interruptions. A man comes to wash the windows, but he begs them to go right ahead with their singing. He hears so many songs around that building they don't mean a thing to him. Benny, also a song writer, must rush in to tell them about his newest hit, a dashing romantic number called "Hello, Tokio!" They can't help that much, either.

Now Paul has arrived and they are all ready to run over "June Moon" with Maxie if they can manage a few minutes of quiet. They get this when the window cleaner finally gets on the outside of the window and stays there. Now Maxie and the boys plunge into "June Moon," with Fred leading the singing:

"Summer winds are sighing in the trees, my dear;
I am sure I know what makes them sigh;
They are sad on moonlight nights like these, my dear;
They are lonely for you, same as I.
Sweetheart, how can you resist their plea,
And the moon you used to share with me?

June Moon, shining above,
Will my true love come soon?
June Moon, I am so blue;
I know that you long for her, too.
Sweet nightbird, winging aloft,
Singing a soft love tune,
Tell her to come to me here,
To me and her dear June Moon."

Just as they have finished the song Edna Baker comes timidly through the door. Fred is surprised and it may be a little disturbed to see Edna, but his manner is cordial. The excitement of the song is still with him.

Edna is properly impressed by what she has heard of "June Moon." It's beautiful. It's wonderful of Fred to have finished it. After the others have discreetly withdrawn and Fred and Edna are left alone she hesitantly calls his attention to his having overlooked a chance to kiss her and is a little eager to know what has kept him from seeing her so long. She has worried for fear he was sick or something. But, of course, if it has only been because he was busy, that's understandable. Still, it has been two Sundays since they went anywhere together. They used to have such nice Sundays.

But, as Fred explains, he has to work when Paul feels like it. "Music writers don't keep no hours," he explains, professionally. "They work when they're inspired. And it ain't just writing the songs that takes time. You have to go around places, and keep in contract with the other boys, so you get new notions. You got to keep getting new notions in this game."

A fuller confession is finally forced from him when Fred admits that he has been going about quite a lot of places where music is heard and that he and Paul have not always been alone. Mrs. Sears has been along and—sometimes, Mrs. Sears' sister. But she isn't much of anybody. Just a sister who can't be left home alone because she's timid.

EDNA—Does she know about—me, Fred?

FRED—Huh?

EDNA—Didn't you ever tell her about—me?

FRED—Well, you see, we just—it's only business, and there hasn't nothing like that come up.

EDNA—What's she like, Fred?

FRED—I don't know. She—

EDNA (*hard at work*)—A girl like she has probably got lots of beautiful clothes. She probably makes little me look like nothing.

FRED—That part don't matter. It wouldn't make no difference to me if she had all the clothes in the world. Or if she was bare, either.

EDNA—Is she—very pretty?

FRED—Yah, she—I hardly ever noticed if she was pretty or not.

EDNA—What's her name?

FRED—Miss Fletcher.

EDNA—I mean her first name.

FRED—I believe they call her Eileen.

EDNA—That's a beautiful name. It's a lot nicer than mine, don't you think?

FRED—It's just a different name.

EDNA—Is she blonde or brunette?

FRED—Both—I mean she's red-headed. That is, I never paid much attention.

EDNA—How old is she?

FRED—I don't know.

EDNA—Older than I am?

FRED—A little bit, I guess. I guess she must be. She's been on the stage.

EDNA (*putting across a little mild horror*)—Honestly, Fred?

FRED—Yah, but don't think—I mean, that don't mean anything.

EDNA—Oh, Fred, you want to be careful! Because you take a woman like she, that's close to forty or more—

FRED—She ain't forty.

EDNA (*conceding two years*)—Well, thirty-eight. And she sees a young boy who almost any woman would be proud to win your affections, and there isn't anything she might not stoop to, to entangle you.

FRED—There won't no woman untangle me.

EDNA—You can't tell, Fred—the most terrible things can happen. There was a near friend of mine, a man, and he was acquainted with a count, an international count, and he came here to New York and one night they went on a wild party and he fell in love with a beautiful chorus girl from the Metropolitan Opera Company—I forget the name of the opera. And he bought her pearls and diamonds, and in less than a week's time he found out they was both married. That's just what could happen to you, dear.

FRED—Who found out who was married?

EDNA—Both of them were married—the count and the girl.

FRED—He must have been a fine count, not to know he was married.

EDNA—Fred, doesn't it cost an awful lot of money when you go around to all these places—or do they take you?

FRED—Well, that part's going to be all right, because as soon as they take our song I'll get what they call an advance royalties. And of course after it's a big hit I'll have plenty of money.

It is Fred's plan, the minute he gets any money, to pay Edna back the little loan he had from her. It makes him uncomfortable owing a girl money—especially a girl. Edna isn't worried. She'd be glad to give Fred everything she has, but it doesn't look as if she'd have much from now on. Her job at the dentist's is no more. She had mixed up a couple of appointments and one man had his bones scraped when he didn't expect it and the bones didn't really need scraping.

Edna is pretty unhappy about losing her job, but she doesn't care any more about it when Fred kisses her again and asks her to wait in the reception room while they are singing "June Moon" for Mr. Hart. Then perhaps they can go some place and have a soda or something.

Mr. Hart is pretty rushed when he does come and the audition does not go as well as it might. Benny, the "Tokio" boy, tries to steal Mr. Hart's attention. The window cleaner is in and out most inopportunely. Even Mr. Hart's mind is not exclusively on the song.

For one thing, being just back from this swing around the West, Mr. Hart is not at all comfortable about the Mexican situation. There may be, and again they may not be, trouble. But, if there should be trouble—then the first one in with a good stirring war song is going to clean up. It's just a tip.

Now Ned Wayburn is on the wire. And now George Gershwin is reported waiting in the anteroom. This is particularly exciting news. Mr. Hart goes out. Benny goes out. The window cleaner goes out. Everybody goes out to have a look at George—everybody except Maxie. He will wait until George comes to him.

Now Lucille Sears and Eileen Fletcher have arrived. Eileen has come to see Mr. Hart, but she hasn't any idea of letting it appear that she has. She much prefers to meet him accidentally. It is Lucille's idea that it will have to be very accidental. She hasn't much faith in Hart's continuing interest in Eileen—the way he went away, and the way he acted after he got away. He certainly did not exactly keep the wires hot while he was gone.

"He wrote to me every place he went," insists Eileen.

"Yah, if you call picture postcards writing."

"He was busy most of the time. It was a business trip."

"He certainly sent you a beautiful view of the Detroit Athletic Club. (EILEEN *glares at her.*) And that new waterworks in Cleveland. A man that didn't care about you would have sent a picture of the *old* waterworks. He's kind of a Latin type. Hot-blooded."

"You can say all you want to. Just the same, when he finds I've been going out with Stevens he's going to be insanely jealous. You watch him."

"Well, maybe. But he didn't even wire you for a date tonight. It's the first time he hasn't done that."

"He's taking it for granted. That's even better."

Now Fred and Paul are back, and still excited. They hope Eileen's right—that she and Lucille have brought them luck, and Fred is prepared, if Mr. Hart buys the song, to stage a celebration for the four of them.

Eileen gets her wish. Mr. Hart runs plump into her without expecting it. The meeting flusters him a little, but he soon recovers. Eileen tries to put him at his ease by recounting the wonderful time she has been having showing Mr. Stevens the city. Fred admits that he has not known Miss Fletcher long, but they certainly are good friends. Which seems to give Mr. Hart an idea. He is more anxious than before to hear "June Moon." Let them hunt up Maxie and get right at it.

Lucille is still anxious about Eileen's plans respecting Fred Stevens and the Hart complication. If Hart should buy the song and Fred should give a party, what is Eileen going to do about it? Eileen is going to decide that later. She can fix anything with Fred, he's that far gone he will believe anything.

Lucille is also anxious that the song shall be a hit, although she knows that even if it is Paul is so far behind on his royalties that it will mean little or nothing to her. "He could write 'Madame Butterfly' and it wouldn't even get me a new girdle," says she.

In line with which confession Lucille admits thinking seriously of letting another man help her. She has met an old sweetheart, Ed Knowlton, and Ed, after a drink or two, had wanted to help her right away. He is married and has a couple of kids, but he isn't happy. He can't get rid of his wife because her uncle or somebody owns the business. But he wants Lucille to be happy.

"I don't know what to do," Lucille admits to Eileen. "You and I look at things different. But Ed's so nice. The things he says —they make me feel young again. And it's such a relief to talk to a man that hates music!"

Fred rushes back into the room. Mr. Hart has taken the song! His first song is about to be published! And they're making him out a check for two hundred and fifty dollars!

The good news is shortly confirmed by Mr. Hart himself. He's quite proud of Fred. "What do you think of this young man?" he asks Eileen. "Making good in his first attempt?"

"It's wonderful."

"Yes, indeed!" chimes in Lucille.

HART—And Paul, too. He's written a nice little melody. Did you get your check, Stevens?

FRED—No, sir. Not yet.

HART—Goldie'll bring it to you.

MAXIE (*crossing to his own office*)—Well, thought you people would be on your way by this time.

EILEEN—We are waiting for Fred's check!

MAXIE—I'll bet you are. (*He leaves.*)

FRED—Mr. Hart! We were all planning on going some place tonight, to celebrate the success of the song. We'd love to have you come along with us, if you can. (*A moment of embarrassment.* EILEEN *waits.*)

HART—Well, now, I'd like to do that, but I'm very sorry. (HART *starts talking to Fred, but shifts his gaze to* EILEEN.) You see, I just got back from this trip, and I'm tied up with Mr. Goebel tonight.

FRED—Oh, that's too bad.

EILEEN (*with some meaning*)—Yes, it is.

HART—I'm sure you'll have a wonderful time. Can't tell you how much I'd like to be along. But of course, business comes first. (*A very beautiful young lady enters. Her name is* MISS RIXEY.)

MISS RIXEY—Hello, Joe. Am I late?

HART (*after clearing his throat*)—Miss Rixey, isn't it?

MISS RIXEY (*puzzled at this reception*)—What?

HART—Ah—they told me you were coming.

MISS RIXEY (*coming right up to him*)—You knew damn well I was coming.

HART (*still trying to cover up*)—Did you bring those orchestrations?

MISS RIXEY (*holding up a bundle which obviously contains two bottles of liquor*)—You mean this?

HART (*sunk by this time; grabs her by arm and rushes her into his office*)—Ah—just step into my office and we'll talk business.

MISS RIXEY—Listen, Joe, that driver of yours is so damn dumb—

HART (*loudly*)—Yes, we publish that! Right this way!

LUCILLE (*airily, when they are gone*)—Well, well, well!

FRED—It's too bad he can't go, but the four of us can have a good time.

EILEEN (*recklessly*)—Have a good time! You bet we can! We're going to have the best time any crowd ever had! Aren't we, Freddy boy? (*Throws her arms around him and kisses him.*)

FRED—We sure are, girlie!

GOLDIE (*coming on*)—Here's your check, Mr. Stevens.

PAUL—Great!

EILEEN—Hooray! Here's the check! (*She takes it.*)

FRED—Just in time!

EILEEN—Two hundred and fifty dollars! You've just got to give me a great big kiss!

LUCILLE—Oh, you two!

EILEEN—Do you love me?

FRED—You bet I do!

LUCILLE—Where'll we go for dinner?

PAUL—I want a good steak.

EILEEN—What about the Park Casino?

LUCILLE—Oh, fine! I've never been there! I hear it's marvelous.

EILEEN—They've got the most wonderful band! You'll love it, Freddie boy!

FRED—I will if you're along!

EILEEN—I'm going to be, don't you worry about that! Wherever you are, that's where I'm going to be!

FRED—That suits me all right!

LUCILLE—Come on, everybody!

PAUL—Don't forget we got to stop at the Astor!

EILEEN (*waving the check*)—I should say not! We're not going to forget that, are we, Freddie boy?

FRED—You bet we aren't! (*They are gone;* GOLDIE *alone is left. She picks out some songs from the shelves.* EDNA, *the girl he left behind him, peeps in, then enters.*)

EDNA—Do you know if they've heard Mr. Stevens's song yet? I mean "June Moon"?

GOLDIE (*pretty hard-boiled*)—Yah. They did.

EDNA (*starting brightly forward*)—Was it all right? Did they like it?

GOLDIE (*surveying her*)—They took it.

EDNA (*in pleased excitement*)—Really! Where are they? Still in there?

GOLDIE—Not any more. They've all gone.

EDNA—What?

GOLDIE—They went out just a couple of minutes ago.

EDNA—Mr.—Stevens too?

GOLDIE—Yah. Mr. Sears and the two girls, too.

EDNA—Oh! . . . Thank you very much. (GOLDIE *takes a moment to look her up and down, then goes.* EDNA *stands stockstill for a moment, stunned. The door opens; the window cleaner returns, sponge still in hand. He looks at* EDNA *a bit curiously; the scrutiny is more than she can stand. She rushes out.*)

THE CURTAIN FALLS

ACT III

A month later, in the music room at Goebel's, Benny, the author of the ill-fated "Tokio," is telling Goldie, the patient filing clerk, a part of his troubles. He was robbed of "Tokio" by a certain party who heard him play over the song and went and wrote "Hello, Shanghai!" What's worse, Maxie insists the stolen number is the better of the two because Shanghai is farther away than Tokio! So far as Benny is concerned, he is through with this Goebel-Hart outfit. Let them get along without him if they can—they and their cheap "June Moon" hit. The oldest idea in the world a hit! And Benny writes a great novelty, but no one will listen to it. It sounds like a tough break.

Paul Sears is in looking for Fred Stevens. Paul has been worried about Fred. Here they have an order for a lot of new numbers, after the hit of "June Moon," and Stevens doesn't seem to want to work. Mr. Hart is also worried about Stevens, but he has enough other troubles to occupy him most of the time. One of them is Benny.

Benny has a new song. "The title is 'Give Our Child a Name,' " he explains eagerly, to the impatient Mr. Hart. "It'll make 'June Moon' sound like a dirge. It's a couple that give birth to a little one in two-four tempo."

"It won't do you any good knocking Stevens' number."

"I ain't knocking his lousy number, but get this, Mr. Hart—"

He is at the piano in a single jump and has just started—

"Should a father's carnal sins
Blight the life of babykins?
All I ask is give our child a—"

when the missing Fred appears, with Eileen. They have been out buying clothes for Fred, Eileen explains. That's why they are late. They're sailing Saturday, which is a little frightening to Fred. He would really like to put it off a month. But Eileen, he explains, wants to be on the "Riveer" in the season.

"Well, I hope they don't take you at Monte Carlo," cheerily warns Hart.

"If they don't take us there we can go somewhere else." Fred is sure of that.

Mr. Hart is gone before Fred can take up with him a little matter that Eileen is urging—a matter of getting a further advance, it now appears.

Eileen—Don't forget—you're to ask him for a thousand dollars advance on each of them.

Fred—But that's too much! I've borrowed thirty-five hundred dollars off them already on "June Moon"—maybe more than my royalties will amount to altogether.

Eileen—Don't be ridiculous! That number will still be selling when you're dead.

Fred—I won't care so much then.

Eileen—Your children will. (Fred *is embarrassed.*) Don't you want children, dear?

Fred—I don't get along with them very well.

Eileen—You would with your own.

Fred—No. I figure I'd get along better with other people's, because they'd go home once in a while.

Eileen—We needn't think of that now. Let's just think of you and me, all alone on that big boat.

Fred—We won't be alone. The fella said it would be pretty near full.

Eileen—But we don't have to see anybody. A bride and groom don't generally go around much—they're supposed to be so awfully in love.

Fred—I'll want to eat once in a while.

Eileen—They'll serve us in our cabin.

Fred—It'll be kind of close quarters. Maybe I could go in the dining room and order you a meal sent up.

Eileen—And leave me all alone? I'd be scared to death.

FRED—It's just as dangerous in the dining room as the bedroom. If the ship sinks, pretty near all the rooms will be under water.

EILEEN—Let's not think about such things. Just think of the pleasant side, London and Paris—I'm glad we're going to Paris first, so I can get some clothes.

FRED—Clothes? What have you been buying?

EILEEN—They're all right for the ship, dear, but not the Riviera. Don't you want to be proud of me—the way I look?

FRED—But if you're going to stay in your cabin all the time you won't need nothing but a Mother Hubbard. (MAXIE *comes in.* EILEEN *automatically starts to go.*)

MAXIE—Well! All ready for the big trip?

FRED—Pretty near. The boat sails Saturday.

MAXIE—I don't know what you want to go to Europe for.

EILEEN (*bristling*)—Why not?

MAXIE—Because he's never been there. A song writer never goes anywhere for the first time—they're always going back to places. Back to Indiana—back, back to Baltimore.

EILEEN (*annoyed*)—Fred, are you going to talk to Mr. Hart?

FRED—Yes, ma'am.

EILEEN—Well, this should be a good time. (*She goes, in about medium dudgeon.*)

FRED—I'd like to be going back, back to Schenectady, but Eileen's got her heart set on Europe.

MAXIE—I hear it's quite a place.

FRED—Yes, I guess so. I was kind of excited about it at first, but now I don't know— I don't want to go bad. I'm kind of tired, I guess—the way we been going it lately. I'm kind of behind on my sleep.

MAXIE (*appraisingly*)—But you've been having a lot of fun. All those night clubs.

FRED—I did at first—dancing and everything—but now my feet's so sore I have to take a bath every day. You might as well take a whole bath as just your feet. And they ache so I can't sleep in them. Gosh, I'm so tired all the time. I don't have time to sleep anyway. We shop till the stores is closed, and then we get dressed up for dinner and the evening. If I don't get some rest soon I'll have a nervous break-up. And everything costs so much. Eileen wants a taxi if she's only going in the other room.

MAXIE—This trip to Europe—that's going to be kind of expensive, too, ain't it?

FRED—Yes. I always thought I'd save my money, if I ever got any.

MAXIE—You picked out a thrifty girl, all right.

FRED—I kind of get thinking sometimes, maybe a man like I that's just breaking in, maybe he shouldn't get married so soon, especially a woman that's got to have so many clothes. Sometimes I think it would be better if I hadn't got engaged.

MAXIE (*feeling his way*)—I read of a case once, in Michigan, where a man was engaged to a girl and didn't marry her.

FRED—I didn't read that. Have you got the clippings?

MAXIE—No. But my memory's pretty good. For instance, I remember a mighty nice little girl that was here to see you one time. I even remember her name—Miss Baker.

FRED (*nervously*)—Maxie, you haven't seen her or anything, have you?

MAXIE—Me? No. Why?

FRED (*uneasily*)—I guess I shouldn't be thinking of her at a time like this—

MAXIE—Are you?

FRED—I don't know. Sometimes I— (GOLDIE *enters, bound for those same old music shelves. It is a welcome interruption so far as* FRED *is concerned.*)

FRED—I got to find Paul. I got to do some work. (*He withdraws.*)

Maxie is seriously concerned about Stevens. As seriously concerned as Maxie can be about anything. He admits as much to Goldie. Goes even further and admits that he has already done something about it. He has got in touch with Edna Baker.

Maxie might have admitted even more, but Lucille Sears bustling into the room at the moment stops him. This is "a new Lucille, patently. She wears a gorgeous red dress, topped off with a coat of the same material, trimmed in white fur. But it's not only the clothes. She has that note of assurance that only the perfectly dressed woman can have."

But Lucille is not altogether comfortable in her mind. She starts visibly when Maxie suggests that she looks like a bride herself. Nor does Eileen's enthusiasm over the new dress help a great deal, when she comes. Lucille is frankly conscious and fearfully afraid of what Paul may think. And say. And do.

Paul is naturally suspicious at sight of the new finery, but more easily mollified than Lucille expects, for when she intimates that she has bought the outfit on credit, he thinks he will probably be able to take care of it when payment is due.

But Paul has another problem in his mind. He is not entirely satisfied with the way things have been going with young Stevens. Eileen has the boy so high in the air he and Fred can hardly work at all, and he has come to think a lot of Fred. Besides, is it right for Eileen to be taking him on this European trip? Or for her to be spending his money the way she is? It strikes Paul as a sort of dirty trick, especially when he remembers Hart—and everything.

LUCILLE—You ought to have more sense.

PAUL—Just the same, I don't feel right about it. And the way she's throwing his money around—like it was confetti. Spending every nickel she can get on herself! Clothes, clothes—

LUCILLE—You can't go to Europe in a life belt.

PAUL—Do you know what she spent in one afternoon, yesterday? Close to four hundred dollars. He pretty near cried when he told me. And I don't blame him. He's too nice a kid.

LUCILLE—She doesn't spend that every day.

PAUL—She shouldn't have spent it at all. You should have had more sense than to let her.

LUCILLE (*flaring a little*)—How could I stop her? I wasn't there.

PAUL—Yes, you were! You were with her all afternoon.

LUCILLE (*quickly covering herself*)—Oh, yes. I thought you meant the day before.

PAUL—It was Sunday, the day before.

LUCILLE—Yah— I just got mixed up, that's all.

PAUL—Anyhow, something ought to be done about it. She's got him in debt enough.

LUCILLE (*nervously*)—I'll talk to her about it. (*Starts out.*) Don't you say anything to her. Don't say anything about— I mean, what she spent yesterday afternoon. I'll go and talk to her. (*She gets away.*)

When Edna Baker arrives in search of Maxie she finds the music room occupied principally by Benny Fox. And she finds Benny still trying desperately to get some one to listen to his new song, "Give Our Child a Name." Edna, being timidly uncertain about a lot of things, has no chance of stopping him, so she thinks perhaps she should be going. But Benny holds her.

BENNY—Wait—you want to hear a great song? You know who I am, don't you? I'm Benny Fox, the hit writer. I write words and music both. I'm like Berlin, only more pathetic. Now I gotta new one. It's about a couple that have a baby without benefit to a clergyman, and you can dance to it. (*He plays it.*)

"Should a father's carnal sins
Blight the life of babykins?
All I ask is give our child a name—I mean a last name.
I don't ask to share your life,
Live with you as man and wife;
All I ask is give our child a name—not just a first name."

(MAXIE *comes on.*) Hello, Maxie. I'll start over so you can get this. "Should a father's carnal sins—"

MAXIE (*looking at* EDNA)—Wait a minute! Isn't this—Miss Baker?

EDNA—And you're Mr. Schwartz.

MAXIE—Correct!

BENNY—Come on, Maxie! Get a load of this! "Should a father's carnal sins—"

MAXIE—Go back to your cell! We want to talk!

BENNY—But she wants to hear this number!

MAXIE (*gets an idea*)—Listen! You don't know who she is.

BENNY—No.

MAXIE—Well! Remember what happened to "Tokio." (*It's a case of the burnt child.* BENNY *scoots out, throwing a look back at* EDNA *as he goes.*)

MAXIE—My, but I'm glad to see you!

EDNA—It's nice of you to say so, anyway.

MAXIE—I guess it was kind of nervy of me, calling you up that way. Hope you didn't mind.

EDNA—Why—no. I—I thought it was very friendly.

MAXIE—Of course it ain't really any of my business exactly, but—nobody else was doing anything, so I thought I would. Probably you can guess who it's about.

EDNA—Tell me about him! What's happened? What's happened to him?

MAXIE—Do you mind if I ask a question? I think I know the answer.

EDNA—What?

MAXIE—You're in love with him, aren't you? (EDNA *turns away.*) You know, you can tell me. I'm for you—I want to help you. You do—love him? (EDNA *nods.*) Enough to keep him from—ruining himself?

EDNA—How do you mean?

MAXIE—He's engaged to be married. You know that?

EDNA—I—supposed that was it.

MAXIE—But he's not happy. He's not in love with her.

EDNA (*breaking out*)—I can't do anything! He doesn't love me! He never did!

MAXIE—Somebody's got to do something. He's not a fellow that can think for himself. They left that out.

EDNA—Oh, why did you make me come here? I shouldn't have done it—I don't know why I did! I've been trying every way to forget him—I went away, and I didn't see anybody, and then I went around with lots of people—it only made it worse. I kept wanting to call him up, and once I did, only—I hung up before he could come to the telephone.

MAXIE—Let me bring him in here.

EDNA—No, no! I don't want to talk to him! I mustn't!

MAXIE—But he's in trouble. And you're the only one that can help him.

EDNA—He don't want to see *me!*

MAXIE—Let me tell him you're here. It can't do any harm. (EDNA *is silent.*) You needn't answer. Only promise me one thing.

EDNA—What?

MAXIE—No matter what happens, come and see me afterwards. Will you? (EDNA *nods.*) The second door on the left, down that hall. (MAXIE *goes.* EDNA *is alone for a moment. Two moments, even. Then a pretty stirred* FRED *comes on.*)

FRED—Hello, Eddie.

EDNA—Hello.

FRED—I'm awful glad to see you, Eddie! Gee, but I'm glad to see you!

EDNA—I didn't really come to— I mean, it was Mr. Schwartz that made me talk to you.

FRED—My, but it's great to see you again. I didn't know how great it would be.

EDNA—I'm glad to see you, too, Fred. I'm glad you're well and that you're going to be—happy.

FRED—I been thinking about you, Eddie—an awful lot, lately. I been waking up in the morning, thinking about you.

EDNA—Are you waking up in the morning again, Fred?

FRED—I been going to call you up to tell you about it. We

used to have a lot of fun together. (*Eagerly.*) Remember that day in Van Cortlandt Park when I lost my watch and that little boy found it?

EDNA—And you gave him a nickel.

FRED—It was a dime. And he said, "Keep it and buy your wife a radio set." He thought we was married. (*He laughs, as though trying to induce a mood of merriment in* EDNA.)

EDNA—I remember.

FRED—You was embarrassed, all right. You got red.

EDNA—Any girl would.

FRED—And then coming back we forgot to change at Seventy-second Street. That is, you forgot. I didn't know any better.

EDNA—I just wasn't thinking.

FRED—We had to go all the way down to Times Square. That's when we saw the flea circus.

EDNA—You said one of the fleas reminded you of a man in Schenectady.

FRED—Yeah. Perry Robinson. He always walked like he'd just picked up a nail. (FRED *drops the pretense and comes out with it.*) Eddie, did Maxie say anything to you? About me?

EDNA (*in agony*)—He said you were going to be married, Fred. I should have congratulated you.

FRED (*suddenly*)—I don't want to any more, Eddie! I know it now! I don't want to!

EDNA—Don't say that, Fred! Don't! Don't say it unless you mean it! I couldn't stand it!

FRED—But I do mean it, Eddie! I mean it more than anything in the— (EILEEN *comes on. You might have guessed it.*)

EILEEN (*rather gayly*)—I'm sorry.

FRED (*making up his mind*)—No—don't go away. This is—Miss Fletcher.

EILEEN (*appraisingly*)—Hello.

FRED—And this is Miss Baker. She's the little girl—I mean, I used to know her when—

EDNA (*who can't stand it*)—I'll be going if you don't mind. Good-bye, Fred.

FRED—No—look! Don't go away!

EDNA—Yes, I must! I—good-bye, Miss Fletcher! (*She rushes off.* FRED *hesitates for a second; then starts out after her.*)

Fred would have followed Edna if Eileen had not stopped him. Just what does he mean by acting that way? One would think

Miss Baker was the girl he was going to marry in place of her!

Fred frankly confesses now that he doesn't want to go on. He doesn't want to get married.

Whether he does or not, Eileen does not intend to give him up. He can't get out of an obligation that easily—just by saying he is through. Didn't he beg Eileen to marry him? Knowing that she was engaged to another man at the time. Worse than that, he has made her love him and now he wants to leave her. Is that honorable?

Honorable? The suggestion is an inspiration to Fred.

"Honorable?" he repeats, fervently. "That's just what I got to be. That's why I can't marry you."

"What do you mean?"

"I mean I got to marry another girl, to save her from—from worse than death."

"That little kid?"

"Yes."

"You mean you've got her in trouble?"

"Yes! That's it!"

"I don't believe you. I'm going to call her back."

"No! No! You mustn't tell her that," Fred cries.

"Why not?"

"I—I want to surprise her."

There is scorn in Eileen's look as she surveys him pityingly. "Did you think I was going to fall for any story like that?" she demands. "I'm the one you're engaged to and I'm the one you're going to marry."

It is a crestfallen Fred that Paul Sears faces when he breaks in upon this scene. Eileen is as smilingly triumphant as circumstances warrant and feels safe in leaving the men together.

Fred doesn't feel like working. Perhaps he will feel more like it in the morning. Besides, he has to go get his passport. He had planned to get it yesterday, but he had to go shopping with Eileen. Now Paul remembers. And Fred must have had a swell time running around with two women all day.

Two women? There weren't two. Only one. Only Eileen!

From which it develops that Lucille had not been one of the party. Nor can she explain why she lied about it when she was asked where and when she got her new gown.

Now Eileen is in and ready to defend her sister. The dress? Well, she bought it for Lucille if Paul wants to know. And Lucille hadn't told him for fear he wouldn't let her take it.

Where was Lucille the disputed afternoon? Well, she went to a matinee—with an old friend. On Monday? To the Palace? Yes? Who was on the bill? Who were the headliners?

LUCILLE (*panic in her voice*)—I don't see what difference that makes.

PAUL (*not raising his tone*)—You—dirty—lying—double-crosser!

EILEEN—That's not true.

LUCILLE (*stopping* EILEEN)—Keep still! I'm sick of the whole thing! (*She faces* PAUL.) Yes! . . . Yes, if you want to know! . . . Yes and to hell with you! Did you think I was going to wait around forever for you to give me the things I wanted? God knows I waited long enough! And then—I just didn't wait any longer, that's all. What do you know about that? Huh? What do you know about that? (PAUL *is stunned. Turns slowly away.*) So that's the way that stands! (*She takes a step toward the door; breaks into sobs.* EILEEN *goes to her; puts her arm around her.*)

FRED—But—but you mean to say that when you were married to *him*— (*He takes a moment, trying to realize it. Then, to* EILEEN.) But *you* must have known she was doing it!

EILEEN—What? Why—no, I didn't.

FRED—Yes. You said you bought her the dress.

PAUL (*a scornful laugh*)—Known she was doing it! She put her up to it!

EILEEN—That's not true!

PAUL—No? Well, then I'll tell you something that is true!

EILEEN—Don't you believe him, Fred!

PAUL—And thank God I've got the courage to tell you at last!

EILEEN—He's just a liar, that's what he is! I tell you he's a liar!

FRED—Why, what is it?

PAUL—You didn't know your fiancée had a lover, did you?

FRED—What?

EILEEN—I tell you it's a lie! He's just trying to separate us!

PAUL—Am I?

EILEEN—He's just making it up!

PAUL—She told you she was engaged to be married! Well, she wasn't. He was her lover, and he kicked her out, and that's why she took up with you! I'd have told you long ago, if I hadn't been a coward!

FRED (*staggered, turns to* EILEEN)—Is this true?

EILEEN (*in final realization that the game is up*)—Of course it is, you little fool!

FRED—Gosh!

EILEEN—That's probably a pretty big shock to those fine up-stage morals of yours.

FRED—Then I been going around all this time with a—bad woman?

EILEEN—And now have we both got permission to go, or does somebody else want to speak? (*Spotting* EDNA, *who has been brought on the scene by* MAXIE.) Maybe your little girl friend would like to say a few words?

FRED—If she does, she'll say them to me. And I'll know I can believe them, too.

EILEEN—I'm sure you'll understand each other. What's more, you're probably the only two people in the world that would. Come on, Lucille. (*She surveys the lovers.*) I want to come and visit that child of yours—next month. (LUCILLE *and* EILEEN *go.* PAUL *has dropped into a chair, his head buried in his hands.*)

FRED (*turning to where* EDNA *and* MAXIE *stand*)—Eddie, I—I don't have to marry her.

EDNA—I'm so happy, Fred.

FRED—I'm sorry, Paul, about—everything.

PAUL—That's all right. I'm glad if I helped fix things for you. I should have told you long ago. (*He goes.*)

FRED—Only look! I've still got the ticket for the boat, and it says, "Frederick M. Stevens and Wife." And I wonder if the steamship allow you to change your wife?

MAXIE—Yes. If you don't do it in midstream.

EDNA—If your wife is the right kind she won't let you take her on an expensive trip. She'll make you put everything into a home. I don't mean a big home—just a little bungalow would do.

FRED—Bungalow! A bungalow for two! That'd be a great title!

MAXIE—And I've got a great tune! (MAXIE *goes into "Button Up Your Overcoat."* FRED *is enchanted—to him it is something that* MAXIE *has composed on the spur of the moment. He starts improvising words.*)

FRED—"In a bungalow for two,
Where we can bill and coo—"

THE CURTAIN FALLS

MICHAEL AND MARY

A Comedy in Three Acts

By A. A. Milne

WHEN Mr. Milne first wrote "Michael and Mary" it was designed as one of those flashback dramas that have, since "On Trial" set the pattern sixteen years ago, often proved exciting and satisfying theatre entertainment.

Mr. Milne had begun his romance in the present when the son born to Michael and Mary Rowe was facing a marriage, or at least a love problem of his own. Certain things he said then caused Michael and Mary to review their own lives in retrospect and as they sat looking backward what they saw was enacted on the stage.

But while he was at work something happened to change Mr. Milne's mind regarding the technique to be employed, and the play was altered to its present form.

Also the first title was "This Flower," taken from a quotation of Shakespeare's "King Henry V"—"Out of this nettle, danger, we pluck this flower, safety," though Michael had substituted "self-respect" for "safety."

Once there was some thought of calling the piece "The Adorable Criminals," but Mr. Milne was quick to protest. He had not forgotten the impudence of the film men who had changed "The Dover Road" to "The Little Adventuress." Finally, after many conferences, "Michael and Mary" was agreed upon.

The play was sent, act by act, from the work room of the author in London to the office of Charles Hopkins in New York. Mr. Hopkins has been to Milne much the same sort of help and inspiration that Charles Frohman was to Barrie in the old days. Before "Michael and Mary" he had produced successfully two other Milne comedies, "The Ivory Door" and "The Perfect Alibi." Both these plays achieved long runs, largely because of their popular appeal, partly, no doubt, because the Hopkins Theatre is small (seating no more than 299 persons) and the expense of its maintenance therefore appreciably less than that of most Broadway theatres. It is a happy combination of author and producer, vastly appreciated by a constantly growing Milne-Hopkins public in New York.

"Michael and Mary" was produced on December 13 and ran well into the summer with very little seasonal decline in the interest of its audiences.

At the play's beginning the meeting of Michael Rowe and Mary Weston occurs one May morning in 1905 in one of those recessed galleries of the British Museum in which it is often easy to escape briefly from the observation of such visitors as may be wandering about.

Mary is sitting huddled up on a broad bench placed in an aisle between showcases, crying quietly. "She is young, not more than twenty, too forlorn now to look as pretty as she might, shabbily dressed in the middle-class fashion of 1905. She herself is negatively middle-class. She has been 'brought up nicely' but you feel that she might use the wrong words now and then, although her voice is too gentle ever to offend you, however middle-class, in moments of emotion, her mode of speech may become."

Michael, coming quickly around the corner of an alcove, becomes suddenly aware of Mary. He had not expected to find a stranger on that particular bench. He stops awkwardly, trying to appear interested in the showcases. Michael "is young, happy, obviously intelligent, shy in an emergency, but not for that reason tongue-tied; rather specially well-dressed today in a first-of-the-season flannel suit and straw hat. In fact it is clear that he is meeting somebody, and wishing she wouldn't always be late."

After considerable restless fidgeting, and a good deal of anxious looking up and down the corridor, Michael decides he would like to sit down, too, if Mary doesn't mind. When her attitude suggests that she does mind, or feels at least that she should pretend to mind, Michael becomes quite chattily apologetic. So much so that Mary soon comes to accept him as harmless and rather interesting.

Michael is so happy at the moment that he feels he must talk with someone. Presently he has confessed that he is there to meet someone; that the someone is a young woman in whom he is interested; that he has, in fact, given some thought to marriage but, when it comes to that, what could he marry on?

Mary is a little bitter on the subject of marriage. Nor does she agree that it all depends on the person you marry. How can anyone know a person one has no more than taken out to lunch? Or dinner? And noticed that he or she behaves quite well in such surroundings? You can't really know a person by just meeting him.

It is Michael's idea that meetings and marriages are a good deal a matter of chance anyway. Like being the one unfortunate in thousands hit by a motor car. Luckily it's always the other fellow who gets run over.

"Not always," sighs Mary, after a noticeable pause.

"I say, *you* haven't been run over, have you?" demands Michael, quite concerned, "you know what I mean?"

MARY (*violently*)—Never you mind about *me*. I didn't want to talk to you, did I? I didn't try to, did I?

MICHAEL—Oh, Lord, no, I began it. You see, the hereditary weakness of the Rowes is that they simply cannot stand about on one leg. They must sit down. And we couldn't sit on the same seat and not say anything to each other, could we? It's all right in a train, where you can gaze into the middle distance, and wonder if you've packed your toothbrush, but sitting right up against a wall—I say, you aren't crying? No, I say, you mustn't, not on my birthday.

MARY (*breaking down altogether*)—Oh, what can I do? What can I do? I can't just die.

MICHAEL (*sliding along the seat and taking her hand*)—Look here, you're not going to die. Hold tight on to that. You're *all* right. Say to yourself, "I'm all right now because I've found somebody and I'm going to talk it over with him." Whatever it is, it will help you to talk it over with somebody.

MARY (*pulling away her hand and getting up*)—Yes, I'm all right now. Good-bye, I'm glad you're happy.

MICHAEL (*putting out his hand to stop her*)—No, I say, look here—

MARY (*striking the hand away*)—Oh, I hate you, I hate you all —*horrible* men! Let me go!

MICHAEL (*bowing in his best manner*)—I beg your pardon. (*He stands on one side.*)

MARY—Horrid *gentlemen! He* was a gentleman, too. He behaved beautifully at lunch.

MICHAEL—Oh!—Oh! Now I see— And then you—married him?

MARY—And then I married him. (*She drops down on to the seat again.*)

MICHAEL (*looking at her*)—I didn't think of you as married.

You're so young. (*After a pause.*) You really are? That sounds caddish, but I mean if he was that sort of man—

MARY—I can't show you the wedding ring because I pawned it a month ago— What do you think I got for it?

MICHAEL—Oh, don't! This is horrible.

MARY—Half a crown. It looked like gold, but it wasn't gold. Just gilt-edged— Same as him.

MICHAEL (*more to himself than to her*)—I always wonder how any woman can marry any man. I should be terrified if I were a woman.

Mary's story is the not unusual one of the girl in the shop who meets a man who behaves nicely at lunch and ends by marrying him. After a time Mary's husband tired of married life and left her. Left her with a humorous letter to remember him by, because Mary's husband was by nature a funny man.

"Dear Mary," she reads Michael from the letter in her bag, "Good-bye to England, Home and Beauty. I'm off to Philadelphia in the morning." (*That's a quotation, so it's funny, explains* MARY.) "Sorry I can't stop, but we really don't suit each other. I like them plumper and covered with diamonds and rubies. You'll find another man easy enough, and if you like to marry him I shan't forbid the bands. I was always fond of music." (*That's another funny bit, about the bands, notes* MARY.) "Hoping this finds you as well as it leaves me at present, Your Loving Husband, Harry. P.S. My address is a coat and trousers so I'm afraid I can't leave it to you."

It is a funny letter, Mary agrees, but she has not been quite able to appreciate it at its funniest. Since then she has tried to go back to the shop but there was no place for her. She has tried other shops, also, without success. Now, like many others, she is sitting on a bench telling a hard luck story to a sympathetic listener without a penny in her purse. Wasn't it clever of her to empty the purse?

"Aren't I doing it well?" Mary demands, her voice following an ascending scale of hysteria.

"If you're not telling me the truth then there's no truth in the world, and nothing matters," solemnly declares Michael.

There isn't much to the rest of the story, except that Mary has that day been turned out of her lodgings; that she is utterly alone and utterly destitute and that what she had planned to do that night need not be frightening if one does not think about it.

Michael *is* thinking about it, and very seriously, when Violet Cunliffe appears on the scene. Violet is the girl Michael has been waiting for. There is a difference between Mary and Violet—"between Mary and the Real Thing."

"Mary herself feels it; you can see her stiffen," reports the author, "you can see Violet stiffen, too, just for a moment; or no—you can't see it. That is not her way. She lets her glance wander coolly, appraisingly over Mary and all at once we (and Mary) realize what a common little thing Mary is. Even so, Mary is a woman, and Violet knows it; one man again to two women; and Mary has been crying, and will therefore win—and Violet knows it. But she will carry it off; see how gallantly she does it."

Violet is quite casual with Michael, and a little cool and aloof as Michael tries awkwardly to introduce her to Mary, or Mary to her.

As for Mary, she is on her feet now and ready to leave. She would go, even though Michael insists that she shall not. Everything is quite all right with her, Mary snaps, defiantly. All that she had told Michael was a lie. That's how she makes her living.

But Michael can see that she is lying now. Mary is desperately in need, Michael explains to Violet. She's absolutely starving, even though she may say she isn't. It would be a fine thing, thinks Michael, if they were all to go to lunch together! Vi could help Mary a lot, if she would!

VIOLET (*to* MARY)—Isn't he doing it badly? Men are so funny like that. (*To* MICHAEL.) Too sweet of you to ask me, Michael, but I'm afraid I'm engaged. Do take Miss—your friend—out instead.

MARY (*doing her best to live up to* VIOLET)—I'm engaged, too.

MICHAEL (*angrily*)—What's the matter with you all? (VIOLET *again seems to share a secret with* MARY *as to the absurd stupidity of men.*) You're lunching with *me*. It was all arranged.

VIOLET (*shaking her head at him in amusement*)—Oh, no, Michael. That was yesterday. Don't you remember? We had a delightful lunch. I'm meeting somebody else here today. (*To* MARY.) It's a great meeting-place, the British Museum, isn't it, Miss— I do wish I knew your name. Or is it a secret?

MARY (*like a servant giving her name to her employer*)—Weston.

VIOLET (*graciously*)—Thank you. Michael, let me introduce you to your friend, Miss Weston. (*To* MARY.) This is Mr.

Michael Rowe. Well, I must fly. (*Looking at her watch.*) Gracious, I'm nearly half an hour late. (*To both, with a smile.*) Good-bye! Have a good lunch!

MICHAEL (*in a last desperate attempt to explain the unexplainable*)—Vi!

VIOLET (*as she goes*)—Can't stop a minute, dear boy. *I'm* absolutely starving, too.

All suggestion of a smile has gone from Violet's face as she turns and leaves them. Michael is bewildered and troubled. And Mary is determined that she, whose pride is quite as important as that of Violet, will not be the gainer by this unhappy situation. Michael can write Violet and explain everything. And she (Mary) will take nothing from him.

"If that's pride it's nothing to be proud of," suggests Michael, quietly. "It's like the wedding ring he gave you—pretending to be gold. You know, if the house is on fire and a woman refuses to be saved in her nightgown, she isn't being modest, she's being shameful and horrible. If *you* were wrecked in mid-Atlantic, would you refuse to be rescued until you had been introduced to the captain, and paid him for the use of his boat? Well, you're shipwrecked now, and my sail has just come over the horizon. Thank God for it."

Mary is quite impressed now. Michael, she discovers, is not a silly boy, but a man. And Michael is suddenly full of plans. He is not, he insists, a little sharply, in love with Miss Cunliffe, so Mary need not worry about that.

Michael has two hundred pounds in the bank and rooms in Islington. (It's a cheapish part of London, and Lamb used to live there.) He is trying to be a writer, but if he doesn't earn anything for a year he can still live on half his balance. And Mary can live on the other half, if she will!

They are young enough to do anything, says Michael, Mary 20 and he 23, and they have a year certain to do it in. He knows he has something in the way of brains to work with, even if his father, who looks upon writing as just an excuse for shirking a real job of work, doesn't think so. Aside from that he has nothing but a fountain pen with a gold nib. "A nib, mark you, of solid gold; a golden nib indeed, as you will see one day."

"And you're going to give *me* half of all you have in the world?" demands Mary incredulously.

"Don't keep on saying 'all you have in the world,'" pleads Michael, "as if it included a couple of yachts and a coal mine.

I'm going to give you the extremely small sum of 100 pounds—on certain conditions."

MARY—I'm glad there are conditions. (*Eagerly.*) Make them hard.

MICHAEL—Well, naturally, I shall want to know how you're getting on. So the first condition is that we meet once every week—let's make it Tuesday, because today's Tuesday—and have the cheapest possible dinner together (*hastily*)—or lunch, if you prefer it—and tell each other what sort of luck we've had in the last week. Agreed?

MARY (*happily*)—Yes.

MICHAEL—The second is—well, as a matter of fact I think that's all. Now it's your turn, Mrs. Weston. Make any conditions you like.

MARY—May I really?

MICHAEL—Of course.

MARY—Well, Weston is my maiden name. Mary Weston. So I'm either *Miss* Weston or Mrs. —— Do you mind if I keep to the Weston? I hate the other so—and I haven't got a wedding ring.

MICHAEL—Good idea. But now I'm going to make another condition. On the seventh Tuesday from now we have the cheapest-possible-dinner-but-one, and formally drop the "Mr." and "Miss." Agreed? (*She nods.*)

MARY—Now my second condition. Don't give me 100 pounds. Give me whatever it is every Tuesday. One pound something.

MICHAEL (*a sudden suspicion in his mind*)—You swear faithfully to *come* every Tuesday?

MARY—Yes. (*After a pause.*) Thank you. That was awfully sweet of you.

MICHAEL—What?

MARY—Knowing I should come if I had all the money at once, and being afraid I mightn't if I had to come for it each week. (*They looked at each other for a moment.*)

MICHAEL—Oh, well, but it's obvious.

MARY—I shan't forget. (*Timidly.*) There *was* one other—

MICHAEL—Fire away.

MARY—Could I—just once—just this once—just kiss your hand?

MICHAEL (*horribly embarrassed*)—Oh, please, please—

MARY (*snatching it and kissing it*)—Thank you. (*She begins to cry, utterly without control.*)

MICHAEL (*getting up and smacking her in a friendly way on the back*)—Come on, let's go and have that lunch.

THE CURTAIN FALLS

Fifteen months later the Rev. Simon Rowe, Michael's father, walks into his son's living room at Islington. It is a comfortable room, furnished largely with Michael's own things.

Simon Rowe is "a tall man and ungainly, a craggy, uncomfortable man, with human loves and desires and tenderness which have never settled down happily with his religion. He has an ugly, clean-shaven face, not without attraction, for you can conceive it the face of a man who would die for his beliefs. He loves Michael, but he can never forget that he is responsible for him, and to his God. To be a father at all is difficult; to be a father and a clergyman almost impossible; and so Michael and he have come to dread each other's company, knowing there can never be any real friendship between them. At least Michael knows this, but poor Simon Rowe always hopes that next time will be different."

Mrs. Tullivant, Michael's landlady, who is "forty-five, a big, friendly, kindly creature with almost a barmaid's allowance of fair hair, which is always on the verge of coming down," has brought the Rev. Rowe to his son's room and is eager to make such report of the young man as will do him credit.

Michael, says Mrs. Tullivant, spends a good share of his time in writing, and very good pieces, too, she judges from what she has read of them. Michael gets paid for them, too. At least there was one about Horace, the Tullivant infant, for which Michael received three guineas. With that money Michael and "his lady" had a celebration, Mrs. Tullivant reports. They had gone to the restaurant in which Mr. Tullivant is employed as a waiter and they had a grand time.

Mrs. Tullivant is also pleased to explain that young Mr. Rowe's "lady," the mention of whom worries the Rev. Rowe considerably, is none other than her second floor front. Mrs. Tullivant had had a gentleman lodger in that second floor front, but when he moved out and she had suggested to Mr. Rowe that he might have a friend who would like to move in, Mr. Rowe was off like a shot and when he came back he brought Miss Weston with him, much to Mrs. Tullivant's surprise.

"But there she was, the friend he came back with," she chortles, amiably, "and couldn't be more sweet; a clergyman's daughter herself, I daresay, and there's my eight and six regular every Saturday."

ROWE—I see. (*His mouth is very tight, and the atmosphere, even by Mrs. Tullivant, is unmistakeable.*)

MRS. TULLIVANT (*who is having none of it*)—Excuse me, sir, but you don't.

ROWE—I beg your pardon?

MRS. TULLIVANT (*firmly*)—Nothing of that sort goes on in *my* house.

ROWE—I didn't say anything.

MRS. TULLIVANT—Not say, but gave a look as much as to say.

ROWE—I assure you—

MRS. TULLIVANT—You can't deny, sir, that you drew an inference.

ROWE—Well, I admit I wondered—

MRS. TULLIVANT—That's it, sir, you wondered, which is why I felt called upon to answer. And speaking as a mother of five to a clergyman, which is free and open, I say that Mr. Rowe has slept upstairs and Miss Weston has slept downstairs every night.

ROWE—Really! I think we had better—

MRS. TULLIVANT (*now thoroughly worked up*)—If this wasn't my house which is respectable, and Mr. Rowe wasn't Mr. Rowe which is a gentleman, and Miss Weston wasn't Miss Weston which is a lady, I won't say there mightn't be comings and goings in the night which I wasn't aware of, being in my own bed and asleep when not attending to Horace which is in arms. But Mr. Rowe being Mr. Rowe—

ROWE (*to himself*)—Dear me, what a peculiar woman.

MRS. TULLIVANT (*annoyed*)—Yes, sir, we all have our peculiarities. You may have noticed that you have a slight cast in one eye yourself, sir, but I don't feel called upon to mention it, being none of my business and sorry for you.

ROWE (*candidly*)—You're quite right, Mrs. Tullivant, I have. I always hoped that nobody noticed it.

MRS. TULLIVANT—Well, that's frank of you, sir, and I *shouldn't* have noticed it, but for your saying what you did. And now I'll be frank too. I *am* peculiar. There's women as near this doorstep as would surprise you who wouldn't mind what went on in their house, but I'm not one of them. And being a peculiar woman, as you pointed out, sir, I say you have no cause to be thinking wicked things of your son.

ROWE—No, no, I'm sure you're right. (*To himself.*) But it's an anomalous position.

Mrs. Tullivant is not at all sure what an anomalous position may be, so she repeats her assertion that one room is on the second floor and the other on the third. Yes, Mr. Rowe and Miss Weston do breakfast together, but "if they never share anything more come-together than a coffee pot" Mrs. Tullivant seems convinced no great harm will be done.

Michael bursts upon them a moment later. Bursts is the word, because Michael is aglow. Sight of his father, however, serves for the moment to subdue him. Michael is as pleased as may be to see his father, and would have him stay to tea, but the Rev. Rowe is too hurried for that.

Now Mrs. Tullivant has left them and the subject of the Rev. Rowe's conversation with her, respecting the young woman in the second floor front, has come up.

Father is first concerned as to whether Miss Weston is or is not a lady. Michael isn't sure. He hasn't asked her lately. Probably not, seeing her father was a draper.

The fact that the Rev. Rowe's father also was a draper makes this sound a bit like a family insult, though Michael disclaims that intention.

"I'm sorry, father," Michael apologizes, "somehow you always seem to draw out the worst in me. But your question was an impossible one. Quite honestly I can think of no reasonable way of answering it. If I said yes it would mislead you. If I said no it would mislead you. Well, perhaps that is an answer in itself.

ROWE—I think I understand. Her father was not actually a draper?

MICHAEL—He may have been. Whatever he was, he's dead. So is her mother.

ROWE—She is alone in the world?

MICHAEL—Entirely.

ROWE—That puts a great responsibility on you, Michael.

MICHAEL (*gravely*)—I have known that for some time.

ROWE (*after a pause*)—Perhaps I may be allowed to ask without impertinence—Are you in love with her?

MICHAEL (*from the bottom of his heart*)—Oh, my *God,* yes!

ROWE (*standing up in cold anger*)—I don't wish to remind you again of my cloth, but if you cannot—

MICHAEL (*standing up and letting himself go*)—Oh, damn your cloth! It can sit in the presence of the abominations of the world, the horrible cruelties of the world, the conditions under which forgotten women suffer and unwanted children are born, and then dares to stand up and censure *me,* who have tried to do good, because I call on my God to witness that I love this—lady.

ROWE—That is not seriously advanced as an argument to which I am to reply?

MICHAEL (*dropping back into his chair*)—No, it's a joke. A screaming joke.

The Rev. Rowe recovers poise after a moment devoted to contemplating the scene from the window and returns to the statement of an important decision. He feels that, with all respect for Miss Weston, Michael should do something about her. He loves her. She probably loves him. But can Michael afford to marry?

"Yes," answers Michael, "I think, generally speaking, one can afford anything if one wants it badly enough. Life's pretty exciting anyhow; it would just be more exciting. And I'm hoping, of course, to do better as I go on."

The Rev. Rowe is doubtful. His own marriage, on eighty pounds a year, was a struggle. He is still paying for the bringing up of his children. He is still very poor. He could not help Michael. Furthermore, he feels that "a young man unable to support the responsibilities of marriage, yet unwilling to forego its pleasure," should look for a partner of his own class. If, however, Michael is convinced of his own love, and of Miss Weston's, then the Rev. Rowe would exact a promise that either Michael shall marry Mary or leave her before it is too late, before he has broken her life and dishonoured his own.

MICHAEL (*to himself*)—Oh, isn't it difficult, isn't it difficult!

ROWE—Is it too much to ask of my son?

MICHAEL—Oh, if you knew how much it is!

ROWE—And are you afraid of the responsibilities of marriage? There is no peace and lasting happiness to be found in pleasure, my son. There must be responsibility and struggle and danger (*His voice takes on the eloquence and beauty of the words he quotes.*) "where the immortal garland is to be run for, not without dust and heat."

MICHAEL (*looking up suddenly*)—Danger! (*His father's eyes are on him.*) Danger! You've said it! I'll give you a quotation, too. "Out of this nettle danger, we pluck this flower—" self-respect. That's it! That's the way. Yes, I promise. Marriage or—farewell to Islington. It's the only way. Why didn't I think of it before? Father, you're a genius!

ROWE (*ignoring whatever of this he doesn't understand*)—My dear boy, it was so obvious.

MICHAEL—No, no, it's very subtle.

ROWE (*getting up*)—Well, I must be going after my train. Thank you, Michael, you have made me very happy.

MICHAEL (*to himself*)—I ought to have seen it all along. Idiot!

ROWE (*feeling in his pockets*)—I had brought it along in any case, thinking it might be useful, but now, of course— (*He puts a five pound note on the table.*)

MICHAEL (*in sudden remorse*)—Oh, *no*, father, *no!*

ROWE—So many young people forget that marriage demands capital as well as income—if it's only for the ring and the marriage fees. So they begin their married life in debt and never get out of it. Well, even five pounds helps. At least it will buy the ring— (*He passes it across to his son.*)

MICHAEL (*in horror*)—Do you mean to say that you specially brought that for me and had it in your pocket all the time, when I was being so— (*Shaking his head.*) No, you mustn't. You don't know. I couldn't take it.

ROWE—Dear Michael, don't be absurd. Just a little tip to my own son. You aren't too old for that, are you?

MICHAEL—No, not too old, but—you don't know. Besides I know what five pounds means to you.

ROWE (*putting it back on the table*)—Well, I shall leave it here. From the moment that I went into the Bank yesterday and asked Mr. Barnes for a new five pound note, the money was yours, not mine.

MICHAEL—Look here, you swear it isn't a bribe or a reward or anything like that? I mean you did it for me anyhow before you knew about—her?

ROWE—Dear Michael, use your common sense. Do I carry five pound notes about with me in the ordinary way? (MICHAEL *shakes his head with a smile.*) And did I know anything about Miss Weston until I came here?

MICHAEL—No—right. (*He puts the note in his pocket.*) Thank you, dear. (*He gives a little laugh.*) It's awful cheek to say it, but however many other commandments I may break, I do *honour* you, father. There's something about sheer goodness that always gets me. Mind you, I disagree with you profoundly about everything under the sun, sometimes you irritate me intensely—and—and yet (*with a little ashamed laugh*) I believe I love you. Good-bye.

With his father gone Michael is not long giving the three signal taps on the floor that brings Mary hurrying up the stairs, a steaming teapot in her hands. A happy Mary, "a beautiful Mary, and still a gentle Mary. We should not despise her now, even if Miss Cunliffe were here, too."

And now Michael is able to release the enthusiasm which his father had checked. Chapman and Hall, publishers, have taken his book! They've agreed that it is a first novel of the most distinct promise! And though they quibbled, as business men will, about any advance, insisting that there is never very much sale for a first novel, they offered fifty pounds on account of a ten per cent royalty.

Mary is quite awed at the thought of the fifty pounds.

"What did you do?" she demands, excitedly. "Go on your knees and say, 'Thank you, kind Mr. Chapman, bless you, dear Mr. Hall!' "

"No, I didn't say anything," reports Michael. "But something in my chair suddenly husked out, 'Make it a hundred and crash like gentlemen.' "

"Michael!"

"I was so surprised that I fainted. When I came around I heard Chapman speak out loud and bold, 'Well, well, take a hundred if you must,' and Hall said, 'And you'd better have 15 per cent over 5,000'; and I said, 'And you take the Crystal Palace, dear old Hall, and Chapman had better have the St. George's Swimming Baths.' And after this mutual exchange of gifts we parted. Now who says I'm not a business man?"

It was the typing that did it, Michael is convinced. And the typing was Mary's. Done on the typewriter she had secretly bought and helped by the typing lessons she had secretly taken. But that was Mary's greatest pleasure; the knowledge that she was helping.

MICHAEL (*suddenly*)—I can't eat. It's choking me. I want to talk to you. (*He pushes away his plate.*)

MARY—Yes, Michael.

MICHAEL (*looking at her*)—Mary, you know, don't you, that I love you?

MARY—I didn't know, Michael. There was that Miss Cunliffe. (*He shakes his head.*) And then—but these last few months I have wondered sometimes.

MICHAEL—Do you love me, Mary?

MARY—Always. Always from that first day. You knew,

didn't you? (*He shakes his head.*) I'm glad I didn't show it too plainly. And yet I was so proud of loving you. Will you say again that you love me?

MICHAEL—I just love you.

MARY (*with a deep sigh*)—Whatever we do, nothing can take that away.

MICHAEL (*hurriedly*)—If once I kiss you, my darling, that's the end of everything. Do you understand? (*She nods.*) Well, now I want to try and explain something to you, but it's difficult. And first I want you to understand that I love you and honour you and respect you so deeply, with my whole heart, that nothing I say could ever take away from that. You will understand, won't you, that we're in a difficult position, and that if I say things which seem to be—which I put awkwardly, that—that it's just that I'm not putting them very well.

MARY—Oh, Michael, how can you doubt?

MICHAEL—Well, now then. You're married to this horrible man, and so you can't marry me. And I suppose some people would say that since you ought to be able to divorce him, and you can't because you don't know where he is, then there is no harm in our living together. And religious people would say that, if we can't get married properly, then there is wickedness in living together. And the Law doesn't say anything, except that if we had children they would be illegitimate.

MARY—Children, Michael? Oh, I would love to have a son! Can I just think about him for a little? (*She thinks about him.*)

MICHAEL—I've been thinking this and that way and all around it, for weeks and weeks, almost thinking of nothing else, wondering what to do. Because I had a sort of feeling that I had only to ask you to live with me and you would. There, that's the thing I was going to say badly and I said it. But is it true?

MARY (*waking up from her dream*)—What, Michael?

MICHAEL—That you would have come to me any time if I had asked you.

MARY (*nodding*)—Yes.

MICHAEL—I thought so. And I thought that you'd just do it out of gratitude, and I should be a cad to ask you.

MARY—No. Well, you see I can't really tell you if I should have done it out of gratitude, because I should have done it out of my great love for you, because you wanted it.

MICHAEL—Anyhow, you would have done it, so it was really left to me to decide, and I wanted to ask you so badly, and I didn't dare. Because—oh, I don't suppose I'm any better than any other man, but I wanted to be good to you, and I'd taken you under my care and you were so young. What could I do?

MARY—I knew I could trust you from that first day.

MICHAEL—That's just it. You trusted me.

Michael tells Mary of his father's visit and of the promise he had made him. That he would marry her if she would have him. But, as Mary points out, she is already married! How can she marry Michael?

In quite the ordinary way, Michael insists. Not in a church, perhaps, but in a registry office. What's bigamy? Only a word. What's illegal? Another word to frighten them. And words are going to be Michael's slaves.

"I don't understand," confesses Mary. And then, with hope in her voice, she suddenly asks: "Do you mean my first husband is dead? Or didn't he marry me properly? Oh, Michael! Is it?"

"I don't know," admits Michael, almost gaily. "He may be dead. Or he may have married somebody else before you—and left her. Or you may be his legal wife. Perhaps we shall never know. But that's nothing. It's outside us. Marry me. Pledge yourself to me for ever and for ever, as I pledge myself to you. Whatever the law is, whether the marriage is legal or illegal, the pledge is binding on *us*. We can't do more, Mary. And somehow I feel that to run the danger means that we're doing our best to live decently, to keep our self-respect. We're not just coming together carelessly for the moment's pleasure—we're earning our happiness."

MARY (*apparently casually, after thinking this out*)—What happens to you if you commit bigamy—if they find you out?

MICHAEL—They send you to prison.

MARY—For marrying two people?

MICHAEL—Yes—if the first one's alive.

MARY (*smiling to herself*)—I think it's a wonderful idea, Michael. Of course I'll do it.

MICHAEL (*in sudden horror*)—Mary! You *don't* think—(*commandingly*) *I'm* doing this. It's always supposed to be the man who's to blame. That's the law. I shall tell them I persuaded you, lied to you, said your husband was dead. I'm the one.

MARY (*with a smile*)—Oh, no, Michael. *I'm* having the two husbands. When shall we get married?

MICHAEL (*violently*)—No, no, *no!* You've got to promise first that you're leaving it all to me. Good God, to think of them putting *you* in prison! Shutting you up, ordering you about, putting their hands on your shoulders! *You!* It would be nothing for *me*. Promise! Quick! (*And* MARY *sees how much worse it would be for him if it were she who went to prison.*)

MARY—All right, Michael. I promise. But couldn't we both go?

MICHAEL—If we could go together! But then it wouldn't be prison. (*To himself, alarmed by the awful possibility of* MARY *in prison.*) I wonder. Perhaps I'm silly about the whole thing. But—

MARY—No, no, my darling. You're right, absolutely right. It's a fine way out. And the fact that we can be punished for it—

MICHAEL—That *I* can. Don't forget.

MARY (*wistfully*)—Oh, Michael, Michael! Do you think I shall like them to take you away from me?

MICHAEL (*remorsefully*)—I'm sorry, my darling. It will be worse for you, of course—ought we? Shall we? Well, we're in it together. Shall we risk it?

MARY (*nodding*)—Yes, Michael.

MICHAEL—Then will you marry me, Mary?

MARY (*nodding*)—Yes, Michael. (*He gives a deep sigh and holds out his hands to her.*)

THE CURTAIN FALLS

ACT II

It is thirteen years later. In the sitting room of Michael's flat in Chelsea, a pale grey room with most of the upholstery in pinks and mauves; a room in which "the general effect is one of quiet comfort and an absence of fuss"; Michael and Mary are sitting reading. She has the evening paper, he a book. "Obviously they are having an evening at home, for he is in a smoking jacket and she in something less than an evening frock."

"Michael is older by the lines in his face, but hardly looks his 37 years; Mary, also thirteen years older than when we saw her last, shows it even less than he, now that her hair and her skirts are short. Indeed you might almost think them a newly married couple in the late twenties. There is an air of happy content about them."

Suddenly Mary is excited by something she has found in her

paper. She would show it to Michael, but it is a little difficult to get him away from his story. (The hero he is following had just found a collar stud he had lost a hundred and seventy-five pages back.) Finally Michael is willing to pay some attention to Mary and then he discovers that what she has found is a picture of Mrs. Michael Rowe, wife of the well-known writer!

It is the first time that Mary has appeared in the illustrated papers. This is a story on the short or long hair question, a symposium of what "well-known people say." And there is a quotation from Mr. Rowe, too.

" 'Mr. Rowe speaks with authority,' " Michael reads, " 'for his wife, who was a Miss Weston before her marriage, is a lovely example of the new fashion which suits her *petite* features to perfection.

" 'Being engaged in a canteen while her husband was gallantly serving his country on the battlefront,' " continues Michael, " 'with the 16th Bedfordshires, in which regiment he rose to the rank of captain, and having followed the example of those of her fellow workers who had already sacrificed their luxurious tresses, Mrs. Michael Rowe, who has a charming flat in Chelsea, found that—' and so on. In other words you cut your hair off because it kept getting into the soup, and then found that you couldn't grow it again. Well, it's all good for trade."

"How rather disgusting of you," insists Mary.

"I am disgusting. That's why I'm so popular."

"I meant about my hair."

"I adore your hair," protests Michael, blowing a kiss in Mary's direction. "Come here and I'll rumple it for you."

The arrival of the post puts a stop to playfulness for in the post there is an expected letter from David. Rather an important letter, seeing that it is a report of things that happened in a certain cricket match the first day David wore trousers.

"I love him in trousers," interpolates Mary, as Michael pauses in reading the letter.

" 'And I caught their captain,' " Michael reads. " 'A high one and I had to run for it, but I caught it.' Very lucidly explained. I hope you understand, Mary."

"Of course I do."

" 'My 35 was top score. Carter made 20, he was next, and it was my very first match for the school, and it wasn't his because he's older. I was the youngest. You did say a penny a run, didn't you, so that's 2/11. I wish it had been 3/–; it would have been, if I'd made one more. And, Binks, I was top again in class this week—' "

There is more to the letter including an accounting of such financial credits as would be puzzling to anyone but a proud father; a request for a bloodhound; a further bargaining for a penny a run for at least the first eleven matches and assurances of much love.

Now Mary has taken the letter and read it for herself and glowed a bit with happiness.

"Darling David!" she murmurs. And then to Michael: "How proud are you?"

"Never before in the history of the world," lazily answers David's father, "has a man been told that his son made top score in his first match on the very day when for the first time he saw his wife's photograph in the evening paper. That's the sort of man I am."

"Are you happy, darling?"

"Terribly. I've got the prettiest wife, the most heavenly son and the most comfortable flat in London and I've just had the best dinner."

Come to think of it, the dinner wasn't all that it might have been. It is the maid's night out.

Which suggests to Michael that perhaps the Rowes should expand a bit. At least to the extent of having more than one servant.

But Mary is not in agreement with Michael in this. She must go on being economical for Michael. Something might happen. Mary wants to feel safe.

True, they have been able to save quite a bit. First a hundred pounds; then two hundred; then five. Now they have a thousand. But can they ever feel safe?

Michael and Mary have just agreed that whatever they do is for David, and Michael has insisted that when David goes to public school they shall have a butler, even if they have to sack him at the beginning of each term, when the doorbell rings.

The caller would probably be Ferguson, Michael thinks. Ferguson wants to borrow a book and he is the kind that would take a long time about it. Especially if Mary is there. So he sends Mary to her room to wait until Ferguson has left.

The caller isn't Ferguson. He is a stranger. "An over-polite, middle-sized man in the late forties, with a waxed mustache, and something of a military air, as if he were a retired sergeant who had become a shop-walker; yet both his 'smartness' and his 'oiliness' have something wrong about them, something which makes you feel uncomfortable, as if they do not really belong to him."

The stranger has asked to see Captain Rowe. Michael has asked him in to find out the nature of his inquiry. The stranger, it now appears, is in search of a long lost niece. He has seen the picture of Mrs. Michael Rowe in the evening paper and she has so greatly reminded him of his niece, who was Mary Weston, that he was impelled to call and see if she were the same. His name is George Weston and he has not seen his niece, Mary, since she was a little girl with long curls.

Mrs. Rowe, Michael assures Uncle George, has no uncles living and therefore cannot be his niece. The caller, however, is persistent. It is altogether unlikely that he was ever spoken of in the family as an uncle, seeing that he was what one might speak of as a bad egg, and left home when he was very young. Now that he has returned, and particularly as he knows he is carrying in his heart the seeds of a deadly disease he is naturally anxious to discover some of his kinfolk before Death, the Great Master, comes to claim him.

MICHAEL—Oh, I say. That's bad luck.

PRICE—One could not have knocked around the world as I have done, Mr. Rowe, without paying for it. I have no complaint against the Fates, the Three Sisters, no complaint but one. To whom can I leave the fortune so hardly earned? I have lost touch with my few relations. Are they alive? Are they dead? Who can say? And then I open my paper, and I see—can it be my niece?—The name? The likeness? Mr. Rowe, George Weston would not have been doing his duty as an uncle and a citizen if he had not come around to inquire. So George Weston has come. If he is mistaken, pardon his intrusion. He can but withdraw.

MICHAEL (*impressed by this*)—I see. Well, it's very— Of course you are quite right from your point of view but I really don't think my wife— Would your niece recognize you?

PRICE—I think so, Mr. Rowe. I think we should recognize each other. But I am content to leave it in her hands. I am not trying to force myself on you. If she prefers to disown—

MICHAEL—There is no question of that, but I still think you've made a mistake. However, it is for my wife to say. (*He goes to the door.*) Mary! Just come a moment, darling. (*He waits at the door for her, and as she comes in says)*—This is a Mr.—

MARY (*seeing him*)—Harry!

PRICE (*with a horrible satisfaction*)—Mary. I thought so. Mary.

MICHAEL—Harry? Oh, my God!

MARY (*running to him*)—Michael, Michael. (*She clings to him.*)

MICHAEL—It's all right, darling.

MARY—It's him! He's come back. Hold me! Keep me!

MICHAEL (*holding her*)—It's all right, darling.

PRICE (*with a bow*)—Harry Price, at your service. Husband of the affectionate lady now in your arms. Tut-tut-tut. What would the Bishop say?

MICHAEL (*releasing Mary*)—Just a moment, darling. (*He puts her down in a chair and goes up to Price.*) Mr. Price, when I first heard your name fifteen years ago, I promised myself that if I ever met the cad who owned it, I would punch him in his filthy face, and go on punching him in his face, as long as we could both stand up. I'm older now, and life doesn't seem so simple. But let me warn you seriously that you're due for it, and that at the very least provocation you'll get it. So be careful.

PRICE (*retreating uneasily*)—No, no, no. No roughness, Mr. Rowe. Remember my weak heart. Mary, you wouldn't let him be *rough,* would you?

MARY—You mustn't. It wouldn't do any good. You mustn't think of *him.* It's David we must think of. (MICHAEL *flashes a warning look at her.*)

PRICE—Now, now, that's not fair, Mr. Rowe. Don't frown at Mary. She's telling me nothing I didn't know. I found out all about David, and all about everything before I came. I've had a busy twenty-four hours, Mary dear. Only landed in Liverpool yesterday with 3.17.6 in the pocket, got to London, picked up evening paper, found I'd come into a fortune, consolidated fortune, came around to my friend Mr. Rowe's flat to claim fortune. Quick work.

MARY—Michael! (*She puts out a hand to him. He gives it a little reassuring pat.*)

MICHAEL—It's all right, darling.

PRICE—It's all right, Mary. Mr. Rowe is going to see reason. Harry Price knows when he isn't wanted. Just this matter of the little fortune to be arranged, and then Harry Price goes off. The Rowes never see him again. Ah, well! The best of friends must part.

MICHAEL—You've been abroad a good deal lately, Mr. Price?

PRICE—Landed in Liverpool yesterday. (*With a sudden shiver.*) Christ! To think if I hadn't! What I might have missed!

MICHAEL—I was just going to tell you what you might have missed. Prison. In England people go to prison for blackmail.

PRICE (*coolly*)—And for bigamy?

Michael is firm. Not a cent will the pathetic Mr. Price get! Michael will see Mr. Price damned first. Nor can he be moved by any of the results that Mr. Price so graphically pictures. Let him go to court. He will get twenty years for blackmail. Michael may get one for bigamy.

"And now outside, Mr. Price," concludes Michael, threateningly. "I'm still longing to punch you in the face, and if I'm going to prison for a year and then have to wait nineteen years for you to come out this seems my last opportunity. So don't hang about."

"Look here, you can't do this." Price turns pleadingly to Mary. "Mary! Make him see reason. He's got no right to treat you like this. And his poor little son—"

"You're quite right, Michael."

"Now, look here, Mr. Rowe. I'll go back to America—"

"You're hanging about, Price."

"And say five hundred. I don't want to be hard on you."

"Get out!"

"She's not worth five hundred, eh? I see what it is. You *want* her to go to prison. You want to get rid of her. Got some other little bit of skirt in your eye. That is? (MICHAEL *jumps at him.*) Now then, now then, no roughness! A-a-a-ah!"

Michael has hardly started for Price when the latter suddenly collapses and falls to the floor, his head behind the sofa. Michael bends over him anxiously. Price is dead.

Michael's first thought is that he has killed Price. In his heart he wanted to kill him, and Price is dead. Mary will not have it that way. Price, even when she knew him, had always complained of his heart. She thought then it was just an excuse for not working.

Anyway, Price is dead. He did not hit his head on anything, and there is no blood about. But he is dead. So nothing will have to be done about that. The doctor will know how he died. The police will want to know, too.

Who is Price? How did he come there? Why did he and Michael quarrel?

MICHAEL—An inquest. They'll ask questions. Who is he? It will all come out. Well—who is he?

MARY (*in a whisper*)—The man I married.

MICHAEL—Yes—I always wanted to kill him—and now I've killed him.

MARY—No, Michael, no!

MICHAEL—Well, now it's out. We took the risk, and now we're going to pay.

MARY—I'm ready.

MICHAEL—There's David.

MARY—David! Oh!

MICHAEL—I was too happy. That's how it always is. (*Suddenly in a voice of anguish.*) Oh, God! I see the gates of Hell opening for you and David. Everything gone. And we were all so happy together.

MARY—Think of the happiness we have had, Michael. And it's because of what we did that we have had that happiness. Because we kept our self-respect, because we knew that this might come, and weren't afraid of it. Whatever is coming now, we have had those years. Whatever is coming, we love each other.

MICHAEL (*gently*)—I'm not complaining, my darling. God knows I've had more happiness than I ever deserved. And if you forgive me, I regret nothing.

MARY—Forgive! Oh, Michael! (*He kisses the top of her head and goes to the door.*)

MICHAEL—I suppose I'd better ring up the police.

MARY—I suppose so.

MICHAEL (*hesitatingly*)—Yes. (*He opens the door, goes slowly out and comes slowly back again.*) No.

MARY—What is it?

MICHAEL—No. Let's fight for it.

MARY—Fight?

MICHAEL—Lie.

MARY—Oh! (*Sadly.*) Oh, Michael! We seem to have done so many things that we oughtn't to have done.

MICHAEL (*shouting suddenly*)—I don't know what's right and I don't care what's right, but I'd damn my soul a thousand time to save *you,* Mary. (*Gently.*) And David—because he was part of you.

MARY—I hate telling lies somehow. It isn't goodness. It's just a sort of feeling.

MICHAEL—It's to save, not to hurt.

MARY—To save ourselves.

MICHAEL—My God—as if I cared about myself! (*Suddenly.*) Come on! I'm going to do it. There's a chance for us. (*Holding out his hand.*) I haven't lost you, Mary?

MARY (*with a wistful smile*)—You ought to know.

MICHAEL—Come on, then. (*He takes her hand and leads her to the sofa.*) Now. (*He looks at his watch.*) It's 9:30. I suppose they'll know more or less when he died. We'll say 9:35, and we didn't know what to do at first, and didn't ring up until 9:40. That gives us ten minutes. At 9:40 I ring up, and by then we've got a complete story ready for them, of who he is and how he came here. And how he died. Ten minutes. Now then. Who is he?

Little by little they try to construct a plausible case. They mustn't bring Mary into it at all, for one thing. If the police were to start investigating from that angle—no, Price must be a stranger. Perhaps a beggar? A threatening beggar? No, for then he would have stopped at other places first.

Suppose they had been out and this fellow had followed them? But if they had been out, where would they have been?

Michael might have gone out to mail a letter, and when he came back—no, there's the girl below. She would have seen him. That's too dangerous!

But time is pressing! They must think of something! And Michael just can't think properly.

"Oh, God, if you ever helped me to make up a story, help me now!" he prays. And then, as he smiles at Mary, Michael adds: "Go on, darling. It's you who will give it to me."

It is Mary's idea that they should stay as near the truth as possible. Michael is agreed to that so long as they keep Mary out of it.

Why did Price come? He came because he saw Mary's picture in the paper. That's where he got the name, and the address. Probably he called himself a fellow author and pretended to be an admirer of Michael's books! Michael let him in and then he became threatening! But there must be no hint of blackmail—Michael let him in and then found he was a fraud—

A great light breaks in upon Michael! Why author? Why not soldier?

MICHAEL—Old soldiers. London's full of them. Sixteenth Bedfordshires. Had a friend in the 16th probably. Came here as a man in my Company. Gave the friend's name, vaguely remembered the face. Asked him in. Found out he was a fraud—that's easy now—told him to clear out. He won't. I go to ring up the police. He tries to stop me. I push him out of the way—Got it! (*With a long sigh of relief.*) Oh, thank God!

MARY (*wistfully*)—He won't mind our lying, will He?

MICHAEL (*slowly, looking at her*)—I think He would forgive *you* anything.

MARY—What is the time?

MICHAEL—9:37.

MARY—Shall we ring up now?

MICHAEL—No, no, no! We must get this absolutely right, so as to be sure of it. Now then, Mary. A dress rehearsal. Think yourself back to where we were. The bell has just rung, and I think it's Ferguson, and I told you to go to the bedroom.

MARY (*getting up*)—Yes.

MICHAEL—Now, from now on you just behave perfectly naturally, taking the cues from me. You know nothing except what you hear, see or are told *now*.

MARY—Yes. Let's see. I said that I should probably go to bed, didn't I? (*Saying it naturally.*) I shall probably go to bed.

MICHAEL (*smiling*)—I shall tell him you have, but don't you dare to.

Word by word, scene by scene, speaking both for himself and the mythical Stranger, Michael constructs an alibi. The man came to the door; called Michael Captain Rowe; claimed to be a fellow named Cameron; a member of Michael's company; the 16th Bedfordshires; wounded at Mametz.

"Let's see," Michael asks the Stranger, "Cameron was an electrician, wasn't he, before the war? Then a signaller? What platoon? Oh, yes, the Ninth." But the Ninth—now he has an offer of a job at Hull if— It isn't Cameron at all! Granger was the man Michael was thinking of. Looks a little like this fellow! That's the reason he was taken in! "You'd better get out, Cameron, if that's your name—"

But Cameron won't go. He becomes threatening to him. As Michael starts towards the phone to call the police he pushes Cameron aside. He falls! And there he is back of the sofa! Michael calls Mary! She finds him bending over the body of the dead man. He tells her hurriedly what has happened. Shall they send for the doctor? No, the police! Because they don't know who the man is! Now they are sitting together on the sofa, their hands clasped.

MARY—It's difficult, waiting, isn't it?

MICHAEL—Yes—waiting to go in at cricket—waiting to go over in France.

MARY (*with a shudder*)—Waiting for a telegram to say you're killed.

MICHAEL—Nothing can be worse than the war.

MARY—Nothing. You're alive. Nothing else really matters. (*They are silent again.*)

MICHAEL—The day we decided to get married—my father came—do you remember? (*Mary nods.*) He quoted those glorious lines of Milton's— *You* know— "I cannot praise a fugitive and cloistered virtue, unexercised and unbreathed—where that immortal garland is to be run for, not without dust and heat." I said I'd give him another quotation. From Shakespeare. "Out of this nettle danger, we pluck this flower—self-respect." Shakespeare said "this flower, safety." But it wasn't safety I was looking for. Something better than that. You said just now that we'd kept our self-respect; well that's what I wanted us to do, and we did it, didn't we?

MARY—I think so, Michael.

MICHAEL—And now the danger is really here, we are trying, after all, to pluck "this flower, safety." I thought I'd gone one better than Shakespeare. I haven't, you see.

MARY—We must fight a danger. We can't just sit down and be overwhelmed by it.

MICHAEL—Yes, but how? How shall we feel when we're safe? Safe for always now. Now he's dead. Were you right when you said at once that you hated lying? I hate it, too. Is that the answer—that Safety isn't worth it at the cost of what we are going to do? Which flower shall we pluck? Safety or self-respect? Are they both growing there? Can we have both?

MARY (*in a low voice*)—I don't know.

MICHAEL—We go into the witness box. We take an oath. "I swear by Almighty God—"

MARY—Michael!

MICHAEL—Well, I think I can spare *you* that. But *I* shall have to go. I will do it gladly—but will it hurt *you* too much? To see me there. To hear me there.

MARY (*in a low voice*)—I don't know, Michael.

MICHAEL—Sweetheart, my very lovely darling, I am just at your service. If you wish it, even if you aren't quite sure, but think you wish it, we will tell the truth, the whole truth, unashamed, and let happen what ever will happen. (*He waits. For a little while she doesn't answer.*)

MARY (*after a silence*)—When you were out of the room, I read David's letter again.

MICHAEL (*remembering*)—Oh, David, David.

MARY—I imagined him—hurt, bewildered, understanding so little, only that something had happened, as if the sun had gone in on his birthday, and the world was cold, suddenly. Never quite the same again.

MICHAEL—No.

MARY—I suppose we were selfish about David; he ought never to have been born; but I did want him so. And now I feel he's something sacred. All the debts we owe must be paid to him. We have to put him first—before ourselves, before each other, before the truth, before everything.

MICHAEL—Yes. (*With a deep sigh.*) Yes.

MARY—We must be very good to him—afterwards.

The front door bell has rung. Michael and Mary stand up. For just a second they are in each other's arms. Mary has decided she had rather be waiting there with Michael and not in her room.

Now the police have arrived. Sergeant Enderby, followed by Dr. Roberts, "a neat, quick, laconic man of 35 or so, with a black, tooth-brush mustache."

The doctor's examination is perfunctory. The man is dead. There is no evidence of external violence. It will be all right to have the body removed. Three policemen bring in the stretcher. One of them, Officer Cuff, is told to remain. Cuff, "an honest-looking, round-faced, romantic countryman," sits down with a notebook and pencil.

Michael's story is told substantially as he rehearsed it. Occasionally the sergeant puts in a question, as importantly as possible, as when Michael speaks of the man as having given his name as Cameron.

"Taking a risk, wasn't he?" interposes the sergeant. "Mightn't have been a Cameron in your company at all."

"Were you in France, sergeant?" asks Michael, after a pause.

"No, sir. Had to have *some* police in London."

"Of course. But, you see, you go into action, say 120 strong, come out 50, pick up a draft of 60, turn 'em around three times and go into action again, come out 70, pick up another 40, turn 'em around twice and go into action again—and so on forever. Difficult to remember all their names two years afterwards."

"I see, sir, but if he'd never been in the army, would he know that?"

"That's true. Unless one of his friends had tried it and got away with it."

"Of course, there's a lot of this old soldier stuff going about," concludes the sergeant. "They soon pick up the trick of it."

Soon the sergeant is finished with Michael. Now he would like to see Mrs. Rowe. And perhaps Michael will just write down what he has told the sergeant.

"You'll be told about the inquest," warns the sergeant.

MICHAEL—Right. (*He goes to the door and then comes back slowly.*) I say, I'd be most awfully obliged if you could keep my wife out of it—I mean, out of the inquest. She didn't see the man at all until he was dead, and I called to her. I thought at first he'd just fainted.

SERGEANT—She wasn't here when he came in?

MICHAEL—No. She was in her bedroom. *I* let him in—our servant's out for the evening. I shouted out to her to get a meal of some sort ready—that was when I thought he was genuine—and then I called to her again to bring smelling salts, and she came in with them. Then we found he was dead, and I rang up, she—she wanted to stay with me.

SERGEANT—I see.

MICHAEL—I mean, of course see her now, and ask her anything you like.

SERGEANT—If that's so, sir, looks as though she won't have much to tell us.

MICHAEL—Well, you'll hear. Of course, I'm in your hands entirely. But if you *could* spare her the ordeal of the inquest I should be— I don't know if you're married? Anyway I expect you understand.

SERGEANT—That's all right, sir. I'll do what I can.

MICHAEL—Thanks very much. I'll fetch her. (*He goes out and we hear him calling to her.*)

SERGEANT (*to* CUFF)—Well, and what do *you* think of it all?

CUFF (*humorously—but also half hopefully—prepared to believe anything*)—I think 'e was 'er first 'usband, to 'oom she's lawfully married, and 'e called unexpectedly and started something, and they poisoned 'im together, with a subtle poison which South American injuns use for their arrows.

SERGEANT—Ha-ha-ha! (*He laughs heartily for a moment and* CUFF *joins him respectfully.*) Yes, well, that's enough of that, Cuff. (*In friendly contempt.*) You've been reading William le Kewx again. (*He takes out his pencil and notebook and gets back to business.*)

THE CURTAIN FALLS

ACT III

Into Michael's room in the house in Chelsea, in 1929 ("a room furnished with books around the walls; a comfortably untidy room"), burst young David Rowe. David is 22, "a tall, nice-looking, cheerful young man, who is obviously no fool."

It is about 10:30 o'clock in the morning and David is quite plainly excited about something. Whatever it is he would share it evidently with his father and mother. He calls loudly for "Binks" and "Bubbles," but there is no response, save from Miss Welby, Michael's secretary, a "quiet, efficient, not ill-looking" woman of thirty-five. "For years David has been trying to turn her into a human being, but she insists on maintaining her official attitude."

Miss Welby is also looking for Mr. Rowe, who is wanted on the 'phone. Miss Welby will say 'phone and not telephone, as she should, but David doesn't seem to be able to do anything about that. Neither is he exactly successful in extracting a smile, much less a laugh, from her.

"Good-bye, Ermyntrude," David calls impudently, as Miss Welby continues her search for Mr. Rowe. "Go and ring yourself up on the 'phone and send yourself a 'gram. God save us, Binks and I spend all our time trying to educate you, and you don't *help* us, woman. (*She goes, with a slam of the door.*) And don't be rough. In my young days ladies *were* ladies."

Michael is in a second later and Miss Welby has delivered her message. It is to warn Mr. Rowe that Sergeant Cuff would like to see him at 12.

"Michael is 47 now, but still doesn't look it. However, we shall find that he is undoubtedly older, even though he is neither bald, nor gray."

Sergeant Cuff, Michael explains to David, is a police sergeant, not a soldier. A police sergeant who was marked, in a way, by the early reading of detective fiction. Since then he has made a fad of constructing and reconstructing plots. Michael met Cuff the time "a fellow died on him," as David puts it. They had been, in a way, friends ever since. Cuff is always coming around with some new and ghastly plot to talk over.

David, upon his father's inquiry, admits that he is feeling particularly gay this morning. He has had a lively night, dancing and dancing, drinking and drinking—within limits—according to the custom of the time. The custom puzzles David.

"Tell me," he demands of his father, "why are you the devil of a fellow if you like drinking alcohol, and the devil of a prig if you don't?"

"That's the one thing I don't know, David."

"The drink problem is a very difficult one," David goes on. "It has two aspects. One I have already mentioned. The other is this: Why, if you happen to like beer, do you have to become a Roman Catholic and shout the good news all over Sussex?"

"That, as you say, is the question," agrees Michael.

"This opens up the general problem. Why are the things you like doing, continually being done by the people you don't like?"

"In other words," concludes Michael, "why is one so much nicer than everyone else."

David is gay, but restless. There is evidently something on his mind. Part of it presently comes off. He is waiting, it seems, for Romo.

MICHAEL (*considering*)—Romo. (*Shaking his head.*) Conveys nothing. Which of the many?

DAVID—Rosemary for remembrance.

MICHAEL—Oh, yes! At least I think I—no, no, that's wrong. It was distinctly a Susan you were walking out with in the spring.

DAVID (*smiling at* MICHAEL *affectionately*)—I suppose you and Bubbles, having obtained the coöperation and consent of your respective Papas and Mamas, got solemnly engaged to each other, and were allowed five minutes alone in the drawing-room together, after promising that you would be careful with the aspidistra and only kiss each other once?

MICHAEL (*also smiling*)—Well, no, it wasn't quite like that. (*His mind wanders back to the past.*) It's a funny world. (*There's a profound reflection for you.*) We hear a lot about the unkind way in which Victorian children were brought up, and how much more wisely and kindly we bring our children up today. But the clever, good, kind Georgian parents of today were the Victorian children of yesterday, so that *their* bringing up doesn't seem to have done them much harm. In fact, I doubt if anybody who condemns the Victorian method would point triumphantly to himself as a horrible example of it. Funny, isn't it?

DAVID—Then the only answer is that it doesn't much matter *how* you're brought up. I don't believe that.

MICHAEL—No, but the "how" may go down deeper than we think. Not "with a bicycle on your fourth birthday" or "without," but—well, "with love" or "without."

DAVID—Honestly, Binks, were you and your father as fond of each other as we are? As intimate?

MICHAEL—Are we intimate? (DAVID *looks away.*) We have jokes together, we are on delightfully friendly, casual terms, but do you tell me any more than I told my father—of whom I was afraid, to whom I never made a joke? (DAVID *is silent.*) Come on, old boy. You're nervous and excited, and you're saying, "Shall I tell Binks now, or shan't I? Oh, no, I can't," and you're spoiling your own morning and mine. Out with it.

DAVID—You devil! How did you know?

MICHAEL—Oh, come! *I'm* not a fool. Aren't you glad?

DAVID—Would *your* father have known if you had something on your mind?

MICHAEL—Ah, perhaps that's it. He wouldn't. One up for the modern system. Well, go on.

DAVID (*after a little silence*)—Romo and I got married this morning.

MICHAEL (*after a long pause*)—Why so suddenly?

DAVID—It's a little hard to explain. Bravado. Disgust. I don't know. Well, a sort of gesture, I suppose.

MICHAEL—You might *try* and explain. Disgust of what?

DAVID—D'you know Coggers?

MICHAEL—No, what is it?

DAVID—A damned lousy cad.

MICHAEL—Oh! No, I don't.

DAVID—We were at a cocktail party, the day before yesterday. They were all talking—being terribly modern and advanced and —oh, my God, how futile. Romo and I were supposed to be having a gay and happy time. I didn't dare to look at her in case she was enjoying it. This fellow Coggers was holding forth, about the absurdity of marriage and the curious old-fashioned fetish of chastity. All the usual stuff. I suppose he saw that I wasn't so terribly amused as the others were all trying to be, and just to annoy, because he knows that you and I are rather—rather specially friends, he said, "Doubtless even the moral Michael Rowe"

—that's because you don't write the muck that he and his friends write—"doubtless even he has condescended to at least one bastard."

MICHAEL (*in anguish*)—David!

DAVID—It's all right, Binks. I knew that if *ever* there was a man—I got up and put my glass down. He said "Another, David?" with a foul smile that seemed to bring all the rest of the room in, and I said, "No, you'll want it all yourself," and I hit him—just one. And then I said, "I've been wanting to do that for a long time. Thanks for giving me the excuse," and I walked out—all white and trembling, Binks. I'd forgotten Romo, I'd forgotten everything, except that I wanted to get out of that damned house. And there, beside me suddenly on the doorstep, was—Romo. She said nothing, and we walked away; and then she said, "Thank you, David," and I said, "Will you marry me at once, as soon as we possibly can?" and she said, "I should like to do that, David," and —we're married.

Romo, David reports, has gone to tell her people. Then she is coming for David. How are they going to live? Well, David has found himself a job in a second-hand bookshop where he will have a chance to "begin at the bottom and work sideways."

"And so in one afternoon you become a man," says Michael, a little wistfully.

"If you like, Binks."

"Are you really in love with her?"

"I don't know," admits David, consideringly. "We'd always been just friends, that's all. But it seems impossible now that she shouldn't always be there."

"That's good enough. Thank you very much for telling me all this, David."

Of course, "Bubbles" must be told, but before that is done there is something that Michael has to say to David, too, when his mother comes. Then Romo is announced.

Romo is—"but who can describe a modern girl? Save for those subtle, indescribable differences they all look the same. Just by that much is she different."

Michael is obviously pleased with Romo. And quite glad to tell them why. For the last two or three years, David has been bringing a succession of attractive females home. Michael has never been quite sure of their names, but as each has, in a way, passed in review he and Mary have paused and made comment. Sometimes it has been, "Oh, no, no!" Sometimes, "Well, I'm not so sure," and once they had both said, "Ah!" That was when Romo came.

Romo is very proud of Michael's admission. And a little excited. There are many things to think of. For one, so far as Romo can make out, she has been turned out of her home. When she had told her father what had happened he had acted quite badly about it. Kept on referring to David as "a lot of young puppies" until Romo, out of respect for her new husband, if nothing else, was forced to pack her things, put them in her car and leave.

The car is outside, with the things. They have until Sunday night. They will start on their honeymoon and let the car decide where they shall go. That settled, there is something else Romo wants to know.

ROMO—David, why did you want to marry me so suddenly?

DAVID—Because I love you.

ROMO (*shaking her head*)—I think you're going to love me tremendously. But that wasn't it. Why, David?

DAVID (*after a pause*)—I've got a confession to make.

ROMO—A very bad one?

DAVID—It is rather. (*Solemnly.*) I believe I'm early Victorian.

ROMO—What a nice thing to be.

DAVID—I'm not really modern—

ROMO—I wonder sometimes if any of us are; if it isn't just an invention of the newspapers and the novelists.

DAVID (*surprised*)—Coggers—the dirty swine—

ROMO—Yes, but there've always been dirty swine in the world.

DAVID—Well, but I mean, I believe I'm really old-fashioned. Conservative. (*With a shy laugh.*) I believe I should like going to church on Sunday with my family—through the fields.

ROMO—Then why don't you?

DAVID—I don't mean this family. I mean— (*He looks at her shyly.*)

ROMO (*with a smile*)—I'll make a note of it.

DAVID—Oh, Romo, I felt so sick of cleverness suddenly, and sneers—easy sneers at goodness— I think when I went out of that house I could almost have joined the Salvation Army straight away, if there'd been anyone in a blue jersey and a tambourine outside. Luckily there wasn't. But there was somebody just as good waiting for me, and I said to myself, "That's what I want—Romo. I'm safe with her. We'll be good together."

ROMO—Thank you for thinking so, David.

DAVID—I'm respectable. That's what's the matter with me really, though nobody guesses. I don't like irregular things. I'm—

ROMO—Public school, University, and M.C.C.

DAVID—That's about it, I'm afraid. The perfectly normal, respectable young man.

ROMO (*looking at him lovingly*)—Shall I tell you what you really are?

DAVID—Yes.

ROMO—Very, very young. (*She kisses him lightly.*) My David.

Now Michael and Mary are back. "Mary still refuses to look as if David were her son. But she is pretty solemn at the moment, because of the story that Michael has to tell them. It is a story that Michael has always known he must tell David some time, but each time he has tried he has found a perfectly good excuse for not doing it. There were so many things to be considered.

"In my father's age," explains Michael, "almost everything you wanted to do was wrong; in this age almost nothing you want to do is wrong. I came right between the two—when one still felt that right was right and wrong was wrong, but one didn't quite know which was which. It made it difficult."

Romo is sitting in the arm chair, and David on the arm of it. Michael and Mary are on the sofa, holding hands, as they have sat many times since the day the story concerns.

"You'll think we're a strange house," Michael begins, speaking to Romo. "Well, we are. I'll tell you how. David, you've said some funny things this morning. 'Mr. Rowe's gift of irony'—it has been a very ironical morning. Now I'll tell you the story of Michael and Mary . . . It begins in the British Museum in 1905. I was twenty-three. I had gone there . . ."

Slowly the curtain falls. The audience has heard that story already. Michael is just finishing as the curtain rises again. David has moved away from Romo and is sitting by himself, looking on the floor. Romo has her eyes on Michael.

MICHAEL—I think I did it well—acted well. You see, a writer gets into the way of taking his imagination seriously. To me the man lying there *was* Cameron, the pretended Cameron. I doubt if the police really suspected anything, but he was a clever fellow that sergeant, and he made Mary tell her story too. There's one thing, David, that you and I can say together. Whatever dangers threaten us, whatever evil surrounds us, this we know: that Mary will never let us down. She told her story. Before she began I knew that we were safe. Then there was the inquest. The sergeant kept his word and only I went into the box. I took the oath, I gave my evidence. I swore by Almighty God . . . I didn't like that. (MARY *slips her hand into his.*) They had found out his name—not Price, luckily—the name he had last used. He had just landed from America, as he said—the truth for once. They didn't follow him up any farther, and of course the verdict was "Death from natural causes" . . . We were safe. That is our story—as it ended there ten years ago. But now there are two things more to be said. First: after this man's death, Mary and I could have been married again, legally. Second: many years later, when this new law came in, we could, being married legally, have made your birth what is called legitimate. All that seemed to me, seems to me still, an infinitesimally small thing. In as far as I have offended against my God, the sanction of the Law cannot better my account with Him, and, indeed, it seems to me almost indecent to invoke it. But in as far as I have offended against you, David, I am in your hands. It is for you to say. (*There is a long silence.* MICHAEL *and* MARY *sit hand in hand, as they sat once before, waiting for the verdict—this time of their son.* DAVID *looks at* ROMO, *awkwardly, unhappily, but she will not meet his eyes. She keeps her head down, so that he cannot see her face, but you can see her hands clench and tighten. With a long sigh,* DAVID *gets up, gives a half-defiant look at* ROMO *and goes across to the sofa. He raises the joined hands of* MICHAEL *and* MARY, *goes on one knee and kisses them.*)

DAVID—I don't think I have any more to say.

ROMO (*jumping to her feet*)—Isn't he a fine son! Isn't he a fine son! Aren't you proud of him?

MICHAEL (*softly*)—Yes.

DAVID (*surprised at her outburst*)—Romo!

ROMO—Oh, David, David, if you had failed me! If you had failed me, I should have walked out on you; yes, I should. I was just clenching my hands and saying, "Oh, let him understand! Let him understand! He's so young!"

DAVID—I was afraid *you*—I mean you've been absolutely let in for all this—

ROMO—Oh, David, how little you understand me!

DAVID—Well, you don't seem to know much about me and Binks and Bubbles, if you thought for a moment—

ROMO—How little we understand each other! Well, let's begin now. (*To* MARY.) I'm afraid I shan't be a wife like you. I don't expect they've been making them lately. But I won't let David down. That I promise. (*She holds out her hands.*)

MARY (*with a smile*)—I think I'll have that kiss now. I've been wanting it rather badly.

ROMO (*kissing her and then holding her at arm's length*)—When I think of my silly little life—and yours—what you've been through. It's all somewhere, I suppose—not in your face—(*she shakes her head*)—in your heart. (*Eagerly, suddenly.*) Life *is* fun, isn't it? I mean the frightening things are fun, and the unknown things are fun—and everything? (MARY *nods.*) Well, come on, David, let's have a dash at it.

DAVID—Right.

ROMO (*going to* MICHAEL)—I like your stories, Michael Rowe. (*She gives him a happy little laugh.*) I like your wife. I like your son. (*She gives him a little, quick kiss.*) See you again shortly—very shortly. We may sponge on you for a bed Sunday night.

MARY—Oh, do. That will be lovely.

DAVID—I was wondering about that.

ROMO—And then on Monday, while my husband is working, I shall look for lodgings—in Islington or somewhere.

MARY—Don't be absurd!

MICHAEL—No, she's right, I expect.

ROMO—Michael Rowe knows. (*She gives him a little pat and goes to* MARY, *taking her hand.*) Come and see me down.

They are gone now and David and Michael are facing facts and emotions a little consciously, but understandingly. David doesn't want a thing changed. Not a thing. Of course things will be different from now on. David hates leaving the old home, knowing that. But there is the new home, David's home, to consider now.

"It's cheek," ventures David, "but—I do honour you, father."

"That makes me very proud," answers Michael. "Good-bye, my David."

David goes, covering such confusion as he may feel by joking with Miss Welby, who has come to bring Michael's work to him.

For a moment Michael is alone. There is a great relief in his face as he turns to his work. Then Mary comes. He'll not get much work done this morning.

There is happy relief in Mary's expression, too. The story has been told at last. There is no more doubt now as to how David would take it.

"Thank God he's got somebody to hold on to," Michael says. "He'll have bad moments, I expect, poor David."

They are silent for a little while and then Mary sighs. "Well, the story is ended now. It has been fun writing it together. What shall we write next?"

"Just the love story of Grandmama and Grandpapa sitting before the fire together."

"Oh, we aren't as old as all that," smiles Mary.

"Old," protests Michael with spirit, "I feel twenty-three again. I want to go to the British Museum with you, and have dinner at that funny little place, and— Oh, let's do something perfectly idiotic together. What shall it be?"

For a moment the plan is halted. Sergeant Cuff is calling, and the sergeant has interesting news for them. It's about an old friend of theirs.

The police, Sergeant Cuff reports, in running down a criminal gang of counterfeiters, has come upon a young woman, Sallie Winter by name, who, pleading that she never had had a chance, and being able to prove it, has excited the interest of the police.

Sallie Winter, it further appears, was married to that self-same Walker who had died in Rowe's flat in 1905!

"I don't like leaving a story unfinished," admits Sergeant Cuff. "We'd met the man Walker once in your flat, and now we'd met him again. I said to myself, 'You've left your mark in one or two other places, my lad, if I'm not mistaken. Let's have a look for you.' Account of being my duty, you see, sir, and account of being my pleasure, as you might say. So I had a look for him between times."

"Yes," encourages Michael, trying not to show his interest.

CUFF—That man! Price, his name was. Harry Price. Well, I'm not so sure of that. Perhaps I'm not far enough back yet, but Price he is when I first begin to hear of him—remember the Brides in the Bath case?

MICHAEL—Yes.

CUFF—Well, that's the sort of man Price was. I can't go so far as to put a murder on him, but I have my opinion about that.

MARY—Oh!

MICHAEL (*thinking of* MARY)—How horrible!

CUFF—Yes, sir. Well, I've got him pretty well taped out now.

I'm on to what looks like his first marriage—1905. Mary West. Or Westall. By tonight I daresay I shall know all about *that*. I don't seem to hear of him before owe-five, but of course, you never know.

MICHAEL (*to himself*)—You never know.

CUFF—Well, sir, of course I'm not a great author like you, but in a manner of speaking I write stories too, and I like 'em rounded off, same as you do, I expect.

MICHAEL—Yes—yes.

CUFF (*getting up*)—Well, that's how it is, sir—madam—and I knew you'd be interested, seeing that you were acquainted with the party. I'll let you know if anything else transpires.

MICHAEL—Thank you, Cuff. We *are*—very much interested.

CUFF—Well, good day, sir, good day, madam. By your leave, sir.

So the story isn't ended after all.

"How silly to think we can say, 'Here a new chapter begins,'" muses Michael. "Eternal life! It is here with us now—in this world. All that we have been. All that we have done, lives on forever."

Mary's thoughts are of the girl, Sallie Winter. If it hadn't been for Michael she might have been a Sallie Winter! But Michael knows better than that. Anyway, he's glad Price is dead. Glad he killed him—if he did kill him!

The story may all come out now. Michael has often wondered if it ever would. And if it does Cuff will probably report what he finds, however friendly he may feel toward Michael. Cuff is the artist type. He would put his job first.

If the story does come out it isn't the death of Price that will count. It is the perjury the law won't like. Michael knows that. The Law takes perjury rather seriously.

But "men do it in the divorce court every day," Mary insists, scornfully.

"Yes," admits Michael, "that's why it doesn't matter. Everybody knows that they're only saying, 'Look at me being a perfect gentleman.' What I said was, 'Look at the Law being a perfect ass. I've fooled it.' The Law doesn't like that. As Cuff says, it has to be respected."

MARY (*after a pause*)—If they do send you to prison, what would it be?

MICHAEL—Extenuating circumstances, like poor Sallie Winter? Six months? About that?

MARY—Six months? Away from you.

MICHAEL—It was more than that in the war sometimes.

MARY (*violently*)—It will be *nothing* like the war! That awful war! Nothing!

MICHAEL (*comfortingly*)—Oh, my darling, nothing! We can pretend it *is* the war over again, and then how easy it seems. No danger, no uncertainty—the world's shortest and most painless war for wives.

MARY—Yes, I shall be all right, Michael— I don't feel unhappy. I'm sure we've been right all through. I wouldn't change any single thing we've done.

MICHAEL—Nor would I—now. But, honestly, I'm not sorry to pay. It seems to make us really safe at last. Spiritually safe. It is a lovely flower, Mary, and now at last we have plucked it.

MARY (*nodding*)—Now that David is safe.

MICHAEL—Yes. Now let come what may. (*He gets up and sits next to her on the sofa.*) There's been a lot of talk today about young David. I suppose you do know, Mary, that, as much as I love him, I love your little finger—(*he picks it up and fondles it*)—your funny little finger, more than the whole of David's body?

MARY (*very gently*)—I think I do know, Michael. (*She looks at his hand, and says with a meaning look which he cannot mistake.*) You've got a funny little finger, too.

THE CURTAIN FALLS

DEATH TAKES A HOLIDAY

A Drama in Three Acts

Adapted by Walter Ferris

(From the Italian of Alberto Casella)

THE original version of "Death Takes a Holiday," which reached this country some years back, was in the nature of a fairly rollicking comedy. The playgoing and playwriting Italians are much more inclined to laugh at the gaunt and cadaverous fellow who rattles around in his bones than they are to take him seriously as a messenger come to call mortals to a life beyond the life we know.

It was not until Lee Shubert had contracted for the script and turned it over to Walter Ferris for revision that the play began to assume the character and form in which it was later to win its success. Mr. Ferris is an educator and playwright of some experience, being the author of "The First Stone" which Eva Le Gallienne produced at the Civic Repertory Theatre in 1927.

When the drama was first thought to be in playable form it was tried out with some misgiving—once by a Little Theatre group near New Haven, I believe, and once by a stock company in Cincinnati. After each trial there were revisions of the script.

Finally, when it had shaken down to its present form, it was played in Washington, in Pittsburgh and in Philadelphia, where it enjoyed a success as one of the offerings of the Professional Players' group, a subscription organization banded together to promote better class productions.

In December the play was brought to the Ethel Barrymore Theatre in New York. Its reception was friendly but not particularly enthusiastic. The public's interest steadily increased, however, until this fantastic drama was listed with the popular successes of the season.

At the play's opening, in Duke Lambert's castle in Italy, it is nearing midnight in late October. The great hall of the castle is dimly lighted, but outside in the garden a bright moonlight is flooding tall cyprus trees. The great hall opens directly into the garden, with steps leading to three large French windows at back. At the top of the steps there is a marble bench.

It has been a weird sort of night. Its strangeness has been noticed by the servants, Cora and Fedele. Repeatedly shadows have been seen to cross the face of the moon and reports have come that the Duke has had an accident with his car.

An exaggerated report, the Duke is glad to admit presently, as he and Alda, "a woman of 28, slender, beautiful," enter the hall. They had been close to an accident but something had happened just at the instant it seemed that they must crash. Alda is a little disappointed. She had a feeling there might have been something wonderfully interesting the other side of that crash.

The Lamberts are entertaining guests and now these begin to assemble. Stephanie Lambert, the hostess, "a dark, rather mysterious-looking woman of forty, with a rich, husky voice," is with them. One is the Princess of San Lucca, "a fair, sweet woman"; another the Baron Cesarea, "bluff and red-cheeked at seventy-five, with a merry eye."

These, too, have also been worrying. Both cars have been driven too fast. Including the one that was ahead with the young people in it—Corrado and Grazia. Drive as fast as he did, the Duke could not keep up with the young people.

Corrado himself was worried, he admits, when he brings in another group of guests. These include Rhoda Fenton, "a handsome, straightforward English girl of twenty-four," and Eric Fenton, "a tall, intelligent-looking Englishman." Corrado is the son of the Duke and Stephanie, "a dark, beautifully mannered man of twenty-two, with a lightly dissipated face."

Apparently this has been a night for accidents and miraculous escapes. Corrado, too, had been blinded by a mysterious shadow and had not seen a cart on the road in front of him until he was fairly upon it.

"Just at that second some instinct told me to swerve," he says.

"And we made a slight parabola at seventy miles an hour on one most inadequate wheel," adds Eric Fenton.

"With a fifty-foot drop below—"

"One inch more and all the king's horses and all the king's men couldn't have found the pieces."

Yet through all this Grazia, who has stopped behind in the garden, dreamed on complacently. They all wondered at that. And yet it was Grazia's wish that they drive fast—and faster still.

"I believe her exact remark was that if we *did* go fast enough we might reach the illimitable, whatever that is," reports Eric.

The cart in the road, it transpires, was the same one that figured in Duke Lambert's adventure. He had actually struck it. And yet, though the driver must have been hurled fifty feet through the air, he was no more than slightly winded and the car was not even scratched. Certainly they are each and severally entitled to drink to their escapes this night.

"Well, happy days!" suggests Eric.

"And a beautiful woman to love," adds the Baron.

CORRADO—And a beautiful woman to love *us*. It's not much good without that. (*Pause. He comes down.*) You know, I'm wondering . . . if our cart driver *had* broken his neck. . . . I mean, what do you suppose comes after that? . . . Where could he be now?

BARON—It might be well to give that a little attention if you're going to keep up this speed.

STEPHANIE (*lightly*)—The poor carter would be gathered into the heart of God.

ALDA—Yes, but where . . . Olympus, the Elysian fields . . . the Pearly Gates?

ERIC (*smiling*)—I fancy he would be driving a superb team of mules down a perfect road, with a barrel of wine and an amiable wife waiting at the end. . . . That is, if he could choose. . . . All ideas of Heaven are really wish-images, aren't they?

DUKE—In that case a woman would look forward to a perfectly appointed boudoir, and the entrance of a perfectly satisfactory love.

ALDA—How well you know us.

BARON—Ha . . . sounds like *my* entrance.

ALDA—Have you a lurid past, dear?

BARON—I've lived harder than any of you. We knew how, in my time.

ALDA (*smiling*)—And were you a tremendous lover?

BARON (*pleased*)—Five beautiful creatures depended on me, all at one time, for their pleasure . . . and profit.

DUKE—Good Lord! Think of the fatigue!

BARON—And I kept them all happy, too. No man's enough for that, nowadays.

CORRADO (*to* RHODA)—This is no place for a young girl, Rhoda. Shall we dance?

RHODA (*rises*)—I'd love to. (*They exit.*)

ALDA (*to* BARON)—Oughtn't you go to bed, darling?

BARON (*rising*)—Bed? Certainly not. I'm feeling younger, I don't know why.

ALDA—I think you ought to go. It's been a tiring day.

BARON—So it has. Dashing about all over the place. Felt about eighty-seven at dinner time. Thought I wouldn't last much longer. Now I'm about sixty.

The Princess of San Lucca is worried about Grazia, who is her daughter. Grazia is doubtless perfectly safe in the garden, but it has been rather an unusual night and the girl has not seemed just herself of late. Perhaps, when she marries Corrado—

Grazia comes from the garden. "She is a lovely girl of 18, charming and gentle, but oddly remote." She is, she assures her Princess mother, quite all right. And there has been nothing to worry about, really. Yet even Grazia is willing to admit the night has been unusual.

"It's the strangest night I've ever known," she admits to the Duke. "Didn't you feel it? All the time on the drive there were shadows running over the fields. And yet there weren't any clouds in the sky to make shadows. Didn't you notice?"

"By Jove . . . . there weren't."

"It was just your imagination, Grazia," insists the Princess.

"I had forgotten how silent and swift a shadow can be," Grazia goes on. "I felt as though there were wings somewhere about. And we seemed to be flying, too."

Both the Duke and Corrado are anxious that Grazia should give some thought to marrying Corrado. Corrado wants her to set a day for their wedding. Even the Princess joins with the happy suggestion that they could be quite ready in a month.

"We could spend the winter on the Riviera, and in Egypt and Greece. You know how much you want to see the Ægean Isles."

But Grazia puts them off. She is not ready for marriage yet.

"You know I love you all, and want to please you. But don't you see, I'm not ready."

"But why, Grazia?"

"That life is too . . ."

She pauses, as though she were searching her thoughts. "There's a kind of happiness I want to find first, if I can."

"Aren't you happy with me?" Corrado demands.

"Yes, dear . . . But that isn't quite what I mean. (She looks at them helplessly.) I wish I knew how to tell you. (She turns to the garden.) There is something out there . . . which I must find first."

Leaving them Grazia goes into the garden alone, and leaves a constrained silence behind her, which the Baron manages to break by calling attention to himself. Especially to his legs. For some unaccountable reason they seem to be getting younger. Not a creak in a single knee and he, who never expected to dance again, carries the Princess away to the ballroom.

Corrado is still anxious about Grazia, he confesses to his mother, and eager for her love. But to gain it must he turn saint? And live only for poetry? And music? . . . Still, there is no use cursing his luck. . . .

The weird happenings of the night continue. A telephone message from the relatives of a lady who was expected to die at any minute reports that the patient has taken food and wants to get up.

A moment later a loud shriek comes from the garden and Grazia, "her hair in disorder, her face convulsed with terror, appears in the central window." She is still screaming as Corrado reaches her, and she half swoons in his arms.

It is a moment before they can arouse Grazia, and then her account of what has happened is halting and uncertain.

"I . . . don't . . . know . . . what it was. . . . There was something cold . . . and terrible. . . . Oh, Mother."

She clings to her mother as Corrado kneels before her.

"It's all right, Grazia. You are safe now."

"I was sitting by the fountain," the girl goes on; "watching the shadows . . . in the garden . . . dreaming. I could hear your voices . . . and the music. . . . It was all so peaceful . . . and so beautiful. . . . That I didn't want to come in . . . I thought . . . in a moment I am going to feel something important . . . some happiness. I felt a world about to open. . . . And then . . . Oh!"

"Go on, Grazia."

"And then . . . an icy wind seemed to touch me. . . . But it wasn't a wind, because all the leaves were still."

"Oh, Grazia!"

"I felt someone behind me . . . running. . . . There wasn't any sound . . . but I felt someone running. . . . . And I saw . . ."

"What did you see?" demands the Duke.

"A . . . shadow . . . an enormous darkness. . . . And yet it wasn't a shadow, because I could see the sky and moon through it. . . . Oh, Corrado!"

"It's all right, Grazia."

Gradually Grazia is quieted. It probably has been the wild ride that has disturbed her, the Duke suggests, and the danger. Sleep is what she needs most. A room shall be prepared for her that she may rest quietly until morning. Meantime Eric and Corrado will search the grounds. There may have been a prowler—

But even the most careful search fails to reveal anyone in the garden. Certainly the mysteries do pile up.

Now the house is quiet and Fedele reports everything in readiness for the night. All have gone to their rooms, save the Duke. He thinks he will sit up and keep an eye on the garden. Only the table light is burning.

Then, in the silence, "a presence is felt, rather than seen, standing above the steps in the garden."

DUKE (*startled*)—Who, who's there? (*Rises.*) Who's there. (*Turns swiftly and takes gun from table drawer.*) Speak up, or I'll shoot! (DUKE *lifts his gun and pulls the trigger. The gun does not even click. He tries to fire again with the same result. A tall, black shadow moves forward through the window. The* DUKE *falls back in terror.*

(*The shadow is Death. His head is covered by a hood. From his shoulders a long black cloak falls. His face appears like the mask of death. His hands are gloved. He speaks in a rich voice which has a curious quality of ironic humor.*)

SHADOW—I beg you not to be afraid.

DUKE (*gasping*)—Who . . . who . . . are you?

SHADOW (*in an amused tone*)—I don't wonder you ask. I suppose, as a caller, I *am* unusual, even unique.

DUKE (*lifting the gun*)—You stand back! (*The* SHADOW *lifts his hand and lowers it slowly. With the motion the* DUKE *lowers his gun.*)

SHADOW—It's quite useless against me. (*The* SHADOW *comes down.*) Break your gun. (*The* DUKE *does this, his eyes on the* SHADOW. *The bullets fall on the floor.*) Now pull the trigger. (*The* DUKE *pulls the trigger. The gun clicks audibly.*) You see, it works now. I should have let you shoot, but I was afraid it might waken your household and interfere with my plans. (*The* DUKE *gasps. This is nearly too much for him. The* SHADOW *regards him. His voice is amused.*) You seem badly shaken, but I suppose it's natural. You are the only person who has ever faced me like this whose alarm was not justified.

DUKE (*hoarsely*)—Who . . . who are you?

SHADOW—Ah, I beg your pardon. I've been so interested in my reception that I have forgotten to explain. (*He hesitates.*) I'm afraid it will be difficult. Perhaps you had better sit. (*The* DUKE *starts to sit on the divan. The* SHADOW *indicates a chair.*) No, here . . . Your back may need support.

DUKE (*sitting*)—Is this some horrible masquerade? If it is . . .

SHADOW (*with a laugh*)—No, strange as it may seem this is my natural appearance. That is, to you. In justice to myself I ought to say that my true appearance is somewhat more attractive than this, but unfortunately I can appear to man only as he imagines me to be. (*The* DUKE *gasps. The* SHADOW *goes to him.*) That seems incredible, doesn't it? But then, the whole thing is incredible. . . . I'm afraid, my dear fellow, you will have to make a considerable effort. You see, I am not of your world. (*The* DUKE *shrinks from him as the* SHADOW *sits on the opposite side of the table.*) I am . . . how shall I describe it? A sort of . . . vagabond of space. Think, if you can, of infinity. That may help. Think of limitless reaches of light, and limitless reaches of darkness. Think of sound that goes whispering on forever. You see, if you are to grasp this you will have to discard your usual formulas. For instance, at one moment I am touching the evening star with my shadow and plucking some mortal on the earth by the sleeve. . . . Do I make myself clear? (*He looks at the* DUKE *who is staring, fascinated.*) Evidently not. I told you it would be difficult. (*He rises.*) You see, I am . . . or I was until I crossed your threshold . . . Death. (*The* DUKE *leaps to his feet.*) Ah, I thought it might give you a shock. But please be assured. I am not on my usual mission tonight. Quite the contrary. If I were, do you think we should be chatting like this? Instead I should have lain beside you for a moment on your bed, or breathed on your hair as you passed by. I have already stood beside one of you, tonight, without harm . . . that lovely girl in the garden. (*He has moved beside the fireplace.*)

DUKE—Ah . . . then it was you!

SHADOW—Yes. I didn't intend her to see me. She appears to be remarkably sensitive and aware. The rest of you, if I may say so, have been less acute. I have, you know, been with you all evening.

DUKE—Oh . . . then that explains . . .

SHADOW—Several things. Your son, I thought, was rather desperate tonight. If I had been playing my proper rôle I should have taken him and those charming young people in the car . . . regretfully, I assure you. I positively had to hold his wheels on the edge of that precipice.

DUKE—You . . . held . . .

SHADOW—Yes . . . quite. And I brought your flying cart driver to earth. I was absent-minded for a moment or I shouldn't have allowed that accident. But really, you and your son ought not to drive like that, when I am . . . myself.

DUKE (*recovering*)—You saved . . .

SHADOW (*with a laugh*)—Amusing, isn't it? Death in the rôle of guardian angel. But I did. Doesn't that reassure you that I have no . . . er . . . lethal intentions?

DUKE—It does, rather. (*The* DUKE *has recovered his poise and his breath. He is getting used to this strange visitor.*)

SHADOW—That's better. In a moment we shall be, I trust, quite good friends. But perhaps you had better sit again. There are a few more unusual details. (*The* DUKE *sits on the divan. The* SHADOW *follows and sits beside him, the* DUKE *drawing back.*) I am about to take a holiday. Again that sounds incredible, doesn't it? Even to me. Think of it . . . for the first time in history there will be no murders, no fatal accidents. No man will even die in his bed. Not a leaf will fall, or a star from heaven. Nothing will decay, nothing crumble. There will be only life, and growth . . . a sort of cosmic springtime. . . . (*He sits contemplating this as though in awe, then laughs.*) But don't be alarmed. It can't go on long, or there would be a serious overcrowding. Of course, that could be remedied by another world war, but that gives me so much work. I shall take three days only, and crowd as much as possible into them. After that I must go back.

DUKE (*in a more normal tone*)—But why are you doing this?

SHADOW—For a number of reasons. . . . For one thing, to discover why men fear me as they do.

DUKE—Don't you know? (*The* SHADOW'S *tone changes suddenly. An inner intensity makes itself felt.*)

SHADOW—How should I know, who have never experienced a mortal sensation? What could terror mean to me, who has nothing to fear? Or pity, when I must not pity? Or kindness, or aspiration, or love? These are only words to me, whose meaning I am curious to discover. (*He pauses a moment. His tone is light.*) In particular I should like to know something of love. It appears to be a potent force which makes men do quite mad things. . . . It is the word most often on the lips of man when he goes with me, unless he is old and spent with life. (*He pauses again. There is a sudden return of his intensity.*) And there is another reason. Can you conceive how weary I am of always being misunderstood? . . . I see things that are gracious, and young, and fragrant; and sometimes I desire them, with a vague and aching tenderness. . . . But if I come too near . . . if they feel the presence of my shadow, a horror comes upon their minds. (*He rises with an intense, restless movement.*) Can you conceive how lonely I am, when there is nothing that doesn't shun me, that doesn't shrink as I come near?

DUKE (*slowly*)—Yes, of course . . .

SHADOW (*intensely, as though to himself*)—There is something here . . . to be known and felt . . . something desirable that makes men fear me and cling to their life. I must know what it is! (*He pauses abruptly.*) In short, my dear sir, I wish to live a complete life in the space of three days.

It is not going to be an easy thing to accomplish, Death admits. But he is quite sure it can be done, and that the attempt will prove most interesting, if the Duke will help.

First Duke Lambert is to invite Death to spend the three days at Villa Happiness as one of the guests. As a mortal, of course. Death will become quite a man of the world.

In fact he will become, as he thinks it over, that same Prince Sirki of Vitalba Alexandri whom Duke Lambert is expecting. The Prince, Death is pained to inform his host, will not appear. The Prince and Death had met professionally earlier in the evening.

Fortunately Prince Sirki was not known to Duke Lambert's other guests or to his family, and his substitute can, therefore, be quite freely introduced as the Prince himself.

"And please understand," the Shadow adds, comfortingly, "that my presence in your house will not be a menace, but a protection."

"Oh, thank you."

"On one condition, on which I shall insist."

"Yes?"

"I am to be Prince Sirki . . . no other. I shall be a mortal, and I must be treated as a mortal, in every particular. I require that no one under this roof, and no one who may visit you shall show repulsion or fear, on pain of my instant displeasure. . . . I will have nothing distasteful on my holiday. If anyone violates my command, I shall leave, instantly, as a mortal and return as . . . (*He nods his head significantly.*)

"I understand, Your Highness."

And now Death is deeply impressed with the possibilities of his adventure. There is something suggesting hysteria in his speech as he continues, speaking as though to himself.

"And so I am at last to become a mortal! . . . I shall feel

blood in my veins . . . warm blood of life. I shall feel my desire becoming flesh and my hunger taking the fire of blood. . . . I shall know what you know, and feel what you feel. When I take flowers in my hand they will not wither. And youth will not run from me with terrified eyes. (*He makes a movement of intense restlessness, as though his inner pressure were near agony.*) My hunger shall be appeased for an hour . . . my hunger that is as old as time. . . . And those that I love need not . . . be afraid, not afraid! (*He laughs with insane intensity.*) No. . . . No . . . I am beside myself. . . . My holiday is just caprice . . . a mad joke I play with life. . . . Ha, ha . . . what a monstrous, what a sublime joke. . . . (*He draws himself up with a mocking laugh.*) I, Death, do hereby take on the world, the flesh and the Devil! (*With an effort the Shadow masters himself.*) Forgive me, my friend. My sense of humor overcame me for a moment. . . . And now shall we begin our interesting experiment?"

There is still the matter of the appearance of this new Prince Sirki. What shall his face be like? It cannot bear the likeness of Death that men have come to fear. Death will borrow the Lamp of Illusion, which so softens the lines of ugly and forbidding things as to make them quite acceptable to those mortals who cannot bear to face life as it really is. With the aid of the Lamp of Illusion he will change his entire person.

"I think your guests will not find me unattractive," he says, "and you will not find me a poor masquerader! Expect me soon. . . . You are to be distinguished among hosts, sir. None has entertained Death before, and lived."

With a bound Death has disappeared in the garden. Immediately there are shots fired outside and Corrado's voice can be heard calling excitedly to Eric Fenton to stop the fleeing intruder.

The Duke is terrified. He commands that Corrado shall cease this particular pursuit. One by one, the guests rush in from their sleeping rooms. The shots have terrified them. Nor is their confused state of mind helped any by the Duke's strange attitude toward their pursuit of the prowler they believe they have seen.

Still the Duke will not satisfy their curiosity beyond the confession that he has had a most extraordinary experience and that the danger they feared has passed. Grazia is safe. That's all that matters.

And now they must be prepared to help him receive another guest. Prince Sirki of Vitalba Alexandri will be with them shortly. And, if they would please their host, they will be very careful in their treatment of the Prince.

"Treat him as a Prince and a gentleman always. This is more important than I can tell you. And, above all, you mustn't be afraid."

"But why should we be afraid?"

"He might be offended, don't you see?" The Duke is taken off guard, but he pulls himself quickly together. "You must be gay and laugh with him," he continues, "and no matter what happens, you must never shun him, or protest . . . or run . . . It would be no good if you did. . . . You can't run from . . ."

Duke Lambert checks himself sharply, and before the growing fear of his guests can take form Prince Sirki is announced.

(*The* SHADOW *enters in the fatigue uniform of a grand duke of Russia. As he enters the Lamp of Illusion begins to glow on the wall. He wears a great coat and cap, and a monocle in his eye. He hands his cap to* FEDELE *and comes down the steps. He clicks his heels and bows. The women curtsey and the men bow. All the guests are astonished and delighted at his distinguished appearance.*)

One by one the guests are presented to the distinguished newcomer. They accept the honor formally, perhaps a bit hesitantly, but without conscious fear.

To the ladies Death is gracious and courtly, as pleased with their trust of him as they with his interest in them. The Baron Cesarea he is most pleased to meet—at last. And the Baron is equally pleased to report that not only is he indebted to Prince Sirki for an exciting evening, but also for the fact that with the Prince's appearance, his rheumatism has disappeared and he feels young enough to take up statesmanship again.

With the introductions over the Prince would put them all at their ease.

"Please make no change in your plans because of my sudden appearance," he begs of them. "I should like to join in your pleasures, if I may, and enjoy the hours with you. I beg you not to make a stranger of me."

DUKE—Will Your Highness have a little refreshment?

SHADOW—Refreshment? (*The word is evidently strange. He accustoms his mind to it.*)

DUKE—A glass of wine?

SHADOW (*doubtfully*)—Oh, yes, a glass of wine.

DUKE—Corrado . . . (CORRADO *brings a glass of wine. The* SHADOW *considers it, smiling.*)

SHADOW—I have never tasted wine . . . of your country. . . .

May I drink to this delightful household? I believe this is one of your customs, is it not?

DUKE—It is, yes. And may I thank you for myself and my guests?

SHADOW (*lifting his glass*)—To this household . . . to life . . . and to all brave illusion. (*He sips and starts to hand the glass to* CORRADO *when he reconsiders and drinks more.* CORRADO *starts to take the glass.*) Wait a minute. (*He finishes the wine. The* SHADOW *stands as though weighing the effect. His face lights with a curious smile.*) I think I shall enjoy your wine. It goes pleasantly in my veins.

DUKE (*smiling*)—It is often a consolation.

SHADOW—Ah, I see. One of the handmaids of illusion.

FEDELE—The rooms are ready, Your Grace. (*He exits.*)

SHADOW—My rooms?

DUKE—Yes. At your pleasure.

SHADOW—Then, if you will forgive me, I think I will go now. (*He smiles again secretly.*) I have not slept, for ages, and I feel curiously tired. (*He bows to the group.*) Good night, my friends. My holiday begins most agreeably.

(*All bow and murmur "Good night, Your Highness." As the* SHADOW *turns to cross, the* PRINCESS *and* GRAZIA *enter, left. The* SHADOW *pauses suddenly, his eyes on* GRAZIA.)

DUKE—Your Highness, may I present the Princess of San Lucca, and her daughter, Grazia. . . . Prince Sirki.

(*The* PRINCESS *bows, murmuring "Your Highness." The* SHADOW *and* GRAZIA *stand as though they had heard nothing. Then the* SHADOW *bows and stands aside as the* PRINCESS *and* GRAZIA *pass,* GRAZIA *and the* SHADOW *holding each other's eyes. The* SHADOW *starts to exit, he takes a few steps, looks back at* GRAZIA, *then exits as the curtain falls.*)

ACT II

It is 9 o'clock in the evening of the third day following the arrival of Prince Sirki at the Villa Happiness. The main hall of the castle is the same, but in the garden outside there have been noticeable changes. "The flowers and vines appear more profuse and brilliant; they seem crowding into the room."

In an adjoining room there is music, and the gay laughter of a happy crowd. Corrado, resplendent in evening dress, is quite inclined to sink dully into a chair when he comes from the ballroom. Baron Cesarea, who follows him out, is quick to note Corrado's attitude and inclined to wonder at it, seeing that it is a glorious night and that he himself is feeling "a very blade of a fellow."

As for Prince Sirki, he is positively a sensation, the Baron admits. The women crowd about him, the men envy him his successes.

Presently the Prince joins these two. He is in the full dress uniform of a grand duke and very impressive. He, too, has felt the need of a breath of fresh air.

"I am not used to this mixture of perfume and warm flesh," His Highness confesses. "It is . . . disturbing."

"But such a pleasant disturbance," chortles the Baron. "Ah, I wish I knew the secret of your popularity!"

"It is quite simple," the Prince replies. "Suggest that you have great depths of wisdom and great depths of passion, which no one has really discovered. They will come flocking."

A moment later Sirki has grown philosophical in seeking to learn from the Baron what it is that men prize most in life.

SHADOW—What is this thing of great price that dignifies our life, and makes it dear?

BARON—It is very flattering of you to ask. . . .

SHADOW—I have been joining in your games and in your dances. I have won some bits of metal at a little wheel. (*He tosses a purse of gold on the table.*) It seems to me that we are like children, playing with toys, passing the time while we wait for something . . . for that thing of great price. Beneath this play I hear the voice of a deep hunger, unsatisfied. For what? Can you tell me?

BARON—Philosophers have never agreed about the ultimate good.

SHADOW (*a little impatiently*)—I am asking you as a person.

BARON—Why, in my own case, I have had two aims . . . love and power.

SHADOW—Power! I have power, but that is a lonely thing. I thought this good was something to be shared.

BARON—Of course, men have chosen other things . . . religion, for instance. They have even died for that.

SHADOW—Yes, I have known many of them. They died in defense of their own opinion. But at least they were not afraid.

BARON—I used to say, in my young days, that I would die for love. I often threatened it.

SHADOW (*impatiently*)—It seems to me that men have not

begun to discover the magnificence of their life. . . . To breathe the perfumed air of a garden! To feel one's strong body moving in the sun! To feel thought flashing on the mind, and emotion like a glowing fire in the soul! . . . There is splendor here, if one can find it. (*He gestures toward the garden.*) Out there is the night, crowded with beauty! And we herd inside, feverish over little games. Why?

BARON (*slyly*)—Haven't you found that only lovers care to be alone in the night?

SHADOW—Perhaps that's it. Perhaps that beauty is too great to be borne, unless it is shared. . . . Tell me, Baron . . . you see I am a little strange to your ways . . . how does one find that love, or know when one has found it?

BARON (*slyly*)—The language of eyes and lips is universal, is it not, Your Highness?

SHADOW (*sternly*)—I am serious.

BARON—Why, one meets a beautiful creature . . . preferably a beautiful creature . . . and something electric passes between you. Then there is the prelude of talk, long or short. (*He laughs.*) I remember that once coming down stairs in a room much like this, and finding a lovely girl sitting alone, I stopped, and our eyes met. After a long look I stepped to the wall, dimmed the lights, and a moment later she was in my arms. A divine creature!

SHADOW (*drily*)—Again that sounds like playing with toys.

BARON (*gently*)—I am speaking of affairs, of course. There was one whom I loved, with whom I could share . . . anything. But she died.

SHADOW—Yes, I remember. The Countess Sfortza.

BARON (*quickly*)—You knew her?

SHADOW—I met her, just once, toward the end of her life.

The Prince finds himself interested but not seriously perturbed by the Baron's report of the strange things that have been happening in the world the last few days. There is the case of the man who threw himself from the Eiffel Tower yet picked himself up, unhurt. Poor fellow! He is at least entitled to a letter of condolence, agrees the Prince. And there is the curious situation existing on the Algerian front, where there is a war going on. Not a shot fired in three days. But that, Sirki explains, is but temporary. Men's sacred privilege of blowing each other to bits will be restored shortly to them.

The Baron's reminiscences flow on. He is reminded, by a drink of Corrado's cognac, of the nights and nights he had sat up as a young man drinking and talking of love and religion.

But why religion *and* love, the Prince demands. Aren't they the same—two words with the same meaning?

"Of course they are," the Baron agrees, a bit flustered by the Prince's logic. "Of course they are. What a magnificent mind you have. And what a lover you must be!"

"Ah . . . if I had the time!" the Prince muses. Then, lifting his glass, he offers a toast. "My dear Baron, let us drink to three things: To beauty, to love, and to ecstasy that is their child."

And now, his manner having become suddenly curt as he realizes that Grazia and her mother have not yet come and the hour grows late, Prince Sirki leaves them. The "bits of metal" he has won he gives them to pass on to their favorite charities.

The Baron has also gone in search of further ballroom adventures and Eric Fenton has drifted in. He, too, is disturbed—uncomfortably disturbed by the chill that comes over him whenever Prince Sirki is around. Eric has noticed, too, that Duke Lambert is not altogether happy; nervous and as watchful, in fact, as though he were awaiting something that might happen. And what did the Duke mean by that unfinished sentence, when he said: "You can't run from . . ."

Both Eric and Corrado are determined to learn the answer. Duke Lambert, looking strained and grave as he joins them, evades their queries as to the cause of his apparent worry. And warns them to be extremely careful this particular evening not to let anyone see that they are worried.

"Be . . . be particularly friendly with the Prince," the Duke adds. "It's his last evening and I want it pleasant."

The Princess Marie has arrived. Grazia is not with her. Yet Grazia must not miss this evening. The Duke is almost insistent on that point. Which excites the suspicions of the Princess as well as the others.

"Lambert," she demands, "what is all this mystery about?"

"Mystery?"

PRINCESS—Yes. You all seem concerned about something. Who is this man?

DUKE (*slowly*)—Prince Sirki. . . .

PRINCESS—I feel that you are concealing something.

DUKE—Please, Marie.

PRINCESS—And Grazia has been very strange these past three

days. . . . Restless . . . and almost exalted. I think she is attracted to this man. And if there is any reason why she should not be . . .

CORRADO (*desperately*)—They're all fascinated!

DUKE—No. . . . No, they couldn't be. . . .

PRINCESS—Why?

DUKE—I mean . . . nothing could come of it. He wouldn't encourage them. And, Marie, it's his last evening. He goes at midnight.

CORRADO—Why at midnight?

DUKE (*off guard*)—That's his natural . . . That is . . . it's a whim of his, just whim, nothing more.

PRINCESS—I wish you might be frank with me. As it is I think I must forbid Grazia to come.

DUKE (*sharply*)—Don't do that!

CORRADO—Do keep her at home, Princess.

DUKE (*desperately*)—You mustn't! It might be . . . (*He pauses, then speaks earnestly.*) Marie . . . I love Grazia, almost as much as you do. If any harm threatens her I shall know. What I am doing is for the best . . . for all of us. Please believe that I would give my life for Grazia.

CORRADO—We all would.

PRINCESS—Then there is no reason why she should not come?

DUKE—None.

PRINCESS (*after a pause*)—Very well. I must take your word, of course.

CORRADO—I'll take care of her, Princess.

PRINCESS (*gives Corrado wrap*)—Thank you, dear; and will you telephone for her to come?

CORRADO—Yes, of course.

The wonders of the evening expand. The Baron's recovery of his middle youth continues to delight him and surprise his friends, particularly his lady friends.

Eric Fenton and Mme. Alda are likewise disturbed, but it is mostly nerves with them. Neither has been able to sleep. Both are conscious of a strange, mysterious influence associated with Prince Sirki, yet neither is able exactly to define it.

There are many things that have not been explained. The lamp that is kept burning even through the day, for one. When Alda asked Sirki about that, she reports, he merely smiled and answered that it was "a bit of decoration to give *couleur de rose* to my adventure."

Even Rhoda Fenton has not been without fears and strange misgivings respecting the Prince. "I've felt like praying all day," she confesses to Alda. And even as she confesses she notices with a start that roses which had been put in a bowl the day the Prince arrived have not withered at all.

"And one of the gardeners said this morning that things were growing as he never saw them," she continues. "He said that not a leaf had fallen. . . . Alda . . . the vines . . . are trying to burst their way into the house. . . . What does it mean?"

Before Alda can attempt an adequate answer, and before Rhoda can follow up an impulse to run, Prince Sirki is with them. Alda curtseys and passes him on the stairway. But Rhoda is held. Nor can she get away by advancing the excuse that she has left her pearls lying on a table and fears a servant may be tempted. Pearls have little value in the country from which the Prince hails.

He has, His Highness admits, been observing the athletic Rhoda for some time and favorably.

"You move as freely as an unhurrying wind," he tells her. "It is a delight to watch. And there is something about you of the freshness of the morning star."

"Oh, Your Highness!"

SHADOW (*smiling*)—You know, it is peculiarly refreshing to me to be near some one who is so very fit.

RHODA—Why?

SHADOW—Well, the oddness in that is a little obscure. But, believe me, it is there.

RHODA—Your Highness so often speaks in riddles.

SHADOW—Yes. A game I play for my amusement. You see, I have known so much of illness that I take a singular interest in all young and budding life . . . in vigor, in bloom. It quite stirs me. (*He stands as though listening to his sensations.*) Yes, it undoubtedly stirs me.

RHODA (*breathlessly, after a pause*)—Oh, please don't stop!

SHADOW—In what key shall I go on?

RHODA—Say anything!

SHADOW—Very well, Miss Fenton, what is love?

RHODA (*startled*)—Love?

SHADOW—Yes, love. The thing of which you are thinking so earnestly, just now.

RHODA (*hesitant*)—Why . . .

SHADOW—Tell me. Don't be afraid. What does it mean to you?

RHODA—Why . . . to find some . . . some splendid man, who loves you, too . . .

SHADOW (*smiling*)—Like myself, perhaps?

RHODA—Yes. And . . . and to live with him . . . the rest of your life.

SHADOW—Thank you. You have done bravely. (*The* SHADOW *is speaking with a growing intensity.*) But . . . if the rest of one's life were only a few days . . . or a few hours . . . would that be enough to justify . . . love?

RHODA (*frightened*)—You mean . . . if one of them should . . .

SHADOW (*continuing*)—And if, after those few hours, they should go a great way off, where they should live like two beams of light . . . with the swiftness and clarity of light. Would that be enough?

RHODA (*frightened*)—Your Highness . . . I don't understand!

SHADOW (*intensely*)—Suppose . . . when their bodies had clung together for an hour that they must live, for the rest of time, like two thoughts, communing together in pure silence. Would you choose such love? Have you enough courage? (*He is looking into her eyes with burning directness.* RHODA *draws back with a smothered cry. He stops her with a laugh, then takes her hand.*) No, I must not frighten you. I have your answer.

RHODA—What have I said?

SHADOW—A great deal. You see, my dear, yours is only a vague calling of the blood, the effect of exercise and open air. . . . Very beautiful, no doubt, and prophetic of a healthy human race, but . . .

RHODA (*brokenly*)—Oh, Your Highness . . . I have disappointed you!

SHADOW—It is my fault. I asked too much. (*He bows in dismissal.*) I hope you find your pearls quite safe, Miss Fenton. (*She starts away.*) And . . . when we next meet do not be afraid. Those who know me best have found that there is nothing to fear.

Rhoda has gone, but Alda has returned. And now she, in turn, is listening, entranced, to the subtle and disarming compliments of the Prince. Soon she is willing to confess that he is "the most fascinating . . . the most compelling . . . the most royal man" she has ever met.

"You are an interesting woman, Alda," the Prince returns.
"Am I?" she queries, earnestly.
"Shall I tell you what you are?"
"Yes."

SHADOW—You have lost many illusions, but you cling to one, hoping it is not an illusion. Do you know what it is?

ALDA—Yes.

SHADOW—You have sought experience, but none has satisfied you, yet. You long for something wild . . . overpowering, to sweep you beyond thought.

ALDA (*faintly*)—Yes.

SHADOW—Shall I read you further? You are an open book to me.

ALDA—Yes.

SHADOW—I have been listening to the sound of you. On the surface there are many little sounds, graceful and charming. And beneath, one simple and primitive sound. I am hearing it now. (*He is exerting all his charm.*) Shall I go on?

ALDA (*closing her eyes*)—Yes.

SHADOW—You do not know who I am, and my mystery attracts you, and stirs your desire. I can see it now, throbbing in your blood . . . I can see it rising like a throb in your throat. (ALDA *puts one hand quickly to her throat. She is now a bird caught by a snake's eyes.*)

ALDA—Oh . . .

SHADOW (*with sinister intensity*)—The unknown is drawing you. I wonder . . . if I were to tell you who I am . . .

ALDA (*faintly*)—Who . . . are you?

SHADOW—Ah, could you bear that, you, a mortal?

ALDA (*shrinking*)—A mortal?

SHADOW—I wonder if your passion is great enough. You desire me now. You are quivering at the thought of my touch. I can feel you calling to me. If I were to kiss you. (*He kisses her.*) Ah . . . now you are caught up into the dark current of my being. Shall I call you back, or will you go on . . . and on?

ALDA (*half swooning*)—On . . .

SHADOW (*triumphantly*)—Ah . . . then I *can* feed your desire!

ALDA—Yes.

SHADOW—You do desire me?

ALDA—Yes.

SHADOW—How much?

ALDA—More than life itself.

SHADOW—I wonder . . . You are not afraid?

ALDA—No.

SHADOW—Let me see. (*He lifts her face.*) Look into my eyes! Look deep! What do you see there?

ALDA (*fearfully*)—Shadows!

SHADOW—Look into that shadow. Let your thought go to its wildest reach. . . . I *will* you to know who I am.

ALDA (*in sharp fear*)—No . . . no!

SHADOW (*intensely*)—You, who were not afraid! You desired me as a mortal, say my immortal name and see if you desire me still!

ALDA (*near fainting*)—I . . . can't!

SHADOW—Say it!

ALDA—Oh . . . pity me!

SHADOW—Say it!

ALDA—You are . . . Oh . . . (*She screams and falls in a half faint on the sofa. He laughs in sardonic bitterness.*)

SHADOW (*rising after a pause*)—Ah . . . it wasn't love with you, only passion. You were flaming, but at the sound of my name lust grew cold, and that is not the measure of love. You're not great enough for me, Alda. I am looking for a response you could never give. I am searching for someone who knows, and is not afraid.

ALDA—Oh . . . oh . . .

SHADOW (*after a pause, in a changed tone*)—Forgive me, I had to do this. There was something I wanted to know, and you have told me. (*He takes a few restless steps.* ALDA *watches him fearfully. He speaks half to her and half to himself, with a deep intensity.*) I wanted to know and feel so much! And I have . . . a lifetime, many lifetimes, in three days. Because I was so avid of life my senses have drained it. (*He takes a rose from the bowl.*) Even this flower . . . No one will ever know its fragrance like I have. None could know . . . but Death. (ALDA *rises and rushes fearfully from the room. He is so absorbed that he doesn't notice.*) But there is another flower . . . more fragrant than this . . . which I haven't plucked. I've been afraid! But I *must* pluck it. Until then I haven't lived. And I will not end these days in failure.

Grazia has at last arrived. She comes from the garden "dressed in white, looking lovely and buoyant," and she is most happy in her greeting of His Serene Highness. She even would accept lightly his protest that she is far too formal in her attitude toward him and agrees to call him by one of his many given names—Boris, maybe—and permit him to call her Grazia.

"You make it sound like music," Grazia confesses.

"It is music," answers the Prince. "It has overtones that go singing on and on. . . . But they are not sad. They're full of grace and light."

"Your Highness is being very kind tonight."

"I wonder if I am being . . . *kind,*" His Highness mutters. His face is contracted with pain.

The Duke has returned, bringing with him Major Whitred, a veteran of the Legion, and as he switches on the lights he is worried at the sight of the Prince and Grazia so intimately concerned with their own thoughts.

That Grazia is happy is shown by the buoyancy with which she curtseys and leaves them when the Duke reports that her mother has been looking anxiously for her.

Major Whitred, "a lean, tanned, distinguished soldier about 40; dressed in the uniform of the Foreign Legion, his breast covered with medals," confesses that he has been awfully anxious to meet Prince Sirki, and the Prince admits that he has not been unmindful of the Major's desire.

As a matter of fact, as the Prince recalls the circumstances, they have nearly met on numerous occasions. And, for his part, he is always ready to meet a soldier and a good fellow.

DUKE—I think you'll find the Major a man after your own heart, Your Highness. Like yourself, his job has taken him to all parts of the world. (*The* DUKE *exits.*)

SHADOW—I've known a good many legionaires, but usually on the field.

MAJOR—Quite so, sir. We generally stay there.

SHADOW—That, also, has not escaped my notice.

MAJOR (*laughing*)—We're a mad lot, I'm afraid. It's a wonder I'm still here. Been nodding good morning to Death for a long while, now. I've stood uncomfortably close to him, several times.

SHADOW (*smiling*)—Why do you say "uncomfortably close" when you have so often sought a closer acquaintance?

MAJOR (*with a laugh*)—Well, hardly that. I suppose it's the danger that's attractive. I don't mean to say one's never afraid. Personally I'm often petrified. Of course, most of the legionaires are trying to say good-bye. They've got into trouble, or a woman's gone back on them. They've messed things up, somehow. But no matter how glad we'd be to get out, we always feel a bit chilly when the Old Man comes to fetch us, don't we?

SHADOW (*haughtily*)—I beg your pardon? The Old Man? Oh, yes . . . the Old Man. (*He laughs suddenly.*) Sit down, Major. (*They sit.*) You do not know how funny that is. Tell me . . . what do your friends in the legion expect to find when they say good-bye?

MAJOR—Why . . . six feet of earth, I should think . . . and a good rest. And no more parades.

SHADOW—Is that all?

MAJOR—Well, of course they'll be safe from the women.

SHADOW—Safe! . . . Oh, I see. It appears, then, that love makes a man either wish to live or to die.

MAJOR—That's about it. As for what comes after, fighting chaps don't think much about it. Better leave mysteries like that alone, don't you think?

SHADOW—But they are never left alone. Fear is the proof of that. And religion builds fantastic pictures to still that fear and to make life seem less hard. But has it never occurred to you, Major, that death may be only more simple than life, and perhaps more desirable?

MAJOR (*after a pause*)—Odd, you should say that. You know, sometimes, when I've been in a tight place, I've had a curious sort of inspiration. It may have been just the excitement, of course, the intoxication of danger.

SHADOW—Perhaps it was revelation.

MAJOR (*slowly*)—Yes. And once I had a curious dream when I was wounded. I was standing alone, at the top of the world, on an icy peak, and all the mysteries seemed clear to me. I knew all truth for a moment, and was utterly content. Since then I have felt that death may be a high adventure, a magnificent discovery . . . a glorious freedom. (*He is rather embarrassed at saying this.*)

SHADOW—Permit me to say, you are a very fortunate man.

MAJOR—I suppose it's the unknown that bothers us . . . and the parting. Personally, there isn't anyone who cares very much when or where I go. But usually there is.

SHADOW (*after a pause, struck by some thought*)—The parting! Yes . . . when someone must be left behind. (*He rises, bows formally, indicating that the audience is over.*) Thank you, Major, this has been very interesting. We shall meet again, of course.

MAJOR—Happy to meet you any time.

The Major has gone. Duke Lambert, still worried, finds a match now in Sirki. His Highness is also greatly troubled. Something that he had not foreseen has happened, and to meet the difficulty he must again demand the fullest understanding and the most complete coöperation from his host. Again the Prince warns that there must be no interference with what he is obliged to do.

Prince Sirki is, he confesses, in love. Though he laughs sardonically as he confesses it, the muscles of his face are taut with strain.

"I, who am called the destroyer of life, now wish to love and cherish life . . . to hold it tenderly . . . and passionately." His laughter is sardonic.

"But . . . do you love . . . a mortal?" fearfully demands the Duke.

"I said . . . passionately. . . . Does that indicate a bloodless ghost?"

DUKE—But . . . Your Highness . . . what will happen when you . . .

SHADOW—You think perhaps I am being cruel. . . .

DUKE—This is . . . horrible . . .

SHADOW (*intensely restless*)—Perhaps I am being cruel. . . . I don't know. . . . But isn't that proof of my mortality? Does your mortal lover think and weigh? He plunders where he can, knowing that there will be an end. Does it matter if that end is one day or ten years?

DUKE (*in agony*)—But it is fatal to love you!

SHADOW—Have you forgotten that tonight I must go, with empty hands?

DUKE—Are you sure?

SHADOW (*austerely*)—I am an expert at . . . conclusions . . . my friend. (*He considers the* DUKE. *His voice is strained and sharp.*) Don't look at me with that fear in your eyes! I tell you it is I who am afraid! (*He laughs wildly.*) This is what my caprice has brought me to. I came to sip and taste your pleasures, to find what meaning they had that makes you cling to life. And I have found it. . . . It is love, and the hope of winning love. And now I am caught and bound, until this borrowed blood of mine is aching with an intolerable pain. (*He laughs again.*) I, who was invincible, have found a stronger thing than I!

DUKE—Will you tell me . . . who?

SHADOW (*suddenly*)—No, I will not tell you. But understand this, clearly. I will not be thwarted. I should not wish to repay your kindness with disaster, but, I warn you, no one must hinder me. Is that clear?

DUKE (*swallowing hard*)—Yes.

SHADOW—Thank you.

Sirki has gone back to the garden, leaving Duke Lambert agitated and fearful. When he is joined by Corrado and the Baron he is forced almost to the point of breaking his word in his effort to warn them of the situation with which they are all faced.

Prince Sirki has confessed his love of a guest in that house. So much the Duke tells them. More than that they cannot know. Of what the terrible significance of his statement may be they must remain in ignorance. And they must do something to try and stop His Highness. . . . Let Corrado stay close to Grazia; let the Baron keep near Alda. That's all that any of them can do.

Corrado finds the instructions not easy to carry out. With the Duke and the Baron returned to the party Corrado meets Grazia as she comes from the garden, walking as though in a dream. When she speaks it is as though from a great distance. "Her voice is gentle, but as impersonal as pure sound."

Grazia is not interested in the entertainment. She is not interested, at the moment, in Corrado, nor in his impassioned desire to keep close to her because he loves her and fears for her safety.

Grazia asks to be left alone. She is not afraid. She is quite calm. She is waiting for someone—but there is no danger. Only happiness—something that she has been waiting for for a long time.

"Please don't be unhappy, Corrado," she pleads at sight of his misery. "I love you, in some way, in some way I can't make clear. If I didn't feel so far away I should be in your arms, crying, and holding you close to me. I want to do that, but I think I never shall."

Grazia is trembling a little with the cold. She would send Corrado for her cloak. When he is reluctant to leave her, even for so short a time, she puts her arms about his neck and kisses him. But even as he clings to her, trembling, protesting his consuming love, she dismisses him.

When Corrado has left her Grazia looks after him for a moment and then slowly mounts the steps and sits on the bench. "Presently the Shadow approaches, slowly, from the garden." Now he stands looking down at her.

SHADOW—Why are you not with the guests? (*In a limpid, happy tone.*)

GRAZIA—For the same reason that you're not, I think.

SHADOW—You say that so simply, as though you knew.

GRAZIA—I do know.

SHADOW—It's strange. . . . We hardly need to speak, do we?

GRAZIA—Thoughts are so much clearer than words.

SHADOW—Then perhaps you can tell me what I've been doing in the garden?

GRAZIA—I think I can . . . almost.

SHADOW—Tell me. I want to hear it from your lips. (GRAZIA *speaks slowly with a curious clarity and simplicity of voice.*)

GRAZIA—I think you have been holding life in your hands, as I do sometimes. . . . I think you have been a little afraid of its beauty.

SHADOW (*trembling*)—Ah, you do know! You wonderful, exquisite child! (*He kneels and takes her hand.* GRAZIA *seems hardly breathing as she looks up into his face.*) I have been walking in a garden that was full of you, and under a sky that sang of you. . . . Your laughter was in a wind that went by and touched my hair. . . . I knelt by a yellow flower, and out of its heart came a sound that was your voice. I put my ear to the ground, and heard your footsteps moving toward me, across the world. All the earth was trembling under your little feet. I stood looking at the sky, and the night was illumined by the knowledge of you . . . and I was *shaken.*

GRAZIA (*as though from a distance*)—And ever since I saw you, I have been shaken. . . . Oh, what is this that has happened? Who . . . are you?

SHADOW (*trembling*)—Sirki . . .

GRAZIA (*shaking her head*)—I don't mean that . . . you seem to come from a distant place . . .

SHADOW—I do come from far away . . . but . . .

GRAZIA—When I'm with you I see depths in your eyes that are like the worlds I visit in sleep . . . and beneath your words there is a sound that I've heard in dreams, and sometimes when there is a storm in the mountains . . . and when you leave me the light goes from the sky. (*She gives a little, shaken laugh.*) You seem like the mystery that is just beyond sight and sound . . . always just beyond my reach. . . . Something that draws . . . and frightens me. (*The* SHADOW puts his arms about her. His voice is shaken with emotion.)

SHADOW—Oh, Grazia . . . Grazia . . . don't be afraid of me!

. . . I am Sirki who loves you! More than any man could love you! I am Sirki, who needs your warmth and your beauty more than any man could need them. I say your name over and over, until its music runs through all my being. . . . Your hands are white jasmine flowers in the sun. (*He covers her hands with kisses.* GRAZIA *is near to fainting.*) Grazia . . . listen to me. I am a great power, and I am humble before you . . . and to-night I must go back to my . . . distant kingdom.

GRAZIA (*far away*)—Will you take me? (*The impact of her words is startling. He rises as though shocked beyond speech.*)

SHADOW—Take . . . you . . .

GRAZIA—Yes. I should be so unhappy, alone.

SHADOW—Take . . . you . . . (*With sudden intensity.*) No . . . no! Don't tempt me. (*He lifts her and takes her in his arms.*) But, Grazia, give me one hour of you! Let me hold you once, and feel your life. You are the meaning of beauty that I must know. Grazia, let me hold you, and feel that ecstasy . . . and know that I have lived!

GRAZIA—Oh, my love, my love!

SHADOW—My little love!

Their lips cling together in a long kiss and slowly they walk up the steps and into the garden. Duke Lambert, coming from the house, sees them as they disappear and is terrified. Corrado, following his father, bringing Grazia's cloak, insistently demands to know where she is and why he should be kept back from going to her.

Now Corrado knows it is Grazia that Sirki meant, and he feels that Sirki is cruel. Surely, they must save Grazia from this stranger some way! Nor is he content with the Duke's insisting that if there were anything that could be done he would not now be there impotently protesting his helplessness.

Now Stephanie has come. And Grazia's mother. Now Eric and the Major. And demanding to know what is happening and why? Finally the Duke tells them. He speaks with difficulty and there is no trace of conviction in his voice.

DUKE—Grazia . . . and Prince Sirki . . . have gone into the garden. . . . There is nothing to be alarmed about.

CORRADO (*after a pause*)—But you're alarmed, Father, you're terrified. I must know why.

PRINCESS—Lambert, let me go to her!

DUKE—No . . . no . . . wait!

CORRADO—Then I'll go. (*He starts away.*)

DUKE (*shouting*)—I forbid you to move! (*They stand facing one another.*)

CORRADO—Then tell me why I can't go. (*Comes down to table.*) Give me your reason.

DUKE—I can't . . .

CORRADO—Grazia's in some danger, I know it.

PRINCESS—Where have they gone?

DUKE—No!

CORRADO—You *will* tell me, or by God I'll kill him.

DUKE (*in sudden hysteria*)—You can't kill him. . . . But he can kill us. If he but puts out his hand, all of us . . .

CORRADO—Who is this prince?

DUKE—You don't know what you're asking.

CORRADO—And I don't care. I only know that Grazia's in danger.

DUKE—You're risking your life, and I'm risking mine.

CORRADO—What's your life or mine? You said you would die for Grazia.

DUKE—I would, if that would save her.

CORRADO—Then tell me what you know!

STEPHANIE (*suddenly*)—No, Lambert, no!

PRINCESS (*moaning*)—Save Grazia! Save Grazia!

DUKE (*after a pause*)—Very well, I'll tell you. . . . He said if I reveal his secret he will leave instantly as Sirki, and return as . . . Steel yourselves, if you are to hear it. . . . He is not Prince Sirki. He is one who waits . . . The one whom all men dread. (*Hysterically.*) His Majesty . . . *Death* . . . amusing himself, on a holiday!

PRINCESS—Grazia . . . Grazia . . . (*She starts toward the garden as the curtain falls.*)

ACT III

The evening has worn on. It is 11:30. The Duke, Stephanie, Baron Cesarea, Eric, Major Whitred and Corrado are all in the great hall of the castle, "looking as though they had been staring at Death for hours."

"If only he would come, if he *must* come, and get it over with," Eric voices the sentiment of all the watchers.

"And bring Grazia," adds the tortured Corrado.

The waiting grows tense. Duke Lambert recalls again, as he

has done many times, the warning that when the Prince appears he must be treated and thought of only as Prince Sirki.

Major Whitred thinks perhaps if they all would go and leave him to meet the Prince alone it would be better. He is, after all, rather used to that experience.

It would do no good, the Duke is convinced. And Stephanie is sure that if any of them should show fear now it would mean the gravest danger to the Duke, who has revealed the secret.

Eric Fenton finds some comfort in the thought that seeing they have been facing the enemy for two hours in their minds it may not be so difficult when he does come.

"Much easier, of course," the Major agrees. "There's something inspiring in danger when it's right in front of you. I wonder if it's because we really know that—that what's beyond is inspiring, too?"

Baron Cesarea, too, discovers a helpful philosophy to fit his own case.

"I thought I'd found my youth again," he muses, "but it was only his holiday. I'd stopped dying, that's all. Now my holiday's over. Tomorrow I'll be older than ever. I might as well go with him tonight."

The Major is certain they will all have the proper courage to meet whatever comes.

"Do you know, I think we may all be wrong to be afraid," the soldier ventures. "I talked with him tonight about dying, and he said, 'Has it ever occurred to you that death may be only simpler than life, and infinitely more kind?' "

"He said . . . that?" demands the Duke.

"Yes. And when he spoke I had a curious feeling that somehow he knew."

"Now there is a sudden silence and a movement of fear as the Shadow is seen approaching from the garden. He enters slowly and considers the group. Their attempt to meet him bravely indicates that they know who he is. The shadow carries on his arm his black cloak which he throws over the back of a chair."

His Highness faces the Duke. There is a note of disappointment in his voice.

"So, you have broken your promise," he says.

"I was desperate, sir. It was my son's life against my promise. I had no choice." The Duke's explanation is halting.

"I am not used to these distinctions," calmly answers Sirki.

"It was my life or my son's, sir. If you insist on the penalty, I am ready."

Steadily, sadly, Prince Sirki studies the group. Before his gaze Stephanie sinks weakly upon the divan.

"I see. You had no choice. I thought we should part as friends, with kindly remembrances, but now my shadow has come between us."

Presently they speak of Grazia. She has not come in. There is terror in the Duke's voice as he ventures the fear that—already—

"I am Sirki, for a few moments still," the Prince reminds them. As His Highness sinks into a chair by the table, "in evident pain of spirit," Duke Lambert sees the suffering in his face. Something like wonder and satisfaction creep into his exclamation:

"Ah, now *you* are suffering," he says.

"What do *you* know of suffering?" wearily demands the Prince.

DUKE—I've known something of it these past three days.

SHADOW—Yes, of course. I've been so absorbed in my own trouble that I forgot. And yet I have not forgotten. My own pain has taught me what human suffering can be. (*He rises and walks about like a caged lion.*) This is the end of my holiday. In a few moments I shall be summoned and my wild prank will be over. I thought I could be a mortal and yet greater than any mortality. I had not reckoned with the power of love. Now I have looked at the sun, and I am blinded. I have lost my way!

DUKE—And must we lose Grazia?

SHADOW (*laughing*)—The irony of this is magnificent. I am the Lord of endings. And now I am caught in my own net. Men are sad because I am in the world, and there must be an end and a frustration. And in a few moments I shall be what I was, and for me there will be an end . . .

DUKE—But you . . . you are above loss and pain.

SHADOW—Am I, and still a mortal? I thought tonight that I had reached the end of my experiment. I had found love. But it was not the end. Beyond that I have found the pain of the loss of love . . . if I must lose it. . . .

DUKE—But it *must* be lost to you.

SHADOW—Why?

DUKE—Because you are . . .

SHADOW—Death. . . . (*His tone becomes light, ironical.*) My dear Duke . . . thank you for defining the problem. I have been talking a little wildly, but you have brought me back to earth. The situation is this: You do not wish to give up Grazia . . . neither do I. It is as simple as that, and as profound as the sadness of all parting.

They plead with Sirki in the name of Grazia's friends, and of her mother. Princess Marie joins her pleas to theirs—that he shall give Grazia back to them. And still he reasons against them, pits their sadness against his immeasurable regret, their ignorance against his knowledge, their childish fears, their supreme interest in their own needs, against the perfect love which casts out fear.

"I tell you to go with me now, in love, would be triumph, not death, as it is known to you." His voice vibrates with conviction.

It is the Duke who makes the final plea. The Prince has come as a guest to that house. There is a code which holds among men which requires that one shall not violate good faith. Shall not the Prince respect that code?

"There are worlds between us, and I cannot reach your minds." There is a terrible intensity in the Prince's tone. "You ask me to make this sacrifice as a man, when my desire is greater than a man could know. You ask me to give up love, when I long for love with a surpassing hunger. . . . You are in terror and I am in agony. (*He buries his face in his hands, then looks up.*) Why do men fear my coming? I do not see how they can bear their lives. Their courage is magnificent. I am proud to have worn the garment of this flesh."

Duke—Your Highness, we are not answered. You have ten minutes more of life, and after that . . . What can you give Grazia?

Shadow—Sleep perhaps, and the release of dreams. And beyond that . . . (*He pauses hopelessly.*) There are no words by which to tell you.

Duke—But that is death to us . . . and to her.

Shadow—A word you have been taught to fear. A symbol of the unknown. And because of that word you would keep her from me?

Princess—Your Highness, because she is dear to us.

Shadow—But even now she is not yours. The shadowy places of the imagination are her home. It is such a simple step from her world to mine.

Duke (*desperately*)—But Grazia doesn't know who you are.

Before you do this monstrous thing, won't you tell her and let her choose?

SHADOW—Ah . . . (*He covers his face in his hand, suddenly.*) Even Grazia was born to fear this face. She would die with me now, as Sirki. But to choose Death as a lover . . . No . . . No . . . I will not!

DUKE (*imploringly*)—But you gave me your word . . .

SHADOW (*ironically*)—My word . . . I remember. I said that no harm should come to this house.

DUKE—Or to the one you loved. . . .

SHADOW—But I am doing her no harm, if you only knew.

DUKE (*pressing his advantage*)—But you gave me your word!

SHADOW—And you think me bound by that?

DUKE—I do . . . as an honorable man would be bound.

SHADOW (*bitterly*)—Because I assumed your flesh, must I assume your weakness, too?

DUKE (*earnestly*)—Then pity our weakness. Be as generous as you are great. You came in search of human experience. Compassion, sir, is the highest emotion man can know . . . I have seen compassion struggling in you. We have come to beg the life of Grazia. (*There is a pause. The* SHADOW *broods a moment, then makes a gesture of resignation. His tone is ironical and bitter.*)

SHADOW—So . . . Again I am caught by my own folly. I gave myself life, not knowing the force that is in life, not the force that is in love. I gave myself life, and with it the little rules by which it is lived. And now I, Death, must bow to life. (*He laughs with wild bitterness.*) What a sublime joke! . . . What a monstrous and bitter comedy! (*His laughter ceases. He speaks in a light ironical tone.*) My dear Duke, you have all risked your lives for Grazia. I must not be outdone for courage.

Slowly the Prince turns and goes toward the garden. He lifts his hand. Presently Grazia appears "walking as though in a dream."

"Your Highness, did you call?" Again her voice comes as though from a distance. She passes her mother without hearing her exclamations of joy at her daughter's reappearance. She stands now facing Prince Sirki.

Gradually Grazia becomes conscious of her mother's protests that she should not startle them so, she should not run away in the night—

But, Grazia answers, she was quite safe with Sirki. She will always be safe with him. She must always stay with him. Even if, as her mother says, he is going away to a distant country, she would not be happy if she did not go with him.

"He's kind, mother, and more tender than anyone I've known; even more tender than you. I've found the happiness I've looked for so long."

"Why are you all so strange?" she goes on, "and why is it so dark? I wish you would be happy with me. I've found my love. There ought to be lights . . . and music . . ."

It is nearing midnight. Their pleas are redoubled, and still strange to Grazia. Sirki is resigned. Nothing that can be done now, he feels, can make any difference. Yet he will make the confession he has promised. Slowly he puts on his black cloak.

"So my mortal experience must have the usual ending," he mutters, as though to himself. "I, too, must have my parting."

Now he stands before Grazia. "His voice is austere in his renunciation. It is agony for him to speak."

SHADOW—Grazia . . . I came to this house as a jest . . . and made love to you as a jest. (GRAZIA *looks at him her smile unchanged.*)

GRAZIA—You are trying to destroy my love . . . because they wish it. . . . It was not a jest.

SHADOW (*sharply*)—Grazia . . . don't smile so! It's true. (*He turns to the group.*) Some one tell her, quickly . . . while there's time. . . . Corrado, she is cold. Take her in your arms and give her warmth! (CORRADO *goes to* GRAZIA. *He can hardly speak.*)

CORRADO—Grazia— (*She doesn't look at him.*) Grazia . . . don't you hear me?

GRAZIA (*far away*)—Yes . . . I hear.

CORRADO—Won't you stay . . . with me?

GRAZIA—I can't, Corrado. But I shall always love you.

CORRADO (*helplessly*)—Oh . . . Oh, God! (*He turns away.*)

SHADOW—Princess . . . call her to you, or she's lost.

PRINCESS—Grazia, my darling . . . come back to me! (*She looks at* GRAZIA, *who stands smiling at the* SHADOW, *then turns away, in helpless terror.*) Oh . . . she's lost . . . she's lost. (*There is a silence of tense fear. After a moment the* SHADOW *goes to her. His tone is full of pain.*)

SHADOW—Listen, Grazia, while there is time. I mustn't take you with me. You must stay here, with those who love you. If you went with me you could never come back to them again. I am going far away, to a land that would be all strangeness and mystery to you. . . . Grazia, do you hear?

GRAZIA—Yes, I hear.

SHADOW—Then, why don't you draw away?

GRAZIA—Why must you say these things to me? They can make no difference.

SHADOW (*desperately*)—You don't understand. . . . My holiday is over. . . . I am going . . . at once.

GRAZIA—I am ready.

SHADOW—No . . . you can't go with me!

GRAZIA—Yes, I can. Shall we go now? (*She goes closer to him, with a happy gesture, and takes his hand.*)

SHADOW—But you don't know who I am!

GRAZIA—You are my love. (*A slight pause, then the* SHADOW *turns to the* DUKE.)

SHADOW—You heard? Do you wish me to speak and destroy this . . . happiness?

DUKE (*unsteadily*)—You must!

SHADOW (*with a gesture of longing and tenderness*)—Grazia, my little love, it was not a jest! (*He turns slowly and stands before the Lamp of Illusion, then makes a sudden movement of his arms and the Lamp goes out. In the brief darkness he covers his head with the hood of his cloak and mounts the stairs, where the green light strikes his face which is now the mask of death.*) Good-bye, my friends. Remember that there is only a moment of shadow between your life and mine. And when I call, come bravely through that shadow, and you shall find me only your familiar friend. (*He makes a gesture of farewell to* GRAZIA.) Good-bye, Grazia. Now you see me as I am.

GRAZIA (*her smile unchanged*)—But I have always seen you like that. You are not changed.

SHADOW (*in astonishment*)—You have seen me like this! (GRAZIA *goes and stands at the foot of the steps.*)

GRAZIA—Yes. You seem beautiful to me. (*She mounts the steps and stands beside him.*)

SHADOW (*triumphantly*)—Then there *is* a love which casts out fear, and I have found it. (*A chime of bells begins, and the leaves begin to fall.*) And love is greater than illusion, and as strong as death. (*He stands with his arm about her, as the leaves fall and the bells peal. At the stroke of twelve there is a sudden and complete darkness.*)

THE CURTAIN FALLS

REBOUND

A Comedy in Three Acts

By Donald Ogden Stewart

AT least three comedies have been born of the interesting meeting of Arthur Hopkins, producer, Philip Barry, playwright and Hope Williams, society amateur, in December, 1927.

On that occasion the play was Barry's "Paris Bound." Madge Kennedy was the star and Miss Williams, lifted from the ranks of the socially exclusive Comedy Club, played a chief comedy rôle—that of a chatty and witty society matron of the younger set.

The year following Barry wrote a second comedy, "Holiday," that Miss Williams might have a rôle suited to her talents in which Mr. Hopkins could feature her. Added to the cast of "Holiday" were two other society rôles which the producer thought should be, or at least could be, most effectively played by amateurs to the manor born. He engaged Donald Ogden Stewart, humorist, and Barbara White to play them, the characters being those of Nick and Susan Potter, also smartly flippant members of the junior set.

Then it occurred to Mr. Stewart that he could do what Mr. Barry had done and carry the Potters into another play that should also have a part for Miss Williams. Hence we have in "Rebound" Lester and Elizabeth Crawford and Elizabeth's sister, Sara Jaffrey, entangled in another romance.

"Rebound" reveals the adventure of two young people who catch each other on the rebound from other and, at the time, seemingly more vital love affairs.

As the play opens it is 9 o'clock Monday morning, which is departure time at the Crawfords' country place near New York. The week-end is over. The guests are having their going-away breakfasts, the table being set for six. At the moment no one is down save Liz Crawford.

"Liz is thirty-one, good-looking, smartly dressed in tweeds. She carries the happy assurance of one who has always done the right thing. She has gone to the right schools and married the right husband. Life to her has become fairly simplified into the business of keeping her husband happy and running a household . . ."

The first week-end guest to join Liz at table is Lyman Patterson. "He is forty-three and the very successful, very wealthy head of Patterson & Co., a young but powerful Wall Street banking house."

Lyman has had a lovely visit, but is eager to get back to his office. Not even the lure of this fine October morning nor the urging of his hospitable hostess can tempt him to stay over another day.

Lester Crawford, who is next to appear, "is thirty-four, good-looking, and may best be described by the word 'nice.' Groton and Harvard have turned out a good product, not particularly exciting but very pleasant."

Having slept the sleep of a 36-hole golfer, and feeling particularly amiable this morning, even the news that Liz's mother is coming on the 9:28 fails to disturb Les. He can even recall good-naturedly that a couple of love-birds, either Bill and Evie, or perhaps Sara and Johnnie, were talking in the garden as late as 3 A.M.

There is considerable speculation concerning the heart affairs of that absent four. Will Bill and Evie hit it off? Will Johnnie marry Sara, or won't he? Neither Liz, nor Les, nor Lyman can quite agree on the probabilities.

They are still wondering when Sara Jaffrey joins them. "Sara is twenty-eight and not as good-looking or 'smart' as her sister Liz. And Sara's entrance is particularly unimpressive because she is holding her nose with a large handkerchief."

Sara, it shortly appears, is having a nosebleed. Why, she doesn't exactly know. Nor can she guess. Nor can they. Rather silly to be having a nosebleed so early in the morning, but there it is. A piece of ice held at the back of Sara's neck fixes the nosebleed.

Still if it isn't the nosebleed it is something else. Now Sara has heard for the first time that her mother is coming. She is not exactly thrilled by the news. Inclined, rather, to consider a means of escape. Perhaps Lyman would marry her! He wouldn't have to tell anybody.

"I'll live at the Martha Washington and only come out nights," Sara promises.

"I should want to tell everybody," gallantly responds Lyman.

LYMAN—I seem to have heard of a young man named Johnnie.

LES—Yes—what about this 3 A.M. garden stuff?

SARA—I went to bed at 11:00, darn it—and you know it.

LES—Yes, you did!

SARA—I did. Was Johnnie getting away with something in the garden? Oh, the dirty little mouse! Who with—Evie?

LIZ—Well, it certainly wasn't with me.

LES—Say, did we get a nice little rise out of sister or didn't we? What's the matter, Sara—in love or something?

SARA—Shut up. Was it really Johnnie?

LES—I don't know.

SARA—Honestly, you would think that Evie'd got enough men without snaking him.

LIZ—It wasn't Johnnie.

LES—Of course it wasn't. It must have been Bill, the great lover.

LIZ—Poor Bill!

SARA—Love does terrible things to good men.

LIZ—Well, it serves him right.

LES—And wait till he marries her.

SARA—I'm waiting.

LYMAN (*getting up*)—Excuse me, Liz—I think I'll get ready to go on in.

LES (*Rises.*)—Be right with you, Lyman.

SARA—Don't you really think you could marry me, Lyman?

LYMAN—I'm sure I could.

SARA—I make a wonderful raspberry whip.

LES (*to* LYMAN)—It's a crime we have to go.

SARA (*calling after them*)—Just look through his bag, Les, to see that he hasn't taken any towels.

LIZ—Don't say things like that to Lyman, Sara. It embarrasses him.

SARA—I know. I love to embarrass Lyman. He's so darned rich.

LIZ—Well, that isn't the way girls get married.

SARA—Oh, you and your getting married.

LIZ—Suit yourself, dearie. You're 28 now. You can vote.

SARA—Liz, that's an awful mean thing to say. You know I'm having a rotten time.

LIZ—What about Johnnie? (*She indicates* JOHNNIE *by a nod of her head toward the upstairs room.*)

SARA (*with a slightly mocking laugh*)—Oh, we sat around and kidded about his career. Lord, the careers I've had to listen to. I know all about practically every career now except plumbing. I suppose that will come, too. Thank God, Johnnie has a sense of humor about his.

LIZ—Is Johnnie going to stick to architecture?

SARA—Architecture of the Ritz bar.

LIZ—It is a good excuse to live in Paris.

SARA—Lord, I wish I was going to Paris.

LIZ—With Johnnie?

SARA—With anybody. With Lyman. Do you suppose Lyman wants a good mistress? Mistress and general housework, with Thursday nights off?

LIZ—You might do a lot worse than marry Lyman, kid.

SARA—There you go again. Liz, you know I couldn't marry Lyman. We don't speak the same language at all.

LIZ—That isn't so important.

SARA—Well, there certainly wouldn't be much point to my marrying Lyman for his money. Why can't I find somebody like Les?

LIZ—It's a shame Bill's being wasted on Evie. Do you really think Johnnie will come through?

SARA—You don't seem to want him to, very much.

LIZ—I can't imagine Johnnie as a husband.

SARA—Oh, you just don't like him. We get along awfully well.

LIZ—When does he sail?

SARA—This afternoon.

LIZ—Are you going in with him?

SARA—He hasn't mentioned it.

LIZ—Oh, sure—he'll ask you.

SARA—I doubt it. You've been very sweet, darling, you and Les. You've worried and you've got me beaux and you've done your best—but I guess I'll just have to live with my canaries and my music—and my dear sweet old mother, the so and so.

Sara is perfectly frank about her mother. To escape, and be free, on a boat— Sara would elope. She would elope with Johnnie, with anybody.

Now Bill Truesdale has come to breakfast. "He is twenty-seven, handsome, nonchalant, sure of himself."

Bill is also a good deal of a kidder. Much like Sara that way. They have a grand time kidding each other. And giving each other occasional verbal digs covered by their kidding. Sara centers her attacks this morning on Evie and the possibilities of an understanding between Bill and Evie. Also the lateness of the hour that certain people choose for conversations in a garden.

Bill, however, is not fussed. He retired at 1. Evie retired at 1. At least he had said good night to Evie at 1.

"And when you say 'good-night' to them they go straight to bed," ventures Sara.

No, Bill doesn't get the garden stuff at all. But he is, he admits, a little worried about Sara and Johnnie. Johnnie is all right —but—

"Well, Bill," says Sara, being serious when she says it, "you all make me a little sick. Just because Johnnie wears red neckties and can't shoot an 83— We can't all of us marry Bills, you know."

BILL—Now you're talking.

SARA—I'm not apologizing for Johnnie.

BILL—Yes, you are. You're defensive. You're too good a girl for him, Sara.

SARA—Of course I am, Bill. I deserve you.

BILL—Well, I wouldn't say that.

SARA—Of course not. But supposing I don't love you, Bill? Supposing I love Johnnie?

BILL—You don't love Johnnie.

SARA—All right. But supposing I do?

BILL—Love doesn't make you lose your standards.

SARA—No.

BILL—No. Now take Evie and me—

SARA—I was just going to suggest that.

BILL—How do you mean?

SARA—Why, what could I mean? You're perfect and Evie's perfect.

BILL—You don't like Evie.

SARA—Oh, I adore Evie.

BILL—Well, anyway, here's my point. I've got faults—

SARA—Oh, Bill!

BILL—And Evie's got faults.

SARA—Evie?

BILL—What faults?

SARA—None. Go ahead.

BILL—And we're in love. But it isn't sappy love.

SARA—Sappy love?

BILL—You know—that's what love does to some people—they just go sappy. And so help me, God, if Evie ever went like that—

SARA—You needn't worry about Evie.

BILL—Well, I hope not. God, I hate sappy people.

Sara—Do you mean Johnnie's sappy?

Bill—Well, he might go sappy on you.

Sara—I don't think I would like that either.

Bill—Of course you wouldn't. You've got too much stuff.

Sara—I don't think you're right about Johnnie.

Bill—Maybe not.

Sara—And I'll tell you another thing, Bill. I may marry Johnnie.

Bill—No— (*Shaking his head.*) Uh, uh. Do you want to make a bet?

Johnnie Coles walks in before the bet can be registered. "In contrast to Bill he might be termed 'not regular.' His hair is never combed and his clothes never seem to fit. There lurks about him a slight suggestion of careless madness and irresponsibility."

Johnnie is complacently content. He is wearing one of Bill's ties, and also a pair of Bill's socks. But, he boasts, he sticks to his own purple underwear. Which, Bill reveals, he won as a poetry prize at Williams.

Bill finishes his breakfast very quickly after Johnnie arrives and is soon gone to complete his going-to-town plans. Which gives Sara and Johnnie a good chance to talk. Bill, Johnnie admits, gets fearfully on his nerves at times.

Sara is going to miss Johnnie a lot while he is in Europe. And Johnnie is going to miss Sara. They get on so well together. Johnnie is going to Paris and Sara's mother is coming. Johnnie doesn't care much for Sara's mother, either.

"She wants me to go out to Pasadena with her for the winter," reports Sara. "Know any nice people in Pasadena? Lovely climate. Sunshine. Perpetual sunshine. Perpetual drives with mother. Today we'll go through the orange country, Sara. Well, well, real oranges. Real oranges, mother. Real orange blossoms."

What would Sara do, Johnnie wonders, if she were free of her mother. Sara doesn't know, but she thinks it would be called matricide. Johnnie has been wondering, seriously, what Sara, free of Mrs. Jaffrey—

Evie Lawrence is the last one in for breakfast. She is "twenty-four, beautiful, slow-moving, sure of herself and her physical hold over men. Her predominant characteristic, aside from her beauty, is her selfishness."

Evie is tired, and evasive as to why she is tired. Sara jabs queries at her and Evie parries them successfully, if a little heavily. Evie's nerves are taut. She is not going abroad, as Sara thought. Evie is so sick of visiting she could scream. Visiting is all she has done for three years. Also she would like to know now what train is the first she can get into town.

Sara has gone to inquire about the trains for Evie when Lyman Patterson comes back. He understands why Evie is not feeling quite up to the mark. It was nearly 4 o'clock, as Lyman recalls it, when they retired. And still they had not settled everything.

LYMAN (*walking up and down*)—There are one or two things that have occurred to me this morning.

EVIE—Oh, let's not talk any more.

LYMAN (*after a moment*)—In the first place, you must realize that this affair with Bill is just that—an "affair." I am sure of it. You would be very foolish to marry Bill, and you know it. You don't love Bill.

EVIE—Lyman, please!

LYMAN—And in the second place I don't care a hang whether you love me or not. I'll make you love me. I'm not worried about that. You said—

EVIE—Oh, what difference does it make what I said.

LYMAN—You said that you thought you could learn to love me. That's enough for me. You may think that love is important—and it is. But there are a lot of other factors in a marriage like this—

EVIE—Oh, I don't know.

LYMAN—One more thing. Don't you worry about this being a success. That's my lookout.

Lyman and Les have said their good-byes and left for town. Bill Truesdale is trying to cheer Evie. Why she should be low when her fiancé feels so fit Bill can't understand. But Evie has something to tell Bill. Evie loves Bill—but she can't marry him—

Why Evie can't marry Bill would probably have been told if Mrs. Jaffrey had not at the moment appeared in the doorway. "She is the mother of Liz and Sara and is what might be described as a rich sea lion."

Finding Bill and Evie in each other's arms Mrs. Jaffrey is pleased. That means a wedding and she adores weddings. She will come to this one if she has to fly. Evangeline will make a beautiful bride and William is her favorite young man.

Evie has started for the train and Bill has insisted on going to the station with her. For the first time Mrs. Jaffrey has had a real good look at Sara.

MRS. JAFFREY—Well, Sara! How are you?

SARA—I'm all right, mother.

MRS. JAFFREY—Is that friend of yours—that Johnnie person—still here?

SARA—He's sailing this afternoon.

MRS. JAFFREY—Good. Well, Evangeline and William do not look to me like two people who are going to get married. Evangeline had better marry somebody before long.

SARA (*a little belligerently*)—Why?

MRS. JAFFREY—Well, for one thing, she's had too many beaux. And, for another, she's getting along.

SARA—My God, mother—she's twenty-four.

MRS. JAFFREY (*with a condescending smile*)—Yes, dear.

SARA—Yes, supposing Evie were twenty-eight or thirty and weren't married? What difference would it make?

MRS. JAFFREY—None, dear—none. Is that a spot on your dress?

SARA (*without looking*)—No. What difference would it make? Answer me that, mother.

MRS. JAFFREY—Now, Sara, don't get so excited. See those lovely trees—

SARA—See the moo-cow and the sheep-sheep. What difference does it make if a girl never gets married? She's just as good a girl, isn't she? How does marriage make her any better?

MRS. JAFFREY—You'll know, dear.

SARA—I'll know—I'll know what?

MRS. JAFFREY—When you're married, dear.

SARA—I'll know what when I'm married? A man? A baby?

MRS. JAFFREY—Sara, I would rather you didn't talk that way.

SARA—Well, I'm just asking you. Supposing I never get married—what difference does that make? Am I any different?

MRS. JAFFREY—Yes.

SARA—How?

MRS. JAFFREY—I say you'll know. And I'll say, furthermore, that your sister and I will be very disappointed—

SARA—Disappointed? But why? Am I a failure if I don't get

married? You got married, didn't you? That was a success, I suppose—with father now wandering alone all over Europe—

MRS. JAFFREY—Sara! Will you let me finish?

SARA—And I'm a failure because the right man doesn't happen to ask me to become his wife. Well, what if I am? I can't go around asking men to marry me. I'm what I am—and if they don't like it, that isn't my fault. Oh, I'm sick of the whole damn business. You're all so terribly unfair.

MRS. JAFFREY—Sara, I don't wish to discuss this with you in your present mood. I have just had a very long and difficult trip and I should think that you would sometimes have a little consideration for others besides yourself.

SARA—Well, how about a little consideration for me?

MRS. JAFFREY—Sara, if you ever have a baby of your own, you'll know what it is you're saying. The years I gave up everything for you—

SARA—Oh, my God—*that* again!

MRS. JAFFREY—Sara! (MRS. JAFFREY *exits.*)

SARA—Oh, damn her. (*She throws herself into a chair and begins to cry.*)

Johnnie is surprised and a little distressed to find Sara in tears. But he soon has jollied her into a good humor again, partly with his clowning, which takes her mind away from the irritations of meeting mother. Does Johnnie really want to know what mother was talking to Sara about? Johnnie does, but some other time. He has just remembered something he has to do before he gets on the boat.

Bill Truesdale is back from seeing Evie to the station, as depressed as a lover might reasonably be expected to be. They are a pair, these two, but Sara is more inclined to laugh than to be sunk, as Bill is.

"What is there about me, Bill, that makes me so completely irresistible?" asks Sara.

"I don't know," confesses Bill.

SARA—Sometimes it bothers me—this strange power I have over men.

BILL—Yes.

SARA—Why, I'm just Sara, that "IT" girl.

BILL—And I'm Bill the Great Lover.

SARA—Any conquests today, Great Lover?

BILL—No, today's been sort of an off-day.

SARA—What's the matter? Isn't the old sex appeal working?

BILL—Sex appeal? (*He laughs.*)

SARA—You seem sunk, Truesdale.

BILL—Do I? That's strange.

SARA—Anything wrong?

BILL—No. Everything's fine. Perfect.

SARA—What's the matter?

BILL—Well, it seems that the engagement of Miss Evangeline Lawrence to Mr. William Truesdale was just a big joke.

SARA—Bill—no!

BILL—The Great Lover has been given the air.

SARA—Oh, Bill—this is too terrible.

BILL—Dandy, isn't it?

SARA—I'm so sorry. Oh, I'm so sorry.

BILL—Thanks, Sara. We can go to the wedding together.

SARA—Who?

BILL—It seems she's marrying a Mr. Lyman Patterson.

SARA—No. That's awful, Bill.

BILL—No, it isn't. It's dandy. Fine and dandy.

SARA—Bill—you poor dear.

BILL—I'm all right.

SARA—She's really going to marry Lyman?

BILL—Sure. Why not? A girl tells you she loves you—oh, what the hell? I don't know.

SARA—Want a drink, Bill?

BILL—No, thanks.

SARA—She couldn't have loved you.

BILL—She must have. I'm Truesdale, the Great Lover.

SARA—Well, well—isn't everything just daisy!

BILL—Wonderful.

SARA—We must do something about this fascination of ours, Bill.

BILL—We might bottle it.

SARA—Sara and Bill. The success twins.

BILL—Cleopatra and Casanova.

SARA—I'm a little worried about myself. It isn't right that one woman should have so much.

BILL—I know.

SARA—Now I wish men would think of me as a human being instead of always—*that.*

BILL—It's terrible.

SARA—If they would only talk to me about books and flowers.

What is it, Bill? Is it something about us? Something in our voices?

BILL—It must be.

SARA—Still, I don't know. Sometimes, I think maybe it's just the way I play the saxophone. Tell me, it isn't that, Bill. Tell me, I've got to know. Tell me, it isn't just the way I play the saxophone? (*She sees that* BILL *is very downhearted and she walks over to him and puts her hand on his shoulder.*) I'm really awfully sorry, Bill—awfully sorry.

BILL—Thanks, Sara.

THE CURTAIN FALLS

ACT II

Six months later, in the living room of a hotel suite in Paris, Bill Truesdale is completing a morning toilet by tying a tie the while he looks under the furniture for his shoes, and lets a valet in at the door.

It is about noon of a beautiful April day, but neither the day nor the weather help Bill's French appreciably. He is forced finally to call Sara in order to tell Alphonse, whose name is really Pierre, that he (Bill) is shy a pair of shoes and that he would like to have a dinner coat pressed and mended.

Sara is also slightly confused when she comes from the adjoining bedroom, attired in a trousseau negligee. Sara is perfectly willing to tell Pierre anything that Bill thinks might be helpful, but she would prefer to begin with easy sentences first.

Sara manages finally to make Pierre understand that it is shoes and not huntsmen that she means when she orders a couple of chasseurs, which is as much of a relief to Pierre as it is to the Truesdales.

"Ah, oui—les chaussures," explodes Pierre. *"Je les ai pris en ban pour la cirage et malheureusement la femme de chambre les a mis dans la chambre d'un monsieur et madame au sixième, mais je les chercherai toute de suite si vous les attendez un petit instant."*

"What was that?" demands Bill, incredulously.

"Well," explains Sara, "it seems that on the sixth of the month all of the orphans in this district are taken for their annual picnic and outing in honor of the discovery of radium by Madame Curie— (*To* PIERRE.) Madame Curie, *n'est ce-pas?*

"Madame?"

"Yes, Madame Curie, and so your shoes have been borrowed to complete a float representing the friendship between France and America. Either that, or he says that he never saw your shoes. Now what was the next question?"

Sara and Bill have been married a month today and are very happy. They love each other desperately and this anniversary is an occasion to be celebrated. That, too, has been arranged. Sara's father is coming for lunch at 12 to meet Bill. It is nearly 12 now.

Bill figures that he will just have time to amble over to the bank and get the mail. Sara doesn't like the idea. Mr. Jaffrey is due any minute. Why must Bill go now? Or is he expecting another letter from Evie?

There have been letters from Evie, it transpires, and Sara has read most of them. Pretty dull, she found them.

Bill isn't greatly pleased at the idea of having his mail read. People don't read other people's letters, says he. If it comes to that, counters Sara, husbands don't correspond with their old girls, either.

"I'm not corresponding," snaps Bill. "I haven't answered any of her letters."

"You haven't? Oh, Bill, you ought to. Let me answer them."

"Well, I'm not going to. I don't give a damn about Evie."

"All right. Let's not quarrel about it, anyway. Hurry back, Bill. I've a surprise for you."

They are in each other's arms now, with one good-bye kiss calling for another.

"And when you come back," promises Sara, "I'll have on my surprise. Oh, Bill, this is so exciting—oh, I love you so very much—oh, Bill, hurry right back—and look out for taxicabs—and don't speak to French girls—and bring me something—and love me very much."

Bill is at the bank and Sara has not had a chance to change into anything, when Liz Crawford is announced. Liz and Les docked that morning from the *Ile de France* and Liz is overjoyed to see her sister. For the next few minutes the air is filled with reports and reminiscence of things associated with Sara's and Bill's wedding.

There is much talk of the wedding pictures and how funny everybody looked in them. And there is barely time to get in a word about father's coming to lunch (and won't the Crawfords stay?), and mother's warning that is to call Sara by phone from New York at noon, before Lester arrives.

Les is also full of congratulations and gossip. He had stopped at the bank, and who do they suppose he had met there? Lyman and Evie! Another honeymoon couple. But they're sailing back on the *Majestic* next day.

Sara is not surprised. Evie had written Bill that they were coming some time. Everybody has been most anxious to know whether Bill and Evie have met, Sara reports.

"I don't know what people expect me to do," she admits, "foam at the mouth, or something?"

Sara is much too happy for anything like that. She and Bill have had a grand time and everything is lovely, including the anniversary dress she has bought for four thousand francs for Bill's surprise. Why should she worry about Evie?

The Crawfords have gone back to their hotel, after promising to meet Sara and Bill and Mr. Jaffrey at dinner, when the phone operator announces the call from New York. It is a typical eighty-five-dollar-a-minute exchange of news.

"Hello . . . Hello, mother. Isn't this wonderful? I can hear you perfectly . . . I say I can hear you perfectly . . . What . . . Oh, well, you see, I haven't had a minute to write . . . honestly. How are you? . . . oh, yes . . . Yes . . . Oh, that's too bad . . . That's too bad . . . That's too bad. . . . Well, I'm fine . . . Yes, mother, but I haven't had a chance to write. Bill's fine . . . He's gone for the mail . . . No, I didn't. It probably was forwarded to Rome . . . Oh, yes, of course I did . . . of course I did, mother. I telephoned her but she was out . . . Aunt Julia and Uncle Lawrence were out, too. We left cards . . . No—Cousin Mabel has gone to Florence. . . . Yes, we left cards there, too . . . Yes . . . Well she looked all right to me . . . I thanked her for the water pitcher, anyway. I'll write her a note . . . Yes . . . today . . . But, mother, I haven't had any time."

It is during the phone call that a knock on the door is followed by the appearance of Henry Jaffrey, Sara's father. "He is 50, well-dressed, pleasant, with the red nose and face of a man who hasn't been quite sober for twenty years."

Sara interrupts her conversation with her mother long enough to wave a greeting and returns to it to report the arrival. The news, however, apparently calls for no more than a polite acknowledgment at the other side of the ocean.

Sara and her father are happy in this meeting. It is a little difficult for him to think of Sara as a married woman, and he is ever so anxious to meet his new son-in-law. Anxious, too, to hear about the wedding. And about his other daughter, Liz, and Les, and the party they are all to have that night.

Sara is a little anxious about Bill, disappointed that he is not there to greet father. But he surely will be along any minute now.

Mr. Jaffrey has brought a couple of presents he thought might be acceptable. A string of pearls for Sara and a little something for Bill that can be delivered later.

Now, while Sara is getting into the anniversary dress, that she may have it on when Bill comes, Mr. Jaffrey calls the bar on the phone and orders champagne cocktails that they may be ready for the celebration. He is also a little curious about this Bill person.

"Tell me, who is this Bill?" he calls. "Do I know him?"

SARA—I don't think you would, father. He comes from Minneapolis. Andover—Yale—Bankers' Trust—

MR. JAFFREY (*finishing the sentence*)—and heaven is the next stop. He's found that.

SARA—What a flatterer. Really, father. Oh, I know you'll love Bill. He's a sort of combination of you and Lincoln and Washington and Apollo—

MR. JAFFREY—In the Bankers' Trust Company? (SARA *enters from bedroom.*)

SARA—This is our Spirit of Kansas City number. Like it, monsieur?

MR. JAFFREY—I'm not much of a judge, my dear, but I would say that I have rarely seen a more beautiful dress—or mannequin.

SARA (*sitting down*)—I hope Bill likes it. He's terrible about clothes. The only dress he ever noticed was the one we got engaged in and he keeps wondering why I don't wear that all the time. Bill doesn't really know very much about anything, father.

MR. JAFFREY—No men do. And they know less as they get older.

SARA—Except you, father. You know more than all the men in the world.

MR. JAFFREY—I'm sure I do. But that's because I happened to become your father, dear. It has been a great education.

SARA—I must have been a horrible little girl.

MR. JAFFREY—You were. I spent most of your girlhood wondering whether to drown you or myself.

SARA—I'm glad you didn't do either. Don't you think I've improved?

Mr. Jaffrey—I hope not. I was very fond of that little girl.

Sara—With all her faults?

Mr. Jaffrey—With all her faults. I don't ever want her to change.

Sara—What do you mean—"change"? It's what you've always put at the end of your letter. "Don't ever change." How could I change, father?

Mr. Jaffrey—I'll tell you, my dear. I want you always to be the Sara I knew as a child. That Sara had many rare qualities. My urging you not to change was a sort of prayer. When I learned you were to be married I tried to write you about this. I tried to say marriage is a compromise in which some people sometimes sacrifice qualities from which they should never part. They lose grace. I don't want that to happen to you. That's what I meant when I said, "Don't change, my dear, don't ever change!"

A phone call to the Bankers' Trust brings the information a moment later that Mr. William Truesdale has been there, but has left. Sara is still trying to find out just when Bill had left as the curtain falls.

An hour and a half later, their lunch finished, coffee and brandy on the table in front of them, Sara and Mr. Jaffrey are trying valiantly to convince each other that they have had a lovely visit, a nice luncheon and a good talk. At least Mr. Jaffrey is trying to convince Sara that he feels that way about it. But Sara, plainly hurt at Bill's failure to report, is also plainly worried. Something might have happened to Bill—

Once or twice Sara tries to get her father to go. There is no need of his staying longer. Mr. Jaffrey prefers to remain. He is ever so interested in the things that Sara has told him; interested in the people she and Bill have met; interested in the things they have done. It may be something of a struggle for him to keep the conversation ball going, but with the help of the brandy Mr. Jaffrey manages it. He is greatly surprised when he looks up and sees that Sara, breaking a little under the strain, is crying. His comforting assurance that he knows Bill is all right is heartening but not at all convincing. Sara still can't understand why Bill doesn't come. And she is ever so frightened.

Then the telephone rings—a little more persistently than usual, and Mr. Jaffrey answers it. Bill is calling. Now Sara is at the phone and Bill is hearing a lot of things.

SARA (*taking receiver from father*)—Well, what a washout you turned out to be. I know. It's been nice to have known you. Where do you want your suitcase sent? No. Not a message. I've had it. Yes, father's here. Come around some time and meet your father-in-law. Get to know your wife's family. Who's that with you—the beautiful Evie? I thought as much. How—oh, hello, Evie. Well, isn't this lovely. Brides of a feather—brides of a feather gather no moss. Hello, dear. I'm crazy to see you. Why don't you and Bill come around some time? Come on up now. Oh, I know—the telephone service is terrible. Of course, he couldn't get me. Why, of course, I'm not angry at him. Come on over here. I'm dying to see you. Bring Bill with you. Yes. Good-bye, dear. (*Hangs up.*)

MR. JAFFREY—Is everything all right, dear?

SARA—Oh, great. Everything's just dandy. Bill ran into an old friend and forgot about lunch. They must have had a good time. I like to see young people have a good time. Well, I'm glad he isn't run over. No, I'm not. I wish he had been. It would have served him right. Father, I'm so sorry. Please forgive him.

MR. JAFFREY—Of course. I'm afraid, though, that I really can't wait—

SARA—Of course not. He doesn't deserve to meet you. You were a darling, though— I can't thank you enough.

MR. JAFFREY—You've thanked me, dear.

SARA—I'm sorry I was such dull company, father.

MR. JAFFREY—But you weren't.

SARA (*Crosses to telephone.*)—Well, I might have a little letdown now. Let's have some wine, father. Let's celebrate—Bill's triumphant return. He who was lost— (*At the telephone.*) The bar, please. Yes, hello—this is Madame Truesdale in room 184. *Oui.* Would you please send up some champagne? Yes. I don't know. For three people— (*To father.*) Can't you possibly stay?

MR. JAFFREY—Not possibly.

SARA (*at telephone*)—For three people—two ladies and a gentleman. Very cold for a very cold gentleman, and send up extra glasses. Thank you. (*To father.*) Oh, I wish you could stay.

MR. JAFFREY—So do I, dear.

SARA—I'd like you to meet Bill's idea of a wonderful girl. My God—what a wonderful girl. Oh, father—he's been so naughty—you will forgive him, won't you? (*He opens his arms and she goes to him.*)

Mr. Jaffrey—Let's both forgive him—what do you say? Good-bye.

Sara—God bless you, father. You are so sweet. See you tonight.

Mr. Jaffrey (*Kisses her.*)—Good-bye, daughter. Tell Bill I'm sorry I couldn't wait. You're still my daughter?

Sara—Do you think so?

Mr. Jaffrey—I'm afraid so. Always stay that way, won't you? Promise your father. Good-bye, dear.

Sara—I promise. Good-bye, and we'll see you tonight, father.

Mr. Jaffrey must have passed Johnnie Coles in the hall, so quickly does the latter's appearance follow on the former's departure. Johnnie Coles! Of all people! And at this particular time! The thought fills Sara with a wild sort of excitement that for the moment puzzles Johnnie. He is willing to share the spirit of this anniversary occasion, so long as Sara is sure Bill will not object, but he finds it a little difficult to understand just how it happens that Sara, a happily married woman, as she asserts, is preparing to celebrate with no husband present. Still Sara repeats that marriage is great and should be tried by all.

Johnnie, too, has had news of Evie and Lyman Patterson. They are not, according to his informants, getting on so well. Somebody who saw them in Berlin was of the opinion that Evie looked quite unhappy. Johnnie will be interested to see Evie. Understanding how it is that Sara has actually asked Bill to stop and bring her back with him is not so easy. This is a new Sara drinking champagne with him. She seems, at the moment, he says, a little distrait.

Sara—You never liked Bill, did you, Johnnie?

Johnnie—Why, Sara!

Sara—I could tell from your letter. You didn't want me to marry him, did you?

Johnnie—Well, Sara—this is a little embarrassing, to say the least.

Sara—Don't be silly, Johnnie. We're awfully old friends. I loved your letter—it was the only one that was honest.

Johnnie—I was a bit drunk, I imagine, when I wrote it.

Sara—Backing out?

Johnnie—No, I meant everything I said.

Sara—It's funny, the way things have happened, isn't it? Here— (*She starts to pour.*)

JOHNNIE—Hey, you'll get me frightfully stewed. How do you mean, funny?

SARA—Oh, I don't know. I'm still awfully fond of you—Johnnie. I think I sort of got to depend on you and haven't got over it yet.

JOHNNIE—S'mutual, kid. (*A pause.*) Judas!

SARA—What?

JOHNNIE—Nothing. I'll tell you some day.

SARA—Tell me now—give it to me as a wedding present.

JOHNNIE—I gave you a wedding present. It cost $78.

SARA—I wrote you a polite note.

JOHNNIE—A very dull note.

SARA—I know. But I didn't know what the present had cost.

JOHNNIE—It was the first dull note I'd ever had from you. I don't think my letter deserved it.

SARA—It didn't.

JOHNNIE—Listen, Sara. (*He is interrupted by the sound of laughing outside the door. Enter* BILL *and* EVIE, *arm in arm.*)

SARA—Well, well, enter Evie. (JOHNNIE *and* SARA rise. SARA *and* EVIE *kiss each other.*)

BILL—Hurrah—the war's over.

They are all talking at once, now. The conventional and hurried queries and answers of a first meeting of friends after a separation of weeks. Out of the jumble of words Evie emerges smilingly and goes to the piano to play "Am I Blue?"

Bill manages to get in a word of explanation with Sara. "Dear, please forgive me," he says, as he kisses her. "I feel like a snake."

"It was all right," Sara smiles back. "I had a lovely lunch with father—and a talk with Johnnie."

"Evie wanted to show me a shop—we bought you something."

"Father brought you something."

They are all drinking now. All except Evie. She continues to play "Am I Blue?" and now she is singing the chorus. Sara offers a toast: "To Evie and Lyman." They drink that, and when no one goes on Sara offers another toast: "To Bill and that lucky girl, Sara."

"Lucky Bill, I say," croons Evie.

"Oh, Evie—how sweet!" murmurs Sara.

Evie is singing and Sara is helping with the chorus.

"Am I blue?
Ain't there tears in my eyes telling you?

Am I blue?
You'd be, too, if each plan with your man done fell through.
Am I blue?"

Lyman Patterson breaks into the celebration, a little awkwardly. He had expected Evie back at the hotel. Evie offers no explanation of why she was not there.

Lyman is glad to take part in Sara's and Bill's celebration, or says he is. Marriage is fine, admits Lyman, though Evie has not been feeling particularly well. They are sailing Saturday on the *Majestic.*

Bill has an idea. Why shouldn't Lyman and Evie wait a couple of weeks longer? Then they could all go home together. That would be great! Evie thinks so, too. Even Sara agrees, but not with anything that might be mistaken for enthusiasm. Lyman agrees to see if he can arrange a change of bookings, and Evie kisses him sweetly as a reward for his interest.

Now Johnnie Coles is at the piano, playing "I May Be Wrong." Bill and Evie are dancing. Sara stands at the piano watching them as she sings the words of the song, with Johnnie and the others chiming in:

SARA— "I may be wrong."
JOHNNIE—"She may be wrong."
SARA— "I think you're wonderful!"
JOHNNIE—"I think you're swell."
SARA— "I may be wrong."
JOHNNIE—"She may be wrong."
BILL— "I think you're marvelous."
EVIE— "I think you're swell."
SARA and
EVIE— "I like your style, say, I think it's marvelous;
"I'm all wrong, so how can I tell—
"All my shirts are unsightly—all my ties a crime.
"You came along. I think you're wonderful."

Bill and Evie are still dancing. Sara and Johnnie are at the piano. Lyman, a little bored, is looking on.

THE CURTAIN FALLS

ACT III

Back in the Crawfords' dining room the following September, Johnnie Coles, evidently considerably perturbed, is pacing the floor. Johnnie and Liz Crawford are the first home from a dancing party. It is near morning and Liz has scrambled eggs for the expected crowd.

The eggs are getting cold and Johnnie is getting nervous. Nor can Liz drag him out of his gloom. Nor Les Crawford, who is the next one in. Johnnie just refuses to be cheered.

The dancing party has been a success so far as Liz is concerned, but she is free to confess that she doesn't like the way Bill and Evie carried on. If she were Lyman Patterson she certainly would do something about it. Liz is worried, too, on Sara's account. Sara has put up with a good deal since she and Bill came home on the same boat with Lyman and Evie, and she is beginning to look pretty well sunk.

When Sara arrives she is almost as gloomy as Johnnie Coles, and nothing in the line of Lester's kidding, usually so effective in cheering Sara, is of any help to her.

Now Evie and Bill have arrived, arm in arm and laughing happily. It has been a great party so far as they are concerned. Let Johnnie Coles spread gloom. Let Sara and Lyman sit out most of the dances if they will, Bill and Evie have had their good time in spite of all. Evie, for one, has never laughed so much in her life. In fact, she and Bill are in such rare form that she is sure they can even cheer Johnnie Coles, if they can find him. They go to the living room to try.

"Who was that attractive couple?" asks Sara, as Bill and Evie disappear.

"I'm sorry, Sara, I should have introduced you," Les apologizes. "I thought of course you knew each other. That was a Mr. William Truesdale, your husband, you know."

SARA—Oh, yes—my husband.

LES—A very attractive young man, too. Married to Liz Crawford's sister, Sara. Very interesting girl—Sara. Plays the flute beautifully, they say.

SARA (*Rises.*)—Don't. (EVIE *is playing the piano in the living room.*)

LES—Don't what?

SARA—Les, why did I marry Bill?

Les—Now don't talk that way. Wait till you've been married ten years.

Sara (*Crosses to table.*)—Oh, my God—is this going to go on for ten years?

Les (*cheerfully*)—Sure. Twenty. Thirty.

Sara—No, it's not.

Les—Bill's all right, kid.

Sara—Les, I'm licked.

Les—Sara.

Sara—No, but what can I do?

Les—For God's sake, use your head, girl. Don't be silly. Bill's only human.

Sara—That's just it. Why should anyone human prefer me to Evie?

Les—Sara—you're talking like a perfect damn fool.

Sara—I know it.

Les—Well, snap out of it.

Sara—And Bill is to keep on with Evie?

Les—That doesn't mean anything.

Sara—No, it doesn't mean anything. It doesn't mean anything that I'm being constantly humiliated? That everywhere I go I find them together? That she shows him off to me as she did just now? That she brushes his hair and straightens his tie and keeps crooning her damn songs to him? The man I married? That doesn't mean anything?

Les—It's just one of those affairs.

Sara—An affair—I hate the word. Les, I don't see why marriages have to end up in a series of affairs. Holding hands with somebody else's husband. Tea at the Prince George. Why can't marriage be clean? Why can't two people love each other? Good God, Les—I love Bill. I'll give Bill everything I've got.

When Bill comes back Sara tries a little desperately to talk with him; to tell him that she is unhappy, that his attitude toward her, and more particularly his attentions to Evie, have made her unhappy, and that she doesn't want to go on being unhappy.

Bill's defense is that Sara is foolish; that her criticism of Evie is silly; that he is not happier with Evie than he is with her and that she is making much out of nothing. Even her tears are silly to Bill. There is nothing he can do but leave her to pull herself together.

Sara has dried her eyes and regained some sort of command of herself when Johnnie Coles brings his troubles to her. Johnnie has been crying, too. He has come to realize the great mistake he made a year before when he went to Europe without Sara and left her to marry Bill. Now Johnnie would rectify that mistake. He knows now that he loves Sara. He knows that Bill does not love her. If he did he could not treat her as he does. Johnnie wants Sara to come away with him. He is on his knees, his head in her lap, pleading his great need of her when Sara stops him.

SARA—Johnnie, dear, please get up. Please get up. I can't bear to see you on your knees. Get up, Johnnie, dear. (*He rises and she puts him into a chair.*) Sit there. And promise me something.

JOHNNIE—Sara!

SARA—Promise me you will never go on your knees to anyone again. People don't understand. I understand.

JOHNNIE—I love you so.

SARA—I understand. I've just been on my knees. But people don't want that. They don't want that.

JOHNNIE—I love you so.

SARA—I know you do, dear. But love mustn't make you beg. Oh, Johnnie, we've both been so wrong. I've just been begging for love, too. I didn't realize how wrong that was until I saw you on your knees. We aren't beggars, Johnnie. Forgive me if that hurts. I wouldn't hurt you for the world. But you have made me see.

JOHNNIE—But I belong to you, Sara.

SARA—I don't want you to, Johnnie. Please understand. I don't want anyone to belong to me. I want you to belong to yourself.

JOHNNIE—I don't understand. I don't understand.

SARA—I know, Johnnie. But you will. That's all I can say. That was all my father could say to me when I didn't understand. Love is a compromise, he said—love is a compromise in which people sometimes lose grace. I understand now. I've lost grace, Johnnie. That must never happen to you, dear. You're much too fine.

JOHNNIE—But what's to become of you, Sara? What's to become of you?

SARA—I don't know, Johnnie. But I know I'm going to be all right. You've done something for me—I don't quite understand yet—but I feel strangely free, as though I had wakened from a bad dream. I feel whole again. You've given me back something, dear. You've given me back something. I shall always remember you for that, and love you.

JOHNNIE (*Rises.*)—Good-bye, Sara.

SARA—Don't feel sorry. You're what counts. You, yourself—don't need people—you've got yourself.

JOHNNIE—I think I'd better go.

SARA—Good-bye, Johnnie—you dear, dear person. (*She kisses him.*) God bless you.

There is elation in Sara's voice when Liz finds her sitting alone a moment later. She sees her way clear now. She knows what to do. She wants to see Bill right away. She wants to give him a message from her father. She wants—

LIZ—Sara, will you talk sense?

SARA—Yes. Oh, Liz—haven't I been too disgusting?

LIZ—No. What have you done?

SARA—What have I done? What have I done? I've groveled. I've begged. I've felt sorry for myself. I've cried about myself.

LIZ—Oh, come on now, dear.

SARA—But I have, Liz. I can see it all, now.

LIZ—What, what of it?

SARA—What of it? Oh, Liz, everything of it. I've had no pride. I've had no courage. I've been humble. I've been meek. I've taken insults from people. I've let people walk over me. I've let Evie Patterson walk over me. Evie Patterson that—oh, I must see Bill.

LIZ—Now wait, dearie—

SARA—Wait? But for what? (LESTER *enters.*)

LIZ—Les, talk to Sara.

LES—I'd love to. How well you look this evening, Miss Ferguson.

SARA—It's morning.

LES—Why, so it is.

SARA—It's morning. It's a new day. That's allegorical, isn't it?

LES—It certainly is.

SARA (*Rises.*)—Oh, Les. This is so wonderful.

LES—What?

SARA—It's all come back to me.

LES—Well, that's great. What's come back to you?

SARA—Everything. My sense for one thing.

LES—You don't mean to say it's the old Sara?

SARA—I think so.

LES—Well, well—glad to see you back. We've certainly missed you. Have a nice trip?

SARA—An awful trip.

LIZ—We got your post card.

LES—Tell us all about it.

SARA—Well, the first day out I fell in love with one of the sailors. (BILL *and* EVIE *enter, laughing.*)

BILL—Say, where's old man Johnnie? We miss him terribly in there. No gloom at all. Got to have gloom. First thing you know we'll all be having a good time.

EVIE—That would never do.

LES—You're just in time. Sara's telling about her trip.

EVIE (*to* BILL)—Look at that tie. Come here.

BILL—No, don't.

EVIE—Come here. (*She fixes his tie.*)

SARA—Well, as I was saying, I fell in love with one of the sailors. Did I ever tell you about love, Les?

LES—No. Tell us about love.

SARA—Love is a wonderful thing. Love makes birds sing. Love makes the grass grow. Love is good for colds in the head, la grippe, neuralgia, headaches, constipation, that tired feeling—

BILL—Sara, that isn't funny—

SARA—I'm being heckled! My friends, this brand of love has done wonders. I know of a little girl who took one bottle and it went right to her knees—

LES—Look out, kid.

SARA (*Rises.*)—Now, take a cheaper kind of love—our No. 4 brand—for unfortunate young husbands. One swallow of this and they see their old girls again—two swallows and they forget their wives—

EVIE—Bill, I think that's enough.

BILL—Sara!

Now Bill and Evie have walked out of the room arm in arm, leaving Sara staring after them a little triumphantly. It is a fairly cheap thing she has done, she admits, and she has no intention of going noble on them, but there is something that she has to have out with Bill, and this is the time.

"I know what's on your minds," Sara tells them. "I know just what a divorce would mean to all of you. But marriage isn't that important. Marriage isn't more important than something inside of me that's been dying. Nothing is. Something's happened to me—that's all I can say. I'm not going to be any what's-her-name—the wife who walked out and slammed the door. I'm not going to walk out—at least, I don't think I am. I'll stick. This marriage is something I got myself into and I'd like to see it through—if Bill will give me a chance. But I've got to see it through on different terms."

Les is sure Sara is right, but he thinks perhaps this is not just the time—

Bill is back and alone. He has come to have a serious talk with Sara. There are things, says Bill, that he does not expect his wife to do. And there are a lot more things, adds Sara, that a wife doesn't expect her husband to do.

Never again, says Bill, does he want to see Sara act as she had just acted before people. Her making fun of Evie may not have been so bad, but making fun of Bill, and of love, of their love—that hurt! Bill can't understand Sara. One minute she is crying for love and the next minute she is making a joke about it. She must have been drunk.

SARA—Would you like to know what love has done to me, Bill? It has made me a small person. A weak and cowardly person.

BILL—Sara!

SARA—I based my whole life on our marriage. I clung to it like a greedy child. I loved you. My one fear was losing you. I became resentful and bitter and churlish. I snarled at Evie. I cursed at you. And tonight I turned beggar. I begged you to love me.

BILL—Sara, don't say that. Don't say that.

SARA—But it's true, Bill. I did beg for your love—I'll never beg again. I'm not even sure that I want it.

BILL—Sara, this is all new to me. I can't make you out. I had no idea that I was really hurting you. I thought you were being unreasonable about things that didn't count. And, believe me, Sara, they didn't count. Nothing really matters to me except you. I've been a fool, Sara. I've been a fool. Maybe I've really lost you. I can't believe it, but maybe I have. But, Sara—let's try again. Let me try again. I love you, and you're all that I love. Let me try again.

SARA—I saw love tonight, Bill. I saw it for the first time and I know now that love is dependent, poignantly dependent. It needs so much from the loved one. It was the need I felt for you tonight when I went begging.

BILL—Sara!

SARA—The need has gone now, Bill. It's strange that anything so overpowering could vanish so suddenly, but it has, Bill, it has. I'm alone again. But I'm not lonely. My love doesn't need you any longer.

BILL—But I need you, Sara—for the first time, I need you. Perhaps it's the first time I have really loved you, but I do love you, Sara, I do love you. Oh, let's try again, Sara. Please, please try again.

SARA—I think love can be grand, Bill, but I don't want ours if it's to be anything less than grand. I don't want it.

BILL—But it can be grand. It will be grand. Let's try, Sara, let's try.

SARA—All right, Bill. We'll try.

BILL—Sara! Sara! (*They embrace.* EVIE *enters.*)

EVIE—Oh!

BILL (*turning*)—Excuse us, Evie.

EVIE—Why, certainly. (*She exits.*)

BILL—Exit, Evie.

SARA—Enter Sara.

BILL—They embrace.

CURTAIN

THE PLAYS AND THEIR AUTHORS

"The Green Pastures." A fable play in eighteen scenes by Marc Connelly, adapted from the stories of Roark Bradford's "Ol' Man Adam an' His Chillun." Copyright, 1929, by the author. Copyright and published, 1930, by Farrar & Rinehart, Inc., New York.

As a collaborator with George S. Kaufman on "Dulcy," "Merton of the Movies" and "Beggar on Horseback," Marc Connelly has made several previous appearances in these volumes. He is a Pennsylvanian, born in McKeesport in 1891. Had his education from the public schools and Trinity Hall, and became a newspaper reporter at the usual comparatively early age. Came to New York with the lyrics for a musical comedy and when the piece failed stayed on. Wrote "The Wisdom Tooth" by himself and "The Wild Man of Borneo" with Herman Mankiewicz.

Roark Bradford was born in Lauderdale county, Tennessee, in 1896. His schooling continued variously until the war, when he was assigned with a detachment of coast artillery to Panama. Starting overseas in November, 1918, they ended the war on him. He taught gunnery at Mississippi Agricultural and Mechanical College for a time and then went into newspaper work, first in Atlanta, then in New Orleans, where he became Sunday editor of the New Orleans *Times Picayune*. His success as a writer of short stories of Negro life has earned him comparison with DuBose Heyward and Joel Chandler Harris. His "Child of God" won the O. Henry Prize in 1927, and his "Ol' Man Adam an' His Chillun," "This Side of Jordan" and "Ol' King David and the Philistine Boys" are popular.

"The Criminal Code." A drama in three acts by Martin Flavin. Copyright, 1929, by the author. Copyright and published, 1929, by Horace Liveright, New York.

Martin Flavin has the past season experienced his most active period as a playwright, and his most successful as well. In 1923 he came quickly and promisingly to notice with the production of a play called "Children of the Moon" in New York. It was what is frequently spoken of as a highbrow success. He was not successful in realizing his promise after that, though two of his plays, "Service for Two" and "Lady of the Rose" reached production. This year, however, he came early with "The Criminal Code," followed a few weeks later with a splendid college play which failed of popular support called "Crossroads," and later a comedy, "Broken Dishes," which had been tried out of New York as "Shucks." The latter half of the year he spent profitably in Hollywood writing scenarios for the talking pictures. Mr. Flavin is a Californian, born in San Francisco in 1883. He was a business man in Chicago before he took to writing.

"Berkeley Square." A fantastic drama in three acts by John Balderston, suggested by a short story by Henry James entitled "A Sense of the Past." Copyright, 1929, by the author. Copyright and published, 1930, by the Macmillan Company, New York.

John Balderston, who has a middle name, Lloyd, presented to him by his father, has devoted most of his working years to the newspapers. Born in Philadelphia, in 1889, after he was through with the public schools and had had two years at Columbia University, he became New York correspondent of the Philadelphia *Record*. In 1915 he went to London as a free lance war correspondent, became associated with the McClure Syndicate and represented the United States Committee on Public Information over there during 1918-19. He was made the editor of the *Outlook* in London in 1920 and the chief London correspondent of the New York *World* in 1923. His writing for the stage, previous to his contribution of "Berkeley Square," was confined to "A Morality Play for the Leisure Classes." He is also author of a war book, "The Genius of the Marne." In writing "Berkeley Square" Mr. Balderston acknowledges the assistance of J. C. Squire of London.

"Strictly Dishonorable." A comedy in three acts by Preston Sturges. Copyright, 1929, by the author. Copyright and published, 1929, by Horace Liveright.

Preston Sturges was born in Chicago but they took him to Europe as a boy and he lived there seven years. As a matter of record he was living in Riga, Latvia, which sounds terribly foreign, when he was 14, and it was there that he wrote a song called

"Winky" that gained considerable family circulation. He came back to America in 1914 with a fixed intention of doing something about a theatre career. The war held him up for a time, he doing service as an aviator. When he got back to the theatre, he held several positions as a stage manager, working for the company that produced "Œdipus Rex" at the Century Theatre and later for Brock Pemberton when he produced "Goin' Home" and "Hotbed." About this time Mr. Sturges wrote a comedy called "The Guinea Pig" and produced it himself. Many people liked it. Then he wrote "Strictly Dishonorable." Mr. Pemberton and Antoinette Perry staged it and the play achieved the first outstanding success of the season. This having been attended to, Mr. Sturges got himself married and went back to Europe on a wedding tour. Song writing is still his avocation. Recently he has produced three bearing the titles "My Cradle of Dreams," "After the Rain" and "Lonely."

"The First Mrs. Fraser." A comedy in three acts by St. John Ervine. Copyright, 1929, by the author. Copyright and published, 1930, by the Macmillan Company, New York.

St. John Greer Ervine became, in a way, an international critic of the drama when he spent the season of 1928-29 in America as the guest critic of the New York *World.* He has been devoted to the theatre for many years, both in Dublin, where he at one time directed the Abbey Players, and in London, where he served as dramatic critic at different times of the *Labour Leader,* the *Daily Citizen,* the *Weekly Dispatch,* the *Morning Post* and the *Observer.* He was with the *Observer* from 1919 to 1923, and returned to that berth following his seven months in New York. He was a lieutenant in the Royal Dublin Fusiliers during the war, being wounded in 1918 and invalided home. He has written many plays, several novels and two books on the theatre, "The Organized Theatre" and "How to Write a Play." His plays best known in America are "John Ferguson," which established the success of the Theatre Guild; "Jane Clegg," which followed, the second season; "Mixed Marriage," "Mary, Mary, Quite Contrary," which David Belasco produced; "The Magnanimous Lover," a short piece prominent in the repertory of the Abbey Players; and now the very successful "The First Mrs. Fraser." With this last success Mr. Ervine has retired temporarily from dramatic criticism and is devoting himself to writing and lecturing. He was born in Belfast, Ireland, in 1883.

"The Last Mile." A tragedy in three acts by John Wexley. Copyright, 1929, under the title "All the World Wondered," by the author. Copyright and published, 1930, by Samuel French, New York.

To try to classify John Wexley as a writing man is to discover that if he belongs to any group it is that which includes the adventurers and the wanderers. He is another with Jack London, Jim Tully and Carl Sandburg. He has been many places and seen many things, and he will not be 28 years old for several months. He was born in New York. He went to school in New York, and helped his father in his trade as a roofer. On his own he has been many kinds of workmen, a waiter, a bellboy, a salesman, a floorwalker, a stoker, an actor. He has always had an interest in the theatre, because Maurice Schwartz of the Yiddish Art Theatre is his uncle on his mother's side. He has played in Yiddish in his uncle's company. He played briefly with Eva Le Gallienne's Civic Repertory company, and when "The Last Mile" was produced he was playing a small part in Leo Bulgakov's revival of Gorky's "At the Bottom." In the old days of the Washington Square Players Wexley wrote three one-act plays for them, "Rules," "Machine Gun" and "What Is Your Desire?" "Rules" was a prison play. Wexley had long thought of extending it. His ambition to do so was whetted when he read Robert Blake's account of a day of execution in a death house printed in the *American Mercury*. This was a sketch in dialogue form called "The Law Takes Its Toll." When the Canon City prison mutiny followed, the play took form in the Wexley mind. He thought of it then as a drama that should be called "All the World Wondered," after a line in Tennyson's "Charge of the Light Brigade." During the weeks of preparation Wexley visited and studied conditions in the Illinois state penitentiary at Joliet and New York's "big house" up the river at Sing Sing.

"June Moon." A comedy in three acts by Ring W. Lardner and George S. Kaufman. Copyright, 1929, by the authors. Copyright and published, 1929, by Charles Scribner's Sons, New York.

Ring Lardner, having devoted his writing time to newspaper work, various syndicates, a series of short stories and numerous sketches, has not gone in seriously for playwriting until recently.

Last season he wrote a comedy which finally saw production under the title of "Elmer the Great," and stood by during the preparation of "The Love Nest," which Robert Emmet Sherwood made out of a Lardner story. He was born in Niles, Mich., in 1885, graduated from the public schools and Armour Institute, Chicago, and took up newspaper work, first in South Bend, Ind., and later in Chicago. He worked on most of the Chicago papers, finishing with a considerable service on the *Tribune,* his last stay in the sporting department of that paper being for six years. He is the author of many volumes of short stories, including "The Young Immigrunts," "You Know Me, Al," "How to Write Short Stories," is the father of four boys, and he lives in East Hampton, L. I.

George Kaufman is a familiar of these pages, having contributed to no less than five previous volumes of "The Best Plays." With his inclusion as Mr. Lardner's collaborator herein he will have been listed with this particular selection of best play writers six times out of the nine years that have passed since he made his début with Marc Connelly in the 1921-22 volume with "Dulcy." His record, therefore, has been generously outlined in other volumes. He was born in Pittsburg in 1889, and has been in newspaper work since he was 20, starting as a contributor to the columns of the humorists and finishing as dramatic editor of the New York *Times,* a position he still holds.

"Michael and Mary." A comedy in three acts by A. A. Milne. Copyright, 1929, by the author. Copyright and published, 1930, by Chatto and Windus, London, 1930.

Alan Alexander Milne has been placed in one previous volume of this theatrical history. "The Dover Road," a comedy concerned with the would-be divorcees escaping from London to Paris, was included in the 1921-22 book. Mr. Milne began writing plays in 1918, with a piece called "Wurzel-Flummery." In America he may be remembered for his "Belinda," at one time in the repertory of Ethel Barrymore; "The Truth About Blayds," which was almost a success the same year he wrote "The Dover Road"; his "Mr. Pim Passes By," which is still in the repertory of the Theatre Guild; "The Perfect Alibi," which achieved a season's run in New York, and "The Ivory Door," which did nearly as well. Mr. Milne was graduated from Trinity College, Cambridge, in 1903, was for many years editor of *Punch* and has written numerous novels.

"Death Takes a Holiday." A fantastic drama in three acts by Walter Ferris, adapted from the Italian of Alberto Casella. Copyright, 1928, 1930, by Walter Ferris. Copyright and published, 1930, by Samuel French, New York and London.

Walter Ferris is an educator whose avocation for several years has been playwriting. His best-known achievement, prior to the production of "Death Takes a Holiday," was a drama called "The First Stone," which Eva Le Gallienne included in the repertory of the Civic Theatre the season of 1927-28. This play was based on a short story by Mary Heaton Vorse, and had a Cape Cod setting. Born in Green Bay, Wis., in 1882, Mr. Ferris got his B.A. from Beloit College, 1905, a B.D. from Yale, 1909. He was an instructor in English at Yale from 1911 to 1917 and headmaster of the Roxbury School from 1917 to 1924. He is married and lives in Cheshire, Conn.

Alberto Casella was for five years in the war. There the idea for "Death Takes a Holiday," known in its original Italian as "La Morte in Vacanza," was born. First, he told Mme. Berta Cutti of the Society of Italian Authors, he wanted to write a play about a state of mind. It was while he was toying with this inspiration that his acceptance of Death as a human came to him. "Do you know," he said to Mme. Cutti, "that divine immortal was a living reality to me in the trenches? Now in one form, now in another. Occasionally we felt His Highness was actually on a vacation when his handmaid, Illusion, had us fast in her clutches . . . think of it! . . . many a time he wilfully overlooked a comrade . . . later coming back to escort someone else out of a tired, bleeding world. . . . He often seemed human to me." When Casella had finished the play Mme. Cutti translated it and submitted it first to John Barrymore. John liked it but could not play it. Norman-Bel Geddes had it for a time and contemplated a production. Then Lee Shubert, looking for serious plays for his newly formed playgoers' leagues in Chicago and Philadelphia, bought it and set Walter Ferris at work making the adaptation that was later successfully played. There were many adaptations before everybody was satisfied.

"Rebound." A comedy in three acts by Donald Ogden Stewart. Copyright, 1929, by the author.

Donald Ogden Stewart is the type of humorist and writer who gathers his material where he finds it, and if the fields he is occupying are not fertile he seeks those that are. Thus, as a traveler, after he had graduated from Yale with an A.B. in 1916, and served as seaman, quartermaster and chief quartermaster in the war, he capitalized his travels in "Mr. and Mrs. Haddock Abroad" and "Mr. and Mrs. Haddock in Paris." Interested in amateur theatricals, he agreed to give his talent to the world as a professional when Arthur Hopkins offered him a place in Philip Barry's "Paris Bound." From this experience he was inspired to try playwriting and produced "Rebound," built around the personality of Hope Williams, a fellow player with him in the Hopkins company. Mr. Stewart was born in Columbus, O., in 1894. His books include "A Parody Outline of History" and "Aunt Polly's Story of Mankind." He continued his adventures as an actor by playing a part in his own play, "Rebound."

PLAYS PRODUCED IN NEW YORK

June 15, 1929—June 15, 1930

(Plays marked with asterisk were still playing June 15, 1930)

BORROWED LOVE

(13 performances)

A comedy in four acts by Bide Dudley. Produced by John Osborne Clemson at the Times Square Theatre, New York, June 17, 1929.

Cast of characters—

Robert Carroll....................Jerome Collamore
Tom Bradford....................Barry O'Neill
John Carter....................Richard Gordon
Grace Carter....................Mary Fowler

Act I.—Interior of a Box Office in a Chicago Theatre. Acts II, III and IV.—Living-Room Carter Home in North Chicago, Near the Lake Front.

John Carter, suffering physically from an attack of flu, conceives the plan of interesting his wife, Grace, in another man. They select Tom Bradford, a theatrical manager, who is interested in the adventure. Carter, however, finds that he cannot go as far as he liked and plans to make it possible for Mrs. Carter to divorce him and marry Bradford. Confessing the plan, he learns that Mrs. Carter and Bradford have never been more to each other than friends, that she still loves her husband, sick or well, and that a famous New York specialist hopes to make him well.

HOT CHOCOLATES

(219 performances)

A colored revue by Andy Razaf, music by Thomas Waller and Harry Brooks. Produced at the Hudson Theatre, New York, June 20, 1929.

Principals engaged—

Jazzlips Richardson	Three Midnight Steppers
Jimmie Baskette	Baby Cox
Paul Bass	Edith Wilson
Paul Meers	Thelma Meers
Eddie Green	Margaret Simms
Billy Marey	Louise Higgins
Billy Higgins	Madeline Belt
Dick Campbell	Dolly McCormick
	Jubilee Singers

Staged by Leonard Harper.

KEEP IT CLEAN

(16 performances)

A musical revue in thirty-eight scenes by Jimmy Duffy and Will Morrissey; music by Lester Lee, Jimmy Duffy, Harry Archer, Benny Ryan, James Hanley, Clarence Gaskill, Violinsky, Charles Tobias and Harry Converse. Produced by William Duffy and John Hickey, Jr., at the Selwyn Theatre, New York, June 24, 1929.

Principals engaged—

Will Morrissey	Midgie Miller
Jimmy Duffy	Edith Murray
Ted Marcel	Pauline Gaskins
Jim Harkins	Rosemary Ryder
Jimmie O'Brien	Mlle. Amerique
Douglas Stanbury	Karol Kane
Frank Farnam	Helen Gleason
Don Kennelly	Mae Dailey
Jimmie Carr's orchestra	Market Dancers

Staged by Mr. Morrissey and Russell Markert.

BAMBOOLA

(34 performances)

A colored musical comedy by D. Frank Marcus, music by Mr. Marcus and Bernard Maltin. Produced by Irving Cooper at the Royale Theatre, New York, June 26, 1929.

Cast of characters—

Eb..... *The "Harmonizers"* .....Robert Ecton
Jeb..... *The "Harmonizers"* .....Oliver Foster
Ned..... *The "Harmonizers"* Charles Lawrence
Fred..... *The "Harmonizers"* ...Claude Lawson
Rhodendra Frost.....Mercedes Gilbert
'Lije Frost.....Monte Hawley
Sheila Nesoit.....Hilda Perleno
Samson Frost.....Percy Winters

Ludlow Bassom....................................George Randol
Anna Frost....................................Isabell Washington
Deputy Sheriff....................................Ray Giles
Sambo....................................John Mason
"Dusty"....................................."Dusty" Fletcher
Stage Doorman....................................Ray Giles
First Pedestrian....................................Cora Merano
Second Pedestrian....................................Ruth Krygar
J. Quentin Creech, the Star....................................Billy Andrews
Myrtle Wyms, the Soubrette....................................Billy Cortez
Tom Gin, "The Chief Comedian"....................................Brevard Burnett
"The Song Bird"....................................Revella Hughes
Anna's Maid....................................Cora Merano
The Preacher....................................Ray Giles

Staged by Sam Rose.

Parts I and II.—In and Around the Frost Home in Savannah and the Jackson Theatre, New York.

EARL CARROLL'S SKETCH BOOK

(400 performances)

A musical revue in forty-four scenes by Earl Carroll, music and lyrics by E. Y. Harburg and Jay Gorney. Produced by Mr. Carroll at the Earl Carroll Theatre, New York, July 1, 1929.

Principals engaged—

Will Mahoney	Dorothy Britton
William Demarest	Dorothy Carroll
Don Howard	Patsy Kelly
Coly Worth	Gracie Worth
George Givot	Phelps Twins
Three Sailors	Frances Joyce
Omar	Grace Du Faye

Staged by Mr. Carroll, Edgar MacGregor and Leroy Prinz.

SHOW GIRL

(111 performances)

A musical comedy revue by William Anthony McGuire, based on the novel by J. P. McEvoy, music by George Gershwin, lyrics by Ira Gershwin and Gus Kahn. Produced by Mr. Ziegfeld at the Ziegfeld Theatre, New York, July 2, 1929.

Principals engaged—

Jimmie Durante	Ruby Keeler
Joseph Macauley	Barbara Newberry
Eddie Foy, Jr.	Harriet Hoctor
Frank McHugh	Noel Francis
Calvin Thomas	Doris Carson
Austin Fairman	Caryl Bergman
Lou Clayton	Sadie Duff
Eddie Jackson	Kathryn Hereford
Matthew Smith	Blaine Cordner

Staged by Mr. Ziegfeld, Bobby Connelly and Albertina Rasch.

BEDFELLOWS

(47 performances)

A farce comedy in three acts by Louise Carter. Produced by Bernard Levey for Lloyd Productions, Inc., at the Waldorf Theatre, New York, July 1, 1929.

Cast of characters—

Mrs. Barbara Yost.................................Jane Marbury
Ruth Yost.................................Betty Lee Carter
Felix Cornwall.................................Hal K. Dawson
Elinor Charlot.................................Anne Bronaugh
Sarah.................................Helen O'Donnell
Dorothy Cornwall.................................Lee Smith
Jack Charlot.................................John Vosberg
Robert Rodgers.................................Robert Lowing
Dr. Bim.................................Geoffrey Bryant
Henry Smith.................................William Gunthy

Acts I, II and III.—Cornwall Living Room.
Staged by Bernard W. Suss.

BROADWAY NIGHTS

(40 performances)

A musical revue in twenty-four scenes with music by Sam Timberg, Lee David and Maurice Rubens, lyrics by M. Jaffe. Produced by the Messrs. Shubert at the 44th Street Theatre, New York, July 15, 1929.

Principals engaged—

Dr. Rockwell	Odette Myrtil
Frank Gaby	Laura Lee
Harry Conley	Peggy Cornell
Joe Phillips	Rita Owen
Harry Stockwell	Ruth Gormly
Sam Raynor	Vivian Hunter
George Dobbs	Lillian Lane
Hoyt Meredith	Margaret Merle
George Schiller	Jeanne Walton
Eddie Shubert	Mary Manson
Archie Foulke	Hale Girls
King, King and King	Foster Girls

Staged by Busby Berkeley and Stanley Logan.

FREDDY

(63 performances)

A comedy in three acts by C. Stafford Dickens. Produced by Murray Phillips at the Lyceum Theatre, New York, July 16, 1929.

Cast of characters—

George Gommery.............................C. Stafford Dickens
Parker.......................................Lawrence H. Cecil
Jane Gommery...................................Beatrice Terry
Freddy Hall..................................Raymond Walburn
Andrew Toomley..................................Hubert Druce
Hollis.....................................Cecilia Radclyffe
Queenie Mellish..................................Vera Neilson
Acts I and III.—The Gommerys' House in the Country. Surrey.
Act II.—Queenie Mellish's Apartment in Town.
Staged by C. Stafford Dickens.

George and Jane Gommery, married, fall out of love with each other and in love with somebody else. George takes up with Queenie Mellish, actress, or tries to. Jane fastens on Freddy Hall, who doesn't want at all to be loved by her. To get himself out, Freddy claims Queenie is his mistress, which causes some confusion. After a while George and Jane resume and Freddy and Queenie are threatened with an affair of their own.

NOW-A-DAYS

(8 performances)

A drama in three acts by Arthur F. Brash. Produced by William A. Brady at the Forrest Theatre, New York, August 5, 1929.

Cast of characters—

Jean Wing.......................................Peggy Shannon
Paula Newhall....................................Mayo Methot
Barbara Herford...................................Irene Blair
Martin..A. O. Huhan
Sheldon Lunt.......................................Jack Boehn
Boyd Butler....................................Melvyn Douglas
George Chatfield..................................Walter Smith
Mrs. Fisher..................................Beverly Sitgreaves
A Stranger......................................Edward Pawley
Mr. Huntington...............................Duncan Penwarden
Acts I and III.—Living Room in the Home of the Herfords. Act II.—At Mrs. Fisher's.
Staged by Jessie Bonstelle.

Jean Wing is a flapper, Barbara Herford a nice girl and Paula Newhall hard-boiled and ruthless. Discussing men Barbara admits her love of Boyd Butler, a hero sober, a bad boy drunk. Paula wagers $50 she can get Boyd for her own. To win, Paula twits Boyd into drinking, takes him to a questionable boarding house where he gets into a fight with a bootlegger. During the fight Paula strikes the bootlegger with a bottle, killing him, and runs away. Barbara gets Boyd away, but he is dug out by a detective and is about to be arrested when Paula reappears, confesses and kills herself.

* IT'S A WISE CHILD

(356 performances)

A comedy in three acts by Laurence E. Johnson. Produced by David Belasco at the Belasco Theatre, New York, August 6, 1929.

Cast of characters—

Mrs. Stanton.......................................Helen Lowell
Alice Peabody.......................................Olga Krolow
Bertha.......................................Leila Bennett
Bill Stanton.......................................George Walcott
Roger Baldwin.......................................Humphrey Bogart
Joyce Stanton.......................................Mildred McCoy
James Stevens.......................................Minor Watson
G. A. Appleby.......................................Harlan Briggs
Cool Kelly.......................................Sidney Toler
Otho Peabody.......................................Porter Hall
Acts I, II and III.—The Living Room in the Stanton Home.
Staged by David Belasco.

Joyce Stanton, engaged to the middle-aged banker, G. A. Appleby, fancies herself in love with the younger and handsomer Roger Baldwin. Having been told that no man would think of marrying a girl who has borne a child by another lover, Joyce boldly tells G. A. that she is about to become a mother. The banker promptly releases himself from his engagement, but so, in a way, does Roger Baldwin, too. Then Joyce discovers her true love is and always has been the family lawyer, James Stevens.

JERRY-FOR-SHORT

(64 performances)

A comedy in three acts by William A. Grew. Produced by Eugene Productions, Inc., at the Waldorf Theatre, New York, August 12, 1929.

Cast of characters—

Betty Hartwell.......................................Lorna Carroll
Bascom Jenkins.......................................Cameron Mathews
John Hartwell.......................................Fiske O'Hara
Geraldine Jenkins.......................................Patricia Quinn
Robert Manners.......................................Joseph Fay
Minerva Manners.......................................Marie Louise Dana
Cyril Forbish.......................................John Brewster
Mary.......................................Dorothy Greene
Perkins.......................................Harold Bolton
Anthony La Vere.......................................Don Costello
Acts I, II and III.—Living Room of John Hartwell's Home in Westchester.
Staged by William A. Grew.

The Hartwells, newly rich, are in Westchester County, New York, trying to buy their niece, Betty, in love with the high-toned Robert Manners, a place in society. They acquire the Jenkinses, father and daughter, as butler and social secretary. Westchester society snubs them until word comes from England that Jenkins has come into a title. Then society flocks to the Hartwells and Mrs. Manners tries to hasten the marriage of Betty and Robert. Word that the title story was a mistake breaks everything off. Mrs. Manners finally accepts Betty for herself alone.

MURRAY ANDERSON'S ALMANAC

(69 performances)

Revue in twenty-eight scenes, book by Noel Coward, Rube Goldberg, Ronald Jeans, Paul Gerard Smith, Harry Ruskin, John McGowan, Peter Arno and Wynn; music by Milton Agar and Henry Sullivan; lyrics by Jack Yellen. Produced by Almanack Theatrical Corporation at Erlanger's Theatre, New York, August 14, 1929.

Principals engaged—

Jimmie Savo	Trixie Friganza
Roy Atwell	Eleanor Shaler
Fred Keating	Helen Thompson
Jack Powell	Stella Power
William Griffith	Billie Gerber
George Christie	Eleanor Terry
Warren Lassiter	Frances Mann
Franc Lassiter	Norma Maxine
Charles Barnes	Rita Glynde
Roy Rice	Anita
Frederick Carpenter	Henrietta
Reeder Boss	Helen Royal
Charles Royal	Mary Werner

Staged by John Murray Anderson, William Holbrook and Harry Ruskin.

DINNER IS SERVED

(4 performances)

A comedy in three acts by Alan Mowbray. Produced by Miller and Powell at the Cort Theatre, New York, August 15, 1929.

Cast of characters—

Flossie..Gaby Fay
Mary Bishop..............................Beatrice Hendricks
John Barron................................Edward Emery

Jack Hamilton....................................Hugh Huntley
Billy Bishop.....................................Alan Mowbray
Acts I, II and III.—In Billy Bishop's House in the Country.
Staged by Mr. Mowbray.

Mary Bishop is disappointed because her husband, Billy Bishop, is not more ardent as a lover. She thinks to excite his interest in his home work by diverting his attention to Flossie, the maid. As it turns out Billy, weighing the wisdom of Jack Hamilton, surprises Mary with his ardor and Flossie takes up temporarily with Edward Emery, Mary's father.

GETTING EVEN

(5 performances)

A comedy in thirty-four episodes by Nathaniel Wilson. Produced by the author at the Biltmore Theatre, New York, August 19, 1929.

Cast of characters—

Veronica Mathilda McConnell....................Georgia Clarke
Dorothy Ruth....................................Louise Kirtland
Patrick ....James T. Ford
Mary..Lydia Wilmore
Mrs. McBride (Dorah)............................Lalive Brownell
Mrs. Reddin (Theresa)...........................Grace M. Murray
Monica..Dorothy Guthern
Joe ....Patrick Glasgow
Mathews...Arthur Harless
Mr. Johnston....................................Eugene Kane
Mrs. Johnston...................................Ann Jordan
Leo Grub..Percy Kilbride
Raymond Brooks ....Lon Carter
Carl Remick ....Ward Soladar
Clyde Remick....................................Stanley Whitman
Freddie Leavitt.................................Norman Stewart
Raymond Hill....................................Edmund MacDonald
Tom Costello....................................Eddie Mann
A Nurse...Roberta Bellininger
A Doctor ....Donald Thompson
A Quack...Robert Vose
A Captain of Police ....Roger Bacon
Scenes in and About the McConnell Home, New Rochelle, the Hotchkiss Home, the Johnston Home and Camp and a Hospital.
Staged by Mr. Wilson.

Veronica McConnell, following the death of her mother, tries to make her own living. In pictures her honor is threatened. As a maid of all work she is employed by the Johnstons, disciples of a higher spiritual life. When Mrs. Johnston finally dies, Mr. Johnston wants to marry Veronica, but she is already married and dies in a hospital as a result of an abortion, convinced no good can come of a person's trying to get even with the world.

A NOBLE ROGUE

(9 performances)

An operetta by Kenyon Scott. Produced at the Gansevoort Theatre, New York, August 19, 1929.

Cast of characters—

Jules Le Blanc....R. A. Rose
Celeste Beauregard....Cecil Carol
Colonel Mulford....Frank Howson
Señorita Velasquez....Melba Marcelle
Grambo....Esteban Cerdan
Madame Le Blanc....Nanette Flack
Major Villere....Robert Hobbs
Captain Lockyer....Gordon Richards
Virginia Mulford....Marguerite Zender
Evalina....Helen Heed
Jean Lafitte....Robert Rhodes
Captain Dominique You....William Balfour
Captain O'Shaughnessy....Alfred Heather
Alphonse....Jimmie Carr
François....Andre Borice
Rina....Marie La Verni
Louise....Irma Friend
Señor Antonio....Barry Devine
Rancher....Lionel Sainer

Act I.—Patio of the Café Mespero, New Orleans. Act II.—Camp of Jean Lafitte.

Staged by the author.

The romance of Virginia Mulford, daughter of the Old South, and Jean Lafitte, romantic buccaneer, during the War of 1812. Jean wins.

GAMBLING

(152 performances)

A drama in four acts by George M. Cohan. Produced by the author at the Fulton Theatre, New York, August 26, 1929.

Cast of characters—

Sheridan....Harry Lillford
Connelly....Harold Healy
Draper....George M. Cohan
Freelock....Robert Middlemass
Lewis....Dan Carey
Carlysle....Neil Stone
Dorothy....Isabel Baring
Braddock....Douglas MacPherson
Mazie....Mary Philips
Brennan....Charles Johnson
Marie....Kathleen Niday
Gaylor....Theodore Newton
Martin....Ernest Fox
Mason....Mark Sullivan
Buddy....William Gillard
Maid....Mary Fox

Captain....................Jack Williams
Knowles....................Jack Leslie
Wayne....................Duke Keeley
Attendant....................Joseph Halsey
Messenger....................Irving Jackson
Mrs. Cromley....................Lydia MacMillan
Chief....................Edward F. Nannary
Miss Daly....................Jane Thomas

Act I.—Al Draper's New York Home. Act II.—Dorothy's and Mazie's Apartment. Act III.—Draper's Gambling House. Act. IV.—Knowles' Office.

Staged by Sam Forrest.

Al Draper, gambler, has a letter from his adopted daughter that she has sailed suddenly from Europe; that she is accompanied by a young man named Braddock and that they are temporarily in hiding. Before Draper can learn more, the police report the discovery of the dead body of the girl in an obscure hotel. She has been killed, apparently, by a blow in the face. In an effort to track down the murderer after the police fail, Draper makes friends with two women friends of Braddock's, Mazie and Dorothy. Just as he hopes to fasten the crime on some one known to them, Braddock confesses.

SOLDIERS AND WOMEN

(64 performances)

A drama in three acts by Paul Hervey Fox and George Tilton. Produced by Lew Cantor at the Ritz Theatre, New York, September 2, 1929.

Cast of characters—

Kiroth....................Lota
Khitmagars....................{ Sarat Lahiri / Frank De Silva
Captain Clive Branch....................Derek Glynne
Captain Luke Arnold....................Leonard Mudie
Surgeon-Major Reynolds....................Clifford Walker
Hendrich Rathje....................Edward Fielding
Colonel John Ritchie....................Montague Shaw
Lieutenant Donaldson....................G. P. Huntley, Jr.
Brenda Ritchie....................Violet Heming
Helen Arnold....................Verree Teasdale
Lieutenant Mason....................Reginald Sheffield
Trooper Delehanty....................Robert Bunce Williams
Trooper Wilson....................Basil Hanbury
Marta....................Ruth Rickaby
General Sir Charles Conant, K.C.B., K.C.S.I.. D.S.O....A. E. Anson

Acts I, II and III.—In an Obscure Military Outpost in Baluchistan, Northern India.

Staged by Joseph H. Graham.

Brenda, wife of Col. John Ritchie, bored by the monotony of her life at the British military post in Baluchistan, achieves a passion for the handsome young Captain Clive Branch. Repulsed by Branch, who admits his love for the wife of Captain Arnold, Brenda seeks revenge by shooting Branch. In the dark she kills Arnold instead. Circumstances point to the probable guilt of Branch and Brenda gloats over his plight until she is herself uncovered as the murderess by the astute General Sir Charles Conant.

GREAT SCOTT

(16 performances)

A comedy in three acts by Howard E. Kock. Produced by L. A. Safian at the Forty-ninth Street Theatre, New York, September 2, 1929.

Cast of characters—

Molly Scott....................................Ethel Strickland
Annie Simpson....................................Mary Roth
Jake Scott....................................Walter Horton
Lem Scott....................................Millard F. Mitchell
Delancey Scott....................................Ray Harper
Ruth Watson....................................Adele Ronson
J. H. Watson....................................Dean Raymond

Acts I and III.—Kitchen of the Scott Home. Act II.—Outer Office of the Watson Can Company.
Staged by Albert Bannister.

Delancey Scott, given a college education by his hard-working father, returns from his graduation full of theories and book learning. Neither his father nor his dumb brother Lem think much of his knowledge, but his mother is his friend. Delancey goes to work in the mill with his father and brother, stirs the men to strike, wins the hand of the daughter of the mill owner and finally works things out fine for everybody, thanks to his education.

SWEET ADELINE

(234 performances)

A musical comedy in fifteen scenes by Oscar Hammerstein, 2d, music by Jerome Kern. Produced by Arthur Hammerstein at Hammerstein's Theatre, New York, September 3, 1929.

Cast of characters—

Sergeant Malone....................................Thomas Chadwick
August....................................George Raymond
Dot....................................Violet Carlson
Emil Schmidt....................................Robert Fischer

Addie....Helen Morgan
Nellie....Caryl Bergman
Lulu Ward....Irene Franklin
Dan Ward....Robert Emmett Keane
Tom Martin....Max Hoffmann, Jr.
Ruppert Day....Charles Butterworth
Doctor....Jack Gray
Orderly....Tom Thompson
Colonel....Martin Shepard
Gus....Gus
Will....Will
James Day....Robert Chisholm
Sam Herzig....Harry Vokes
Eddie....Wally Crisham
Sid Barnett....John Seymour
The Sultan....Len Mence
The Jester....George Djimos
Maizie O'Rourke....Helen Ault
Head Carpenter....William Shepard
Props....Martin Shepard
George....Borrah Levinson
Jerry Beall....Jerry Jarnegan
Young Blood....Jackson Fairchild
Gabe Case....Ben Wells
A Cabby....Tom Rider
Old Sport....Harry Esmond
Doc....George Magis
Jim Thornton....Jim Thornton
Hester Van Doren Day....Sally Bates
Willie Day....Peter Bender
George Smith's Girl Band....Frances Flanigan, Polly Fisher, Josephine Rice, Mabel Thilbault, Gertrude Clave, Laura Mutch

Act I.—Scene 1—Schmidt's Beer Garden, Hoboken, 1898. 2—A Hospital Tent Near San Juan Hill, Cuba. 3—Kitchen Entrance to the Schmidt Home. 4—Under the Stage of the Olympia Burlesque Theatre, the Bowery. 5—Stage and Auditorium. Act II.—Scene 1—Corridor in Front of Parterre Boxes, a Broadway Theatre. 2—McGowan's Pass Tavern. 3—Summer. (a) A Horse Car. (b) A Hansom. 4—Hoffman House Bar. 5—Jim's Sloop. 6—Madison Square Garden. 7—The Stage of Madison Square Garden Roof. 8—On Fort George Hill. 9—Alongside the *Lucania.* 10—A Broadway Theatre.

Staged by Reginald Hammerstein and Danny Dare.

Addie, daughter of Emil Schmidt, who runs a beer garden in Hoboken, is a great favorite of the customers because of her talent for singing songs that cause them to cry in their beer. Addie loves Tom Martin of the steamship St. Paul, but when Tom joins the navy for the Spanish-American War it is Nellie Schmidt he favors. Addie takes to the stage, is a hit and finally makes Broadway. Later she discovers she loves James Day, who backs her show.

THE COMMODORE MARRIES

(40 performances)

A comedy in three acts by Kate Parsons, suggested by Smollett's "Peregrine Pickle." Produced by Arthur Hopkins at the Plymouth Theatre, New York, September 4, 1929.

Cast of characters—

Fawcett....................................Harry A. Huguenot
May Day....................................Seifert C. Pyle
A Man from Pickle's....................................Jack Byrne
Watch....................................Leslie Hunt
Mr. Hatchways....................................Charles D. Brown
Cookie....................................K. Nambu
Commodore Trunnion....................................Walter Huston
Anna....................................Eva Williams
Perry Pickle....................................Joseph A. Donohue
Ira Pickle....................................Caryl Gillin
Mrs. Pickle....................................Ethel Intropidi
Miss Pickle, Afterwards Mrs. Trunnion............Eda Heinemann
Mrs. Fibtree....................................Lida Kane
Mrs. Calano....................................Lizzie Rechelle
Doctor Dill....................................James Macdonald

Acts I, II and III.—The Main Room of Commodore Trunnion's House.

Staged by Arthur Hopkins.

Commodore Trunnion, retired from the navy, refuses to give up the sea. His house is fitted out like a ship and he retains certain members of the crew, including his mate, Mr. Hatchways, to live with him. When the Commodore marries Miss Pickle, trouble starts. Humoring his wife because he believes she is to bear him a son, Trunnion is woefully disappointed by her failure to do so. Convinced later that she is a cheat in other ways, the Commodore forces Mrs. Trunnion to walk the plank and resumes his gay old seadog bachelor ways.

SCARLET PAGES

(72 performances)

A drama in three acts by Samuel Shipman and John B. Hymer. Produced by A. H. Woods at the Morosco Theatre, New York, September 9, 1929.

Cast of characters—

Laura Hutchinson....................................Elizabeth Council
Frederick Stoner....................................David Higgins
Mary Bancroft....................................Elsie Ferguson
Leonard Barnes....................................Donald McClelland
Robert Lawrence....................................Robert Williams
Nora Mason....................................Claire Luce
Mrs. Mason....................................Jean Adair
John Remington....................................Lee Baker
Richard Trainor....................................J. Moy Bennett
Officer Callahan....................................William Burnett
Clerk of the Court....................................Archie Sayre
Carlotta Cordez....................................Francesca Hill
Judge Graham....................................John Costello
Nellie Burke....................................Sue Moore
James McGowan....................................Henry Pemberton
Thomas Britton....................................Elmer Cornell
Sister Veronica....................................Gilberta Faust

Valerie..Lilly Marne
Asst. to the District Attorney........................{ John Martin / Jack Fifer }
Court Stenographers..............................{ Albert Hall / Glen Snyder }
Court Attendants...................................{ A. Reno / John Moran }

Act I.—The Private Office of Mary Bancroft, New York. Act II.—A Courtroom. General Sessions. Act III.—The Living Room of Mary Bancroft's Home.

Staged by Ira Hards.

Mary Bancroft, New York's greatest criminal lawyer, agrees to take the case of Nora Mason, charged with the murder of her father, when she learns the girl's justification for the crime. At the trial, when the District Attorney is about to convince the jury that no father would attack his daughter, Nora's mother admits that Nora is an adopted daughter. Demanding the records, the District Attorney learns that Mary Bancroft is the girl's real mother and agrees to suppress the fact. Mary insists that it be made public. Nora is freed. Forced to decide between her real and her foster mother Nora stays temporarily with the foster mother.

HOUSEPARTY

(177 performances)

A drama in three acts by Kenneth Phillips Britton and Roy Hargrave. Produced by George C. Tyler and A. L. Erlanger at the Knickerbocker Theatre, New York, September 9, 1929.

Cast of characters—

Alan Bradford..................................Roy Hargrave
Ronald Evans..................................Edward Woods
Sally Andrews...............................Penelope Hubbard
Florence....................................Harriet MacGibbon
Hortense Pfeiffer.............................Betty Lawrence
Mrs. Milligan...............................Annie Sutherland
Mrs. White.......................................Julia Hay
Mrs. Rutherford............................Louise Mackintosh
Edward Canby.................................Charles Cromer
Darrow Jenckes...............................Matthew Smith
Doris Callander.................................Helen Dodge
Malcolm F. R. White, M.A...................Edward J. LeSaint
Bill Warren...................................Waldo Edwards
Chick Smith.....................................Charles Dill
Marianne Guion................................Edith Hargrave
Bob Davis...Billy Quinn
Betty Creeling.................................Cynthia Rogers
James..Lawrence Bolton
Students.........Richard Ewell, John Mercer, Wm. C. Haskell, Edward Whitner and Everett Miller
Houseparty Guests..........Helen Oursler, Beatrice Holtby, Dorothy Harris, Lois Benson and Betty Stoddart

Acts I, II and III.—Library of a Fraternity House at Williams College, Williamstown, Massachusetts, During House Parties.

Staged by Harry Wagstaff Gribble.

During an afternoon tea dance at a Williams College fraternity house Alan Bradford is accused by Florence, one of the town girls, of being the father of her expected infant. Florence admits a reasonable doubt but is determined to disgrace Roy unless he raises $10,000 for her. In grabbing her by the throat to prevent an outcry Roy accidentally knocks Florence into the fireplace, where a heavy andiron falls on her head and kills her. Panicky with fear Roy hides the body in a cupboard and thereafter suffers mental tortures until he is forced to a confession. Tried and acquitted, he still is haunted with visions of the accident until his loyal roommate, Ronald Evans, helps him snap out of it.

REMOTE CONTROL

(79 performances)

A drama in three acts by Clyde North, Albert C. Fuller and Jack T. Nelson. Produced by A. L. Jones and Morris Green at the Forty-eighth Street Theatre, New York, September 10, 1929.

Cast of characters—

Walter Brokenchild	Frank Beaston
Dorothy Doyle	Louise Barrett
Ralph Shugart	Hobart Cavanaugh
Helen Wright	Patricia Barclay
Charles Golden	Arthur Pierson
Moran	William Foran
Bert Rupert	Donald Kirke
Doctor A. P. Workman	Edward Van Sloan
Agnes Joyce	Consuelo Flowerton
Betty Blair	Alice Davenport
Lorraine Winthrop	Mimi Lehmann
Beatrice Allen	Raleigh Kennedy
May Prescott	Audrey Berry
June Carter	Claire Nolte
Pete	George Leach
Joe	Michael Markham
Ed	William Honohan
Jack	Dave Abrams
W. L. Oakwood	George Lessey
Sergeant Devine	Lawrence Leslie
Burke	Harold Woolf
Slattery	James V. Nolan
Professor Murrey	Al Ochs
Ruth	Polly Clarke

Larry Funk's WPH Nut Crackers
Acts I, II and III.—The Radio Studio of WPH, Chicago.
Staged by Clyde North.

Walter Brokenchild, announcer for Station WPH, Chicago, agrees to let six Junior League girls broadcast a part of their "Follies" program. During the broadcasting holdups invade the studio and rob the girls of their jewels. Brokenchild, seeking to do a little amateur detective work, is about to fasten a motive on

Dr. Workman, spiritualist, when the doctor is killed at the microphone. Brokenchild is accused of the murder, loyally defended by his secretary-sweetheart, Helen Wright, and eventually cleared. It was the Ghost gang.

MURDER ON THE SECOND FLOOR

(45 performances)

A drama in three acts by Frank Vosper. Produced by A. H. Woods at the Eltinge Theatre, New York, September 11, 1929.

Cast of characters—

Hugh Bromilow....................................Laurence Olivier
Lucy Timson...Voila Lyel
Sylvia Armitage...................................Phyllis Konstam
Joseph Reynolds...................................Charles Brown
Mrs. Rose Armitage...............................Florence Edney
Edward Armitage...................................O. B. Clarence
Jam Singh...George Probert
Miss Snell...Drusilla Wills
A Police Constable................................Henry Warwick
A Police Inspector................................John R. Turnbull

Act I.—The Sitting Room of Mrs. Armitage's House in Bloomsbury, London. Acts II and III.—The Stairs and Landing of the Second Floor of Mrs. Armitage's House.

Staged by William Mollison.

Hugh Bromilow, living in a Bloomsbury boarding house, London, in search of atmosphere for use in his playwriting, is dared by the landlady's daughter to prove that he can, as he says, write just as good a mystery play as any being produced in the West End. Bromilow, sitting at the side of the stage with the girl, Sylvia Armitage, begins the recital of a story, using the characters of the lodgers in the house. As he talks his play takes shape, a drug conspiracy is revealed, one lodger is killed by another and most of the rest of them are suspected of having committed the crime. The plot proves in the end to be that of Bromilow's newest play, produced the night before.

PORGY

(34 performances)

A folk play in three acts by Dorothy and DuBose Heyward. Revived by the Theatre Guild at the Martin Beck Theatre, New York, September 13, 1929.

Cast of characters—

Maria . . . Georgette Harvey
Jake . . . Wesley Hill
Lily . . . Dorothy Paul
Mingo . . . Richard Huey
Annie . . . Ella Madison
Sporting Life . . . Percy Verwayne
Serena . . . Rose MacClendon
Robbins . . . Morris McKenny
Jim . . . Peter Clark
Clara . . . Edna Thomas
Peter . . . Hayes Pryor
Porgy . . . Frank Wilson
Crown . . . Jack Carter
Crown's Bess . . . Evelyn Ellis
A Detective . . . Frederick Smith
Undertaker . . . Leigh Whipper
Scipio . . . Wallace Hill
Simon Frazier . . . A. B. Comathiere
Nelson . . . Wayland Rudd
Alan Archdale . . . Erskine Sanford
The Crab Man . . . Leigh Whipper
The Coroner . . . Garrett Minturn
Policemen . . . Felix Jacoves, Walter Warner

Act I.—Scene 1—Catfish Row in Charleston, S. C. 2—Serena's Room. Act II.—Scene 1—Catfish Row. 2—A Palmetto Jungle. 3—Catfish Row. 4—Serena's Room. Act III.—Catfish Row.
Staged by Reuben Mamoulian.

See "The Best Plays of 1927-28."

A COMEDY OF WOMEN

(5 performances)

A comedy in three acts by Leo de Valery. Produced by Mr. De Valery at the Craig Theatre, New York, September 13, 1929.

Cast of characters—

Evy . . . Hilda Heywood Howe
Julia . . . Ethel Allen
May Wilson . . . Ruth Fallows
Mrs. Blanche Potter . . . Jane Allyn
Pierre Preval . . . Leo de Valery
Carmen Rodriguez . . . Jean Downs
Mrs. Van Kerkelaer . . . Theresa Maxwell Conover
Alice Elliott . . . Mary Hayes
Hortense Smith . . . Madeleine King
Miss Edwards . . . Ethel Mason
Mr. Elliott . . . Leslie T. Peacocke
Prince Paoli . . . John Buckler
Dolores . . . Marion Steeve
Mabel . . . Margaret Gollins
Aphrodite . . . Elizabeth Day

Acts I, II and III.—Preval's Park Avenue Apartment in New York City.
Staged by Edward Elsner.

Pierre Preval, desired of many women, suffers their blandishments patiently for two hours and then escapes by eloping with Alice Elliott.

THE SEA GULL

(63 performances)

A drama in four acts by Anton Tchekov, translated by Constance Garnett. Produced at the Civic Repertory Theatre, New York, September 16, 1929.

Cast of characters—

Medvedenko (Semyon Semyonovitch)..............Harold Moulton
Masha (Daughter of Shamraev)...................Eva Le Gallienne
Sorin (Pyotr Nikolayevitch).........................Paul Leyssac
Konstantin Gavrilovitch Treplev.......................Robert Ross
Yakov...Herbert Shapiro
Nina (Milailovna Zaretchnaya)..............Josephine Hutchinson
Polina Andreyevna...................................Leona Roberts
Dorn (Yevgeny Sergeyevitch).........................Walter Beck
Shamraev (Ilya Afanasyevitch)......................Egon Brecher
Trigorin (Boris Alexeyevitch).....................Jacob Ben-Ami
Irina (Nikolayevna Arkadina, Madame Treplev)......Merle Maddern
A Man Cook...David Kerman
A Housemaid.....................................Elisabeth Shelley

Act I.—Part of the Park on Sorin's Estate. Act II.—Lawn in Front of Sorin's House. Acts III and IV.—The Dining Room in Sorin's House.

Staged by Miss Le Gallienne.

See "The Best Plays of 1928-29." The Repertory company, under Eva Le Gallienne's direction, also revived Ibsen's "The Master Builder," Sierra's "The Cradle Song," and Molière's "The Would-be Gentleman" the week of September 16.

A STRONG MAN'S HOUSE

(24 performances)

A drama in three acts by Lee Wilson Dodd. Produced by John Tuerk at the Ambassador Theatre, New York, September 16, 1929.

Cast of characters—

John McGarrick.................................A. G. Andrews
Simeon Fitch...................................Robert Strange
Janet Hale...Mary Nash
Roy Hamerman......................................Lester Vail
Dr. Bull...Charles Horn
Sam Hamerman...................................Howard Lang
Bill Dunkhorst.................................Robert W. Craig
Allen..Ray Collins
Calkins..Ross Hertz

Acts I, II and III.—"Sam's Castle," Near Paris, State of Illiana, U. S. A.

Staged by Lionel Atwill.

Janet Hale accepts employment as a professional nurse in the home of the millionaire, Sam Hamerman, with the avowed intention of inducing Roy Hamerman, son and heir, to marry her. Her schemes are furthered by the elder Hamerman, who distrusts his son as a dreaming mollycoddle who takes after his dead mother. Hamerman dies, Janet and Roy are married. Learning of the conspiracy Roy insists that Janet shall go through with her bargain and she in time comes to recognize him as the really strong man in the house and is glad to accept and endorse his ideals.

HAWK ISLAND

(24 performances)

A melodrama in three acts by Howard Irving Young. Produced by Thomas Kilpatrick at the Longacre Theatre, New York, September 16, 1929.

Cast of characters—

Tom Austen.....................................Joseph Granby
Harriet Cooper.....................................Olga Lee
Gregory Sloane.....................................Clarke Gable
Stella Wayne.....................................Helen Joy
Anthony Bryce.....................................Charles Halton
Louise Hollister.....................................Frances Kain
Paul Cooper.....................................Henry O'Neill
Barker.....................................Sumner Gard
Madeline Austen.....................................Mary Fowler
Donald Parish.....................................A. J. Herbert
Sally Rogers.....................................Elaine Temple
Lynn Rogers.....................................N. R. Cregan
Captain Westover.....................................Walter F. Scott

Acts I, II and III.—Study in Gregory Sloane's Summer Home on Hawk Island off the New England Coast.

Staged by Mr. Young.

Gregory Sloane, host to a house party on a rugged island off the coast of Maine, is bored to desperation by the crime talk inspired by one of his guests, a detective-story novelist. To prove an argument and stir some excitement Sloane and the novelist arrange a fake murder. The novelist is shot and the evidence against Sloane is conclusive. When the novelist returns to the house after dark prepared to explode the hoax he is actually shot and killed by a husband with whose wife he has been philandering. The evidence still points to the innocent Sloane. The conclusion is satisfying.

PHILADELPHIA

(32 performances)

A melodrama in three acts by S. John Park. Produced by Ashcraft Productions, Inc., at the Mansfield Theatre, New York, September 16, 1929.

Cast of characters—

District Attorney Jennings..........................J. P. Hopkins
John Bradshaw..........................Jack Motte
Robert Crawford..........................Walter Regan
Mrs. B. J. Miller..........................Lita Torgerson
Nellie Densford..........................Eleanor Hayden
Slicer..........................Tewks O'Dare
Inspector Brennan..........................Walter Ayers
1st Aid Hospital Interne..........................Del McDermid
Sadie Watkins..........................Kitty Robinson
Judge Densford..........................William Walcott
Coroner..........................Ernest Pollock
1st Detective..........................Ralph Morehouse
2nd Detective..........................Frank Lengel
Acts I, II and III.—Law Offices of the Firm of Bradshaw and Crawford.
Staged by S. John Park.

John Bradshaw, Philadelphia's crookedest lawyer, has accepted $25,000 from Robert Crawford, law student, and taken him into partnership. Suspecting that he is being cheated, Crawford starts an investigation that exposes Bradshaw as a tool of Philadelphia's gangdom. During the investigation Bradshaw is shot. His body is being rifled by Crawford and others when he comes to life, thanks to his bullet-proof vest. Crawford is not discouraged. He goes on exposing crooks, even to the highest higher ups.

FIESTA

(39 performances)

A drama in three acts by Michael Gold. Produced by Experimental Theatres, Inc., at the Provincetown Playhouse (Garrick), New York, September 17, 1929.

Cast of characters—

Chato..........................Charles McCarthy, Jr.
Pablo..........................Allen Nagle
Tomas..........................Harold Garry
Ignacio..........................Edward Segal
Isidro..........................Arnold Mirante
An Old Peon..........................Paul Dorn
A Peon..........................Martin Glee
Rafaela ....Ruth Chorpenning

Aurelio..David Fields
Miguel...William Martin
Don Felipe...Jack La Rue
Dona Luisa...Beverly Sitgreaves
Don Jesus..Warren Colston
Don Enrique...Carl Benton Reid
Guadalupe..Virginia Venable
Santiago..George Tobias
Uncle Pepe..Keith Stillman
Amador..David De Sisto
Sheriff..Josef Lagarovici
Tombola Woman..Virginia Rose
A Dancing Girl..Sophia Delza
Fiesta Ensemble.......Henry Petersilie, Benjamin Taly, Philip Roll, Sidney Kline, George Buyante, Albert Rosen, Leon S. Birnbaum, Charles Sardisco, Anthony Grey, Donald McHenry, Kemble Knight, Eugene Grossman, Richard de Merino, Lillian Okun, Maide Huneker.
Dancers....Anita Case, Esther Junger, Brana Ghorn, Darly Urritia, Malie Urritia.

Acts I and III.—Main Room of Rancho la Loma. Act II.—Scene 1—The Plaza of the Town. 2—A Place in the Woods.

Staged by James Light.

Don Enrique is a patriotic revolutionist who returns to his ranch imbued with the doctrines of Señor Tolstoy, whom he hopes to emulate. He brings with him Guadalupe, war orphan, 15 years old and beautiful, who symbolizes Mexico to him. He hopes to refine and educate Guadalupe and through her convince his peons of their possibilities. His mother, Dona Luisa, considering him visionary, advises Guadalupe to forget Enrique and run away to the fiesta. His brother, Don Felipe, follows after and seduces the girl. Enrique, enraged, seeks to kill his brother but the bullet hits a peon instead.

STREET SINGER

(191 performances)

A musical comedy in two acts by Cyrus Wood and Edgar Smith; lyrics by Graham John; music by John Gilbert, Nicholas Kempner and S. Timberg. Produced by Busby Berkeley at the Shubert Theatre, New York, September 17, 1929.

Cast of characters—

Mabel Brown...Jane Alden
Ronnie...Nick Long, Jr.
Claire...Ruth Shields
Manager of Cafe Royal....................................Phil Reep
Colonel Brown...Ed Garvie
Muriel...Peggy Cornell
Waiter...Jack Kelley
Annette...Nell Kelly
Louis..Harry K. Morton
Picot...Andrew Tombes
Doorman..Walter Johnson
First Tourist...Don Cortez

Second Tourist....................................Frank Gagen
A Lady....................................Kay Ross
John....................................Cesar Romero
Suzette....................................Queenie Smith
George....................................Guy Robertson
Prefect of Police....................................Frank Lalor
First Agent of Police....................................Bentley Stone
Second Agent of Police....................................Larry Hogan
The Baron....................................Jimmy Lyman
Erminie....................................Audrey Maple
Jean Baptiste....................................Phil Reep
Manager of Folies Bergere....................................Walter Johnson
Theatre Attendant....................................Jimmy Lyman
Louise....................................Marian Palmer

Act I.—Foyer of the Cafe Royal in Paris. Act II.—Scene 1—Reception Room in George's Summer Place. 2—Foyer of the Folies Bergère. 3—Green Room of the Folies Bergère.

Staged by Busby Berkeley.

George, rich and amorous, meets Suzette, a beautiful but poor flower vendor, and becomes sufficiently interested to want to make a lady of her. Suzette not only becomes a lady but also a leading dancer at the Folies Bergère. George almost loses her at the appointed time, but recovers her for the finale.

* STRICTLY DISHONORABLE

(321 performances)

A comedy in three acts by Preston Sturges. Produced by Brock Pemberton at the Avon Theatre, New York, September 18, 1929.

Cast of characters—

Giovanni....................................John Altieri
Mario....................................Marius Rogati
Tomaso Antiovi....................................William Ricciardi
Judge Dempsey....................................Carl Anthony
Henry Greene....................................Louis Jean Heydt
Isabelle Parry....................................Muriel Kirkland
Count Di Ruvo....................................Tullio Carminati
Patrolman Mulligan....................................Edward J. McNamara

Act I.—The Speakeasy of Tomaso Antiovi on West 49th Street, New York. Acts II and III.—A Rear Apartment Upstairs Over the Speakeasy.

Staged by Mr. Pemberton and Antoinette Perry.

See page 147.

THE CROOKS' CONVENTION

(13 performances)

A farcical satire by Arthur Somers Roche. Produced by Irving Lande at the Forrest Theatre, New York, September 18, 1929.

Cast of characters—

Alice Jones....................................Helene Dumas
Edward J. Harrington..........................Joseph Sweeney
Steve..Pat Kane
Judge Console..................................O. T. Burke
Bill...John O. Hewitt
Abigail Hart................................Louise Perine
James J. Timmons ....William Thompson
Noah Withers.....................................Will Marsh
Senator Stevens, "Big Bill".................Joseph Burton
Sergeant McConnell...........................Frank Horton
"Revival" Hunt...................................Stuart Fox
Smith.......................................Charles Slattery
Robert Gildad...................................Leo Donnelly
Reed Harmon................................Gay B. Kingston
The "Yellow Kid".................................Tom Blake
Tim Doonan...................................James T. Ford
Jack Manners....................................John Burkell
"Big Jennie"....................................Eleanor Hicks
Badger Kate.....................................Kay Mallory
Lifting Nell....................................Natalie Frees
Jake Sternberg..............................Milton C. Herman
Sam Raynor...................................John O. Hewitt
Mazarin......................................J. Carroll Naish
Ballot Box Sam..................................Frank Horton
Captain Jennings.................................Clifton Self

Act I.—The Office of Mr. Harrington. Acts II and III.—A Ballroom in the Ritz-Plaza Hotel.
Staged by Leo Donnelly.

The leading crooks of the country, in convention assembled, are converted to a better life by "Revival" Hunt at about the same time leading citizens organize to combat a crime wave. As a result of the crooks' conversion the country is thrown into a state of turmoil. There is no work for the police, banks close for lack of business, the churches have no sinners to save and even the home is threatened. When the crooks go back to work the country returns to normal.

CAPE COD FOLLIES

(30 performances)

A musical revue in twenty-eight scenes, book and lyrics by Stewart Baird, music by Alexander Fogarty. Produced by Cape Cod Playhouse at the Bijou Theatre, New York, September 18, 1929.

Principals engaged—

L'Estrange Millman	Ellen Love
Corbet Morris	Dorothy Llewellyn
David London	Doris Glaenzer
Peter Joray	Kathryn Hayman
Cecil Clovelly	Vera Hurst
William Watson	Betty Barr
Bobby Fulton	Mary Rose

Douglas Beddingford	Peggy Ellis
Kenneth Burton	Norma Mason
Thornton Boatwright	Justine De Paul
Lloyd Nolan	Elvira Jones

Staged by Stewart Baird, dances by John Lonergan.

ROPE'S END

(100 performances)

A melodrama in three acts by Patrick Hamilton. Produced by Lee Shubert at the Theatre Masque, New York, September 19, 1929.

Cast of characters—

Wyndham Brandon..............................Sebastian Shaw
Charles Granillo..............................Ivan Brandt
Sabot..............................John Trevor
Kenneth Raglan..............................Hugh Dempster
Leila Arden..............................Margaret Delamere
Sir Johnstone Kentley..............................Samuels Lysons
Mrs. Debenham..............................Nora Nicholson
Rupert Cadell..............................Ernest Milton

Acts I, II and III.—Rooms in Mayfair, London, Shared by Brandon and Granillo.
Staged by Reginald Denham.

Wyndham Brandon and Charles Granillo, Oxford students, strangle the son of Sir Johnstone Kentley for the thrill of the crime. They drag the body to their rooms, crowd it into a chest and invite a party of guests for tea, including the dead man's father and aunt. Tea is served from the top of the chest in which the body reposes. One guest, Rupert Cadell, also slightly erotic, gradually fastens the crime upon the hysterical boys and prepares to see them hanged.

NIGGER RICH (THE BIG SHOT)

(11 performances)

A comedy in three acts by John McGowan. Produced by Lee Shubert at the Royale Theatre, New York, September 20, 1929.

Cast of characters—

Denning..............................Roderick Maybee
Eddie Perkins..............................Spencer Tracy
Blake..............................Don Beddoe
Mrs. Mason..............................Adelaide Hibbard
Helen Page..............................Elvia Enders
Mike Kelly..............................Eric Dressler
Joe Burns..............................John A. Butler

Nina Welman....................................Helen Flint
Ray Cole....................................Franklyn Fox
Gunny Jones....................................Richard Taber
Martin....................................Rikel Kent
Tucker....................................William Lemuels
Gates....................................Gene West

Acts I and III.—The Dugout Club, New York City. Act II.—A Sitting Room in a Suite at the Ritz-Carlton Hotel.
Staged by John McGowan.

Mike Kelly, a hero in war, a "heel" in peace, after sponging for years on his friends, particularly "Gunny" Jones, wins a stake backing a race horse. He moves to the Ritz, assumes the high hat, forgets his friends, steals his former colonel's girl and flies high until a market crash strips him of everything he has. He wanders, down and out, back to the Dugout Club for ex-service men, makes over his insurance to "Gunny" and kills himself.

SWEETHEARTS

(17 performances)

A comic opera in two acts by Harry B. Smith and Fred de Gresac, music by Victor Herbert. Produced by the Jolson Theatre Musical Comedy Company at the Jolson Theatre, New York, September 21, 1929.

Cast of characters—

Sylvia, Princess of Zilania....................................Gladys Baxter
Prince Franz....................................Charles Massinger
Liane.................................... Genevieve Naegele
Mikel....................................Richard Powell
Paula....................................Flavia Arcaro
Lieutenant Karl....................................Paul Davin
Hon. Percival Slingsby....................................Wm. J. McCarthy
Petrus Van Tromp....................................Detmar Poppen
Aristide Caniche....................................Lee Daly
Jeanette....................................Wee Griffin
Clairette....................................Mary Thurman
Babette....................................Edith Artley
Lisette....................................Lisette Braddock
Toinette....................................Florence Cazelle
Nanette....................................Ethel Lynne
Captain Louvent....................................Roland Tudor
First Footman....................................Donald Catlin
Second Footman....................................Bronek Wrobleski
Coquette....................................Lucyle Keeling
Disdainful Girl....................................Frances Baviello
Village Belle....................................Sally Galbreaith
Military Girl....................................Frances Moore
Heralds.................................... { Cecilia Stockdale / Lucyle Keeling

Act I.—Courtyard of the Laundry of the White Geese, Bruges, Belgium. Act II.—The Royal Hunting Lodge, Zilania.
Staged by Milton Aborn.

Sylvia, Princess of Zilania, was hidden as a babe in a tulip bed, found by Paula, the laundress, and reared as a commoner. Prince

Franz, wandering through the laundry, comes upon Sylvia, loves her and is frightfully glad to discover later in the evening that she is of royal blood.

SWEET LAND OF LIBERTY

(8 performances)

A melodrama in two acts by Philip Dunning. Produced by A. L. Erlanger and George C. Tyler at the Knickerbocker Theatre, New York, September 23, 1929.

Cast of characters—

Flossie Brendell	Anne Forrest
Jack Richards	Ralph Theodore
Charlie Hunter	George Barbier
Muserve	Thomas Coffin Cooke
Joseph J. Davis	John Sharkey
Patrolman Russ	J. J. Hyland
Dan	Joseph Woodburn
Buckley	Robert Lynn
War Veteran	Wilton Lackaye, Jr.
Nevens	James Keane
Franklin Baker	Hermann Lieb
Mrs. Molly Richards	Dorothy Blackburn
Little Jackie	Bobbie Steele
Otis	Joseph Crehan
Mrs. Hunter	Elsa Ryan
Newton	Robert Harrison

Act I.—Charlie Hunter's Place. Act II.—Upstairs.
Staged by Philip Dunning.

Charlie Hunter and Jack Richards, liquor dealers, are witness to the murder of Muserve, Federal prohibition agent. Both agree to tell what they saw to the grand jury. Before either can testify Hunter is threatened with prosecution under the Jones law and Richards is shot in the back. The game goes on, with Hunter deciding to go out of business and fight the mess of crooks in office, including the district attorney.

GEORGE WHITE'S SCANDALS

(161 performances)

Musical revue in two acts, by W. K. Wells and George White; music and lyrics by Cliff Friend, George White and Irving Caesar. Produced by Mr. White at the Apollo Theatre, New York, September 23, 1929.

Principals engaged—

George White	Frances Williams
Willie Howard	Evelyn Wilson
Eugene Howard	Carolyn Nolte
Ernest Charles	Jean Scott
Jim Carty	Claire Scott
Jack White	Vada Alexander
Harry Morrissey	Margaret Manners
Fred Lyon	Sue Elliott
Jack Durant	Alice Kerwin
Mitchell and Durante	Lesley Storey
Elm City Four	Youda Wood
Ted and Sally	Abbot Dancers

Staged by George White; Abbott Dancers directed by Florence Wilson.

THE LOVE EXPERT

(16 performances)

A comedy in three acts by John Kirkpatrick. Produced by Gustav Blum in association with A. T. Jones at Wallack's Theatre, New York, September 23, 1929.

Cast of characters—

Mr. Jackson....................................Halliam Bosworth
Mrs. Jackson....................................Mabel Montgomery
Mary Jackson....................................Natalie Wykes
Minnie Belle Carter....................................Anna Thomas
Miss Alice....................................Helen Holmes
Tom Jones....................................Earl McDonald
Chester Wade....................................Owen Cunningham
Tony....................................William Lovejoy
Mrs. Wade....................................Janet Merle
O'Riley....................................Lawrence O'Brien

Acts I, II and III.—Living Room of the Jackson Home on the Outskirts of a Small City.
Staged by Gustav Blum.

Mary Jackson writes to the Love Expert of her local paper, Miss Alice, asking advice as to whether she (Mary) should marry Chester Wade or Tony. Miss Alice calls to make a personal investigation, taking Tom Jones, reporter, with her. Miss Alice expects to marry Tom, but Tom likes Mary better and takes her away from both her other suitors.

THE CHERRY ORCHARD

(14 performances)

A drama in four acts by Anton Tchekov. Translation by Constance Garnett. Revived by the Civic Repertory Theatre, New York, September 23, 1929.

Cast of characters—

Lopahin (Yermolay Alexevevitch)....................Donald Cameron
Dunyasha....................Ria Mooney
Epihodov (Semyon Pantaleyevitch)....................Jacob Ben-Ami
Firs....................Sayre Crawley
Madam Ranevsky (Lubov Andreyevna)....................Merle Maddern
Anya....................Josephine Hutchinson
Varya....................Eva Le Gallienne
Charlotta Ivanovna....................Leona Roberts
Gaev (Leonid Andreyevitch)....................Paul Leyssac
Semyonov-Pishtchik....................Walter Beck
Yasha....................J. Edward Bromberg
Trofimov (Pyotr Sergeyevitch)....................Harold Moulton
A Tramp....................Robert Ross
A Stationmaster....................Robert H. Gordon
A Post-Office Clerk....................Herbert Shapiro

Acts I and IV.—A Room in the House. Act II.—The Open Country. Act III.—Living Room.

Staged by Eva Le Gallienne.

In addition to the Tchekov drama the Civic Repertory company this week also presented Tchekov's "The Sea Gull," Sierra's "The Cradle Song," Molière's "The Would-be Gentleman," and Ibsen's "The Master Builder."

SUBWAY EXPRESS

(271 performances)

A drama in three acts by Eva Kay Flint and Martha Madison. Produced by Edward A. Blatt at the Liberty Theatre, New York, September 24, 1929.

Cast of characters—

Mrs. Zlotnick....................Charlotte Weinstein
Mr. Zlotnick....................Louis Jospey
Sidney Zlotnick....................Herbert Schwartz
Harold Zlotnick....................Jackie Winston
Mr. Cotton....................William T. Hays
Mrs. Cotton....................Maude Nolan
Miss Smith....................Janet Gay
Mrs. Delaney....................Ann Weston
Thomas Delaney....................George Offerman, Jr.
First Sheik....................Anthony Pawley
Second Sheik....................Arnold Preston
First Flapper....................Helen Mack
Second Flapper....................Gloria May Kelly
Young Man....................Edward Everett Hale, 3rd
Young Girl....................Virginia Stone
Workman....................Peter Barbier
First Sailor....................Thomas Linker
Second Sailor....................Garland Kerr
Dale Tracy....................Dorothy Peterson
Edward Tracy....................Jack Lee
Whitney Borden....................Edward Pawley
Herman Stevens....................J. Hammond Dailey
George Mason....................Arthur Hughes
Officer O'Toole....................Gordon Hamilton
Mr. Perkins....................William DuPont

Mrs. Perkins....................................Minnie Stanley
Ben..Sam LeRoy
Morris..Alexander Micone
Newsboy...Sidney Salkow
Officer Mulvaney...............................Barton McLane
Tony..George Colan
Zippi...Alberto De Stefanis
Blonde..Virginia Otis
Clarke..Wall Spence
Mrs. Wolf.......................................Marie Offerman
Mrs. Samuels....................................Blanche Collins
Harlem Lady.....................................Elizabeth Taylor
Bogart..Henry Schaefer
Helen...Jeska Thompson
Dot...Dorothy Patten
Mrs. Mullen.....................................Mary Pettes
Motorman..William Pawley
Conductor.......................................Frank B. Miller
Inspector Hannen................................Edward Ellis
Detective Cobb..................................Bernard Thornton
Dr. Blum..George LeSoir
Mr. Anderson....................................Charles Newsom
Mechanic..Garland Kerr

Acts I, II and III.—Interior of a Subway Car.
Staged by Chester Erskin.

Edward Tracy and Whitney Borden, partners in a stock brokerage firm, board a subway train at Park Place, New York, accompanied by Dale Tracy, Edward Tracy's wife, and Herman Stevens, a clerk. Shortly afterward, when Borden objects to a drunken man's attentions to Mrs. Tracy, there is a fight, the lights go out, there is a pistol shot and policemen rush in. Edward Tracy is found shot through the heart. Investigation proves the broker was electrocuted before the pistol was fired. Inspector Hannen takes over the investigation, suspects Borden, who admits his love for Mrs. Tracy, and finally fastens the crime on an outsider.

MANY WATERS

(110 performances)

A drama in three acts by Monckton Hoffe. Produced by Charles B. Cochran and Arch Selwyn at the Maxine Elliott Theatre, New York, September 25, 1929.

Cast of characters—

ACT I
Scene 1—Theatreland

James Barcaldine................................Ernest Truex
Mabel Barcaldine................................Marda Vanne
Compton Schloss.................................Ronald Simpson
Secretary.......................................Marjorie St. Aubyn
Henry Delauney..................................Aubrey Dexter

Scene 2—Years Ago at Earl's Court Exhibition

An Old Gentleman................................Paul Gill
Another Old Gentleman...........................F. B. J. Sharp

A Youth..Lawrence Ireland
Mabel Wingrove..Marda Vanne
James Barcaldine..Ernest Truex

Scene 3—A Registry Office

A Charwoman..Margaret Yarde
A Junior Clerk..Horace Sequiera
A Man..Aubrey Dexter
Mabel Wingrove..Marda Vanne
James Barcaldine..Ernest Truex
A Woman..Mariel Bruce
A Registrar..Harold B. Meade

ACT II

Scene 1—The Barcaldines' Flat (Twenty Years Later)

Freda Barcaldine..Maisie Darrell
James Barcaldine..Ernest Truex
Mabel Barcaldine..Marda Vanne
Philip Sales..Lawrence Ireland
Dolly Sales..Marjorie St. Aubyn
Edith..Violet Penule
Stanley Rosel..Francis L. Sullivan

Scene 2—The Plaza Club (On the Same Night)

Captain Bovill..Aubrey Dexter
A Waiter..Harold B. Meade
Freda Barcaldine..Maisie Darrell
Godfrey Marvin..Robert Douglas

Scene 3—The Barcaldines' Flat (An Hour Later)

James Barcaldine..Ernest Truex
Philip Sales..Lawrence Ireland
Mabel Barcaldine..Marda Vanne
Dolly Sales..Marjorie St. Aubyn
Freda Barcaldine..Maisie Darrell

Scene 4—The Barcaldines' Flat (A Few Months Later)

Mabel Barcaldine..Marda Vanne
James Barcaldine..Ernest Truex
A Nurse..Mariel Bruce
Another Nurse..Gwendoline Hill
Edith..Violet Penule
Dr. Sangster..Paul Gill
Dr. Hinchcliffe..F. B. J. Sharp

Scene 5—Rosel's Office (Four Weeks Later)

Typist..Gwendoline Hill
Clerk..Pete Warren
Stanley Rosel..Francis L. Sullivan
Doris Rosel..Margaret Yarde

Scene 6—Bankruptcy Buildings (The Same Day)

James Barcaldine..Ernest Truex
The Registrar..F. B. J. Sharp
Official Receiver..Ronald Simpson
Mr. Clinchpole..Paul Gill
Mr. Everitt..Horace Sequiera
Stanley Rosel..Francis L. Sullivan
Associate..Harold B. Meade
An Usher..Robert Douglas

ACT III

Scene 1—St. James Park

Mabel Barcaldine..Marda Vanne
James Barcaldine..Ernest Truex
Ticket Collector..Paul Gill

Scene 2—Theatreland

Mabel Barcaldine..Marda Vanne
James Barcaldine..Ernest Truex
Henry Delauney..Aubrey Dexter
Compton Schloss..Ronald Simpson

Staged by Leon M. Lion.

Henry Delauney, producer, and Compton Schloss, author, are arguing the question of salable plays. Delauney holds for the Cinderella type of romance. Schloss believing a better type of drama, with plots that are honestly patterned after life, would sell as well to the public and be more creditable to the producer. Mr. and Mrs. James Barcaldine, an average middle-class couple, are drawn into the discussion. They decide in favor of Cinderella. There being no romance, no great variety in their own lives, they like to have their imaginations stirred in the theatre. The scene flashes back to the meeting of the Barcaldines and brings them through a succession of domestic adventures and tragedies to the present.

MOUNTAIN FURY

(13 performances)

A drama in three acts by David Davidson, Jr. Produced by Ack-Rud Enterprises, Inc., at the President Theatre, New York, September 25, 1929.

Cast of characters—

John....................Edwin T. Jones
Ezra....................Jack Roseleigh
Fenicle....................Barry Macollum
Deacon Brown....................Stephen Wright
Myra....................Mary Miner
Bill Strunk....................Frederick B. Manatt
Sheriff Harmon....................Carleton Macy
Paul Harmon....................Herbert Ashton, Jr.

Acts I, II and III.—The Large Room in the Cabin of the Browns, on the Top of Brushy Mountain, in the Alleghanies.
Staged by E. J. Blunkall.

Myra loves Paul, the sheriff's son. Myra's father hates the sheriff. Always has and always will. Wants Myra to marry Bill Strunk, villain. Bill and Paul fight in the dark. Fenicle, a light-witted lad, loving Myra, kills Bill and clears the way for Paul.

SEE NAPLES AND DIE

(62 performances)

A comedy in three acts by Elmer Rice. Produced by Lewis Gensler at the Vanderbilt Theatre, New York, September 24, 1929.

Cast of characters—

A Small Chess-Player....................Gregory Dniestroff
A Bearded Chess-Player....................S. Sarmatoff

Basil Rowlinson....................................Horace Cooper
Angelo De'Medici...................................Rinaldo Schenone
Lucy Evans...Beatrice Herford
Hugo Von Klaus.....................................Walter Dreher
Charles Carroll....................................Roger Pryor
Luisa..Rose Rolanda
Hjordis De'Medici..................................Margaret Arrow
Kunegunde Wandl....................................Margaret Knapp Waller
Nanette Dodge Kosoff...............................Claudette Colbert
Carriage Driver....................................Edward Maurelli
Ivan Ivanovitch Kosoff.............................Pedro De Cordoba
Stepan...Albert West
Mary Elizabeth Dodge Norton........................Lucille Sears
General Jan Skulany................................Marvin Kline
Fascist Guards.....................................{ Ulisse Mattioli / Joseph Pierantoni }

Acts I, II and III—The Terrace of the Albergo Pensione de'Medici, at Capo di Sorrento, on the Bay of Naples.
Staged by Elmer Rice.

Nanette Dodge and Charles Carroll quarrel in Paris when Nanette breaks her engagement to Charles and marries Ivan Kosoff, a fraying Russian of title. Charles runs away to Sorrento and takes up with Kuney Wandl. Nanette follows after to explain to Charles that she was forced into the marriage with the Russian to save her sister; that she is about to be divorced and that she still loves Charles. Charles thinks Nanette is kidding him, but learns differently when a pair of revolutionists shoot Ivan.

SCOTLAND YARD

(27 performances)

A drama in six scenes by Denison Cliff. Produced by A. H. Woods at the Sam H. Harris Theatre, New York, September 27, 1929.

Cast of characters—

Capt. John Leigh, D.S.O. ....Paul Cavanagh
Doctor Deon..Raoul de Tisne
Sister Cecilia.....................................Andre Corday
Lieut. Graves......................................Stapleton Kent
Hargest..C. Haviland Chappell
Gates..Charles Row
Lady Xandra Usher..................................Phoebe Foster
Lord St. Arran.....................................Frederic Worlock
Lady St. Arran.....................................Marga La Rubia
Sir Clive Heathcote................................A. P. Kaye
Kent Heathcote.....................................Bramwell Fletcher
Charles Fox..Gerald McCarthy
Sir Dennis O'More..................................Edward Rigby
Clerk..Frederick Sutton
Superintendent Drewe...............................Byron Russell
Chief Inspector Yorke..............................Stapleton Kent
MacKillop..Byron Russell
Rudge..Robert Vivian

Scene 1—The Laboratory of Dr. Deon, in the Convent-Hospital

of the Sisters of the Cross, at St. Cyr, Near Paris. 2—The Embassy Club, London. 3—Sir John Usher's Chamber in the Bank of England. 4—Lady Xandra's Bedroom at Castle St. Arran, Pevensey. 5—Sir John's Chamber in the Bank. 6—A House boat on the Thames, Near Henley.

Capt. John Leigh, D.S.O., picked up on a battlefield in France, finds himself being discharged with a new face from the hospital of a famous plastic surgeon in St. Cyr. It is the face of Sir John Usher, chairman of the Board of the Bank of England, who was hurled into the same shellhole with Leigh. Thinking Usher dying Leigh had taken his wallet as a means of identification. In the wallet was the picture. Capt. Leigh, before going to war, was known to Scotland Yard as the cleverest thief in England. When he takes Usher's place at the bank he also discovers himself married to Usher's bride of a day, who loves him. The fact that he also loves her saves the Bank of England from being robbed of a million sterling. Usher turns up alive.

CANDLE LIGHT

(128 performances)

A comedy in three acts by Siegfried Geyer, adapted by P. G. Wodehouse. Produced by Gilbert Miller at the Empire Theatre, New York, September 30, 1929.

Cast of characters—

Marie..Gertrude Lawrence
Prince Rudolf Haseldorf-Schlobitten................Reginald Owen
Josef..Leslie Howard
Baron Von Rischenheim..........................Robert English
Baroness Von Rischenheim........................Betty Schuster
Liserl..Rita Vale
A Waiter......................................Ralph Roberts
Koeppke.......................................Jack Carlton

Acts I, II and III.—The Prince's Apartment in Vienna.
Staged by Gilbert Miller.

Josef, valet to Prince Rudolf Haseldorf-Schlobitten, thinking his master gone for the evening, invites a lady whose voice enchants him over the telephone to call. He is making progress with the lady when the Prince unexpectedly returns and, sensing the situation, decides to change coats and places with his man to help along the adventure. Josef is distressed but willing. The lady, it later transpires, is a parlor-maid masquerading as her mistress, who is really interested in the Prince.

DIVIDED HONORS

(40 performances)

A drama in three acts by Winnie Baldwin. Produced by K. A. L. at the Forrest Theatre, New York, September 30, 1929.

Cast of characters—

Mary Lane....................................Doris Freeman
Kenneth Stewart....................................Guido Nadzo
Angela Bannerman....................................Jane Kim
Anna....................................Jeanne DeMe
Vina Chase....................................Glenda Farrell
Detective-Sergeant Scott....................................Philip Heege
Police Officer....................................Richard Bowler
Police Officer....................................Edgar Henning
Acts I, II and III.—Living Room in Kenneth Stewart's Apartment.
Staged by William B. Friedlander.

Kenneth Stewart, writer, loving Angela Bannerman and being loved by his adopted sister, Mary Lane, gets tight and when he awakes finds that he has inadvertently married Vina Chase. Angela, to clear the situation, induces Kenneth to say that he will give up both his wife and his adopted sister when somebody shoots Angela dead. Vina takes the blame, is acquitted and, realizing that Mary Lane is the wife for Kenneth, fades gracefully out of the picture on her way to Europe.

A HUNDRED YEARS OLD

(39 performances)

A comedy in three acts by Serafin and Joaquin Quintero. English translation by Helen and Harley Granville-Barker. Produced by Gilbert Miller at the Lyceum Theatre, New York, October 1, 1929.

Cast of characters—

Manuel....................................Arthur Lewis
Carmen Campos....................................Georgia Harvey
Dona Marciala....................................Katherine Grey
Don Evaristo....................................Fred Tiden
Papa Juan....................................Otis Skinner
Dona Filomena....................................Octavia Kenmore
Eulalia....................................Mary Howard
Trino....................................Hardie Albright
Currita....................................Mary Arbenz
Rosa....................................Veronica Rey
Antonon....................................Charles Dalton
Alonso....................................Gerald Hamer
Acts I, II and III.—Papa Juan's House in Andalusia.
Staged by James Whale.

Papa Juan del Monte, preparing for the celebration of his hundredth birth anniversary, insists on running things his own way. All his relatives and descendants shall be invited, whatever their station, whatever their failures, moral or financial. He also deftly directs the romance of two of his great grandchildren, Trino and Currita.

LADIES LEAVE

(15 performances)

A comedy in three acts by Sophie Treadwell. Produced by Charles Hopkins at the Charles Hopkins Theatre, New York, October 1, 1929.

Cast of characters—

Hannah....................Jane Hazzard
Dr. Arpad Jeffer....................Charles Trowbridge
J. Burnham Powers....................Walter Connolly
Zizi Powers....................Blyth Daly
Philip Havens....................Henry Hull
Irma Barry White....................Catharine Calhoun Doucet
A Masseur....................William Stern
Jessie....................Vera Mellish
Barbara....................Katharine Lyons
Hilda....................Athene Taylor
Acts I, II and III.—Living Room of the New York Apartment of J. Burnham Powers.
Staged by Charles Hopkins.

Zizi Powers, restless and love starved, listens to the advice ot Dr. Jeffer, a Viennese expert, and decides to live freely. She takes Philip Havens, her husband's young assistant, as lover, but still her problem is not solved. Finally she runs away to Vienna in search of further advice from Dr. Jeffer.

THE CRIMINAL CODE

(173 performances)

A melodrama in prologue and three acts by Martin Flavin. Produced by William Harris, Jr., at the National Theatre, New York, October 2, 1929.

Cast of characters—

A Waiter....................Walter Colligan
Martin Brady....................Arthur Byron
Lew....................Dan Poole
A Girl....................Bessie Belmont
An Officer....................Frank Barnes
Robert Graham....................Russell Hardie
Mr. Nettlefold....................Burr Caruth

Dr. Rinewulf....................................Walter Kingsford
Laboratory Assistant............................Martin Perkins
MacManus..Thomas Findlay
Captain Gleason.................................Leo Curley
Simpkins..Edwin E. Vickery
Runch...William Franklin
A Negro...Norman Miller
Jim Fales.......................................Joseph Mackin Nerney
Miss Brady......................................Ethel Griffies
A Clerk...Charles Day
Mary Brady......................................Anita Kerry
Galloway..Henry Crossen
Kurtz...Dan Poole
Stolper...Frank Barnes
Mr. Sheridan....................................Carroll J. Davis
Jerry...Murray Bennett

Prologue—Office of the State's Attorney. Act I.—Scene 1—Prison Laboratory. 2—Jute Mill. 3—Mess Hall. 4—Cell. 5—Warden's Office. Act II.—Scene 1—Warden's Living Room. 2—Warden's Office. Act III.—Scene 1—Warden's Living Room. 2—Warden's Office. 3—Dungeon. 4—Inner Wall. 5—Warden's Office.

Staged by William Harris, Jr.

See page 71.

AMONG THE MARRIED

(44 performances)

A comedy in three acts by Vincent Lawrence. Produced at the Bijou Theatre by Philip Goodman October 3, 1929.

Cast of characters—

Ethel Mills.....................................Katherine Wilson
Helen Robinson..................................Peggy Allenby
Bill Minot......................................Edward Leiter
Brandt..Royal C. Stout
Joe Robinson....................................John Junior
Jack Mills......................................Frank Morgan

Acts I, II and III.—The Living Room of the Mills' Home.

Staged by Vincent Lawrence.

Ethel Mills, in love with her husband, is attracted to Bill Minot, her golf club champion. When she hears her husband has been flirting with a Spanish actress in town she refuses to be disturbed. But when she finds her best friend, Helen Robinson, and her husband together in her room she rebels and sends for Minot to be even. In the end the Mills family, unhappy but hopeful, agrees to continue living together, but with the understanding that the double standard shall prevail.

TOWN BOY

(3 performances)

A comedy in three acts by Marie Baumer. Produced by Charles Harris at the Belmont Theatre, New York, October 4, 1929.

Cast of characters—

Ma Keck....................Jane Ellison
Pete....................Millard F. Mitchell
Pa Keck....................Guy Hitner
Molly Keck....................Ruth Easton
Charlie Brownwell....................Tom Douglas
Ben Davis....................Ralph Bellamy
Myra Spoonhour....................Margaret Watson
Liphe Crawley....................Thad Gray
Mrs. Crawley....................Ada Barbour
Jim Henley....................Allen Lee
Mrs. Henley....................Joan Sudlow
Dave....................John Clubley
Alice....................Vaugn Hansen
Elsie....................Desiree Harris
Johnny....................Robert Porterfield
Dirk....................David Pritchard
Mrs. Hawkins....................Maud Sinclair
Mr. Lancer....................Larry Johns
Lee....................Lon Carter
Joe Farrell....................James Depillo

Act I.—Scene 1—In a Buggy. 2—Back Living Room of the Keck House. Acts II and III.—The Same.

Staged by William Keighley.

Molly Keck, a country girl working in a Pennsylvania town, takes Charlie Brownwell, her town beau, out to meet her folks. The folks find Charlie even funnier than he finds them. Baited by big, strong Ben Davis, Molly's country lover, Charlie tries to prove his courage by fighting Ben. Charlie is badly beaten, but his courage and his weakness win Molly completely.

KARL AND ANNA

(49 performances)

A drama in four acts by Leonhard Frank, translated by Ruth Langner. Produced by the Theatre Guild at the Guild Theatre, New York, October 7, 1929.

Cast of characters—

A Guard....................Charles C. Leatherbee
Karl....................Otto Kruger
Richard....................Frank Conroy
First Prisoner....................Claude Rains
Second Prisoner....................Philip Leigh
Supervisor....................Herbert J. Biberman
Another Guard....................Robert Norton
Marie....................Ruth Hammond
Anna....................Alice Brady
Marie's Sister....................Gale Sondergaard
Sister's Husband....................Larry Fletcher

Act I.—Russian Prison Camp on the Border Between Russia and Asia. Acts II, III and IV.—Anna's Kitchen-Living Room in Berlin.

Staged by Philip Moeller.

Karl and Richard, fellow prisoners in a Russian camp, pass the lonesome days and nights talking of Anna, Richard's young wife.

Karl, learning of Anna's most intimate ways, escapes prison the day he saves Richard's life from the guards and makes his way to Berlin and to Richard's apartment. There he tries to convince Anna that he is Richard himself, greatly changed by his three years in prison. Anna knows differently, but accepts Karl because of a sudden, overwhelming love for him. A year later she is to bear Karl's child when Richard comes back. He would kill Karl but Anna objects. Karl and Anna go away together.

MADEMOISELLE BOURRAT

(26 performances)

A drama in four acts by Claude Anet. Produced by the Civic Repertory Theatre, New York, October 7, 1929.

Cast of characters—

Mademoiselle Bourrat.......................Josephine Hutchinson
Madame Bourrat.................................Alma Kruger
Celestin.......................................Robert Ross
Julie..Agnes McCarthy
Louisa...Paula Miller
Monsieur Bourrat...............................Paul Leyssac
Caroline Bourrat de Vermaud....................Florida Friebus
Madame Bourrat de Vermaud......................Leona Roberts
Monsieur Allemand..............................Harold Moulton
Monsieur Le Cure...............................Egon Brecher

Acts, I, II, III and IV.—The Bourrats' House Near Valleyres.
Staged by Eva Le Gallienne.

Mlle. Bourrat has grown up in ignorance of the facts of life but keenly maternal. Innocently she accepts the advances of the gardener and when her condition becomes known cannot understand her horrified and harshly dictatorial mother's determination to keep the situation hidden from the world. Mlle. Bourrat suffers great unhappiness but is finally in a measure triumphant.

HER FRIEND THE KING

(24 performances)

A comedy in three acts by A. E. Thomas and Harrison Rhodes. Produced by L. Lawrence Weber at the Longacre Theatre, New York, October 7, 1929.

Cast of characters—

Tornetti.......................................William Dorbin
Scarlotti......................................Henry Morrell
Count Churak...................................Charles Esdale

Georges (Ex-King of Constantia-Felix)..........William Faversham
Princess Lydia..........Katharine Kohler
Miss Bridgerton..........Daisy Atherton
Mrs. Alfred Hastings..........Ara Gerald
Prince Otto..........Hugh Sinclair
A Maid..........Peggy Hovenden
Phelps..........Edmund Dalby

Act I.—A Salon at the Chateau de Beaulieu Near Lake Geneva, Switzerland. Acts II and III.—Living Room of Mrs. Hastings' Villa, Hotel de Russe, Delice les Bain.
Staged by F. Gatenby Bell.

Georges, former king of Constantia-Felix, meets again during his exile a rich American widow, Mrs. Alfred Hastings, to whom he had on a previous occasion been romantically attracted. Mrs. Hastings works to assist in the restoration of the King and is rewarded by his stipulation that she shall share the throne with him.

THE HOUSE OF FEAR

(48 performances)

A mystery farce in three acts by Wall Spence. Produced by Ray Productions, Inc., at the Republic Theatre, New York, October 7, 1929.

Cast of characters—

The Intruder..........Frank Thomas
Madame Zita..........Effie Shannon
Gerald..........Maury Tuckerman
Peggy Walker..........Barbara Gray
Paula Knox..........Lea Penman
Dr. Jack Ladd..........Harry Worth
Craig Kendall..........Gordon Westcott
Morton..........Clay Clement
Buddy Bronson..........Cecil Spooner
Finnegan..........James McLaughlin

Acts I, II and III.—An Old Mansion Near New York.
Staged by Elmer H. Brown.

Madame Zita is determined to clear her son, escaped from Sing Sing after having been imprisoned for murder. At a house party held in the former home of a spiritualistic medium, Madame Zita organizes a series of séances and other nerve tests that result finally in forcing a confession from the real murderer.

MLLE. MODISTE

(48 performances)

Musical comedy in two acts by Henry Blossom, music by Victor Herbert. Revived by the Jolson Theatre Musical Comedy Company at the Jolson Theatre, New York, October 7, 1929.

Cast of characters—

Henry De Bouvray, Comte de St. Mar.............Detmar Poppen
Capt. Etienne De Bouvray.........................Robert Rhodes
Hiram Bent.......................................Richard Powell
Gaston...———
General Le Marquis de Villefranche.............Wm. J. McCarthy
Lieut. Rene Le Motte..............................Roland Tudor
Francois...Lee Daly
Mme. Cecelie.......................................Flavia Arcaro
Fanchette...Edyth Artley
Nanette...Florence Caselle
Marie Louise......................................Lucyle Keeling
Bebe..Frances Baviello
Mrs. Hiram Bent...............................Bernice Mershon
Fifi...Fritzi Scheff

Act I.—Mme. Cecelie's Hat Shop, Rue de la Paix, Paris. Act II.—Scene 1—Comte de St. Mar's Private Dining Room. 2—"The Charity Bazaar" in the Garden of the Chateau de St. Mar

Staged by Milton Aborn

The adventure of Hiram Bent of Keokuk, Ia., who manages to be of considerable assistance to a Parisian milliner without becoming involved in the usual comic opera plot.

JENNY

(111 performances)

A comedy in four acts by Margaret Ayer Barnes and Edward Sheldon. Produced by William A. Brady, Jr., and Dwight Deere Wiman at the Booth Theatre, New York, October 8, 1929.

Cast of characters—

John R. Weatherby...............................Guy Standing
Cole...Robert Lowe
Eustace Wade......................................Lewis Martin
Cissy Weatherby...............................Katherine Emmet
Prince Dimitri Miranoff.......................Coburn Goodwin
Jack Weatherby....................................Ben Lackland
Nora Gerrish...Joyce Carey
Alec Ames.......................................Charles Brokaw
Jenny Valentine......................................Jane Cowl
Angela Weatherby..................................Helen Brooks

Acts I, II and IV.—Home of John R. Weatherby, Greenwich, Conn. Act III—Jenny's Cabin in the Canadian Woods

Staged by Frederick Stanhope

Jenny is an actress who, visiting in Connecticut, is attracted to the rose garden of John R. Weatherby and later to John R. himself. She finds him being unmercifully ridden by a shallow wife and a trio of ungrateful children and determines to help him. Luring him to her camp in the Canadian woods, Jenny tricks John into staying for a month. At the end of that time she returns home with him, frankly tells the Weatherby family what she has done and walks out. The emancipated John R. follows after, leaving the family wondering.

JUNE MOON

(273 performances)

A comedy in three acts by Ring Lardner and George S. Kaufman. Produced by Sam H. Harris at the Broadhurst Theatre, New York, October 9, 1929.

Cast of characters—

Fred M. Stevens.....Norman Foster
Edna Baker.....Linda Watkins
Paul Sears.....Frank Otto
Lucille.....Jean Dixon
Eileen.....Lee Patrick
Maxie.....Harry Rosenthal
Goldie.....Florence D. Rice
A Window Cleaner.....Frank Conlan
A Man Named Brainard.....Emil Hoch
Benny Fox.....Philip Loeb
Mr. Hart.....Leo Kennedy
Miss Rixey.....Margaret Lee

Prologue—In a Parlor Car. Act I.—Paul Sears' Place. Acts II and III.—Room at Goebel's.

Staged by George S. Kaufman.

See page 236.

FIRST MORTGAGE

(4 performances)

A drama in three acts by Louis Weitzenkorn. Produced by W. P. Farnsworth and H. M. Hayman at the Broadhurst Theatre, New York, October 10, 1929.

Cast of characters—

Elmer Gray.....Walter Abel
Elmer's Wife.....Beatrice Hendricks
Elmer's Father.....Dodson Mitchell
Elmer's Mother.....Josephine Morse
Elmer's Aunt.....Dorothy Walters
Elmer's Sister.....Sara Haden
Elmer's Brother-in-Law.....Richard Abbott
Mr. Tarbot.....Walter O. Hill
Mr. Hofnagle.....Maxwell Driscoll
Dan.....Ely Solomon
Bill.....Ray Earles
Grocery Boy.....Frank Burton
Gracie Turner.....Leona Maricle

Acts I, II and III.—Elmer's House. The Porch. High Falls, N. J.

Staged by Jose Ruben.

Elmer Gray grows restless and unhappy under the strain of his life in a New Jersey suburb. He buys his home on the partial payment plan and discovers that in place of owning it the home owns him. When his wife goes home to her mother to have her baby Elmer slips his moral moorings and flirts around with Gracie Turner, a neighborhood charmer. With Mrs. Gray returned, the baby having died, and the old routine of installments and disappointments facing Elmer again, he seeks release by burning down his house only to discover that his father is quite willing to build him another. Thus he is left with only the thought of Gracie Turner's nearness to cheer him.

LADIES DON'T LIE

(12 performances)

A comedy in three acts adapted by Herman Bernstein from the German of Paul Frank. Produced by Radiant Productions, Inc., at the Gallo Theatre, New York, October 10, 1929.

Cast of characters—

Peter..Joseph Allenton
Hannah..Maria Ziccardi
Edgar..Richard Sterling
Ralph..Dodd Mehan
Philip..Charles Richman
Dr. Quantner..Wallace Erskine
Lackey..Frank Hilliard
Mathias..Walter Cartwright
Pilot..Stanley DeWolf
Thea..Spring Byington
Acts I, II and III.—The Dining Hall of the Romedius Villa.
Staged by Edward Sargent Brown.

Thea, former wife of Philip and Ralph, and sweetheart of Edgar, swoops down out of the sky and lands on a desert island these three have selected as a place of escape from all women. After stirring all three to action of one sort and another, Thea is content to fly away again with her newest masculine interest, the aviator. She just didn't want to be forgotten.

BONDS OF INTEREST

(24 performances)

A comedy in a prologue and three acts, translated by John Garrett Underhill from the Spanish of Jacinto Benevente. Produced by Walter Hampden at the Hampden Theatre, New York, October 14, 1929.

Cast of characters—

Leander.....................................Charles Quigley
Crispin.....................................Walter Hampden
The Innkeeper.............................C. Norman Hammond
First Inn Servant...........................Stephen Irving
Second Inn Servant..........................Francis Dears
Harlequin...................................Tom Gomez
The Captain.................................Louis Polan
Dona Sirena.................................Mabel Moore
Columbine...................................Elinor Harriot
Laura.......................................Jeanne Clark
Risela......................................Evelyn Goodrich
Polichinelle................................Ernest Rowan
The Wife of Polichinelle....................Caroline Meade
Silvia......................................Ingeborg Torrup
Pantaloon...................................Etienne Girardot
The Doctor..................................Cecil Yapp
The Secretary...............................Gordon Hart
First Constable.............................Murray D'Arcy
Second Constable............................Howard Galt

Act I.—A Plaza in a City. Act II.—The Garden of Dona Sirena. Act III.—A Room in Leander's House.
Staged by Claude Bragdon.

Leander and Crispin, a gentleman and his valet, living by their wits and escaping the law by various subterfuges, invade a small town in Spain and trick themselves, through Crispin's cleverness, into a comfortable state of being. In the end Leander, turning moral and sentimental at the same time, wins Silvia, the beautiful daughter of the rich Polichinelle.

THE NUT FARM

(40 performances)

A comedy in three acts by John C. Brownell. Produced by John Henry Mears at the Biltmore Theatre, New York, October 14, 1929.

Cast of characters—

Mrs. Barton.................................Helen Henry
Willie Barton...............................Wallace Ford
Robert Bent.................................Louis Kimball
Ezra Sliscomb...............................Sam Coit
Helent Bent.................................Natalie Schater
Agatha Sliscomb.............................Louise Huntington
Hamilton T. Holland.........................Edward Keane
J. Clarence Biddeford.......................Graham Velsey
Harold Van Horton...........................Mortimer LePey
Hilda.......................................Mabel Marden

Acts I, II and III.—Living Room in the Bent Home, Southern California.
Staged by Harry MacFayden.

The Barton family of Newark, N. J., coming into a little money when Robert Bent, son-in-law, sells his store, plan to buy a nut farm in California and live peacefully thereafter. But Helen Bent falls under the influence of a crooked moving picture director, and the family funds go into the production of a picture. Little Brother Willie Barton, however, knows something about pictures, and when it looks as though everything was smashed he ups and fixes the picture so cleverly it even pleases Sid Grauman.

DEEP CHANNELS

(4 performances)

A comedy in three acts by J. W. Von Barre and Paul Krafft. Produced by Mr. Von Barre at the Waldorf Theatre, New York, October 18, 1929.

Cast of characters—

Peter	Robert M. Hicks
Karl	Jesse W. Le Roy
Marie	Angie Allen
Dr. Mueller	Stephen Clark
Baron Von Sturm	Jack Soanes
Greta	Frances Johnson
Martha	Helen Spring
Meena	Elizabeth Delmore Ferris
Ghekko	Alfred Fink

Acts I, II and III.—Drawing Room of the Baron's Home.
Staged by Joseph Soraghan and Herschel Mayall.

Greta Von Sturm, finding herself agitated in the presence of her strong young groom, Karl, is puzzled. When she permits Karl to kiss her they are overseen by Marie, the maid, who hoped to marry Karl. Her dream shattered, Marie jumps off the cliff. Then Greta gives herself to Karl. Still happiness eludes her and she decides to marry Dr. Mueller, who is less agitating but much safer.

THE MIDDLE WATCH

(29 performances)

A farcical comedy in three acts by Ian Hay and Stephen King-Hall. Produced by Arch Selwyn and Charles B. Cochran at the Times Square Theatre, New York, October 16, 1929.

Cast of characters—

Marine Ogg	Alfred Wellesley
Ah Fong	George Carr
Captain Randall (Royal Marines)	Robert Mawdesley

Fay Eaton....................................Dodo Watts
Flag Lieutenant....................................T. W. Sleigh
Marjorie....................................Venetia Dormer
Nancy Hewitt....................................Enid Menhinick
Commander Baddeley (Royal Navy)..............Michael Shepley
Charlotte Hopkinson..............................Madge Whiteman
Admiral Sir Hercules Hewitt, K.C.B....................Fred Kerr
Mary Carlton....................................Ruth Abbott
Lady Hewitt....................................Annie Esmond
A Sailor....................................James Carter
Captain Maitland (Royal Navy)..................John Boyne Rowe
Corporal Duckett (Royal Marines)..................George Carr
Act I.—Scene 1—Captain's Lobby. 2—Captain's Cabin. Night. Act II.—Captain's Lobby. Act III.—Captain's Cabin. On Board H.M.S. *Falcon.*

Fay Eaton, engaged to marry Marine Captain Randall of H.M.S. *Falcon,* dines with him on board, together with her chum, Mary Carlton, a visiting American girl. The engine of the picket boat breaks down and the girls are obliged to stay the night on the ship. Captain Maitland, attracted to Mary, graciously gives the girls his cabin, but the ship is ordered suddenly to sea and the admiral of the fleet comes aboard. He also wants the captain's cabin. Much confusion in pajamas before morning.

LOLLY

(29 performances)

A comedy in three acts by Fanny Heaslip Lea. Produced by the New York Theatre Assembly at the Assembly Theatre, New York, October 16, 1929.

Cast of characters—

Laura Carroll....................................Elinor Bedford
Jeff Robertson....................................John Brewster
Daniel Gaylord....................................Hugh Miller
Mrs. Hoyt....................................Mary Thayer
Mr. Hoyt....................................Howard Claney
Lolly Carroll....................................Mary Young
Waiter....................................Alvin Kerr
Walt Rolland....................................Harvey Sayers
Louis Shane....................................Daniel Coxe
Francine Delmar....................................Betty Sherwood
Mrs. Fairfax....................................Eileen Douglas
Miguel De Castro....................................Alberto Carrillo
Act I.—Club Deauville. Acts II and III.—Lolly's Apartment.
Staged by Walter Greenough.

Lolly Carroll, a gay lady of frustrated dreams of romance, threatens to lose her head over a Spanish gigolo. It is all her daughter Laura, 19, can do to keep Lolly straight. She manages it with the aid of Dan Gaylord, back home after twenty years in South America. It transpires that Dan is not only Lolly's lost romance but also Laura's father.

THE CHANNEL ROAD

(60 performances)

A comedy in three acts by Alexander Woollcott and George S. Kaufman. Produced by Arthur Hopkins at the Plymouth Theatre, New York, October 17, 1929.

Cast of characters—

Pierre....................William Young
The Widow Beauvais....................Marie Bruce
Corporal Kleinert....................Paul W. Dorn
Private Schwartz....................Bjorn Koefoed
Private Rosenberg....................Edmund Loewe
Dr. Courtois....................Edgar Stehli
Therese....................Anne Lubow
Dorfman, Private....................Martin Noble
Henri Le Fevre....................Seldon Bennett
The Count De Mallett....................R. C. Johnsrud
Mademoiselle Elise De Mallet....................Edith Van Cleve
Madame Le Fevre....................Peggy Conway
Sister Celeste....................Mildred Beverly
Sister Caroline....................Juana Allraum
Madeleine Rousset....................Anne Forrest
Lieutenant Engel....................Siegfried Rumann
The Fiddlers....................Louis Schmidt, Louis Kruger

Acts I, II and III.—The Main Room of a Roadside Inn in Normandy. December, 1870.

Staged by Arthur Hopkins.

In this version of De Maupassant's "Boule de Suif" Madeleine Rousset, prostitute, finds herself crowded into a diligence that is carrying a quartet of haughty French aristocrats and two sisters of charity from Rouen to Dieppe after the disaster of Sedan in the Franco-Prussian war. At a roadside inn where the party stops for the night Madeleine is admired and desired by Lieutenant Engel, the Prussian officer in command of the army of occupation. Refusing the Prussian her favors the party is held. Various bribes are offered Madeleine to break her resolution, but she does not yield until her sympathies are variously aroused. When the party makes ready to resume its journey, the aristocrats are sent back to Rouen. Only Madeleine and the sisters of mercy are permitted to proceed.

GREAT DAY

(36 performances)

A musical comedy by William Cary Duncan and John Wells, music by Vincent Youmans, lyrics by William Rose. Produced by Mr. Youmans at the Cosmopolitan Theatre, New York, October 17, 1929.

Cast of characters—

Pete....................Frank Daley
Tom....................Ken Pulsifer
Richard....................Bob Burton
Ida May....................Letha Burson
Kitty....................Blanche Le Clair
Carolyn....................Kitty Coleman
Phil Randolph....................Billy Taylor
Susie Totheridge....................Ethel Norris
Emmy Lou Randolph....................Mayo Methot
Henry White }
Babe Jackson }....................Miller and Lyles
Pepita Padilla....................Vanessi
Carlos Zarega....................John Haynes
Jim Brent....................Allan Prior
Judge Totheridge....................Walter C. Kelly
Mazie Brown....................Maude Eburne
Charlie....................Vincent Simonin
Lantern Man....................Hugh Chilvers
Lijah....................Lois Deppe

Act I.—Scene 1—The Randolph Plantation. Near New Orleans, La. 2—The Levee. 3—The Spanish Casino. Act II.—Scene 1—The Levee. 2—On the Mississippi. 3—The Cornfield. 4—The Randolph Homestead.

Staged by R. H. Burnside and Frank M. Gillespie; dances by Le Roy Prinz.

Emmy Lou Randolph, forced to sell her plantation, goes to work for the purchaser, Carlos Zarega, who turns the place into a casino near New Orleans. Jim Brent, engineer, loves Emmy Lou and hates Carlos, who seeks to do her wrong. Jim Brent hates Carlos so much, in fact, that finally he pitches him into the Mississippi flood, which leaves Emmy Lou practically free to marry Jim.

MAGGIE THE MAGNIFICENT

(32 performances)

A comedy in three acts by George Kelly. Produced by Laurence Rivers, Inc., at the Cort Theatre, New York, October 21, 1929.

Cast of characters—

Katie Giles....................Mary Frey
Etta....................Joan Blondell
Margaret....................Shirley Warde
Mrs. Reed....................Marion S. Barney
Mrs. Buchanan....................Mary Cecil
Ward....................Frank Rowan
Elwood....................James Cagney
Mrs. Groves....................Doris Dagmar
House Boy....................Rankin Mansfield
Burnley....................J. P. Wilson
Stella....................Frances Woodbury
Mrs. Winters....................Ellen Mortimer

Acts I and II.—Living Room in the Home of Mrs. Reed. Act III.—Downstairs Reception Room at the Home of Mrs. Demarest.

Staged by George Kelly.

Margaret Reed, being the daughter of an artist father, who died while she was an infant, finds herself in later life completely out of sympathy with her mother and her mother's people. When she snubs her tippling aunt, there is a family quarrel during which Mrs. Reed slaps her daughter's face. Margaret thereupon leaves home and goes to live with the wealthy people by whom she is employed as a social secretary. Later there is a reconciliation of sorts and Margaret's mother comes to understand something of her daughter's higher ambitions.

LADIES OF THE JURY

(88 performances)

A comedy in three acts by Fred Ballard. Produced by A. L. Erlanger and George C. Tyler at Erlanger's Theatre, New York, October 21, 1929.

Cast of characters—

THE JURY

Mrs. Livingston Baldwin Crane........................Mrs. Fiske
Lily Pratt..Claire Grenville
Cynthia Tate......................................Eunice Osborne
Mayme Mixter......................................Hallie Manning
Mrs. Dace...Elsie Keene
Mrs. Maguire......................................Marie Hunt
Jay J. Pressley...................................George Farren
Spencer B. Dazey..................................Sardis Lawrence
Alonzo Beal.......................................J. H. Stoddart
Tony Theodophulus.................................Vincent James
Steve Bromm.......................................Walter Kinsella
Andrew MacKaig....................................George Tawde

THE OTHERS

Judge Fish..Wilton Lackaye
Halsey Van Stye...................................Dudley Hawley
Rutherford Dale...................................C. W. Van Voorhis
Dr. Quincy Adams James, Jr........................William Lorenz
Art Dobbs...Al Roberts
Mrs. Gordon (Yvette Yvet).........................Germaine Giroux
Evelyn Snow.......................................June Mullin
Susanne...Vanda Curci
Clerk of the Court................................Edward Powell
Court Reporter....................................Virginia Murray

Act I.—County Court House at Rosevale, New Jersey. Acts II and III.—The Jury Room.

Staged by Harrison Grey Fiske.

Mrs. Livingston Baldwin Crane dutifully fulfils her civic duty by becoming a member of the jury trying Yvette Gordon for the murder of Mr. Gordon. Having satisfied her curiosity as to the conduct of the trial by its frequent interruption, Mrs. Crane finds herself in opposition in the jury room to the other eleven members of the jury who would vote Mrs. Gordon guilty. With some craft and more tact Mrs. Crane, at the end of the second day, has brought the jury around to her way of thinking and a verdict of not guilty is announced.

STRIPPED

(24 performances)

A drama in three acts by Jane Murfin. Produced at the Ambassador Theatre, New York, October 21, 1929.

Cast of characters—

Caroline....................................Jessie Royce Landis
Jefferson....................................J. H. Brewer
Austin Goodwin....................................Vernon Kelso
M'sieu Lazov....................................Lionel Atwill
Henry Snyder....................................Charles Millward
Helene Galli....................................Thelma Hardwick
M'sieu Orlando....................................Mario Majeroni
Mrs. Pringle....................................Christine Compton

Acts I and III.—Living Room of Goodwin Residence. Act II.—Library of M. Lazov's Residence on Long Island.

Staged by Lionel Atwill.

M'sieu Lazov is suspected of being the former Crown Prince of Georgia, which he disproves. He is also accused of having stolen the crown jewels, which he also disproves. But when he is named as the lover of a certain Caroline Goodwin, wife of Austin Goodwin, the charge sticks. The jewels, it transpires, were stolen by Helene Galli, the mistress of Mr. Goodwin. When she is stripped they are revealed hidden in her undies.

ABRAHAM LINCOLN

(8 performances)

A drama in six scenes by John Drinkwater. Revived by William Harris, Jr., at the Forrest Theatre, New York, October 21, 1929.

Cast of characters—

A Chronicler....................................J. Colvil Dunn
Stone....................................Thomas Irwin
Cuffney....................................Harold Kennedy
Susan....................................Florence Short
Mrs. Lincoln....................................Edith Spencer
Mr. Lincoln....................................Frank McGlynn

Tucker.....Forrest Davis
Hind.....Thomas Vaiden
Price.....Conrad Cantzen
Macintosh.....Penwood Batkins
White.....Frank Ginter
Seward.....Gerald Cornell
Jennings.....William B. Randall
Hawkins.....Duncan Cherry
Hay.....Dwight George
Second Clerk.....Albert Durand
Messenger.....Robert Parsons
Salmon Chase.....John C. Hickey
Montgomery Blair.....John Hanley
Simon Cameron.....Herbert Curtis
Caleb Smith.....Joseph Reed
Burnett Hook.....William Norton
Gideon Wells.....Alfred Moore
Mrs. Goliath Blow.....Mary Horne Morrison
Mrs. Otherly.....Jennie A. Eustace
William Custis.....Charles H. Moore
Stanton.....John O'Meara
General Grant.....Albert Phillips
Aide to General Grant.....George Williams
Dennis.....Perry Corson
Soldier.....Daniel Clark
William Scott.....Theodore Fetter
General Meade.....James S. Barrett
General Lee.....William Corbett
John Wilkes Booth.....Thomas Spaulding
Doctor.....Charles Brill

Synopsis: Scene 1—Lincoln's Home at Springfield, 1860. 2—Seward's Room in the White House, Washington. 3—Another Room in the White House. 4—Cabinet Room in the White House. 5—General Grant's Headquarters Near Appomattox, April, 1865. Scene 6—A Small Lounge Back of the Boxes in Ford's Theatre.

Staged by Gerald Cornell, originally directed by Lester Lonergan.

See "The Best Plays of 1919-20."

NAUGHTY MARIETTA

(16 performances)

A comic opera in two acts by Rida Johnson Young; music by Victor Herbert. Revived by the Jolson Theatre Musical Comedy Company at the Jolson Theatre, New York, October 21, 1929.

Cast of characters—

Captain Richard Warrington.....Roy Cropper
Lieut. Governor Grandet.....Herbert L. Watrous
Etienne Grandet.....Louis Templeman
Sir Harry Blake.....Wesley McCloud
Silas Slick.....Richard Powell
Rudolfo.....James S. Murray
Florenze.....Wm. J. McCarthy
Marietta D'Altena.....Ilse Marvenga
Lizette.....Eulalie Young
Adah.....Lydia Van Gilder
Fanchon.....Wee Griffin
Felice.....Frances Baviello
Graziella.....Ruth Sharpe
Indian.....Edward Taylor

East Indian..Hobson Yound
Knife Grinder..Bernie Sager

Act I.—A Public Square in New Orleans. Act II.—Scene 1—A Marionette Theatre. 2—Ball-Room of the Jeunesse Club.

Staged by Milton Aborn.

A TAILOR-MADE MAN

(8 performances)

A comedy in four acts by Harry James Smith. Revived by W. R. Kane, Inc., at the Gallo Theatre, New York, October 21, 1929.

Cast of characters—

Mr. Huber..Maurice Franklin
Mr. Rowlands..Foster Williams
Peter..Thomas Shearer
Dr. Gustavus Sonntag..Kenneth Rowland
Tanya Huber..Mary Vance
John Paul Bart..Grant Mitchell
Pomeroy..Anthony Blair
Mrs. Stanlaw..Minna Gale Haynes
Mr. Stanlaw..John Maurice Sullivan
Corinne Stanlaw..Katherine Standing
Mr. Fitzmorris..Norman Wendell
Mrs. Fitzmorris..Genevieve Frizzell
Bobby Westlake..John Keating
Dick Carroll..Charles Conrad, Jr.
Kitty Dupuy..Lotta Linthicum
Bessie Dupuy..Mary Farren
Mr. Jellicot..Harry Green
Abraham Nathan..Frank Burbeck
Miss Shayne..Mary Louise White
Mr. Grayson..Charles Carey
Mr. Whitcombe..Norman Wendell
Mr. Russell, Mr. Cain, Mr. Flynn, Labor Delegates.....John Boone, Frank Hetterick, Charles Douglas

Acts I and IV.—Tailoring Establishment of Mr. Huber. Act II.—Reception Room at the Stanlaws'. Act III.—Offices of the American Oceanic Shipbuilding Corporation.

Staged by Robert Stevens and Priestly Morrison.

John Paul Bart is a tailor who dreams of doing the things Napoleon left undone. The night he comes into temporary possession of a dress suit, a fur-collared coat and two $50 bills he sets out to prove that clothes at least make some men over. At a grand ball he proves the sensation of the evening, and though his bubble later bursts he has attracted such attention that he is materially helped on toward fortune.

HARLEM

(16 performances)

A drama in three acts by William Jourdan Rapp and Wallace Thurman. Revived by Edward A. Blatt at the Eltinge Theatre, New York, October 21. 1929.

Cast of characters—

George Williams....................................Clarence Taylor
Mazie Williams...Ivy Neely
Arabella Williams...................................Edna Wise Barr
Ma Williams.....................................Elizabeth Williams
Cordelia Williams.................................Alma Smithe
Pa Williams......................................Alonzo Fenderson
Basil Venerable................................William McFarland
Jasper Williams...........................Emory S. Richardson
Effie..Marie Richardson
Jimmie..Ossie Lyles
Thaddeus Jenkins.......................................Sam Davis
Ippy Jones..Hillis Walters
Mary Lou..Leonore Winkler
Roy Crowe..Alston Burleigh
Briggs..Herbert Ellis
Loving Joe......................................Joe Reddick, Jr.
Tim...Gertrude Mae Hill
Honey...Ruth David
Sleepy..C. Thornton
Babes.......................................Allen B. Walker, Jr.
Lou..Louise Renault
Fats..Stanley Wolcot
Pinky...Alonzo Balue
Row..Rae Blanks
Jack..Jackie Barry
Tom..Wallace Edenboro
Bee..Blanche Jones
Reggie....................................Reggie Fenderson, Jr.
Flo...Florence Miller
Mars..Margie Foster
Ironsides..Milton Greene
Hip...Alonzo Freide
Ruth..Ruth Carle
Maybe..Mary L. Payne
Tim..T. Gordon Van Nieff
Slim...Robert Bonner
Rex...Rex Goreleigh
Hot-Stuff Man...................................Milton J. Williams
Kid Vamp.......................................Ernest R. Whitman
Dr. Vodeo.......................................F. Barclay Trigg
Detective Sergeant Palmer........................Cornelius Roddy
Officer Sam...Nat Cash
Janitress..Helen Nelson
Janitress' Daughter...................................Nonie Simmons

Acts I and III.—Living Room of the Williams' Railroad Flat in Harlem. Act II.—Roy's Apartment.

Staged by Chester Erskin.

See "The Best Plays of 1928-29."

WEEK-END

(11 performances)

A comedy in three acts by Austin Parker. Produced by Bela Blau, Inc., at the John Golden Theatre, New York, October 22, 1929.

Cast of characters—

Phillipe...Alfred Hesse
Skip Penney..Grant Mills

Clare Penney....................................Margaret Mower
Brett Laney....................................Warren William
Arthur....................................Bruce MacFarland
Marie....................................Frances Kelly
Chris Chapman....................................Hugh O'Connell
Marga Chapman....................................Vivienne Osborne
Acts I, II and III.—The Living Room of the Penneys' House in Barbizon, France.
Staged by Worthington Miner.

Skip Penney and Brett Laney were war-time buddies. At a week-end party at the Penneys' in Barbizon, France, ten years after the war, Brett discovers that Skip still loves Marga Chapman; that he, Brett, also loves Marga Chapman; that Marga is married to an amiable alcoholic she is about to throw over; that when Skip and Marga go to a certain hotel to talk things over he must believe they did just that and nothing else. Mrs. Penney doesn't believe Skip; Mr. Chapman doesn't believe Marga. Mr. Chapman shoots himself nobly and Brett Laney comforts Mrs. Chapman.

BUTTON, BUTTON

(5 performances)

A comedy in three acts by Maurice Clark. Produced by Herman E. Shumlin, in association with H. C. Potter and George Haight, at the Bijou Theatre, New York, October 23, 1929.

Cast of characters—

Mrs. Patience Boynton-Woodhouse....................Anne Shoemaker
Mr. George Woodhouse....................................John Westley
Maudie....................................Mary Gildea
Josie....................................Shirley O'Hara
Emery....................................Harry Cooke
"Button"....................................Lynne Overman
Rita Weed....................................Alison Skipworth
Phœbe Weed....................................Justine Chase
Ed....................................Harry Selby
Al....................................Reginald Fife
Acts I, II and III.—In the Living Room of the George Woodhouse Home in Englewood, N. J.
Staged by Maurice Clark and H. C. Potter.

"Button" Woodhouse, the difficult younger son of the Woodhouse family, is discharged from one of the sanitariums to which he has been assigned because of an alleged weak and uncertain mentality. Invading the home of his brother George, "Button" is soon convinced that he is the only really sane person on the premises. By one farcical means and another he puts all his pestering relatives to rout.

THE SILVER TASSIE

(51 performances)

A drama in four acts by Sean O'Casey. Produced by the Irish Theatre, Inc., at the Irish Theatre, New York, October 24, 1929.

Cast of characters—

Sylvester Heegan....................Sean Dillon
Mrs. Heegan....................Emma Conrow
Simon Norton....................Edward O'Connor
Susie Monican....................Margaret Barnstead
Mrs. Foran....................Kitty Collins
Teddy Foran....................Ralph Cullinan
Harry Heegan, D.C.M....................Sherling Oliver
Jessie Taite....................Allyn Gillen
Barney Bagnal....................David Keating
Kevin Kearney....................John Ferris
The Croucher....................Schuyler MacGuffin
1st Soldier....................James Metcalfe
2nd Soldier....................John Ferris
3rd Soldier....................Ned Lane
4th Soldier....................Ralph Cullinan
The Corporal....................Francis Kennelly
The Visitor....................Abram Gillette
The Staff Wallah....................L. H. Dennison
1st Stretcher-Bearer....................Pendleton Harrison
2nd Stretcher-Bearer....................Harry Wallace
3rd Stretcher-Bearer....................John Wynne
4th Stretcher-Bearer....................Dajalna Montana
1st Casualty....................Patrick Glasgow
2nd Casualty....................Leonard Austin
Surgeon Forby Maxwell....................Bertram Millar
The Sister of the Ward....................Ennis Clare

Act I.—Room in Heegan's Home, Dublin. Act II.—Somewhere in France. Act III.—Ward in a Hospital. Act IV.—Room in Premises of Avondale Football Club.

Staged by Miceal Breathnach.

Harry Heegan, home from the wars on leave, helps the Avondale football club win the silver tassie, emblematic of the championship, for the third successive time. Returned to the wars he takes with him a memory of Jessie Taite's love and kisses. At the front Harry develops a growing hatred of war and when he suffers a wound that cripples him for life his hatred turns to a bitterness that becomes tragic at home when he is forced to sit helplessly by and see his best friend take Jessie from him.

THE BOOSTER

(12 performances)

A comedy in three acts adapted by Nat Reid from the Viennese of Nertz and Friedmann. Produced by Y-DNA, Inc., at the Bayes Theatre, New York, October 24, 1929.

Cast of characters—

Maurice Koppler....................................Lester Bernard
Rebecca Koppler....................................Jean Newcombe
Zorah Koppler....................................Beatrice Miller
Leo Von Friessheim....................................Ben Laughlin
Jacob Stieglitz....................................Sam Wright
David Stieglitz....................................William McFadden
Mr. Blau....................................Rosalie Wincott
Mrs. Mary Malone....................................Josephine Deffry
Helen Strauss....................................Helena Rapport
Daffie....................................Kitty Clark
Acts I, II and III.—The Koppler Apartment, New York.
Staged by Victor Morley.

Maurice Koppler and Jacob Stieglitz, having been friends for a lifetime, are interested in the romance of their children, Rebecca and David. Jacob, in his effort to make a successful doctor of David the first year after the latter's graduation from medical school, takes to advertising him flamboyantly. The effect is nearly to ruin both David's chances and his romance. They succeed in muffling Jacob just in time.

THE GHOST PARADE

(13 performances)

A melodrama in three acts by Hadley Waters. Produced by Charles K. Gordon at the Lyric Theatre, New York, October 28, 1929.

Cast of characters—

Major Gilbert Ainslee....................................Oswald Marshall
Lizzie....................................Catherine Proctor
Suma Singhi....................................Clarence Derwent
Helen Ainslee....................................Joan Blaine
Capt. Bruce Grey....................................Evan Thomas
Joan Beggs....................................Ann Johnson
Lt. "Billy" Ayers....................................Donald Blackwell
District Commissisoner John Kent....................................Stuart Casey
Chandra....................................W. Wana Singh
Natives..........K. P. Howwa, Wm. Coray, John De Silva, Lou Kintum, C. White, L. Boucari
Acts I, II and III.—Headquarters of Major Ainslee, in an Old Temple in the Mountains of Northern India.
Staged by Charles K. Gordon.

Major Gilbert Ainslee, in command of a far-flung post of the British army in Northern India, is occupying a slightly haunted temple from which there emerge strange sounds and through which there occurs from time to time a parade of ghostly figures. As it transpires, the ghosts are hired to keep up the mystery while the thrifty old major and certain others smuggle in arms and ammunition and sell them to the jolly old tom-tom beating and frequently uprising natives.

A WONDERFUL NIGHT

(125 performances)

Operetta with score by Johann Strauss, book adapted from "Die Fledermaus," by Fanny Todd Mitchell. Produced by the Messrs. Shubert at the Majestic Theatre, New York, October 31, 1929.

Cast of characters—

Latzo Garbo..........Bartlett Simmons
Footman at Grunewald's..........Robert Irving
Mme. Agout..........Sarah Brown
Kathie..........Mary McCoy
Mathilda Grunewald..........Gladys Baxter
Leo..........Charles Chesney
Max Grunewald..........Archie Leach
Doctor Von Lubke..........Joseph Lertora
Bochmeister..........Hal Forde
Frieda..........Dorothy Kane
Prince Koslofsky..........Allan Rogers
Frau Hickenlooper..........Sallie Stembler
Countess Malakoff..........Peggy Udell
Baroness Von Pogenhardt..........Julia Barker
Marquise De Montmarte..........Gretchen Wilson
Countess Vichy..........Thalie Hamilton
Countess Perrier..........Anna May Denehy
Lady Buttonshire..........Marian Alden
Madame De Chaumont..........Rosalind Wishon
Baroness Metelier..........Georgia Gwynne
Madame De Esplanade..........Mabel Ellis
Duchess De Montparnasse..........Marion Gillon
Princess Fleur De Lys..........Virginia Bethel
Alfred..........M. Varrelle
First Flunkey..........Robert Smith
Second Flunkey..........Ray Wright
Third Flunkey..........Trueman Gaige
Fourth Flunkey..........Charles Townsend
Richard Lowen..........Robert Burk
Blatz..........Solly Ward
A Keeper..........Arthur Wood
Messenger..........George Smith

Act I.—Scene 1—The Prater Café. 2 and 3—At the Grunewalds'. Act II.—At Prince Koslofsky's. Act III.—In the Jail.

Staged by José Ruben and Chester Hale.

A free adaptation of the story of Max, who is granted one night's respite after being sentenced to jail. He spends the night at a ball given by Prince Koslofsky, where he flirts with his own wife when she is introduced to him as a masked Hungarian countess. Previous versions have been called "Night Birds" and "The Merry Countess."

BERKELEY SQUARE

(229 performances)

A drama in three acts by John L. Balderston. Produced by Gilbert Miller and Leslie Howard at the Lyceum Theatre, New York, November 4, 1929.

Cast of characters—

Maid....Irene Howard
Tom Pettigrew....Brian Gilmour
Kate Pettigrew....Valerie Taylor
The Lady Anne Pettigrew....Alice John
Mr. Throstle....Tarver Penna
Helen Pettigrew....Margalo Gillmore
The Ambassador....Fritz Williams
Mrs. Barwick....Lucy Beaumont
Peter Standish....Leslie Howard
Marjorie Frant....Ann Freshman
Major Clinton....Charles Romano
Miss Barrymore....June English
The Duchess of Devonshire....Louise Prussing
Lord Stanley....Henry Warwick
H.R.H. the Duke of Cumberland....Robert Greig

Act I.—Scene 1—Five O'Clock, October 23rd, 1784. Scene 2—Five O'Clock, October 23rd, 1928. Scene 3—Continuous with Scene 1. Act II.—Scenes 1 and 2—Night. A Few Days Later, 1784. Act III.—Scene 1—Afternoon in 1784. A Week Later. Scene 2—Continuous with Scene 1, but in 1928.

Acts I, II and III.—In the Morning Room of a House of the Queen Anne Period in Berkeley Square, London, in the Years 1784 and 1928.

Staged by Gilbert Miller and Leslie Howard.

See page 108.

CORTEZ

(8 performances)

A comedy in three acts by LeRoy Clemens and Ralph Murphy. Produced by Jack Linder at the Mansfield Theatre, New York, November 4, 1929.

Cast of characters—

Steve....Richard K. Keith
Sancho....Juan Villasano
José....John Philip Ryder
Mickey O'Day....Thomas V. Gillen
Miguel....Clyde Veaux
Lorin X. Pendelton....George W. Barbier
Nancy Helton....Dorothea Chard
Diane Meredith....Helen Baxter
J. Stanwood Drexel....Walter Fenner
J. W. Temple....William Jeffrey
Smithers....Edward Kay
Señor Don Hernando Cortez y Romero....Lou Tellegen
Felipe....Robert Harrison
Gin Long....T. Kunihara

Myrtle..Eugenie Reid
Locke..Maxwell Driscoll
Chauffeur..Monroe Bennett
Spanish Troubadors..Lipari Trio

Act I.—Headquarters of Enterprise Films, Inc., on Location in the Sonora Valley, Mexico. Act II.—The Castello of Cortez. Act III.—Living Room of Diane Meredith's Bungalow, Hollywood, California.

Staged by Ira Hards.

Don Hernando Cortez, a Spanish gentleman with a grievance against the Mexicans, rounds up a moving picture company making scenes in the Mexican hills and carries its leading players away to his castle in Sonora. There he loves Diane Meredith, the leading woman, who pretends to like him in the hope that she can thus save her company. Released by Don Hernando the company returns to Hollywood, the señor follows after and there really wins Diane.

WHITE FLAME

(8 performances)

A drama in three acts by Robert Lillard. Produced by James Kenney at the Vanderbilt Theatre, New York, November 4, 1929.

Cast of characters—

Logan..William Walcott
Hinkley..Joseph Sweeney
Don Marlowe..Kenneth Harlan
Hope Richardson..Sydney Shields
Aunt Dora Marlowe..Molly Pearson
Irene..Doratha Duckworth
Marilyn Marlowe..Helen Dodge
Mrs. Huggins..Frances Kennan
Audrey..Edith King
Dudley Blackstar..George MacQuarrie
Sonny Marlowe..Warren MacCallum

Acts I, II and III.—The Living Room of the Old Marlowe House in Brooklyn.

Staged by Karl Nielsen.

Don Marlowe, being blinded by his youthful loves, fails to see that Hope Richardson is really the wife for him. He tries two others, but after a period of years have elapsed and both these marriages have turned out unhappily, Marlowe, at the instigation of his infant son, turns to Hope and finds his happiness.

MAKE ME KNOW IT

(4 performances)

A comedy in three acts by D. Frank Marcus. Produced by Wallace Davis at Wallack's Theatre, November 4, 1929.

Cast of characters—

Hot Dog Vender....Allen Gillard
Willie Weaver....James Dunmore
"Hop" Abbott....Napoleon Whiting
Joe Nippy....Charles L. Hawkins
Policeman....Philip Martin
Eb Sneedy....Brevard Burnett
Tagger Daly....Leo Bailey
Georgia Peach....Julia Moses
A Sweet Mama....Edna Ellington
Another....Marion Fleming
Mirandy....Ollie Burgoyne
Jenny....Florence Lee
"Noisy" Knowles....George Howe
Jack Riggs....Claude Hopkins
Nate Sawyer....Walter Duke
Mrs. Sophie Crouch....Enid Raphael
Ezra Gaines....Paul C. Floyd
"Bulge" Bannon....A. B. Comathiere
Mona Bannon....Vivienne Baber
George Gaines....Barrington Guy
Rev. Washington Stubbs....Louis Schooler
Dr. Julian Robbins....Lorenzo Tucker
Another Policeman....Takapia Hire

Act I.—Scene 1—A Thoroughfare. 2—"Bulge" Bannon's Home. Act II.—Scene 1—"Bulge" Bannon's Home. Act III.—Scene 1—The Regent Political Club. 2—A Room in a Roadhouse. 3—"Bulge" Bannon's Home.

Staged by D. Frank Marcus and Sam Rose.

A panorama of Negro life in which a political boss seeks to elect a black to office and thus defeat the villainous white who has been holding up the Negroes.

THE FORTUNE TELLER

(16 performances)

A comic opera in three acts by Harry B. Smith; music by Victor Herbert. Revived by the Jolson Theatre Musical Comedy Company at Jolson's Theatre, New York, November 4, 1929.

Cast of characters—

Musette / Irma / Lieut. Feodor....Tessa Kosta
Fresco....Detmar Poppen
Count Berezowski....Wm. J. McCarthy
Sandor....Charles E. Gallagher
Ladislas....Roy Cropper
Boris....Harry Hermsden
Pompom....Charlotte Woodruff
Vaninka....Dene Dickens
Rafael....Amy Alexander
Waldemar / Prompter....Bernie Sager
General Korbay....Leslie McLeod
1st Detective....Francesco Yannelli
2nd Detective....Edward Taylor
Gardener....James Carwin

Lieutenant....................................Hobson Young
Act I.—Garden of the Opera House. Act II.—Grounds of the Chateau of Count Berezowski. Act III.—Camp of the Hungarian Army, Near Buda-Pesth.
Staged by Milton Aborn.

"The Fortune Teller" was first produced the season of 1898-99 introducing Alice Nielsen as a star. She sang the triple rôle later in London.

BITTER SWEET

(159 performances)

An operetta in three acts by Noel Coward. Produced by Florenz Ziegfeld and Arch Selwyn, by arrangement with Charles B. Cochran, at the Ziegfeld Theatre, New York, November 5, 1929.

Cast of characters—

ACT I.—SCENE 1

Parker....................................Trevor Glyn
Dolly Chamberlain....................................Audrey Pointing
Lord Henry....................................Patrick Ludlow
Vincent Howard....................................Max Kirby
The Marchioness of Shayne....................................Evelyn Laye
Nita....................................Joan Stanbrough
Helen....................................Constance Perrin
Jackie....................................Cecile Maule-Cole
Scene—Lady Shayne's House in Grosvenor Square, 1929.

SCENE 2

Sarah Millick....................................Evelyn Laye
Carl Linden....................................Gerald Nodin
Mrs. Millick....................................Isabel Ohmead
The Hon. Hugh Devon....................................Tracy Holmes
Scene—The Millicks' House in Belgrave Square, 1875.

SCENE 3

Carl Linden....................................Gerald Nodin
Lady Devon....................................Kathleen Lambelet
Mrs. Millick....................................Isabel Ohmead
The Hon. Hugh Devon....................................Tracy Holmes
Sir Arthur Fenchurch....................................Charles Mortimer
Sarah Millick....................................Evelyn Laye
The Marquis of Steere....................................Donald Gordon
Lord Edgar James....................................Richard Thorpe
Lord Sorrel....................................Hooper Russell
Mr. Vale....................................Leslie Bannister
Mr. Bethel....................................Anthony Neville
Mr. Proutie....................................Douglas Graeme-Brooke
Victoria....................................Marjorie Raymond
Harriet....................................Audrey Pointing
Gloria....................................Nancy Brown
Honor....................................Isla Bevan
Jane....................................Winifred Talbot
Effie....................................Vesta Sylva
Scene—The Ballroom of the Millicks' House in Belgrave Square, 1875.

ACT II

Waiters—Cleaners:
Piccolo...Peter Donald
Lotte...Zoe Gordon
Freda..Nancy Barnett
Hansi...Dorothy Debenham
Gussie...Sylvia Leslie
Carl Linden...Gerald Nodin
Manon (La Crevette)...................................Mireille
Captain August Lutte...............................Desmond Jeans
Herr Schlick.......................................Charles Mortimer
Sari Linden..Evelyn Laye
Lieutenant Tranisch....................................Louis Miller
Scene—Herr Schlick's Café in Vienna, 1880.

ACT III

Burley..Albert Chapman
The Marquis of Shayne...............................John Evelyn
Mrs. Bethel (Effie)......................................Vesta Sylva
Mr. Bethel..Anthony Neville
Mrs. Vale (Jane)....................................Winifred Talbot
Mr. Vale..Leslie Bannister
Mrs. Proutie (Gloria)...............................Nancy Brown
Mr. Proutie.................................Douglas Graeme-Brooke
The Duchess of Tenterton (Victoria).............Marjorie Raymond
The Duke of Tenterton...............................Donald Gordon
Lady Sorrel (Honor).......................................Isla Bevan
Lord Sorrel...Hooper Russell
Lady Edgar James (Harriet)........................Audrey Pointing
Lord Edgar James....................................Richard Thorpe
Sir Hugh Devon......................................Tracy Holmes
Lady Devon...Jane Moore
Madame Sari Linden......................................Evelyn Laye
Vernon Craft.....................................Cunningham Glen
Cedric Ballantyne.................................Paul Spender-Clay
Bertram Sellick.......................................Hugh Cuenod
Lord Henry Jade.......................................George Woof
Accompanist...Eddie Lisbona
Scene—Lord Shayne's House in London, 1895.
Staged by Noel Coward.

Dolly Chamberlain, promised in marriage to one man and in love with the leader of a jazz band, confides in her aunt, the Marchioness of Shayne, thus inspiring the older woman to relate as a warning the story of her own love adventures as a young woman. These show her eloping with her music teacher, Carl Linden, who is afterward killed in a Viennese café when he resents an insult to his wife. Mme. Linden later becomes a great prima donna and marries the Marquis of Shayne.

BROKEN DISHES

(178 performances)

A comedy in three acts by Martin Flavin. Produced by Marion Gering at the Ritz Theatre, New York, November 5, 1929.

Cast of characters—

Jenny Bumpsted....................................Eda Heinemann
Myra Bumpsted....................................Ellen E. Lowe
Mabel Bumpsted....................................Etha Dack
Elaine Bumpsted....................................Bette Davis
Cyrus Bumpsted....................................Donald Meek
Bill Clark....................................Reed Brown, Jr.
Sam Green....................................Art. Smith
Rev. Dr. Stump....................................J. Francis-Robertson
A Stranger....................................Duncan Penwarden
Quinn....................................Josef Lazarovici

Acts I, II and III.—Living Room in the Bumpsted Home, in a Small Mid-Western Town.

Staged by Marion Gering.

Jenny Bumpsted has ruled her family with a high hand for a good many years. Rebellion does not appear until Elaine, the youngest daughter, decides that she wants to marry Bill Clark, the delivery boy for Bascom's store. Elaine enlists the help of her henpecked father, Cyrus, and he, emboldened abnormally after he has drunk two or three cups of hard cider, proves a tower of strength. As a final gift of the gods the girlhood lover of Mrs. Bumpsted, about whom she has boasted all her married life, turns out to be a crook.

CAPONSACCHI

(39 performances)

Drama in three acts by Arthur Goodrich and Rose A. Palmer, based on Browning's "Ring and the Book." Produced by Walter Hampden at the Hampden Theatre, New York, November 5, 1929.

Cast of characters—

Giotti....................................Robert C. Schnitzer
Melchior....................................Stephen Irving
Andrea....................................Francis Dears
Montini....................................John F. Roche
Pope Innocent XII....................................Moffatt Johnston
Guido Franceschini....................................Ernest Rowan
Caponsacchi....................................Walter Hampden
Tommati....................................Gage Bennett
Venturini....................................Louis Polan
Scalchi....................................Gordon Hart
Gherardi....................................Dallas Anderson
Pietro Comparini....................................Franklin Salisbury
Violante Comparini....................................Caroline Meade
Pompilia....................................Ingeborg Torrup
Canon Conti....................................Cecil Yapp
Governor of Arezzo....................................C. Norman Hammond
Archbishop of Arezzo....................................Edwin Cushman
Margherita....................................Mabel Moore
Salvatore....................................Edward Ross
Peppina....................................Ada Cavagna

Innkeeper at Castelnuovo.......................S. Thomas Gomez
His Servant.......................................Edward Ross
Marinetta.....................................Evelyn Goodrich
Guard at Castelnuovo........................Robert C. Schnitzer

Prologue—A Court of Justice at the Vatican. February, 1698. Act I.—Carnival, Arezzo. Act II.—Scene 1—Caponsacchi's Cell, Arezzo. 2—Street Outside Guido's Palace. Arezzo. 3—Inn at Castelnuovo. Act III.—Scene 1—Court of Justice at the Vatican. Pietro's Villa. Rome. Epilogue—Court of Justice at the Vatican.

Staged by Walter Hampden.

See "The Best Plays of 1926-27."

CROSS ROADS

(28 performances)

Drama in three acts by Martin Flavin. Produced by Lewis E. Gensler at the Morosco Theatre, New York, November 11, 1929.

Cast of characters—

Patricia...Sylvia Sidney
Barbara..Mary Morris
Duke...Franchot Tone
Tony..Irene Purcell
David..Malcolm Duncan
Michael...Eric Dressler
A Girl..Dennie Moore
Jep...Oscar Polk
Mamie..Anna Borden
Dora..Peggy Shannon
A Man..Herbert Heywood
Cronin...Orrin Burke

Act I.—The '05 Bench. Act II.—Scene 1—The Sig House. 2—The '05 Bench. Act III.—Scene 1—Gamma House. 2—The '05 Bench.

Staged by Guthrie McClintic.

Michael is tired of medical school and in love with Patricia, an attractive co-ed. Michael wants to quit school and marry Patricia. Patricia, being foresighted, refuses to agree. Michael, disturbed and unhappy, picks up a waitress and spends the night with her at a road house. The place is raided, scandal follows and Michael is threatened by the waitress's father. Patricia, smarting under Michael's charge that she isn't human, tries to even matters by going with the college rake, but changes her mind. Michael, saved by the confession of the waitress, recovers Patricia and they decide to finish school.

THUNDER IN THE AIR

(16 performances)

Drama in three acts by Robins Millar. Produced by Lee Shubert in association with Laura D. Wilck at the Forty-ninth Street Theatre, New York, November 11, 1929.

Cast of characters—

Dorothy Stanes....................Jeannette Sherwin
Rev. Arthur Stanes....................Leonard Willey
Gibbs....................John Bramall
James Harding....................Wilfrid Seagram
Major Vexted....................J. Fisher White
Mrs. Vexted....................Henrietta Crosman
Miss Newton....................Edith Harcourt
Pamela Bentley....................Selena Royle
A Soldier....................Robert Haslam
Anna....................Judith Haneman
A Boy....................Freddie Stange

Acts I, II and III.—Living Room of Major Vexted's House Outside London.

Staged by Laura D. Wilck and F. Cowles Strickland.

Ronald Vexted, soldier, has been dead ten years. His family, with friends, on the occasion of his birth anniversary, hold an experimental spiritualistic séance. Later Ronald appears as a materialized spirit to different members of the family and to his intimates, but always in the form and habit in which each remembers him best. Thus the theory is advanced that the dead live as long as they are remembered. Ronald, having been something of a rotter in life, continues something of a rotter after death. His ghost is finally laid.

HEADS UP

(144 performances)

A musical comedy in two acts; book by John McGowan and Paul Gerard Smith; music by Richard Rodgers; lyrics by Lorenz Hart. Produced by Aarons and Freedley at the Alvin Theatre, New York, November 11, 1929.

Cast of characters—

Martha Trumbell....................Janet Velie
Peggy Pratt....................Alice Boulden
Rex Cutting....................John Hundley
Larry White....................John Hamilton
Betty Boyd....................Betty Starbuck
Georgie....................Ray Bolger
"Skippy" Dugan....................Victor Moore
Captain Denny....................Robert Gleckler
Mary Trumbell....................Barbara Newberry
Jack Mason....................Jack Whiting
James Clarke....................Lewis Parker
Bob } Harry }....................Atlas and LaMar
Carson....................Louis Delgado
Dillon....................Richard Macaleese

Phil. Ohman at the Piano.

Act I.—Scene 1—Garden of Mrs. Trumbell's Home at New London. 2—Dock. 3—"Skippy's" Galley Aboard the *Silver Lady*. 4—Yacht Club. Act II.—Scene 1—Water Front. 2—Headquarter's

Office, U. S. Coast Guard, New London. 3—Aboard the *Silver Lady*. 4—An Island. 5—Mrs. Trumbell's Home.
Staged by George Hale.

Mary Trumbell is interested in Lieutenant Mason of the coast guard the time the Trumbell yacht is being used by Captain Denny in a rum smuggling enterprise unknown to Mary's mother. "Skippy" Dugan, the cook, is aware of Captain Denny's racket but is unable to speak his mind, having been promised this and that if he does. When pursuit grows hot the captain burns the yacht which grows hotter.

OTHER MEN'S WIVES

(23 performances)

A comedy in three acts by Walter Hackett. Produced by Edgar Selwyn at the Times Square Theatre, New York, November 12, 1929.

Cast of characters—

Maitre D'Hotel....................................Armand Cortez
Angela Worthing....................................Dorothy Hall
Anthony Peel....................................Hugh Sinclair
The Maid....................................Claiborne Foster
Reginald De Brett....................................Percy Ames
Gendarme....................................Walter Armin
Sir John Deptford....................................John G. Spacey
Sam Worthing....................................Harvey Stephens

Acts I, II and III.—In a Private Sitting Room in a French Seaside Hotel Near Le Touquet.
Staged by Edgar Selwyn.

Lady Deptford's sister (the maid) has gone to a roadside inn near Le Touquet hoping to buy back her ladyship's diamonds from certain parties before their loss is discovered by Sir John, who might suspect the worst. At the inn sister becomes involved with a couple of would-be elopers, Angela and Anthony. When there is danger of scandal and interference from the gendarmes, Angela and the maid change rôles and this helps the maid fascinate Anthony and save Angela, too.

WINTER BOUND

(39 performances)

A drama in nine episodes by Thomas H. Dickinson. Produced by the Provincetown Playhouse at the Garrick Theatre, New York. November 12, 1929.

Cast of characters—

Eunice MacKail....................................Hume Derr
Emily Fullbright....................................Marie Goff
Tim Lockwood....................................Warren Colston
Tony Ambler....................................Aline MacMahon
Jimmy Hollister....................................Richard Abbott
Philip Martin....................................Otto Hulett
Chet Williams....................................Willard Robertson

In the Main Room of Tony Ambler's House in Connecticut. Scene 1—Indian Summer. 2—Early Frost. 3—Wind and Rain. 4—Deep Snow. 5—February Thaw. 6—A Late Cold Snap. 7—March Comes in Like a Lion. 8—Broken Branches. 9—Promise of Spring.

Staged by James Light.

Tony Ambler, seeking freedom in a man-ruled, sex-burdened world, induces Emily Fullbright to retire with her to a farm in Connecticut, there to prove by doing it that women are sufficiently resourceful to take care of themselves. So far as Tony is concerned the experiment proves successful, but after the strain of lonesome winter months the more feminine Emily runs to the arms of Chet Williams, a neighboring farmer, and later marries him. No woman, decides Emily, can live contrary to nature's laws whatever her ideals. On top of Emily's desertion Tony hears that Jimmy Hollister, a boy who has come to worship her, has been run over by the freight train he was trying to board to get away from her.

VENEER

(31 performances)

A drama in three acts by Hugh Stange. Produced by Harry L. Cort and Charles H. Abramson at the Sam H. Harris Theatre, New York, November 12, 1929.

Cast of characters—

Ethel....................................Ruth Hunter
Pete....................................Harold Waldridge
Maysie Bedell....................................Jeanne Greene
Skeets....................................John Kane
Charlie Riggs....................................Henry Hull
Miss Gordon....................................Edith Shayne
George Lawrence....................................William Roselle
A Girl....................................Marion Grant
Allie Smith....................................Joanna Roos
A Student....................................Robert Sinclair
A Young Man....................................Ranald Savery
Callahan....................................Jack C. Connolly
Ling....................................Richard H. Wang

Act I.—Scene 1—Corner of the Palace Dance Hall. 2—Uptown Branch of the Public Library. 3—Boat-Deck of the *Hendrick Hudson,* Act II.—Scene 1—Callahan's Pavilion at Coney Island. 2—Furnished Apartment. 3—Booth in Sam Yong's Oriental-American Restaurant. 4—Public Library. Act III.—Scene 1—Palace Dance Hall. 2—The Apartment.

Staged by Hugh Stange.

Charlie Riggs, boastful ne'er-do-well, sees Allie Smith in a branch library on Washington Heights, New York. Charlie picks up an acquaintance with Allie, telling her stories of his great travel adventures when he was in the navy. Acquaintance ripens into intimate friendship. Charlie and Allie take a two-room apartment and set up housekeeping at Allie's expense while Charlie is waiting for his great chance. Three months later Charlie is bored with the experiment. The fact that Allie is to have a baby does not restrain him. He takes her savings and leaves. Allie kills herself.

QUEEN BEE

(21 performances)

A comedy in three acts by Louise Fox Connell and Ruth Hawthorne. Produced by Joseph B. Glick at the Belmont Theatre, New York, November 12, 1929.

Cast of characters—

Margaret Talbot	Charlcie Hedge
Elaine Stevens	Eleanor Phelps
Briggs	William Stone
Roger Hyde	Warren Parker
John Talbot	Brian Donlevy
Gilbert Blake	Ian Keith
Janice Blake	Gertrude Bryan

Acts I, II and III.—Living Room in the Gilbert Blake Home, Westchester.
Staged by Allan Dinehart.

Janice Blake, restless and dictatorial, taxes the patience of her amiable husband and then turns for further diversion to his best friend, John Talbot. She pauses long enough in her affair with John to shatter the romance of her younger sister, Elaine, and Roger Hyde. Janice's husband happens to overhear a part of her proposal to John and leaves her. So do John and the others.

YOUR UNCLE DUDLEY

(96 performances)

A comedy in three acts by Howard Lindsay and Bertrand Robinson. Produced by A. L. Erlanger and George C. Tyler at the Cort Theatre, New York, November 18, 1929.

Cast of characters—

Mabel Dixon Church.............................Beatrice Terry
Ethelyn Church.................................Eleanor Hayden
Janet Dixon.................................Mrs. Jacques Martin
Cyril Church..................................William Haworth
Dudley Dixon..................................Walter Connolly
Christine Sederholm...........................Ellen Southbrook
Charlie Post...................................George Barbier
Robert Kirby.......................................James Bell
Acts I, II and III.—Living Room in the Home of Dudley Dixon.
Staged by Howard Lindsay and Bertrand Robinson.

Dudley Dixon is the popular type of small-town man who neglects his own business but is highly successful with all important civic movements. He finally acquires a collection of loving cups but is about to lose his own business. Ridden ragged by a shrewish sister to whom he owes money, Dudley hopes to be rid of her when her daughter wins a singing contest and uses the $5,000 prize for study abroad. When the prize is withheld from the girl, Dudley manages to borrow the money, rid his home of its disturbers and marry Christine Sederholm, his Swedish sweetheart.

A LEDGE

(16 performances)

A drama in three acts by Paul Osborn, suggested by a short story by Henry Holt. Produced by the New York Theatre Assembly at the Assembly Theatre, New York, November 18, 1929.

Cast of characters—

Louis.......................................Pickering Brown
Dr. Cecil Lander............................William Randall
Richard Legrange..............................Leonard Mudie
George Veranger.............................Augustin Duncan
Geoffry Clarke..................................Gage Clarke
Mary Veranger............................Marguerite Borough
Janet Parker..................................Miriam Stuart
Apps..James S. Barrett
Rossiter...Jack Regan
Acts I and III.—Library of the Legrange Home. Act II.—Office of the Executive Board.

Mary Veranger, out of love with her aging husband, plans to elope with his secretary, Geoffry Clarke. Geoffry steals a package of bonds from the Veranger safe, gives them to Mary for safe keeping and she, not knowing what the package contains, asks her good friend, Richard Legrange to keep them for her. Richard, a Veranger partner and long suspected by the older man of being in love with Mary, discovers what the bonds are and, thinking to save Mary, admits their theft. His partners decree that, in punishment, he shall walk a narrow ledge around the corner of their building twenty stories from the ground. He will fall, they figure, and his death be attributed to suicide. But Richard does not fall. He lives to discover that Geoffry is the thief and that Mary knows now it is Richard she loves.

A PRIMER FOR LOVERS

(24 performances)

A farce in three acts by William Hurlbut. Produced by Herman Gantvoort at the Longacre Theatre, New York, November 18, 1929.

Cast of characters—

Virginia Beechmore....Dorothy Mortimer
Elkin Beechmore....Robert Warwick
Walters....Joseph Greene
Lucy Elliott....Ann Mason
Jessica Featherston....Alison Skipworth
John Elliott....Charles Laite
Marguerite Brace....Rose Hobart
Ned Jacques....Gavin Muir
Katie....Gwen DeLany

Acts I and III.—Drawing Room of the Beechmores' House. Act II.—Scene 1—Sitting Room Between Elkin's and Virginia's Bedroom. 2—Boudoir to Marguerite's Bedroom.
Staged by William P. Adams.

At a more or less riotous house party near New York, Elkin Beechmore arranges a rendezvous with Marguerite Brace. Marguerite swallows an overdose of sleeping potion by mistake and her place is taken in the dark by Lucy Elliott. Lucy is desperately in love with Beechmore while her husband John is quite as crazy about Mrs. Beechmore. Jessica Featherston, sophisticated dowager, is the amused recipient of numerous confidences and true romance finally involves Ned Jacques and Marguerite Brace.

ROBIN HOOD

(16 performances)

A romantic opera in three acts by Harry B. Smith, music by Reginald DeKoven. Revived by the Jolson's Theatre Musical Comedy Company at the Jolson Theatre, New York, November 18, 1929.

Cast of characters—

Robert of Huntington (Afterwards Robin Hood)........Roy Cropper
Sheriff of Nottingham..........................William Danforth
Sir Guy of Gisborne..............................John Cherrie
Little John.......................................Greek Evans
Will Scarlet..............................Charles E. Galagher
Friar Tuck..............................William J. McCarthy
Alan-A-Dale....................................Muriel Alcock
Lady Marian Fitzwalter.............................Olga Steck
Dame Durden...................................Ida Brooks Hunt
Annabel.......................................Dorothy Seegar

Act I.—A Market Place in Nottingham. Act II.—Sherwood Forest. Act III.—Courtyard of the Sheriff's Castle. England in the time of Richard I.

Staged by Milton Aborn.

IT NEVER RAINS

(185 performances)

A comedy in three acts by Aurania Rouverol. Produced by Hyman Productions at the Republic Theatre, New York, November 19, 1929.

Cast of characters—

Mabel Rogers.......................................Ann Dere
Savannah.......................................Tululah Wesley
Henry Rogers.....................................Jack Bennett
Jimmy Rogers.....................................Carl J. Julius
Norleen Sears....................................Pauline Drake
Clara Donovan....................................Fay Courtenay
Walter Donovan.....................................Phil Kelly
Dorothy Donovan....................................Sidney Fox
Dane Lawson....................................Abram Gillette
Margaret.......................................Marjorie Lytell
Gale...Tululah Wesley
Mary..Audree Workman

Acts I, II and III.—Room at the Rogers Bungalow, Just Outside Los Angeles, Cal.

Staged by Paul Martin.

Henry Rogers, Californian, sells his friend and guest, Walter Donovan, from the East, a piece of rare California real estate. The Donovans are pleased, young Dorothy Donovan is in love with Jimmy Rogers, and everything is lovely until it is discovered that the real estate deal looks crooked. Then the war. In the end it turns out a good investment and the love of the young people is permitted to ripen.

CLAIRE ADAMS

(7 performances)

A drama in eight scenes by Daniel N. Rubin. Produced by Tom Weatherly at the Biltmore Theatre, New York, November 19, 1929.

Cast of characters—

Claire....................................Mildred MacLeod
Gene Adams....................................Charles Starrett
Clyde Price....................................Buford Armitage
Jack....................................Earl McDonald
Leah....................................Thelma Booth
Cramer....................................Edward Broadley
Ted Roper....................................Charles Ritchie
Doyle....................................E. M. Johnstone
Brent....................................Frank Charlton
Vincent....................................Jack McGann

Scene 1—Claire's Home, Waco. Scenes 2, 3, 4, 6—Gene Adams' Apartment, New York. Scenes 5, 7, 8—Clyde Price's Apartment, New York.

Staged by Priestley Morrison.

In Waco, Texas, Gene Adams, reporter, and Clyde Price, who has inherited a plantation, want to marry Claire. She loves Gene, and marries him when he agrees to move to New York. Three years later Claire is blue and disgusted and Gene isn't getting on. Clyde Price, back from Paris, has little trouble winning Claire this time. Six months later, when Clyde deserts her, Claire takes up with his cousin, Ted Roper. When Clyde returns again to taunt her Claire inspires Ted to stab him to death. Claire and Ted are on their way to jail and Gene Adams is telephoning the story to his paper at the play's end.

SHERLOCK HOLMES

(45 performances)

A drama in four acts by William Gillette and Arthur Conan Doyle. Revived by George C. Tyler and A. L. Erlanger at the New Amsterdam Theatre, New York, November 25, 1929.

Cast of characters—

Sherlock Holmes....................................William Gillette
Doctor Watson....................................Wallis Clark
John Forman....................................Brinsley Shaw
Sir Edward Leighton....................................Byron Russell
Count Von Stahlburg....................................Alfred Ansel
Professor Moriarty....................................John Miltern
James Larrabee....................................Montague Shaw
Sidney Prince....................................William Postance
Alfred Bassick....................................J. Augustus Keough
Jim Craigin....................................William H. Barwald
Thomas Leary....................................Herbert Wilson
"Lightfoot" McTague....................................Henry Lambert
John....................................Fred Tasker
Billy....................................Burford Hampden
Parsons....................................Donald Campbell
Alice Faulkner....................................Peg Entwistle
Mrs. Faulkner....................................Dorothy Peabody Russell
Madge Larrabee....................................Roberta Beatty
Therese....................................Kate Byron

Mrs. Smeedley....................................Rose Kingston
Act I.—Drawing Room at the Larrabees. Act II.—Scene 1—Moriarty's Underground Office. 2—Sherlock Holmes' Apartments. Act III.—Stepney Gas Chamber. Act IV.—Dr. Watson's Room.
Staged by William Postance.

Mr. Gillette first produced "Sherlock Holmes" in November, 1889, revived it in 1907 and again in 1912. This "hitherto unpublished episode in the career of the great detective, showing his connection with the strange case of Miss Faulkner," relates the adventures attending the roundup of Professor Moriarty and his gang of crooks, including James and Madge Larrabee, who were holding Miss Faulkner in the expectation of collecting blackmail.

THE GAME OF LOVE AND DEATH

(48 performances)

A drama in three acts by Romain Rolland. Translation by Eleanor Stimson Brooks. Produced by the Theatre Guild at the Guild Theatre, New York, November 25, 1929.

Cast of characters—

Sophie de Courvoisier....................................Alice Brady
Claude Vallee....................................Otto Kruger
Jerome de Courvoisier....................................Frank Conroy
Lazare Carnot....................................Claude Rains
Denis Bayot....................................Sidney Paxton
Lodoiska Cerizier....................................Laura Straub
Chloris Soucy....................................Anita Fugazy
Crapart....................................Charles Henderson
Horace Bouchet....................................Alan Willey
Citizens of the Republic—
Timoleon....................................Robert Norton
Doucin....................................William Earle
Peau d'Ane....................................Lizbeth Kennedy
Others in the Play—Katherine Randolph, Kitty Wilson, Clinton Corwin, Frank De Silva, Paul Farber, Henry Fonda, Leopold Gutierrez, Daniel Joseph, Charles C. Leatherbee, P. Lapouchin, Hughie Mack, Lionel Stander, Mike Wagman, J. E. Whiffen.
Fifer....................................Frank Petrie
Drummer....................................Irwin Young
Acts I, II and III.—The Drawing Room of the de Courvoisier House in Paris in the Late Afternoon of a Day Towards the End of March, 1794.
Staged by Rouben Mamoulian.

Jerome de Courvoisier, a level head among the excited Girondists of the French revolution in 1794, discovers that his wife Sophie, much younger than he, is not only harboring Claude Vallee, a fugitive from the guillotine, in their home but that Sophie and Claude love each other. Courvoisier, refusing to join the radicals at the sacrifice of his principles, is given two passports by Carnot, his old friend. He turns the passports over to his wife and her lover and nobly prepares to meet his death. Sophie, reinspired by this sacrifice, sends Vallee to his freedom alone and remains behind to share her husband's fate.

THE PATRIARCH

(15 performances)

A drama in three acts by Boyd Smith. Produced by Joseph E. Shea at the Forty-ninth Street Theatre, New York, November 25, 1929.

Cast of characters—

Sarah Gaunt....................Cissie Loftus
Joe Gaunt....................Howard Phillips
Abner Gaunt....................William Courtleigh
Jeff Tanner....................Max Von Mitzel
Lem Gaunt....................A. L. Bartolot
Leah Tanner....................Marian Grant
Act I.—Gaunt Sitting Room. Act II.—Scene 1—Bald Eagle Knob in the Alleghenies. 2—Gaunt Sitting Room. Act III.—Gaunt Sitting Room.
Staged by F. Cowles Strickland.

Abner Gaunt, a strong man and just, has become the patriarch of his mountain community, a lord of the land dispensing justice and settling disputes. Abner's youngest son, Joe, kills his brother, Lem, in a quarrel over Leah Tanner, and Abner is forced to pronounce sentence of death on his best beloved.

MENDEL, INC.

(216 performances)

A comedy in three acts by David Freedman. Produced by Lew Cantor at the Sam H. Harris Theatre, New York, November 25, 1929.

Cast of characters—

Mendel Marantz....................Alexander Carr
Zelde....................Lisa Silbert
Lillian....................Helen Dumas
Mimi....................Evelyn Gaile
Jakie....................Master Lester Salkow
Bernard Shnaps....................Joe Smith
Sam Shtrudel....................Charles Dale
Bessie Kvitch....................Anna Chandler
Milton Kahn....................Joseph Striker
Oscar Gassenheim....................Elliott Roth
Zigmund Gassenheim....................Morris Freeman

Nathan Krause....................................Richard Clark
Halibut....................................William B. Calhoun
A Woman....................................Bertha Byrt
The Marshal....................................Ralph Sanford
An Engineer....................................Ted Athey
Acts I and II.—Home and Business Place of Mendel Marantz. Act III.—Mendel's New Home.
Staged by Lew Cantor.

Mendel Marantz, a kindly but visionary inventor, despite the secret help of his daughter, manages finally to get himself and his affairs in such a jam that Mrs. Marantz has to go to work to support the family. Mendel stays home, does the housework and continues working on his invention, destined to make housekeeping a pleasure in place of a task. The invention turns out better than anyone except the audience anticipated.

SALT WATER

(87 performances)

A comedy in three acts by Dan Jarrett. Produced by John Golden at the Golden Theatre, New York, November 26, 1929.

Cast of characters—

John Horner....................................Frank Craven
Marion Potter....................................Una Merkel
Sam Bowen....................................Claude Cooper
Percival Todd....................................Alan Goode
Pansy Horner....................................Edythe Elliott
Hattie Horner....................................Patricia O'Hearn
Jim Quirk....................................James C. Lane
Harrison Davis....................................Robert Burton
Nick Dominick....................................William Edmunds
Doctor Price....................................Henry Lawrence
Buddy Holt....................................George Spelvin, Jr.
Acts I, II and III.—The Home of John and Pansy Horner at Snag Harbor.
Staged by John Golden.

John Horner has but one ambition in life: He wants to own and captain a salt water ship as his father and grandfather had done before him. When he and his practical wife, Pansy, have jointly saved $5,000 John plans to invest it in a boat and, with his partners, sail south in search of cargoes and adventure. Pansy, hoping to keep John home, has already taken the money to buy the Snag Harbor ferry. John is furious, and in the midst of his fury the ferry bumps into her wharf and burns up. Separation threatens when John learns an insurance company is to replace the ferry and decides to captain the new boat if Pansy will let him.

HOW'S YOUR HEALTH

(47 performances)

A comedy in three acts by Booth Tarkington and Harry Leon Wilson. Produced by Lyle Andrews and R. H. Burnside at the Vanderbilt Theatre, New York, November 26, 1929.

Cast of characters—

Miss Pusey....................................Eleanor Shaler
Francis....................................John Carmody
Lawrence Satterleigh....................................Roy Atwell
Dr. Pepper....................................Donald Brian
Sam Catterson....................................Herbert Corthell
Miss Helen McCoy....................................Virginia O'Brien
Miss Mary Hickson....................................Virginia Eastman
Jimmie....................................Eddie Morgan
A Pirate....................................Robert Spencer
A Pierrette....................................Phyllis Rae
A Columbine....................................Rita Glynde
A Folly....................................Elinor Millard
A Harlequin....................................Floyd English
Acts I and III.—Lawrence Satterleigh's Apartment, New York City. Act II.—In the Apartment of Helen and Mary.
Staged by R. H. Burnside.

Lawrence Satterleigh, convinced that he has at least one foot in the grave, is induced to go to a party and forget his troubles. At the party he meets Helen McCoy, who is pretty, goes rakish and practically wrecks the evening, much to the distress and concern of his friends, Dr. Pepper, and Sam Catterson.

TOP O' THE HILL

(15 performances)

Drama in three acts by Charles Kenyon. Produced by Felix Young at the Eltinge Theatre, New York, November 26, 1929.

Cast of characters—

Sally Lawrence....................................Claudia Morgan
Mrs. Lawrence....................................Virginia Hammond
Howard Lawrence....................................Sidney Booth
Billy Lawrence....................................Lester Vail
Ann Leicester....................................Katherine Wilson
Dolly....................................Georgia Lee Hall
Sandy Dunn....................................Charles D. Brown
Acts I, II and III.—A Hotel in San Francisco, Dignified, Exclusive and Slightly Victorian.
Staged by C. Worthington Miner.

Ann Leicester, prominent picture star, engaged to the socially prominent Billy Lawrence, is exposed by the hard-boiled politician, Sandy Dunn. Ann, under the name of Maizie Ryan, had lived for two years as a girl in Russian Rosy's place in San Francisco, seven years before she met Lawrence, and had, during most of that time, been Dunn's mistress. Her refusal to go back to Dunn brings about the exposure, but Lawrence is game and refuses to give Ann up.

* SONS O' GUNS

(231 performances)

A musical comedy by Fred Thompson and Jack Donahue; music and lyrics by Arthur Swanstrom, Benny Davis and J. Fred Coots. Produced by Connolly and Swanstrom at the Imperial Theatre, New York, November 26, 1929.

Cast of characters—

Jimmy Canfield	Jack Donahue
Mary Harper	Shirley Vernon
Hobson	William Frawley
Arthur Travers	Milton Watson
Carl Schreiber	Barry Walsh
Bernice Pearce	Mary Horan
General Harper	Richard Temple
Billswater	Eddie Hodge
Parker	Robert Dohn
Oswald	Alfred Bardelang
Marie	Ann Karyle
Jeanette	Gwendolyn Milne
Joan	Marion Chambers
Colette	Frances Markey
Irene	Isobel Zehner
Major Archibald Ponsonby-Falcke	David Hutcheson
Pierre	Raoul de Tisne
A British Officer	Charles E. Bird
A British Tommy	Joseph Spree
U. S. A. Captain	Harry Holbrook
U. S. A. Bugler	Charles Dodson
A German Prisoner	Robert Dohn
A German Prisoner	Alfred Bardelang
Yvonne	Lily Damita

The Action of the Play Takes Place in 1918-19.
Staged by Bobby Connelly; ballets by Albertina Rasch.

Jimmy Canfield, rich and more or less worthless, is forced into the war only to find that his former valet is now his rough top sergeant. His adventures are unhappy, especially after he falls in love with Yvonne. Accused of being a spy and jailed, Jimmy escapes and practically wins the war single-handed.

THE HUMBUG

(13 performances)

A drama in three acts by Max Marcin. Produced by Mr. Marcin at the Ambassador Theatre, New York, November 27, 1929.

Cast of characters—

Professor Justin Forbes............................P. R. Scammon
Lawson Coombs..............................Wheeler Dryden
Roger Loft......................................Paul Harvey
Mrs. Theresa Forndyce..........................Corinne Ross
Dr. Norman Ware................................King Calder
Wilson Romer...................................John Lyons
Mrs. Valerie Loft...............................Kay Strozzi
Louise.......................................Dorothy Lyons
Dr. Alexis Collender...........................John Halliday
Nora...Myrtle Stanton
Mr. Dobbs......................................Jack Bennett
Mrs. Dobbs...................................Margaret Doty
Alice Trask.................................Eleanor Griffith

Act I.—Scene 1—Rostrum of the American Academy for the Advancement of Science and Art. 2—Sitting Room in the Home of Roger Loft. Act II.—The Home of Dr. Alexis Collender. Act III.—Scene 1—Loft's Home. 2—Rostrum of the American Academy.

Staged by Max Marcin.

Dr. Alexis Collender, hypnotist, specializes in the subjugation of women attractive to him, causing them, under his spell, to leave husband or fiancé at his command. Collender needs votes if he is to get into the Academy for the Advancement of Science. Dr. Ware opposes his candidacy. So does Dr. Loft. Collender, having hypnotized Dr. Ware's fiancée, Alice Trask, also places Mrs. Loft under his power. Ware finally pretends to be hypnotized by Collender and when commanded to pull the trigger of a revolver does so with good effect, killing the hypnotist seducer.

* FIFTY MILLION FRENCHMEN

(229 performances)

A musical comedy in two acts by Herbert Fields; music and lyrics by Cole Porter. Produced by E. Ray Goetz at the Lyric Theatre, New York, November 27, 1929.

Cast of characters—

Michael Cummins...............................Jack Thompson
Billy Baxter..................................Lester Crawford
Marcelle Fouchard...............................Dorothy Day
Louis.......................................Ignatio Martinetti

Joyce Wheeler....................Betty Compton
Emmitt Carroll....................Thurston Hall
Gladys Carroll....................Bernice Mershon
Peter Forbes....................William Gaxton
Looloo Carroll....................Genevieve Tobin
Sylvia....................Fifi Laimbeer
May De Vere....................Evelyn Hoey
Mrs. De Vere....................Gertrude Mudge
Mr. Ira Rosen....................Robert Leonard
Mrs. Rosen....................Annette Hoffman
Junior....................Larry Jason
Violet Hildegarde....................Helen Broderick
Boule De Neige....................Billy Reed
Oscar....................Lou Duthers
Mons. Pernasse....................Mario Villani
Le Sahib Roussin....................Jean Del Val
The Grand Duke Ivan Ivanovitch of Russia........Mannart Kippen
Joe Zelli....................Jean Del Val
Maitre D'Hotel....................Oscar Magis

Prologue—Foyer, Cocktail Room and Bar at the Ritz, Paris. Act I.—Scene 1—The American Express Co., Rue Scribe. 2—A Bookstall. 3—Cafe de la Paix, Place de L'Opera. 4—On the Boulevard. 5—Racetrack at Longchamps. Act II.—Scene 1—Lounge of Hotel Claridge. 2—Corridor at the Claridge. 3—Zelli's. 4—Les Halles. 5—Chateau Madrid.

Staged by Edgar M. Woolley; dances by Larry Ceballos.

Peter Forbes, rich and wild, glimpses Looloo Carroll in Paris and thereafter wagers his friend, Michael Cummins, that within a month, and without the aid of his letter of credit, he, Peter, will become engaged to Looloo. Peter strips himself of funds, takes on a job as guide and thereafter pursues the amused and interested Looloo until he wins his wager.

THE SILVER SWAN

(21 performances)

A musical comedy by William S. Brady and Alonzo Price; music by H. Maurice Jacquet. Produced by Herman Gantvoort at the Martin Beck Theatre, New York, November 27, 1929.

Cast of characters—

Lieut. Berthold....................Robert Roltner
Adolf....................David D. Morris
Lieut. Walther....................Alexander Leftwich, Jr.
Lieut. Erich....................Walter Munroe
Seppel....................Harry Miller
Denise....................Laine Blaire
Hortense Zorma....................Alice MacKenzie
Gurlitt....................Robert G. Pitkin
Alexandrine....................Ninon Bunyea
Capt. Richard Von Orten....................Edward Nell, Jr.
Tiger....................Paul Joyce
Princess Von Auen....................Lina Abarbanell
Gabrielle....................Vivian Hart
General Von Auen....................Florenz Ames
Marie....................Lucille Constant
Theresa....................Jill Northrup

Lieut. Karl....................................William Dillon
Act I.—The Garden of The Silver Swan. Act II.—Scene 1—Room in The Silver Swan. 2—Hortense Zorma's Dressing Room. 3—Garden of The Silver Swan.
Staged by Alonzo Price and Leroy J. Prinz.

Capt. Richard Von Orten thinks he is in love with Hortense Zorma, leading lady of an opera troupe living at The Silver Swan, until he meets Gabrielle, the new ingénue. Thereafter he is kept busy singing, explaining and avoiding intrigues inspired or directed by the Princess Von Auen.

YOUNG SINNERS

(229 performances)

A comedy in three acts by Elmer Harris. Produced by the Messrs. Shubert at the Morosco Theatre, New York, November 28, 1929.

Cast of characters—

Constance Sinclair....................................Dorothy Appleby
Mrs. Sinclair....................................Hilda Spong
Butler....................................Edward Forman
Elsa Hemplemeyer....................................Vera Amazar
Baron Von Konitz....................................Carlos De Valdez
Bud Springer....................................Robert Beyers
Gene Gibson....................................Raymond Guion
John Gibson....................................Edward Donnelly
Trent....................................Arthur Bowyer
Manager of an Apartment House....................................Edward Racey
Alice Lewis....................................Faye Marlyn
Tom McGuire....................................John Harrington
Maggie McGuire....................................Gwyn Stratford
Little Tim....................................Arthur Scanlon
Act I.—Scene 1—Sinclair Home, Florida. 2—Gene's Apartment. Acts II and III.—Living Room, Gene's Camp, Adirondacks.
Staged by Stanley Logan.

Gene Gibson, embittered and wild at 20, is turned over by his millionaire father to Tom McGuire, a professional man-builder. McGuire whips Gene into submission, takes him to the Adirondacks to complete the cure and sends for a girl to keep him company. Constance Sinclair, hearing of the girl's assignment and being herself in love with Gene, manages to substitute for the professional entertainer. Gene, however, grown moral as well as healthy, refuses to take Constance's advances seriously, declaring he will wait until she is 18 and marry her honorably. On interference by their parents Gene gets a moving picture job and runs away with Connie, to Iowa, where a girl's of age at 17.

CHARM

(4 performances)

A comedy in three acts by John Kirkpatrick. Revived by Sam Bacon at Wallack's Theatre, New York, November 28, 1929.

Cast of characters—

Mrs. Wilson.....Mabel Montgomery
Mrs. Harper.....Elizabeth Rathburn
Joe Pond.....Kenneth Dana
Mr. Harper.....William Balfour
Ida May Harper.....Ann Thomas
Mr. Lester.....Guy Wellington
Klein.....Carlton Emory
"Doc" Garfield.....Gay B. Kingston
Mrs. Paxton.....Sammie Harris
Mr. Paxton.....George Lydecker
Babe.....Winnie Worth
Violet.....Annie Laurie Jaques
Claude.....Walter Speakman
Miss Mildred.....Virginia Fairfax

Acts I, II and III.—Harper Sitting Room.
Staged by Edgar Henning.

As "The Book of Charm" Mr. Kirkpatrick's comedy was produced by Rachel Crothers at the Comedy Theatre, New York, September 3, 1925. See "The Best Plays of 1925-26."

THE AMOROUS ANTIC

(8 performances)

A farce in three acts by Ernest Pascal. Produced by Sam H. Harris at the Theatre Masque, New York, December 2, 1929.

Cast of characters—

Sena Balsam.....Phoebe Foster
Percival Redingote.....Alan Mowbray
Harlow Balsam.....Frank Morgan
Emily Gunning.....Vera Neilson
A Model.....Harry Clarke
Another Model.....Mortimer Lepey

Acts I and III.—Studio of Harlow and Sena Balsam. Act II.—Percival Redingote's Studio.
Staged by Ernest Pascal.

Sena Balsam, modernist painter, induces Percival Redingote, sculptor, to pose for her. During the posing both feel a controllable but positive biological urge toward each other and agree, dispassionately, that a consummation of their passion is necessary to their artistic growth. Harlow Balsam, playwright and

Sena's husband, quite understands the conclusions of his wife and his best friend, but something urges him to protest. He even goes so far as to plead with Sena that she at least postpone the adventure, which she agrees to do. This, naturally, makes Percival fearfully mad. But there isn't anything much that he can do about it.

THE MERRY WIDOW

(16 performances)

A musical comedy in three acts by Victor Leon and Leo Stein; music by Franz Lehar. Produced by the Jolson Theatre Musical Comedy Co. at the Jolson Theatre, New York, December 2, 1929.

Cast of characters—

Sonia (The Merry Widow)........................Beppe De Vries
Vicomte Camille De Jolidon........................Roy Cropper
Marquis De Cascada........................Francesco Yannelli
M. De St. Brioche........................Paul Catlin
General Novikovich........................William Phite
M. Khadja........................Clarence Harvey
Nisch........................W. J. McCarthy
Prince Danilo........................Evan Thomas
Baron Popoff........................Richard Powell
Natalie........................Dene Dickens
Olga........................Mary Patterson
Lo-Lo........................Wee Griffin
Fi-Fi........................Lizette Braddock
Do-Do........................Amy Alexander
Zo-Zo........................Ethel Lynn
Jou-Jou........................Frances Bariello
Frou-Frou........................Eleanor Gilmore
Clo-Clo........................Helen Etheridge
Margot........................Mary Thurman
Willie........................Bernie Sager
Head Waiter........................Leslie McLeod

Act I.—Marsovian Embassy in Paris. Act II.—Grounds of Sonia's House Near Paris. Act III.—Maxim's Restaurant, Paris.

Staged by Milton Aborn.

Sonia and the Prince Danilo quarreled when Sonia married. They meet again in Paris, where the Prince is a member of the Marsovian embassy and Sonia is a rich widow. Danilo swears he will never give Sonia a chance to jilt him a second time and Sonia thinks he will. She proceeds with confidence and then they go into the waltz. This is the beginning of the end.

WHIRLPOOL

(3 performances)

A drama in three acts by William Jourdan Rapp and Walter Marquiss. Produced by the American Playwrights at the Biltmore Theatre, New York, December 3, 1929.

Cast of characters—

Mrs. Schultz....................................Dorothy Walters
Bill Dugan....................................Francis Pierlot
Rev. James Gregg....................................Edward Leiter
Alice Gregg....................................Louise Quinn
Ethel Fraylin....................................Ruth Mero
Arthur Wilson....................................Bentley Wallace
Henrietta Blodgett....................................Eleanor Wells
Henry Potter....................................Willard Dashiell
Jason Crane....................................Halliam Bosworth
Mrs. Sarah Pryor....................................Kate McComb
Father Patrick Ryan....................................Bernard Craney
Howard McCarl....................................John Vosburgh
Charles Black....................................Cecil Holm

Acts I, II and III.—Pastor's Study in the First Protestant Church of Kingstown, Illinois.

Staged by Edwin H. Morse.

Rev. James Gregg, seeking to do God's work in an Illinois mining town, finds himself variously handicapped. His wife is out of sympathy with his work and what it pays. He feels himself falling in love with the president of the Young People's society, who wants to marry another boy, and finally he is attacked by the community boss, representing Capital, who is loudly opposed to Labor, represented by striking miners. The Rev. Gregg winds up by giving his wife her freedom and going on to another parish to work alone.

HEADQUARTERS

(15 performances)

A melodrama in three acts by Hugh Stange. Produced by Sidney Wilmer, Walter Vincent and Alfred E. Aarons at the Forrest Theatre, New York, December 4, 1929.

Cast of characters—

John Brophy, Sergeant....................................John Sharkey
Patrick Kelly, Sergeant....................................William Gargan
Harry Donovan....................................Stanley Lindahl
Monahan....................................D. J. Hamilton
Donald S. Smith....................................Donald Foster
Wm. B. Regan, Inspector....................................William Farnum
Richard Condon....................................George Baxter
Doreen Regan....................................Mildred Mitchell
Mimi Sharon....................................Lea Penman
Lydia Dale....................................Florence Johns
Herbert Stanislaws....................................George Fisher
Marty Sanford....................................Harry Sherwood
A Man....................................Sam Lawlor
His Wife....................................Elaine Ivans
Doorman....................................Lane Stanley
Brown....................................Ray Clifford
Williams....................................Lawrence O'Brien
August Krag....................................Robert Toms
Jones....................................J. Wilson

Commissioner Fritzmorris............................Harry Hanlon
Police Photographers..............William Meehan, Eugene Farrell
Finger Print Experts................Arthur Leonard, George Hunt
Dr. Jeremiah Harlow............................Royal Thayer
Mechanic Dunn..................................George Collignon
Capt. Hogan....................................Arthur Hammil
Isadore Lipwitz................................Samuel Levene
High School Party—Betty Manning, Isabel Manning, Mell Efrid, Arthur Leonard, Eugene Farrell, Marjorie Manning and George Hunt.

Act I.—Scene 1—Inspector Regan's Office. 2—Section of 70th Street. Act II.—Scene 1—Richard Condon's Study. 2—Boudoir of Mimi Sharon. Act III.—Richard Condon's Study

Staged by Jo Graham.

Inspector Bill Regan, called upon to investigate the murder of his wife, Mimi Sharon, picture star, and Richard Condon, picture actor, is forced to accept circumstantial evidence connecting his daughter, Doreen, with both crimes. Doreen had been in Condon's rooms taking dictation the night of the murder and Mimi Sharon was found in a hideaway next door. At the last minute proof is found that Doreen is innocent and a hired slayer guilty.

THE LIVING CORPSE

(33 performances)

A tragedy in three acts by Leo Tolstoy. Produced at the Civic Repertory Theatre, New York, December 6, 1929.

Cast of characters—

Anna Pavlovna..................................Alma Kruger
Nurse..Mary Ward
Sasha..Florida Friebus
Maid...Mary Sarton
Victor Michailovitch Karenin...................Donald Cameron
Lisa (Elizabeth Andreyvna).....................Josephine Hutchinson
Afremov..Harold Moulton
Fedya (Feodor Vasilyevitch Protasov)...........Jacob Ben-Ami
Ivan Markarovitch..............................J. Edward Bromberg
Nastasia Ivanovna..............................Leona Roberts
A Young Army Officer...........................Herbert Shapiro
A Musician.....................................Sayre Crawley
A Gypsy Girl...................................Ruth Wilton
Masha..Rita Romilly
A Gypsy Man....................................David Turk
Gypsy Choir Leader.............................Theodore Zarkevitch
Gypsy Musicians..........Paul Zamulenko, Constantine Shevtchenko
A Doctor.......................................Walter Beck
Stackov..David Kerman
Butkevitch.....................................Blake Scott
Koratkov.......................................Arnold Moss
Footman..Lee Hillery
Footman..Gordon Wallace
Anna Dimitrievna Karenina......................Eva Le Gallienne
Prince Sergei Dimitrievitch Abrezkov...........Paul Leyssac
Waiter...Robert Lewis
Ivan Petrovitch Alexandrov.....................Egon Brecher
Lackey...Leonard Farley

Voznesensky....................................Joseph Kramm
Petushkov....................................Gordon Wallace
Innkeeper....................................David Turk
A Drunken Woman....................................Ria Mooney
Innkeeper's Assistant....................................William Steinhorn
Artemyev....................................Robert H. Gordon
Policeman....................................Henry Howard
Examining Magistrate....................................Walter Beck
Melnikov....................................Herbert Shapiro
Clerk....................................Mooney Diamond
Court Attendant....................................Robert Ross
A Young Lawyer....................................David Turk
A Lady....................................Elizabeth Shelly
An Army Officer....................................Joseph Kramm
Petrushin....................................J. Edward Bromberg
A Doctor....................................Robert Lewis

Act I.—Scene 1—Dining Room at Protasov's. 2—At the Gypsies'. 3—Dining Room. 4—A Room at Afremov's. Act II.—Scene 1—Mme. Karenina's Drawing Room. 2—A Furnished Room, Fedya's Lodgings. 3—A Private Room in a Second-Class Restaurant. 4—Drawing Room at Lisa Protasov's. Act III.—Scene 1—A Dirty Room in a Low-Class Restaurant. 2—Office of Examining Magistrate. 3—A Corridor of the District Courthouse. In Moscow at the End of the Nineteenth Century.

Staged by Jacob Ben-Ami.

This play, known also as "Redemption," was first given in an English translation in 1918, Arthur Hopkins the producer and John Barrymore playing the chief part. It was later revived by Morris Gest and Edgar Selwyn (1928) with Alexander Moissi playing the chief part in German. It is the tragedy of Fedya, a sensitive soul, who takes to drink to ease his tortured soul and leaves Lisa, his wife, to save her the contamination of his presence. He would give Lisa a divorce, but cannot stand the degradation of submitting the necessary evidence. He tries suicide and lacks the requisite courage. He makes it appear that he has made way with himself. Years later, his story being overheard, he is summoned to court as a witness against Lisa, who has remarried. Realizing that the case is going against Lisa, he finally succeeds in fatally shooting himself.

DIANA

(8 performances)

Drama in four episodes by Irving Kaye Davis. Produced by L. Lawrence Weber, in association with Hugh Ford, at the Longacre Theatre, New York, December 9, 1929.

Cast of characters—

FIRST EPISODE
Paul Dilworth's House in Paris

Hedwig....................................Janet McLeay
Broadley....................................Henry Vincent

Maurice..Boris Batt
Andre Chapelle...Jerome Lawler
Henri Geroux...Alan Devitt
North Carolina Pendleton...................................Louise MacKintosh
West Virginia Pendleton....................................Edythe Tressider
Marquis de Guiche..Harold Webster
Hugo Neumann...Charles Quigley
Paul Dilworth..John Craig
Peterkin...Margaret McCauley
Dolores..Edna Gertrude Hagan
Victorine..Ludmilla Toretzka
George Luft..Jefferson de Angelis
Ilya Polonsky..Nicolai Oulukanof
Diana..Mary Nash

SECOND EPISODE
Diana's Studio

Mme. Beuvais...Jean Newcombe
Mme. Dubois..Josie Intropodi

THIRD EPISODE
"The Laughing Mask" Café in Moscow

Mulikovski... Nicholas Grey
Misha..Nicholas Gelikhovsky
Grigori Yessnikoff...Sergei Shishkin

FOURTH EPISODE
Diana's Apartment in Nice

Bob Stevens..Carleton Hildreth

Staged by Hugh Ford.

Diana Bolton, having reached the peak of her dancing career in Paris, where she and her two children are living under the protection of Paul Dilworth, is attracted by Hugo Neumann, a youthful and gifted pianist. Quarreling with Dilworth she establishes a dancing studio in which Neumann is much at home. The pianist's fancy being diverted from Diana to her favorite pupil, Hedwig, and her children being killed in an accident, a second rearrangement of her menage becomes necessary. Diana harkens to the call of the Soviets and goes to Russia to dance. Here she meets and marries a young Russian poet, Ilya Polonsky. Neglected by Polonsky she takes refuge in an apartment in Nice, scorns an engagement in vaudeville as degrading to her art and goes to her accidental death when a trailing scarf she is wearing on an automobile ride becomes entangled in the wheels and strangles her. (Founded on the life of Isadora Duncan.)

THE NOVICE AND THE DUKE

(28 performances)

Shakespeare's comedy, "Measure for Measure," rearranged in modern dress and setting by Olga Katzin. Produced by Walter Greenough for the Theatre Assembly at the Assembly Theatre, New York, December 9, 1929.

Cast of characters—

Vincentio, the Duke....................Leslie Palmer
Angelo....................Leo G. Carroll
Escalus....................Maurice Cass
Claudio....................Leonard Mudie
Lucio....................Hugh Miller
Provost....................Charles Hampden
Friar Peter....................George Coulouris
Elbow....................James S. Barrett
Froth....................Wynn Young
Pompey....................A. P. Kaye
Valet....................Alvin Kerr
Isabella....................Anne Shoemaker
Francisca....................Thais Lawton
Mariana....................Constance Hope
Juliet....................Sheelagh Hayes
Mistress Overdone....................Thais Lawton

Scene 1—A Private Room in the Palace. 2—A Street. 3—A Cloister. 4—An Audience Chamber. 5—A Street. 6—A Private Room. 7—A Prison. 8—A Garden. 9—A Prison. 10—The City Gate in Vienna.

Staged by Olga Katzin.

The story of the Duke's successful attempt to trap Angelo, the adulterer, by leaving him in charge of affairs in Vienna. Angelo's first case is that of a youth whose sister is a probationary nun. Angelo insists the nun shall give herself to him to save her brother. The Duke, made privy to the demand, conspires with Isabella, the nun, to trap Angelo and thus convict him of the crime for which he would have convicted the youth.

FAMILY AFFAIRS

(7 performances)

A comedy in three acts by Earle Crooker and Lowell Brentano. Produced by Arthur Hopkins and L. Lawrence Weber at the Maxine Elliott Theatre, New York, December 10, 1929.

Cast of characters—

Roger Wheaton....................Joseph McCallion
Janet Wheaton....................Elaine Temple
Yeager....................Cecil Clovelly
Charles Wheaton....................Frank Elliot
Estelle Wheaton....................Billie Burke
Horace Parker....................Edmund George
"Silks" Lee....................Leona Boutelle
Audrey Ainsworth....................Audrey Ridgwell
Paul Savelle....................Bruce Evans

Acts I, II and III.—The Living Room of the Wheaton Home in the East Sixties, New York.

Staged by Arthur Hopkins.

Estelle Wheaton, aware for two years that her husband, Charles, has maintained a Park Avenue apartment for Audrey

Ainsworth and that her son Roger has been paying the expenses of "Silks" Lee, a chorus girl, decides on a drastic adventure to save her men folk and her home. She invites both mistresses to the Wheaton home for a week-end, and includes her debutante daughter's far from satisfactory fiancé and a supposed gigolo for herself. If the family must retrench, Estelle explains, what better way than to have all the family affairs under one roof? As a result of one wordy evening's experience the affairs are satisfactorily adjusted. "Silks" Lee comes through nobly to marry Roger and the debutante daughter falls in love with the gigolo, who isn't.

* MICHAEL AND MARY

(232 performances)

A comedy in three acts by A. A. Milne. Produced by Charles Hopkins at the Charles Hopkins Theatre, New York, December 13, 1929.

Cast of characters—

Mary....................Edith Barrett
An Attendant....................Peter Lang
Michael....................Henry Hull
Violet....................Katherine Standing
Mrs. Tullivant....................Alice Belmore Cliffe
The Rev. Simon Rowe....................David Glassford
Mary's Uncle....................Vernon Kelso
Inspector Enderby....................Leonard Willey
Dr. Roberts....................Robert Vivian
"P. C." Tuff....................Harry Beresford
A Policeman....................Emile Littler
David....................Alan Willey
Miss Welby....................Hilda Plowright
Romo....................Helen Claire

Act I.—Scene 1—At the British Museum. 2—The Room in Islington. Act II.—The Flat in Chelsea. Act III.—The House in Chelsea. London, 1905 to 1929.

Staged by Charles Hopkins.

See page 272.

RED RUST

(65 performances)

A drama in three acts by V. Kirchon and A. Ouspensky. Adapted by Virginia and Frank Vernon. Produced by the Theatre Guild at the Martin Beck Theatre, New York, December 17, 1929.

Cast of characters—

Bezborodov....................Lionel Stander
Lutikov....................George Tobias
Andrei....................Harry M. Cooke
Petrossian....................Elliot Sullivan
Pimples....................Lee Strasberg
Besseda....................Albert Angell
Terekhine....................Herbert J. Biberman
Voznesienski....................Spenser Kimbell
Piotr....................Lutha Adler
Supervisor....................Charles Peyton
Vassili....................Ackland Powell
Nina....................Gale Sondergaard
Fenia....................Florence House
Varvara....................Virginia Berry
Lenov....................William Challee
Lisa....................Ruth Nelson
Fedor....................Franchot Tone
Olga....................Ruth Chorpenning
1st Old Woman....................Helen Plaut
2nd Old Woman....................Lizzie Rechelle
1st Passerby....................Wells Richardson
2nd Passerby....................Charles Peyton
3rd Passerby....................Frank Verigun
Youth....................Joseph Kleima
Beggar....................Thomas Fisher
Peddler....................George Shoemaker
Mania....................Eunice Stoddard
Loukitch....................Curtis Arnall
Secretary....................Charles Peyton
Zavialov....................Harry Wilson
Nikolai....................Boris Korlin

Act I.—Scene 1—Room in a Student's House in Moscow in 1927. 2—Gymnasium. 3—Terekhine's Room. Act II.—Scene 1—Red Square. 2—Room in a Student's House. Act III.—Scene 1—Student's Room. 2—Terekhine's Room.

Staged by Herbert J. Biberman.

Terekhine, achieving prominence and some influence with the Soviet through his successes in the revolution, proceeds thereafter to run things with a high hand, eventually to the irritation of the more decent members of his "cell." When Nina, one of the women Terekhine has taken, is found dead and Terekhine reports that she killed herself, the cell expels him on the charge of having forced by his own brutality Nina's act. The higher council sets aside the expulsion, but the cell later tricks Terekhine into a confession and proceeds to punish him.

INSPECTOR KENNEDY

(43 performances)

A drama in three acts by Milton Herbert Gropper and Edna Sherry. Produced at the Bijou Theatre, New York, December 20, 1929.

Cast of characters—

Wong..Goo Chong
Ada..Eve Kohl
Gilbert Mortover..Walter Watson
Barbara Dean..Margaret Mullen
Matthew Carroll..Don Merrifield
Dwight Mortover..Henry Herbert
Mrs. Wemble..Valerie Bergere
Tony Carroll..Maurice Burke
Charlie Dunn..Carroll Ashburn
Detective Reilly..Abbott Adams
Officer Smith..Felix Figman
Officer Thomas..Lawrence O'Sullivan
Dr. Gray..C. Russell Sage
Byrne..Maurice Barrett
Inspector Kennedy..William Hodge
Detective Rorke..William Cullen

Acts I, II and III.—Study in the Home of Dwight Mortover on East 68th Street, New York.
Staged by William Hodge.

Dwight Mortover, an aged importer who has also dealt in narcotics, tries to induce his secretary, Barbara Dean, to marry him. When he is repulsed Mortover plans to be even by killing himself and making it appear that Tony Carroll, Barbara's fiancé, committed the crime. He sets the scene, provides the circumstantial evidence and is fatally shot. Inspector Kennedy, with a reputation for shrewdness, takes the case and unravels it within a few hours, despite the fact that no fewer than four of Mortover's intimates confess to having shot him. The shooting had been craftily done through a hole in the ceiling by one who had a duplicate of the pistol found on Tony.

HALF GODS

(17 performances)

A drama in two acts by Sidney Howard. Produced by Arthur Hopkins at the Plymouth Theatre, New York, December 21, 1929.

Cast of characters—

Stephen Ferrier..Donn Cook
Hope Ferrier..Mayo Methot
Ada..Elizabeth Goodyear
Dennis..Paul Porter
Rush Bigelow..Walter Regan
Judge Sturgis..Walter Walker
Helena Grey..Dorothy Sands
Dr. Mannering..Edward Reese
First Policeman..Robert Bunce Williams
Second Policeman..Philip Beveridge
Pauline..Laura Hamilton
First Porter..Arthur Shaw
Second Porter..Hal K. Dawson

Third Porter..Thaddeus Clancy
Dr. Wolheim..Siegfried Rumann
First Detective..Arthur Shaw
Second Detective..Hal K. Dawson

Act I.—The Ferriers' Flat. The Bedroom. 2—Living Room. 3—Dr. Mannering's office. 4—Room in Back of Helena Grey's Bookshop. 5—Long Island Police Station. Act II.—Scene 1—Judge Sturgis' Private Office. 2—The Ferriers' Flat. The Living Room. 3—Pauline's Sitting Room. 4—The Ferriers' Flat. The Bedroom. New York.

Staged by Arthur Hopkins.

Hope and Stephen Ferrier, eight years married, the parents of two healthy children, are beginning to get on each other's nerves. Stephen objects to trailing Hope through her social campaigns. Hope resents Stephen's various preoccupations. Several times they come close to separation. It is a psychoanalyst's opinion that Stephen is an "infantile extrovert" and Hope an "intuitive introvert." The day Hope would start for Reno and a divorce the German specialist attending her children openly questions her right to leave, intimates that her only value to the world is that of a mother and a breeder of men and dares her to violate these obligations. Later Stephen, opposing Hope, is slapped for his pains and Hope promptly knocked down for the slap. This paves the way to a better understanding.

METEOR

(92 performances)

A comedy in three acts by S. N. Behrman. Produced by the Theatre Guild at the Guild Theatre, New York, December 23, 1929.

Cast of characters—

Ann Carr..Lynn Fontanne
Douglas Carr..Douglass Montgomery
Phyllis Pennell..Shirley O'Hara
Sherman Maxwell..Martin Berkeley
Curtis Maxwell..Lawrence Leslie
Dr. Avery..Edward Emery
Raphael Lord..Alfred Lunt
Mullin..Leonard Loan
A Butler..Charles McClelland

Act I.—Living Room in Dr. Avery's House in a Small University Town in Massachusetts. Acts II and III.—Living Room in Raphael Lord's House on Fifth Avenue, in New York City.

Staged by Philip Moeller.

Raphael Lord, a supreme egoist, marries Ann Carr, the daughter of a college professor, tires of and abandons his studies and goes to New York to give his career wings and acquire power.

Within five years he is many times a millionaire, his prophetic vision helping vastly in his speculations. When failure threatens the most colossal of his enterprises and his wife leaves him Lord is still undaunted. He has depended too much upon his genius, he concludes. Now he will give his great mind completely to his career and refashion it to meet greater and greater successes.

BABES IN TOYLAND

(32 performances)

A musical comedy by Glen MacDonough; music by Victor Herbert. Revived by the Jolson Theatre Musical Comedy Company at the Jolson Theatre, New York, December 23, 1929.

Cast of characters—

Uncle Barnaby....................Wm. Balfour
Frances....................Frances Moore
Adele....................Adele Savoye
Tom Tom....................Marcella Swanson
Hilda....................Mona Moray
Gonzorgo....................Barry Lupino
Roderigo....................Rupert Darrell
The Widow Piper....................Jayne Waterous
Bo Peep....................Margaret Byers
Jill....................Wee Griffin
Peter....................Helen Rae
Bobby Shaftoe....................Barry Lupino, Jr.
Jack....................Mary Thurman
Sallie Waters....................Eleanor Gilmore
Curly Locks....................Martha Gale
Tommy Tucker....................Evelyn Brown
Simple Simon....................Frances Baviello
Little Red Riding Hood....................Ethel Lynne
Miss Muffett....................Helen Etheridge
Boy Blue....................Dene Dickens
Jane....................Betty Byron
Alan....................Frank Gallagher
1st Dandy....................Frank Yanelli
2nd Dandy....................Don Catlin
Contrary Mary....................Leotabel Lane
Inspector Marmaduke....................W. J. McCarthy
Master Toymaker....................Dean Raymond
Grumio....................Chester Herman
Max....................Frank Yanelli
The Brown Bear....................Bernie Sager
The Baby Bear....................Barry Lupino, Jr.
The Giant Spider....................Jos. Schrode
A Fairy....................Gene Dickens
Santa Claus....................Louis Diamond

Act I.—Scene 1—Contrary Mary's Garden. 2—Garden Wall. 3—The Spider's Forest. 4—The Floral Palace of the Moth Queen. Act II.—Scene 1—Christmas Tree Grove in Toyland. 2—A Street in Toyland. 3—The Master Toymaker's Workshop. 4—Exterior of the Master Toymaker's Castle. Act III.—The Courtyard of the Toyland Palace of Justice.

Staged by Milton Aborn.

Uncle Barnaby is a miser and Jane and Alan stand in the way of his acquiring a fortune. But despite all the things he can do, and all the other things he can think he would like to do, the children escape and the fair, square justice of Toyland sees them safely through to a life that shall be happy ever after.

TOP SPEED

(102 performances)

A musical comedy in two acts by Guy Bolton, Bert Kalmar and Harry Ruby. Produced by Bolton, Kalmar & Ruby, Ltd., at the 46th Street Theatre, New York, December 25, 1929.

Cast of characters—

Tad Jordan..Harland Dixon
Daisy Parker..Sunny Dale
Bellows..Lloyd Pedrick
Gerry Brooks..Paul Frawley
Elmer Peters..Lester Allen
Molly..Laine Blaire
Pete Schoonmaker..Lon Hascall
Virginia Rollins..Irene Delroy
Babs Green..Ginger Rogers
Chauffeur..Ken Williams
Shirley..Shirley Richards
Mr. Rollins..Theodore Babcock
Vincent Colgate..Sam Critcherson
Spencer Colgate..John T. Dwyer
Waiter at the Yacht Club........................George Del Drigo
Souvenir Storekeeper..William Hale

Act I.—Scene 1—Terrace of Onawanda Lodge. 2—Bench Near the Lodge at Dawn. 3—Main Lounge, Onawanda Lodge. Act II.—Scene 1—Border Line Yacht Club. 2—In the Woods. 3—Bedroom in Onawanda Lodge. 4—Regatta Ball.

Staged by John Harwood; dances by John Boyle.

Gerry Brooks and Elmer Peters, brokers' clerks, are at a Thousand Islands resort posing as millionaires. They meet and fascinate a couple of millionaires' daughters, Virginia Rollins and Babs Green, and flirt the evening through with both the girls and the ever-present menace of exposure. The sheriff wants Elmer for having caught fish in a fish hatchery and Gerry almost takes a bribe in a boat race. Everything is cleared up by 11:15.

WOOF, WOOF

(45 performances)

A musical comedy in two acts by Estelle Hunt, Sam Summers and Cyrus Wood; music and lyrics by Edward Pola and Eddie

Brandt. Produced by Demarest and Lohmuller, Inc., at the Royale Theatre, New York, December 25, 1929.

Cast of characters—

Stage Manager.................................William Plunkett
Babe Birdy.....................................Helen Goodhue
Monty Fleming..................................Al Sexton
Tommy Clair....................................Jack Squires
Elmer Green.........................."Sunkist" Eddie Nelson
Chosty...Olive Fay
Susie Yates....................................Louise Brown
Henry..George Haggerty
Mrs. Clair.....................................Madeline Grey
Colonel Penny..................................Louis Casavant
Virginia Lee Penny.............................Gladyce Deering
Harv McDaniel..................................Andrew Mack
Al Stafford....................................Edwin Walter
Sugar Betty Ann................................Martha Copeland
Dude...Arthur Bryson
Sluefoot.......................................U. S. Thompson
Soapy Blake....................................John Kennedy

Act I.—Scene 1—Back Stage. In the Wings. 2—Dressing Room Corridor After Performance. 3—Tommy Clair's Home in New Jersey. 4—"Tree Top Inn," Along Hudson. Act II.—Scene 1—Auto Camp on the Outskirts of Mobile. 2—Corridor of a Hotel in Mobile. 3—Training Camp Near Mobile. 4—Pari Mutuel Betting Booths at the Track in Mobile. 5—On the Course.

Staged by Leonide Massine.

Susie Yates, attractive girl from a small town, is in New York trying to get a stage job. A millionaire orchestra leader, Tommy Clair, is eager to help Susie if she will put herself in his hands (and arms). Monty Fleming, a poor but honest dancer, offers marriage but not much else. Monty wins in a dance.

RICHELIEU

(88 performances)

A drama in four acts by Sir Edward Bulwer-Lytton, in a new version by Arthur Goodrich. Produced by Walter Hampden at the Hampden Theatre, New York, December 26, 1929.

Cast of characters—

Gaston, Duke of Orleans........................Louis Polan
Count De Baradas...............................Moffat Johnston
Clermont.......................................S. Thomas Gomez
Marion De Lorme................................Caroline Meade
Sieur De Beringhen.............................Gordon Hart
Chevalier De Mauprat...........................Ernest Rowan
First Gamester.................................Clark Hundley
Huguet...C. Norman Hammond
François.......................................Charles McCarthy, Jr.
Joseph...Cecil Yapp
Cardinal Richelieu.............................Walter Hampden
Julie De Mortemar..............................Ingeborg Torrup
One of the Twenty..............................Edwin Cushman

Another of the Twenty....................................Gage Bennett
Louis XIII....................................Dallas Anderson
Duran....................................Robert C. Schnitzer
First Guard....................................Stephen Irving
Second Guard....................................Harold Williams
First Secretary of State....................................Edwin Cushman
Second Secretary of State....................................Gage Bennett
Third Secretary of State....................................Franklin Salisbury
Courtiers, Gamesters, Soldiers, Conspirators, Ladies of the Court, etc.

Act I.—Scene 1—At the House of Marion De Lorme. 2—At Cardinal Richelieu's Palace. Act II.—Scene 1—At Adrien De Mauprat's House. Afternoon of the next day. 2 and 3—At Cardinal Richelieu's Palace. Act III.—Scene 1—At the House of Marion De Lorme. 2 and 3—The Gardens of the Louvre.

Staged by Walter Hampden.

A shortened version of the Bulwer-Lytton classic from which asides and soliloquies are cut and the chief dramatic scenes drawn more closely together.

DEATH TAKES A HOLIDAY

(180 performances)

A drama in three acts adapted by Walter Ferris from the Italian of Alberto Casella. Produced by Lee Shubert at the Ethel Barrymore Theatre, New York, December 26, 1929.

Cast of characters—

Cora....................................Florence Golden
Fedele....................................Thomas Bate
Duke Lambert....................................James Dale
Alda....................................Ann Orr
Stephanie....................................Olga Birbeck
Princess of San Luca....................................Viva Berkett
Baron Cesarea....................................Wallace Erskine
Rhoda Fenton....................................Lenore Sorsby
Eric Fenton....................................Roland Bottomley
Corrado....................................Martin Burton
Grazia....................................Rose Hobart
His Serene Highness, Prince Sirki, of Vitalba Alexandri
Philip Merivale
Major Whitred....................................Frank Greene

Acts I, II and III.—Great Hall in the Castle of Duke Lambert.

Staged by Lawrence Marston.

See page 310.

SEVEN

(35 performances)

A drama in seven episodes, by Frank J. Collins. Produced by James Cooper at the Republic Theatre, New York, December 27, 1929.

Cast of characters—

Heloise....................Beverly Sitgreaves
Captain Otis....................Robert Strange
Saunders....................Preston Foster
Jake....................Millard F. Mitchell
Carroll....................Del Cleveland
Griffin....................Alan Davis
Charlerois....................Armand Cortes
Huston....................Tom Douglas
La Comtesse de Villette....................Suzanne Caubaye
Liane....................Helene Gunther
Colonel Bayne....................George Lessey

The Seven Episodes Take Place in the Salon of the Château Villette, Somewhere on the Western Front, in the Spring of 1918.

Staged by Lionel Atwill.

There are seven aviators in the Second Pursuit squadron of the American forces. They are quartered in the Château Villette somewhere on the western front shortly after America has entered the Great War. One by one they go to their deaths. Among the replacements is Huston, a boy of 21, who enlisted with the Harvard unit. His nerves snap and in an effort to revive his interest in life the beautiful Countess de Villette gives herself to him the night he should have been undertaking a dangerous bombing mission. Learning next day that his captain had held up the order at the Countess's request, Huston, bitterly reproachful, flies to his own death.

* THE FIRST MRS. FRASER

(207 performances)

A comedy in three acts by St. John Ervine. Produced at the Playhouse, New York, December 28, 1929.

Cast of characters—

Ninian Fraser....................John Halloran
Mabel....................Emily Hamill
James Fraser....................A. E. Matthews
Janet Fraser....................Grace George
Philip Logan....................Lawrence Grossmith
Murdo Fraser....................Eric Elliott
Alice Fraser....................Annabella Murray
Elsie Fraser....................Carol Goodner

Acts I, II and III.—Janet Fraser's Flat in Knightsbridge.

Staged by Grace George.

See page 204.

CITY HAUL

(77 performances)

A comedy in three acts by Elizabeth Miele. Produced by Gil Boag at the Hudson Theatre, New York, December 30, 1929.

Cast of characters—

Hopkins..Lawrence Bolton
Brady..Lynn Root
Shafer..Harold Bolton
Jackie..Buddy Schubert
Bill Henderson..J. Anthony Hughes
Timothy MacHugh, the Mayor..Herbert Rawlinson
Dr. Andrew Sprague..John Stokes
Dora MacHugh..Dorothy Lebaire
Tony Scaranza..Henry Sherwood
Mrs. Carl Bolton..Mathilda Baring
Rev. Dr. Cruse..Arthur Cole
Rev. Dr. Miller..Reginald Fife
Mark Moore, Police Commissioner..Charles Slattery
Mrs. Harrison Leeds..Ann Winston
Mrs. Mary Malone..Lizzie McCall
Edwards..Donald Kellogg
Kelly..Ben Roberts
Dan Kelly..Doan Borup
Fisher..Gene Miller
Roy Conway..C. E. Smith
Mary Burns..Adelaide Kendall

Acts I, II and III.—The Mayor's Office in the City Hall.
Staged by Harry Wagstaffe Gribble.

Timothy MacHugh, mayor of an Illinois city, accepts graft as a part of the political game, grabbing the bigger part of any city funds that pass through his hands. Also a large slice of tax money. His daughter Dora is in love with his secretary, Bill Henderson, who has served a prison term, having been framed for robbery. MacHugh forbids the marriage, but is glad to reconsider when Henderson is instrumental in saving MacHugh when the reform forces trace down the tax money theft.

THE UNSOPHISTICATES

(8 performances)

A comedy in three acts by Harry Delf. Produced by Mr. Delf at the Longacre Theatre, New York, December 30, 1929.

Cast of characters—

Mistress Brewster..Molly Pearson
John Bradford, Elder..John T. Doyle
Prudence Brewster..Nydia Westman
John Bradford..Vernon Rich
Barbara Sewell..Helen Baxter
A Magistrate..J. H. Brewer
Mullens..John C. Hickey
Chilton..Robert Robson
Mistress Chilton..Catherine Hayden
Smith..William Thompson
Mistress Smith..Enid Gray
Brasher..Harry Hammel
Clark..Jerome Kennedy
A Neighbor..John Martin
Mistress Winthrop..Margaret Arrow

Humility....................................Frances Hess
Faith....................................Marion Morse
A Cooper....................................John Baldwin
Priscilla....................................Gene Hynd
Hope....................................Margaret Mitchell
A Fiddler....................................Martin Noble
Mary....................................Peggy Pitou
Mistress Jones....................................Florence Morse
Margaret....................................Mabel Marden
Mistress Freeman....................................Frances A. Hess
Phyllis....................................Gertrude Flynn
A Young Lad....................................Robert Hess
Peter....................................Philip Roll
Thomas....................................Hayden Bodycombe
William....................................Patrick Glasgow
Rogers....................................John Wynne

Acts I, II and III.—In the House of Mistress Brewster, at New Plymouth, in the Year 1622.

Staged by Ralph Murphy.

John Bradford, Sr., is convinced that his son, John, Jr., 17, should wed with Prudence Brewster, 16, and thus hurry along the population of the Puritan settlement of New Plymouth in the year 1622. Mistress Brewster, mother of Prudence, favors delay on the plea that the young people know nothing of life and are much too young to marry. Mistress Brewster changes her mind, however, when she discovers that the young people have been courting, so John and Prudence are wed. Not, however, until Barbara Sewell, a saucy newcomer to the colony, demonstrates the facts of life to John, is the marriage threatened with successful consummation.

DAMN YOUR HONOR

(8 performances)

A comedy in four acts by Bayard Veiller and Becky Gardiner. Produced by Vincent Youmans at the Cosmopolitan Theatre, New York, December 30, 1929.

Cast of characters—

La Tour....................................John Halliday
Governor Waring....................................Frederic Worlock
Cydalyse Waring....................................Jessie Royce Landis
Michel Du Fresne....................................Peggy Shannon
James Coleman....................................Alan Campbell
British Officer....................................J. Malcom Dunn
Diablo....................................Adin Wilson
Captain Gains....................................Frederick T. Forman
Rigaud....................................Curtis Karpe
Beluche....................................William B. Mack
Dominique....................................James T. Ford
Gambio....................................Harry D. Southard
Guy....................................Richard Curtis
Negro Servant....................................James Brown

Act I.—Beach on Baratavia. Act II.—Scene 1—Governor Waring's Garden. 2—La Tour's House. Act III.—Mrs. Waring's Boudoir. Act IV.—The Ship.

Staged by Bayard Veiller and Becky Gardiner.

La Tour, a bold, handsome buccaneer in 1812, steals the money of Governor Waring and the jewels of the governor's wife, Cydalyse. After noting the beauty of Cydalyse and falling in love with her, he determines to return the jewels. Posing as an American army captain he brings the jewels to Cydalyse, is almost captured, believes he has been betrayed by his love and climbs boldly into her chamber to be revenged. (Hence the title.) Away again on his ship La Tour's sailors mutiny and sail for safer waters. When he is free he would about ship and return for his love but finds that unnecessary. Loving him, Cydalyse has crept aboard and wants to stay.

WAKE UP AND DREAM

(136 performances)

An English revue in two acts by J. H. Turner; music and lyrics by Cole Porter. Produced by Arch Selwyn, in association with C. B. Cochran, at the Selwyn Theatre, New York, December 30, 1929.

Principals engaged—

Jack Buchanan	Jessie Matthews
William Stephens	Tilly Losch
Toni Birkmayer	Tina Meller
Dave Fitzgibbon	Jean Barry
Lance Lister	Marjorie Brooks
Claude Newman	Wyn Clare
Roy Mitchell	Frances Shelley
A. B. Imeson	Greta Wood
Douglas Phillips	Ann Barberova
Gomez Trio	Mary Tomlinson

Staged by Frank Collins; dances by Tilly Losch, Jack Buchanan and Max Rivers.

THE PLAYBOY OF THE WESTERN WORLD

(27 performances)

A comedy by J. M. Synge. Produced at the Irish Theatre, New York, January 2, 1930.

Cast of characters—

Christopher Mahon..............................Sean Dillon
Old Mahon..............................Jess Sidney
Michael James Flaherty..............................Royal Dana Tracy
Margaret Flaherty..............................Betty Murray
Widow Quin..............................Grania O'Malley
Shawn Keough..............................George Mitchem

Philly Cullen.....Francis Kennelly
Jimmy Farrell.....J. S. McLaughlin
Sara Tansey.....Ann Mitchel
Susan Brady.....Alice Erhardt
Honor Blake.....Frances Kennan
Nellie.....Cele McLaughlin
A Bellman.....R. S. Plowden
Some Neighbors——Barbara Robins, Kathleen Baddeley, Walter Murphy, Bernard Cahill.
Acts I, II and III.—Near a Village on a Wild Coast of Mayo.
Staged by Miceal Breathnach.

The adventure of Christopher Mahon the time he flayed his "da" with a loy and came to a distant place to boast of his crime as no less than a murder and bask in the great heroism with which the simple folk, particularly the females, of the countryside received him. The unexpected appearance of the murdered man served somewhat to discomfit the braggart only to make a greater romancer than ever in the end.

WATERLOO BRIDGE

(64 performances)

A drama in two acts by Robert Emmet Sherwood. Produced by Charles Dillingham at the Fulton Theatre, New York, January 6, 1930.

Cast of characters—

Kitty.....Cora Witherspoon
A Military Policeman.....Hannam Clark
Gertrude.....Eunice Hunt
An Officer.....George G. Wallen
A Sergeant Major.....Alexander Frank
A Sergeant.....Douglas Garden
Myra.....June Walker
A Sailor.....William Evans
An Australian.....Allen Fagan
A Civilian.....Herbert Saunders
Roy Cronin.....Glenn Hunter
A Constable.....David Post
Mrs. Hobley.....Florence Edney
A Laborer.....George Spelvin
His Wife.....Margaret Searls
Act I.—Scene 1—Waterloo Bridge, London. 2—Myra's Room in Mrs. Hobley's Lodging House. Act II.—Scene 1—Myra's Room. 2—Waterloo Bridge.
Staged by Winchell Smith.

Roy Cronin, an upstate New York boy who enlisted with the Canadians the first year of the war, is walking across Waterloo Bridge, London, in 1917, when he trips over the suitcase belonging to Myra, an American chorus girl who, since the war, has divided her time between street walking and serving as a farmerette. In the acquaintance that follows, Myra, discovering that Roy still holds to his illusions regarding good women, refuses to disillusion him. Roy accepts Myra as a good girl and wants to help her. Finding out the truth, he still wants to help. Going back to war, he leaves Myra an assignment of his pay.

CHILDREN OF DARKNESS

(79 performances)

A tragi-comedy in three acts by Edwin Justus Mayer. Produced by Kenneth Macgowan and Joseph Verner Reed at the Biltmore Theatre, New York, January 7, 1930.

Cast of characters—

Mr. Snap, Under-Sheriff of London and Middlesex..Walter Kingsford
First Bailiff..........Albert Bees
Mr. Cartwright..........J. Kerby Hawkes
Mr. Fierce..........Richard Menefee
Jonathan Wild, the Great..........Charles Dalton
Count La Ruse..........Basil Sydney
Laetitia..........Mary Ellis
Lord Wainwright..........Eugene Powers
Bailiffs..........Joseph Skinner, William Plunkett

Acts I, II and III.—Room in the House of Mr. Snap, Adjoining Newgate Prison, London.
Staged by Edwin Justus Mayer.

Among the paying guests of Mr. Snap, under-sheriff of London and Middlesex, and chief jailer of Newgate prison in 1725, are the Count La Ruse and Jonathan Wild, thieves; Mr. Cartwright, poet, and Lord Wainwright, poisoner. Laetitia, the jailer's daughter, loves La Ruse, desperately, and when he seeks to break her hold upon him, takes up with Mr. Cartwright by way of bringing La Ruse back. La Ruse and Mr. Snap conspire to rob Jonathan Wild the day of his hanging, on pretense of buying him a pardon. With freedom in sight, La Ruse, convinced by Laetitia of his worthlessness and the hopelessness of any attempted reform, takes his own life, leaving the money he has stolen to the poet. Laetitia falls then to Lord Wainwright.

SO WAS NAPOLEON

(Sap from Syracuse)

(25 performances)

A farce by Jack O'Donnell and John Wray. Produced by Robert V. Newman and Arnold Johnson at the Sam H. Harris Theatre, New York, January 8, 1930.

Cast of characters—

Hartley Hopkins....................Grant Mills
Belle Cherry....................Frances Crossey
Adolph....................Frank Dae
Littleton Looney....................Hugh McConnell
Sam Henderson....................Paul Byron
George Pope....................Lloyd Russell
Earl Truesdale....................Roland Wilson
Florence Goodrich....................Mary Murray
Bells....................Spencer Bentley
Solomon Hycross....................Granville Bates
Dolly Thornton....................Ruth Donnelly
Pedro Zaballa....................Sidney Riggs
Countess de Bouchard....................Elsa Ersi
Senator Halpin....................Jack Rafael
Commodore Barker....................Louis Frohoff
Beauvais....................Albert Gesse
Juju....................Czara Romanyi
R. Walter Tulliford....................Oliver Holmes
A Detective....................Marcel Rousseau
A Gendarme....................George Spelvin
Another Gendarme....................Joseph Spelvin

Act I.—Scene 1—Ante-Room of a Private Dining-Room, Onondaga Hotel, Syracuse, N. Y. 2—Promenade Deck. S.S. *Leviathan.* Act II.—Drawing Room of the Countess De Bouchard's Suite, S.S. *Leviathan.* Act III.—Countess De Bouchard's Chateau at Nice.
Staged by John Hayden.

Littleton Looney, a sap about town in Syracuse, inherits $18,000 from an aunt and decides to take a trip to Europe. Certain kidding members of the Syracuse Chamber of Commerce tender Looney a farewell banquet, give him a horseshoe of artificial roses and speed him on his way by wiring the captain of the *Leviathan* that the Syracusan is a great personal friend of all the big New York politicians, from Al Smith down. On the ship Looney is made much of by the captain and the passengers. Among others he meets the Countess de Bouchard, who owns nickel mines in Bolivia, and lets her think him a great mining engineer. In the last act he is accidentally able to save the Countess' mines and marry the Countess.

AT THE BOTTOM

(72 performances)

A new version of Maxim Gorki's "Night Lodging," adapted by William L. Laurence. Produced by Leo Bulgakov Theatre Associates, Inc., at the Waldorf Theatre, New York, January 9, 1930.

Cast of characters—

The Baron....................Carroll Ashburn
Kvashnya....................Welba Lestina
Bubnov....................Victor Killian
Andrei....................John Wexley
Nastya....................Barbara Bulgakova

Anna..Elsa Lazareff
Satin..Richard Hale
The Actor..E. J. Ballantine
Michael Kostilyev.......................................Ian Wolfe
Vaska..Walter Abel
Natasha..Anne Seymour
Luka..Edgar Stehli
Alyoshka...Lewis Leverett
Vasilisa..Mary Morris
Abramka...Louis John Latzer
The Tatar..Ari Kutai
The Grizzly..Trevor Bardett
Acts I, II and IV.—A Flop-House in a Large Provincial Town, Central Russia. Act III.—Courtyard of the Flop-House.
Staged by Leo Bulgakov.

The text of Gorki's study of a group of Russia's poorest poor, the inhabitants of a "flop-house," is here put into the American vernacular. Previous New York productions have been one in English in December, 1919, by Arthur Hopkins, called "The Lower Depths," and the Moscow Art Theatre production in February, 1923.

PHANTOMS

(56 performances)

A melodramatic satire by A. E. Snitt and L. Sand. Produced by Louis A. Safian at Wallack's Theatre, New York, January 13, 1930.

Cast of characters—

Wing Sang..Edward Colebrook
Alfred Burke...Arnold Daly
Chick Crane...Hal Clarendon
Charles Wright...Harold Kennedy
Betty Jackson...Dennie Moore
Arnold Jackson..Theodore Scharfe
Tom Power...Raymond Barrett
Janet Wright...Margery Swem
Andrew Gordon...Ray Harper
Inspector Phido Prance..............................Edwin Redding
Officer Sylvester.......................................Knox Herold
Acts I, II and III.—In the Reception Room of the Combined Residence and Gambling Establishment of Alfred Burke and Charles Wright, New York City.
Staged by Monroe Bennett Hack.

Alfred Burke, proprietor of a gambling house, is killed in the first act and many people are suspect. Becoming involved in their own mystery, the authors turn to burlesque in the second act, with the entrance of Phido Prance, detective. A bit of romance was associated with the desire of Andrew Gordon to marry Janet Wright.

NANCY'S PRIVATE AFFAIR

(136 performances)

A comedy in three acts by Myron C. Fagan, produced by Mr. Fagan at the Vanderbilt Theatre, New York, January 13, 1930.

Cast of characters—

Billy Ross....................Stanly Ridges
Norah....................Julie Cobb
Sally Lee....................Diantha Pattison
Nancy Gibson....................Minna Gombell
Donald Gibson....................Lester Vail
Mrs. Jane Preston....................Beatrice Terry
Peggy Preston....................Marian Grant
Henri....................Albert Ferro
Sir Guy Harrington....................Gavin Muir

Act I.—Living Room in the Gibson Home, Westchester. Acts II and III.—Living Room in Sally Lee's Home, Long Island.
Staged by Myron C. Fagan.

Nancy Gibson, loving Donald, her husband, dearly, is distressed when she realizes that she is losing him to a pert young person named Peggy Preston. Her friends tell Nancy that she is partly to blame, in that she has permitted herself to become a frump. Let her fix herself up and get back in the competition. Nancy takes off her horn-rimmed spectacles and gets a hair wave. She also hires a moving picture actor to follow her about and pretend to be a diamond king. As a result Peggy Preston leaves Donald Gibson for the phony diamond merchant and Donald begs the privilege of remarrying Nancy.

THE PRINCE OF PILSEN

(16 performances)

A musical comedy by Frank Pixley; music by Gustav Luders. Revived by the Jolson's Theatre Musical Comedy Company at the Jolson Theatre, New York, January 13, 1930.

Cast of characters—

François....................Robert O'Connor
Edith Adams....................Alice Wellman
Cook's Courier....................Melvin Redden
Jimmy....................Wee Griffin
Arthur St. John Wilberforce, Lord Somerset....................Denis Gurney
Mrs. Madison Crocker....................India Cox
Hans Wagner....................Al Shean
Nellie Wagner....................Vivian Hart
Lieut. Tom Wagner....................Joseph Toner
Carl Otto, the Prince of Pilsen....................Roy Cropper

Sidonie....................................Marjorie Seltzer
Sergeant Brie....................................Carl Dews
Dene....................................Dene Dickens
Frances....................................Frances Baviello
Premiere Danseuse....................................Mona Moray
American Girls { Boston....................................Dene Dickens
Baltimore....................................Mona Moray
New Orleans....................................Frances Baviello
Chicago....................................Clara Martens
New York....................................Leonore Brody }

Act I.—Garden of the Hotel Internationale. Act II.—Scene 1—Court of the Hotel Internationale. 2—Lane Adjacent to the Hotel. 3—Floral Fete. 4—Corridor in the Hotel Internationale. 5—Court of Hotel.

Staged by Milton Aborn.

This story of the Cincinnati brewer who is mistaken for the Prince of Pilsen during a visit to Germany with his family was a popular musical comedy in the middle nineties, with the late John Ransome featured in the comedy rôle.

* STRIKE UP THE BAND

(175 performances)

A musical comedy in two acts by Morrie Ryskind (based on a libretto by George S. Kaufman); music by George Gershwin, lyrics by Ira Gershwin. Produced by Edgar Selwyn at the Times Square Theatre, New York, January 14, 1930.

Cast of characters—

IN THE STORY

Timothy Harper....................................Gordon Smith
Richard K. Sloane....................................Robert Bentley
Horace J. Fletcher....................................Dudley Clements
Myra Meade....................................Ethel Kenyon
Mrs. Grace Draper....................................Blanche Ring
Anne Draper....................................Doris Carson
Joan Fletcher....................................Margaret Schilling
Jim Townsend....................................Jerry Goff
Two Men About Town....................................{ Bobby Clark
Paul McCullough }
Doctor....................................Maurice Lapue

IN THE DREAM

Colonel Holmes....................................Bobby Clark
Gideon....................................Paul McCullough
Doris Dumme....................................Marion Miller
Herr Konrad....................................Maurice Lapue
Suzette....................................Ethel Britton
Soisette....................................Virginia Barnes
Sergeant....................................Walter Fairmont
Premiere Danseuse....................................Joyce Coles

Red Nichols and Orchestra.

Act I.—Scene 1—In Front of the Horace J. Fletcher Chocolate Works. 2—The Main Office. The Dream—Scene 1—Main Office.

2—Private Office. 3—Gardens of Mr. Fletcher's Home. Act II.—Scene 1—Switzerland. 2—Mr. Fletcher's Private Office. 3—Reception Hall.
Staged by Alexander Leftwich; dances by George Hale.

Horace J. Fletcher, a self-made American business man in the chocolate trade, becomes considerably exercised over a protest filed by Switzerland against the duty Congress puts on imported milk chocolate. Suffering a minor stroke, Horace is given, by the doctor, a powder which sets him dreaming. He sees himself as the general of an American army in Switzerland trying to arrange a battle or two with the Swiss. The war ends in confusion when Col. Holmes of the American forces learns to yodel and is thus put in possession of the enemy's secret calls to arms.

EVERYTHING'S JAKE

(76 performances)

A comedy in three acts by Don Marquis. Produced by the New York Theatre Assembly at the Assembly Theatre, New York, January 16, 1930.

Cast of characters—

Clem Hawley.....Charles Kennedy
Hennery Withers.....Walter Vonnegut
Al, the Bartender.....Edward Donnelly
Jake Smith.....Thurston Hall
Autoist.....Harry Selby
Mildred Smith.....Eleanore Bedford
"Ma" Smith.....Jean Adair
Will Van Heysen.....Benjamin Hoagland
Lady Ambrose.....Catherine Willard
Barker.....Mel Efird
Hotel Flunkey.....Alvin Kerr
Edwards.....Marius Underwood
Countess of Billhorn.....Ethel Morrison
Waiter.....Paul Dorn
First Domino Player.....Pendleton Harrison
Second Domino Player.....Mitch Hutchinson
Mother Michaud.....Regine De Valat
Pierre.....William Barry
Chef.....George Freedley
Louise.....Marie Dalba

Prologue—Jake Smith's Tavern at Baycliff, L. I. Acts I and III.—Sitting Room of the Smith's Hotel Suite in Paris. Act II.—Scene 1—Sidewalk Café in Paris. 2—Lady Ambrose's Apartment.
Staged by Walter Greenough.

Jake Smith, having made a fortune bootlegging at Baycliff, L. I., is induced by Ma Smith and his daughter, Mildred, to take them to Paris. For his own entertainment he also takes his pals, Clem Hawley (The Old Soak); Al, the bartender, and Hennery

Withers along. In Paris Jake is vamped by Lady Ambrose, an ex-American chorus girl married to an English title. Getting too much liquor aboard, Clem Hawley and Al the bartender call on Lady Ambrose determined to free Jake from her clutches. Jake's fortune is swept away in a bank crash while he is away from home, but Ma saves enough from the wreck to start him on a new bootlegging project.

JOSEF SUSS

(40 performances)

A drama in five scenes, adapted by Ashley Dukes from the novel "Power" by Lion Feuchtwanger. Produced by Charles Dillingham, in association with J. C. Williamson, Ltd., at Erlanger's Theatre, New York, January 20, 1930.

Cast of characters—

General Remchingen............................Cyril Raymond
Councillor Weissensee............................Ralph Truman
Manager of the Casino............................Harold Webster
Karl Alexander (Later Duke of Wurtemberg)........Malcolm Keen
Marie Auguste (Later Duchess of Wurtemberg)....Yolande Jackson
An English Lord............................Robert G. Rendel
Josef-Suss Oppenheimer ("Jew Suss")..........Maurice Moscovitch
The Rabbi Gabriel............................Stanley Drewitt
A Courier............................Victor Esker
Nicolas............................J. C. Dunn
Binder............................Horace Pollock
A Rabbi............................Alexander Sarner
Deputy President Sturm............................H. McKenzie Rogan
Magdalen............................Maureen Shaw
Dom Bartelemy Pancorbo............................Vincent West
Graviella............................Beyrl Walkly
Naemi............................Janet Morrison

Scene 1—The Pump Room at Wildbad in 1737. 2—Audience Room in Suss's House in Stuttgart. 3—Ballroom in Suss's House. 4—Keep of Suss's Castle in the Forest of Hirsau. 5—Throne Room in the Ducal Castle of Ludwigsburg.

Staged by Reginald Denham.

Josef-Suss Oppenheimer, doing Karl Alexander a good turn at the gaming tables in the pump room at Wildbad, is later rewarded with the confidence of his patron when Karl Alexander becomes Duke of Wurtemberg. As a member of the Duke's cabinet Josef-Suss is instrumental in bringing to his boudoir the daughter of Councillor Weissensee. The Councillor, in revenge, leads the Duke to the forest castle in which Suss has hidden his own daughter, the beautiful Naemi. Naemi, attacked by the Duke, falls to her death from the walls of the keep, and Josef-Suss, to be avenged, foments an uprising of the citizens against his amorous patron, going gratefully to his own death later.

THE CHALLENGE OF YOUTH

(24 performances)

A drama in three acts by Ashley Miller and Hyman Adler. Produced by Hyman Adler at the Forty-ninth Street Theatre, New York, January 20, 1930.

Cast of characters—

Nancy Summers....................................Ann Thomas
Horace Bronson (Hod)..........................William Lovejoy
Aunt Joanna (Mrs. Jermyn)........................Helene Mitchel
Stephen Adams.................................Harold De Bray
Geraldine..Evelyn Adler
Walden Ames...................................Walter Pearson
Desire Adams.....................................Alma Merrick
Wade Block (Fatty)...............................Frank Johnson
Tilly...Lottie Salisbury
Billy...James Jackson
Tommy...Jerome Samuelson
Lois..Lois Michel
Bobbie...Bobbie Del Rio

Acts I, II and III.—The Home of Professor Adams, an Educator of Importance Who Lives in a Small New England College Town.
Staged by Hyman Adler.

Desire Adams, a victim of the sex curiosity of her college set, gives herself to Horace Bronson following a wild petting party in her own home. Her father, a college professor, discovers his daughter's lapse of morals, is properly horrified but paternally loyal. He is prepared to quit the school and the community to still the scandal, when Desire decides to marry the young man.

THE CHOCOLATE SOLDIER

(25 performances)

A musical comedy by Rudolph Bernaur and Leopold Jacks, adapted by Stanilaus Stange; music by Oscar Straus. Revived by the Jolson's Theatre Musical Comedy Company at the Jolson Theatre, New York, January 27, 1930.

Cast of characters—

Nadina Popoff..................................Alice Mackenzie
Aurelia Popoff.....................................Vera Ross
Mascha...Vivian Hart
Lieutenant Bumerli.............................Charles Purcell
Captain Massakroff............................William C. Gordon
Louka..Frances Baviello
Stephan..Wee Griffin
Colonel Kasimir Popoff..........................John Dunsmure
Major Alexius Spiridoff..........................Roy Cropper

Act I.—Nadina's Boudoir in Popoff's House, in a Small Town Near the Dragoman Pass, Bulgaria. 1885. Acts II and III.—Courtyard, Gardens and Exterior of Popoff's House.
Staged by Milton Aborn.

The musical version of Bernard Shaw's "Arms and the Man," last sung in New York in December, 1921, at the Century Theatre, with Donald Brian and Testa Kosta in the chief rôles.

THE WOMEN HAVE THEIR WAY

(25 performances)

A comedy in three acts by Serafin and Joaquin Quintero, adapted by Harley and Helen Granville-Barker. Produced at the Civic Repertory Theatre, New York, January 27, 1930.

Cast of characters—

Don Julian Figueredo.......Egon Brecher
Santita.......Mary Ward
Adolfo Adalid.......Donald Cameron
Dieguilla.......Paula Miller
Concha Puerto.......Leona Roberts
Guitarra.......J. Edward Bromberg
Pilar.......Ria Mooney
Angela.......Josephine Hutchinson
Pepe Lora.......Robert Ross
Dona Belen Zurita.......Merle Maddern
Juanita La Rosa.......Eva Le Gallienne
Don Cecilio.......Sayre Crawley
Young Peasant Girl.......Elizabeth Shelly
Sacristan of San Antonio.......Walter Beck

Acts I, II and III.—The Home of Don Julian, a Priest of a Small Town in Andalusia.

Preceded by—

THE OPEN DOOR

By Alfred Sutro

Cast of characters—

Sir Geoffrey Transom.......Donald Cameron
Lady Torminster.......Eva Le Gallienne

Scene—The Drawing-Room of Lord Torminster's Cottage by the Sea
Staged by Eva Le Gallienne.

Adolfo Adalid, a handsome young lawyer of Madrid, has business which keeps him for a few days in a small town in Andalusia. Here, where the women outnumber the men five to one, getting a husband is a serious business. Looking upon Adolfo and finding him fair, the women of the village determine that he shall marry their chief beauty, Juanita La Rosa. Thereafter Adolfo finds himself being tricked or forced into frequent contacts with Juanita, which he resents. Yet, when Pepe Lora grows jealous, and Dona Belen, Juanita's guardian, grows suspicious of Adolfo's attentions to her ward and would send him away, Adolfo discovers that he is in love and doesn't want to leave. Which is as the women planned it. . . . "The Open Door" is an old-time one-acter written by Alfred Sutro in which Lady Torminster steals downstairs to talk things out with Sir Geoffrey Transom, who loves her, the wife of his best friend. They leave the door open as a sop to convention.

SARI

(15 performances)

A musical comedy in two acts by Julius Wilhelm and Fritz Greenbaum, English adaptation by C. S. Cushing and E. P. Heath; music by Emmerich Kalman. Produced by Eugene Endrey at the Liberty Theatre, New York, January 29, 1930.

Cast of characters—

Pali Racz	Boyd Marshall
Laczi Racz	J. Humbird Duffy
Sari Racz	Mitzi
Klari Racz	Gloria Frey
Joska Fekete	David D. Morris
Juliska Fekete	Marybeth Conoly
Gaston (Count Irini)	Jack Squires
Cadeaux	Bernard Jukes
Count Estragon	Eduardo Ciannelli
Pierre	Pat Clayton

Act I.—Courtyard of Pali Racz's Home in Lorinczfalva, Hungary. Act II.—Paris Home of Count Irini.
Staged by Mitzi Hajos; dances by Albertina Rasch.

"Sari" was first produced by Henry W. Savage at the Liberty Theatre, New York, the same theatre in which it was revived, in January, 1916. The cast then included, in addition to Mitzi, Van Renssalear Wheeler, Blanche Duffield, J. Humbird Duffy and Harry Davenport.

RECAPTURE

(24 performances)

A drama in three acts by Preston Sturges. Produced by A. H. Woods at the Eltinge Theatre, New York, January 29, 1930.

Cast of characters—

Mrs. Stuart Romney.....Cecelia Loftus
Rev. Outerbridge Smole.....Hugh Sinclair
Monsieur Remy.....Gustave Rolland
Gwendoliere Williams.....Glenda Farrell
Monsieur Edelweiss.....Joseph Roeder
Auguste.....Meyer Berenson
Henry C. Martin.....Melvyn Douglas
Patricia Tulliver Browne.....Ann Andrews
Capt. Hubert Reynolds, D.S.O.....Stuart Casey
Madame Pistache.....Louza Riane

Acts I and III.—Lobby of the Bellevue-Superbe-Palace Hotel, at Vichy, France. Act II.—Bedchamber of the Villa Lune de Miel.
Staged by Don Mullaly.

The Henry C. Martins meet, five years after their divorce, at a hotel in Vichy. Mr. Browne is there with a week-end friend, the former chorus beauty, Gwendoliere Williams, and the former Mrs. Browne (Patricia Tulliver Browne) is traveling with Capt. Hubert Reynolds, whom she expects shortly to marry. Henry Martin, at sight of his former wife, feels all his old love for her revived and insistently proposes that they run away to the nearby villa in which they spent their honeymoon and there try to recapture the careless rapture of their first love. The adventure proves successful so far as Mr. Browne is concerned, but Mrs. Browne knows that she will never love Henry again. At the earnest pleading of the chorus girl, who really loves him, Mrs. Browne agrees to try and go through with a remarriage for Henry's happiness, but that day she steps into an uncertain elevator in the hotel, which crashes to the basement and she is killed.

GEN. JOHN REGAN

(30 performances)

A comedy in three acts by George A. Birmingham (Canon Hannay). Produced at the Irish Theatre, New York, January 29, 1930.

Cast of characters—

Horace P. Billing.....John F. Clearman
Timothy Doyle.....George Riddell
Mary Ellen.....Nelly Neil
Sergt. Colgan.....Francis Kennelly
Constable Moriarty.....George Mitchem
Thaddeus Golligher.....Walter Murphy
Maj. Kent.....A. Trevor Bland
Dr. Lucius O'Grady.....Herbert Ranson
Mrs. Gregg.....Anne Mitchell
Inspector Gregg.....James Metcalfe
Mrs. DeCourcy.....Eileen Burns
Father McCormack.....Jess Sidney

Tom Kerrigan....................................Bernard Cahill
Lord Alfred Blakeney..............................W. M. Bellis
Acts I and III.—The Market Square of Ballymoy. Act II.—Coffee Room of Doyle's Hotel.
Staged by Joseph Augustus Keough.

Horace Billing, a forward young American from South Bend, Ind., determines to stir up the sleepy town of Ballymoy, Ireland, in which a stalled motor has stranded him. As a start he announces to the simple-minded natives that he has come to see that proper honor is done one Gen. John Regan, hero of Bolivia, who was born in Ballymoy. Where is the statue of Gen. Regan? There being no Gen. Regan, there is quite reasonably no statue, but the Ballymoy citizens, led by Dr. Lucius O'Grady, decide that there should be. Therefore they immediately start a fund to provide a statue. With this they purchase a stone carving from a friendly mortician and arrange an elaborate unveiling program, when they discover that there is no Gen. Regan. True, there isn't, admits Dr. O'Grady, but there may be. Which pleases Billing so much that he gives the town $25,000 for a new pier.

MANY A SLIP

(56 performances)

A comedy in three acts by Edith Fitzgerald and Robert Riskin. Produced by Lew Cantor at the Little Theatre, New York, February 3, 1930.

Cast of characters—

Patsy Coster....................................Sylvia Sidney
Ted Coster...Tom Brown
Smithy...Maude Eburne
Emily Coster...................................Dorothy Sands
Jerry Brooks.............................Douglass Montgomery
William Coster................................Malcolm Duncan
Stan Price...................................Elisha Cook, Jr.
Act I.—Home of William Coster in Boston. Act II.—Living Room in the Home of Patsy and Jerry. Act III.—The Apartment of Stanley Price.
Staged by Robert Riskin.

Jerry Brooks and Patsy Coster, loving each other in a Greenwich Village apartment, agree that, as Jerry insists, marriage is all wrong and a sure death to love. But after a time Patsy decides that she wants to be married and confesses her situation to her flighty mother, Emily Coster. Emily, being experienced and shrewd, leads Jerry to believe that he is about to become a father, and, being an honorable young man, he insists on marrying Patsy.

They are married, but when Jerry discovers the deception he runs away. He is brought back, first by his own desire and second by Patsy's confession that this time the baby rumor is true.

REBOUND

(114 performances)

A comedy in three acts by Donald Ogden Stewart. Produced by Arthur Hopkins at the Plymouth Theatre, New York, February 3, 1930.

Cast of characters—

Liz Crawford....................................Corinne Ross
Lyman Patterson............................George MacQuarrie
Marta...Anne Lubow
Les Crawford...........................Donald Ogden Stewart
Sara Jaffrey...............................Hope Williams
Bill Truesdale..................................Donn Cook
Johnnie Coles..............................Robert Williams
Evie Lawrence.............................Katherine Leslie
Mrs. Jaffrey....................................Ada Potter
Pierre..Pierre D'Ennery
Jules...Edward La Roche
Henry Jaffrey.................................Walter Walker

Acts I and III.—Dining Room in the Country Home of Les and Liz Crawford, Near New York. Act II.—Living Room of a Hotel Suite in Paris.

Staged by Arthur Hopkins.

See page 343

DISHONORED LADY

(127 performances)

Drama by Margaret Ayer Barnes and Edward Sheldon. Produced by Gilbert Miller and Guthrie McClintic at the Empire Theatre, New York, February 4, 1930.

Cast of characters—

Madeleine Cary...........................Katharine Cornell
Marquess of Farnborough.......................Francis Lister
Lawrence Brennan................................Paul Harvey
Jose Moreno...............................Fortunio Bonanova
Richard Wadsworth..........................Harvey Stephens
Rufus Cary......................................Fred L. Tiden
Rosie Walsh.....................................Ruth Fallows
Ella...Brenda Dahlen
Sims...Lewis A. Sealy
Riley..Edwin Morse
Albert...Jimmy Daniels

Act I.—Scene 1—Living Room of Jose Moreno's Apartment on West 49th Street, New York City. 2—Library of Rufus Cary's House on Washington Square. Act II.—Scene 1—Mr. Cary's Library. 2—Moreno's Living Room. Act III.—Mr. Cary's Library.

Staged by Guthrie McClintic.

Madeleine Cary, neurotic and restless, is periodically drawn toward men. Having met Jose Moreno, an Argentinian cabaret artist, in Paris, she calls on him at his apartment, when she hears he is in New York and stays the night. Six months later Madeleine is desperately in love with Lord Farnborough, but Jose Moreno refuses to release her from her technical obligation to him. Thereupon Madeleine poisons Jose, is charged with the crime, tried and acquitted. Her men folk, including her father, after standing by her through the trial and perjuring themselves in her defense, thereafter quit her precipitately and Madeleine is left unhappily free and deserted.

THE BOUNDARY LINE

(37 performances)

A drama in three acts by Dana Burnet. Produced by A. L. Jones and Morris Green at the Forty-eighth Street Theatre, New York, February 5, 1930.

Cast of characters—

Dorothea Fenway............................Katherine Alexander
Margaret Larson............................Winifred Lenihan
Allan Fenway............................Otto Kruger
Sarah............................Doris Sanger
Elbert............................Lew Payton
Gussie............................Marie Simpson
Elija Horton............................John T. Doyle
Fifi Hodge............................Miriam Sears
Peter Sturgis............................Charles Trowbridge
George Hodge............................John Butler
Reggie Vane............................Houston Richards
Sam............................B. E. Blanchard

Acts I and III.—Living Room of the Fenway Home Near Bluefields, N. Y. Act II.—Meadow.
Staged by Dana Burnet and Morris Green.

Allan Fenway, idealist poet, has gone cheap magazine and saved enough money to buy a place in suburban New York, at the insistence of his practical wife, Dorothea. Having acquired the place, Dorothea insists that it shall be fenced in, even though the fence will cut off a neighbor's right of way to a brook. Allan, who believes that all boundaries, physical or spiritual, are crippling to the spirit, opposes the fence, but Dorothea wins. As a result of a court action refusing an injunction to the irate neighbor, the fence is built, the neighbor is prepared to go into a shotgun protest, suffers a stroke of apoplexy and dies. Allan, defeated and unhappy, takes to the road with a company of passing campers. Dorothea takes on the sympathetic and somewhat amorous attorney who fought her fence case in court.

OUT OF A BLUE SKY

(17 performances)

A comedy in three acts adapted by Leslie Howard from the German of Hans Chlumberg. Produced by Tom Van Dycke at the Booth Theatre, New York, February 8, 1930.

Cast of characters—

ON THE STAGE

Property Man	Otis Sheridan
Electrician	Earl Redding
Stage Manager	Tammany Young
Lottie	Willa Grey
Stage Director	Gregory Ratoff
Play Reader	William Gargan
Joe	Martin Noble
Paul	Ben Kamsler
Treasurer	Stanley Wood

IN THE AUDIENCE

Dr. Friedrich Neumann	Reginald Owen
Gabriela Neumann	Katherine Wilson
Paul Rana	Warren William
Jessica Wenderoth	Eleanor Terry
Sonia Lanser	Tanya Amazar
Alexander Sonnholz	William Haskell
Lewis Leitner	Lee Crowe
Irate Spectator	J. Gibbs Penrose
Ellie	Joan Graham

The Action Takes Place at the Stadttheatre in Vienna.
Staged by Leslie Howard.

The Stage Director of the Stadttheatre in Vienna finds himself after his audience has gathered with neither company nor play. He recruits a company by calling for volunteers from the audience and they make up a play as they go along. It happens that the man who insists on playing the lover (Paul Rana) is really in love with the lady (Gabriela Neumann) who plays the wife. They therefore carry on their affair under the very nose of the lady's husband (Dr. Neumann) to the end of the play.

IT'S A GRAND LIFE

(25 performances)

A comedy by Hatcher Hughes and Alan Williams. Produced by A. L. Erlanger and George C. Tyler at the Cort Theatre, New York, February 10, 1930.

Cast of characters—

Austin Tyler..Cyril Scott
Helen Tyler..Mrs. Fiske
Jean Tyler..Leona Beutelle
Timmy Tyler..Andrew Lawlor, Jr.
"Doc" Burdette..Raymond Van Sickle
Nikolas Van Tyle..Gene Gowing
Major Richard Dale..Robert Barrat
Mercedes Dale..Germaine Giroux
Validia Sierra..Virginia Venable
Dr. Moran..William Lorenz
Reporter on the New York *Times*..C. W. Van Voorhis
Reporter on a Tabloid..Walter Kinsella
Joseph..Edward Powell
A Trained Nurse..Elsie Keene

Acts I, II and III.—Living Room of the Tylers' Park Avenue Apartment.

Staged by Harrison Grey Fiske.

Helen Tyler holds her Park Avenue home together by ignoring the moral lapses of its members. She refuses to divorce her husband, Austin, even though he has long maintained a collection of mistresses. She shuts her eyes to her daughter's affair with a married man and accepts as her son's wife the chorus girl he marries, even though she knows the girl had formerly been one of Mr. Tyler's favorites. Her final sacrifice is to permit another of her husband's attachments to have her baby in the Tyler home.

RITZY

(32 performances)

A comedy in three acts by Viva Tattersall and Sidney Toler. Produced by L. Lawrence Weber at the Longacre Theatre, New York, February 10, 1930.

Cast of characters—

Edgar Smith..Mr. Truex
Nancy Smith..Miss Hopkins
Tillie..Katharine Renwick
Mr. Peabody..J. H. Brewer
Louella McKenzie..Josephine Evans
Maude Mooney..Effie Afton
Oscar Mooney..John Junior
Charlie McKenzie..Sydney Riggs

Acts I, II and III.—One Room and Bath at the Georgian Hotel in New York City. The Residence of Mr. and Mrs. Smith.

Staged by Sidney Toler.

The Edgar Smiths think they have inherited $200,000 when Mrs. Smith's Uncle Peter dies in Mexico. Edgar immediately gives up his job and Mrs. Edgar gives away all her clothes. They give a party in celebration of their good fortune and then walk out on their guests when they are invited to a snooty society couple's apartment for cocktails. The report of Uncle Peter's fortune proves fictitious and the Smiths sink quickly back to normal, but are cheered in the end when Edgar gets his job back at more than double his former salary.

RIPPLES

(55 performances)

A musical comedy in two acts by William Anthony McGuire; music by Oscar Levant and Albert Sirmay; lyrics by Irving Ceasar and Graham John. Produced by Charles Dillingham at the New Amsterdam Theatre, New York, February 11, 1930.

Cast of characters—

Herman Dutcher....Arthur Cunningham
Honus....William Kerschell
Malcolm Fairman....Edward Allen
Ripples....Dorothy Stone
Richard Willoughby....Charles Collins
Mrs. Willoughby....Mrs. Fred Stone
Rip....Fred Stone
Mary Willoughby....Paula Stone
John Pillsbury....Andrew Tombes
Jane Martin....Kathryn Hereford
Mrs. John Pillsbury....Althea Heinly
Corporal Jack Sterling....Eddie Foy, Jr.
State Trooper....J. Marshall Smith
State Trooper....Dwight Snyder
State Trooper....Ray Johnson
State Trooper....Del Porter
Sergeant Banner....Charles Mast
Mrs. Sterling....Pearl Hight
Peggy....Millicent Bancroft
Little Billie Sheer....Paul Paulus
Lollipop....Colonel Casper

Act I.—Scene 1—The Van Winkle Inn in the Catskills. 2—Outside the Inn. 3—Cottages of Rip and the Sterlings. 4—Catskills at Sunrise. 5—Exterior of the Headquarters of State Troopers. 6—Colonial Room in Mrs. Willoughby's Country House. Act II.—Scene 1—Woodland on the Willoughby Estate. 2—Tree in Sleepy Hollow. 3—Interior of the Headquarters of State Troopers. 4—Ballroom of the Willoughby Residence.

Staged by William Anthony McGuire; dances by William Holbrook.

Rip Van Winkle, great-great-grandson of the original Rip, is as big a liar and as steady a drinker as his famous ancestor. He drinks himself to sleep in the Catskills and awakes to find himself surrounded by dwarfs. They turn out to be bootleggers, hired for size to fool the state troopers. Ripples, Rip's daughter, thinks she loves Trooper Sterling, but finds out it is the rich Richard Willoughby who holds her heart.

NINE-FIFTEEN REVUE

(7 performances)

Tunes and comedy sketches selected from the works of twenty composers and writers. Produced by Ruth Selwyn at the George M. Cohan Theatre, New York, February 11, 1930.

Principals engaged—

Van Lowe	Paul Kelly
Helen Gray	Oscar Ragland
Mary Murray	Earl Oxford
Michael Tripp	Margaret Merle
Diane Ellis	Fred Keating
Wally Crisham	Michon Bros.
Gracella and Theodore	Lynne Dore
Harry McNaughton	Charles Lawrence
Frances Shelley	Nan Blackstone
Lovey Girls	Don Voorhees and His Orchestra.

Staged by Alexander Leftwich; dances by Busby Berkeley and Leon Leonidoff.

JOSEPH

(13 performances)

A comedy in three acts by Bertram Bloch. Produced by John Golden at the Liberty Theatre, New York, February 12, 1930.

Cast of characters—

Potiphar....Ferdinand Gottschalk
Neris....Ara Gerald
Pharaoh....Douglas Dumbrille
Pharaoh's Guard....Michael Markham
Thetis....Catherine Cooper
Jezra....Sidney Murray
First Guard....George Ertell
Second Guard....Thomas Lewis
A Slave Dealer....H. H. McCullum
Joseph....George Jessel
Deborah....Ann Teeman
An Old Slave....Harold Hartzell
Slave Girl....Lois Hazzard
Ashtahoolum....Curtis Jenkins
First Jailer....Julian Noa
Second Jailer....Robert Burton
Prison Superintendent....Selden Bennett
King's Baker....Tom Post
King's Butler....Ted Athey
A Prison Slave....Lackaye Grant
Palace Guard....Michael Markham
Second Guard....John Cameron

Act I.—Potiphar's Garden. Act II.—Scene 1—The Garden. 2—Prison Cell. Act III.—Scene 1—The Cell. 2—An Ante-Room in Pharaoh's Palace.

Staged by George S. Kaufman.

A freely modernized version of the Biblical story in which Joseph, sold into slavery, organizes Potiphar's slaves and is made his head man. When he is sought by the amorous Mrs. Potiphar and spurns the lady's offer, she denounces him as her would-be seducer. Thrown into prison preparatory to being hung Joseph shows his jailer how he can turn a handsome profit by organizing his prisoners into a work gang and irrigating the land. Called finally to interpret Pharaoh's dream, Joseph is given his liberty and wide powers.

* TOPAZE

(141 performances)

A comedy in three acts by Marcel Pagnol, adapted by Benn W. Levy. Produced by Lee Shubert at the Music Box, New York, February 12, 1930.

Cast of characters—

Topaze....................Frank Morgan
Ernestine Muche....................Mildred Mitchell
Muche....................Hubert Druce
Tamise....................Harry Davenport
Le Ribonchon....................Cornelius Vezin
Suzy Courtois....................Phœbe Foster
Baroness Pitart-Vergniolles....................Catherine Doucet
Castel-Benac....................Clarence Derwent
Butler....................Cornelius Vezin
Roger de Berville....................Nicholas Joy
First Stenographer....................Aldeah Wise
Second Stenographer....................Dauna Allen
Officer....................Cecil Clovelly
An Old Man....................Alf Helton

PUPILS AT PENSION MUCHE

Cordier....................Warren McCullum
Durant-Victor....................Freddie Stange
Pitart-Vergniolles....................Peter Boylan
Seguedille....................Harry Murray
Tronche-Bobine....................James McGuire
Jusserand....................George Canto-Janis
Bertin....................James Guiname
Blondet....................Richard Offer
Bleriot....................Eddie Wragge
Mentez....................Martin Postal

Act I.—Classroom in the Pension Muche. Act II.—Small Salon at the Home of Suzy Courtois. Act III.—Office of M. Castel-Benac.
Staged by Stanley Logan.

Topaze, an unremittingly honest teacher in the Pension Muche, refuses to alter the report card of a dumb pupil to please a rich mother and the headmaster of the school. He is discharged and is taken up by the city's biggest grafter. Discovering that he is being used as a dummy to rob the citizens, Topaze threatens to expose his employer, but decides to hold his tongue when he is given his degree as a Doctor of Moral Philosophy. The new honor so changes the character of Topaze that he immediately becomes a bigger grafter than his employer, and takes over both the latter's business and his mistress.

* THE LAST MILE

(140 performances)

A tragedy in three acts by John Wexley. Produced by Herman Shumlin at the Sam H. Harris Theatre, New York, February 13, 1930.

Cast of characters—

Fred Mayor.......................................Howard Phillips
Richard Walters.......................................James Bell
"Red" Kirby.......................................Hale Norcross
Vincent Jackson.......................................Ernest Whitman
Eddie Werner.......................................George Leach
Drake.......................................Don Costello
John Mears.......................................Spencer Tracy
O'Flaherty.......................................Herbert Heywood
Peddie.......................................Orville Harris
Principal Keeper Callahan.......................................Ralph Theadore
Harris.......................................Richard Abbott
Tom D'Amoro.......................................Joseph Spurin-Calleia
Father O'Connors.......................................Henry O'Neill
Evangelist.......................................Clarence Chase
Frost.......................................Bruce Macfarlane
Brooks.......................................Albert West

Act I.—Late May. It Is Evening. Act II.—Two Weeks Later. It Is Late Afternoon. Act III.—Six Hours Later. It Is Night. The Scene Is the Death-House of the Keystone State Penitentiary at Keystone, Oklahoma.

Staged by Chester Erskin.

See page 175.

THE INFINITE SHOEBLACK

(80 performances)

A drama in three acts by Norman MacOwan. Produced by Lee Shubert at the Maxine Elliott Theatre, New York, February 17, 1930.

Cast of characters—

Andrew Berwick.......................................Leslie Banks
Lizzie.......................................Molly McIntyre
Ralph Mayne.......................................Donald Blackwell
Mrs. Willis.......................................Essex Dane
Mary.......................................Helen Menken

Dr. Ralston....................................Norman MacOwan
Brig. General Driver..............................Walter Plinge
Egyptian Waiter..................................Taeb-Boucari
A.V.A.D..Mary Roth
A Nurse..................................Elisabeth Upthegrove
1st R.F.A. Officer............................Oswald Marshall
2nd R.F.A. Officer..........................Victor Barrington
An Australian Officer..........................Michael Stark
A French Infantry Officer....................Joseph Romantini
A French Artillery Officer.....................Roman Arnoldoff
A French Girl....................................Anne Linwood
1st Infantry Officer..............................Arthur Gilmore
2nd Infantry Officer.........................Clement O'Loghlen
R.F.C. Officer...............................Philip Cary Jones
Capt. Chesney.................................Robert Harrigan
A.P.M..Robert Donaldson
Mrs. Smart...............................Frances Ross Campbell

Act I.—Edinburgh March, 1914. Act II.—Cairo, June, 1916. Act III.—Edinburgh, 1920.

Staged by Leslie Banks and Norman MacOwan.

Andrew Berwick, a poverty stricken honor student in Edinburgh, preparing for his actuary examinations, is asked to trade examination papers with a failure, for a sum of money. Andrew spurns the bribe heatedly, until he finds a fainting lady on his doorstep and falls in love with her. Her name is Mary, and she is fleeing from her professorial father's house because she is tired of being educated and wants to live, live, live. To save Mary's life, Andrew takes the bribe money and sends her into Spain. When next they meet, the second year of the war, Mary is living in sin with a general in Cairo. Andrew fights to reclaim her soul, wins her to marriage, motherhood and respectability, and then loses her when she dies following the birth of her baby.

* APRON STRINGS

(136 performances)

A comedy in three acts by Dorrance Davis. Produced by Forrest C. Haring at the Bijou Theatre, New York, February 17, 1930.

Cast of characters—

John Olwell.......................................Frank Monroe
Hester...Josie Intropidi
Mrs. Olwell.......................................Maidel Turner
Inez Wakefield...................................Ethel Intropidi
Barbara Olwell......................................Audray Dale
Daniel Curtis.......................................Roger Pryor
Ezra Hunniwell..............................Jefferson De Angelis

Acts I, II and III.—In the Olwell Living Room in a Thriving Metropolis Within Motoring Distance of Chicago.

Staged by Earle Boothe.

Daniel Curtis, a most upright young man, has been brought up and carefully guarded by his mother, Pansy Pomeroy, who ran a column of advice for many readers. When she dies she arranges that her influence shall live after her by leaving a letter covering every probable major event in his life to be delivered to him by the executor of her estate. When Daniel marries he reads the letter on marriage and thereafter treats his bride with such tender solicitude that she runs away from him, insisting that he is a fish. Daniel follows and, after his attorney has succeeded in getting one or two drinks of liquor into him, asserts his manhood and reclaims his wife.

THE COUNT OF LUXEMBOURG

(16 performances)

A musical comedy by Willner and Bodansky, adapted by Glen MacDonough; music by Franz Lehar. Produced by the Jolson's Theatre Musical Comedy Company at the Jolson Theatre, New York, February 17, 1930.

Cast of characters—

Pierre....Hobson Young
Juliette....Trudy Mallina
Raymonde....Carl Dewes
Anatole Brissard....J. Chas. Gilbert
Foyot....Clif Heckinger
Nicolai....Maurice Holland
Coralie....Helen Cowan
Sidonie....Alice O'Donnell
Count of Luxembourg....Roy Cropper
Mentschikoff....Ralph Brainard
Pelegrin....Ivan Arbuckle
Paulovitch....Chas. Carver
Grand Duke Rutzinoff....Florenz Ames
Angele Didier....Manila Powers
Registrar....Hobson Young
Fanchot....Frances Baviello
Mimi....Wee Griffin
Princess Kokozeff....Elizabeth Crandall

Act I.—Brissard's Studio in the Latin Quarter, Paris. Act II.—Reception Room. Palace of the Grand Duke.

Staged by Milton Aborn.

MEI LAN-FANG

(41 performances)

China's greatest actor in a series of one-act plays selected from his extensive repertory. Directed by F. C. Coppicus for the China Institute of America at the Forty-ninth Street Theatre, New York, February 17, 1930.

Première program—

"The Suspected Slipper," a story of the T'ang dynasty.

Duel scene from "Green Stone Mountain," a play of the Ming dynasty.

"The End of the 'Tiger' General," a story from the Ming dynasty.

"The Ruse of the Empty City," from "The Three Kingdoms," Han dynasty.

"The King's Parting with His Favorite," a play of the Ts'in dynasty.

Miss Soo Yong, mistress of ceremonies.

SIMPLE SIMON

(135 performances)

A musical comedy by Ed Wynn and Guy Bolton; music by Richard Rodgers; lyrics by Lorenz Hart. Produced by Florenz Ziegfeld at the Ziegfeld Theatre, New York, February 18, 1930.

Cast of characters—

Bert Blue (Bluebeard)	Paul Stanton
Fingy	Alfred P. James
Jack Horner / Gilly Flower (Jack and Jill)	Will Ahern / Bobbe Arnst
Simon	Ed Wynn
Policeman	Anthony Hughes
Elaine King (Cinderella)	Doree Leslie
Olee King (King Cole)	Lennox Pawle
Otto Prince	Hugh Cameron
Jonah (Genii)	Master George Offermann
Popper	Gil White
Tony Prince (Prince Charming)	Alan Edwards
Telescope Operator	Benn Carswell
Sal	Lee Morse
Jewel Pearce	Helen Walsh
Gladys Dove	Hazel Forbes
Captain in Dullna Army	Douglas Stanbury
The Horse	Joseph Schrode / Pete La Della
The Giant Head	Frank De Witt
The Frog	William J. Ferry
Premiere Danseuse	Harriet Hoctor
Miss Hazel	Hazel Forbes
The Hostess	Helen Walsh
The Hat Saleslady	Marion Dodge
The Perfumery Girl	Vila Milli
The Photography Girl	Blanche Satchel
The Soda Fountain Girl	Caja Eric
The Manicure Girl	Mildred Ivory
Nona Goyne	Virginia McNaughton
Little Boy Blue	Mary Coyle
Red Riding Hood	Helen Walsh
Wolff	Clementine Rigeau / Elaine Mann
Goldylocks	Agnes Franey / Virginia McNaughton
Puss in Boots	Patsy O'Day
Hansel	Elsie Behrens
Gretel	Mabel Baade
Jazz	Bobbe Arnst
Cat and the Fiddle	Marie Conwal
Cow	Gladys Pender
Dog	Dorothy Patterson

Dish..Lois Peck
Spoon...Neva Lynn
Bo-Peep...Dolores Grant
Old Lady in the Shoe....................................Frieda Mierse
Miss Muffet...{Georgia Payne
Caja Eric}
The Fairy Goddesses.....................................{Blanche Satchel
Marion Dodge}
Snow Queen..Pirkko Alquist
Rapunsel..Hazel Forbes

Act I.—Scene 1—Coney Island. Scene 2—Ferrymen Alley. Scene 3—The Boundary Line Between Dullna and Gaylreia. Scene 4—The Hunting Room in King Cole's Palace. Scene 5—The Forest at Christmas. Scene 6—The Fairyland Ball. Act II.—Scene 1—The Corner Drug Store in Dullville (Chief Village of Dullna). Scene 2—Outside the Walled City. Scene 3—The Kissing Forest. Scene 4—Inside the Citadel of King Otto's Palace. Scene 5—Ferryman Alley.

Staged by Zeke Colvan; dances by Seymour Felix.

Simon, a simple-minded news dealer in Coney Island, sells papers but doesn't read them. He much prefers fairy stories. Thus it happens that one night when he is poring over his favorite book he sleeps and dreams of exciting adventures with all his Mother Goose heroes and heroines.

THOSE WE LOVE

(77 performances)

A drama in three acts by George Abbott and S. K. Lauren. Produced by Philip Dunning at the John Golden Theatre, New York, February 19, 1930.

Cast of characters—

Julia Aiken...Madaleine King
Eloise Hart...Natalie Potter
Clifford Aiken..John Stokes
Valerie Parker..Helen Flint
Frederick Williston.....................................George Abbott
Jake..Percy Kilbride
May Williston...Armina Marshall
Rickie..Edwin Phillips
Evelyn..Josephine Hull
Mr. Blake...Charles Waldron
Helen...Elizabeth Taylor
Ashton Copeland...G. Albert Smith
Bertie Parker...Franklyn Fox
Daley...Joseph Crehan
A Stranger..J. Ascher Smith

Acts I, II and III.—In the Willistons' Home in Westchester.
Staged by George Abbott.

Frederick and May Williston, he a writer, she a composer, weather the hard years of their marriage successfully. When their son, Rickie, goes to boarding school, they separate temporarily for the good of their work. During one such separation, Mr. Williston flirts mildly with Valerie Parker. Mrs. Williston, making certain suspicious discoveries, gives Mr. Williston a chance to explain, which he eludes by lying. Mrs. Williston thereupon leaves him. This time the Valerie Parker attraction proves too strong to resist. Afterward Williston is remorseful, but Mrs. Williston is unforgiving, until Rickie's future is threatened. Then there is a hopeful adjustment.

THE PLUTOCRAT

(101 performances)

A comedy in three acts by Arthur Goodrich, based on Booth Tarkington's novel of the same name. Produced by Mr. and Mrs. Coburn at the Vanderbilt Theatre, New York, February 20, 1930.

Cast of characters—

Albert Jones.................................Theodore St. John
Luigi..James Moore
Lawrence Ogle...............................Fairfax Burgher
Mrs. Tinker..................................Ivah Wills Coburn
Olivia Tinker...................................Emily Graham
Madame Momoro..............................Suzanne Caubaye
Hyacinthe Momoro..............................John Brewster
Earl Tinker...........................Charles Douville Coburn
Mr. Wackstle................................William R. Randall
Mr. Weatherwright..................................Lark Taylor
"Doc" Taylor...Billy Fay
Sir William Broadfeather.........................Walter Edwin
Lady Broadfeather..................................Iseth Munro
Cayzac..Armand Cortes
A Waiter..John Gray
Prince Karno....................................James La Curto

Act I.—Smoking Room of S.S. *Duumvir*. Acts II and III.—Balcony Room in Hotel at Bindar on the Edge of the Sahara.
Staged by Charles Coburn and Arthur Goodrich.

Earl Tinker, an Omaha packer, taking the Mediterranean tour with his wife and daughter, behaves after the manner of the boastful American business man of fiction, is modestly vamped by Mme. Momoro, a French woman, and comes through the experience with his moral principles and his heart of gold intact. Miss Tinker, starting the trip with a lively loathing for Lawrence Ogle, a snobbish New York playwright, ends by becoming engaged to marry him.

THE APPLE CART

(88 performances)

A political extravaganza in three acts by George Bernard Shaw. Produced by the Theatre Guild at the Martin Beck Theatre, New York, February 24, 1930.

Cast of characters—

Pamphilius....................................Thomas A. Braidon
Sempronius....................................Rex O'Malley
Boanerges, President of the Board of Trade.........Ernest Cossart
Magnus, the King....................................Tom Powers
Alice the Princess Royal..........................Audrey Ridgewell
Proteus, Prime Minister............................Claude Rains
Nicobar, Foreign Secretary.......................Morris Carnovsky
Crassus, Colonial Secretary.......................George Graham
Pliny, Chancellor of the Exchequer...................John Dunn
Balbus, Home Secretary..........................William H. Sams
Lysistrata, Powermistress-General................Helen Westley
Amanda, Postmistress-General................Eve Leonard-Boyne
Orinthia.....................................Violet Kemble Cooper
The Queen.....................................Marjorie Marquis
Mr. Vanhattan, the American Ambassador.......Frederick Truesdell

Act I.—Office in the Royal Palace. Act II.—(An Interlude) Orinthia's Boudoir. Act III.—The Terrace of the Palace. Time—The Future.

Staged by Philip Moeller.

Magnus, King of England, finds himself in conflict with his progressive cabinet, led by the Prime Minister. The cabinet demands that Magnus shall relinquish the right of veto. His Majesty, much the superior of his ministers in debate, defeats their argument but bows to their power. He will, he agrees, abdicate the throne. But he will also, as a private citizen, continue to fight them. He will stand for Parliament from Windsor. Rather than face this potentially disturbing situation, the ministers withdraw their demands.

THE INTERNATIONAL REVIEW

(95 performances)

A revue in two parts by Nat N. Dorfman and Lew Leslie; music and lyrics by Dorothy Fields and Jimmy McHugh. Produced by Lew Leslie at the Majestic Theatre, New York, February 25, 1930.

The principals—

Gertrude Lawrence	Harry Richman
Florence Moore	Jack Pearl

Argentinita	Anton Dolin
Moss and Fontana	Jans and Whalen
Bernice and Emily	Radaelli
Esther Muir	Robert Conche
Livia Marracci	Berinoff and Eulalie
Rosemary Deering	Robert Hobbs
McCann Sister	Richard Ryan
Babe La Valle	Chester Hale Girls

Staged by Lew Leslie and E. C. Lilley; dances by Busby Berkeley, Harry Crosley.

GALA NIGHT

(15 performances)

A comedy in three acts by Laurence Eyre. Produced by Hunter Williams at Erlanger's Theatre, New York, February 25, 1930.

Cast of characters—

Max....Mortimer Browning
Rudi Telcs....Robert E. Lowes
Pierre Durand....Louis Rousseau
Naliv....Demetrius Vilan
Zita....Josephine Schlenk
Mme. Karpovna....Madge Lacey
Mme. Vincini....Harriet Wood
Mlle. Clement....Maida Clewley
Fogarisi....Charles Carey
Toros....Cyril Charles
Arpad Panna....George MacEntee
Intendant Andrassy....George Lessey
Luti Bender....Desiree Tabor
Drina Andrassy....Eve Cassanova
Czinka Lazzlo....Jules Epailly
Stefi....Frank Garletts
Paval Zala....James Rennie
Heinrich Stolzer....France Bendtsen
Irma Lazzlo....Adele Klaer
Mitzi Stolzer....Beverly Bayne
Waiter....Charles La Torre
Assistant Waiter....Frank Taylor
Maritska....Ethel Porter
Nicholas....George Hoyt

Acts I and III.—Salon of the Suite Assigned to the Conductors of the Opera House. Act II.—Paval Zala's Apartment.
Staged by Joseph Mullen.

Paval Zana, a popular tenor at the opera, is pursued by so many women his adventures become farcical. He finally eludes them all but Irma Lazzlo.

THE SEA GULL

(5 performances)

A drama in three acts by Anton Chekhov. Revived by the Leo Bulgakov Associates at the Waldorf Theatre, New York February 25, 1930.

Cast of characters—

Masha....Dorothy Yokel
Simeon Medvedenko....Ian Wolfe
Constantine Treplev....Lewis Leverett
Peter Sorin....E. J. Ballantine
Yakov....Boris Marshalov
Nina Zarechny....Barbara Bulgakova
Paulina....Elza Lazareff
Dr. Dorn....Carroll Ashburn
Irina Arkadina....Mary Morris
Shamraev....Victor Kilian
Boris Trigorin....Walter Abel
Housemaid....Evelyn Hill
Cook....Robert Parsons

Act I.—In the Park of Sorin's Estate. Act II.—The Lawn in Front of Sorin's House. Act III.—Dining Room in Sorin's House. Act IV.—A Room in Sorin's House.

* THE GREEN PASTURES

(125 performances)

A fable play by Marc Connelly. Produced by Laurence Rivers, Inc., at the Mansfield Theatre, New York, February 26, 1930.

Cast of characters—

Mr. Deshee....Charles H. Moore
Myrtle....Alicia Escamilla
First Boy....Jazzlips Richardson, Jr.
Second Boy....Howard Washington
Third Boy....Reginald Blythwood
Randolph....Joe Byrd
A Cook....Frances Smith
Custard Maker....Homer Tutt
First Mammy Angel....Anna Mae Fritz
A Stout Angel....Josephine Byrd
A Slender Angel....Edna Thrower
Archangel....J. A. Shipp
Gabriel....Wesley Hill
The Lord....Richard B. Harrison
Choir Leader....McKinley Reeves
Adam....Daniel L. Haynes
Eve....Inez Richardson Wilson
Cain....Lou Vernon
Cain's Girl....Dorothy Randolph
Zeba....Edna M. Harris
Cain the Sixth....James Fuller
Boy Gambler....Louis Kelsey
First Gambler....Collington Hayes
Second Gambler....Ivan Sharp
Voice in Shanty....Josephine Byrd
Noah....Tutt Whitney
Noah's Wife....Susie Sutton
Shem....Milton J. Williams
First Woman....Dinks Thomas
Second Woman....Anna Mae Fritz
Third Woman....Geneva Blythwood
First Man....Emory Richardson
Flatfoot....Freddie Archibald
Ham....J. Homer Tutt
Japheth....Stanleigh Morrell
First Cleaner....Josephine Byrd
Second Cleaner....Florence Fields
Abraham....J. A. Shipp

Isaac.....Charles H. Moore
Jacob.....Edgar Burks
Moses.....Alonzo Fenderson
Zipporah.....Mercedes Gilbert
Aaron.....McKinley Reeves
A Candidate Magician.....Reginald Fenderson
Pharaoh.....George Randol
The General.....Walt McClane
First Wizard.....Emory Richardson
Head Magician.....Arthur Porter
Joshua.....Stanleigh Morrell
First Scout.....Ivan Sharp
Master of Ceremonies.....Billy Cumby
King of Babylon.....Jay Mondaaye
Prophet.....Ivan Sharp
High Priest.....J. Homer Tutt
The King's Favorites.....Leona Winkler, Florence Lee, Constance Van Dyke, Mary Ella Hart, Inez Persand
Officer.....Emory Richardson
Hezdrel.....Daniel L. Haynes
Another Officer.....Stanleigh Morrell

Part I.—Scene 1—Sunday School. 2—A Fish Fry. 3—A Garden. 4—A Roadside. 5 and 6—A Private Office. 7—Another Roadside. 8—A House. 9—A Hillside. 10—A Mountain Top. Part II.—Scene 1—Private Office. 2—Mouth of a Cave. 3—Throne Room. 4—Foot of a Mountain. 5—A Cabaret. 6—Private Office. 7—Outside a Temple. 8—Another Fish Fry.

Staged by Marc Connelly.

See page 33.

* FLYING HIGH

(122 performances)

A musical comedy in two acts by B. G. DeSylva, Lew Brown and John McGowan; music by DeSylva, Brown and Henderson. Produced by George White at the Apollo Theatre, New York, March 3, 1930.

Cast of characters—

Eileen Cassidy.....Grace Brinkley
Bunny McHugh.....Pearl Osgood
Tod Addison.....Oscar Shaw
Gordon Turner.....Henry Whittemore
Tim.....Bob Lively
Judy Trent.....Dorothy Hall
"Sport" Wardell.....Russ Brown
Pansy Sparks.....Kate Smith
"Rusty" Krause.....Bert Lahr
Major Watts, M.D.....Fred Manatt
Mr. Henry.....Robert Lewis
Mr. Charles.....Jack Bruns
The Gale Quadruplets.....Jane, Jean, Joan and June

Act I.—Scene 1—Roof of an Apartment House in Manhattan. 2—In Front of the Apartment House. 3—Canteen at Newark Airport. 4—Medical Examiner's Office. 5—Flying Field. 6—In Front of the Canteen. Act II.—Scene 1—Waiting Room at the Newark Airport. 2—Outside the Waiting Room. 3—An Anteroom. 4—In Front of Major Watts' Office. 5—Flying Field at Midnight. 6—Flight.

7—In Front of the Reception Hall. 8—Reception Hall at the Flying Field.

Staged by Edward Clark Lilley; dances by Bobby Connelly.

Tod Addison, an ace among the mail flyers, hopes to break a record of one kind, or perhaps another, but while his ship, primed and loaded, is at rest, his mechanic, "Rusty" Krause, crawls into the pilot's seat and starts off. Thereafter Rusty is kept in the air long past record time, because he doesn't know how to bring the ship to earth. Eventually, meaning near the close of the evening, Tod manages to fly for a record, and thus is able to marry Eileen Cassidy, whom he met when he landed on a New York roof in the first act.

MARCO MILLIONS

(8 performances)

A comedy by Eugene O'Neill. Revived by the Theatre Guild at the Liberty Theatre, New York, March 3, 1930.

Cast of characters—

Christian Traveller....Vincent Sherman
Magian Traveller....Sanford Meisner
Buddhist Traveller....Martin Wolfson
A Mohammedan Captain....Albert Van Dekker
A Corporal....Harry Wise
Princess Kukachin, Granddaughter of Kublai....Sylvia Field
Marco Polo....Earle Larimore
Donata....Helen Tilden
Tedaldo, Paal Legate to Acre....Louis Veda
Nicolo, Marco's Father....Frederick Roland
Maffeo, Marco's Uncle....Harry Mestayer
A Dominican Monk....Walter Coy
A Knight Crusader....Philip Foster
A Papal Courier....Sydney Little Mansfield
One Ali Brother....Harry Wise
Older Ali Brother....Martin Wolfson
Prostitute....Therese Guerini
A Dervish....John Henry
An Indian Snake Charmer....John Henry
A Buddhist Priest....Vincent Sherman
Chamberlain....Philip Foster
Kublai, the Great Kaan....Sydney Greenstreet
Chu-Yin, a Cathayan Sage....Henry Travers
Boatswain....Albert Van Dekker
Ghazan, Kaan of Persia....Sanford Meisner
Donata's Father....John C. Davis
Messenger from Persia....Paul Yost
A Buddhist Priest....Vincent Sherman
A Taoist Priest....Francis Ward
A Confucian Priest....Harry Wise
A Moslem Priest....Thomas Mackay

Staged by Rouben Mamoulian.

See "The Best Plays of 1927-28."

THE SERENADE

(15 performances)

A musical comedy by Harry B. Smith; music by Victor Herbert. Produced by Jolson's Theatre Musical Comedy Company at the Jolson Theatre, New York, March 4, 1930.

Cast of characters—

The Duke of Santa Cruz.....Forrest Huff
Dolores.....Lorna Doone Jackson
Alvarado.....Greek Evans
Romero.....Charles E. Galagher
Lopez.....Roy Cropper
Colombo.....John Cherry
Inez.....Olga Steck
Gomez.....William White
The Colonel.....Hobson Young
Captain Anselmo.....Carl Dews
Senora Valdez.....Elizabeth Crandall
Isabella.....Wee Griffin
Juana.....Frances Baviello

Acts I and III.—Duke's Castle in the Mountainous Region of Spain. Act II.—Senora Valdez School for Girls and Barracks of Spanish Dragoons.

Staged by Milton Aborn.

THE PLAYERS FROM JAPAN

(15 performances)

A repertory from the modern Japanese theatre adapted and directed for the American stage by Michio Ito. Produced by the Japanese Theatre Association at the Booth Theatre, New York, March 4, 1930.

Cast of characters in "Koi-No-Yozakura"—

Kanebo.....Issaku Izumi
Hiyakashi.....{ Hidichi Iwata / Yaisuke Kikuchi }
Anma.....Koryo Yamada
Yopparai.....Kiyoshi Mimasu
Tsujura Uri.....Miss Sumako Okada
Shinnai Nagashi.....Chozo Onada
Jingoro.....Hajime Mori
Tuwa.....Tokujiro Tsutsui
Nagoya.....Minoru Yamanaka
Murasame Tayu.....Miss Kazue Ueno
Takao Tayu.....Miss Tsuyako Misono
Konohana Tayu.....Miss Momoyo Chigusa
Yakko.....Miss Sumiko Susuki
Haha.....Koryo Yamada
Kanjotori.....Tokuji Tsuji
Jingoro.....Hajime Mori
Ningyo.....Miss Momoyo Chigusa

Staged by Michio Ito.

The opening bill of the Japanese players consisted of three short plays, "Koi-No-Yozakura" (Romance in Cherry Blossom Lane), "Kage-No-Chikara" (The Shadow Man), and "Matsuri" (Festival). The first tells of a poor sculptor who worships a handsome Geisha girl, and, being unable to afford her, makes a life-sized statue of her which comes to life in his barn-like studio. The second is a drama of the Samurai, in which Chuji, son of an honored warrior killed by the Lord of the Province for daring to speak to him without permission, is taught by Enzo, the Shadow man, how to fight so that he may later avenge his father's death and the abduction of his sweetheart. The third is a holiday festival in ancient Tokio.

A GLASS OF WATER

(9 performances)

A comedy in three acts by Eugene Scribe. Produced at the Laboratory Theatre, New York, March 5, 1930.

Cast of characters—

Queen Anne of England..........................Maria Germanova
Lady Churchill, Duchess of Marlborough..............Emily Floyd
Henry St. John, the Viscount Bolingbroke..........Charles Kradoska
Arthur Masham......................................Britton Diller
Abigail Churchill................................Angela Mulinos
The Marquis de Torcy (Ambassador of Louis XIV)..Richard Gaines
Thompson..Karl Swenson
Lady Albemarle.................................Frances Williams
Lord Harley, Earl of Oxford........................William Post
Lady Abercrombie..................................Elaine Howe

Acts I, II and III.—The Action Takes Place in London, in St. James' Palace.
Staged by Maria Germanova.

A duel of wits at the court of Queen Anne of England in which Bolingbroke and the Duchess of Marlborough play principal rôles and romantic Queen Anne thinks she is desperately in love with Arthur Masham, who unfortunately prefers Abigail.

LAUNCELOT AND ELAINE

(25 performances)

A dramatization of the Tennyson "Idyll" by Edwin Milton Royle. Revived by Round Table Productions, Inc., at the President Theatre, New York, March 8, 1930.

Cast of characters—

Sir Gawain....................George Christie
Sir Modred....................Albert Phillips
Sir Launcelot....................Frank M. Thomas
Prince Arthur....................J. W. Austin
Voice of Lyonesse....................Sara Perry
Lady Margaret....................Ann Anderson
Lady Vivian....................Marie Chambers
Lady Ysolde....................Helen Oursler
Lady Beatrice....................Myrta Bellair
Lady Rosmond....................Prunella Bodkin
Queen Guinevere....................Selena Royle
Dumb Servitor....................Harold Vizard
Sir Lavain....................Sherling Oliver
Sir Torre....................Adin Wilson
Elaine....................Josephine Royle
Lord Astolat....................Charles Hammond
Hermit....................Lionel Adams

Prologue—Glen in the Trackless Wastes of Lyonesse. Act I.—Queen's Garden in King Arthur's Court. Acts II and III.—Courtyard of the Castle of the Lord of Astolat. Act IV.—Sunken Garden of Arthur's Palace.

Staged by Calvin Thomas.

See "The Best Plays of 1921-22."

THIS MAN'S TOWN

(8 performances)

A drama in three acts by Willard Robertson. Produced by George Jessel at the Ritz Theatre, New York, March 10, 1930.

Cast of characters—

Tom....................Paul Byron
Swede....................Arvid Paulson
Buck....................Willard Robertson
Cleo....................Betty Brenska
Hazel....................Mary Howard
Doctor....................Max Von Mitzel
Bill Post....................Pat O'Brien
A Marine....................Clyde Franklin
A Sailor....................Harold Morgan
A Salvation Army Worker....................Caroline Newcombe
George....................Jethro Warner
Ida Anders....................Viola Frayne
Murphy....................Edwin Stanley
Felice Pelangio....................Antonio Salerno
Antonio Fantana....................Eduardo Ciannelli
Eddie Anders....................Walter Glass
Peanuts....................Vincent Yorke
Havanna....................Jerome Lesser
Carrie....................Constance Cummings
Mack....................George Neville
McKenna....................Walter Newman
Pete....................Joseph Slayton
Ben....................Joseph Kennedy
Dot....................Dorothea Scott
Jean....................Eugenia A. Herman
Gypsie....................Lulu Stone
Georgie....................Betty de Pascue
Clara....................Marjorie Main

Gus....................Emmett Shakelford
Fitz....................William E. Morris
Lieutenant of Police....................Len D. Hollister
Wagner....................Lewis Gordon
Rosso....................Samuel Levine
Medical Examiner....................W. L. Douglas
Rooney....................John Burkell
Babe....................Lois Shore
Smith....................Milton C. Herman
Connor....................Charles C. Wilson

Acts I, II and III.—In and Around a Lunch Wagon.
Staged by Lester Lonergan.

Eddie Anders, framed by Antonio Fantana, dope peddler and proprietor of the Ritz Diner, does his stretch in prison and, getting out, calls on Fantana for a settlement. It is New Year's eve and Fantana, in addition to his other worries, is arranging for the bumping off of a detective or two. There are three murders during the evening, including that of Fantana. When he refuses to settle with Anders, the boy shoots him. Bill Post, reporter, working on the story, fixes it so Anders goes free.

PENNY ARCADE

(24 performances)

A drama in three acts by Marie Baumer. Produced by William Keighley and W. P. Tanner at the Fulton Theatre, New York, March 10, 1930.

Cast of characters—

Bum Rogers....................Ackland Powell
George....................Don Beddoe
Mrs. Delano....................Valerie Bergere
Angel....................Eric Dressler
Happy....................Millard F. Mitchell
Joe Delano....................Paul Guilfoyle
Mitch McKane....................Frank Rowan
Sikes....................George Barbier
Myrtle....................Joan Blondell
Harry Delano....................James Cagney
Jenny Delano....................Lenita Lane
Nolan....................Martin Malloy
Dugan....................Ben Probst
Dick....................Harry Gresham
Mabel....................Desiree Harris
Fred....................Jules Cern
Vivian....................Annie-Laurie Jaques
Mr. James....................Edmund Norris
Rose....................Lucile Gillespie
Jim....................John J. Cameron
Anna....................Eleanor Andrus
Bob....................Marshall Hale
Jack....................William Whitehead
Johnson....................Harry Balcom

Acts I, II and III.—In and Around Mrs. Delano's Penny Arcade in an Amusement Park Near New York.
Staged by William Keightley.

Angel, working for Mrs. Delano in a turn-the-crank picture exhibit in an amusement park, is in love with Jenny, the Delano daughter. Jenny's brother Harry, trying to be a bootlegger, has a run-in with Mitch McKane, racketeer, and shoots McKane. Jenny is witness to her brother's act and keeps quiet until Mrs. Delano tries to pin the crime on Angel. Then Jenny protests and justice is done.

THE BLUE GHOST

(112 performances)

A mystery comedy in three acts by Bernard J. McOwen and J. P. Riewerts. Produced by Jimmie Cooper at the Forrest Theatre, New York, March 10, 1930.

Cast of characters—

Dr. De Former.............................Bernard J. McOwen
Mr. Gray.............................Leslie King
Jasper.............................Nate Busby
Inspector Wise.............................Douglas Cosgrove
Frank Host.............................King Calder
Florence Waller.............................Lyle Stackpole
The Stranger.............................Stephen Clark
Acts I, II and III.—Home of Dr. De Former on Harlan Cliff—Somewhere in California.
Staged by Stephen Clark.

Murder has been done and practically everybody's hair has been standing on end in the castled home of Dr. De Former. The periodical appearances of a Blue Ghost are responsible. Inspector Wise goes out to investigate. His discoveries reveal the comic fear of Jasper, a Negro servant, and the fact that Dr. De Former and Frank Host love the same leading woman. It is proved conclusively in the end that Jasper has been drinking.

VOLPONE

(8 performances)

A comedy in three acts adapted by Stefan Zweig from the original of Ben Jonson. Revived by the Theatre Guild at the Liberty Theatre, New York, March 10, 1930.

Cast of characters—

1st Servant.............................Burton McEvilly
2nd Servant.............................Martin Wolfson
3rd Servant.............................Sydney Little Mansfield

Singer....Vincent Sherman
Singer....Paul Yost
Singer....Donald Smith
Singer....Walter Franklyn
Mosca (The Gadfly)....Earle Larimore
Volpone (The Fox)....Sydney Greenstreet
Slave....John Henry
Voltore (The Vulture)....Frederick Roland
Corvino (The Crow)....Henry Mestayer
Corbaccio (The Raven)....Edgar Kent
Canina....Helen Tilden
Colomba (The Dove)....Sylvia Field
Maid to Colomba....Lucille Banner
Servant to Corbaccio....John C. Davis
Leone, Captain to the Fleet (The Lion)....Albert Van Dekker
Captain of Sbirri....Philip Foster
Sbirri....George Cotton, Walter Coy, Alan Blaine, Donn Sylvester, Harry Wise, Thomas Mackey, Clifford Odets, Fred De Veau
Judge....Sanford Meisner
Judge's Clerk....Lucian Scott
Court Attendant....Vincent Sherman
Court Attendant....Francis Ward
Priest....John C. Davis

Act I.—Volpone's Bedroom. Act II.—Scene 1—Corvino's House. 2—Corbaccio's House. 3—Volpone's Bedroom. Act III.—Scene 1—Audience Chamber of the Senate. 2—Volpone's Bedroom.

Staged by Philip Moeller.

See "The Best Plays of 1927-28."

LOVE, HONOR AND BETRAY

(45 performances)

A drama in three acts adapted by Fanny and Frederic Hatton from the French of A. Antoine. Produced by A. H. Woods at the Eltinge Theatre, New York, March 12, 1930.

Cast of characters—

The Young Man....Robert Williams
The Husband....Mark Smith
The Woman....Alice Brady
The Lover....Clark Gable
The Doctor....Wilton Lackaye
The Chauffeur....George Brent
The Young Girl....Glenda Farrell

Act I.—Scene 1—Cemetery. 2—Living Room. Act II.—Scenes 1 and 3—Cemetery. 2—Living Room. 4—"The Love Nest." Act III.—Cemetery.

Staged by Don Mullaly.

The shades of the three men principally concerned with the love life of one woman arise in a cemetery and grow reminiscent. One is a boy who had killed himself when the woman had jilted him. One is the fat millionaire she married. He died of shock when she threatened to return to him after spending some time with her lover. One is the lover in question who is completely done in physically by her impassioned devotion to him. The woman is decorating all three graves and trying to take a broad-shouldered chauffeur away from her daughter at the play's end.

THE RIVALS

(28 performances)

A comedy in three acts by Richard Brinsley Sheridan. Revived by George C. Tyler at Erlanger's Theatre, New York, March 13, 1930.

Cast of characters—

Sir Anthony Absolute....................John Craig
Captain Jack Absolute....................Rollo Peters
Faulkland....................Pedro De Cordoba
Bob Acres....................James T. Powers
Sir Lucius O'Trigger....................Fiske O'Hara
Fag....................Percival Vivian
David....................George Tawde
Thomas....................Dann Malloy
Mrs. Malaprop....................Mrs. Fiske
Lydia Languish....................Margery Maude
Julia Melville....................Betty Linley
Lucy....................Georgette Cohan

Act I.—Scene 1—A Street in Bath. 2—Dressing Room in Mrs. Malaprop's Lodgings. 3—Captain Absolute's Lodgings. Act II.—Scene 1—North Parade. 2—Mrs. Malaprop's Lodgings. 3—Acres' Lodgings. Act III.—Scenes 1 and 3—Mrs. Malaprop's Lodgings. 2—North Parade. 4—King's Mead Fields.

Staged by Harrison Grey Fiske.

A revival made noteworthy principally by the fact that Mrs. Fiske appeared for the first time in New York as Mrs. Malaprop, although she had played the part on tour for four or five years.

A MONTH IN THE COUNTRY

(71 performances)

A comedy by Ivan Turgenev. Produced by the Theatre Guild at the Guild Theatre, New York, March 17, 1930.

Cast of characters—

Herr Shaaf....................Charles Kraus
Anna Semenova....................Minna Phillips
Natalia Petrovna....................Alla Nazimova
Mikhail Aleksandrovich Rakitin....................Elliot Cabot
Lizaveta Bogdanovna....................Eda Heinemann
Kolia....................Eddie Wragge
Aleksei Nikolaevich Bieliaev....................Alexander Kirkland
Matviei....................Louis Veda
Ignati Ilich Spigelski....................Dudley Digges
Viera Aleksandrovna....................Eunice Stoddard

Arkadi Sergieich Islaev........................John T. Doyle
Katia..Hortense Alden
Afanasi Ivnych Bolshintsov....................Henry Travers

Acts I and III.—The Drawing Room. Acts II and IV.—The Garden. 1840.

Staged by Rouben Mamoulian.

Natalia Petrovna, grown restless through contemplation of her dull husband and a dull routine on his estate, accepts gratefully the platonic love offered by her husband's good friend, Mikhail Rakitin, but is not stirred by it. When, however, her eyes first rest upon the new tutor engaged for her son, one Aleksei Bieliaev, she realizes that romance has at last come to Russia. When her young ward, Viera, also falls in love with Aleksei, Natalia is furiously jealous. But when she finally confesses her passion to Aleksei, the boy embarrassedly admits that he is greatly honored, but decides he had better run right back to Moscow. Which he does. Mikhail also leaves. And Natalia resumes the dull routine of her life.

THE ROYAL VIRGIN

(8 performances)

A drama by Harry Wagstaffe Gribble. Produced by W. P. Tanner at the Booth Theatre, New York, March 17, 1930.

Cast of characters—

Robert Cecil, Lord Burleigh......................Murray Kinnell
Sir Walter Raleigh..............................Charles Francis
A Gentleman.....................................Milton Parsons
The Countess of Nottingham......................Veree Teasdale
Henry, Earl of Southampton......................Wilfrid Seagram
Elizabeth, Queen of Great Britain and Ireland........Thais Lawton
The Countess of Rutland.........................Vivienne Osborne
Robert Devereux, Earl of Essex....................Hugh Buckler
A Gentlewoman...................................Marcia Hanan
A Gentlewoman...................................Nancy De Silva
Lieutenant of the Tower..........................Milton Parsons

Act I.—Scene 1—Anteroom. 2—Council Chamber. Act II.—Scene 1—Garden. 2—Queen's Boudoir. 3—Audience Chamber. Act III.—Scene 1—Queen's Boudoir. 2—Tower of London. 1601.

Staged by Harry Wagstaffe Gribble.

A drama fashioned by Mr. Gribble from John Banks' play, "The Earl of Essex, or the Unhappy Favorite," (1682); and two later versions done by Henry Brooke and Henry Jones (1748). Loosely follows the historical episodes of the fall of Essex as Elizabeth's favorite, culminating in his being sentenced to death, with Elizabeth's discovery of his secret marriage to the Countess of Rutland as a motivating jealousy. Elizabeth repents and would pardon Essex at the last, when she discovers that she has been tricked by her messenger, the Countess of Nottingham, but her pardon arrives too late.

MAYFAIR

(8 performances)

A drama in three acts by Laurence Eyre. Produced by Richard Herndon at the Belmont Theatre, New York, March 17, 1930.

Cast of characters—

Atkins....................Stapleton Kent
Stanislaus....................Hugh Millar
Mr. William Danvers....................Arthur Hohl
Gregory Muir....................Derek Glynne
Rosamund, Lady Clarges....................Chrystal Herne
"Bertie" Lord Clarges....................Frederick Worlock
Evie Traynor....................Elaine Temple

Acts I and III.—Boudoir of Lady Clarges. Act II.—Cabin on Lord Clarges' Private Yacht.
Staged by Laurence Eyre.

Lord Clarges, more in love with his career than with his wife, would sacrifice her to William Danvers if necessary in order to control Danvers' influence in the appointment of a new ambassador to Rome. Lady Clarges, however, prefers to give her favors to Gregory Muir, an under secretary, and thus deliberately fails her husband and sees him carted back to his former post in Peru.

THE MATRIARCH

(23 performances)

A drama in three acts by G. B. Stern. Produced by Lee Shubert at the Longacre Theatre, New York, March 18, 1930.

Cast of characters—

Sophie Maitland....................Paula Sabina
Mrs. Mitchell....................Violet Ley
Oliver Maitland....................Hesketh Pearson
Anastasia (The Matriarch)....................Constance Collier
Wanda Rakonitz....................Inez Bensusan
Toni Rakonitz....................Jessica Tandy
Simson....................E. A. Walker
Susan Rakonitz....................Georgina Wynter
Danny Maitland....................Derrick De Marney
Val Power....................Dorothy Dunkels
Maximilian Rakonitz....................Earle Grey
Otto Solomonson....................Albert V. Edwards
Louis Rakonitz....................George Cross
Felix Rakonitz....................Alan Keith

Elsa Rakonitz.................................Laura Smithson
Isaac Cohen.................................Abraham Sofaer
Gerald Rakonitz.................................Henry Lewis, Jr.
Prologue—1902: Cottage in Cornwall. Acts I and II.—1921: Drawing-room in Holland Park. Act III.—1927: Studio in Chelsea.
Staged by Frank Vernon.

Sophie Maitland, childless representative of the Rakonitz family, adopts the illegitimate son of her vagabond husband, Oliver Maitland, and presents him to her mother, Anastasia Rakonitz, the matriarchal head of the family, as her own. Twenty years later Danny Maitland has been accepted as a Rakonitz and is about to be inducted into the jewelry business when the family fortunes crash. Thereafter the younger generation of the Rakonitz family come through to take charge. In the end Toni, keenest of the girls, forswears a budding desire to marry Danny, now known as a Gentile and a Maitland, to become "the new Matriarch."

I WANT MY WIFE

(12 performances)

A comedy by B. M. Kaye. Produced by Murray Phillips at the Liberty Theatre, New York, March 20, 1930.

Cast of characters—

Parker.................................Jerome Collamore
Dr. Pemberton.................................Edward Fielding
Miss Mathilde Macaulay.................................Marion Abbott
Mrs. Cecelia Bordon.................................Spring Byington
Janet Macaulay.................................Patricia Barclay
Hartley Rossiter.................................Alan Davis
Farquhar Yoots.................................Gerald Oliver Smith
Alfred Towder.................................Herbert Yost
Mrs. Fairchild.................................Gladys Lloyd
Act I.—Living Room in Mrs. Bordon's House in New York. Acts II and III.—Living Room in Alfred Towder's House. Scarsdale, New York.
Staged by Ralph Murray.

Cecelia Bordon's brother Alfred, having suffered one attack of amnesia that kept him in Philadelphia for three weeks, is susceptible to psychic influences. Alfred is also heir to a million dollars if he marries within a certain period. Cecelia, having met a psycho-theorist, is convinced that if she can implant the marriage idea in Alfred's mind, before she puts him to sleep with a powder, he will wake up in love with Janet Macaulay. The scheme is tried and it works. Alfred is finally convinced. Then another girl appears from Philadelphia with a marriage certificate. She had married Alfred during his previous lapse.

HAMLET

(5 performances)

A repertory of Shakespeare's plays. Revived by the Chicago Civic Shakespeare Society at the Shubert Theatre, New York, March 24, 1930.

Cast of characters—

Claudius, King of Denmark....................William Courtleigh
Hamlet..Fritz Leiber
Horatio..John Burke
Polonius...Philip Quin
Laertes.....................................Lawrence H. Cecil
Rosencrantz..................................Thayer Roberts
Guildenstern...................................Grant Gordon
Osrick.......................................Charles Desheim
Marcellus.......................................Robert Allen
Bernardo......................................Ralph Menzing
Francisco....................................Wilfred Mallory
A Grave-Digger...............................Robert Strauss
Another Grave-Digger..........................Claudius Mintz
First Player..................................James Neill, Jr.
Second Player................................Charles Desheim
A Priest.....................................Wilfred Mallory
Ghost of Hamlet's Father..........................Hart Jenks
Gertrude, Queen of Denmark..................Virginia Bronson
Ophelia...Marie Carroll
Player Queen......................................Vera Allen

Scene—Denmark, Near the Castle of Elsinore.

MACBETH

(4 performances)

Cast of characters—

Duncan, King of Scotland..........................John Burke
Malcolm...Robert Allen
Donalbain....................................Charles Desheim
Macbeth...Fritz Leiber
Banquo...Hart Jenks
Macduff....................................William Courtleigh
Lennox.......................................Wilfred Mallory
Ross..Lawrence H. Cecil
Fleance...Marie Carroll
Seyton..Ralph Menzing
A Doctor...Philip Quin
A Sergeant....................................James Neill, Jr.
A Porter.......................................Robert Strauss
A Murderer.....................................Thayer Roberts
Another Murderer..............................Claudius Mintz
First Witch.....................................John Forrest
Second Witch..................................Kathryn Collier
Third Witch..................................Virginia Stevens
A Gentlewoman.....................................Vera Allen
Lady Macbeth................................Virginia Bronson

Scene—In Scotland: and Chiefly at Macbeth's Castle.

TWELFTH NIGHT

(2 performances)

Cast of characters—

Orsino, Duke of Illyria....Hart Jenks
Sebastian....Grant Gordon
Antonio....John Burke
A Sea Captain....Ralph Menzing
Curio....Charles Desheim
Valentine....Robert Allen
Sir Toby Belch....Lawrence H. Cecil
Sir Andrew Ague-Cheek....James Neill, Jr.
Malvolia....Fritz Leiber
Fabian....Robert Strauss
Clown....Thayer Roberts
First Officer....Wilfred Mallory
Second Officer....Claudius Mintz
Olivia....Kathryn Collier
Viola....Vera Allen
Maria....Virginia Bronson
Plays Staged by Fritz Leiber.

During this engagement Mr. Leiber and his associates also revived "The Merchant of Venice," "Taming of the Shrew," "Richard III," "King Lear," "As You Like It," "Twelfth Night" and "Julius Cæsar."

THE OLD RASCAL

(72 performances)

A comedy by William Hodge. Produced at the Bijou Theatre, New York, March 24, 1930.

Cast of characters—

Frederic Tipperman....Edmund Dalby
Olga Kimble....Margaret Mullen
Harry Allen....David Morris
Julia May....Judith Windsor
Eddie Afburn....Donald Kirke
James Hart....Douglas Wood
Mrs. Joe Adams....Alice Fisher
Alfred Ledge....Hermann Lieb
William Prigman....John Martin
Joe Adams....William Hodge
Photographer....Maurice Barrett
Effie Ames....Francez Dumas
Acts I, II and III.—Reception Room of Joe Adams' Suite in a Prominent New York Hotel.
Staged by Maurice Barrett.

Joe Adams, retired jurist, angry with the crusading Mrs. Adams because she has smashed up his wine cellar in the West, comes to New York with a spree and eventual marital freedom in mind.

Mrs. Adams, planning to forestall her husband's advantage, precedes him to the wicked city, falls in with crooked lawyers and pays $50,000 to have her husband compromised, in order that the divorce testimony may favor her. Joe, in New York, gets tight, is doped by his valet, who is one of the gang, and passes out. The conspirators bring in a brunette in pajamas who gets into bed with Joe, and a photograph is taken. Next morning old Joe is considerably surprised to find his bed crowded. He is variously threatened by the blackmailers but is smart enough to outwit them and a compromise of sorts with Mrs. Adams follows.

DEAR OLD ENGLAND

(23 performances)

A satirical farce in three acts by H. F. Maltby. Produced by E. F. Bostwick, Inc., at the Ritz Theatre New York, March 25, 1930.

Cast of characters—

Foreword	Jack Soanes
Lady Shoreham	Gladys Hanson
Mrs. Kirkpatrick	Kitty Bingham
Lord Tottenham	Reginald Carrington
Lady Tottenham	Violet Besson
Ursula Shoreham	Mary Vance
Mr. Burrows	Edward Rigby
Mr. Raky	Tracy Barrow
Hector Burrows	Reginald Sheffield

Acts I, II and III.—The Home of Lady Shoreham, Somewhere on the Sussex Downs, Not a Thousand Miles from Brighton.
Staged by E. F. Bostwick.

Following the Great War, many aristocratic English families were literally dispossessed. Many took cover wherever they could find it. On waste land in Sussex a village grew up containing, among others, Lady Shoreham, her daughter Ursula, and a goat, and Lord and Lady Tottenham living in abandoned tram cars. Ursula Shoreham, accepting a position as scullery maid at the Towers, the ancient Shoreham home, attracts the son of the bounder Burrows, who has bought the place. Young Burrows insists on rescuing the aristocratic Cinderella and finally succeeds.

MAURICE CHEVALIER

(18 performances)

A recital of songs by the French Disseur. Presented by Charles Dillingham at the Fulton Theatre, New York, March 30, 1930.

I.—Duke Ellington and His Cotton Club Orchestra. Introducing Henry Wetzel and Alias Berry in Their Harlem Dance Specialties. Mr. Ellington Will Play a Program of Selections from the Following Numbers in Impromptu Rotation: "Awfully Sad," "Mississippi Dry," "St. Louis Blues," "Black Beauty," "When You're Smiling," "Dear Old Southland," "Jas O'Mine," "The Mooche," "Swampy River," "East St. Louis Toodle," "Come Along, Mandy," "Liza."

II.—Eleanor Powell, Dancing Star from "Follow Thru."

III.—Maurice Chevalier, in a Program of His Songs in French and English.

HOUSE AFIRE

(16 performances)

A comedy in three acts by Mann Page. Produced by Arthur Fisher at the Little Theatre, New York, March 31, 1930.

Cast of characters—

Mary Ogden	Florence Earle
John Ogden	John Hazzard
"Doc"	William B. Mack
Ann Elliott	May Collins
Willie	John Hazzard, Jr.
Mrs. Geo. Humphrey	Beatrice Colony
Mrs. Baxter	Marie Haynes
Miss Davis	Doris Freeman
George Humphrey	Earle Mitchell
Walter Elliott	Charles Laite
Chief Herb Brown	Chas. W. Ritchie
Betty Morrison	Betty Blythe
Billy Morrison	William McFadden
Telka	Virginia Dawe

Acts I and III.—Ogden Home in Rockport, New Jersey. Act II.—Elliotts' Apartment in Town.

Staged by Clifford Brooke.

Ann Elliott has no love of the country. Her husband, Walter, is fond of gardens, lawn mowers and such, but Ann much prefers to live in the city where there is life. Therefore Ann is pleased when the Elliott suburban home burns down. In town she spends most of the insurance money for new gowns and gay times. Then the insurance company, grown suspicious, seeks her arrest as an incendiary. Looks tough for Ann until the fire is charged and proved against another.

BROADWAY SHADOWS

(16 performances)

A comedy in three acts by Willard Earl Simmons. Produced by Theatres Productions, Inc., at the Belmont Theatre, New York. March 31, 1930.

Cast of characters—

Mary Weston....................................Lucille Fenton
Richard Alan...................................Howard St. John
Dapper Jim Weston..............................Leo Dawn
Mickey Dugan...................................Frank H. Fey
Camille De Varville............................Madja Torre
Mrs. Roberta Ross..............................Adele Gilbert
Sneaky...Jack Goodman
Marge Gray.....................................Linda Carlon
Sylvia Fenton..................................Alfreda Sill
John Douglas Alan..............................Lawrence C. Phillips
Lois Weston....................................Baby Marie Polizzotto
Ruby Hudson....................................Mona Zavin

Acts I, II and III.—Furnished Apartment in the West Seventies.
Staged by W. E. Simmons.

Richard Alan, in a jam at home over a raised check, runs out and rents himself an apartment in the seventies. Meets Mary Weston, whose husband is an ex-convict. Richard marries Mary in spite of everything. Jim, the convict, comes back, threatening everybody, but is shot in the back by one of Mary's girl friends, who has heard there is a reward on Jim's head, dead or alive. Which makes everything fine and dandy for somebody.

TROYKA

(15 performances)

A drama in three acts adapted by Lulu Vollmer from the Hungarian of Imre Fazekas. Produced by Laura D. Wilck at the Hudson Theatre, New York, April 1, 1930.

Cast of characters—

The Captain....................................Weldon Heyburn
Natascha.......................................Zita Johann
Ivan...Albert Van Dekker
1st Soldier....................................William Parke
Semion...Jack Roseleigh
Avinov...Philip Leigh
Izeff..George Casselberry
Selivenoff.....................................Ray Earles
Bogulieff......................................Martin Noble
Koska..Lewis Milne
Bolotoff.......................................George Bratt
Vassely..Frank Dae
Pushkin..Eugene Brominski
Gustoff..William G. Edwards
Sienko...William House
2nd Soldier....................................Tony Mack
Kuroff...Edward Hartford
Dymov..Walter Dreher
A Man..Mel Tyler

Acts I, II and III.—Semion's Cabin in the Prison Camp on the island of Sakhalin, Siberia.
Staged by Lemist Esler.

Natascha, an orphan on the island of Sakhalin, Siberia, is adopted by one of the prisoners, Semion. Later Semion and

Natascha live together, with Ivan as a cabin mate. Ivan also loves Natascha, but being an honest doctor of philosophy he denies his love until the revolution frees all prisoners. Then Ivan tries to get Semion to go back to his wife and children in Moscow and leave Natascha to him. Semion, now realizing that Natascha is his true mate, refuses to go. Whereupon Semion and Ivan fight, Semion is killed and Natascha runs away with a Russian army captain. Life certainly is full of surprises.

THEY NEVER GROW UP

(24 performances)

A comedy in three acts by Humphrey Pearson. Produced by the New York Theatre Assembly at the Theatre Masque, New York, April 7, 1930.

Cast of characters—

Martha Ware....................................Kathryn March
Maud Holbrook..................................Anne Sutherland
Emma...Florence Auer
Peter Holbrook.................................Edwin Maynard
Andrew Ware....................................Otto Kruger
Hawley...Claude Cooper
Joe Santano....................................Edward Colebrook
Tonia Cordoba..................................Mary Fowler
Haggerty.......................................H. H. McCollum
Gannon...Jack Bennett
Major Peeler...................................George Le Soir

Act I.—Scene 1—Corner of the Library in the Home of Andrew Ware in San Diego. 2—Barroom of Cantina de Santano, Tecade, Mexico. Acts II and III.—Living Room of Andrew Ware's Ranch House in the Cuyamaca Mountains of Southern California.

Staged by Walter Greenough.

Andrew Ware, a big business success in his thirties, grows fearfully weary of making frying pans and growing rich. Cursed with a nagging wife, he craves romance and adventure, reads western cowboy stories to and with his chauffeur, and finally runs away from a bridge tea at home across the line into old Mexico. There he meets Tonia Cordoba, deportee, who is trying to get back into the States. Andrew agrees to help Tonia and ends by falling in love and running away with her to South America, after the nagging Mrs. Ware has agreed to divorce him.

JONICA

(40 performances)

A musical comedy in two acts by Dorothy Heyward and Moss Hart; music by Joseph Meyer; lyrics by William Moll. Produced by William B. Friedlander at the Craig Theatre, New York, April 7, 1930.

Cast of Characters—

A Nun....Julia Baron
The Abbess....Mabel Gore
Jonica....Nell Roy
A Woman....Clara Thropp
Millie....Dorothy Murray
Benjamin Flood....Bert Matthews
A Pullman Porter....Charles Doyle
A Pullman Conductor....Larry Beck
Barney Morton....Earle S. Dewey
Fanchon....Joyce Barbour
Mr. Burdick....George S. Shiller
Don Milan....Jerry Norris
Officer Quinn....Harry T. Shannon
Mary Alice....June O'Dea
Mrs. Emma Ross-Benton....Madeline Gray
A Butler....Larry Beck
Orchestra Leader....Ralph Hertz
Betty....Priscilla Gurney
Peggy....Ruth Goodwin
Mabel....Irene Swor
A Dancer....Pal'mere Brandeaux
A Dancer....Mlle. Daudet
Peter....Jack Stillman
Wilma and Earlyne....Wallace Sisters

Act I.—Scene 1—Room in a Convent Near Buffalo, N. Y. 2—A Railroad Station. 3—Interior of a Sleeping Car. 4—Plaza of the Berkerley Apartments, New York. 5—Barney Morton's Apartment. Act II.—Sun Parlor of Mrs. Ross-Benton's Home, "Whippoorwill Lodge," in Connecticut.

Staged by William B. Friedlander; dances by Pal'mere Brandeaux.

Jonica leaves the convent to travel alone to New York, where she is to be an attendant at the wedding of her friend, Mary Alice. On the train Jonica's experiences include meeting a drunken fat man and a lively show girl named Fanny. It happens, not unexpectedly, that both have something to do with the wedding party and that the bachelor dinner for the groom and the final rehearsals for the wedding are both scheduled to take place at the home of Mrs. Ross-Benton in Connecticut. The editor cannot remember just why. Finally it appears that Don Milan is the groom's best man and that he has loved Jonica for years and years, if not longer.

LIVE AND LEARN

(5 performances)

A drama by Lincoln Kalworth. Produced by Michael Kallesser at Wallack's Theatre, New York, April 9, 1930.

Cast of characters—

Harold Fuller.......................................Alden Chase
Mabel Fuller.......................................Lois Jesson
Mrs. Donnelly.......................................Selma Hall
Dorothea Robinson.......................................Felicia Howard
Frederick Manning.......................................Ned Reese
Annette Roberts.......................................Beatrice Nichols
Mr. Robinson.......................................William S. James
Taxi Driver.......................................Richard Curtis
Acts I, II and III.—"Love-Bird Bungalow," Leonia, New Jersey.
Staged by Richard Irving.

Harold Fuller eloped with Mabel three days before she was to make her début as a concert singer and finds himself at the end of three years a bit fed up with her strict economies and domestic ambitions. Soon Harold acquires the habit of inviting Annette Roberts, a model, out to the house for a series of gin parties. Mabel rebels and leaves. Harold marries Annette. A few years later, after Mabel has had a fine success as a singer in Europe, she returns to find Harold and Annette breaking up the furniture. She buys Annette off and gets Harold started right again, because, as she explains, he is the only baby she ever had.

* HOTEL UNIVERSE

(72 performances)

A psychological drama in one act by Philip Barry. Produced by the Theatre Guild at the Martin Beck Theatre, New York, April 14, 1930.

Cast of characters—

Pat Farley.......................................Glenn Anders
Tom Ames.......................................Franchot Tone
Hope Ames.......................................Phyllis Povah
Lily Malone.......................................Ruth Gordon
Alice Kendall.......................................Ruthelma Stevens
Norman Ross.......................................Earle Larimore
Ann Field.......................................Katherine Alexander
Felix.......................................Gustave Rolland
Stephen Field.......................................Morris Carnovsky
Two Hours Upon the Terrace of a House in the South of France, Near Toulon.
Staged by Philip Moeller.

A party of American friends are visiting Ann Field, who has been nursing a slightly demented father in a villa on the shores of the Mediterranean near Toulon. Grown depressed and moody, partly by reason of the strangeness of the place, which at one time was a small hotel about which legends of strange happenings had grown up, partly by the recent suicide of a young boy they all had known well, the party becomes severally and individually introspective. Finally, inspired by the strange visionings of Ann's father, each is carried back in memory to certain outstanding happenings in his or her youth. The adventures serve to clear their several minds and return the party to a normal outlook.

* THREE LITTLE GIRLS

(72 performances)

A musical comedy in three acts by Herman Feiner and Bruno Hardt-Warden; adapted by Marie Hecht and Gertrude Purcell; music by Walter Kollo; lyrics by Harry B. Smith. Produced by the Messrs. Shubert at the Shubert Theatre, New York, April 14, 1930.

Cast of characters—

THE PROLOGUE, 1846

Wendolin....................................Charles Brown
Attendant....................................Tom Houston
Baron Von Rankenau....................................Edward Lester
Beate-Marie....................................Natalie Hall
Baron Von Biebitz-Biebitz....................................Raymond Walburn
Count Von Rambow....................................John Goldsworthy
Hendrik Norgard....................................Charles Hedley

THE PLAY—ACT I.—1868—Additional Characters

Mrs. Munke....................................Lorraine Weimar
Kunz....................................Stephen Mills
Otto Kunz....................................Harry Puck
Beate....................................Natalie Hall
Marie....................................Bettina Hall
Annette....................................Martha Lorber
Karl Norgard....................................Charles Hedley
Fritz Von Tormann....................................Rollin Grimes
Franz Walden....................................George Dobbs

ACT II

Von Hoffenstein, Chamberlain to H.S.H. Prince Von Hochberg
Raymond O'Brien
H.S.H. Prince Von Hochberg....................................Tom Houston

ACT III.—1880

Charlotte.................................... Thelma Goodwin
Little Marie....................................Frances Hess
Little Hans Norgard....................................Buddy Proctor
Mademoiselle....................................Mary Bell
Marie....................................Margaret Adams
Elsa....................................Lillian Lane
Hans Von Kursten....................................John Edwards
Mme. Morrosini....................................Bettina Hall
Escamillo....................................Cario Ferretti

Staged by J. J. Shubert.

Beate-Marie and Hendrik Norgard, who love each other, are separated in 1846. Beate-Marie is forced to marry Count Von Rambow to save the family fortunes. In 1868 Beate, daughter of

Beate-Marie, and Karl, son of Hendrik, meet and love but are also separated. Love, however, triumphs.

* UNCLE VANYA

(71 performances)

A comedy by Anton Chekhov, as adapted by Rose Caylor. Produced by Jed Harris at the Cort Theatre, New York, April 15, 1930.

Cast of characters—

Marina....................Kate Mayhew
Michael Astroff....................Osgood Perkins
Ivan Voinitski (Uncle Vanya)....................Walter Connolly
Sonia....................Joanna Roos
Alexander Serebrakoff....................Eugene Powers
Ilya Telegin....................Eduardo Ciannelli
Helena....................Lillian Gish
Mme. Voinitskaya....................Isabel Vernon
A Servant....................Harold Johnsrud

Act I.—The Garden of the Serebrakoffs' Country Estate. Acts II and III.—In the House. Act V.—Vanya's Study.
Staged by Jed Harris.

See "The Best Plays of 1928-29."

VIRTUE'S BED

(71 performances)

A comedy drama in three acts by Courtenay Savage. Produced by Lohmuller and Emery, Inc., at the Hudson Theatre, New York, April 15, 1930.

Cast of characters–

Sonia....................Czara Romanyi
May....................Audree Workman
Lucia....................Dorothy Diane
Madame Delange....................Vera G. Hurst
Hamid....................Sarat Lahiri
Major Harry Austin....................Robert Strange
Eileen Gregory....................Ara Gerald
Casey....................Doris Covert
Hilary Benson....................A. J. Herbert
Jenkins....................Joseph Greene
Madame Clara Northrup....................Camilla Crume
The Honorable Patricia Walls....................Shirley Gale
Winnie St. Johns....................Valerie Dade
Sir Eric Ramsey....................J. Kerby Hawkes
Alice Chamberlain....................Ethel Remey
Donald Chamberlain....................Albert Hayes

Act I.—Roof of Madame Delange's House, North Africa. Acts II and III.—Eileen Gregory's House, Near London.
Staged by Jo Graham.

Eileen Gregory, lured into a life of shame, and shipped to North Africa, continues in that profession until she inherits a considerable sum of money. Then, bent on becoming respectable, she goes to London and succeeds in establishing herself in society. Everything lovely until Major Harry Austin, old admirer and patron of Eileen's, turns up and exposes his old friend's deceit. Eileen faces the scandal, tells her virtuous friends what she thinks of them and their ways, and gives up her social position, with the Major standing more or less nobly by.

LADY CLARA

(28 performances)

A comedy in three acts by Aimee and Philip Stuart. Produced by the Messrs. Stuart at the Booth Theatre, New York, April 17, 1930.

Cast of characters—

Tudor....................Roland Hogue
Earl of Drumoor....................T. Wigney Percival
Countess of Drumoor....................Lenore Chippendale
Justin Kerr....................Stuart Casey
Clara Gibbings....................Florence Nash
Yolande Probyn....................Nora Swinburne
Errol Kerr....................Terence Neill
Mr. Gallagher....................John Gray
Acts I, II and III.—The Sitting Room of Errol Kerr's Flat, in St. James', London.
Staged by Rollo Wayne.

Clara Gibbings discovers, on the death of her mother, that she (Clara) is the illegitimate daughter of the Earl of Drumoor. Clara has been brought up as a barmaid and her mother, who owned several public houses, has left her a considerable sum of money. She has social ambitions, however, and conceives the scheme of forcing Errol Kerr, a nephew of the Earl of Drumoor, to marry her to stop a family scandal she otherwise will uncover. Errol agrees, under protest, and the family is ready to accept Clara. Seeing how sporting they are she hasn't the heart to insist and goes back to her own class.

PENAL LAW 2010

(19 performances)

A drama in three acts by Alexander Gerry and Augusta Greely. Produced by Alexander Gerry at the Biltmore Theatre, New York, April 18, 1930.

Cast of characters—

Roger Stuart, Jr. .... Frank Milan
Roger Stuart, Sr. .... John MacFarlane
Montague Williamson .... Maynard Burgess
Raymond Miller .... Spencer Kimbell
Dora Sandrey .... Janet McLeay
Thomas Mason .... Cecil Holm
Lenora Wharton .... Helene Mitchell
Margory Wharton .... Jean Colbert
Lucy Van Dam .... Gertrude Flynn
Miriam Andrews .... Tululah Westley
Maid .... Gertrude Perry
Mrs. Sandrey .... Florence Pendleton
Peter Dawson .... Worthing Romaine
1st Attendant .... Richard Brandlon
2nd Attendant .... Abraham Gillette
Court Clerk .... Jud Langill
Court Stenographer .... Irving Morrow
D.A.'s Assistant .... Ranald Savery
District Attorney Hendricks .... Anthony Baker
Judge Hawley .... Albert C. Henderson
Mrs. Mason .... Brita Heurlin

Act I.—Scene 1—Home of the Stuarts in Westchester, New York. 2—Roger Stuart's Bedroom. Act II.—Same as Scene 1, Act I. Act III.—Trial Term of the Criminal Court in New York County.
Staged by Augusta Greely.

Roger Stuart, Jr., is a rising young lawyer. He has just won his first important case by convicting a man on circumstantial evidence. In the Stuart home, in Westchester, Dora Sandrey is one of those pretty parlor maids who, in the theatre, either have been or are about to be seduced. The chauffeur, a married man, is guilty in this instance, but Dora accuses Roger, the young master. Because Dora is under 18, Roger is arrested, tried and convicted, also on circumstantial evidence, at which moment both the chauffeur and Dora's real age are exposed.

DORA MOBRIDGE

(9 performances)

A drama in three acts by Adeline Leitzbach. Produced by Louis Isquith at the Little Theatre, New York, April 19, 1930.

Cast of characters—

Ellin Mobridge .... Florence Gardner
Dora Mobridge .... Louise Carter
George Hartley .... Allen B. Nourse
Herbert Mobridge .... Jack Halliday
Will Mobridge .... Halliam Bosworth
Judge Barrett .... Joseph Eggenton
Alice Barrett .... Alice Davenport
Mrs. Hartley .... Isabelle Winlocke
Mr. Thomas .... Hamilton Christy
Dr. Bryce .... Bruce Morgan
Mr. Wallace .... Thomas M. Reynolds
Madam Van Doran .... Maude Richmond

Acts I, II and III.—Dora Mobridge's Home, Glendale, N. J.
Staged by J. Kent Thurber.

Dora Mobridge, a generous and helpful friend and neighbor, is highly respected and greatly loved in the town of Glendale, N. J., until she inherits $400,000 and, in order to get the money, is obliged to admit that she was a foundling and was brought up by the landlady of a house of ill repute in Milwaukee. Despite her fine record, Glendale turns against Dora. So does her only begotten son. But she has the money and brighter prospects at the play's end.

SIR HARRY LAUDER

(9 performances)

Annual trans-continental tour of the Scotch comedian. Under the direction of William Morris. At the Jolson Theatre, New York, April 21, 1930.

Mr. Lauder's selection of songs was made from the appended list:

"Flower of the Heather"
"I Love a Lassie"
"When I Get Tae Scotland"
"Roaming in the Gloaming"
"Ta! Ta! Ma Bonnie Maggie Darlin' "
"Waggle o' th' Kilt"
"Saftest o' th' Family"
"The End of the Road"
"She's Ma Daisy"
"Nice t' Get Up in th' Morning"
"Hame o' Mine"
"When I Meet McKaye"
"Just Got Off th' Chain"
"Somebody's Waiting for Me"
"Doughie the Baker"
"Cronies o' Mine"

Acts from vaudeville included in the Lauder program: Eno troupe of Japanese jugglers; Fitzgerald and Hoag, "The Hollywood Horse"; Stella Powers, prima donna; Arnaut Brothers, "Two Loving Birds," and Don Julian, continental cartoonist.

ROMEO AND JULIET

(16 performances)

A tragedy by William Shakespeare. Revived by the Civic Repertory Theatre, Inc., at the Civic Theatre, New York, April 21, 1930.

Cast of characters—

Escalus, Prince of Verona....................Jacob Ben-Ami
Paris....................Blake Scott
Montague....................Harold Moulton
Capulet....................Walter Beck
An Old Man....................Joseph Kramm
Romeo....................Donald Cameron

Mercutio....................................J. Edward Bromberg
Benvolio....................................Robert F. Ross
Tybalt....................................Robert H. Gordon
Friar Lawrence....................................Sayre Crawley
Friar John....................................Joseph Kramm
Balthasar....................................Arnold Moss
Samson....................................Herbert Shapiro
Gregory....................................Robert Lewis
Peter....................................Burgess Meredith
Abraham....................................Lee Hillery
An Apothecary....................................Howard da Silva
Page to Capulet....................................Amy Chandler
Page to Paris....................................Gordon Wallace
Page to Mercutio....................................Vernon Jones
An Officer....................................David Turk
Lady Montague....................................Mary Ward
Lady Capulet....................................Merle Maddern
Juliet....................................Eva Le Gallienne
Nurse to Juliet....................................Leona Roberts
1st Watchman....................................Henry Howard
2nd Watchman....................................Robert Lewis
3rd Watchman....................................David Kerman
Drummers....Burgess Meredith, Gordon Wallace, Mooney Diamond
Pages—May Sarton, Virginia Stevens, Mooney Diamond, Burgess Meredith, Gordon Wallace, William Steinhorn
Dancers—Florida Friebus, Renee Orsell, Irene Sharaff, Ruth Wilton, Estelle Scheer, Lee Hillery, Frederick Giuliano, Henry Howard

Act I.—Scene 1—Public Place in Verona. 2—Street. 3—Capulet's House. Act II.—Scene 1—Capulet's Orchard. 2—Outside Friar Lawrence's Cell. 3—Street. 4—Capulet's Garden. 5—Outside Friar Lawrence's Cell. 6—Public Place. Act III.—Scene 1—Friar Lawrence's Cell. 2—Hall in Capulet's House. 3—Balcony, Juliet's Room. 4—Friar Lawrence's Cell. 5—Hall Capulet's House. 6—Juliet's Room. Act IV.—Scene 1—Hall in Capulet's House. 2—Juliet's Room. 3—Street in Mantua. 4—Outside Friar Lawrence's Cell. 5—Churchyard; in it a Monument Belonging to the Capulets. Scene—Verona and Mantua.

Staged by Eva La Gallienne.

A slightly altered acting version, in which certain scenes, notably that at the end of the play, which frequently has been cut following the death of Juliet, are restored.

LITTLE ORCHID ANNIE

(16 performances)

A comedy in three acts by Hadley Waters and Charles Beahan. Produced by Myra Furst at the Eltinge Theatre, New York, April 21, 1930.

Cast of characters—

Ruth Davis....................................Jane Allen
Oswald Reynolds....................................Franz Bendtsen
Madge King....................................Kitty Kelly
Vi Mudgeon....................................Leona Maricle
Bud Condon....................................Spencer Bentley
Evelyn Walsh....................................Mary Murray
Daniel Michael Paul Flynn....................................James Norris
Madame Elaine....................................Maude Odell
Annie Westlake....................................Betty Lawrence

George Graham.............................Walter Davis
Myron C. Kuppenheimer.....................Frank Wilcox
Mrs. Flynn................................Jane Corcoran
Blanche...................................Lois Parker
Harry Clifford............................Eddie Dean
Patrick O'Connell.........................Robert B. Williams

Act I.—Showroom in the Wholesale Dress House of Madame Elaine, Inc. Act II—Annie's Duplex Apartment. That Night. Act III—The Same. Christmas Morning. Time—Present.
Staged by Frederick Stanhope.

Annie Westlake, model, is neither very beautiful nor very dumb, but awfully appealing. Rich men vie with each other in trying to make her comfortable and happy. Georgie Graham gives her tips on Bethlehem Steel, Kuppy Kuppenheimer buys her jewels and Rolls-Royces. With the money she sends Danny Flynn to Yale. The night Georgie and Kuppy both decide to spend the night with Annie, Dan announces that he is really Annie's husband—and proves it. There is a fight; the police come, and Dan is ready to quit, until Annie convinces him that everything she has done has been for him.

ROOM 349

(15 performances)

A drama in three acts by Mark Linder. Produced by Loyalty Productions, Inc., at the National Theatre, New York, April 21, 1930.

Cast of characters—

Mr. Ripley................................Juan Villasana
Philip "Buffalo Phil" Spitzel.............Gordon Westcott
Louis "Speed" King........................Murray Alper
Archie "Buck" Bauman......................Dave Manley
Peter "Poker Pan" Tyler...................Larry Oliver
Myrtle....................................Shelly Claire
Jonesy....................................Charles H. Henderson
Hotel Manager.............................Wallace King
Lefty.....................................Richard Keith
Patricia Counahan.........................Lida Kane
Joseph "Sandy" Tully......................Jack Hartley
Sergeant McGillen.........................Walter Wilson
Bell Boy..................................David Hughes
Babette Marshall..........................Inez Norton
Toots Thornton............................Helen Shipman
Counselor Arthur Adler....................Richard Warner
District Attorney Farrell.................G. Swayne Gordon
Clerk of the Court........................George Spelvin
Judge William Gibbon......................Kirk Brown
Harold Stromberg..........................Roy D'Arcy
Frankie "Dago" Lombardi...................Clyde Veaux
Joe Curley................................Jos. H. Weber

Act I.—Scene 1—Corridor on the Third Floor of a New York Hotel. 2—Room 349. Act II.—Criminal Court. Act III.—Scene 1—Room 349. 2—Criminal Court.
Staged by Victor Morley.

Harold Stromberg, super-racketeer, has decided to marry Babette Marshall and get away from "all this," meaning gambling and drinking and the racket in general. That night he sits in a stud poker game in room 349, Royal Hotel, grows peevish when luck is against him; quarrels with one gunman who is put out of the game, and with a gambler who is left in. Stromberg is finally shot through the heart, apparently from the fire escape, and dies. The host of the evening ("Sandy" Tully) is accused of the murder, tried and acquitted and the killing remains as much of a mystery as that of Arnold Rothstein, which suggested the writing of the play.

* STEPPING SISTERS

(63 performances)

A farce comedy in three acts by Howard Warren Comstock. Produced by Albert Bannister at the Belmont Theatre, New York, April 22, 1930.

Cast of characters—

Herbert Ramsey....William Corrett
Cecilia Ramsey....Theresa Maxwell Conover
Norma Ramsey....Gertrude Moran
Lucile Dawson....Roselyn Harvey
Regina Chetworth-Lynde....Helen Raymond
Rose La Marr....Grace Huff
Jack Carleton....Frederic Tozere
Rev. Henry Chambers....George McEntee
Mrs. Henry Chambers....Margery Dalton
Mrs. Donaldson....Lorna Elliott
Teddy Donaldson....William Lynn
Mrs. Tremaine....Hope Landin
Jepson....Vernon G. Williams

Acts I, II and III.—Herbert Ramsey's Country Home, Near Patchogue, L. I.
Staged by Albert Bannister.

Cecilia Ramsey, Regina Chetworth-Lynde and Rose La Marr, were, in the old days, spear-toters in a variety of burlesque troupes. None of them is boasting about it today. Cecilia ("Cissie" to her intimates) is married to a wealthy Long Islander and her daughter Norma is doing nicely in society. Norma organizes a benefit and invites the volunteers to rehearse in her home. Then it is that Regina (who used to be Queenie) discovers Cissie. She promises, however, to say nothing. Then along comes Rose (was Rosie) and the worst is threatened. Turns out that Norma knew all the time about her mother and is not the least bit ashamed. In fact she is all set to marry an actor herself.

COURTESAN

(3 performances)

A drama in three acts by Irving Kaye Davis. Produced by Joseph Leone at the President Theatre, New York, April 29, 1930.

Cast—

Alice Trevor..Elsa Shelley
Unseen Characters involved in the Play—Marie, the Maid; Arthur Blandick Ross, Alice's Lover; Dot, Her Friend; Sergei Rikolnikoff, the Pianist; Marjorie Ross, Arthur's Daughter; John Stevens, Alice's ex-Husband; Tommy, Her Six-Year-Old Son; Jimmy McCoombs, Her ex-Lover; Levett, the House Detective
Acts I, II and III.—Alice Trevor's Suite in a New York Hotel.

A monologue in three acts in which the single character manages to translate her adventures with the aid of the telephone and by speaking to certain off-stage characters who never are required to reply. Miss Trevor, having lived with a man of some social distinction for years, is about to be introduced to the family. She leaves for the reception at the end of the first act, returns crushed and depressed at the beginning of the second; seeks understanding consolation from a musician with whom she has been flirting across the court; is made aware that the musician knows she is a kept woman; accepts his invitation to call; resents his acceptance of her on a professional basis; kills him and throws herself from her balcony rather than submit to arrest.

OH, PROFESSOR!

(2 performances)

A comedy in three acts by Edward W. Harris. Produced by the author at the Belmont Theatre, New York, May 1, 1930.

Cast of characters—

Rose..Mary Kay
Frances...Margery Swem
Charles...Wheeler Dryden
Prof. Robert Garati.................................Giuseppe Sterni
J. F. Merrill.......................................Frank Reyman
Joe Cummins...William E. Lemuels
Seth Rosen..Max Von Mitzel
Isabel..Maida Reade
Sam Pratzman..Knox Herold
Prof. E. W. Clark...................................Walter Cartwright
Acts I, II and III.—At the Home of Prof. Garati.
Staged by Giuseppe Sterni and Wheeler Dryden.

Professor Garati, unjustly accused of something or other, resigns his faculty position, marries his secretary, and lets her brother, who is proud of having been a seven-months' baby, invest his savings in a lotion business. The money is lost and the trusting professor is practically sunk when the seven-months' baby and his sister, by playing detective, expose the dean of the college as an adulterer and induce him to give Professor Garati another and a better job.

THE TRAITOR

(17 performances)

A drama in three acts by Charles H. Brown, based on Robert Louis Stevenson's "The Pavilion on the Links." Produced by Mr. Brown at the Little Theatre, New York, May 2, 1930.

Cast of characters—

Frank Cassilis....................................Frank Henderson
Beppo..Guglielmo D'Rosa
Donald...John Lott
Agnes......................................Vera Fuller-Mellish
Robert Northmour...............................Charles Penman
Clara Huddlestone..................................Don Currie
Bernard Huddlestone..............................Fuller Mellish
Acts I, II and III.—Northmour's "Pavilion on the Links" in Northern Scotland.
Staged by Maurice Barrett.

Bernard Huddlestone, a London financier, having gambled with the money belonging to the Italian Carboneri, of which he is a trusted agent, induces Robert Northmour to help him escape, with what is left, to the Northmour pavilion on the Scottish links. Northmour's price is the love of Clara Huddlestone. At the pavilion Clara meets and prefers Frank Cassilis. While the love conflict rages the Carboneri surround the pavilion. Huddlestone finally gives himself up and Northmour decides to go into Italy with the Carboneri. Which leaves practically everything swell for Cassilis and Clara.

LITTLE THEATRE TOURNAMENT

(7 performances)

Conducted by Walter Hartwig, in association with the Manhattan Little Theatre Club, Inc., for four cash prizes and the David Belasco Trophy emblematic of the Little Theatre championship of America, at the Waldorf Theatre, New York, the week of May 5, 1930.

MONDAY, MAY 5

The Make-Up Box Players of Hunter College, Manhattan, present "The Gods Are Wise," by Bryna Rachel Isaacs.

The Cast—

Frea, Lady in Waiting............................May Edelsack
Garulf, Prince of the Frisians, Son of Hildeburh.....Sylvia Herring
Hildeburh, Queen of the Frisians, Wife of Finn....Jeannette Dubin
Oddrun, Lady in Waiting......................Hortense Wittstein
Scene—The Queen's Bower not far from the Great Hall. Finnsburgh. Time—500 A.D.
Directed by Elizabeth-Vera Loeb.

The Central Players of the Central Branch Y.W.C.A., Manhattan, present "The Bridge," by Dorothy Blanchard.

The Cast—

Mrs. Joy..Billie Dunn
Anna Caldwell...............................Elizabeth Schreiber
Jean..Clara Buck
Martin Jackson................................Ben Hawthorne
Donald Joy.......................................Joe Moylan
Scene—A Summer Cottage. Time—Afternoon in the Early Autumn.

The Henry Players of the Playhouse of the Henry Street Settlement, Manhattan, present "The Sisters' Tragedy," by Richard Hughes.

The Cast—

Philippa, aged 28..............................Beulah Kashins
Charlotte, aged 19..............................Sarah Manney
Lowrie, aged 13................................Ruth Hamowitz
Owen, their brother..........................George B. Dowell
John, Charlotte's Fiancé.......................Nathan Hirsch
Scene—The Hall in the Sisters' Home, a Victorian House in the Welsh Hills on an Autumn Afternoon.
Play Staged Under the Direction of Eva M. Fry. Setting designed by Frederick H. Little.

The City College Players of Brooklyn present "The Will," by Sir James M. Barrie.

The Cast—

Mr. Devizes, Sr................................Sol Bloomberg
Robert, Jr., His Son..........................George Breivogel
Surtees, a Clerk.............................Edward R. Simkin
Mrs. Philip Ross...................................Sylvia Lee
Mr. Philip Ross..............................Henry Margulies
Sennet, a Clerk...............................Harry Feldman
Creed, a Clerk................................George Bursor
Scene—England. Time—The End of Queen Victoria's Reign, Then Edward VII's, Then George V's.
Directed by Harry Sikofsky.

TUESDAY, MAY 6

Staten Island Little Theatre, Staten Island, N. Y., present "Legend," by Philip Johnson.

The Cast—

Mrs. Reed..Eva Meyer
Mrs. Walters....................................Betty McCrum
The Rev. Mr. Fallows..........................Irving Hopkins
The Stranger.................................Charles Campion
Scene—Mrs. Reed's Cottage in a Fishing Village on the East Coast of England.
Director, Joseph Latham.

The Town Club Players of the Women's Town Club, Manhattan, present "Bursting the Barriers," by Benjamin Feiner, Jr.

THE ENGLISH MANNER

(After Somerset Maugham)

Sir Frederick..Dudley Brill
Butler..James Amster
Lady Susan..Helen Danzig
Scene—An English Drawing Room.

THE AMERICAN MANNER

(After Eugene O'Neill)

Joe, Conductor on the El..Nathan Fribourg
Jennie, His Wife..Rae Rawitser
Policeman..Harold Wineburgh
Expressman..Harry Walser
Scene—Front Room of a Third Avenue Flat.

THE ITALIAN MANNER

(After Sam Benelli)

Dalgheri..L. Lawrence Stearns
Page..Bessie Stearns
Olivia..Blanche Goldman
Ladies..{ Josephine Kops / Norma Kaufman
Another Page..Florence Curtis
Scene—Ante Room of an Italian Renaissance Banquet Room.
Directed by Benjamin Feiner, Jr., and Henrietta Kiper Morse.

The Association Players Stock Company of the 92nd Street Y.M.H.A., Manhattan, present "Seven Against One," by Maxine Finsterwald.

The Cast—

IN THE CABINET SCENE

Chase..F. Richard Wolff
Arthurs..Lee Bert
Samaris..Stanley A. Joseph
Pistoli..Maxwell Zerner
Bronson..Howard Carde
Smithers..Carl Reissman
Delaney..Saul Trochman
Vagan..Isidore Feil

IN THE PRISON SCENE

First Prisoner..Ben Henring
Second Prisoner..Jack Millstein
Third Prisoner..Abe West
Fourth Prisoner..Harry Singer
Fifth Prisoner..Myron Kraft
Sixth Prisoner..Nat Yanofsky
Eldest Malcombe..Bernard Wallace
Youngest Malcombe..Arthur Stern
First Malcombe..G. Cohn
Second Malcombe..Ralph Krause
Third Malcombe..Harry Kaplan
Fourth Malcombe..Joseph West
Fifth Malcombe..Sidney Stolzenberg
Guard..Gilbert D. Muhlfelder
Guard..Charles H. Weissenbach
Scene—Left—The Secret Meeting Room of Vagan's Cabinet. Right—A Recreation Room in a Prison. Time—Between the Hours of Seven and Eight O'clock.
Produced Under the Direction of Myron E. Sattler. Settings Arranged by Lionel-Gersten Field.

The Sunnyside Playhouse of Sunnyside, Long Island, present "The Road to Rio," by Joseph R. Fleisler.

The Cast—

Dan Adams..Starr Gephart
Jack Curry..David Barr
Lil..Elinor Barr
Bill Burke..Albert Rubenstein
Connors..David Harritan
Scene—Reception Room at the Morgue.
Produced Under the Direction of David Barr.

WEDNESDAY, MAY 7

The Dramatic Society of Cathedral College, Manhattan, present "The Last Man In," by W. B. Maxwell.

The Cast—

Mrs. Judd..Robert Skelly
Mr. Billett..Paul Maher
Mr. Judd..James Ross
Customers..William O'Neill, Thomas Bartley, John Sullivan, George Wallace
The Last Man In..William Kenealy
The Doctor..James Walsh
Scene—The Parlor of a Humble Tavern, in a Poor Street of an English Country Town. Time—The Present.
Directed by Rev. Robert M. Gibson.

The Salon Players of the Salon of Seven Arts, Jackson Heights, L. I., Present "So's Your Old Antique," by Claire Kummer.

The Cast—

Dick Barlow..John Talbot Kimball
Sally, His Wife..Barbara Bruce Tappan
Mrs. Pettis..Ina Brown MacDougall
Mr. Malster..Rexford Kendrick
William, a Chauffeur..Elliott S. Moses
Scene—Dick Barlow's Antique Shop. Time—About Eleven O'clock on a Beautiful May Morning.
Directed by Blanche Talbot Kimball.

The Players of Bronxville, N. Y., present "The House with the Twisty Windows," by Mary Pakington.

The Cast—

James Roper..Dale S. Bartlett
Charles Clive..Edward McGee
Lady Ponting..Kathleen Clements
Heather Sorrell..Ann McGee
Anne Sorrell..Ruth Bretz
Derrick Moore..Edward Zimmer
Stepan..Lawrence Bartlett
Scene—A Cellar of a House in Petrograd, During the "Red Terror."
Charlton Barnes, Director.

The Gardens Players of Forest Hills, L. I., present "Rogues and Vagabonds." Words by Harry B. Smith. Music by Geoffrey O'Hara.

The Cast—

Robin..Henry Porter, Jr.
Sir Thomas Lucy..Alan Hudson
Stalker..John B. Bruns
Bullock..Ted Moir
Will Shakespeare..William Linton
Mary Fytton..Elsie Cropper
Jack Kemp..Walter Claypoole
Tom Green..Fred Kiendl
Audrey Lyle..Loretta Howson
Condell..Andrew Shuman
Richard Burbage..Walter Savell

Doll o' the Fortune....................................Agnes Kiendl
A Lord....................................Frederick Seward
Oldfield....................................E. Ryland Carter
Graig....................................Collyer Elliott
Gamekeeper....................................Cameron Shipp

LADIES AND GENTLEMEN OF THE ENSEMBLE

Frederick Seward	Kimber Seward
Madeleine Van Hagan	Johnnie Mae Welty
Carl Penny	Amy Howell
Leila Savell	Ethel Lee
R. V. Harrington	Mae Ball
Helen Rutledge	Helen Carroll
Conrad B. Taylor	Lyla Wilson
Agnes Viborg	Mabel Shedd
Ted Hager	Robert McCray McKee
Mae Robinson	Frances Moir
Frances Bush	William Roberts
Walter Schallitz	Theresa Sauer
Mabel Claypoole	William Bradshaw
Florence Bennett	Sonja Viborg
J. Gorton Marsh	Helen Shortmeier
Helen Clevenger	Ethel Taylor
George Boyce	Elizabeth Reutermann
Irma Wagner	Lulu J. Clymer
Nixon Lee	Elsie Vandervoort
Frances Pandau	Elspeth Brownell, Accompanist.

Scene—Estate of Sir Thomas Lucy. Stratford-on-Avon. Time—Autumn, 1585.
Under the Direction of Albert S. Howson.

THURSDAY, MAY 8

Wayne Community Players of Goldsboro, North Carolina, present "When the Roll Is Called Up Yonder," by W. Allen Royall.

The Cast—

Fanny Clark....................................W. Allen Royall
Huldah, His Wife....................................Anna Dortch Michaux
Junior, His Son....................................Whiz Smith
Miss Jenny, His Mother....................................Sudie Creech
Claire, Huldah's Friend....................................Janie Burns
Henry Gibbs, Rum-runner....................................Robert Robinson
Nat Green, Patrolman....................................Lloyd Parker
Scene—Living Room of Clark's Home, Ten Miles West of Goldsboro, N. C. Time—Scene 1—Afternoon of a Winter Day, 1928. Scene 2—Evening, Ten Months Later.
Directed by Margaret Kornegay.

Studio Theatre Players, Buffalo, N. Y., present "The Man Who Married a Dumb Wife," by Anatole France.

The Cast—

Master Leonard Botal, Judge....................................Spencer Whedon
Master Adam Fumee, Lawyer....................................David Day
Master Simon Colline, Doctor....................................Sheldon Spangler
Master Jean Maugier, Surgeon and Barber....................................Willis Martyn
Master Serafin DeLaurier, Apothecary....................................Buell Tallman, Jr.
Giles Boiscourtier, Leonard Botal's Secretary..Bernard Hammill, Jr.
A Blind Man....................................Henry Potter
Catherine, Leonard Botal's Wife....................................Ethel O'Dea Meyer
Alison, Leonard Botal's Servant....................................Virginia Butler
Mademoiselle De La Garandiere....................................Helen Gardner
Madame De La Bruine....................................Jane Franklin
Lackeys and Passers-by....Don Tullis, Betty Becker, Margaret Sossaman, Susan Rosengren, Betty Wilcox, Roswell Rosengren.
Scene—House of Judge Leonard Botal, in Paris.
Musical Accompaniment by Charme Allen. Directed by Jane Keeler.
Setting Arranged by Sheldon K. Viele.

The Albany Players of Albany, N. Y., present "The Choice," by Thomas C. Stowell.

The Cast—

Duke of Perigord..............................Thomas C. Stowell
Melusine } His Twin Daughters................ { Faye Smiley
Melisse } { Catherine Cherry
Marco, the Jester.............................Norman R. Sturgis
Manon, Nurse to the Sisters..................Gladys Wilson Boyce
Father Josef..................................Ray Becker
Hugh Carlet...................................Ranulf Compton
Charles, One of Carlet's Soldiers............Reynolds K. Townsend
Scene—A Feudal Duchy Not Far from Orleans, in the tiny France of That Day. 1—A Room in the Great Castle of the Duke of Perigord. 2—The Same, a Half Hour Later. Time—Evening of a Spring Day in the Early 11th Century.
Directed by Thomas C. Stowell. Scenery Designed and Built by Dorothy Lathrop and Paul M. Hewlett.

The Little Theatre of St. Louis, St. Louis, Mo., present "Right of Possession," by Edna Warren.

The Cast—

Clerk of the Court............................Gordon Sommers
Mrs. Howard...................................Eloise Frazier
Miss Harris...................................Irene Deicke
Judge Garland.................................Samuel Goddard
Mr. Lawrence..................................Frank Bacon
Mr. Curtis....................................Percy Ramsey
Mrs. Simmons..................................Adelaide Kalkman
Bonny Simmons.................................Leianna Devlin
Freddy Hargreve...............................Ralph Friedman
Scene—Court of Judge Garland, a Judge of the Juvenile Court.
Directed by Frederick Kitson Cowley. Setting Arranged by F. Ray Leimkuehler.

FRIDAY, MAY 9

Mississippi Agricultural and Mechanical College Dramatic Club, Starkville, Miss., present "A Night at an Inn," by Lord Dunsany.

The Cast—

A. E. Scott-Fortescue (The Toff)..............H. S. Chilton
William Jones (Bill)..........................S. B. Powers
Albert Thomas.................................Newton Townsend
Jacob Smith (Sniggers)........................H. G. Brannon
First Priest of Klesh.........................David Thomas
Second Priest of Klesh........................E. P. Williams
Third Priest of Klesh.........................W. C. Cozine
Klesh...J. A. Ruffin
Scene—A Room at an Inn.
Directed by H. P. Cooper.

The Paravent Players of Providence, R. I., present "Marshal," by Ferenc Molnar.

The Cast—

Edith, the Baron's Wife.......................Pearle Winburg
Maid Servant..................................Mary H. Brigham
Imre Litvay, an Actor.........................Kenneth F. Bruce
Barson San-Friano.............................Jean Bert Pinault
Dr. Janosy, a Physician.......................T. Stewart MacDonald
Scene—Baron San-Friano's Hunting Lodge, Near Budapest.
Directed by Rosalba deAnchoriz Joy.

The Loyola Community Theatre of Chicago, Ill., present "Sun-up," by Lula Vollmer.

The Cast—

Widow Cagle...................................Genevieve Ryan
Ruffe Cagle, Her Son..........................Eugene V. O'Brien
Emmy, His Wife................................Louise Willmarth

Stranger....................................Paul Brenner
Sheriff Weeks....................................J. Paul Ardeeser
Bud, Brother to Emmy....................................Allen Krimbelbine
Scene—Interior of Widow's Cabin in the Mountains of Western North Carolina, Near the City of Asheville. 1—Late Afternoon. September, 1917. 2—Midnight. February. 3—The Same. A Few Hours Later.
Adapted and Directed by Charles S. Costello.

The Morse Players Sponsored by the St. Louis Art League, St. Louis, Mo., present "Eyes," by Maxine Block.

The Cast—
The Grandmother....................................Therese Marie Wittler
Esther....................................Alice Gray Galleher
Max....................................Harold Elbert
Bill Scannell....................................Eugene R. Wood
Directed by Harry R. McClain.

The judges were Percy Hutchinson of the New York *Times*, Marguerite Tazelaar of the New York *Herald Tribune*, William G. King of the New York *Evening Post*, Louise Wilson of the New York *World* and Dan C. Anderson of the New York *Sun*. By unanimous vote they awarded two cash prizes of $200 each for the best unpublished plays presented in the tournament to Maxine Finsterwald's "Seven Against One," presented by the Association Players' Stock Company of the Y.M.H.A., New York, and Maxine Block's "Eyes," presented by the Morse Players of St. Louis, Mo. Two cash prizes of $200 each for the best presentation of previously published plays went to the Studio Players of Buffalo, N. Y., who offered Anatole France's "The Man Who Married a Dumb Wife," and to the Paravent Players of Providence, R. I., for their presentation of Ferenc Molnar's "Marshal." Honorable mention was given Genevieve Ryan for her performance of Widow Cagle in a shortened version of Lula Vollmer's "Sun-up"; to the Henry Street Players of New York for their performance of Richard Hughes' "The Sisters' Tragedy," and to the Salon Players of Jackson Heights, N. Y., for their presentation of Clare Kummer's "So's Your Old Antique." The Belasco cup, emblematic of the Little Theatre championship of the year, went to the Studio Players of Buffalo and "The Man Who Married a Dumb Wife."

LONG-PLAY TOURNAMENT

(7 performances)

Conducted by Walter Hartwig, in association with the Manhattan Little Theatre Club, Inc., for a Samuel French prize of $1,000 and a silver cup awarded by the Theatre Arts Monthly magazine.

MONDAY, MAY 12

The Guild Players of University Settlement, Manhattan, present "The Wooden Idol," a Preposterous Episode in a Prologue and Three Acts, by Leonard White.

The Cast—

IN THE PROLOGUE

A Museum Attendant....Louis Horton
An Elderly Gentleman....Harry Thaler

IN THE PLAY

James Pontifex, Managing Director of Pontifex, Ltd....Harvey Platt
Louisa Pontifex, His Wife....Harriet Ross
Ethel Pontifex, Their Younger Daughter....Bess Soltes
Judith Fison, Their Elder Daughter....Billie Kowit
Gilbert Fison, Their Son-in-law....Sam Weintraub
Hannah Dudgeon, James Pontifex's Sister....Ruth Gottfried
Lord Alfred Wonersh....Emanuel Gottfried
Hon. Adrian Molyneux....Louis Gans
Richard Merryweather, of Arkwright, Merryweather, Ltd....Philip Sloninsky
Tombs, a Servant....Herbert Lizt
Toby, James Pontifex's Clerk....Morris Honig
Scene—Of the Prologue—The Pontifex Museum. Of the Play—Morning Room at Pontifex Hall. Time—The Present.
Directed and Staged by Mrs. J. Glenwood Jones.

TUESDAY, MAY 13

The Thalian Masquers of the Bronx Y.M.H.A., The Bronx, present "Kith and Kin," by Wallace A. Manheimer.

The Cast—

Ma Codner....Dorothy Fowler Gillam
Gene Codner....Samuel Roland
Murray Codner....Mortimer V. Halpern
Ina Codner....Rae D. Negrin
Orrin Codner....John H. Brown
Wilbur Winslow....Charles D. Yuro
Parson Biggs....Emanuel Wieder
Charlie Winslow....Sol Berlad
Bill the Fiddler....Robert Richman
Seth Tucker....Sidney Alter
Mrs. Tucker....Molly Berger
Ben....Kenneth Schiller
Cy....Robert Davis
Fayetta....Esther Marofschick
John....Milton Rubin
Henry....Herman Offer
Elmer....Abraham Menkin
At the Barn Dance....Julian Belin, Sylvia Kleinman, Ruth Silverman, Constance Schrader, Murray Faymen, Benjamin Levitas, Albert Goldstein, Charles Greenwald, Lillian Markowitz, Sylvia Hirsch, Isidore Kleinman, Lou Howitt, Mollie Berger, Sidney Kleinman, Jean Margolis, Mariane Allerhand, Caroline Spellman, Monty Miller, Sylvia Wolfe, George Friedlander.
Act I and III.—Scene 1—The Codner Cabin. 2—The same. That Night. Act II.—The Barn Dance at the Winslows' the Following Evening in the Adirondack Mountains Off the Beaten Track.
Scenery Constructed and Painted by the Masquers Under the Supervision of Abraham Schneiderman. The Dances by Esther Marofschick. Stage Manager, Monty Miller. Directed by Philip Gross.

WEDNESDAY, MAY 14

The Morningside Players of Columbia University, Manhattan, present "The New Freedom," by Marjorie Bartholomew Paradis.

The Cast—

Grover Bainbridge....................John Cocks
Katherine....................May Wolmark
Lida Martin....................Eileen Meyerson
Mrs. Cornell....................Florence Pegram
Zoe Bainbridge....................Elizabeth von Nardroff
Dr. Paul Davis....................Clayton J. Heermance, Jr.
Howard Jameson....................J. F. Foster
Florence Jameson....................Ruth Yates
Kingsley Day....................J. C. Lotterhand
Dottie Parker....................Margaret Smith
Midge Rankin....................Marjorie Patterson
Ethel....................Gerry Raph
A Taxi Driver....................Joseph Davidson

Act I.—The Living Room in the Bainbridge Apartment, Bronxville. A Late Afternoon in June. Act II.—The Same. Eleven Months Later. Act III.—The Westchester Country Club. A Month Later.
Performance Directed by Milton Smith and Elizabeth Van Nardroff.
Settings Designed by Milton Smith, and Built and Painted by Members of the English e6e and Education 162K, Columbia University.

THURSDAY, MAY 15

The Lake Forest Players and The Playwrights Theatre, Chicago, Ill., present "Flying Blind," by Mary Aldis.

The Cast—

George Carrington, a Broker....................Ernst Von Ammon
Marcia, His Wife....................Helen Walton
George, Jr., His Son....................Harry Dickson
Dorothy, His Daughter....................Frances Acher
Henry Tillinghast His Uncle....................Edward H. Pasmore
Caroline Tillinghast, His Aunt....................Evelyn Pasmore
Ellen } ....His Servants.................... { Frances Ambler
Rose } ....His Servants.................... { Mildred Weinberger
Hilda } ....His Servants.................... { Alicia Gordon
Florence Craig, His Wife's Friend....................Virginia Wamboldt
Dr. Felix Hoffman, His Wife's Friend....................M. P. Wamboldt
Sarah Brown, His Wife's Secretary....................Alma Louise Dickson
Liza Hoffman, Ex-wife of Felix....................Martha Wickwire
Isadore Rosenblaum, a Tailor....................Gerald A. Frank
Zabinski, a Labor Leader....................Gregory Thomas

Scene 1—Breakfast Room of the Carringtons' Apartment, Uptown. 8.30 A.M. 2—The Study of Dr. Felix Hoffman. Downtown 3 P.M. 3—The Drawing-room of the Carringtons' Apartment 6 P.M. 4—The Same, After Dinner. 10 P.M. 5—The Same, Late at Night. 12 P.M. The Action Takes Place Between Half-past Eight in the Morning and Half-past Twelve at Night of a Day in Late Winter. Time —The Present.
Director, M. P. Wamboldt. Scenic Director, Sylvia Hamburger.

FRIDAY, MAY 16

The Little Theatre of St. Louis, St. Louis, Mo., Presents "The Twelfth Disciple," by Mary Parmly Koues Sachs.

The Cast—

Prologue....................Elliot Bergfeld
Hillel....................Gordon Sommers
Samuel....................Ralph Friedman
Rachel....................Marion Epstein
First Handmaiden....................Eloise Frazier
Second Handmaiden....................Leianna Devlin
Amos....................Ben Fry
Ezra....................George Wendling
Judas Iscariot....................Charles Dillon
Caiaphas....................Samuel Goddard
Annas....................Bruce McFarlane
First Priest....................Gordon Sommers
Second Priest....................Elliot Bergfeld

Servant to Caiaphas....................................Percy Ramsay
Persons on the Way to the Crucifixion:
A Greek Woman....................................Eloise Frazier
A Greek....................................Percy Ramsay
A Shepherd....................................Ben Fry
A Vendor....................................Maudean Jones-Crane
An Egyptian....................................George Wendling
First Tradesman....................................Elliot Bergfeld
Second Tradesman....................................Gordon Sommers
A Young Maidservant....................................Kathryn Cravens
An Old Woman....................................Adelaide Kalkman
Another Old Woman....................................Irene Deicke

Act I.—Scene 1—A Room in the House of Hillel, Two Days Before the Crucifixion of Jesus. 2—Hillel's Garden Immediately Afterwards. Act II.—An Ante-chamber in the Palace of Caiaphas, the High Priest, Somewhat Later the Same Day. Act III.—Beyond the City on the Road to Golgotha Two Days Later—Good Friday Afternoon. Time—The Action of the Play Takes Place in Jerusalem in the Year 33 A.D.

Directed by Frederick Kitson Cowley. Stage Manager—Archer O'Reilly. Electrician—John Chamberlin. Master of Properties—Ruth Sturgis. The Setting of the Play Is from a Design by F. Ray Leimkuehler. Costumes Designed and Executed by Mrs. Ernest Sachs and Mrs. George C. Smith.

The judges, Lee Foster Hartman of *Harper's* magazine, Carl Carmer of *Theatre Arts Monthly*, J. Kenyon Nicholson of Samuel French & Co., Edith H. Walton of *The Forum* and William G. King of the New York *Evening Post*, by unanimous vote awarded the $1,000 Samuel French prize and the *Theatre Arts Monthly* cup to Marjorie Bartholomew Paradis' "The New Freedom."

* LOST SHEEP

(48 performances)

A comedy in three acts by Belford Forrest. Produced by George Choos and Jack Donahue at the Selwyn Theatre, New York, May 5, 1930.

Cast of characters—

Mr. Harris....................................A. P. Kaye
Mr. Arkwright....................................Edward Cooper
Mrs. Dingle....................................Ruby Hallier
Reverend Wm. Wampus....................................Ferdinand Gottschalk
Mrs. Wampus....................................Cecilia Loftus
Rhoda Wampus....................................Sidney Fox
Mary Wampus....................................Valerie Cossart
Martha Wampus....................................Patricia Calvert
Cabman....................................Edward Broadley
Alfred....................................John Troughton
The Hon. Arthur Topham....................................Harry McNaughton
Eric Bailey....................................Rex O'Malley
Reverend A. A. Bailey....................................Hugh Buckler
First Policeman....................................Walter Plinge
Second Policeman....................................Ronald Dexter

Acts I, II and III.—The Parlour of 32 Pinkney Road, Higher Hampstead, Middlesex, England.

Staged by Marion Gering.

The Rev. William Wampus, Mrs. Wampus and three Wampus daughters are moving from Clapham to Higher Hampstead. They rent a furnished house for temporary shelter. The house formerly was occupied by a notorious woman known as "The Duchess" and six girls. The renting agent, Mr. Harris, thinks if he can restore the house to respectability he can add to its market value. For a day and a night the Wampuses are subjected to amusing and somewhat startling adventures when the gayer young men of the town call to inquire for Mabel and the other girls, and to learn such plans as the Duchess may have for the immediate future. Eric Bailey, son of a vicar, meets Rhoda, the youngest Wampus daughter, thinking her what she isn't at all, and determines to save her from a life of shame. He succeeds, but not without puzzling experiences.

* ADA BEATS THE DRUM

(44 performances)

A comedy in three acts by John Kirkpatrick. Produced by John Golden at the Golden Theatre, New York, May 8, 1930.

Cast of characters—

Ada Hubbard	Mary Boland
Leila Hubbard	Nydia Westman
Ed Hubbard	George W. Barbier
Mr. Sims	Frank Charlton
Jacqueline	Louza Riane
A Cure	Edgar Stehli
Bow-Tie	Hal Thompson
Nadine Wentworth	Natalie Schafer
Alonzo	Marcel Rousseau
Dmitri	Jules Eppailly
Gendarmes	August Aramini N. Gelikhovsky

Staged by Geoffrey Kerr.

Acts I, II and III.—In the Villa Dolores, in the Southwest of France.

Ada Hubbard, hungry for European culture, takes Ed, her husband, and Leila, her daughter, for a fling at the Continent. In the southern part of France the Hubbards rent a villa and wait for company. When none calls Ada manages to round up a pleasant trio, Nadine Wentworth, a poetess; Alonzo, a Spanish painter, and Dmitri, a musician. They eat the Hubbard food and bore Mr. Hubbard to distraction. He gets tight, throws them out of the house, strikes a gendarme and is put in jail. Meantime Leila falls in love with and annexes a trap drummer playing in the Casino orchestra. He was born in Illinois.

THE VIKINGS

(8 performances)

A drama in four acts by Henrik Ibsen. Produced by Richard Herndon at the New Yorker Theatre, New York, May 12, 1930.

Cast of characters—

Ornulf	Richard Hale
Sigurd	Warren William
Dagny	Margaret Mower
Kaare	Robert C. Fischer
Gunnar	Charles Waldron
Hjordis	Blanche Yurka
Thorolf	Edwin Philips
Egil	Richard Jack
Ornulf's Sons	Herschel Cropper Britton Diller O. T. Crawford William Warren William Gear Richard Bowler
Sigurd's Men	Frank Ryan Arthur Row Thomas Rimshart Watkins, Jr.
Hjordis' Men	Chester Leighty Jay Lindsey
Gunnar's Men	Robert Christy John Moran
Hjordis' Ladies in Waiting	Peggy McNaught Evelyn Hill Catherine Meredith Monty Priddy Adele Gilbert Helen Howe

Acts I and IV.—Coast of Norway. Acts II and III.—Gunnar Viking's Hall. During the Reign of King Eric Blood-Axe, in the Eighth Century.

Staged by Blanche Yurka and Thomas Wilfred.

Sigurd, one of the bolder Vikings, has accepted Hjordis' dare that no man shall take her to wife who has not the courage to slay the white bear that guards her chamber. Knowing that his friend Gunnar is much in love with Hjordis, Sigurd first puts on Gunnar's armor. After slaying the bear and possessing Hjordis, Sigurd carries her in her sleep aboard Gunnar's ship. When Hjordis awakes she accepts Gunnar as her lawful mate. Years later, discovering the truth, Hjordis slays Sigurd, expecting their true marriage will be consummated in Valhalla. Sigurd, dying, confesses that he has accepted Christianity and is therefore forbidden the hall of the gods.

GOLD BRAID

(7 performances)

A drama in three acts by Ann Shelby. Produced by Louis A. Safian at the Theatre Masque, New York, May 13, 1930.

Cast of characters—

Abdul..Bruce Adams
Sabena..Loretto Shea
Pvt. Thompson........................Thomas B. Carnahan, Jr.
Linda Rodney..Adele Ronson
Major Rodney..Edward Reese
Mrs. Billings..Marion Abbott
Col. Billings..Jethro Warner
Julio Cortez..Alan Devitt
Quong..Charlie Fang
A Moro..John J. Cameron

Acts I, II and III.—In Major Rodney's Quarters in Camp Malabang, Philippine Islands.
Staged by Gene Gowing.

Linda Rodney, wife of Major Rodney of the Intelligence service, U.S.A., stationed in the Philippines, grows restless and falls out of love with her husband. When the Major insists that she help with his investigation into Moro activities by making love to a Spanish suspect, Julio Cortez, she accepts the assignment, but, falling in love with Julio, refuses to betray him. Accused of disloyalty, Linda leaves her husband, and prepares to return to the U.S.A. and await Julio's coming.

THE TAVERN

(32 performances)

A comedy satire in two acts. Revived by George M. Cohan at the Fulton Theatre, New York, May 19, 1930.

Cast of characters—

The Tavern Keeper's Son........................Theodore Newton
The Hired Girl..Kathleen Niday
The Tavern Keeper........................Robert Middlemass
The Hired Man..Joseph Allen
The Vagabond..George M. Cohan
The Woman..Mary Philips
The Governor..Jack Leslie
The Governor's Wife..Lida Macmillan
The Governor's Daughter..Isabel Baring
The Fiance..Douglas Macpherson

The Sheriff.....Edward F. Nannary
The Sheriff's Men.....Jack Williams / Dan Carey / Manuel Duarte
The Attendant.....Harold Healy
Acts I and II.—In Zacheus Freeman's Tavern.
Staged by Sam Forrest.

See "The Best Plays of 1920-21."

*LET AND SUB-LET

(31 performances)

A farce comedy in three acts by Martha Stanley. Produced by L. A. and J. Hyman, Inc., at the Biltmore Theatre, New York, May 19, 1930.

Cast of characters—

Express Man.....Joe White
Rilla.....Mary Gildea
Dayton.....G. Lester Paul
Margaret Blair.....Gertrude Fowler
Montague Blair.....W. Messenger Bellis
Edward King.....George Dill
William Merritt.....Gordon Richards
Anne Manners.....Frances Sheil
Jane Blair.....Dorothea Chard
Charlie Morse.....Allen Connor
Dole.....Ashley Cooper
Persis Wayne.....Betty Lancaster
O'Brien.....Russell Rockwell
Acts I and III.—Home of Montague Blair. Larchmont. Act II. —Edward King's Bachelor Quarters in New York City.
Staged by Paul Edouard Martin.

Jane Blair, youthful and determined, does not want to go to Europe with her parents. Hiding herself at home Jane leaves a letter saying she has sailed with friends and will meet the family in London. Coming out of hiding Jane learns that her home has been rented to Edward King who wants a summer place for an adopted niece expected from the West. Jane pretends to be the niece, and when the latter arrives manages to park her in the city. Two weeks later the Blairs return and a lot of complications are adjusted, with Jane in Edward's arms.

MILESTONES

(8 performances)

A comedy in three acts by Arnold Bennett and Edward Knoblock. Revived by the Players' Club at the Empire Theatre, New York, June 2, 1930.

Cast of characters—

Prologue, Spoken by....................Edwin Milton Royle
Mrs. Rhead....................Florence Vroom
Rose Sibley....................Dorothy Stickney
Gertrude Rhead....................Beulah Bondi
Thompson....................P. J. Kelly
Ned Pym....................Ernest Cossart
Sam Sibley....................Warburton Gamble
John Rhead....................Tom Powers
Emily....................Selena Royle
Nancy....................Catherine Willard
Arthur Preece....................Herbert Ranson
Footman....................Jay Fassett
Webster....................William H. Sams
Lord Monkhurst....................Gerald Hamer
Muriel....................Audrey Ridgwell
Richard Sibley....................Edmund George
Act I.—Rhead Drawing Room. December, 1860. Act II.—Same. June, 1885. Act III.—Same. June, 1912.
Staged by Henry Stillman.

In 1860 John Rhead, junior partner of Rhead & Sibley, iron masters, is keenly excited about the launching of the first iron steamship and eager that his firm should enter shipbuilding. Because his older partners pooh-pooh his visionary optimism he marries a Sibley daughter, draws out of the firm and becomes a wealthy independent. In 1885 John, grown conservative, is as strongly convinced that the new-fangled metal called steel is but a flash in the pan and refuses to let his daughter marry the inventor. In 1912 Emily Rhead, who had traded her romance for a title, is as strongly set against her daughter marrying the man of her own choosing.

"Milestones" was preceded by a revival of "The Little Father of the Wilderness," a one-act drama by Austin Strong and Lloyd Osborne, originally played by Francis Wilson in 1912.

Cast of characters—

Pere Marlotte....................Francis Wilson
Frere Gregoire....................Gene Lockhart
Louis XV....................Frederick Lewis
Chevalier De Frontenac....................Walter Hampden
Duc de St. Albret....................Jerome Lawler
Captain Chevillon....................John C. King
Monsieur D'Ayen....................Pacie Ripple
Mademoiselle Henriette....................Margalo Gillmore
Duchesse de Fronsac....................Margherita Sargent
Marquise de Segur....................Irene Shirley
Mademoiselle de Chavaniac....................Adele Walker
Madame de Simiane....................Florence Fair
Mademoiselle de Coigny....................Agnes Brady
Madame d'Epernon....................Olga Birkbeck
Comtesse Auguste d'Arenberg....................Essie Emery
Madame Durfort....................Kathleen Lockhart
Mademoiselle de Hautefort....................Joyce Arling
Madame de Sancy....................Jane Hamilton
Mademoiselle de Tremouille....................Emily Graham
Madame Mentpensier....................Marian Sommers

Chief Conotocaurious..............................Augustin Duncan
Chief Monocatootha....................................Loren Stout
First Guard....................................Raymond Thayer
Second Guard............................Lawrence McK. Miller
Duc de Fronsac.................................Henry Mortimer
Marquis de Segur.................................Hannam Clark
Captain La Tour Marbourg.........................Joseph Kilgour
Lieutenant General Dulong........................Frazer Coulter
Marquis de Trinc.................................Wright Kramer
Lieutenant Franval...................................Doan Borup
Major Dubois Martin...........................Edwin T. Emery
Lieutenant Colonel De Fayols.....................George Riddell
Captain De Vrigny..................................Walter Scott
Major De Bedaulx.................................Harry Forsman
Lieutenant Candon...............................Jack O'Donnell
Lieutenant Conde................................John K. Hodges
Major De Gimat...........................George Buchanan Fife
Colonel Mercoeur.................................Reginald Birch
Lieutenant d'Artois...........................George Vandegrift
Cadet Poix.......................................S. Ascher Smith
Footman.......................................Abraham Gillette

An Antechamber at the Palace of Versailles.
Staged by Austin Strong.

SPOOK HOUSE

(15 performances)

A mystery drama in three acts by Joe Byron Totten. Produced by the DeMilt Associated Players at the Vanderbilt Theatre, New York, June 3, 1930.

Cast of characters—

Philip Haynes.....................................John A. Lorenz
Priscilla Lathrop................................Leslie Bingham
Spike Connelly....................................Leo Donnelly
Fingers Tolman...................................James A. Boshell
Grace Gale......................................Dorothy Blackburn
Robert Dyne...............................Edwin Forrest Forsberg
Muriel Dyne..Myrta Bellair
Arthur Joyce......................................Wilfred Lytell
Roberta Dyne.....................................Thelma Marsh
Dick Hammond.......................................Guy Hitner
Tom McCarthy..............................Lawrence O'Sullivan

Acts I, II and III.—Philip Haynes' Home—Known as "Spook House," Westchester County, New York.

Philip Haynes, tenant of the old Bailey house, in which the owner was murdered, hires Spike Connelly, an accredited gunman, to shoot down the rich Robert Dyne while the guests at a Haynes dinner are playing a new game called "Murder." The bullet intended for Dyne hits Haynes instead and the police have a great time clearing up the mystery. It is finally revealed as a plot conceived by young Bailey to uncover the murderer of his father.

* GARRICK GAIETIES

(14 performances)

A revue in two acts. Produced by the Theatre Guild, Inc., at the Guild Theatre, New York, June 4, 1930.

Principals engaged—

Nan Blackstone	Edith Meiser
Albert Carroll	James Norris
Ruth Chorpenning	Cynthia Rodgers
Imogene Coca	Edith Sheldon
Theodore Fetter	Roger Stearns
Edwin Gilcher	Donald Stewart
Hildegarde Halliday	William Tannen
Ray Heatherton	Thelma Tipson
Sterling Holloway	Velma Vavara
Otto Hulett	Mickey Burton
Eve Latour	Ginger Meehan
Kate Drain Lawson	Jo Myers
Philip Loeb	Polly Rose

Staged by Philip Loeb and Olin Howard.

The list of contributors to the book of this, the third edition of the "Gaieties" organized by Theatre Guild juniors, included:

Music by March Blitzstein, Aaron Copland, Vernon Duke, Basil Fomeen, Harold Goldman, William Irwin, Ned Lehak, Everett Miller, Peter Nolan, Willard Robison, Charles M. Schwab and Kay Swift.

Lyrics by Allen Boretz, Ruth Chorpenning, Ira Gershwin, L. Y. Harburg, Sterling Holloway, Paul James, Ronald Jeans, Malcolm McComb, John Mercer, Henry Myers, Louis M. Simon, Josiah Titzell.

Sketches by H. Alexander, Carroll Carroll, Ruth Chorpenning, Leopoldine Damrosch, Gretchen Damrosch Finletter, Landon Herrick, Sterling Holloway, Benjamin M. Kaye, Newman Levy, Dorian Otvos and Louis M. Simon.

* LYSISTRATA

(12 performances)

A farce from the Greek of Aristophanes, adapted by Gilbert Seldes. Produced by the Philadelphia Theatre Association, Inc., at the Forty-fourth Street Theatre, New York, June 5, 1930.

Lysistrata.................................Violet Kemble Cooper
The Guard...Jose Limon
First Old Woman..................................Mary Blair
Second Old Woman.........................Virginia Chauvenet

Third Old Woman....................................Marie Lalloz
Kalonika...Miriam Hopkins
Myrrhina...Hortense Alden
First Athenian Woman.............................Ruth Garland
Second Athenian Woman..........................Helen Savery
Third Athenian Woman..........................Nancy McKnight
Fourth Athenian Woman..........................Ilse Gronau
Fifth Athenian Woman.........................Ernestine Henoch
Sixth Athenian Woman...........................Betty Schlaffer
First Theban Woman.........................Consuelo Flowerton
Second Theban Woman..................................Letitia Ide
First Spartan Woman....................................Lona Dawn
Second Spartan Woman...........................Gloria Braggiotti
First Corinthian Woman..............................Justine Chase
Second Corinthian Woman......................Marion Morehouse
Lampito..Hope Emerson
First Old Man..Ian Wolfe
Second Old Man..................................Houston Richards
Third Old Man.....................................Etienne Girardot
Fourth Old Man...Owen Meech
Fifth Old Man.......................................Conrad Cantzen
President of the Senate.......................Sydney Greenstreet
Clerk..Elliott Sullivan
First Policeman..Lucian Scott
Second Policeman.....................................Howard Wilson
Third Policeman.......................................Newton Whyte
First Senator...Orrin Burke
Second Senator..Paul Haskle
Third Senator..Morton Moore
Fourth Senator..Chester Hammond
Fifth Senator..Thornton Whitney
A Herald from Sparta......................................Eric Dressler
Kinesias...Ernest Truex
First Young Man (Polydorus)........................John Clearman
Second Young Man......................................George Cotton
Third Young Man...Clayton Irving
The Child...James McCallion
Lycon..Albert Van Dekker

Staged by Norman-Bel Geddes; dances by Doris Humphrey and Charles Weidman.

Lysistrata, wife of Lycon, tired of the Peloponnesian wars and the consequent strain upon the family ties, organizes the women of Athens, Sparta, Thebes and Corinth in a wife strike. The women take oath to deny themselves to their husbands and lovers until peace is declared and treaties signed. The women win.

* CHANGE YOUR LUCK

(11 performances)

A colored revue in two parts, book by Garland Howard, music by J. C. Johnson. Produced by Cleon Throckmorton at the George M. Cohan Theatre, New York, June 6, 1930.

Cast of characters—

Big Bill..Alex Lovejoy
Cateye..Jimmy Thomas
Hot Stuff Jackson......................................Garland Howard
Malindy...Alberta Perkins

Profit Jones....................................Sam Cross
Skybo Snowball....................................Speedy Smith
Bandana Babe Peppers....................................Cora La Redd
Romeo Green....................................Sterling Grant
Josephine Peppers....................................Neeka Shaw
Mary Jane....................................Alberta Hunter
Diamond Joe....................................Chick McKenney
Ebenezer Smart....................................Hamtree Harrington
Mathilda....................................Mable Grant
Evergreen Peppers....................................Leigh Whipper
Passionate Sadie....................................Millie Holmes
Rat Row Sadie....................................Emma Maitland
Tack Annie....................................Aurelia Wheeldin
Sisters of Mercy { Dottie....................................Dorothy Embry
Mary....................................Mary Mason
Lil....................................Lillian Cowan }
Hot Popper Henry....................................Henry Davis
Hot Popper Jimmy....................................James Davis
Hot Popper Van....................................Van Jackson
Ansy....................................Bertha Roe
Percolatin Gertie....................................Gertie Chambers
Short Dog....................................Yank Bronson
Charleston Sam....................................Sammy Van
Shake a Hip....................................Louie Simms
Shake a Leg....................................Buster Bowie
Captain Jones....................................J. Lewis Johnson
The Four Flash Devils....................................S. W. Warren, Chas. Gill, Billy Cole, C. P. Wade

Stanley Bennett and His Syncopators.

Act I.—Scene 1—Levee in Sundown, Miss. 2—Street. 3—Sunflower Lane. 4—Evergreen Peppers' Funeral Parlor. 5—Lobby of Sundown Hotel. Act II.—Scene 1—Rat Row. 2—Street in Rat Row. 3—Lawn Fete at Evergreen Peppers'.

Staged by Cleon Throckmorton; dances by Lawrence Deas and Speedy Smith.

A series of songs and dances strung on a plot concerned with an undertaker who fills his formaldehyde cans with liquor and does a very good bootlegging business.

* ARTISTS AND MODELS

(7 performances)

A revue in two acts; music by Harold Stern and Ernie Golden; adapted from an English musical comedy, "Dear Love." Produced by the Messrs. Shubert at the Majestic Theatre, New York, June 10, 1930.

Principals engaged—

George Hassell
Harry Welsh
Halfred Young
Archie Roberts
Pierce and Harris
Kay Simmons
Stanley Harrison
Rath Brothers
Terry Horne
Aileen Stanley
Vera Pearce
Mary Adams
Dolores De Monde
Rosemary Deering
Naomi Johnson
Kay McKay
Miss Florence

Staged by Frank Smithson and Pal'mere Brandeaux.

STATISTICAL SUMMARY

(Last Season Plays Which Ended Runs After June 15, 1930.)

Plays	*Number Performances*	*Plays*	*Number Performances*
Adam's Apple	16	Little Accident, The	303
Bird in Hand	500	Little Show, The	321
Brothers	255	Love Duel, The	88
Camel Through the Needle's Eye	196	My Girl Friday	253
Decision	64	New Moon, The	509
Follow Thru	403	Nice Women	64
Grand Street Follies	93	Night in Venice	175
Hold Everything	413	Perfect Alibi, The	255
Jade God, The	96	Skidding	472
Jonesy	96	Street Scene	601
Journey's End	485	Tired Business Man, The	24
Let Us Be Gay	353	Whoopee	379

PLAYS THAT HAVE RUN OVER 500 PERFORMANCES ON BROADWAY

To June 15, 1930

Plays	*Number Performances*	*Plays*	*Number Performances*
Abie's Irish Rose	2,532	Street Scene	601
Lightnin'	1,291	Kiki	600
The Bat	867	Blossom Time	592
The Ladder	789	Show Boat	572
The First Year	760	The Show-off	571
Seventh Heaven	704	Sally	570
Peg o' My Heart	692	Good News	551
East Is West	680	The Music Master	540
Irene	670	The Boomerang	522
A Trip to Chinatown	657	Blackbirds	518
Rain	648	Sunny	517
Is Zat So	618	The Vagabond King	511
Student Prince	608	New Moon, The	509
Broadway	603	Shuffle Along	504
Adonis	603	Bird in Hand	500

PULITZER PRIZE WINNERS

"For the original American play performed in New York which shall best represent the educational value and power of the stage in raising the standard of good morals, good taste and good manners."—The Will of Joseph Pulitzer, dated April 16, 1904.

In 1929 the advisory board, which, according to the terms of the will, "shall have the power in its discretion to suspend or to change any subject or subjects . . . if in the judgment of the board such suspension, changes or substitutions shall be conducive to the public good," decided to eliminate from the above paragraph relating to the prize-winning play the words "in raising the standard of good morals, good taste and good manners."

The committee awards to date have been:

1917-18—Why Marry, by Jesse Lynch Williams
1918-19—None
1919-20—Miss Lulu Bett, by Zona Gale
1920-21—Beyond the Horizon, by Eugene O'Neill
1921-22—Anna Christie, by Eugene O'Neill
1922-23—Icebound, by Owen Davis
1923-24—Hell-bent fer Heaven, by Hatcher Hughes
1924-25—They Knew What They Wanted, by Sidney Howard
1925-26—Craig's Wife, by George Kelly
1926-27—In Abraham's Bosom, by Paul Green
1927-28—Strange Interlude, by Eugene O'Neill
1928-29—Street Scene, by Elmer Rice
1929-30—The Green Pastures, by Marc Connelly

PREVIOUS VOLUMES OF BEST PLAYS

Selections of the ten best plays of each season since 1919-1920 in preceding volumes of this Year Book of the Drama are as follows:

1919-1920

"Abraham Lincoln," by John Drinkwater. Published by Houghton Mifflin Co., Boston.

"Clarence," by Booth Tarkington.

"Beyond the Horizon," by Eugene G. O'Neill. Published by Boni & Liveright, Inc., New York.

"Déclassée," by Zoe Akins.

"The Famous Mrs. Fair," by James Forbes.

"The Jest," by Sem Benelli. (American adaptation by Edward Sheldon.)

"Jane Clegg," by St. John Ervine. Published by Henry Holt & Co., New York.

"Mamma's Affair," by Rachel Barton Butler.

"Wedding Bells," by Salisbury Field.

"Adam and Eva," by George Middleton and Guy Bolton.

1920-1921

"Deburau," by H. Granville Barker. Published by G. P. Putnam's Sons, New York.

"The First Year," by Frank Craven.

"Enter Madame," by Gilda Varesi and Dolly Byrne. Published by G. P. Putnam's Sons, New York.

"The Green Goddess," by William Archer. Published by Alfred A. Knopf, New York.

"Liliom," by Ferenc Molnar. Published by Boni & Liveright, New York.

"Mary Rose," by James M. Barrie.

"Nice People," by Rachel Crothers.

"The Bad Man," by Porter Emerson Browne. Published by G. P. Putnam's Sons, New York.

"The Emperor Jones," by Eugene G. O'Neill. Published by Boni & Liveright, New York.

"The Skin Game," by John Galsworthy. Published by Charles Scribner's Sons, New York.

1921-1922

"Anna Christie," by Eugene G. O'Neill. Published by Boni & Liveright, New York.

"A Bill of Divorcement," by Clemence Dane. Published by the Macmillan Company, New York.

"Dulcy," by George S. Kaufman and Marc Connelly. Published by G. P. Putnam's Sons, New York.

"He Who Gets Slapped," by Leonid Andreyev. Published by Brentano's.

"Six Cylinder Love," by William Anthony McGuire.

"The Hero," by Gilbert Emery.

"The Dover Road," by Alan Alexander Milne.

"Ambush," by Arthur Richman.

"The Circle," by William Somerset Maugham.

"The Nest," by Paul Geraldy and Grace George.

1922-1923

"Rain," by John Colton and Clemence Randolph.

"Loyalties," by John Galsworthy. Published by Charles Scribner's Sons, New York.

"Icebound," by Owen Davis. Published by Little, Brown & Company, Boston.

"You and I," by Philip Barry. Published by Brentano's, New York.

"The Fool," by Channing Pollock. Published by Brentano's, New York.

"Merton of the Movies," by George Kaufman and Marc Connelly, based on the novel of the same name by Harry Leon Wilson.

"Why Not?" by Jesse Lynch Williams.

"The Old Soak," by Don Marquis. Published by Doubleday, Page & Company.

"R.U.R.," by Karel Capek. Translated by Paul Selver. Published by Doubleday, Page & Company.

"Mary the 3d," by Rachel Crothers. Published by Brentano's, New York.

1923-1924

"The Swan," by Ferenc Molnar. Published by Boni & Liveright, New York.

"Outward Bound," by Sutton Vane. Published by Boni & Liveright, New York.

"The Show-off," by George Kelly. Published by Little, Brown & Company, Boston.

"The Changelings," by Lee Wilson Dodd. Published by E. P. Dutton & Company, New York.

"Chicken Feed," by Guy Bolton. Published by Samuel French, New York and London.

"Sun-Up," by Lula Vollmer. Published by Brentano's, New York.

"Beggar on Horseback," by George Kaufman and Marc Connelly. Published by Boni & Liveright, New York.

"Tarnish," by Gilbert Emery. Published by Brentano's, New York.

"The Goose Hangs High," by Lewis Beach. Published by Little, Brown & Company, Boston.

"Hell-bent fer Heaven," by Hatcher Hughes. Published by Harper Bros., New York.

1924-1925

"What Price Glory?" by Laurence Stallings and Maxwell Anderson.

"They Knew What They Wanted," by Sidney Howard. Published by Doubleday, Page & Company, New York.

"Desire Under the Elms," by Eugene G. O'Neill. Published by Boni & Liveright, New York.

"The Firebrand," by Edwin Justus Mayer. Published by Boni & Liveright, New York.

"Dancing Mothers," by Edgar Selwyn and Edmund Goulding.

"Mrs. Partridge Presents," by Mary Kennedy and Ruth Warren.

"The Fall Guy," by James Gleason and George Abbott.

"The Youngest," by Philip Barry. Published by Samuel French, New York.

"Minick," by Edna Ferber and George S. Kaufman. Published by Doubleday, Page & Company, New York.

"Wild Birds," by Dan Totheroh. Published by Doubleday, Page & Company, New York.

1925-1926

"Craig's Wife," by George Kelly. Published by Little, Brown & Company, Boston.

WHERE AND WHEN THEY WERE BORN

Name	Birthplace	Year
Abbott, George	Hamburg, N. Y.	1895
Adams, Maude	Salt Lake City, Utah	1872
Allen, Viola	Huntsville, Ala.	1869
Ames, Robert	Hartford, Conn.	1893
Ames, Winthrop	North Easton, Mass.	1871
Andrews, Ann	Los Angeles, Cal.	1895
Anglin, Margaret	Ottawa, Canada	1876
Anson, A. E.	England	1879
Arbuckle, Maclyn	San Antonio, Texas	1866
Arliss, George	London, England	1868
Arthur, Julia	Hamilton, Ont.	1869
Astaire, Adele	Omaha, Neb.	1900
Astaire, Fred	Omaha, Neb.	1899
Atwell, Roy	Syracuse, N. Y.	1880
Atwill, Lionel	London, England	1885
Bacon, Frank	California	1864
Bainter, Fay	Los Angeles, Cal.	1892
Barbee, Richard	Lafayette, Ind.	1887
Barrie, James Matthew	Kirriemuir, N. B.	1860
Barrymore, Ethel	Philadelphia, Pa.	1879
Barrymore, John	Philadelphia, Pa.	1882
Barrymore, Lionel	London, England	1878
Bates, Blanche	Portland, Ore.	1873
Bayes, Nora	Milwaukee, Wis.	1880
Beban, George	San Francisco, Cal.	1873
Beckley, Beatrice	Roedean, England	1885
Best, Edna	England	1901
Beecher, Janet	Chicago, Ill.	1884
Belasco, David	San Francisco, Cal.	1853
Ben-Ami, Jacob	Minsk, Russia	1890
Bennett, Richard	Cass County, Ind.	1873
Bennett, Wilda	Asbury Park, N. J.	1894
Berlin, Irving	Russia	1888
Bernard, Barney	Rochester, N. Y.	1877
Bernard, Sam	Birmingham, England	1863

Bernhardt, Sarah	Paris, France	1844
Bingham, Amelia	Hickville, Ohio	1869
Binney, Constance	Philadelphia, Pa.	1900
Blackmer, Sidney	Salisbury, N. C.	1896
Blinn, Holbrook	San Francisco, Cal.	1872
Boland, Mary	Detroit, Mich.	1880
Bordoni, Irene	Paris, France	1895
Brady, Alice	New York	1892
Brady, William A.	San Francisco, Cal.	1863
Breese, Edmund	Brooklyn, N. Y.	1871
Brian, Donald	St. John's, N. F.	1871
Broadhurst, George H.	England	1866
Bryant, Charles	England	1879
Buchanan, Jack	England	1892
Buchanan, Thompson	Louisville, Ky.	1877
Burke, Billie	Washington, D. C.	1885
Burton, Frederick	Indiana	1871
Byron, Arthur	Brooklyn, N. Y.	1872
Cahill, Marie	Brooklyn, N. Y.	1871
Cantor, Eddie	New York	1894
Campbell, Mrs. Patrick	England	1865
Carle, Richard	Somerville, Mass.	1871
Carlisle, Alexandra	Yorkshire, England	1886
Carr, Alexander	Russia	1878
Carter, Mrs. Leslie	Lexington, Ky.	1862
Catlett, Walter	San Francisco, Cal.	1889
Cawthorne, Joseph	New York	1868
Chaplin, Charles Spencer	London	1889
Chatterton, Ruth	New York	1893
Cherry, Charles	England	1872
Churchill, Burton	Toronto, Can.	1876
Claire, Ina	Washington, D. C.	1892
Clarke, Marguerite	Cincinnati, Ohio	1887
Cliffe, H. Cooper	England	1862
Clifford, Kathleen	Charlottesville, Va.	1887
Coburn, Charles	Macon, Ga.	1877
Coghlan, Gertrude	England	1879
Coghlan, Rose	Petersborough, England	1850
Cohan, George M.	Providence, R. I.	1878
Cohan, Georgette	Los Angeles, Cal.	1900
Colbert, Claudette	Paris	1905
Collier, Constance	Windsor, England	1882
Collier, William	New York	1866

Collinge, Patricia ....Dublin, Ireland 1894
Collins, José ....London, England 1896
Conroy, Frank ....London, England 1885
Cooper, Violet Kemble ....London, England 1890
Cornell, Katharine ....Buffalo, N. Y. 1900
Corrigan, Emmett ....Amsterdam, Holland 1871
Corthell, Herbert ....Boston, Mass. 1875
Courtenay, William ....Worcester, Mass. 1875
Courtleigh, William ....Guelph, Ont. 1869
Coward, Noel ....England 1899
Cowl, Jane ....Boston, Mass. 1887
Crane, William H. ....Leicester, Mass. 1845
Craven, Frank ....Boston, Mass. 1880
Crews, Laura Hope ....San Francisco, Cal. 1880
Crosman, Henrietta ....Wheeling, W. Va. 1865
Crothers, Rachel ....Bloomington, Ill. 1878
Cumberland, John ....St. John, N. B. 1880

Dale, Margaret ....Philadelphia, Pa. 1880
Dalton, Charles ....England 1864
Daly, Arnold ....New York 1875
Daniels, Frank ....Dayton, Ohio 1860
Dawn, Hazel ....Ogden, Utah 1891
Day, Edith ....Minneapolis, Minn. 1896
De Angelis, Jefferson ....San Francisco, Cal. 1859
Dean, Julia ....St. Paul, Minn. 1880
De Cordoba, Pedro ....New York 1881
Dillingham, Charles B. ....Hartford, Conn. 1868
Dinehart, Allan ....Missoula, Mont. 1889
Ditrichstein, Leo ....Temesbar, Hungary 1865
Dixey, Henry E. ....Boston, Mass. 1859
Dodson, John E. ....London, England 1857
Dolly, Rosy ....Hungary 1892
Dolly, Jennie ....Hungary 1892
Doro, Marie ....Duncannon, Pa. 1882
D'Orsay, Lawrence ....England 1860
Dressler, Marie ....Cobourg, Canada 1869
Drew, John ....Philadelphia, Pa. 1853
Drew, Louise ....New York 1884
Druce, Herbert ....England 1870
Dunn, Emma ....England 1875
Dupree, Minnie ....San Francisco, Cal. 1875
Duse, Eleanora ....Vigerano, Italy 1859

Eagels, Jeanne	Kansas City, Mo.	1894
Eames, Clare	Hartford, Conn.	1896
Edeson, Robert	Baltimore, Md.	1868
Eldridge, Florence	Brooklyn, N. Y.	1901
Ellis, Mary	New York	1900
Elliston, Grace	Wheeling, W. Va.	1881
Ellinger, Desirée	Manchester, Vt.	1895
Elliott, Gertrude	Rockland, Me.	1874
Elliott, Maxine	Rockland, Me.	1871
Ellsler, Effie	Philadelphia, Pa.	1898
Eltinge, Julian	Boston, Mass.	1883
Emerson, John	Sandusky, Ohio	1874
Errol, Leon	Sydney, Australia	1881
Fairbanks, Douglas	Denver, Colo.	1883
Farnum, Dustin	Hampton Beach, N. H.	1874
Farnum, William	Boston, Mass.	1876
Farrar, Geraldine	Melrose, Mass.	1883
Faversham, William	Warwickshire, England	1868
Fealy, Maude	Memphis, Tenn.	1883
Fenwick, Irene	Chicago, Ill.	1887
Ferguson, Elsie	New York	1883
Fields, Lew	New York	1867
Fields, W. C.	Philadelphia, Pa.	1883
Fischer, Alice	Indiana	1869
Fiske, Minnie Maddern	New Orleans, La.	1867
Fontanne, Lynn	London, England	1892
Forbes, Robertson, Sir J.	London, England	1853
Foster, Claiborne	Shreveport, La.	1899
Foy, Edward Fitzgerald	New York	1854
Frederick, Pauline	Boston, Mass.	1884
Friganza, Trixie	Cincinnati, Ohio	1870
Frohman, Daniel	Sandusky, Ohio	1850
Garden, Mary	Scotland	1876
Gaythorne, Pamela	England	1882
George, Grace	New York	1879
Gillette, William	Hartford, Conn.	1856
Gillmore, Frank	New York	1884
Gillmore, Margalo	England	1901
Gleason, James	New York	1885
Glendinning, Ernest	Ulverston, England	1884
Gottschalk, Ferdinand	London, England	1869

Grey, Jane .... Middlebury, Vt. 1883
Grey, Katherine .... San Francisco, Cal. 1873

Haines, Robert T. .... Muncie, Ind. 1870
Hale, Louise Closser .... Chicago, Ill. 1872
Hall, Laura Nelson .... Philadelphia, Pa. 1876
Hamilton, Hale .... Topeka, Kansas 1880
Hampden, Walter .... Brooklyn, N. Y. 1879
Harding, Lyn .... Newport 1867
Harris, Sam H. .... New York 1872
Hawtrey, Charles .... Eton, England 1858
Hayes, Helen .... Washington, D. C. 1900
Hazzard, John E. .... New York 1881
Hedman, Martha .... Sweden 1888
Heggie, O. P. .... Australia 1879
Heming, Violet .... Leeds, England 1893
Herbert, Evelyn .... Brooklyn, N. Y. 1900
Herbert, Victor .... Dublin, Ireland 1859
Herne, Chrystal .... Dorchester, Mass. 1883
Hitchcock, Raymond .... Auburn, N. Y. 1870
Hodge, William .... Albion, N. Y. 1874
Hopper, DeWolf .... New York 1858
Hopper, Edna Wallace .... San Francisco, Cal. 1874
Holmes, Taylor .... Newark, N. J. 1872
Howard, Leslie .... London, England 1890
Hull, Henry .... Louisville, Ky. 1893
Huston, Walter .... Toronto 1884

Illington, Margaret .... Bloomington, Ill. 1881
Irving, Isabel .... Bridgeport, Conn. 1871
Irwin, May .... Whitby, Ont. 1862

Janis, Elsie .... Delaware, Ohio 1889
Joel, Clara .... Jersey City, N. J. 1890
Jolson, Al. .... Washington, D. C. 1883

Keane, Doris .... Michigan 1885
Keenan, Frank .... Dubuque, Ia. 1858
Keightley, Cyril .... New South Wales, Aus. ... 1875
Kennedy, Madge .... Chicago, Ill. 1890
Kerrigan, J. M. .... Dublin, Ireland 1885
Kerr, Geoffrey .... London, England 1895
Kershaw, Willette .... Clifton Heights, Mo. 1890

Kosta, Tessa	Chicago, Ill.	1893
Kruger, Otto	Toledo, Ohio	1895
Lackaye, Wilton	Virginia	1862
Larrimore, Francine	Russia	1888
La Rue, Grace	Kansas City, Mo.	1882
Lauder, Harry	Portobello, England	1870
Lawton, Thais	Louisville, Ky.	1881
Lawrence, Gertrude	London	1898
Lawrence, Margaret	Trenton, N. J.	1890
Lean, Cecil	Illinois	1878
Le Gallienne, Eva	London, England	1900
Levey, Ethel	San Francisco, Cal.	1881
Lewis, Ada	New York	1871
Lewis, Mabel Terry	London, England	1872
Logan, Stanley	Earlsfield, England	1885
Loraine, Robert	England	1876
Lord, Pauline	Hanford, Cal.	1890
Lorraine, Lillian	San Francisco, Cal.	1892
Lou-Tellegen	Holland	1881
Lunt, Alfred	Milwaukee, Wis.	1893
Mack, Andrew	Boston, Mass.	1863
Mack, Willard	Ontario, Canada	1873
Mackay, Elsie	London, England	1894
MacKellar, Helen	Canada	1896
Mann, Louis	New York	1865
Mantell, Robert B.	Ayrshire, Scotland	1854
Merivale, Philip	India	1886
Marlowe, Julia	Caldbeck, England	1870
Matthews, A. E.	Bridlington, England	1869
Matthison, Edith Wynne	England	1875
Maude, Cyril	London, England	1862
McIntyre, Frank	Ann Arbor, Mich.	1879
McRae, Bruce	India	1867
Meighan, Thomas	Pittsburgh	1879
Melba, Nellie	Melbourne, Australia	1866
Mellish, Fuller	England	1865
Mercer, Beryl	Seville, Spain	1882
Miller, Marilyn	Findlay, Ohio	1898
Mitchell, Grant	Columbus, Ohio	1874
Mitzi (Hajos)	Budapest	1891
Moores, Clara	Omaha, Neb.	1897

Morgan, Helen	Danville, Ill.	1900
Murphy, Tim	Rupert, Vt.	1860
Nash, Florence	Troy, N. Y.	1888
Nash, Mary	Troy, N. Y.	1885
Nazimova, Alla	Crimea, Russia	1879
Nielsen, Alice	Nashville, Tenn.	1876
Nugent, J. C.	Miles, O.	1875
Nugent, Elliott	Dover, O.	1900
Olcott, Chauncey	Providence, R. I.	1862
O'Neill, Eugene Gladstone	New York	1888
O'Neil, Nance	Oakland, Cal.	1875
O'Ramey, Georgia	Mansfield, Ohio	1886
Painter, Eleanor	Iowa	1890
Pawle, Lenox	London, England	1872
Pennington, Ann	Philadelphia, Pa.	1898
Perkins, Osgood	Boston, Mass.	1892
Pickford, Mary	Toronto	1893
Post, Guy Bates	Seattle, Wash.	1875
Powers, James T.	New York	1862
Power, Tyrone	London, England	1869
Rambeau, Marjorie	San Francisco, Cal.	1889
Rathbone, Basil	Johannesburg	1892
Reed, Florence	Philadelphia, Pa.	1883
Rennie, James	Toronto, Canada	1890
Revelle, Hamilton	Gibraltar	1872
Rickard, Amy	Boston, Mass.	1880
Richman, Charles	Chicago, Ill.	1870
Ring, Blanche	Boston, Mass.	1876
Ring, Frances	New York	1882
Roberts, Theodore	San Francisco, Cal.	1861
Robson, May	Australia	1868
Ross, Thomas W.	Boston, Mass.	1875
Ruben, José	Belgium	1886
Russell, Annie	Liverpool, England	1864
Russell, Lillian	Clinton, Iowa	1860
Ryan, Mary	New York	1885
Sanderson, Julia	Springfield, Mass.	1887
Santley, Joseph	Salt Lake City	1889

Sawyer, Ivy ....London, England 1897
Scheff, Fritzi ....Vienna, Austria 1879
Scott, Cyril ....Ireland 1866
Sears, Zelda ....Brockway, Mich. 1873
Segal, Vivienne ....Philadelphia, Pa. 1897
Selwyn, Edgar ....Cincinnati, Ohio 1875
Serrano, Vincent ....New York 1870
Shannon, Effie ....Cambridge, Mass. 1867
Shepley, Ruth ....New York 1889
Schildkraut, Joseph ....Bucharest, Roumania 1896
Sherman, Lowell ....San Francisco, Cal. 1885
Sidney, George ....New York 1876
Sitgreaves, Beverly ....Charleston, S. C. 1867
Skelly, Hal ....Allegheny, Pa. 1891
Skinner, Otis ....Cambridgeport, Mass. 1857
Sothern, Edward H. ....New Orleans, La. 1859
Spong, Hilda ....Australia 1875
Stahl, Rose ....Montreal, Canada 1872
Standing, Sir Guy ....London 1873
Starr, Frances ....Oneonta, N. Y. 1886
Stevens, Emily ....New York 1882
Stone, Fred ....Denver, Colo. 1873
Stone, Dorothy ....New York 1905
Sydney, Basil ....London 1894

Taliaferro, Edith ....New York 1892
Taliaferro, Mabel ....New York 1887
Tanguay, Eva ....Middletown, Conn. 1878
Taylor, Laurette ....New York 1884
Tell, Alma ....New York 1892
Tell, Olive ....New York 1894
Terry, Ellen ....Coventry, England 1848
Thomas, Augustus ....St. Louis, Mo. 1859
Thomas, John Charles ....Baltimore, Md. 1887
Tobin, Genevieve ....New York 1901
Tobin, Vivian ....New York 1903
Toler, Sidney ....Warrensburg, Mo. 1874
Trevor, Norman ....Calcutta 1877
Truex, Ernest ....Denver, Colo. 1890
Tynan, Brandon ....Dublin, Ireland 1879

Ulric, Lenore ....New Ulm, Minn. 1897

Varesi, Gilda	Milan, Italy	1887
Victor, Josephine	Hungary	1891
Wainwright, Marie	Philadelphia, Pa.	1853
Walker, June	New York	1904
Walker, Charlotte	Galveston, Texas	1878
Warfield, David	San Francisco, Cal.	1866
Warwick, Robert	Sacramento, Cal.	1878
Ware, Helen	San Francisco, Cal.	1877
Weber, Joseph	New York	1867
Welford, Dallas	Liverpool, England	1874
Westley, Helen	Brooklyn, N. Y.	1879
Westman, Nydia	White Plains, N. Y.	1906
Whiffen, Mrs. Thomas	London, England	1845
Whiteside, Walker	Logansport, Ind.	1869
Wilson, Francis	Philadelphia, Pa.	1854
Winwood, Estelle	England	1883
Wise, Thomas A.	England	1865
Wood, Peggy	Brooklyn, N. Y.	1894
Wright, Haidee	London, England	1868
Wycherly, Margaret	England	1883
Wyndham, Olive	Chicago, Ill.	1886
Wynn, Ed.	Philadelphia, Pa.	1886
Ziegfeld, Florenz, Jr.	Chicago, Ill.	1867

NECROLOGY

June 15, 1929—June 15, 1930

Sam F. Kingston, manager, 63. For the better part of thirty years a member of Florenz Ziegfeld's business staff. Born Dublin, Ireland. Died New York, June 17, 1929.

Charles A. Stevenson, actor, 77. For many years leading man for Mrs. Leslie Carter. Later played in support of Jane Cowl and Henrietta Crosman. Retired in 1918, after an engagement with "East Is West." Born Dublin, Ireland; died New York, July 2, 1929.

Dustin Farnum, actor, 55. As a legitimate actor gained fame in "The Virginian" and "Arizona." Was one of the first actors of standing to go into pictures. Brother of and co-star with William Farnum. Born Hampton Beach, Me., died New York, July 3, 1929.

John O'Hara, actor, 70. Played character parts for years, succeeding Frank Bacon in rôle of Bill Jones in "Lightnin'." Died St. Kilda, Australia, July 15, 1929.

John W. Ransome, actor, 69. Most widely known for his success as chief German comedian in "The Prince of Pilsen." Gained fame as a young man for his impersonations of "Boss" Croker, politician. Died New York, August 12, 1929.

Grant Stewart, actor and playwright, 63. Career began in England with Rosina Vokes. Played many years in support of the Coghlans, Olga Nethersole, Ethel Barrymore, Annie Russell, Willie Collier and others. Wrote "Caught in the Rain" with Collier, "Arms and the Girl" with Robert Baker. Born England; died Woodstock, N. Y., August 18, 1929.

Cyril Keightley, actor, 53. Gained prominence in New South Wales, South Africa and Egypt in a variety of rôles; played in "Magda" with Nance O'Neill in London, and in "Love Watches" with Billie Burke in America. Variety of parts followed, his last appearance in New York being in "The Trial of Mary Dugan." Born Wellington, N.S.W.; died New York, August 14, 1929.

Leslie Faber, actor, 50. Prominent leading man in England for many years. Played in America in 1906 in "The Hypocrites," in 1911 in "Witness for the Defense" and in 1928 in "The Patriot." Died London, August 5, 1929.

F. F. Proctor, manager, 78. Beginning as an errand boy in a Boston store, becoming proficient as an acrobat by practicing nights in gymnasiums, young Proctor went from vaudeville performer to theatre owner, acquiring a string of playhouses. He was the father of continuous vaudeville. A year before his death he sold his holdings to the RKO interests. Born Dexter, Me.; died Larchmont, N. Y., September 4, 1929.

Jeanne Eagels, actress, 35. Beginning as a child actress in Kansas City, Miss Eagels arose to prominence as a leading woman for George Arliss and won her greatest success as the star of "Rain," which played for four years. Her last year was spent making talkies, of which "Jealousy" is the most successful. Born Kansas City; died New York, October 3, 1929.

Bert C. Whitney, manager, 60. Successful in the production of musical comedy fifteen years ago, and owner of a string of theatres. Brother of Fred C. Whitney, who produced "The Chocolate Soldier." Born Detroit, Mich.; died Toronto, Canada, October 26, 1929.

John Cort, manager, 70. Organized and controlled a circuit of theatres covering the Northwest forty years ago, known as the Northwest Theatrical Association. Was at one time affiliated with the Shuberts in their fight against the so-called Theatrical Trust, and later switched to the Klaw-Erlanger forces. Built Cort theatres in Chicago and New York. Born Newark, N. J.; died Stamford, Conn., November 17, 1929.

Raymond Hitchcock, actor, 58. Prominent as a comedian in musical comedy and later played in straight comedy. Became a star in "The Yankee Consul." Played with success in "King Dodo," "The Red Widow," "The Beauty Shop," and a series of "Hitchy-coo" revues of which he was the chief inspiration and principal producer. He was in the 1921 "Follies" and was playing in "Your Uncle Dudley" in Chicago when he was first stricken with a heart attack. Born Auburn, N. Y.; died Beverley Hills, Cal., November 24, 1929.

Lydia Yeamans Titus, comedienne, 63. Born on sailing vessel between Sydney and Melba. Was headliner thirty years ago in vaudeville, England and the United States. Honored by Edward VII, who gave her a bar pin after hearing her sing "Sally in Our Alley." Daughter of celebrated Annie Yeamans of Australia and an equally famous clown and bareback rider. Spent childhood on "the lot." Acted with Tony Pastor and the original Pat Rooney. Last years in motion pictures. Died, Los Angeles, Dec. 31, 1929.

George Le Maire, comedian, 46. Played in numerous Shubert revues, and one or two "Follies." In vaudeville a member of the team of Conroy and Le Maire for a number of years. Tried producing with "Broadway Brevities." Died New York, January 20, 1930.

Gordon Dooley, comedian, 31. The last of the three Dooley brothers who builded a great popularity as knockabout comedians in vaudeville and later were prominent in all the best Broadway revues. As a member of the vaudeville team of Dooley and Morton he was preparing for a talking picture career at the time of his death. Died Philadelphia, Pa., January 24, 1930.

Fuller Mellish, Jr., actor, 35. Had recently achieved prominence in modern dramas, starting with "What Price Glory," and was making progress in moving pictures at the time of his death. Died Forest Hills, L. I., February 8, 1930.

Frank Burbeck, actor, 74. Appeared in support of practically all the old-time stars and was for years in the companies of Charles and Daniel Frohman. Died New York, February 20, 1930.

Mabel Normand, actress, 35. One stage appearance in "The Little Mouse" in 1924. Thereafter her career was connected with the screen, in which she achieved popularity and prominence. Born Quebec, Canada, 1894; died Monrovia, Cal., February 23, 1930.

A. L. Erlanger, producer, 70. Took to the theatre as a boy, becoming manager of the Euclid Avenue Opera House in Cleveland for Mark Hanna. Later formed an association with Marc Klaw, who knew the law as well as the show business. Together they formed a theatrical syndicate that brought order to the business of booking attractions. Controlled 700 theatres at one time as booking agents, in association with Charles Frohman, Al Hayman and Nixon & Zimmerman of Philadelphia. In his last years, after quarreling with Klaw in 1919, Erlanger devoted time and energy to expanding Erlanger power by the building and acquirement of theatres. Born Buffalo, N. Y., 1860; died New York, March 7, 1930.

Dore Davidson, actor, 80. Old-time leading man, having appeared in support of Fanny Davenport, Booth and Barrett and in many Dion Boucicault comedies. Played in "Blue Bird" and "The Tailor-made Man." In pictures before his retirement. Died New York, March 7, 1930.

Edward F. Albee, vaudeville manager, 72. Left home as a boy to join a circus. Later, in Boston, formed an association with the late B. F. Keith and together they built up the Keith circuit of vaudeville theatres, bringing that form of entertainment out of the more vulgar varieties where it originated; built up tremendous power, became charitably inclined in church matters and a fanatic on clean shows; organized the National Vaudeville Association to protect his business from labor organizations. Sold out to the Radio-Keith-Orpheum circuit in 1928. Born Maine; died Palm Beach, Florida, March 11, 1930.

Marie Studholm, actress, 55. Popular London star of musical comedy, well known in America through appearances in "An Artist's Model," "San Toy," "Lady Madcap," etc. Died London, March 9, 1930.

Fritz Williams, actor, 64. A favorite light comedian for many years, particularly during the seven years he was a member of Daniel Frohman's Lyceum Theatre Stock Company, playing "The Amazons," "The Home Secretary," "The Benefit of the Doubt," etc. Later joined Weber and Fields. Of recent years played prominently in "Our Betters," "Too Many Husbands," "Rain" and "Berkeley Square." Twice elected Shepherd of the Lambs' Club, New York. Born Boston, 1865; died in Lambs' Club grill, April 1, 1930.

Mme. Emma Albani, prima donna, 77. Favorite opera singer for many years, at Covent Garden, London, and the Academy of Music and Metropolitan in New York. William of Germany made her "the first singer of the royal household" and she was a Dame Commander of the Order of the British Empire. Retired in 1912 at a concert in Albert Hall, London, attended by 10,000 persons. Born Canada; died London, April 3, 1930.

Adele Ritchie, actress, 56. Noted for her beauty and as a musical comedy actress, starting with the "Isle of Champagne" at Miner's Theatre, New York, in 1893; prominently cast with Frank Daniels in "The Devil's Disciple" and "The Wizard of the Nile"; played in "A Chinese Honeymoon" and "Florodora," and in vaudeville in "The Girl in the Taxi." Married and divorced Guy Bates Post. Born Philadelphia; died Laguna Beach, Cal., April 24, 1930.

Charles S. Gilpin, actor, 51. Colored star who came to prominence in the colored theatre and later on Broadway playing a short part in "Abraham Lincoln" and becoming a star in Eugene O'Neill's "Emperor Jones." Died Eldredge Park, N. J., May 6, 1930.

William Cressy, actor, 65. For years popular in vaudeville, playing with his wife, Blanche Dayne, in "Without a Will There's a Way," "A City Case," "One Night Only," etc. Was an entertainer with the A.E.F. Died St. Petersburg, Florida, May 7, 1930.

Ben Hendricks, actor, 65. Known thirty years ago as a star in Swedish-American comedies, "Ole Olson," "Yon Yonson," "A Yenuine Yentleman." Started his stage career as the boy in Joseph Jefferson's production of "Rip Van Winkle." Last engagements with "Desert Song" and "Abie's Irish Rose." Had been in pictures. Born Buffalo, N. Y.; died Hollywood, Cal., April 30, 1930.

William J. Ferguson, actor, 85. Played for many years in support of the stars of his time, including Helena Modjeska, Richard Mansfield and Robert Mantell. Was a callboy in Ford's Theatre, Washington, the night Abraham Lincoln was assassinated. Last surviving member of Laura Keene's "American Cousin" company. Had been in pictures for some years. Died Pikesville, Md., May 4, 1930.

Herbert Hall Winslow, playwright, 64. Wrote nearly a hundred plays, including "The Vinegar Buyer" and "Swell Elegant Jones" for Ezra Kendall. Others included "A Rolling Stone," "When Reuben Came to Town" and "The Little Joker." Born Keokuk, Ia., 1865; died Hastings-on-Hudson, N. Y., June 1, 1930.

Fred C. Whitney, theatrical manager, 65. Prominent for years as the producer of musical and dramatic successes, including "The Chocolate Soldier," "Quo Vadis," "When Johnny Comes Marching Home," "Dolly Varden" (for Lulu Glaser) and a road production of "St. Joan." Son of C. J. Whitney, Detroit opera house proprietor, and a brother of the late Bert C. Whitney.

Arthur Lewis, actor, 84. For sixty-two years played in support of leading stars, his last engagement being with Otis Skinner in "One Hundred Years Old." He was prominent in the companies of Sarah Bernhardt, Mme. Rejane, Mary Anderson and was for many years a dependable of the Maude Adams companies. Born England; died New York, June 13, 1930.

INDEX OF AUTHORS

INDEX OF PLAYS AND CASTS